JOURNEYS

A Reading and Literature Program

Revised Edition with Writing Supplement

Arrivals
Teacher's Manual
Test Booklet

Banner
Teacher's Manual
Test Booklet

Cascade
Teacher's Manual
Test Booklet

Delta
Teacher's Manual
Test Booklet

Emblem
Teacher's Manual
Test Booklet

Findings
Teacher's Manual
Test Booklet

JOURNEYS

A Reading and Literature Program

Cascade

Curriculum and Writing

Richard J. Smith

Professor of Curriculum and Instruction,
University of Wisconsin.
Formerly, Director of Reading Development,
Public Schools of Madison, Wisconsin.
Formerly, Reading Coordinator, Public Schools
of Ripon, Wisconsin.

Max F. Schulz

Professor of English,
University of Southern California.

 HARCOURT BRACE JOVANOVICH, PUBLISHERS

Orlando   New York   Chicago   San Diego   Atlanta   Dallas

Acknowledgments

For permission to reprint copyrighted material, grateful acknowledgment is made to the following sources:

Bantam Books, Inc.: "Skateboarding" from *Girlsports* by Karen Folger Jacobs. Copyright © 1978 by Karen Folger Jacobs. All rights reserved.

Dorothy Boles and Triangle Communications Inc.: "The Contest" by Paul Darcy Boles from *Seventeen* ® Magazine. Copyright © 1975 by Triangle Communications Inc. All rights reserved.

The Caxton Printers, Ltd., Caldwell, ID: "Say It With Flowers" from *Yokohama, California* by Toshio Mori.

CBS Radio, a division of CBS Inc.: "A Shipment of Mute Fate" by Les Crutchfield. Copyright © 1953 by Columbia Broadcasting System, Inc. All rights reserved.

Chilton Book Company, Radnor, PA/Scholastic Books, New York, NY: "Our Indian Heritage" (Retitled "Gifts of the Indian") from *The Day They Hanged the Sioux* by C. Fayne Porter. © 1964 by C. Fayne Porter.

Manuela Williams Crosno: "Otero's Visitor" from *New Mexico Quarterly*, Vol. 7, No. 4, November 1937. All rights reserved.

Doubleday & Company, Inc.: "The Meadow Mouse" from *The Collected Poems of Theodore Roethke*. Copyright © 1963 by Beatrice Roethke as Administratrix of the Estate of Theodore Roethke.

The Dramatic Publishing Company: Dramatization by Pat Gray of *The Hobbit* by J. R. R. Tolkien. © MCMLXVIII by The Dramatic Publishing Company. All rights reserved. Printed in the United States of America.

Norma Millay (Ellis): "Portrait by a Neighbor" by Edna St. Vincent Millay from *Collected Poems*. Copyright 1922, 1950 by Edna St. Vincent Millay. Published by Harper & Row, Publishers, Inc.

The Benjamin Franklin Literary & Medical Society, Inc.: "Night Rider" by Steven Otfinoski from *Child Life* Magazine. Copyright © 1978 by The Saturday Evening Post Company, Indianapolis, IN.

Blanche C. Gregory, Inc. and Lilian Jackson Braun: "The Sin of Madame Phloi" by Lilian Jackson Braun. Copyright © 1962 by Davis Publications.

Harcourt Brace Jovanovich, Inc.: Slightly adapted and abridged from "The Promised Visit" by Grey Cohoe in *Design For Good Reading* by Schumacher, et al. Copyright © 1969 by Harcourt Brace Jovanovich, Inc.

Harper & Row, Publishers, Inc.: Text from "Cynthia in the Snow" in *Bronzeville Boys and Girls* by Gwendolyn Brooks. Copyright © 1956 by Gwendolyn Brooks Blakely. "Pete at the Zoo" from *The World of Gwendolyn Brooks*. Copyright © 1960 by Gwendolyn Brooks. "For My Grandmother" from *On These I Stand* by Countee Cullen. Copyright 1925 by Harper & Row, Publishers, Inc.; renewed 1953 by Ida M. Cullen. "Where the Sidewalk Ends" from *Where the Sidewalk Ends: The Poems and Drawings of Shel Silverstein*. Copyright © 1974 by Snake Eye Music, Inc.

v

Critical Readers

We wish to thank the following people, who helped to evaluate materials for this book.

VINCENT AMATO
Norman Thomas High School, New York, New York

WILLIAM A. FEELEY
Bishop Neumann High School, Philadelphia, Pennsylvania

J. L. JOYCE
Sayville Junior High School, Sayville, New York

MICHAEL J. ROMEO
Kearny High School, Kearny, New Jersey

CAROL SCRIGNIOLI
Cherry Hill High School, Cherry Hill, New Jersey

SHELLEY UMANS
Columbia University, New York, New York
Formerly with New York City Public School System, New York, New York

CONTENTS

Woodnotes

Profiles

Perspectives

Winter Thunder

by Mari Sandoz

Vistas

Mosaic

The Hobbit

by J. R. R. Tolkien **463**
Dramatized by Patricia Gray

Turn to page xiv for Outline of Skills
Turn to page xvii for Writing Supplement

OUTLINE OF SKILLS

Literature Skills

Reading Skills

Composition Skills

Writing Supplement

WOODNOTES

Cat-About-Town

James Herriot

It was a mystery. Where did the cat go each night?

Tristan shouted up the stairs from the passage far below.

"Jim! Jim!"

I went out and stuck my head over the banisters. "What is it, Triss?"

"Sorry to bother you, Jim, but could you come down for a minute?" The upturned face had an anxious look.

I went down the long flights of steps two at a time and, when I arrived slightly breathless on the ground floor, Tristan beckoned me through to the consulting room at the back of the house. A teenage girl was standing by the table, her hand resting on a stained roll of blanket.

"It's a cat," Tristan said. He pulled back a fold of the blanket and I looked down at a large, deeply striped tabby. At least he would have been large if he had had any flesh on his bones, but ribs and pelvis stood out painfully through the fur and, as I passed my hand over the motionless body, I could feel only a thin covering of skin.

Tristan cleared his throat. "There's something else, Jim."

I looked at him curiously. For once he didn't seem to have a joke in him. I watched as he gently lifted one of the cat's hind legs and rolled the abdomen into view. There was a gash on the ventral surface through which a coiled cluster of intestines spilled grotesquely onto the cloth. I was still shocked and staring when the girl spoke.

"I saw this cat sittin' in the dark, down Brown's yard. I thought 'e looked skinny, like, and a bit quiet, and I bent down to give 'im a pat. Then I saw 'e was badly hurt and I went home for a blanket and brought 'im round to you."

"That was kind of you," I said. "Have you any idea who he belongs to?"

The girl shook her head. "No, he looks like a stray to me."

"He does indeed." I dragged my eyes away from the terrible wound. "You're Marjorie Simpson, aren't you?"

"Yes."

"I know your Dad well. He's our postman."

"That's right." She gave a half smile, then her lips trembled.

"Well, I reckon I'd better leave 'im with you. You'll be goin' to put him out of his misery. There's nothing anybody can do about . . . about that?"

I shrugged and shook my head. The girl's eyes filled with tears, she stretched out a hand and touched the emaciated animal, then turned and walked quickly to the door.

"Thanks again, Marjorie," I called after the retreating back. "And don't worry—we'll look after him."

In the silence that followed, Tristan and I looked down at the shattered animal. Under the surgery lamp it was all too easy to see. He had almost been disemboweled[1] and the pile of intestines was covered in dirt and mud.

"What d'you think did this?" Tristan said at length. "Has he been run over?"

"Maybe," I replied. "Could be anything. An attack by a big dog, or somebody could have kicked him or struck him." All things were possible with cats because some people seemed to regard them as fair game for any cruelty.

Tristan nodded. "Anyway, whatever happened, he must have been on the verge of starvation. He's a skeleton. I bet he's wandered miles from home."

"Ah well," I sighed. "There's only one thing to do. Those guts are perforated in several places. It's hopeless."

Tristan didn't say anything but he whistled under his breath and drew the tip of his forefinger again and again across the furry cheek. And, unbeliev-

ably, from somewhere in the scraggy chest a gentle purring arose.

The young man looked at me, round-eyed. "My God, do you hear that?"

"Yes . . . amazing in that condition. He's a good-natured cat."

Tristan, head bowed, continued his stroking. I knew how he felt because, although he preserved a cheerfully hard-boiled attitude to our patients, he couldn't kid me about one thing; he had a soft spot for cats.

"It's no good, Triss," I said gently. "It's got to be done." I reached for the syringe, but something in me rebelled against plunging a needle into that mutilated body. Instead, I pulled a fold of the blanket over the cat's head.

"Pour a little ether onto the cloth," I said. "He'll just sleep away."

Wordlessly Tristan unscrewed the cap of the ether bottle and poised it above the head. Then from under the shapeless heap of blanket we heard it again; the deep purring which increased in volume till it boomed in our ears like a distant motorcycle.

Tristan was like a man turned to stone, hand gripping the bottle rigidly, eyes staring down at the mound of cloth from which the purring rose in waves of warm friendly sound.

At last he looked up at me and gulped. "I don't fancy this much, Jim. Can't we do something?"

"You mean, put that lot back?"

"Yes."

"But the bowels are damaged—they're like a sieve in parts."

"We could stitch them, couldn't we?"

I lifted the blanket and looked again. "Honestly, Triss, I wouldn't know where to start. And the whole thing is filthy."

---

1. disemboweled (dĭs'ĭm-bou'əld) v.: The cat's bowels, or intestines, had been almost entirely torn out.

He didn't say anything, but continued to look at me steadily. And I didn't need much persuading. I had no more desire to pour ether onto that comradely purring than he had.

"Come on, then," I said. "We'll have a go."

With the oxygen bubbling and the cat's head in the anesthetic mask, we washed the whole prolapse[2] with warm saline. We did it again and again but it was impossible to remove every fragment of caked dirt. Then we started the painfully slow business of stitching the many holes in the tiny intestines, and here I was glad of Tristan's nimble fingers, which seemed better able to manipulate the small round-bodied needles than mine.

Two hours and yards of catgut[3] later, we dusted the patched-up peritoneal[4] surface with sulfanilamide and pushed the entire mass back into the abdomen. When I had sutured muscle layers and skin, everything looked tidy, but I had a nasty feeling of sweeping undesirable things under the carpet. The extensive damage, all that contamination—peritonitis[5] was inevitable.

"He's alive, anyway, Triss," I said as we began to wash the instruments. "We'll put him on to sulfapyridine and keep our fingers crossed." There were still no antibiotics at that time but the new drug was a big advance.

The door opened and Helen came in. "You've been a long time, Jim." She walked over to the table and looked down at the sleeping cat. "What a poor skinny little thing. He's all bones."

"You should have seen him when he came in." Tristan switched off the sterilizer and screwed shut the valve on the anesthetic machine. "He looks a lot better now."

She stroked the little animal for a moment. "Is he badly injured?"

"I'm afraid so, Helen," I said. "We've done our best for him but I honestly don't think he has much chance."

"What a shame. And he's pretty, too. Four white feet and all those unusual colors." With her finger she traced the faint bands of auburn and copper-gold among the gray and black.

Tristan laughed. "Yes, I think that chap has a ginger Tom somewhere in his ancestry."

Helen smiled, too, but absently, and I noticed a broody look about her. She hurried out to the stockroom and returned with an empty box.

"Yes . . . yes . . . " she said thoughtfully. "I can make a bed in this box for him and he'll sleep in our room, Jim."

"He will?"

"Yes, he must be warm, mustn't he?"

"Of course."

Later, in the darkness of our bedroom, I looked from my pillow at a cozy scene. Sam in his basket on one side of the flickering fire and the cat cushioned and blanketed in his box on the other.

As I floated off into sleep it was good to know that my patient was so comfortable, but I wondered if he would be alive in the morning. . . .

I knew he was alive at 7:30 A.M.

---

2. prolapse (prō-lăps') n.: The organ that had fallen out of place. In this case, the intestines.
3. catgut (kăt'gŭt') n.: The thread used in surgical operations.
4. peritoneal (pĕr'ə-tə-nē'əl) adj.: Of the membrane lining the walls of the abdomen.
5. peritonitis (pĕr'ə-tə-nī'tĭs) n.: Inflammation of the lining of the abdomen.

because my wife was already up and talking to him. I trailed across the room in my pajamas and the cat and I looked at each other. I rubbed him under the chin and he opened his mouth in a rusty meow. But he didn't try to move.

"Helen," I said. "This little thing is tied together inside with catgut. He'll have to live on fluids for a week and even then he probably won't make it. If he stays up here you'll be spooning milk into him umpteen times a day."

"Okay, okay." She had that broody look again.

It wasn't only milk she spooned into him over the next few days. Beef essence, strained broth, and a succession of sophisticated baby foods found their way down his throat at regular intervals. One lunchtime I found Helen kneeling by the box.

"We shall call him Oscar," she said.

"You mean we're keeping him?"

"Yes."

I am fond of cats but we already had a dog in our cramped quarters and I could see difficulties. Still I decided to let it go.

"Why Oscar?"

"I don't know." Helen tipped a few drops of chop gravy onto the little red tongue and watched intently as he swallowed. I was pleased at the way things were going. I had been giving him the sulfapyridine every six hours and taking the temperature night and morning, expecting all the time to encounter the roaring fever, the vomiting, and the tense abdomen of peritonitis. But it never happened.

It was as though Oscar's animal instinct told him he had to move as little as possible because he lay absolutely still day after day and looked up at us—and purred.

His purr became part of our lives and, when he eventually left his bed, sauntered through to our kitchen, and began to sample Sam's dinner of meat and biscuit, it was a moment of triumph. And I didn't spoil it by wondering if he was ready for solid food; I felt he knew.

From then on it was sheer joy to watch the furry scarecrow fill out and grow strong, and as he ate and ate and the flesh spread over his bones, the true beauty of his coat showed in the glossy medley of auburn, black, and gold. We had a handsome cat on our hands.

Once Oscar had fully recovered, Tristan was a regular visitor.

He probably felt, and rightly, that he, more than I, had saved Oscar's life in the first place and he used to play with him for long periods. His favorite ploy was to push his leg round the corner of the table and withdraw it repeatedly just as the cat pawed at it.

Oscar was justifiably irritated by this teasing but showed his character by lying in wait for Tristan one night and biting him smartly in the ankle before he could start his tricks.

From my own point of view, Oscar added many things to our family. Sam was delighted with him and the two soon became firm friends. Helen adored him and each evening I thought afresh that a nice cat washing his face by the hearth gave extra comfort to a room.

Oscar had been established as one of the family for several weeks when I came in from a late call to find Helen waiting for me with a stricken face.

"What's happened?" I asked.

"It's Oscar—he's gone!"

"Gone? What do you mean?"

"Oh, Jim, I think he's run away."

I stared at her. "He wouldn't do that. He often goes down to the garden at night. Are you sure he isn't there?"

"Absolutely. I've searched right into the yard. I've even had a walk round the town. And remember." Her chin quivered. "He . . . he ran away from somewhere before."

I looked at my watch. "Ten o'clock. Yes, that is strange. He shouldn't be out at this time."

As I spoke the front doorbell jangled. I galloped down the stairs, and as I rounded the corner in the passage I could see Mrs. Heslington, the vicar's wife, through the glass. I threw open the door. She was holding Oscar in her arms.

"I believe this is your cat, Mr. Herriot," she said.

"It is indeed, Mrs. Heslington. Where did you find him?"

She smiled. "Well, it was rather odd. We were having a meeting of the Mothers' Union at the church house and we noticed the cat sitting there in the room."

"Just sitting . . . ?"

"Yes, as though he were listening to what we were saying and enjoying it all. It was unusual. When the meeting ended I thought I'd better bring him along to you."

"I'm most grateful, Mrs. Heslington." I snatched Oscar and tucked him under my arm. "My wife is distraught—she thought he was lost."

It was a little mystery. Why should he suddenly take off like that? But since he showed no change in his manner over the ensuing week, we put it out of our minds.

Then one evening a man brought in a dog for a distemper inoculation and left the front door open. When I went up to our flat I found that Oscar had disappeared again. This time Helen and I scoured the marketplace and side alleys in vain, and when we returned at half past nine we were both despondent. It was nearly eleven and we were thinking of bed when the doorbell rang.

It was Oscar again, this time resting on the ample stomach of Jack Newbould. Jack was leaning against a doorpost. Jack was a gardener at one of the big houses. He gave me a huge benevolent smile. "Brought your cat, Mr. Herriot."

"Gosh, thanks, Jack!" I said, scooping up Oscar gratefully. "Where the devil did you find him?"

"Well, s'matter o' fact, 'e sort of found me."

"What do you mean?"

Jack closed his eyes for a few moments before articulating carefully. " 'Thish is a big night, tha knows, Mr. Herriot. Darts championship. Lots of t'lads round at t'Dog and Gun—lotsh and lotsh of 'em. Big gatherin'."

"And our cat was there?"

"Aye, he were there, all right. Sittin' among t'lads. Shpent t'whole evenin' with us."

"Just sat there, eh?"

"That 'e did." Jack giggled reminiscently. "By gaw 'e enjoyed 'isself. Ah gave 'im a drop o' best bitter out of me own glass and once or twice ah thought 'e was goin' to have a go at chuckin' a dart. He's some cat." He laughed again.

As I bore Oscar upstairs I was deep in thought. What was going on here? These sudden desertions were upsetting Helen, and I felt they could get on my nerves in time.

I didn't have long to wait till the

next one. Three nights later he was missing again. This time Helen and I didn't bother to search—we just waited.

He was back earlier than usual. I heard the doorbell at nine o'clock. It was the elderly Miss Simpson peering through the glass. And she wasn't holding Oscar—he was prowling on the mat waiting to come in.

Miss Simpson watched with interest as the cat stalked inside and made for the stairs. "Ah, good, I'm so glad he's come home safely. I knew he was your cat and I've been intrigued by his behavior all evening."

"Where . . . may I ask?"

"Oh, at the Women's Institute. He came in shortly after we started and stayed there till the end."

"Really? What exactly was your program, Miss Simpson?"

"Well, there was a bit of committee stuff, then a short talk with lantern slides by Mr. Walters from the water company, and we finished with a cake-making competition."

"Yes . . . yes . . . and what did Oscar do?"

She laughed. "Mixed with the company, apparently enjoyed the slides, and showed great interest in the cakes."

"I see. And you didn't bring him home?"

"No, he made his own way here. As you know, I have to pass your house and I merely rang your bell to make sure you knew he had arrived."

"I'm obliged to you, Miss Simpson. We were a little worried."

I mounted the stairs in record time. Helen was sitting with the cat on her knee and she looked up as I burst in.

"I know about Oscar now," I said.

"Know what?"

"Why he goes on these nightly outings. He's not running away—he's visiting."

"Visiting?"

"Yes," I said. "Don't you see? He likes getting around, he loves people, especially in groups, and he's interested in what they do. He's a natural mixer."

Helen looked down at the attractive mound of fur curled on her lap. "Of course . . . that's it . . . he's a socialite!"

"Exactly, a high stepper!"

"A cat-about-town!"

It all afforded us some innocent laughter and Oscar sat up and looked at us with evident pleasure, adding his own throbbing purr to the merriment. But for Helen and me there was a lot of relief behind it; ever since our cat had started his excursions, there had been the gnawing fear that we would lose him, and now we felt secure.

From that night our delight in him increased. There was endless joy in watching this facet of his character un-folding. He did the social round meticu-lously, taking in most of the activities of the town. He became a familiar figure at whist drives, jumble sales, school con-certs, and scout bazaars. Most of the time he was made welcome, but was twice ejected from meetings of the Rural District Council who did not seem to relish the idea of a cat sitting in on their deliberations.

At first I was apprehensive about his making his way through the streets, but I watched him once or twice and saw that he looked both ways before tripping daintily across. Clearly he had excellent traffic sense, and this made me feel that his original injury had not been caused by a car.

Taking it all in all, Helen and I felt that it was a kind stroke of fortune which had brought Oscar to us. He was a warm and cherished part of our home life. He added to our happiness.

When the blow fell it was totally unexpected.

I was finishing the evening surgery. I looked round the door and saw only a man and two little boys.

"Next, please," I said.

The man stood up. He had no animal with him. He was middle-aged, with the rough weathered face of a farm worker. He twirled a cloth cap nervously in his hands.

"Mr. Herriot?" he said.

"Yes, what can I do for you?"

He swallowed and looked me straight in the eyes. "Ah think you've got ma cat."

"What?"

"Ah lost ma cat a bit since." He cleared his throat. "We used to live at Missdon but ah got a job as ploughman to Mr. Horne of Wederly. It was after we moved to Wederly that t'cat went missin'. Ah reckon he was tryin' to find 'is way back to his old home."

"Wederly? That's on the other side of Brawton—over thirty miles away."

"Aye, ah knaw, but cats is funny things."

"But what makes you think I've got him?"

He twisted the cap around a bit more. "There's a cousin o' mine lives in Darrowby and ah heard tell from 'im about this cat goes around to meetin's.

I 'ad to come. We've been huntin' everywhere."

"Tell me," I said. "This cat you lost. What did he look like?"

"Gray and black and sort o' gingery. Right bonny 'e was. And 'e was allus goin' out to gatherin's."

A cold hand clutched at my heart. "You'd better come upstairs. Bring the boys with you."

Helen was putting some coal on the fire of the bedroom.

"Helen," I said. "This is Mr.—er— I'm sorry, I don't know your name."

"Gibbons, Sep Gibbons. They called me Septimus because ah was the seventh in family and it looks like ah'm goin' t'same way 'cause we've got six already. These are our two youngest." The two boys, obvious twins of about eight, looked up at us solemnly.

I wished my heart would stop hammering. "Mr. Gibbons thinks Oscar is his. He lost his cat some time ago."

My wife put down her little shovel. "Oh . . . oh . . . I see." She stood very still for a moment, then smiled faintly. "Do sit down. Oscar's in the kitchen. I'll bring him through."

She went out and reappeared with the cat in her arms. She hadn't got through the door before the little boys gave tongue.

"Tiger!" they cried. "Oh, Tiger, Tiger!"

The man's face seemed lit from within. He walked quickly across the floor and ran his big work-roughened hand along the fur.

"Hullo, awd lad," he said, and turned to me with a radiant smile. "It's 'im, Mr. Herriot. It's 'im awright, and don't 'e look well!"

"You call him Tiger, eh?" I said.

"Aye," he replied happily. "It's them gingery stripes. The kids called 'im that. They were brokenhearted when we lost 'im."

As the two little boys rolled on the floor, our Oscar rolled with them, pawing playfully, purring with delight.

Sep Gibbons sat down again. "That's the way 'e allus went on wi' the family. They used to play with 'im for hours. By gaw we did miss 'im. He were a right favorite."

I looked at the broken nails on the edge of the cap, at the decent, honest, uncomplicated Yorkshire face so like the many I had grown to like and respect. Farm men like him got thirty shillings a week in those days and it was reflected in the threadbare jacket, the cracked, shiny boots, and the obvious hand-me-downs of the boys.

But all three were scrubbed and tidy, the man's face like a red beacon, the children's knees gleaming and their hair carefully slicked across their foreheads. They looked like nice people to me. I didn't know what to say.

Helen said it for me. "Well, Mr. Gibbons." Her tone had an unnatural brightness. "You'd better take him."

The man hesitated. "Now then, are ye sure, Mrs. Herriot?"

"Yes . . . yes, I'm sure. He was your cat first."

"Aye, but some folks 'ud say finders keepers or summat like that. Ah didn't come 'ere to demand 'im back or owt of t'sort."

"I know you didn't, Mr. Gibbons, but you've had him all those years and you've searched for him so hard. We couldn't possibly keep him from you."

He nodded quickly. "Well, that's right good of ye." He paused for a mo-ment, his face serious, then he stooped and picked Oscar up. "We'll have to be off if we're goin' to catch the eight o'clock bus."

Helen reached forward, cupped the cat's head in her hands, and looked at him steadily for a few seconds. Then she patted the boys' heads. "You'll take good care of him, won't you?"

"Aye, missis, thank ye, we will that." The two small faces looked up at her and smiled.

"I'll see you down the stairs, Mr. Gibbons," I said.

On the descent I tickled the furry cheek resting on the man's shoulder and heard for the last time the rich purring. On the front doorstep we shook hands, and they set off down the street. As they rounded the corner of Trengate, they stopped and waved, and I waved back at the man, the two children, and the cat's head looking back at me over the shoulder.

It was my habit at that time in my life to mount the stairs two or three at a time, but on this occasion I trailed up-ward like an old man, slightly breathless, throat tight, eyes prickling.

I cursed myself for a sentimental fool, but as I reached our door I found a flash of consolation. Helen had taken it remarkably well. She had nursed that cat and grown deeply attached to him, and I'd have thought an unforeseen calamity like this would have upset her terribly. But no, she had behaved calmly and rationally.

It was up to me to do as well. I adjusted my features into the semblance of a cheerful smile and marched into the room.

Helen had pulled a chair close to the table and was slumped face down against the wood. One arm cradled her head while the other was stretched in front of her as her body shook with an utterly abandoned weeping.

I had never seen her like this and I was appalled. I tried to say something comforting but nothing stemmed the flow of racking sobs.

Feeling helpless and inadequate I could only sit close to her and stroke the back of her head. Maybe I could have said something if I hadn't felt just about as bad myself.

You get over these things in time. After all, we told ourselves, it wasn't as though Oscar had died or gotten lost again—he had gone to a good family who would look after him. In fact, he had really gone home.

And of course, we still had our much-loved Sam, although he didn't help in the early stages by sniffing disconsolately where Oscar's bed used to lie, then collapsing on the rug with a long lugubrious sigh.

There was one other thing, too. I had a little notion forming in my mind, an idea which I would spring on Helen when the time was right. It was about a month after that shattering night, and we were coming out of the cinema at Brawton at the end of our half day. I looked at my watch.

"Only eight o'clock," I said. "How about going to see Oscar?"

Helen looked at me in surprise. "You mean—drive on to Wederly?"

"Yes, it's only about five miles."

A smile crept slowly across her face. "That would be lovely. But do you think they would mind?"

"The Gibbons? No, I'm sure they wouldn't. Let's go."

Wederly was a big village and the ploughman's cottage was at the far end, a few yards beyond the Methodist chapel. I pushed open the garden gate and we walked down the path.

A busy-looking little woman answered my knock. She was drying her hands on a striped towel.

"Mrs. Gibbons?" I said.

"Aye, that's me."

"I'm James Herriot—and this is my wife."

Her eyes widened uncomprehendingly. Clearly the name meant nothing to her.

"We had your cat for a while," I added.

Suddenly she grinned and waved her towel at us. "Oh aye, ah remember now. Sep told me about you. Come in, come in!"

The big kitchen-living room was a tableau of life with six children and thirty shillings a week. Battered furniture, rows of much-mended washing on a pulley, black cooking range, and a general air of chaos.

Sep got up from his place by the fire, put down his newspaper, took off a pair of steel-rimmed spectacles, and shook hands.

He waved Helen to a sagging armchair. "Well, it's right nice to see you. Ah've often spoke of ye to t'missis."

His wife hung up her towel. "Yes, and I'm glad to meet ye both. I'll get some tea in a minnit."

She laughed and dragged a bucket of muddy water into a corner. "I've been washin' football jerseys. Them lads just handed them to me tonight—as if I haven't enough to do."

As she ran the water into the kettle, I peeped surreptitiously around me and I noticed Helen doing the same. But we searched in vain. There was no sign of a cat. Surely he couldn't have run away again? With a growing feeling of dismay, I realized that my little scheme could backfire devastatingly.

It wasn't until the tea had been made and poured that I dared to raise the subject.

"How——" I asked diffidently. "How is—er—Tiger?"

"Oh, he's grand," the little woman replied briskly. She glanced up at the clock on the mantelpiece. "He should be back any time now, then you'll be able to see 'im."

As she spoke, Sep raised a finger. "Ah think ah can hear 'im now."

He walked over and opened the door and our Oscar strode in with all his old grace and majesty. He took one look at Helen and leaped onto her lap. With a cry of delight she put down her cup and stroked the beautiful fur as the cat arched himself against her hand and the familiar purr echoed round the room.

"He knows me," she murmured. "He knows me."

Sep nodded and smiled. "He does that. You were good to 'im. He'll never forget ye, and we won't either, will we, Mother?"

"No, we won't, Mrs. Herriot," his wife said as she applied butter to a slice of gingerbread. "That was a kind thing ye did for us and I 'ope you'll come and see us all whenever you're near."

"Well, thank you," I said. "We'd love to—we're often in Brawton."

I went over and tickled Oscar's chin, then I turned again to Mrs. Gibbons. "By the way, it's after nine o'clock. Where has he been till now?"

She poised her butter knife and looked into space.

"Let's see, now," she said. "It's Thursday, isn't it? Ah yes, it's 'is night for the Yoga class."

1. Why is Jim shocked when he examines the cat?

2. Jim wants to put the cat out of its misery. Why does he change his mind?

3. After the operation, Jim says that he has a "feeling of sweeping undesirable things under the carpet." What does he expect to happen to the cat?

4. Jim and Helen decide to keep the cat, and they work together to make him well. (a) How does Helen help the cat? (b) How does Oscar help himself?

5. What secret aspect of Oscar's personality do Helen and Jim discover?

6. (a) Why do the Herriots decide to return Oscar to the Gibbons? (b) Do you think they made the right decision? Why or why not?

The Personal Narrative

A personal narrative is a true story written by the person who had the experience. Usually, the author appears as a character in the story and narrates, or tells, the story in the first person.

1. James Herriot appears in the story as the character Jim. What pronoun does he use to refer to himself?

2. (a) Who is Helen? (b) Who is Tristan?

3. Herriot has written several books about his experiences as a veterinarian in northern England. Based on this story from his book *All Things Wise and Wonderful,* how do you think Herriot feels about the animals he takes care of? Find details in the story to support your answer.

Activities

1. **Composition.** Write a newspaper advertisement for a lost-and-found column asking for the return of Tiger. Be sure to include a careful description of Tiger's appearance.

2. **Composition.** Write a paragraph telling about your experiences with an unusual animal. (If you have never had a pet, make up one and write about an imaginary event.)

SENTENCE MEANING

Using Quotation Marks

Quotation marks signal that you are reading the exact words a character speaks in a story. These marks set off the direct speech from the rest of the text. Notice that the quotation marks in the following example set off Jim's exact words.

> "Thanks again, Marjorie," I called after the retreating back. "And don't worry—we'll look after him."

When two or more characters are speaking to one another, quotation marks help you determine who is saying what.

> At last he looked up at me and gulped. "I don't fancy this much, Jim. Can't we do something?"
> "You mean, put that lot back?"
> "Yes."

The opening (") and closing (") quotation marks tell you where the exact words of a character begin and where they end. The paragraph indentation tells you that the speaker changes. (The paragraph indentation signals a new speaker only when the quotation before it ends with a closed quotation mark.) The order of quotations helps you determine who is saying what. In the above dialogue, first Tristan is speaking, then Jim, then Tristan again.

► Read the passage below. Jim (I) is speaking to Helen. Then answer the questions that follow the passage.

> "What's happened?" I asked.
> "It's Oscar—he's gone!"
> "Gone? What do you mean?"
> "Oh, Jim, I think he's run away."
> I stared at her. "He wouldn't do that. He often goes down to the garden at night. Are you sure he isn't there?"
> "Absolutely. I've searched right into the yard. I've even had a walk round the town. And remember." Her chin quivered. "He . . . he ran away from somewhere before."

a. Who says, "It's Oscar—he's gone"?
b. Who says, "Gone? What do you mean?"
c. Who says, "I think he's run away"?
d. Who says, "He wouldn't do that"?
e. Who says that he ran away before?

WORD ATTACK

Using a Glossary

You can find the pronunciation, part of speech, and meaning of a word you may not know in the glossary at the back of this book. The words in the glossary are listed in alphabetical order.

Look at the word *lugubrious* in the following sentence:

"And of course, we still had our much-loved Sam, although he didn't help in the early stages by sniffing disconsolately where Oscar's bed used to lie, then collapsing on the rug with a long *lugubrious* sigh."

There is a good chance you are not familiar with this word. When you look it up in the glossary, you will find the following information.

lugubrious (lo͞o-go͞o′ brē-əs) *adj.*: Extremely sad or mournful.

The symbols in parentheses (lo͞o-go͞o′ brē-əs) tell you how to pronounce this word. You can find a key to these symbols at the front of the glossary. The accent mark (′) tells you which syllable to stress. The abbreviation *adj.* means this word is an adjective. Other abbreviations you may see are *n.* for noun, *v.* for verb, *prep.* for preposition, and *adv.* for adverb. After the colon (:) you will find the definition of the word.

---

1. The following words are from "Cat-About-Town." Look up each word in the glossary. On a separate piece of paper, copy the complete glossary entry for each one.
    a. pelvis
    b. abdomen
    c. ventral
    d. emaciated
    e. suture
    f. ancestry
    g. saunter
    h. medley
    i. distraught
    j. despondent

2. From the list of words in Exercise **1,** choose a word to complete each sentence below.
    a. Oscar was quite _____ and sickly; he had little flesh on his bones.
    b. Jim had to _____ the muscle with catgut.
    c. Oscar's coat was a _____ of bright, unusual colors.
    d. Tristan thought that Oscar must have a ginger Tom somewhere in his _____.
    e. Helen and Jim were very sad and missed Oscar deeply; even Sam seemed _____.

Last Cover

Paul Annixter

Father warned, "Half of that little critter has to love, but the other half is a wild hunter."

I'm not sure I can tell you what you want to know about my brother; but everything about the pet fox is important, so I'll tell all that from the beginning.

It goes back to a winter afternoon after I'd hunted the woods all day for a sign of our lost pet. I remember the way my mother looked up as I came into the kitchen. Without my speaking, she knew what had happened. For six hours I had walked, reading signs, looking for a delicate print in the damp soil or even a hair that might have told of a red fox passing that way—but I had found nothing.

"Did you go up in the foothills?" Mom asked.

I nodded. My face was stiff from held-back tears. My brother, Colin, who was going on twelve, got it all from one look at me and went into a heartbroken, almost silent, crying.

Three weeks before, Bandit, the pet fox Colin and I had raised from a tiny kit, had disappeared, and not even a rumor had been heard of him since.

"He'd have had to go off soon anyway," Mom comforted. "A big, lolloping fellow like him, he's got to live his life same as us. But he may come back. That fox set a lot of store by you boys in spite of his wild ways."

"He set a lot of store by our food, anyway," Father said. He sat in a chair by the kitchen window mending a piece of harness. "We'll be seeing a lot more of that fellow, never fear. That fox learned to pine for table scraps and young chickens. He was getting to be an egg thief, too,

and he's not likely to forget that."

"That was only pranking when he was little," Colin said desperately.

From the first, the tame fox had made tension in the family. It was Father who said we'd better name him Bandit, after he'd made away with his first young chicken.

"Maybe you know," Father said shortly. "But when an animal turns to egg sucking, he's usually incurable. He'd better not come pranking around my chicken run again."

It was late February, and I remember the bleak, dead cold that had set in, cold that was a rare thing for our Carolina hills. Flocks of sparrows and snowbirds had appeared to peck hungrily at all that the pigs and chickens didn't eat.

"This one's a killer," Father would say of a morning, looking out at the whitened barn roof. "This one will make the shoats[1] squeal."

---

1. shoats (shōtz) n.: Young pigs that have just been weaned.

A fire snapped all day in our cookstove and another in the stone fireplace in the living room, but still the farmhouse was never warm. The leafless woods were bleak and empty, and I spoke of that to Father when I came back from my search.

"It's always a sad time in the woods when the seven sleepers are under cover," he said.

"What sleepers are they?" I asked. Father was full of woods lore.

"Why, all the animals that have got sense enough to hole up and stay hid in weather like this. Let's see, how was it the old rhyme named them?

> Surly bear and sooty bat,
> Brown chuck and masked coon,
> Chippy-munk and sly skunk,
> And all the mouses
> 'Cept in men's houses.

"And man would have joined them and made it eight, Granther Yeary always said, if he'd had a little more sense."

"I was wondering if the red fox mightn't make it eight," Mom said.

Father shook his head. "Late winter's a high time for foxes. Time when they're out deviling, not sleeping."

My chest felt hollow. I wanted to cry like Colin over our lost fox, but at fourteen a boy doesn't cry. Colin had squatted down on the floor and got out his small hammer and nails to start another new frame for a new picture. Maybe then he'd make a drawing for the frame and be able to forget his misery. It had been that way with him since he was five.

I thought of the new dress Mom had brought home a few days before in a heavy cardboard box. That box cover would be fine for Colin to draw on. I spoke of it, and Mom's glance thanked me as she went to get it. She and I worried a lot about Colin. He was small for his age, delicate and blond, his hair much lighter and softer than mine, his eyes deep and wide and blue. He was often sick, and I knew the fear Mom had that he might be predestined. I'm just ordinary, like Father. I'm the sort of stuff that can take it—tough and strong—but Colin was always sort of special.

Mom lighted the lamp. Colin began cutting his white cardboard carefully, fitting it into his frame. Father's sharp glance turned on him now and again.

"There goes the boy making another frame before there's a picture for it," he said. "It's too much like cutting out a man's suit for a fellow that's, say, twelve years old. Who knows whether he'll grow into it?"

Mom was into him then, quick. "Not a single frame of Colin's has ever gone to waste. The boy has real talent, Sumter, and it's time you realized it."

"Of course he has," Father said. "All kids have 'em. But they get over 'em.

"It isn't the pox we're talking of," Mom sniffed.

"In a way it is. Ever since you started talking up Colin's art, I've had an invalid for help around the place."

Father wasn't as hard as he made out, I knew, but he had to hold a balance against all Mom's frothing. For him, the thing was the land and all that pertained to it. I was following in Father's footsteps, true to form, but Colin threatened to break the family tradition with his leaning toward art, with Mom "aiding and abetting him," as Father liked to put it. For the past two years she had had dreams of my brother becoming a real artist and going away to the city to study.

It wasn't that Father had no understanding of such things. I could remember, through the years, Colin lying on his stomach in the front room making pencil sketches, and how a good drawing would catch Father's eye halfway across the room, and how he would sometimes gather up two or three of them to study, frowning and muttering, one hand in his beard, while a great pride rose in Colin, and in me too. Most of Colin's drawings were of the woods and wild things, and there Father was a master critic. He made out to scorn what seemed to him a passive "white-livered" interpretation of nature through brush and pencil instead of rod and rifle.

At supper that night Colin could scarcely eat. Ever since he'd been able to walk, my brother had had a growing love of wild things, but Bandit had been like his very own, a gift of the woods. One afternoon a year and a half before, Father and Laban Small had been running a vixen through the hills with their dogs. With the last of her strength the she-fox had made for her den, not far from our house. The dogs had overtaken her and killed her just before she reached it. When Father and Laban came up, they'd found Colin crouched nearby holding her cub in his arms.

Father had been for killing the cub, which was still too young to shift for itself, but Colin's grief had brought Mom into it. We'd taken the young fox into the kitchen; all of us, except Father, gone a bit silly over the little thing. Colin had held it in his arms and fed it warm milk from a spoon.

"Watch out with all your soft ways," Father had warned, standing in the doorway. "You'll make too much of him. Remember, you can't make a dog out of a fox. Half of that little critter has to love, but the other half is a wild hunter. You boys will mean a whole lot to him while he's a kit, but there'll come a day when you won't mean a thing to him and he'll leave you shorn."

For two weeks after that Colin had nursed the cub, weaning it from milk to bits of meat. For a year they were always together. The cub grew fast. It was soon following Colin and me about the barnyard. It turned out to be a patch fox, with a saddle of darker fur across its shoulders.

I haven't the words to tell you what the fox meant to us. It was far more wonderful owning him than owning any dog. There was something rare and secret like the spirit of the woods about him, and back of his calm, straw-gold eyes was the sense of a brain the equal of a man's. The fox became Colin's whole life.

Each day, going and coming from school, Colin and I took long side trips through the woods, looking for Bandit. Wild things' memories were short, we knew; we'd have to find him soon or the old bond would be broken.

Ever since I was ten I'd been allowed to hunt with Father, so I was good at reading signs. But, in a way, Colin knew more about the woods and wild things than Father or me. What came to me from long observation, Colin seemed to know by instinct.

It was Colin who felt out, like an Indian, the stretch of woods where Bandit had his den, who found the first slim, small fox-print in the damp earth. And then, on an afternoon in March, we saw him. I remember the day well, the racing clouds, the wind rattling the tops of the pine trees and swaying the Spanish moss. Bandit had just come out of a clump of laurel; in the maze of leaves behind him we caught a glimpse of a slim red vixen, so we knew he had found a mate. She melted from sight like a shadow, but Bandit turned to watch us, his mouth open, his tongue lolling as he smiled his old foxy smile. On his thin chops, I saw a telltale chicken feather.

Colin moved silently forward, his movements so quiet and casual he seemed to be standing still. He called Bandit's name, and the fox held his ground, drawn to us with all his senses. For a few moments he let Colin actually put an arm about him. It was then I knew that he loved us still, for all of Father's warnings. He really loved us back, with a fierce, secret love no tame thing ever gave. But the urge of his life just then was toward his new mate. Suddenly, he whirled about and disappeared in the laurels.

Colin looked at me with glowing eyes. "We haven't really lost him, Stan. When he gets through with his spring sparking he may come back. But we've got to show ourselves to him a lot, so he won't forget."

"It's a go," I said.

"Promise not to say a word to Father," Colin said, and I agreed. For I knew by the chicken feather that Bandit had been up to no good.

A week later the woods were budding and the thickets were rustling with all manner of wild things. Colin managed to get a glimpse of Bandit every few days. He couldn't get close though, for the spring running was a lot more important to a fox than any human beings were.

Every now and then Colin got out his framed box cover and looked at it, but he never drew anything on it; he never even picked up his pencil. I remember wondering if what Father had said about framing a picture before you had one had spoiled something for him.

I was helping Father with the planting now, but Colin managed to be in the woods every day. By degrees he learned Bandit's range, where he drank and rested, and where he was likely to be according to the time of day. One day he told me how he had petted Bandit again, and how they had walked together a long

way in the woods. All this time we had kept his secret from Father.

As summer came on, Bandit began to live up to the prediction Father had made. Accustomed to human beings, he moved without fear about the scattered farms of the region, raiding barns and hen runs that other foxes wouldn't have dared go near. And he taught his wild mate to do the same. Almost every night they got into some poultry house, and by late June Bandit was not only killing chickens and ducks, but feeding on eggs and young chicks whenever he got the chance.

Stories of his doings came to us from many sources, for he was still easily recognized by the dark patch on his shoulders. Many a farmer took a shot at him as he fled and some of them set out on his trail with dogs, but they always returned home without even sighting him. Bandit was familiar with all the dogs in the region, and he knew a hundred tricks to confound them. He got a reputation that year beyond that of any fox our hills had known. His confidence grew, and he gave up wild hunting altogether and lived entirely off the poultry farmers. By September the hill farmers banded together to hunt him down.

It was Father who brought home that news one night. All time-honored rules of the fox chase were to be broken in this hunt; if the dogs couldn't bring Bandit down, he was to be shot on sight. I was stricken and furious. I remember the misery of Colin's face in the lamplight. Father, who took pride in all the ritual of the hunt, had refused to be a party to such an affair, though in justice he could do nothing but sanction any sort of hunt, for Bandit, as old Sam Wetherwax put it, had been "purely getting in the Lord's hair."

The hunt began next morning, and it was the biggest turnout our hills had known. There were at least twenty mounted men in the party and as many dogs. Father and I were working in the lower field as they passed along the river road. Most of the hunters carried rifles, and they looked ugly.

Twice during the morning I went up to the house to find Colin, but he was nowhere around. As we worked, Father and I could follow the progress of the hunt by the distant hound music on the breeze. We could tell just where the hunters first caught sight of the fox and where Bandit was leading the dogs during the first hour. We knew as well as if we'd seen it how Bandit roused another fox along Turkey Branch and forced it to run for him, and how the dogs swept after it for twenty minutes before they sensed their mistake.

Noon came, and Colin had not come in to eat. After dinner Father didn't go back to the field. He moped about, listening to the hound talk. He didn't like what was on anymore than I did, and now and again I caught his smile of satisfaction when we heard the broken, angry notes of the hunting horn, telling that the dogs had lost the trail or had run another fox.

I was restless, and I went up into the hills in midafternoon. I ranged the woods for miles, thinking all the time of Colin. Time lost all meaning for me, and the short day was nearing an end, when I heard the horn talking again, telling that the fox had put over another trick. All day he had deviled the dogs and mocked the hunters. This new trick and the coming night would work to save him. I was wildly glad, as I moved down toward Turkey Branch and stood listening for a time by the deep, shaded pool where for years we boys had gone swimming, sailed boats, and dreamed summer dreams.

Suddenly, out of the corner of my eye, I saw the sharp ears and thin, pointed mask of a fox—in the water almost beneath me. It was Bandit, craftily submerged there, all but his head, resting in the cool water of the pool and the shadow of the two big beeches that spread above it. He must have run forty miles or more since morning. And he must have hidden in this place before. His knowing, crafty mask blended perfectly with the shadows and a mass of drift and branches that had collected by the bank of the pool. He was so still that a pair of thrushes flew up from the spot as I came up, not knowing he was there.

Bandit's bright, harried eyes were looking right at me. But I did not look at him direct. Some woods instinct, swifter than thought, kept me from it. So he and I met as in another world, indirectly, with feeling but without sign or greeting.

Suddenly I saw that Colin was standing almost beside me. Silently as a water snake, he had come out of the bushes and stood there. Our eyes met, and a quick and secret smile passed between us. It was a rare moment in which I really "met" my brother, when something of his essence flowed into me and I knew all of him. I've never lost it since.

My eyes still turned from the fox, my heart pounding. I moved quietly away, and Colin moved with me. We whistled softly as we went, pretending to busy ourselves along the bank of the stream. There was magic in it, as if by will we wove a web of protection about the fox, a ring-pass-not that none might penetrate. It was so, too, we felt, in the brain of Bandit, and that doubled the charm. To us he was still our little pet that we had carried about in our arms on countless summer afternoons.

Two hundred yards upstream, we stopped beside slim, fresh tracks in the mud where Bandit had entered the branch. The tracks angled upstream. But in the water the wily creature had turned down.

We climbed the far bank to wait, and Colin told me how Bandit's secret had been his secret ever since an afternoon three months before, when he'd watched the fox swim downstream to hide in the deep pool. Today he'd waited on the bank, feeling that Bandit, hard pressed by the dogs, might again seek the pool for sanctuary.

We looked back once as we turned homeward. He still had not moved. We didn't know until later that he was killed that same night by a chance hunter, as he crept out from his hiding place.

That evening Colin worked a long time on his framed box cover that had lain about the house untouched all sum-

mer. He kept at it all the next day too. I had never seen him work so hard. I seemed to sense in the air the feeling he was putting into it, how he was *believing* his picture into being. It was evening before he finished it. Without a word he handed it to Father. Mom and I went and looked over his shoulder.

It was a delicate and intricate pencil drawing of the deep branch pool, and there was Bandit's head and watching, fear-filled eyes hiding there amid the leaves and shadows, woven craftily into the maze of twigs and branches, as if by nature's art itself. Hardly a fox there at all, but the place where he was—or should have been. I recognized it in-

stantly, but Mom gave a sort of incredulous sniff.

"I'll declare," she said. "It's mazy as
a puzzle. It just looks like a lot of sticks
and leaves to me."

Long minutes of study passed before
Father's eye picked out the picture's
secret, as few men's could have done. I
laid that to Father's being a born hunter.
That was a picture that might have been
done especially for him. In fact, I guess it
was.

Finally he turned to Colin with his
deep, slow smile. "So that's how Bandit
fooled them all," he said. He sat holding
the picture with a sort of tenderness for a
long time, while we glowed in the
warmth of the shared secret. That was
Colin's moment. Colin's art stopped being a pox to Father right there. And later,
when the time came for Colin to go to art
school, it was Father who was his solid
backer.

Close Up

1. Stan is tough and strong, while his brother Colin is delicate and often sick. What does Stan mean when he says that Mother fears that Colin may be predestined?

2. Find two reasons for Father's objecting to Colin's art.

3. (a) How does the pet fox create tension in the family? (b) Why does Father decide to call the fox Bandit?

4. After Bandit disappears, Colin finds the fox in the woods. (a) How does Bandit show that he still loves Colin? (b) What tell-tale sign shows that Bandit is also a wild hunter?

5. How does Colin maintain his bond with Bandit?

6. (a) Why does Colin's picture of Bandit show Father that they value the same things? (b) Why does this picture make Father respect Colin's talent?

7. Why do you think this story is called "Last Cover"?

The Short Story

A short story is a brief work of fiction about made-up characters and events. Usually the story involves a conflict or problem that must be solved. The *climax* occurs when the conflict reaches its highest point of intensity. The *resolution* occurs when the conflict ends.

1. (a) List the characters in "Last Cover." (b) Which character do you think is the most important? Why?

2. The main conflict in this story is between Colin and Father. What two things does Father want Colin to give up?

3. At what point does this conflict reach its highest point of intensity?

4. How is this conflict resolved?

Activities

1. Work with a group of your classmates to compile a booklet of woodcraft.

2. Many painters have managed to capture the secrets of nature. Bring in some reproductions of nature paintings by an artist whose work you like. You can find reproductions in a book about the artist or in the vertical file at the library. (If you like, you may select one of the following artists: Thomas Hart Benton, John James Audubon, Winslow Homer, or Georgia O'Keefe.)

SENTENCE MEANING

Using Punctuation Marks

Punctuation marks are signals that help you to read sentences. They tell you when to pause and when to come to a full stop. For example, try reading the following sentence without pausing between groups of words.

> "Three weeks before Bandit the pet fox Colin and I had raised from a tiny kit had disappeared and not even a rumor had been heard of him since."

Read the same sentence, taking a slight pause after each comma.

> "Three weeks before, Bandit, the pet fox Colin and I had raised from a tiny kit, had disappeared, and not even a rumor had been heard of him since."

Three punctuation marks signal the end of a sentence or complete thought. These are the period **(.)**, the semicolon **(;)**, and the question mark **(?)**. The period and the question mark tell you to take a long pause before reading the next sentence. The semicolon tells you to take a slightly shorter pause than you would for a period, since it separates thoughts that are closely related.

Two other punctuation marks are the comma **(,)** and the dash **(—)**. They separate groups of words within the sentence and break up the sentence into readable parts. Both tell you to pause before reading the next group of words.

▶ Copy the following sentences on a separate piece of paper. Then find each sentence in the story and add the punctuation marks. (Remember: If you add a period, be sure to capitalize the letter following the period.)

   a. "For six hours I had walked reading signs looking for a delicate print in the damp soil or even a hair that might have told of a red fox passing that way but I had found nothing." (Add , , —)

   b. "I'm not sure I can tell you what you want to know about my brother but everything about the pet fox is important so I'll tell all that from the beginning." (Add ; ,)

   c. "I'm just ordinary like Father I'm the sort of stuff that can take it tough and strong but Colin was always sort of special." (Add , . — —)

   d. "Father wasn't as hard as he made out I knew but he had to hold a balance against all Mom's frothing for him the

thing was the land and all that pertained to it." (Add
, , .)

e. "Wild things' memories were short we knew we'd have to
find him soon or the old bond would be broken."
(Add , ;)

f. "Noon came and Colin had not come in to eat after dinner
Father didn't go back to the field." (Add , .)

WORD ATTACK

Choosing the Meaning That Fits the Context

Many words in English have more than one meaning. When you read, you must choose the meaning that fits the context. For example, the word *run* can mean: (1) a race that runners take part in; (2) a trip or journey; or (3) an enclosed area in which chickens or other fowl are kept. Now look at this sentence.

"He'd better not come pranking around my chicken *run* again."

Only the third meaning of *run* fits this context.

▶ Read each sentence below. From the two meanings following each sentence, choose the meaning that fits the context.

a. "That fox learned to ⎵ne for table scraps and young chickens."
   (1) to feel grief
   (2) to yearn for or desire

b. "From the first, the tame fox had made *tension* in the family."
   (1) strained relationships or uneasiness
   (2) pressure of a gas

c. ". . . Father and Laban Small had been *running* a vixen through the hills with their dogs."
   (1) chasing or pursuing
   (2) moving quickly

d. "It was Colin who felt out, like an Indian, the *stretch* of woods where Bandit had his den."
   (1) a section of a race course
   (2) an unbroken piece of land

e. "On his thin *chops*, I saw a telltale chicken feather."
   (1) a cut of meat
   (2) jaw or cheek

The Meadow Mouse

Theodore Roethke

-I-

In a shoe box stuffed in an old nylon stocking
Sleeps the baby mouse I found in the meadow,
Where he trembled and shook beneath a stick
Till I caught him up by the tail and brought him in,
5   Cradled in my hand,
A little quaker, the whole body of him trembling,
His absurd whiskers sticking out like a cartoon-mouse,
His feet like small leaves,
Little lizard-feet,
10 Whitish and spread wide when he tried to struggle away,
Wriggling like a miniscule puppy.

Now he's eaten his three kinds of cheese and drunk from
     his bottle-cap watering-trough——
So much he just lies in one corner,
His tail curled under him, his belly big
15 As his head; his bat-like ears
Twitching, tilting toward the least sound.

Do I imagine he no longer trembles
When I come close to him?
He seems no longer to tremble.

-II-

20 But this morning the shoe-box house on the back porch is empty.
Where has he gone, my meadow mouse,
My thumb of a child that nuzzled in my palm?——
To run under the hawk's wing,
Under the eye of the great owl watching from the elm-tree,
25 To live by the courtesy of the shrike, the snake, the tom-cat.
I think of the nestling fallen into the deep grass,
The turtle gasping in the dusty rubble of the highway,
The paralytic stunned in the tub, and the water rising,——
All things innocent, hapless, forsaken.

1. Why does the poet describe the mouse as "a little quaker"?

2. (a) How does the mouse change after it eats the three kinds of cheese? (b) Why do you think the poet hopes that the mouse no longer trembles?

3. In the second part of the poem, the mouse has left the shoe-box house. What does the poet fear will happen to the mouse?

4. Reread lines 25–29. How do you think the poet feels about all fragile and helpless creatures?

The Lyric Poem

A lyric poem is a short work in verse that expresses an emotional response to a person, place, object, or idea. Usually, it contains colorful images and comparisons that help create a vivid picture in the reader's mind. For example, "A little quaker, the whole body of him trembling,/His absurd whiskers sticking out like a cartoon-mouse." Many lyric poems are about nature.

1. (a) To what does the poet compare the mouse's feet? (b) To what does he compare the mouse's wriggling movements?

2. (a) How do these comparisons make you feel about the mouse? (b) How do you think the poet feels about the mouse? Why?

3. In line 22, the poet calls the mouse, "My thumb of a child that nuzzled in my palm." On the basis of this image, how do you think the poet feels about the mouse?

4. (a) What five creatures are mentioned in lines 23–25? (b) How are these creatures different from the mouse?

5. This poem is written in *free verse*. This means that there is no regular rhyme or rhythmic pattern. Do you think this makes the poem *more* or *less* effective? Why?

Activities

1. Find a lyric poem about another helpless creature. Read it aloud to your classmates.

2. **Composition.** Use your imagination to complete the following comparisons.
   a. The mouse trembled like _____.
   b. It lapped up the milk like _____.
   c. It scurried across the floor like _____.
   d. Its eyes were as bright as _____.

SENTENCE MEANING

Using Punctuation to Read Sentences in Poetry

Some poetry is written to be read aloud. The poet tells you when to pause, to stop, and to change the pitch of your voice by using punctuation marks.

Commas (,), dashes (—), and semicolons (;) tell you to pause. (Remember to pause slightly longer for a semicolon than for a comma.) Periods (.), question marks (?), and exclamation marks (!) tell you to stop. A question mark also tells you to raise the pitch of your voice. An exclamation mark tells you to say something with emphasis.

1. Read aloud the first eleven lines of this poem, pausing at each comma and stopping at the period.

2. Look at lines 12–16. Which punctuation mark tells you to take a longer pause than you would for a comma?

3. Read aloud lines 17–19. Remember to raise the pitch of your voice at the end of line 18.

4. Look at the second part of this poem. (a) How many times should you pause? (b) How many times should you stop?

WORD ATTACK

Using a Pronunciation Key

In English, many letters stand for more than one sound. For example, the letter *e* may stand for the vowel sound you hear in *beg* or the vowel sound in *be*.

You can find out how to pronounce a word by looking it up in a dictionary or glossary. Following the entry word, you will find diacritical marks in parentheses. For example: rub·ble (rub′əl). These marks tell you how to pronounce each of the letters in the word. The key to these marks is found either at the bottom of the dictionary page or at the front of the glossary.

1. Look up each of the following words in the glossary. On a separate piece of paper, write the diacritical marks you find after each word.
   a. quake
   b. absurd
   c. cartoon
   d. minuscule
   e. shrike
   f. trough
   g. twitch
   h. nuzzle
   i. nestle
   j. paralytic

2. Say aloud each of the words in Exercise **1**. Then answer the following questions.
   a. Does the *a* in *quake* sound like the *a* in *quart* or in *tape*?
   b. Does the *a* in *cartoon* sound like the *a* in *barge* or in *that*?
   c. Does the *i* in *shrike* sound like the *i* in *big* or in *line*?
   d. Does the *c* in *cartoon* sound like the *c* in *court* or in *center*?
   e. Which letter is silent in *nestle*?
   f. Does the *u* in *nuzzle* sound like the *u* in *ugly* or in *use*?
   g. Does the *gh* in *trough* sound like the *gh* in *tough* or in *ghost*?
   h. Does the *ou* in *trough* sound like the *ou* in *cough* or in *count*?
   i. Does the first *u* in *minuscule* sound like the *u* in *minus* or in *minute*?
   j. Does the second *u* in *minuscule* sound like the *u* in *rule* or in *mule*?

Unforgettable Grizzly Bears

George Laycock

**He learned the hard way
that it is a mistake to sneak up
on a grizzly bear.**

Every time a cowboy rode the trails of western Montana around 1902, he scanned the ground for the tracks of a very special grizzly bear. The animal was the biggest and most powerful grizzly in the area, and he had developed what the ranchers considered some very bad eating habits.

This renegade first became known when it caught one front foot in a bear trap. The trap was chained to a heavy log, but the bear dragged it a quarter of a mile into the brush, log and all. When the trapper found his trap, all that it held were the tips of three toes.

After that, the big bear left a recognizable footprint. A rancher would find the track around his corral and say, "Well, Old Two Toes has paid us another visit."

One night Old Two Toes slipped up on a cow camp and swatted a full-grown cow on the head, dropping her dead in her tracks. She didn't even have time to bawl. The bear killed two more cows, then departed at his leisure. He was starting a long career of big trouble for the cow country. At another camp a big bear climbed into the chuck wagon, ate some

of the grub, then reduced what was left to a shambles. He left his mark in the dust beside the wagon. Old Two Toes had struck again.

He went right on striking for several years, adding calves, cows, and colts to his record. He was a specialist at slipping up on a ranch, killing a steer or two, eating what he wanted, then vanishing before anyone discovered his presence. This infuriated ranchers. They organized and raised money for a reward to be paid to the person who killed Old Two Toes.

But chasing the big bear was risky business. One hunter wounded a bear he thought was Two Toes and followed the bloody trail into the mountains. The brush got thicker and thicker, and the hunter was pushing hard. Suddenly a monstrous bear, growling and snorting, rushed out of a thicket and bore down upon him.

There was barely time to get off one fast shot. It only grazed the bear, which swatted the hunter with one of those broad front paws and sent him flying into the brush, where he lay for a long time, knocked out colder than a Popsicle. While he lay there, quiet and peaceful, the bear bent the barrel of his rifle and split the stock. For the rest of his life that bear hunter limped badly when he walked. He had found Old Two Toes—and learned that it is bad medicine to sneak up on a grizzly.

Then one day, far up in the mountains, a wrangler was taking a string of pack horses across a narrow twisting trail. The horses were crowded close to the inside of the trail because on the other side was a cliff that fell straight down to a creek a quarter of a mile below. The pack string was inching around a hairpin curve when on the mountainside above them, Old Two Toes suddenly rose to his full height to see what in the world was going by.

The bear had the advantage. He came rushing down the hillside and the horses panicked. One of them stumbled over the cliff to its death far below. The wrangler and the rest of his horses were milling about, each trying to stay away from the edge of the cliff. The man had his rifle in his hands by the time his horse threw him off. He crawled back from the edge just in time to get off a fast shot at the charging bear. But it took two more shots at close range before the giant bear fell dead at the wrangler's feet. That was the end of Two Toes. He was about fifteen years old and weighed half a ton. The wrangler who killed him was given the $575 reward; he said he wouldn't care to do it again for twice as much.

Grizzly bears and people never have made good neighbors. People seldom want grizzlies coming close to them or their livestock, and the bears would prefer never to see a human. The bears have good reasons for wanting nothing to do with people. Wherever people have found the big, humpbacked beasts, they have tried their best to kill them—sometimes for no reason—and this has gone on since Lewis and Clark first reported the grizzly bears.

As a result, these wilderness bears vanished as farms and ranches pushed them from state after state. Today, with perhaps 1,000 to 1,200 grizzly bears living south of Canada, most of them in Idaho, Wyoming, and Montana, the animal is a threatened one. Grizzlies are still secure in parts of Alaska and northern Canada.

Even if the grizzlies vanish, stories

about them will live on. Some grizzlies have become legends. About a decade before Two Toes was earning his reputation in Montana, Wyoming had a famous grizzly known as "Bloody Paws." Bloody Paws did for sheep what Two Toes did for cattle. This bear was said to have dispatched more than 500 sheep, including fifty-two in a single night.

Then one afternoon, rancher Jack Madden and Bloody Paws surprised each other at short range right in the middle of a mountain trail. Madden's horse promptly threw his rider, then wheeled and raced for the safety of the ranch, carrying the rancher's rifle with him in the saddle scabbard. With lightning speed, Madden unholstered his .44 and emptied it at the grizzly at point-blank range. The bear dropped, only three paces from him. The sheepmen gave Madden a $375 reward.

But perhaps the best known of all renegade grizzly bears was the one that roamed the mountain cattle country of southern Colorado. This one was known as Old Mose. During his career Old Mose was shot and injured many times, but he seemed to lead a charmed life.

Then Jake Ratcliff said he would give Old Mose something to think about, and he and two friends set off into the hills. One afternoon Ratcliff came upon a freshly killed steer. The prints of Old Mose were plain all around it. A strange tingling sensation crept up the hunter's back. The old bear must be close by.

Minutes later, Ratcliff came upon Old Mose in a clump of small trees and began firing at him. But the bear seemed to ignore the bullets. He rushed the man who was causing this pain and side-swiped Ratcliff with a huge paw, lifting him into the air. Ratcliff landed in the brush with the biggest bear he had ever seen all over him. The man knew that if he fought back he was a goner, so he lay as still as he could. After a while the bear stopped clawing and biting him and began to walk away.

But such a bear will often stop and look back. If he sees a spark of life in the enemy, he may rush back to finish the job. Ratcliff made the mistake of slowly moving his head to see if the bear was gone, and found himself staring into the dark eyes of Old Mose, who promptly returned to the attack.

Ratcliff was still living when his companions found him, and he told them what had happened. That night Ratcliff died and word flashed through the ranch country: Old Mose had become a man-killer. Finally, in 1904, another hunter dropped him on the mountainside, and became a local hero.

All of these and many other famous outlaw bears had some things in common. Each had been shot at and wounded. Some had managed to free themselves from traps. It is possible that the pain of old wounds helped cause their cranky dispositions. Left to themselves, perhaps none of these famous grizzlies would have become outlaws.

In recent years there have been several instances of attacks on people by grizzly bears. Most of these attacks did not have to happen. Grizzlies are most likely to attack if a person gets too close when they are feeding or protecting their young, or when they think they have been cornered.

Nobody should think he can outrun a grizzly. Climbing a tree may save you. The next best thing, if you are very close to a grizzly that charges you, is to stand or lie perfectly still—no matter how much nerve it takes. Better yet, never approach a bear, any bear, in the wild. When hiking in grizzly bear country, making noise is a good idea.

Even people attacked by grizzly bears sometimes defend them. One young hiker mauled by a grizzly in a national park argued with rangers to save the bear. He claimed the trouble was his fault. "I was in the bear's territory," he said.

If more people had thought this way there might be more of these magnificent wilderness creatures left today. There might also have been fewer unforgettable renegades.

Close Up

1. (a) How did Old Two Toes get its name? (b) Why did the ranchers offer a reward for Old Two Toes?

2. Why did Bloody Paws become a legend?

3. (a) Why did Old Mose try to kill Jake Ratcliff? (b) What fatal mistake did Ratcliff make?

4. Do you think Old Mose was really a man-killer? Why or why not?

The Essay

An essay is a short composition about one topic. In the essay, the author shares his or her thoughts and feelings about the topic and reaches certain conclusions.

An essay is nonfiction. This means that it gives factual information and tells about events that really occurred.

1. The topic of this essay is grizzly bears. List five facts the essay gives you about grizzlies.

2. According to the author, why have grizzly bears and people never made good neighbors?

3. (a) Why would a grizzly attack a person? (b) What should a person do if attacked by a grizzly?

4. Reread the last two paragraphs of this essay. (a) What conclusion does the author reach about grizzlies? (b) Do you agree with this conclusion? Why or why not?

Activities

1. **Composition.** Write a tall tale about how you escaped from a grizzly.

2. Draw the paw prints of Old Two Toes.

SENTENCE MEANING

Finding Core Parts

The core parts of a sentence express its basic message. The other parts of the sentence provide extra information about this message.

A sentence has at least two core parts—the simple subject and the simple predicate. The simple subject answers the question "Who?" or "What?" The simple predicate either answers the question "Did what?" or is a form of the verb *to be* (*is, are, was, were,* etc.). In the following example, the simple subject is underlined once and the simple predicate twice.

At another camp, the <u>bear</u> <u><u>climbed</u></u> into the chuck wagon.

In some sentences, a third core part completes the action of the simple predicate. In the following example, the third core part is printed in **boldface.**

The big <u>bear</u> <u><u>ate</u></u> the **grub** before vanishing.

---

1. Find the two core parts in each sentence below. Write them on a separate piece of paper. (If the simple subject is a proper name, be sure to include the full name.)
    a. For the rest of his life, the hunter limped badly.
    b. The horses walked near the inside of the trail.
    c. On the mountainside above them, Old Two Toes rose to his full height.
    d. The horse stumbled over the cliff to its death.

2. Find the three core parts in each sentence below. Write them on a separate piece of paper.
    a. Then one day, far up in the mountains, a wrangler took a horse across a narrow trail.
    b. Because of his position on the mountain, the bear had the advantage.
    c. Bloody Paws surprised Jack Madden in the middle of the trail.
    d. With lightning speed, Madden fired the gun at the grizzly at point-blank range.

3. Usually the simple subject is a noun or a pronoun. [A noun is a word that names a person, place, thing, or idea. A pronoun is a word that takes the place of one or more nouns (*I, he, she, it, you, we, they*).] In each of the following sentences, the subject

is a noun. Replace each noun subject with an appropriate pronoun.

a. The cowboy found tracks made by the bear.
b. Old Two Toes swatted a cow in the head.
c. The incident caused a fury in town.
d. The bullet only grazed the bear.
e. Lewis and Clark were the first people to report seeing grizzlies.

WORD ATTACK

Using Guide Words

At the top of a dictionary or glossary page, you will find guide words. They help you to find the page where the word you are looking for is listed. The words, or entries, in a dictionary or glossary are listed in alphabetical order. The two guide words tell you that all the entries that come between these two words can be found on this page.

Suppose you wanted to find the word *renegade* in the dictionary. First you would turn to the *R* listings. Then you would look at the guide words to find the exact page this word is on.

1. Find each of the following words in the glossary. On a separate piece of paper, write the guide words you find at the top of the glossary pages on which the words appear.

   a. scan
   b. corral
   c. grub
   d. swat
   e. shamble

   f. steer
   g. infuriate
   h. cranky
   i. mill
   j. wrangler

2. Imagine the guide words at the top of the page are *major* and *malice*. Which of the following words would fall on this page?

   a. maker
   b. marker

   c. malicious
   d. malfunction

3. Imagine the guide words at the top of the page are *sense* and *sequin*. Which of the following words fall on this page?

   a. sergeant
   b. sequel

   c. separate
   d. segment

Pete at the Zoo

Gwendolyn Brooks

I wonder if the elephant
Is lonely in his stall
When all the boys and girls are gone
And there's no shout at all,
5   And there's no one to stamp before,
No one to note his might.
Does he hunch up, as I do,
Against the dark of night?

For My Grandmother

Countee Cullen

This lovely flower fell to seed;
  Work gently, sun and rain;
She held it as her dying creed
  That she would grow again.

Close Up

1. At first, "Pete at the Zoo" seems to be about an elephant. What does the poet wonder about the elephant?

2. Reread the last two lines of this poem. (a) Whom do you think the poem is really about? Why? (b) What does "hunch up/ Against the dark of night" mean?

3. (a) In the second poem, what has happened to the grandmother? (b) What does the poet mean when he says "she would grow again"?

A Shipment of Mute Fate

Les Crutchfield

A radio play based on a story by Martin Storm

Characters

Chris Warner, a young zoologist

Captain Wood, captain of the *Chancay*

Sanchez, native guide

Mrs. Willis, stewardess

Mr. Bowman, chief steward

Other Crew Members and Passengers

Chris *(narrating):* I stopped on the wharf at La Guaira and looked up the gangplank toward the liner *Chancay*—standing there quietly at her moorings. The day was warm under a bright Venezuela sun—and the harbor beyond the ship lay drowsy and silent. But all at once in the midst of those peaceful surroundings, a cold chill gripped me, and I shivered with sudden dread—dread of the thing I was doing, and was about to

do! (*Pause. Music comes up and dissolves slowly.*) But too much had happened to turn back now. I'd gone too far to stop. (*Sound: Wooden box set on wooden wharf, boat whistles, etc.*)

I set the box down on the edge of the wharf, placed it carefully so as to be in plain sight—and within gunshot—of the captain's bridge. (*Sound: Steps on gangplank; fade.*)

Then I turned and started up the gangplank. I knew what I was going to do—but I couldn't forget that a certain pair of beady eyes was watching every move I made. Eyes that never blinked and never closed—just watched . . . and waited!

(*Sound: Shipboard commotion.*)

Willis (*coming in*): Oh! You startled me, sir! I didn't hear—why . . . (*with relief*) why, it's Mr. Warner!

Chris: Hello, Mother Willis. How's the best-looking stewardess on the seven seas?

Willis (*a bit evasive*): Why, I'm . . . I'm fine, Mr. Warner. (*Hurriedly.*) Nice to see you again.

Chris (*joshing*): Wait a minute! That's a fine greeting after two months.

Willis: Well—it's just that I'm so . . . so busy just now.

Chris: I don't believe a word of it— sailing day's tomorrow. And on the trip down from New York—you said I was your favorite passenger.

Willis: But——

Chris: Here—what's that you're carrying in your apron?

Willis (*obviously nervous*): Oh, it's nothing. Just . . . supplies.

Chris: Supplies? Let's have a look.

Willis: No! Please!

Chris: Why—it's a cat!

Willis (*almost in tears*): It's Clara, Mr. Warner. Mr. Bowman said I had to leave her ashore—and I just couldn't!

Chris: Who's Mr. Bowman?

Willis: The new chief steward. Clara's been aboard with me for two years—and I just can't leave her here in a foreign country. Especially with her condition so delicate and all!

Chris: Yes (*ahem*), I see! I see what you mean. Well, I hope you get away with it.

Willis: You . . . you won't tell anyone?

Chris: Not a soul. As a matter of fact, if I don't get my way with the Captain, you and I may both end up smuggling!

(*Music: Brief transition, dissolves.*)

Captain (*fades in*): Most happy to have had you aboard on the trip down two months ago, Christopher, and I'm very glad you're coming along with us on the run back to New York.

Chris: Thanks, Captain Wood. There is one thing, though. I'm having a little trouble with the customs men here, and I wondered if you——

Captain: I can't do it, Christopher. I cabled your father this morning—told him I'd have done it for you if I possibly could. He sent a request from New York, you know.

Chris: Yes, I thought he would . . . I . . . wired him from upriver last week.

Captain: I hated to refuse—but it's out of the question.

Chris: Captain Wood, I'm afraid I don't follow you.

Captain: Responsibility to the passengers, son. We'll have women and children aboard—and on a liner, the safety of the passengers comes ahead of anything else.

Chris: But with proper precautions!

Captain: Something might happen. I don't know what—but something might.

Chris: You've carried worse things!

Captain: There isn't anything worse—and any skipper afloat'll bear me out. No, son—I simply can't take the chance, and that's final!

(Music: Hit and out.)

Chris *(narrating):* Final! It wasn't final if I could do anything about it. I hadn't come down here to spend two months in that stinking back country and then be stopped on the edge of the wharf! Two months of it—heat, rain, insects, malaria—I'd gone clear into the headwaters of the Orinoco.[1] *(Fading from mike.)* Traveled through country where every step along the jungle trail might be the last one . . . .

(Music: Swells and dissolves. Sound of men on a trail.)

Chris: Oh . . . Sanchez!

Sanchez *(coming toward mike):* Sí, Señor Warner.

Chris: Better start looking for a place to camp. Be dark in a little while.

Sanchez: Sí, Señor—very soon we turn to river, camp on rocks by water. This very bad country.

Chris: This very bad country! You've been saying that for ten days now. Very bad country.

---

1. Orinoco (ôr′ə-nō′kō) n.: A river that starts in Venezuela and runs to the Atlantic Ocean.

Sanchez: Sí, Señor Warner—this very bad country.

Chris: Oh, skip it. For all the luck we've had so far, it might as well be Central Park.

Sanchez: Central Park? I no understand.

Chris: Never mind. If we don't——

(Excited cries of "Bushmaster!" Sounds of scrambling.)

Chris: Here—what's the matter? Quiet now! Sanchez—what's wrong?

Sanchez: There in the path! See? Bushmaster!

(Music: Loud, then fades.)

Chris *(narrating):* Bushmaster! The deadliest snake in the world! Bushmaster—its Latin name was *Lachesis mutus*—Mute Fate! It lay there in the center of the path—an eight-foot length of silent death—coiled loosely in an undulant loop, ready to strike violently at the least movement. Here was the one snake that would go after any animal that walked—or any man. It lay there and watched us—not moving—not afraid—ready for anything. . . . The splotch of its colors stood out like some horribly gaudy floor mat—lying there on the brown background of the jungle—waiting for someone to step on it. Here was what I'd come two thousand miles for . . . a bushmaster!

(Sound: Pistol shot. Music: Up and out sharply as . . .)

Chris: Sanchez! . . . I didn't want that snake killed!

Sanchez: He no killed, Señor—he

A Shipment of Mute Fate **49**

gone. Bushmaster very smart, very quick—see bullet in time to dodge.

Chris: Anyway, he's gone! And the only one we've seen in five weeks!

Sanchez: Oh, we find other. This very bad country.

Chris: Well, lay off that gun the next time. Don't shoot—do you understand?

Sanchez: Why you say no shoot? You want bushmaster.

Chris: Sure—but I want it alive!

Sanchez: Señor Warner—you tell me you want bushmaster, but you no say "alive"!

Chris: You're getting two hundred dollars for it.

Sanchez: For dead man—what is two hundred dollars? Tomorrow we go back to Caracas.

Chris (going away from mike): Sanchez—I'll give you a thousand dollars! (*Music swells, then fades; Chris narrates.*) It cost me fifteen hundred—but three days later, Sanchez brought me the snake in a rubber bag. He was shaking so hard I thought for a moment the thing had struck him. . . .

Sanchez (excitedly): One thing you make sure, Señor Warner. No turn him loose in Venezuela. Because he know I the one who catch him—and he know where I live!

Chris: All right, Sanchez—I'll keep an eye on him.

Sanchez: He know you pay me to catch him. All the time he watch and wait. You no forget that, Señor Warner—because *he* no forget . . . not ever!

(*Music: Loud, then under voice.*)

Chris (narrating): Well, after going through all that trouble and danger—I wasn't going to let a pigheaded ship cap-tain stop me at the last minute! At least not as long as the cables were still in operation between La Guaira and New York. . . .

(*Music: Swells for transition, then cuts as door closes and steps come in.*)

Chris (coming in): Morning, Captain Wood. The boy at the hotel said you wanted to see me.

Captain: That's right, Christopher. Uh . . . sit down. (*Sound of chair.*) Seems you weren't willing to let matters stand the way we left them yesterday.

Chris: Sorry to go over your head, Captain Wood—but I had to. The museum sent me all the way down here for it and I'm not going to be stopped by red tape. This'll be the *only* live bushmaster ever brought to the United States.

Captain: If I had my way . . . but, orders are orders. Got a cable from the head office this morning. All right. Suppose we talk about precautions.

Chris: I'll handle it any way you say.

Captain: It's got to have a stronger box. That crate's too flimsy.

Chris: It's stronger than it looks—and that wire screen on top'd hold a wildcat. But anyway, I bought a heavy sea chest this morning. We'll put the crate inside of it.

Captain: Sounds all right. Got a lock on it?

Chris: Heavy padlock. It's fixed so the lid can be propped open a crack without unlocking it. The snake's got to have air.

Captain: But in dirty weather, that lid stays shut. I'll take no chances.

Chris: Fair enough.

Captain: We'll keep the thing in my

inside cabin, where I sleep. Can't have it in the baggage room. And nobody on board's to know about it.

Chris: Whatever you say, Captain. But we won't have any trouble. After all, it's only a snake—it doesn't have any magical powers.

Captain: I saw a bushmaster in the zoo at Caracas once. Had it in a glass cage with double walls. It'd never move—just lie there and look at you as long as you were in sight. Gave a man the creeps!

Chris: I didn't know they had a bushmaster at the Caracas Zoo.

Captain: They don't *now*. Found the glass broken one morning, and the snake gone. The night watchman was dead. They never found out what happened.

Chris: Well . . . the watchman must've broken the glass by accident.

Captain: The way they figured it— the glass was broken from the inside! *(Pause.)* We . . . sail in four hours.

(Music: Transition . . . to sound of the open sea . . . music background.)

Chris *(narrating)*: Into the Caribbean—with perfect weather, and a sea as smooth as an inland lake. The barometer dropped a little on the third day—but cleared up overnight, and left nothing worse than a heavy swell. But in spite of the calm seas and pleasant weather, I was becoming possessed with an ominous anxiety. I was developing an obsessive fear of that snake! I stayed clear of the passengers pretty much—got the habit of dropping into Captain Wood's quarters several times a day. . . . *(Sound. Door opens and closes. Steps.)*

He kept the heavy box underneath his berth. I'd approach it quietly and shine my flashlight through the open crack. *(Pause. Sound of two or three steps and stop.)*

Never once could I catch that eight-foot devil asleep, or even excited. He'd be lying there half coiled, his head raised a little, staring out of those beady black eyes—waiting. He'd still be like that when I'd turn away to leave. *(Slow steps.)*

Maybe that's what bothered me— that horrible and constant watchful waiting. *(Sound. Door opens.)* What in the name of heaven was he *waiting* for?

(Sound: Door closes.)

Willis *(fading in)*: Well—hello there, Mr. Warner!

Chris: Oh . . . how are you, Mother Willis?

Willis: My, but you and the Captain spend an awful lot of time around this cabin. I'm beginning to think the two of you must have some guilty secret!

Chris: Oh, no, nothing like that, Mother Willis. I don't know about Captain Wood—but I . . . I certainly don't have any guilty secret!

(Music: Transition into sound: Open foredeck of liner bucking a swell.)

Chris: Well! She's running quite a swell out there, Mr. Bowman!

Bowman: Yeah—it's a little heavy, all right, Mr. Warner. Guess a storm passed through to the west of us yesterday when the glass dropped.

Chris: Think it missed us, then, huh?

Bowman: Yeah—that's what the mate figures. Sure stirred up some water, though.

Chris *(laughs)*: This'll put half the passengers in their bunks.

Bowman: Make it great for my department. Two thirds of 'em will want a steward to hold their heads!

Chris: They'll keep Mother Willis so busy she'll—— Hey! Look at that wave!

Bowman: Huh? . . . Great Jehosaphat! We're taking it on the port bow! Hang on!

(*Sound: Wave crashes across the foredeck . . . seems to shake the whole ship . . . and subsides.*)

Chris: Whew! Not another wave that size in sight. That was a freak if there ever was one.

Bowman: You see 'em like that sometimes—even in a calm sea. (*Pause.*) Gotta get topside, Mr. Warner. Wave really smashed into the officers' deck. Probably did some damage. . . .

Chris: Yeah, I suppose . . . *What did you say?*

Bowman: Wheel companionway was open on the port side—bridge cabins musta taken a pretty bad smashing. They're right below the——Say, is something wrong, Mr. Warner?

Chris: No. No—nothing at all, Mr. Bowman. At least . . . I hope not!

(*Music: Attacks and holds under voice.*)

Chris (*narrating*): Of course, I knew it was only one chance in a thousand—but the chances against that freak wave were one in a thousand, too! I stumbled up the companionway and along the passage to the Captain's cabin.

(*Music. . . Sound of door opening.*)

Willis (*surprised, affably*): Oh . . . come on in, Mr. Warner.

Chris: Mother Willis!

Willis: My, isn't this cabin a mess? I'd better get some of these things out to dry.

Chris: Yeah. Well, I just wanted to check—— Where's that box that was under the Captain's bunk?

Willis: Oh, that! I just shoved it out on deck.

Chris: What!

Willis: The desk over there slid into it. It was all smashed.

Chris: But the small box inside of it! What happened to it?

Willis: Oh, they were both splintered, Mr. Warner—broken wide open.

Chris: Oh, no!

Willis: Why, Mr. Warner—you're as white as a sheet!

Chris: Mother Willis—will you go find Captain Wood? Tell him to . . . come down here immediately.

Willis: Well . . . of course, Mr. Warner. (*Going.*) I'll go tell him right away.

(*Sound: Door closes. Sounds as cued under the following:*)

Chris (*narrating*): I pulled open the top drawer of the bureau beside me (*drawer opening*) and took out the Captain's flashlight and a loaded pistol (*drawer closing*). Mother Willis had left a mop standing by the door. I put my foot on the head of it and snapped off the handle (*snap of handle*). Every move I made turned into slow motion. I could hear my own heart beating. Slowly I started to search the cabin. (*Music: Suspense motif.*)

Sodden heaps of clothing were scattered around on the wet, black floor. I punched at them one at a time—holding the gun cocked—the flashlight pointing along the stick. Nothing. I worked around the room—throwing the light into the dark corners, back of the desk, under the bunk. And wherever I turned, I could feel those cold, unblinking eyes at my back—watching and waiting. *(Pause.)* Using the stick, I pushed open the closet door and threw the light inside. Carefully I poked at the boxes and junk on the floor. *(Pause.)* The snake was not in the closet. Inch by inch, I covered the entire cabin—and then at last I realized the horrible truth.

(Sound: Door opening. Music: Up and clip off.)

Captain: Mother Willis just told me, Christopher. *(Door closes.)* So it's happened!

Chris: That's right, Captain. It's happened.

Captain: I see you found the gun. We'd better start searching the cabin.

Chris: Captain Wood, I . . . just finished searching it.

Captain: Then . . . ! *(Pause.)* Women, kids—and that thing loose on board. A thousand places for it to hide. Heaven help us!

(Music: Establish theme for the "search.")

Captain *(fades in)*: There's no use starting to blame anybody now, gentlemen. I didn't call you officers in here to pass judgment. The thing's done—and that's that.

Mate: You're right there, Captain.

Captain: What we *have* got to do is decide how to handle it.

Bowman: It'd be easier if we didn't have to tell the passengers and crew, sir. I've seen panics aboard ship before!

Captain: Yes, I agree with you, Mr. Bowman—but I don't quite see how we can avoid it.

Mate: They gotta right to know! As long as that snake's loose, everybody on board's in the same danger—and they all oughta know about it!

Chris: Captain Wood—that thing is eight feet long. It can't simply crawl into a crack. Why don't we make a quick search of the whole ship before we spread any alarm?

Captain: Yes, I've thought of that, Christopher.

Bowman: As far as I can see, the only place it *couldn't* be is in the boilers or on top of the galley stove.

Mate: It might've crawled overboard.

Captain: We can't count on that. We've got to assume it's on the ship somewhere.

Mate: Yeah, and that could be anywhere. In a coil of rope—or in a pile of clothes.

Bowman: Yes, or under some woman's berth—or a baby's crib.

Mate: Or even in——

Chris: You've already said it! That bushmaster could be anywhere. We've got to do something, and do it fast!

Captain: All right. I think the best idea's to make a quick search first. You agree to that?

(Cast ad-libs assent.)

Captain: Then if we don't find it—we'll have to warn the passengers.

Chris: We've *got* to find it!

(Music: Up and sustained under voice.)

Chris *(narrating)*: Alone in the dim baggage room, I went through the same movements as I had earlier in the Captain's cabin—gun in one hand, flashlight in the other, poking into every dark corner, behind every trunk and box. Since there was no one in the baggage room, I could keep the gun cocked and ready. The rest of those poor devils were having to do the same thing—bare-handed! All over the ship the search went on.

(Music: Up and cut off.)

Woman *(fade in)*: Here, now, Steward! What on earth are you doing, rummaging through my cabin?

Bowman: Just checking up, ma'am!

Woman: Well, I'm sure there's nothing in here that has to be checked.

Bowman: Sorry, ma'am—Captain's orders. It'll only take a few minutes.

Woman: Well, I never heard of such a thing! A passenger simply doesn't have any privacy at all! *(Fading back into music.)* I've traveled on a lot of different lines, but I've certainly never heard of anything so completely high-handed before . . . !

(Music: Up and under voices.)

Mate: Sorry, sir. Wonder if you'd mind moving over to the other rail? I'd like to look through these lockers.

Man: Sure—go ahead. What's the matter . . . you lost something?

Mate: No. No—just looking things over.

Man: Nothing in there but life preservers.

Mate: Yeah—that's right.

Man: You must be getting ready to sink the boat. *(Laughs.)* Gonna collect the insurance, eh? *(Fading.)* Gonna send us all to the bottom! *(Laughs.)*

(Music: Up and out.)

Chris *(narrating)*: But not one of us could find that deadly shape—coiled in some dark corner, or outstretched along a window seat. Not one of us caught a glimpse of that horrid head, with its beady black, watchful eyes. *(Fades.)* It was nearly dark when we met together again in the chart room.

Captain *(fades in)*: Well, gentlemen—there's no other way. We've risked all the time we can. We must warn the passengers!

Mate: How'll we do it, Captain? Call 'em all together in the lounge?

Captain: No. If we did anything like that, we'd be asking for a panic.

Bowman: We'll get one—whether we ask for it or not!

Captain: Pick a few men and go through the cabin decks. Tell 'em individually—*inside their cabins.* Watch for any that act like they might cause trouble—and we'll keep an eye on 'em. Handle the crew the same way.

(Officers ad-lib agreement. Sounds of steps, chairs.)

Captain *(up a bit)*: As soon as you're finished—arm all the deck officers, and start searching again. Our only chance of preventing a panic is to find that snake!

(Music: Sets growing tension, sustains it under voice.)

Chris *(narrating)*: The slow nightmare that followed grew worse by the hour. None of us slept. All the ship's officers not on duty kept on with that endless search. Passengers locked themselves in their cabins, or huddled together in the lounges—knowing all the time that no spot on board could be called safe. Fear was a heavy fog in the lungs of all of us—and every light on the vessel burned throughout the night. Morning came and brought no relief. Terror and tension mounted by the hour.

(*Music: Swells, fades. Sound of woman sobbing.*)

Willis: There now, Mrs. Crane. Go back to your cabin. The horrid thing's probably crawled overboard by now.

Woman: You're just saying that! You're paid to say it! You don't *know!* Nobody does!

Willis: Now, now. Everything's going to be all right.

Woman: If we could only get off the ship, they could fumigate it. Yes! That's what we've got to do! (*Fading from mike.*) We've got to get off the ship!

Willis (*calling excitedly*): Mr. Bowman—she's going to jump.

Bowman (*in distance*): No you don't, lady.

Woman (*distance*): Let me go! (*Sobbing.*)

Captain (*coming in*): Nice work, Mr. Bowman. Get her down to her cabin. And whatever you do—don't turn her loose!

(*Music: Up and under.*)

Man (*fading in*): You never know when it might strike you. You can't put on a coat or move a chair without risking your life. Something's gotta be done. It might be right here in this lounge!

(*Sound: Stir of fearful crowd.*)

Mate (*coming in*): All right, mister—better quiet down and take it easy.

Man: Take it easy, huh? You're a great officer! Why don't you *do* something about it? That thing might be crawling around here right under our feet . . . .

(*Sound: Rise of frightened voices.*)

Mate: I said shut up! Are you trying to start a riot?

Man: I gotta right to talk! I don't want to die! Nobody's gonna tell me what——

(*Sound: Sock in jaw—body falling. Music: Up and back under.*)

Chris (*narrating*): The second night passed and morning came around again—a gray and rainy day that dragged by, and then night came down again—third night of the terror. Again every light burned, and the whole ship seethed in the throes of incipient panic. Faced by a horror they'd never met on the sea before, crew and officers alike were on the verge of revolt. Passengers sat huddled in a trancelike stupor, ready to scream at the slightest unknown sound.

(*Music: Dissolves slowly.*)

Chris: At seven bells, I made my way forward to the chart room, and found Captain Wood bent over a desk.

(*Sound: Door closes. Steps.*)

Captain (*wearily*): Oh . . . hello, Christopher. Come on in and sit down.

Chris (*on edge*): It's got to be *somewhere*, Captain Wood! It's got to be!

Captain: I don't know. You could search this ship for six months, and never touch all the hiding places aboard. If we can only hold out for two more days—we'll be in port.

Chris: What's your home office say?

Captain: Here's the latest wireless from 'em. "Keep calm—and keep coming." Huh! What else *can* we do? How is it below?

Chris: Pretty bad. Anything could happen.

Captain: Yeah, that's why I took the guns away from the men. One pistol shot, and we'd have a riot on our hands.

Chris: The whole thing's my fault, Captain Wood! That's what I can't forget!

Captain: Take it easy, son.

Chris: If there was only some way I could pay for it myself. Alone!

Captain: No—I know how you feel. But it's no more your fault than mine, or the man who asked you to bring that snake back . . . alive. Nobody planned this. You'd better try to get a little sleep.

Chris: Sleep!

Captain: Mr. Bowman made some coffee down in the steward's galley awhile ago. Better go on down and get yourself a cup—then rest for a couple hours.

Chris: Rest—I can't rest!

Captain: Christopher—it's not going to help anything if you stumble through a hatch half-asleep—and break your neck. Go on and get some coffee. One way or another we've got to hold out for two more days.

(Music: Transition, and dissolves. Sound: Door closing and steps under . . . other sounds as cued.)

Chris *(narrating)*: The light was on in the steward's galley—and the coffee-pot was standing on the stove. *(Steps stop.)* It was still warm, so I didn't bother to heat it. *(Pouring.)* I poured out a cup . . . *(steps)*, carried it over, and set it on the porcelain table top in the center of the room. I started to light a cigarette. The door of the pan cupboard beneath the sink was standing slightly ajar, and I happened to glance toward it. I dropped the cigarette and moved slowly backward. I'd found the bushmaster!

(Music: Loud, then continues softly, movement slow and tense.)

Chris: As I moved, the snake slid out of the cupboard in a single sinuous slide—and drew back into a loose coil on the galley floor—never taking his eyes off me. I backed slowly away—waiting any moment for that deadly, slithering strike. How had he known it was me? He'd stayed quiet when Bowman was here. How had he picked the first time in five days that I was without a gun? My hands touched the wall behind me and I stopped, in terror. . . . The call button and door were on the far side of the room. I'd backed into a dead end! I stared at the snake in fascination—expecting any moment the ripping slash of those poisoned fangs. The lethal coils tightened a little—then were still again. *Homo sapiens versus Lachesis mutus*—a man against mute fate. And all the odds were on . . . fate. I knew then that I was going to die!

(Music: Long chord and clip off.)

Chris: I could feel the sweat run down between the wall and the palms of my hands pressing against it. My skin crawled and twitched, and the pit of my stomach was cold as ice. There was no sound but the rush of blood in my ears.

The snake shifted again—drawing into a tighter coil—always tighter. Why didn't the devil get it over with? Then . . . for an instant his head veered away. Something moved by the stove. I didn't dare turn to look at it. Slowly it moved out into my line of vision. It was a cat! The scrawny cat that Mother Willis sneaked aboard in La Guaira!

Cat: *(A low, threatening growl.)*

Chris: Its back was arched, and every hair stood on end. It moved stiff-legged now, walking in a half-circle around the snake. The bushmaster moved slowly and kept watching the cat. He tightened—he was going to strike at any second.

(Sound: Thud of striking snake, and scrape as it recovers.)

Cat: *(Snarl and spit . . . then back to the low growl.)*

Chris: He struck and missed—the cat was barely out of reach. Now she was walking back and forth again. She was asking to die.

(Sound: Thud and recovery.)

Cat: *(Snarl, spit, and back to growl.)*

Chris: Missed again—by a fraction of an inch. He was striking now without even going to a full coil!

(Sound: Thud and recovery.)

Cat: *(Snarl, spit, growl.)*

Chris: Missed! Again and again—always missing by the barest margin. Each time the cat danced barely out of reach—and each time she countered with one precise spat of a dainty paw—bracing her skinny frame on three stiff legs. And then suddenly I realized what she was doing!

(Sound: Thud and recovery.)

Cat: *(Snarl, spit, growl.)*

Chris: The bushmaster was tiring—and one strike was just an instant slow. But in that split second, sharp claws raked across the evil head and ripped out both the lidless eyes. The cat had deliberately blinded the snake!

(Sound: Repeated thuds of struggle.)

Cat: *(Snarling, spitting.)*

Chris: He didn't bother to coil now but slid after her in a fury—striking wildly but always missing. And every strike was a little slower than the last one. Until finally——

(Sound: The thuds change to the frantic scraping of a heavy snake.)

Chris: As the snake's neck stretched out at the end of a strike, the cat made one leap and sank her razor-sharp teeth just back of the ugly head—sank 'em until they crunched bone with tooth and claw. She clung, as the monstrous snake flailed and lashed on the floor . . . striving to get those hideous coils around her, trying to break her hold, to shake off the slow and certain paralyzing death . . . *(sound of cat out)* that gradually crept over him, and at last stilled his struggles forever!

(Pause. Music.)

Chris: I took a deep breath—the first in minutes—the cat lay on her side on the floor, panting—resting from the fight just over. She had a right to rest. That mangy, brave, beautiful alley cat had just saved my life—and maybe others as well. But as I turned toward the stove—I suddenly became very humble. There were three reasons why that cat had fought and killed the world's deadliest snake. And those three reasons came tottering out from under the stove on shaky little legs—three kittens with their eyes bright with wonder and their tails stiff as pokers. Up on the decks, hundreds of passengers would sigh with relief at the news that the days and nights of terror were ended. They could wait a little longer. *(Pause.)* I pulled open the doors of the cabinet and found a can of milk. Then I dropped down on my knees . . . on the floor of the galley.

Close Up

1. (a) How does Chris gain permission to bring the bushmaster on board? (b) Why does he want a live snake?

2. Several characters believe that the snake has almost supernatural powers. (a) Why does Sanchez say, "No turn him loose in Venezuela. Because he know I the one who catch him—and he know where I live!"? (b) According to the Captain, who broke the glass on the bushmaster's zoo cage?

3. (a) What freak accident allows the bushmaster to escape from the chest? (b) When Chris finds the snake in the cupboard, why does he feel that the snake has been waiting for him?

4. The bushmaster backs Chris into a corner and prepares to attack. How is Chris saved?

5. (a) Why is "Mute Fate" an appropriate name for the bushmaster? (b) How does love triumph over mute fate?

The Play

A play is a story that is meant to be performed. Actors take the parts of the various characters. Through the actors' words and actions, you learn what these characters are like and what happens to them during the course of the play. Since "A Shipment of Mute Fate" is a radio play, it has directions for sound effects that help you to visualize what is happening.

1. The main character in this play is Chris. You learn about him in two important ways—from what he tells you directly and from what he says to other characters. (When Chris is speaking directly to you, the audience, the word *narrating* usually appears after his name.) (a) How does Chris feel as he looks at the *Chancay?* (b) Why does he feel this way?

2. Chris tells the Captain that he wants to bring a live bushmaster aboard. (a) What does the Captain tell Chris? (b) How do you know that Chris doesn't plan to accept this decision?

3. A flashback is a look into the past. It tells you about something that happened earlier in the story. (a) Find the flashback in this play. (b) What purpose does the flashback serve?

4. When you read a play, you imagine the words as you think the actors would say them. On page 53, how do you think the actor playing Mr. Bowman would say, "Huh? . . . Great Jehosaphat! We're taking it on the port bow! Hang on!"?

5. (a) Find three directions for sound effects. (b) What does each of these directions help you to visualize?

SENTENCE MEANING

Reading Sentences with Words Left Out

A sentence expresses a complete thought. It consists of at least two parts—the simple subject and the simple predicate. When you read plays, you will find that playwrights often do not have their characters speak in complete sentences. They try to make their dialogue (what the characters say) sound like everyday conversation. When this occurs, you have to fill in the missing parts of the sentence for yourself. For example, Chris says, "Be dark in a little while." The left-out words are "It will." "It will be dark in a little while."

1. Add the word or words necessary to make a complete sentence from each of the following items.
   a. "This very bad country."
   b. "Got a cable from the head office this morning."
   c. "Missed again—by a fraction of an inch."
   d. "The scrawny cat that Mother Willis sneaked aboard in La Guaira."
   e. "Sorry to go over your head, Captain Wood—but I had to."

2. Add the words necessary to make a compound sentence from the following item. [A compound sentence is made up of two complete sentences joined together by a conjunction (*and, or, but*).]

   "Most happy to have had you aboard on the trip down two months ago, Christopher, and I'm very glad you're coming along with us on the run back to New York."

WORD ATTACK

Understanding Contractions

A contraction is a shortened form of two words. These two words have been joined together by leaving out one or more letters. An apostrophe takes the place of the missing letter or letters. For example:

One Letter	More Than One Letter
is + not = isn't	can + not = can't
you + are = you're	he + would = he'd
it + is = it's	she + will = she'll
	they + have = they've

Notice the spelling change in the following special case:

will + not = won't

▶ On a separate piece of paper, write the two words that have been combined to form each of the following contractions.

   a. "*Who's* Mr. Bowman?"
   b. "I *don't* believe a word of it."
   c. "Mr. Bowman said I had to leave her ashore—and I just *couldn't!*"
   d. "*I'd* gone too far to stop."
   e. "*How's* the best-looking stewardess on the seven seas?"
   f. "*You've* carried worse things!"
   g. "There *isn't* anything worse—and any skipper *afloat'll* bear me out."
   h. "*You're* getting two hundred dollars for it."
   i. "Here—*what's* the matter?"
   j. "*It'd* never move—just lie there and look at you as long as you were in sight."

REVIEW QUIZ

1. In "Cat-About-Town," how does Sam, the Herriots' dog, feel about Oscar? Find one detail that supports your answer.

2. How does Oscar show that he remembers Helen?

3. In "Last Cover," why are the boys afraid that Bandit will forget them?

4. How does Colin prove to his father that he also considers nature important?

5. In "The Meadow Mouse," what does the poet fear may happen to the mouse?

6. How is the mouse like "The turtle gasping in the dusty rumble of the highway"?

7. In "Unforgettable Grizzly Bears," why is Old Two Toes easy to track?

8. According to this essay, why don't grizzlies and human beings make good neighbors?

9. In "A Shipment of Mute Fate," Mrs. Willis is kind to a cat and brings it on board. How does her kindness later prevent disaster?

10. Why doesn't the Captain want to tell the passengers that the snake has escaped?

On Sentence Meaning

1. Copy the following item on a separate piece of paper. Then put quotation marks around the exact words of the speaker.

   I'm afraid so, Helen, I said. We've done our best for him but I honestly don't think he has much chance.

2. Copy the following item on a separate piece of paper. Then add a semicolon, two commas, and a period in the appropriate places.

   We'd taken the young fox into the kitchen all of us except Father gone a bit silly over the little thing

3. Which three punctuation marks tell you to stop?

4. Find the three core parts in the following sentence.

   Around 1902, the cowboys rode the trails of western Montana.

5. Make a complete sentence from the following item.

   "Better start looking for a place to camp."

On Types of Literature

▶ Decide whether the following statements are true or false.
   a. A personal narrative is a fictional story.
   b. A short story is only about real-life people and events.
   c. A lyric poem expresses an emotional response to a person, place, object, or idea.
   d. An essay usually provides factual information and tells about events that really occurred.
   e. A play is a story that is meant to be performed.

COMPOSITION

Sentence Combining

You can combine several short sentences into one effective sentence by removing repeated words. For example:

The cat was large.
It was thin. (,)
It was deeply striped. (, and)
becomes
The cat was large, thin, and deeply striped.

Use the first sentence as your base. Then remove the repeated words in the second and third sentences ("It was"). Finally, combine the sentences by using the comma and connecting word in parentheses.

Look at the next example. The repeated words in the second and third sentences are "avoided the edge of the cliff."

The wrangler avoided the edge of the cliff.
The pack horses avoided the edge of the cliff. (,)
The charging bear avoided the edge of the cliff. (, and)
becomes
The wrangler, the pack horses, and the charging bear avoided the edge of the cliff.

▶ Combine each group of three sentences into one sentence. Remember to use the first sentence as your base. Then remove the repeated words in the second and third sentences. Finally, use the commas and connecting word that appear in parentheses.

a. Helen fed the cat milk.
Helen fed the cat strained broth. (,)
Helen fed the cat baby food. (, and)

b. I caught the mouse by the tail.
I brought him inside. (,)
I cradled him in my hand. (, and)

c. Chris feared the bushmaster.
Sanchez feared the bushmaster. (,)
Captain Wood feared the bushmaster. (, and)

d. It was the biggest grizzly in the area.
It was the meanest grizzly in the area. (,)
It was the most powerful grizzly in the area. (, and)

BEFORE GOING ON

Reading for a Purpose

Reading for a purpose helps you improve your comprehension, or understanding. It is a helpful technique to use when reading difficult material. One way to read for a purpose is to look for the answers to specific questions. Another way is to summarize what you have read after each three or four paragraphs. Finally, you should summarize the entire article after you have completed it.

1. Keep the following questions in mind as you read "The Story of Tuffy, the Dolphin Who Was Trained to Save Lives." After you finish reading, write the answers to the questions on a separate piece of paper.
   a. What three specific tasks did the aquanauts perform underwater?
   b. What were Tuffy's two jobs?
   c. Why did the aquanauts pretend to be lost?
   d. Why did Tuffy swim first to Sealab, and then to the lost aquanaut?
   e. Why did Tuffy "bop" the aquanaut over his head?

2. Reread the article using the following procedure.
   a. Reread paragraphs 1 and 2. Write a sentence summarizing them.
   b. Reread paragraphs 3–6. Write one or two sentences summarizing them. Then answer the following questions.
      (1) What was "home" for the aquanauts?
      (2) What tasks did the aquanauts have?
      (3) What tasks did Tuffy have?
      (4) What was Tuffy's most important task?
   c. Reread paragraphs 7–10. Write one or two sentences summarizing them.
   d. Reread paragraphs 11–13. Write one or two sentences summarizing them.
   e. Reread paragraphs 14–17. Write one or two sentences summarizing them.
   f. Write a paragraph summarizing the entire article.

Further Reading

The Story of Tuffy, the Dolphin Who Was Trained To Save Lives

Margaret Davidson

Everyone knows about astronauts—the men who explore outer space. Now people are beginning to hear more and more about aquanauts, the men who explore space underwater.

In the fall of 1965, a group of aquanauts spent forty-five days underwater near the coast of California. They were part of a project called Sealab II. One of the aquanauts looked a little different from the others. No wonder. He was a 300-pound dolphin named Tuffy.

Tuffy spent much of his time in a pen near the top of the water—so he could breathe. Home for the other aquanauts was a big metal capsule called Sealab which rested on the bottom of the ocean.

Every morning the human aquanauts put on their diving suits and left Sealab to swim in the water outside the capsule. They measured the underwater currents. They took pictures of the ocean floor. They put metal tags on the tails of some of the fish that swarmed around. They studied many different underwater plants.

Tuffy had jobs to do, too. He had been trained to be a messenger. When he was working, he wore a special harness. Waterproof bags could be hooked onto it. In those bags Tuffy carried mail and tools and sometimes medicines to the aquanauts below. Up, down, up, down, he swam—the only live link between two very different worlds.

Tuffy had been trained to do another job, too. It was the most important of all. He had been trained to save lives.

The human aquanauts were safe inside Sealab. They had all sorts of comforts there—hot food, water, soft beds, books, even television. But the minute they stepped outside, they entered a strange and dangerous world.

The sun often shone brightly on the top of the water. But it was always dark as night 200 feet below, where the human aquanauts were exploring.

Each aquanaut carried two small tanks of air on his back. That air meant the difference between life and death in this world of water. But what if an aquanaut got lost? What if he couldn't find his way back to the safety of Sealab before his air was used up?

The human aquanauts knew that if this happened they had one last hope. Tuffy. None of the men became lost during the Sealab II project. But they weren't taking any chances. Again and again they ran tests. They pretended to be lost.

A man would hide himself behind a rock or in the middle of a big clump of plants. He would set off a special buzzer he always carried with him. This buzzer could be heard on the surface of the water. "Emergency!" it meant. "A man is lost. We need Tuffy! Fast!"

Seconds later Tuffy would come plunging down through the water. But he wouldn't head for the "lost" aquanaut—not right away. First he would swim to the Sealab capsule. He would slide his snout through a ring. The ring was attached to one end of a long rope. The other end of the rope was hooked to the metal side of Sealab.

Now *creee-eekkkkk*. Tuffy would scan the water with his sonar. Then off he'd swim toward the hiding man, trailing the rope behind him. Seconds later the man would take the ring from Tuffy. Now he could follow the lifeline of rope back to Sealab—and safety. And Tuffy? His job was done. So he would head for the top of the water for a welcome gulp of air.

Usually Tuffy made this roundtrip of rescue in about one minute. Did he always do his job so quickly and so well? Yes . . . except once.

Tuffy was a very smart, very hard-working dolphin. But he was also stubborn. And he loved to eat. So when Tuffy brought the ring to an aquanaut, he was always given a reward. Each man carried a small plastic bag of chopped fish. Tuffy would let the man take the ring. Then the man would squirt some fish into Tuffy's mouth.

But once something went wrong. The aquanaut tugged and tugged, but he couldn't get his bag of fish open. So finally he gave Tuffy a shove. "Move on," he meant.

But Tuffy didn't move on. *Where was his reward? Where was his mouthful of fish? This wasn't the way things were supposed to happen!* Tuffy stared at the man for a moment. He raised one of his flippers and bopped him over the head. *Then the dolphin aquanaut swam on.*

PROFILES

You Can't Take It with You

Eva-Lis Wuorio

Uncle Basil had a fortune, and he planned to keep it.

There was no denying two facts. Uncle Basil was rich. Uncle Basil was a miser.

The family were unanimous about that. They had used up all the words as their temper and their need of ready money dictated. Gentle Aunt Clotilda, who wanted a new string of pearls because the one she had was getting old, had merely called him Scrooge Basil. Percival, having again smashed his Aston Martin,[1] for which he had not paid, had declared Uncle Basil a skinflint, a miser, tightwad, churl, and usurer with colorful adjectives added. The rest had used up all the other words in the dictionary.

"He doesn't have to be parsimonious, that's true, with all he has," said Percival's mother. "But you shouldn't use rude words, Percival. They might get back to him."

"He can't take it with him," said Percival's sister Letitia, combing her golden hair. "I need a new fur but he said, 'Why? It's summer.' Well! He's mingy, that's what he is."

"He can't take it with him" was a phrase the family used so often it began to slip out in front of Uncle Basil as well.

"You can't take it with you, Uncle Basil," they said. "Why don't you buy a sensible house out in the country, and we could all come and visit you? Horses. A swimming pool. The lot. Think what

---

1. Aston Martin: A type of car.

fun you'd have, and you can certainly afford it. You can't take it with you, you know."

Uncle Basil had heard all the words they called him because he wasn't as deaf as he made out. He knew he was a mingy, stingy, penny-pinching screw, scrimp, scraper, pinchfist, hoarder, and curmudgeon (just to start with). There were other words, less gentle, he'd also heard himself called. He didn't mind. What galled him was the often-repeated warning, "You can't take it with you." After all, it was all his.

He'd gone to the Transvaal[2] when there was still gold to be found if one knew where to look. He'd found it. They said he'd come back too old to enjoy his fortune. What did they know? He enjoyed simply having a fortune. He enjoyed also saying no to them all. They were like circus animals, he often thought, behind the bars of their thousand demands of something for nothing.

Only once had he said yes. That was when his sister asked him to take on Verner, her somewhat slow-witted eldest son. "He'll do as your secretary," his sister Maud had said. Verner didn't do at all as a secretary, but since all he wanted to be happy was to be told what to do, Uncle Basil let him stick around as an all-around handyman.

Uncle Basil lived neatly in a house very much too small for his money, the family said, in an unfashionable suburb. It was precisely like the house where he had been born. Verner looked after the small garden, fetched the papers from the corner tobacconist, and filed his

---

2. Transvaal (trăns-väl') n.: The northeast province of the Republic of South Africa.

nails when he had time. He had nice nails. He never said to Uncle Basil, "You can't take it with you," because it didn't occur to him.

Uncle Basil also used Verner to run messages to his man of affairs, the bank, and such, since he didn't believe either in the mails or the telephone. Verner got used to carrying thick envelopes back and forth without ever bothering to question what was in them. Uncle Basil's lawyers, accountants, and bank managers also got used to his somewhat unorthodox business methods. He did have a fortune, and he kept making money with his investments. Rich men have always been allowed their foibles.

Another foible of Uncle Basil's was that, while he still was in excellent health, he had Verner drive him out to an old-fashioned carpenter shop, where he had himself measured for a coffin. He wanted it roomy, he said.

The master carpenter was a dour countryman of the same generation as Uncle Basil, and he accepted the order matter-of-factly. They consulted about woods and prices, and settled on a medium-price, unlined coffin. A lined one would have cost double.

"I'll line it myself," Uncle Basil said. "Or Verner can. There's plenty of time. I don't intend to pop off tomorrow. It would give the family too much satisfaction. I like enjoying my fortune."

Then one morning, while in good humor and sound mind, he sent Verner for his lawyer. The family got to hear about this, and there were in-fights, out-fights, and general quarreling while they tried to find out to whom Uncle Basil had decided to leave his money. To put them out of their misery, he said, he'd tell them the truth. He didn't like scattering money about. He liked it in a lump sum. Quit bothering him about it.

That happened a good decade before the morning his housekeeper, taking him his tea, found him peacefully asleep forever. It had been a good decade for him. The family hadn't dared to worry him, and his investments had risen steadily.

Only Percival, always pressed for money, had threatened to put arsenic in his tea, but when the usual proceedings were gone through, Uncle Basil was found to have died a natural death. "A happy death," said the family. "He hadn't suffered."

They began to remember loudly how nice they'd been to him and argued about who had been the nicest. It was true too. They had been attentive, the way families tend to be to rich and stubborn elderly relatives. They didn't know he'd heard all they'd said out of his hearing, as well as the flattering drivel they'd spread like soft butter on hot toast in his hearing. Everyone, recalling his own efforts to be thoroughly nice, was certain that he and only he would be the heir to the Lump Sum.

They rushed to consult the lawyer. He said that he had been instructed by Uncle Basil in sane and precise terms. The cremation was to take place immediately after the death, and they would find the coffin ready in the garden shed. Verner would know where it was.

"Nothing else?"

"Well," said the lawyer in the way lawyers have, "he left instructions for a funeral repast to be sent in from Fortnum and Mason.[3] Everything of the best. Goose and turkey, venison and beef, oys-

ters and lobsters, and wines of good vintage, plus plenty of whiskey. He liked to think of a good send-off, curmudgeon though he was, he'd said."

The family was a little shaken by the use of the word "curmudgeon." How did Uncle Basil know about that? But they were relieved to hear that the lawyer also had an envelope, the contents of which he did not know, to read to them at the feast after the cremation.

They all bought expensive black clothes, since black was the color of that season anyway, and whoever inherited would share the wealth. That was only fair.

Only Verner said that couldn't they buy Uncle Basil a smarter coffin? The one in the garden shed was pretty tatty, since the roof leaked. But the family hardly listened to him. After all, it would only be burned, so what did it matter?

So, duly and with proper sorrow, Uncle Basil was cremated.

The family returned to the little house as the housekeeper was leaving. Uncle Basil had given her a generous amount of cash, telling her how to place it so as to have a fair income for life. In gratitude she'd spread out the Fortnum and Mason goodies, but she wasn't prepared to stay to do the dishes.

They were a little surprised, but not dismayed, to hear from Verner that the house was now in his name. Uncle Basil had also given him a small sum of cash and told him how to invest it. The family taxed[4] him about it, but the amount was so nominal they were relieved to know Verner would be off their hands. Verner himself, though mildly missing the old man because he was used to him, was

---

3. Fortnum and Mason: A famous store and caterer; a group that supplies food for parties.

4. taxed (tăksd) v.: Accused or blamed.

quite content with his lot. He wasn't used to much, so he didn't need much.

The storm broke when the lawyer finally opened the envelope.

There was only one line in Uncle Basil's scrawl.

"I did take it with me."

Of course there was a great to-do. What about the fortune? The millions and millions!

Yes, said the men of affairs, the accountants, and even the bank managers, who finally admitted, yes, there had been a very considerable fortune. Uncle Basil, however, had drawn large sums in cash, steadily and regularly, over the past decade. What had he done with it? That the men of affairs, the accountants,

and the bank managers did not know. After all, it had been Uncle Basil's money, ergo, his affair.

Not a trace of the vast fortune ever came to light.

No one thought to ask Verner, and it didn't occur to Verner to volunteer that for quite a long time he had been lining the coffin, at Uncle Basil's behest, with thick envelopes he brought back from the banks. First he'd done a thick layer of these envelopes all around the sides and bottom of the coffin. Then, as Uncle Basil wanted, he'd tacked on blue sailcloth.

He might not be so bright in his head but he was smart with his hands.

He'd done a neat job.

1. Uncle Basil's family complains about his stinginess and greed. (a) Why do Aunt Clotilda, Percival, and Letitia need money? (b) How is Basil's greed different from his family's greed?

2. Uncle Basil likes Verner more than he likes the other members of his family. How is Verner different from the other family members?

3. Basil would not have gotten away with his plan if his family had cared more about him and less about his money. What do they say when Verner suggests they buy Basil a better coffin?

4. Throughout the story, Basil's family tell him, "You can't take it with you." How does Basil prove that they are wrong?

Plot

Plot is the pattern of events in a story. Usually, a story doesn't end exactly where it began. The events are ordered to show progress or change and to bring the story to a satisfying conclusion. Often, a *conflict* is introduced early in the story. When this conflict comes to a head, the story reaches its highest point of interest. This high point is called the *climax*. The final solution to the conflict, called the *resolution*, occurs toward the end of the story.

1. The opening situation presents a conflict. (a) What do the family want from Uncle Basil? (b) What does Uncle Basil want?

2. The conflict comes to a head at the funeral. Why is the funeral the climax, or high point?

3. What is the resolution of this story?

Activities

1. Imagine Uncle Basil had left you all his money. List ten things you would do with it.

2. **Composition.** Imagine you are a newspaper reporter, assigned to cover the reading of the letter at Uncle Basil's feast. Write one paragraph telling the story.

RELATIONSHIPS

Understanding Time Order

Time order tells you how events are related in time. A strategy for understanding time order is to pay close attention to words that signal this relationship. Examples of these words are *after, as, before, finally, meanwhile, since, then, until, when,* and *while.* Notice the signal words in *italics* in the following sentences.

> "He'd gone to the Transvaal *when* there was still gold to be found if one knew where to look."

> "The family got to hear about this, and there were in-fights, out-fights, and general quarreling *while* they tried to find out to whom Uncle Basil had decided to leave his money."

---

1. Read each of the following sentences. Then find the signal word that indicates time order in each sentence.
   a. "That happened a good decade before the morning his housekeeper, taking him his tea, found him peacefully asleep forever."
   b. "The cremation was to take place immediately after the death, and they would find the coffin ready in the garden shed."
   c. "The family returned to the little house as the housekeeper was leaving."
   d. "Another foible of Uncle Basil's was that, while he still was in excellent health, he had Verner drive him out to an old-fashioned carpenter shop, where he had himself measured for a coffin."

2. Make a time line for the following events. Just draw a horizontal line across a page. Starting at the left-hand side of the line, place the events on the line in correct time order. (The event that happened first should be at the left-hand side of the line.)
   a. Verner finished lining the coffin with thick envelopes.
   b. Uncle Basil found gold in the Transvaal.
   c. The lawyer read the contents of Uncle Basil's envelope.
   d. Uncle Basil had a coffin built for himself.
   e. Uncle Basil died.
   f. Uncle Basil hired Verner.

3. Why is it important that Uncle Basil's coffin was built before he died?

WORD ATTACK

Understanding Synonyms

A synonym is a word that has the same or almost the same meaning as another word. For example, Uncle Basil is described as a *miser*—a greedy person who loves to hoard money. The words *skinflint* and *tightwad* are both synonyms for *miser*.

1. Which of the following words are synonyms for *miser*? You may use a dictionary to help you.
   a. scrimp
   b. benefactor
   c. cheapskate
   d. spendthrift
   e. squanderer
   f. pinchfist
   g. hoarder
   h. economist
   i. money-grubber
   j. relative

2. Which of the following words are synonyms for *stingy*? You may use a dictionary to help you.
   a. parsimonious
   b. unpleasant
   c. miserly
   d. penny-pinching
   e. generous

3. Why can a miser be described as a *Scrooge*? You may use a dictionary to help you answer.

4. The words *rich* and *wealthy* are synonyms when *rich* is used in a sentence to mean "having much money." In which of the sentences below can you substitute *wealthy* for *rich* without changing the meaning?
   a. Uncle Basil was *rich*; many years ago he had found gold in the Transvaal.
   b. They served a *rich* dessert from Fortnum and Mason.
   c. The family members hoped they would be *rich* after they inherited Uncle Basil's money.
   d. The ornate decoration on the furniture was too *rich* for his taste.
   e. The land yielded a *rich* harvest that year.

The Promised Visit

Grey Cohoe

It had been a long day at Window Rock, Arizona. Now I was on my way home. I'd shoved myself up at dawn and started from Shiprock early that morning to appear for my tribal scholarship interview. I had applied for it in the spring so I could go to school after my graduation from high school. My brother-in-law, Martin, had been considerate enough to lend me his pickup truck. I would still have been there promptly for my appointment, no matter if I'd needed to walk, hitchhike, or crawl the hundred and twenty miles.

The old zigzagging road lined the shadowed flat region, cooling from a day's heat. It was not until now that the evening wind began to form wool-like clouds, building a dark, overcast stretching across my destination. At first, it was obviously summer rain clouds, and even a child could recognize the rolling grayish mesa.[1] The white lane markers rhythmically speared under me as I raced toward home.

I rolled down the window about an inch to smell the first rain that I would inhale this summer. The harsh air rushed in, cold and wild. Its crazy current tangled and teased my hair. The

---

1. mesa (mā′sə) n.: A high plateau; tableland with steep sides.

aroma of the flying wet dirt tensed my warm nose, a smell of rain. Immediately the chill awakened my reflexes. I balanced my body into a proper driving position, according to a statement in the driver's manual. I prepared to confront the slippery pavement.

By now I could sight the flashes of lightning spearing into the horizon, flowing against the dark overcast. I could almost see the whole valley in one flash. The black clouds looked closer and became angrier as I approached their overcast. Being used to the old reservation road, narrow and rough, and well adjusted to the pickup, I drove ahead to meet the first raindrops.

Many people had died along this same highway, never telling us what caused their accidents. Most of these tragedies occurred in bad weather, especially in thunderstorms. Several months ago the highway department stuck small white crosses along the road at each place where an accident victim had been killed. This was to keep a driver alert and aware. The crosses became so numerous that it caused more confusion and more accidents. When a person sees a cross he becomes nervous.

The dark clouds formed themselves into a huge ugly mass. It reminded me of the fearful myths people told about such angry clouds. Their suspicious appearance scared me, making my joints and very soul tremble.

My mother once mentioned a monster that lived in the thunderclouds. Was it only one of my bedtime stories, or was it the killer of all the cross-marked victims?

Another story was told to me by my grandmother. It was told to her by her late son before he passed away in a hos-

pital. He saw a ghost standing in his way on the highway and he drove through the rain-sogged image. He soon ran off the road after being knocked unconscious by the shock.

"Baloney! I shouldn't believe those nonsenses," I scolded myself. "I don't want to be one of those Navajos who is easily aroused by superstitions."

The dark overcast hid my view of the road, and the area around faded away into darkness so I had to turn on the headlights. My face was now tired of being fixed in the same direction, down the long, dirty highway. My eyelids were so weak that they closed by themselves. I should have slept longer the night before. Again I rolled down the window. The cold air poured in, caressing me with its moistened chill. It awoke me completely.

The sudden forceful blow jolted the car and waved it like a rolling wagon. The screaming wind began to knock at my windows. I clung hard to the steering wheel to fight the rushing wind. I slowed almost to a stop and peered out through the blowing dust, at the hood, trying to keep on the road. Flying soil and tumbleweeds crashed against the car. I could not tell what ran beside the highway—a canyon, or maybe a wash. The angry wind roared and blew so strong that the truck slanted. I didn't know how to escape the Wind Monster. I sat motionless, feeling death inside my soul.

And then the car was rocked by falling raindrops as if it were a tin can being battered by flying stones. The downpour came too quickly for me to see the first drops on the windshield. The whole rocky land shook when a loud cracking flash of lightning shot into the nearby ground.

The storm calmed and turned into a genial shower. Then I could see where I was. Through the crystal rain, a green and white-lettered sign showed up in the headlights. LITTLEWATER 12 miles: SHIPROCK 32 miles. At last I felt relieved. I would be home in less than an hour. Never in my life had I ever longed for home so much as on this day. The windshield cleared and the rain had passed.

With the scary storm over, and no longer penetrated by superstition, I felt as if I'd awakened from a nightmare. My hunger, too, was gone, but the crampy stiffness still tightened my body. I didn't bother to stop for a rest. I rushed straight home. I hoped my supper would be waiting. The clouds slid away and it wasn't as late as I'd thought.

By now some twinkling stars appeared over the northern horizon. The round moon cast its light on the soggy ground as the silky white clouds slid by after the rain. The water reflected the light so that the standing water shone like the moon itself. I could see the whole area as if in daylight. I ran the tires through the shallow puddles on the pavement to feel it splash. I imagined myself running and playing along the San Juan River shore. I continued to hasten on, looking for the lights at Littlewater over on the other side of the next hill.

A few electric lights appeared within range of my headlights. Three dull guide lights shone at the store. One larger light showed up the whole front porch. As usual, there wasn't anybody around at this late hour. I slowed to glance at the porch as I passed by. At the same time, as I turned back to the road, I saw a standing object about fifty yards ahead. I had always feared dark objects at night. My soul tensed with a frightening chill as I trembled. I drove closer, telling myself it might be a horse or a calf.

The lights reached the dark image as I approached. Surprisingly, it was a hitchhiker. I didn't think anything about the person. All that came to my mind was to offer someone my help. Then I saw it was a girl.

I stopped a little way past her.

She slowly and shyly walked up to the car window. She was all wet and trembling from the cold air. "Can you give me a lift to Shiprock?" she politely asked in her soft, quivering voice.

"Sure. That's where I'm going, too." I quickly offered the warm empty seat.

She smiled and opened the door. Water dripped to the floor from her wet clothes. She sat motionless and kept looking away from me.

I thought she was just scared or shy. I, too, felt shy, and we didn't talk for a long time. It wasn't until a few miles from Shiprock that I finally started a conversation.

"I guess the people around this area are happy to get such a big rain," I finally dared to utter. "I was supposed to water our farm field tomorrow, but I guess the good Lord did it for me," I joked, hoping she would laugh or say something. "What part of Shiprock are you from?" I questioned her.

"Not in Shiprock. About one mile from there," she carefully murmured, using her best English.

She was dressed in a newly made green-velvet blouse and a long, silky white skirt. She wore many silver and turquoise necklaces and rings. A red and orange sash-belt tightly fitted around her narrow waist. She was so dressed up that she looked ready to go to town or a dance.

Her long black hair hung loosely to her small round shoulders around her face. In the glow from the instrument panel I could tell she was very pretty. Finally, I gathered enough guts to offer her my school sweater. "Here. You better put this on before you catch a cold. I hear pneumonia is very dangerous," I said, as I struggled to take off the sweater.

She kindly took it and threw it around herself. "Thank you." She smiled and her words came out warmly.

I looked at her and she looked at the same time, too. I almost went off the road when I saw her beautiful smile of greeting. She was the prettiest girl I had ever seen. I jerked the steering wheel and the car jolted back onto the highway. We both laughed. From that moment on, we talked and felt as if we'd known each other before. I fell in love and I guess she did, too.

"Where have you been in this kind of bad weather?" I began to ask questions so we could get better acquainted with each other.

"I visited some of my relatives

around Littlewater." She calmly broke her shyness. "The ground was too wet to walk on so I decided to get a ride."

"I've been to Window Rock to get a scholarship to an art school. I started this morning and it isn't until now I'm coming back. I'm late for supper because of the storm."

I knew she was interested in me, too, as she asked me, "Where do you live?"

"I live on one of the farms down toward west from Shiprock. I live with my family next to Thomas Yazzie's place."

"I used to know Thomas and his family when I was very small," she almost cried. "It's always sad to lose friends."

I felt sorry for her losing her friends. Right then I knew she was lonely.

"Where do you live?" I asked, as I looked straight down the lighted road.

She hesitated to answer as if she weren't sure of it. Then she said, "I live about four miles from Shiprock." Then she lowered her head as if she were worried about something I'd said.

I didn't talk anymore after that. Again it was quiet. I kept my mind on the road, trying to forget my warm feelings for her beauty.

The night settled itself across the desert land, making stars and the moon more bright. The night sky and the dampness made me sleepy. I felt in a dreamy, romantic mood. The rain still covered the road. It was too quiet for comfort.

"Let's listen to some music," I interrupted the silence as I turned on the radio. I tuned to some rock music. So now, with the cool night, beating music, and our silence, we drove until she asked me to stop. It was just about a mile over two hills to Shiprock. I stopped where a dirt road joined the highway.

"Is this the path to your place?" I quickly asked before she departed.

"Yes. I live about three miles up this road." She pointed her lips for direction as she placed her hand on the door handle.

"I wish I could take you home, but the road is too wet. I might never get home tonight. Well, I hope I'll see you in Shiprock sometime. By the way, what's your name?" I tried to keep her there awhile longer by talking to her.

She took a long time to say her name. "Susan Billy," she said finally. Then she added, "Maybe I can visit you some of these nights." She smiled as she opened the door and stepped out of the car.

"All right, goodbye." I tried not to show how I felt as I said those last words.

I looked back in the mirror as I dropped over the hill. She stood waving her hand. I felt proud to find someone like her who wanted so much to see me again. I already missed her. Or was she just joking about her visit? Why would she want to visit me at night? I smiled, hoping she'd come very soon.

Before I knew it I was home. I stopped at our garage. The lights in the house were out and the rain had wet the red brick building to a deeper red. I couldn't wait to get into the bed where I could freely think about Susan. I didn't bother to eat or wake my folks. I just covered myself with the warm blankets.

Another sunny morning turned into a cloudy and windy afternoon. Rain clouds brought another chilly breeze as they had two evenings before, when I had gone to Window Rock. I had not forgotten Susan and, deep in my heart, I kept expecting her visit which she had spoken of. Today, though, we had to go to the field to plant new seeds. The cold called for a warm jacket. I glanced around the room where I usually kept my sweater, a maroon-and-gold-colored school sweater. I walked through the house, but I didn't find it. I used my old jacket instead, hoping my sweater was in the car at the hospital where my brother-in-law, Martin, was working.

The movements of my arms and legs, my digging and sowing seeds, were in my usual routine for the last few weeks. I could let my mind wander to Susan while my body went on with its work.

"Are you tired already? What are you thinking about?" My brother asked as I stopped working.

I remembered where I left my sweater. "What time is it?" I asked him, wishing the time for Martin to come home with the pickup were near, but I remembered that our noon lunch wasn't even thought of yet.

"Don't know. I know it's not lunchtime yet," he joked, and kept hoeing the small weeds along the corn rows.

It wasn't until late that evening, about six-thirty, that I was on my way to see Susan. My whole life filled with joy. The dirt road leading off the highway where Susan had stood seemed dried enough for the tires to roll on.

Slowly and very nervously I approached the end of the three miles to her place. I rode over the last hill and stopped at a hogan. The people were still outside, eating their supper under a shadehouse. A familiar man sat facing me from the circle around the dishes on the ground. I was sure I'd seen him someplace, but I couldn't recall where. His wife sat beside him, keeping busy frying some round, thin dough. Three small children accompanied them, two older girls and a child—I couldn't tell whether it was a girl or a boy. I politely asked the man where I could find Susan.

"Their hogans are near, over beyond that rocky hill," he directed me in his unmannered way. His words came from his filled mouth.

"They moved to the mountain several days ago," his wife interrupted, "but I saw a light at the place last night. The husband might have ridden down for their supplies."

Hopefully, I started again. Sure enough, there were the mud hogans, standing on a lonely plateau. As I approached, a man paused from his busy packing and stood watching me.

He set down a box of groceries and came to the car door. I reached out the window and shook his hand for greeting.

"Hello. Do you know where Susan Billy lives?" I asked, pretending I didn't know where to go to find her.

"Susan Billy?" He looked down, puzzled, and pronounced the name as if he'd never heard of it before. After a while of silence, he remarked, "I don't know if you are mistaking for our Susan, or there might be another girl by that name."

My hope almost left me as I explained further. "Two nights ago I gave her a ride from Littlewater to the road over there. She told me she lived at this place."

His smile disappeared and a puzzled, odd look took its place.

"See that old hogan over in the dis-

tance beyond the three sagebrushes?" He pointed to an old, caved-in hogan. "Susan Billy is there," he sadly informed me.

"Good. I'll wait here until she comes back." I sank into the car happily, but why was he looking so shocked or worried?

"You don't understand," he went on, explaining, "she died ten years ago and she is buried in that hogan."

At first I thought it was a joke. I knew how some parents would try to keep their daughters or sons from seeing any strangers. His black hair and light complexion, not so smooth or whitish as Susan's, somehow resembled hers.

Then I knew he was lying. "I loaned her my sweater and I forgot to get it back." I tried to convince him to tell the truth.

He seemed so shocked as he looked more carefully at the old hogan again. "See that red object on one of the logs?" He pointed out that it hadn't been there until recently.

I saw the maroon object. I could instantly recognize my sweater at a distance. My heart almost stopped with the horrible shock. I struggled to catch my breath back. I didn't believe in ghosts until then, but I had to believe my sweater. I had to believe the beautiful girl who had ridden with me, who had promised to visit me. Still, why hadn't she killed me like the rest of her victims? Was it because of my sweater or because of the love we shared?

From that day, I have proven to myself the truth of the Navajo superstitions. I know I shall never get my sweater back, but, on one of these windy nights, I will see Susan again, as she promised. What will I do then?

Close Up

1. Why do the dark clouds make the young man tremble as he drives through the storm?

2. After the storm passes, he feels as though he has awakened from a nightmare. (a) What does he see that suddenly frightens him again? (b) Why is this sight unusual?

3. (a) Why does the man try to keep Susan talking at the road to her house? (b) How does he feel when she says she may visit him some night?

4. (a) What does the young man find out about Susan a few days later? (b) What does his sweater prove?

5. At the end of the story, does the young man still want a visit from Susan Billy? Why or why not?

Suspense

Suspense is the quality of the story that makes you wonder what will happen next. Suspense makes you fear for the fate of one of the characters. One method of building suspense is foreshadowing. **Foreshadowing means that, early in the story, clues are given to hint at what will happen later.** These clues prepare you to accept what finally happens and give you information usually not available to the characters.

1. Early in the story, the young man thinks about all the people who have died along the road. What do his thoughts on death lead you to suspect may happen?

2. (a) What two tales about storms haunt the driver? (b) Why do you think the author includes these tales?

3. Susan Billy tells the man very little about herself. Does this add suspense to the story? Why or why not?

4. At the end of the story, the man finds out who Susan Billy really is. Do you still wonder what will happen to him? Why or why not?

Activities

1. List details that make this story eerie or frightening.

2. **Composition.** Write a paragraph telling what you think the man will do when he meets Susan Billy again.

RELATIONSHIPS

Understanding Cause and Effect

Some people, events, places are connected through a cause-and-effect relationship. **Something—*the cause*—makes something else—*the effect*—happen.** A strategy for identifying a cause-and-effect relationship is noting the special words that signal this connection.

accordingly	consequently	so (so that)
as a result	for	therefore
because	since	thus

Some of those words also signal other relationships. The word *since* can signal either a cause-and-effect relationship or a time-order relationship. For example:

> He stopped the car *since* it was raining heavily. (cause and effect)
> He had been away from home *since* early morning. (time order)

Be sure to look at the context of the whole sentence before you make a judgment.

---

1. Identify the word or words that signal a cause-and-effect relationship in each item below.
   a. He applied in the spring so he could go to school after graduation.
   b. Since he didn't want to believe in superstitions, he thought of something else.
   c. As a result of the rain, the roads were slippery.
   d. He gave her his sweater because he didn't want her to catch pneumonia.
   e. He knew she liked him, for her eyes told him as much.

2. Copy each sentence below on a separate piece of paper. Draw one line under the part of the sentence that shows the cause, and two lines under the part that shows the effect.
   a. What he heard in her voice was love; therefore, he knew she would find him again.
   b. His mind raced ahead to his next meeting with her; accordingly, he lost all track of time.
   c. It was his maroon sweater; thus, he had no choice but to believe in ghosts.
   d. The girl was dead; consequently, he knew his love was hopeless.
   e. Because she loved him, the ghost did not lead him to his death.

WORD ATTACK

Finding Verb Forms in a Dictionary

A verb is a word that expresses an action or a state of being. For example:

Action	State of Being
He *drove* through the rain.	He *was* a high-school student.
She *smiled* at him.	She *looked* beautiful.

A verb also has *tenses* that show time: present, past, and future. A verb has four principal parts which you must know in order to put a verb into the correct tense. These principal parts are the present infinitive, the past, and the past participle, and the present participle.

Present Infinitive	Past	Past Participle	Present Participle
drive	drove	(have) driven	driving
smile	smiled	(have) smiled	smiling
run	ran	(have) run	running

You can use a dictionary to find the spelling of the principal parts of a verb. First, look up the present infinitive form of the verb: *drive*. You will find the following information:

drive (drīv) *v.*: drove, driven, driving

The first word after the abbreviation *v.* is the past, the second is the past participle, and the third is the present participle. Sometimes the past and the past participle are the same. When this happens, you will find two words after the *v.* For example:

smile (smīl) *v.*: smiled, smiling

The past and past participle are both *smiled*.

► Read each of the following sentences. Then write each of the *italicized* verbs in the form indicated in parentheses. You may use a dictionary to help you find the correct spelling.
   a. She was *hitchhike* (present participle).
   b. He *meet* (past) her for the first time that night.
   c. He had *see* (past participle) her up ahead of him.
   d. He had *prepare* (past participle) for the rainy night.
   e. He is *control* (present participle) the car in spite of the storm.
   f. After a while, the clouds *slide* (past) away.
   g. People *tell* (past) of that storm for years.
   h. Many people had *die* (past participle) along that road.

Say It with Flowers

Toshio Mori

**Teruo needed the job,
but he didn't know if he could
lie to the customers.**

He was an odd one to come to the shop and ask Mr. Sasaki for a job, but at the time I kept my mouth shut. There was something about this young man's appearance which I could not altogether harmonize with a job as a clerk in a flower shop. I was a delivery boy for Mr. Sasaki then. I had seen clerks come and go, and although they were of various sorts of temperaments and conducts, all of them had the technique of waiting on the customers, or acquired one eventually. You could never tell about a new one, however, and to be on the safe side I said nothing and watched our boss readily take on this young man. Anyhow we were glad to have an extra hand because the busy season was coming around.

Mr. Sasaki undoubtedly remembered last year's rush when Tommy, Mr. Sasaki, and I had to do everything and had our hands tied behind our backs from having so many things to do at one time. He wanted to be ready this time. "Another clerk and we'll be all set for any kind of business," he used to tell us. When Teruo came around looking for a job, he got it, and Morning Glory Flower Shop was all set for the year as far as our boss was concerned.

When Teruo reported for work the following morning, Mr. Sasaki left him in Tommy's hands. Tommy had been our number-one clerk for a long time.

"Tommy, teach him all you can," Mr. Sasaki said. "Teruo's going to be with us from now on."

"Sure," Tommy said.

"Tommy's a good florist. You watch and listen to him," the boss told the young man.

"All right, Mr. Sasaki," the young man said. He turned to us and said, "My name is Teruo." We shook hands.

We got to know one another pretty well after that. He was a quiet fellow with very little words for anybody, but his smile disarmed a person. We soon learned that he knew nothing about the florist business. He could identify a rose when he saw one, and gardenias and carnations too; but other flowers and materials were new to him.

"You fellows teach me something about this business and I'll be grateful. I want to start from the bottom," Teruo said.

Tommy and I nodded. We were pretty sure by then he was all right. Tommy eagerly went about showing Teruo the florist game. Every morning for several days, Tommy repeated the prices of the flowers for him. He told Teruo what to do on telephone orders; how to keep the greens fresh; how to make bouquets, corsages, and sprays. "You need a little more time to learn how to make big funeral pieces," Tommy said. "That'll come later."

In a couple of weeks Teruo was just as good a clerk as we had had in a long time. He was curious almost to a fault, and was a glutton for work. It was about this time our boss decided to move ahead his yearly business trip to Seattle. Undoubtedly he was satisfied with Teruo, and he knew we could get along without him for a while. He went off and left Tommy in full charge.

During Mr. Sasaki's absence, I was often in the shop helping Tommy and Teruo with the customers and the orders. One day Teruo learned that I once worked in the nursery and had experience in flower-growing.

"How do you tell when a flower is fresh or old?" he asked me. "I can't tell one from the other. All I do is follow your instructions and sell the ones you tell me to sell first, but I can't tell one from the other."

I laughed. "You don't need to know that, Teruo," I told him. "When the customers ask you whether the flowers are fresh, say yes firmly. 'Our flowers are always fresh, madam.' "

Teruo picked up a vase of carnations. "These flowers came in four or five days ago, didn't they?" he asked me.

"You're right. Five days ago," I said.

"How long will they keep if a customer bought them today?" Teruo asked.

"I guess in this weather they'll hold a day or two," I said.

"Then they're old," Teruo almost gasped. "Why, we have fresh ones that last a week or so in the shop."

"Sure, Teruo. And why should you worry about that?" Tommy said. "You talk right to the customers and they'll believe you. 'Our flowers are always fresh? You bet they are! Just came in a little while ago from the market.' "

Teruo looked at us calmly. "That's a hard thing to say when you know it isn't true."

"You've got to get it over with sooner or later," I told him. "Everybody has to do it. You too, unless you want to lose your job."

"I don't think I can say it convincingly again," Teruo said. "I must've said yes forty times already when I didn't know any better. It'll be harder next time."

"You've said it forty times already so why can't you say yes forty million times more? What's the difference? Remember, Teruo, it's your business to live," Tommy said.

"I don't like it," Teruo said.

"Do we like it? Do you think we're any different from you?" Tommy asked Teruo. "You're just a green kid. You don't know any better so I don't get sore, but you got to play the game when you're in it. You understand, don't you?"

Teruo nodded. For a moment he stood and looked curiously at us for the first time, and then went away to water the potted plants.

In the ensuing weeks we watched Teruo develop into a slick salesclerk but for one thing. If a customer forgot to ask about the condition of the flowers, Teruo did splendidly. But if someone should mention about the freshness of the flowers, he wilted right in front of the customers. Sometimes he would splutter. He would stand gaping speechless on other occasions without a comeback. Sometimes, looking embarrassedly at us, he would take the customers to the fresh flowers in the rear and complete the sales.

"Don't do that anymore, Teruo," Tommy warned him one afternoon after watching him repeatedly sell the fresh ones. "You know we got plenty of the old stuff in the front. We can't throw all that stuff away. First thing you know the boss'll start losing money and we'll all be thrown out."

"I only wish I could sell like you," Teruo said. "Whenever they ask me, 'Is this fresh?' 'How long will it keep?' I lose all sense about selling the stuff, and begin to think of the difference between the fresh and the old stuff. Then the trouble begins."

"Remember, the boss has to run the shop so he can keep it going," Tommy told him. "When he returns next week, you better not let him see you touch the fresh flowers in the rear."

On the day Mr. Sasaki came back to the shop we saw something unusual. For the first time I watched Teruo sell some old stuff to a customer. I heard the man plainly ask him if the flowers would keep good, and very clearly I heard Teruo reply, "Yes, sir. These flowers'll keep good." I looked at Tommy, and he winked back. When Teruo came back to make it into a bouquet, he looked as if he had a snail in his mouth. Mr. Sasaki came back to the rear and watched him make the bouquet. When Teruo went up front to complete the sale, Mr. Sasaki looked at Tommy and nodded approvingly.

When I went out to the truck to make my last delivery for the day, Teruo followed me. "Gee, I feel rotten," he said to me. "Those flowers I sold to the people, they won't last longer than tomorrow. I feel lousy. I'm lousy. The people'll get to know my word pretty soon."

"Forget it," I said. "Quit worrying. What's the matter with you?"

"I'm lousy," he said, and went back to the store.

Then one early morning the inevitable happened. While Teruo was selling the fresh flowers in the back to a customer, Mr. Sasaki came in quietly and watched the transaction. The boss didn't say anything at the time. All day Teruo looked sick. He didn't know whether to explain to the boss or shut up.

While Teruo was out to lunch, Mr. Sasaki called us aside. "How long has this been going on?" he asked us. He was pretty sore.

"He's been doing it off and on. We told him to quit it," Tommy said. "He says he feels rotten selling old flowers."

"Old flowers!" snorted Mr. Sasaki. "I'll tell him plenty when he comes back. Old flowers! Maybe you can call them old at the wholesale market, but they're not old in a flower shop."

"He feels guilty fooling the customers," Tommy explained.

The boss laughed impatiently. "That's no reason for a businessman."

When Teruo came back he knew what was up. He looked at us for a moment and then went about cleaning the stems of the old flowers.

"Teruo," Mr. Sasaki called.

Teruo approached us as if steeled for an attack.

"You've been selling fresh flowers and leaving the old ones go to waste. I can't afford that, Teruo," Mr. Sasaki said. "Why don't you do as you're told? We all sell the flowers in the front. I tell you they're not old in a flower shop. Why can't you sell them?"

"I don't like it, Mr. Sasaki," Teruo said. "When the people ask me if they're fresh, I hate to answer. I feel rotten after selling the old ones."

"Look here, Teruo," Mr. Sasaki said. "I don't want to fire you. You're a good boy, and I know you need a job, but you've got to be a good clerk here or you're going out. Do you get me?"

"I get you," Teruo said.

In the morning we were all at the shop early. I had an eight o'clock delivery, and the others had to rush with a big funeral order. Teruo was there early. "Hello," he greeted us cheerfully as we came in. He was unusually high-spirited, and I couldn't account for it. He was there before us and had already filled out the eight o'clock package for me. He was almost through with the funeral frame, padding it with wet moss and covering it all over with brake fern, when Tommy came in. When Mr. Sasaki arrived, Teruo waved his hand and cheerfully went about gathering the flowers for the funeral piece. As he flitted here and there, he seemed as if he had forgotten our presence, even the boss. He looked at each vase, sized up the flowers, and then cocked his head at the next one. He did this with great deliberation, as if he were the boss and the last word in the shop. That was all right, but when a customer soon came in, he swiftly attended him as if he owned all the flowers in the world. When the man asked Teruo if he was getting fresh flowers, Teruo, without batting an eye, escorted the customer into the rear and eventually showed and sold the

fresh ones. He did it with so much grace, dignity, and swiftness that we stood around like his stooges. However, Mr. Sasaki went on with his work as if nothing had happened.

Along toward noon Teruo attended his second customer. He fairly ran to greet an old lady who wanted a cheap bouquet around fifty cents for a dinner table. This time he not only went back to the rear for the fresh ones but added three or four extras. To make it more irritating for the boss, who was watching every move, Teruo used an extra lot of maidenhair because the old lady was appreciative of his art of making bouquets. Tommy and I watched the boss fuming inside of his office.

on three customers at one time, ignoring our presence. It was amazing how he did it. He hurriedly took one customer's order and had him write a birthday greeting for it; jumped to the second customer's side and persuaded her to buy Columbia roses because they were the freshest of the lot. She wanted them delivered so he jotted it down on the sales book, and leaped to the third customer.

"I want to buy that orchid in the window," she stated without deliberation.

"Do you have to have orchid, madam?" Teruo asked the lady.

"No," she said. "But I want something nice for tonight's ball, and I think the orchid will match my dress. Why do you ask?"

"If I were you I wouldn't buy that orchid," he told her. "It won't keep. I could sell it to you and make a profit but I don't want to do that and spoil your evening. Come to the back, madam, and I'll show you some of the nicest gardenias in the market today. We call them Belmont and they're fresh today."

He came to the rear with the lady. We watched him pick out three of the biggest gardenias and make them into a corsage. When the lady went out with her package, a little boy about eleven years old came in and wanted a twenty-five-cent bouquet for his mother's birthday. Teruo waited on the boy. He was out in the front, and we saw him pick out a dozen of the two-dollar-a-dozen roses and give them to the kid.

Tommy nudged me. "If he was the boss he couldn't do those things," he said.

"In the first place," I said, "I don't think he could be a boss."

When the old lady went out of the shop, Mr. Sasaki came out furious. "You're a blockhead. You have no business sense. What are you doing here?" he said to Teruo. "Are you crazy?"

Teruo looked cheerful. "I'm not crazy, Mr. Sasaki," he said. "And I'm not dumb. I just like to do it that way, that's all."

The boss turned to Tommy and me. "That boy's a sap," he said. "He's got no head."

Teruo laughed and walked off to the front with a broom. Mr. Sasaki shook his head. "What's the matter with him? I can't understand him," he said.

While the boss was out to lunch, Teruo went on a mad spree. He waited

"What do you think?" Tommy said. "Is he crazy? Is he trying to get himself fired?"

"I don't know," I said.

When Mr. Sasaki returned, Teruo was waiting on another customer, a young lady.

"Did Teruo eat yet?" Mr. Sasaki asked Tommy.

"No, he won't go. He says he's not hungry today," Tommy said.

We watched Teruo talking to the young lady. The boss shook his head. Then it came. Teruo came back to the rear and picked out a dozen of the very fresh white roses and took them out to the lady.

"Aren't they lovely?" we heard her exclaim.

We watched him come back, take down a box, place several maidenhairs and asparagus, place the roses neatly inside, sprinkle a few drops, and then give it to her. We watched him thank her, and we noticed her smile and thanks. The girl walked out.

Mr. Sasaki ran excitedly to the front. "Teruo! She forgot to pay!"

Teruo stopped the boss on the way out. "Wait, Mr. Sasaki," he said. "I gave it to her."

"What!" the boss cried indignantly.

"She came in just to look around and see the flowers. She likes pretty roses. Don't you think she's wonderful?"

"What's the matter with you?" the boss said. "Are you crazy? What did she buy?"

"Nothing, I tell you," Teruo said. "I gave it to her because she admired it, and she's pretty enough to deserve beautiful things, and I liked her."

"You're fired! Get out!" Mr. Sasaki spluttered. "Don't come back to the store again."

"And I gave her fresh ones too," Teruo said.

Mr. Sasaki rolled out several bills from his pocketbook. "Here's your wages for this week. Now, get out," he said.

"I don't want it," Teruo said. "You keep it and buy some more flowers."

"Here, take it. Get out," Mr. Sasaki said.

Teruo took the bills and rang up the cash register. "All right, I'll go now. I feel fine. I'm happy. Thanks to you." He waved his hand to Mr. Sasaki. "No hard feelings."

On the way out Teruo remembered our presence. He looked back. "Goodbye. Good luck," he said cheerfully to Tommy and me.

He walked out of the shop with his shoulders straight, head high, and whistling. He did not come back to see us again.

Close Up

1. Teruo works hard and is eager to learn the florist business. Explain the following sentence: "He was curious almost to a fault, and was a glutton for work."

2. What does Teruo find out when he asks how to tell the age of the flowers?

3. Tommy tells Teruo he must sell the old flowers. (a) What does Tommy think Teruo's "business" should be? (b) Who is more practical—Tommy or Teruo? Why?

4. (a) Are the flowers Mr. Sasaki sells really old? Why or why not? (b) How does he show kindness to Teruo?

5. Mr. Sasaki says that Teruo doesn't have any business sense. (a) What does the term "business sense" mean? (b) Do you agree with his judgment of Teruo? Why or why not?

6. You may have seen the phrase "Say it with flowers" in an advertisement for a florist. (a) What does this phrase usually mean? (b) What does Teruo try to "say with flowers"?

Dilemma

A dilemma is a situation that involves a choice between two equally unpleasant alternatives. A method of creating suspense in a story is to place a character in a dilemma.

1. Teruo's situation is a dilemma. He will lose his job unless he lies to the customers. What will he lose if he does lie to the customers?

2. (a) How does Teruo feel the first time he lies to someone about the flowers? (b) How does he feel when Mr. Sasaki finds him selling fresh flowers?

3. (a) What forces Mr. Sasaki to fire Teruo? (b) Do you think Teruo wanted Mr. Sasaki to fire him? Why or why not?

4. (a) How does Teruo feel when he is fired? (b) How does he act?

Activities

1. **Composition.** Write a paragraph telling whether you think Teruo did or did not have courage.

2. **Composition.** Pretend that Teruo opens his own flower shop. Think up a name for it and write a newspaper advertisement.

RELATIONSHIPS

Understanding Cause and Effect

A cause is what makes something happen. An effect is what happens. Many ideas and events are connected by a cause-and-effect relationship. For example, Mr. Sasaki hires Teruo *because* the busy season is approaching. The cause is the busy season. The effect is that Mr. Sasaki hires Teruo.

▶ Copy each of the following sentences on a separate piece of paper. Then draw one line under the part of the sentence that is the cause. Draw two lines under the part of the sentence that is the effect.

a. The delivery boy did not say anything about Teruo because he wanted to be on the safe side.

b. Since Tommy was the head clerk, he trained Teruo.

c. Mr. Sasaki was satisfied with Teruo, so he moved ahead his yearly business trip.

d. Because the delivery boy had worked in a nursery, he knew how to tell the age of flowers.

e. Teruo knew the flowers were old, for they were brought in five days ago.

f. Teruo found it hard to say that the flowers were fresh, since he knew it wasn't true.

g. Tommy sold the old flowers so that he could keep his job.

h. Tommy didn't get angry at Teruo, since he felt Teruo was just a "green kid."

i. Mr. Sasaki knew Teruo needed the job; consequently, he gave Teruo a second chance.

j. Teruo persuaded the customer to buy Columbia roses, since they were the freshest of the lot.

WORD ATTACK

Understanding Homophones

Homophones are words that sound alike, but have different spellings and different meanings. For example:

weak—week	so—sew	to—two—too
time—thyme	ewe—you	sell—cell

▶ Choose the correct homophone to complete each sentence below. You may use a dictionary to help you.

a. "... but at the _____ (time, thyme) I kept my mouth shut."

b. "Mr. Sasaki undoubtedly remembered last year's rush when Tommy, Mr. Sasaki, and I had to do everything and had our hands tied behind _____ (hour, our) backs from having _____ (so, sew) many things to _____ (do, dew) at _____ (one, won) time."

c. "When Teruo reported _____ (four, for) work the following morning, Mr. Sasaki left him _____ (in, inn) Tommy's hands."

d. "We got to _____ (no, know) one another pretty well after that."

e. "We soon learned that he _____ (new, knew) nothing about the florist business."

f. "Every morning for several _____ (days, daze) Tommy repeated the prices of the _____ (flours, flowers) for him."

g. "All I do is follow your instructions and _____ (sell, cell) the ones you tell me to ... "

h. "I guess in this _____ (whether, weather) they'll hold a day or two."

i. "When the customers ask _____ (whether, weather) the flowers are fresh, say yes firmly."

j. "... I _____ (no, know) you _____ (knead, need) a job, but you've got to be a good clerk _____ (here, hear) or _____ (your, you're) going out."

Faces

Ted Joans

I want to see faces
                    of all races/winning faces/grinning
                    faces/happy faces/faces that face East
in prayer/faces covered & uncovered with hair/faces
uplifted & proud/faces of joy of being in love/faces
of yesterday,today,Now & tomorrow faces/faces that
5   erased war/faces that destroyed ignorance, disease, &
hunger/faces that face the tasks & won/freedom faces/
freedom faces/faces of one nation and that nation is the
human being congregation of faces/freedom faces/I want
to see faces/I want to see faces/I want to see faces/I want
to face me

Final Curve

Langston Hughes

When you turn the corner
And you run into *yourself*
Then you know that you have turned
All the corners that are left.

Close Up ▶ Do you think it takes courage to come to terms with yourself, to face who you are? Why or why not?

A Running Brook of Horror

Daniel Mannix

Grace Wiley lived in a small house filled with poisonous snakes that wandered around like cats.

It was through my interest in snakes that, while in California, Jule and I had the most terrible experience of our career.

I had first heard of Grace Wiley some years before when Dr. William Mann, then director of the National Zoological Park in Washington, D.C., handed me a picture of a tiny woman with a gigantic king cobra draped over her shoulders like a garden hose. The snake had partly spread his hood and was looking intently into the camera while his mistress stroked his head to quiet him. Dr. Mann told me: "Grace lives in a little house full of poisonous snakes imported from all over the world. She lets them wander around like cats. There's been more nonsense written about 'snake charming' than nearly any other subject. Grace is probably the only non-Oriental who knows the real secrets of this curious business."

Looking at the picture of that deadly creature, I knew what Ruskin[1] meant when he described a snake as a "running brook of horror." Still, I like snakes, and when Jule and I moved into our Malibu house, I made it a point to call on Grace Wiley.

Grace wasn't at the address Dr. Mann had given me. The neighbors had seen some of her pets in the yard and called the police. Grace finally settled outside Los Angeles near the little town of Cypress. After a phone call, I drove out to see her. She was living in a small three-room cottage, surrounded by open fields. Behind the cottage was a big, ramshackle barn where the snakes were kept. Grace was cleaning snake boxes with a hose when I arrived. She was a surprisingly little lady, scarcely over five

---

1. Ruskin: John Ruskin, an English writer who lived from 1819 to 1900.

feet, and probably weighed less than a hundred pounds. Although Grace was sixty-four years old, she was as active as a boy and worked with smooth dexterity. When she saw me, she hurriedly picked up the four-foot rattlesnake who had been sunning himself while his box was cleaned, and poured him into his cage. The snake raised his head but made no attempt to strike or even to rattle. I was impressed but not astonished. In captivity, rattlers often grow sluggish and can be handled with comparative impunity.[2]

Grace came forward, drying her hands on her apron. "Oh dear, I meant to get dressed up for you," she said, trying to smooth down her thatch of brown hair. "But I haven't anybody here to help me with the snakes, except Mother—and she's eighty-four years old. Don't trip over an alligator," she added as I came forward. I noticed for the first time in the high grass a dozen or so alligators and crocodiles. They ranged from a three-foot Chinese croc to a big Florida gator more than twelve feet long. I threaded my way among them without mishap, although several opened their huge jaws to hiss at me.

"They don't mean anything by that, any more than a dog barking," Grace explained fondly. "They're very tame and most of them know their names. Now come in and meet my little family of snakes."

We entered the barn. The walls were lined with cages of all sizes and shapes containing snakes. Grace stopped at each cage, casually lifting the occupant and pointing out his fine points while she stroked and examined him. Grace unquestionably had one of the world's finest collections of reptiles. I watched her handle diamondback rattlesnakes from Texas, vipers from Italy, fer-de-lance[3] from the West Indies, a little Egyptian cobra (the "asp" that killed Cleopatra), and the deadly karait[4] from India. Then I saw Grace perform a feat I would have believed impossible.

We had stopped in front of a large, glass-fronted cage containing apparently nothing but newspaper. "These little fellows arrived only a short time ago, so they're very wild," explained Grace indulgently. She quietly lifted the paper. Instantly a forest of heads sprang up in the cage. Grace moved the paper slightly. At the movement, the heads seemed to spread and flatten. Then I saw that they were not heads but hoods. I was looking at the world's most deadly creature—the Indian cobra.

Man-eating tigers are said to kill 600 natives a year, but cobras kill 25,000 people a year in India alone. Hunters have been mauled by wounded elephants and lived to tell about it, but no one survives a body bite from a big cobra. I have caught rattlesnakes with a forked stick and my bare hands, but I'm not ashamed to say I jumped back from that cage as though the devil were inside—as indeed he was.

Grace advanced her hand toward the nearest cobra. The snake swayed like a reed in the wind, feinting for the strike. Grace raised her hand above the snake's head, the reptile twisting around to watch her. As the woman slowly low-

---

2. impunity (ĭm-pyo͞o′nə-tē) n.: Freedom from injury.

3. fer-de-lance (fĕr′də-lăns′) n.: A large, poisonous snake with brown and gray markings.

4. karait (kə-rīt′) n.: A small, poisonous snake.

ered her hand, the snake gave that most terrible of all animal noises—the unearthly hiss of a deadly snake. I have seen children laugh with excitement at the roar of a lion, but I have never seen anyone who did not cringe at that cold, uncanny sound. Grace deliberately tried to touch the rigid, quivering hood. The cobra struck at her hand. He missed. Quietly, Grace presented her open palm. The cobra hestitated a split second, his reared body quivering like a plucked banjo string. Then he struck.

I felt sick as I saw his head hit Grace's hand, but the cobra did not bite. He struck with his mouth closed. As rapidly as an expert boxer drumming on a punching bag, the snake struck three times against Grace's palm, always, for some incredible reason, with his mouth shut. Then Grace slid her open hand over his head and stroked his hood. The snake hissed again and struggled violently under her touch. Grace continued to caress him. Suddenly, the snake went limp and his hood began to close. Grace slipped her other hand under the snake's body and lifted him out of the cage. She held the reptile in her arms as though he were a baby. The cobra raised his head to look Grace in the face; his dancing tongue was less than a foot from her mouth. Grace braced her hand against the curve of his body and talked calmly to him until he folded his hood. He curled up in her arms quietly, until I made a slight movement; then he instantly reared up again, threatening me.

I had never seen anything to match this performance. Later, Grace opened the cobra's mouth to show me that the fangs were still intact. The yellow venom was slowly oozing over their tips.

If Grace Wiley had wished to make a mystery out of her amazing ability, I am certain she could have made a fortune by posing as a woman with supernatural power. There isn't a zoologist alive who could have debunked her.[5] But Grace was a perfectly honest person who was happy to explain in detail exactly how she could handle these terrible creatures. I spent several weeks with her studying her technique, and now that I understand it I'm even more impressed than I was before.

Although I had kept snakes for many years, I was probably more astonished by Grace's performance than someone who knew nothing about reptiles. My mistake lay in supposing that all snakes are more or less alike. I knew rattlesnakes but I knew nothing about cobras. Although the cobra is intrinsically a far more dangerous snake than the rattlesnake, Grace would never have attempted to handle a diamondback rattler in the manner she handled this cobra. To understand why, you have to know the physical and psychological differences between the two reptiles.

A rattler has two "coils." When he is resting, he lies coiled up like a length of rope with his head lying on the topmost coil and his rattle sticking up in the center of the heap. When he is angry, he rears the upper third of his body a foot or more off the ground, coiling it into an S-shaped design and sounding his rattle continuously. Snake men call this position the "business coil." The rattler is like a coiled spring. He can strike out the full length of the S, inject his venom, and return into position for another strike literally faster than the eye can follow. He cannot strike farther than the raised S,

---

5. debunked her: Shown that she was a fraud.

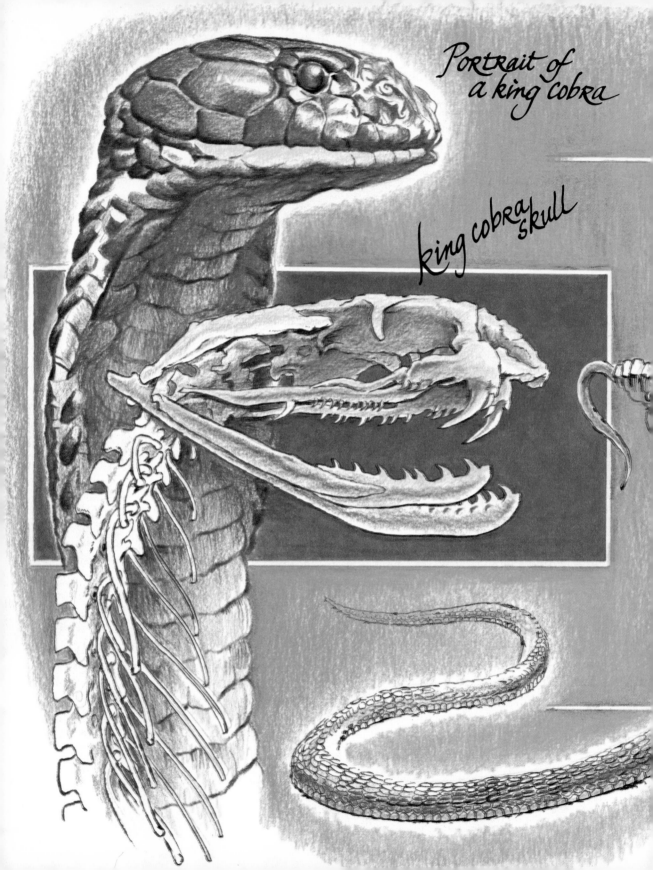

Portrait of
a king cobra

king cobra
skull

A king cobra rearing is taller than a kneeling man

nor will he attack. To attack, he would have to come out of coil and lose his advantageous position. He is like a boxer with his bent arm drawn back for a hay-maker.[6] As soon as his opponent comes close enough, he can let him have it.

A cobra, on the other hand, rears straight upward. If you put your elbow on a table, cup your hand to represent the open hood, and sway your forearm back and forth, you will have a good idea of the fighting stance of a cobra. Your index finger represents the tiny, mouse-like head that does the business. You will see at once that you cannot strike out as far as you could with your arm drawn back. Your range is limited to the length of your forearm. Here is a large part of the secret in handling cobras.

Because of the deceptively coiled S, no one can tell exactly how far a rattler can strike. But with a little practice, you can tell a cobra's range to the inch. Also, the blow of a cobra is comparatively slow. A man with steady nerves can jerk away in time to avoid being bitten. This is exactly what a mongoose does. The mongoose keeps just outside the cobra's range and when he does dart in for a bite, he can jump clear of the blow. A mongoose would stand no chance at all against a rattlesnake.

Another vital difference lies in the method of striking. The rattler does not bite. He stabs with his fangs. A rattler's fangs are very long, so long that they would pierce his lower jaw if he did not keep them folded back against the roof of his mouth. When he strikes, the rattler opens his mouth to its fullest extent, the fangs snap down into place, and the

---

6. haymaker: A blow strong enough to knock someone out.

snake stabs. The fangs are hollow and connect directly with the poison glands in either side of the snake's head. When the snake feels his fangs go home, he instantly discharges his venom deep into the wound. The fangs operate like miniature hypodermic needles and are extremely efficient.

The cobra has no such elaborate apparatus. His fangs are short and do not fold back. Instead of stabbing like the rattler, he must actually bite. He grabs his victims and then deliberately chews while the venom runs down into the wound he is making. These apparently minor distinctions mean the difference between life and death to anyone working with snakes.

When Grace approached a wild cobra, she moved her hand back and forth just outside the snake's range. The cobra would then strike angrily until he became tired. Then he was reluctant to strike again. Grace's next move was to raise her hand over the snake's hood and bring it down slowly. Because of his method of rearing, a cobra cannot strike directly upward (a rattler can strike up as easily as in any other direction), and Grace could actually touch the top of the snake's head. The snake became puzzled and frustrated. He felt that he was fighting an invulnerable opponent who, after all, didn't seem to mean him any harm. Then came the final touch. Grace would put her open palm toward the snake. At last the cobra was able to hit her. But he had to bite and he could not get a grip on the flat surface of the palm. If he could get a finger or a loose fold of skin he could fasten his teeth in it and start chewing. But his strike is sufficiently slow that Grace could meet each blow with the flat of her palm. At last Grace

would be able to get her hand over the snake's head and stroke his hood. This seemed to relax the reptile and from then on Grace could handle him with some degree of confidence.

I don't mean to suggest that this is a cut-and-dried procedure. Grace knew snakes perfectly and could tell by tiny, subtle indications what the reptile would probably do next. She had been bitten many times—she would never tell me just how many—but never by a cobra. You're only bitten once by a cobra.

"Now I'll show you what I know you're waiting to see," said Grace as she put the snake away. "My mated pair of king cobras." Dropping her voice reverently, she added, "I call the big male 'the king of kings.'" She led the way to a large enclosure and for the first time in my life I was looking into the eyes of that dread reptile, the king cobra—or hamadryad.

The common cobra is rarely more than five feet long. Even so, he has enough venom in his poison glands to kill fifty men. Grace's king cobras were more than fifteen feet long—longer than a boa constrictor. The two hamadryads contained enough venom, if injected drop by drop, to kill nearly a thousand human beings. That wasn't all. The hamadryad is the only snake known to attack without any provocation. These fearful creatures have been reported to trail a man through a jungle for the express purpose of biting him. They are so aggressive that they have closed roads in India by driving away all traffic. This is probably because the hamadryads, unlike other snakes, guard their eggs and young, and if a pair sets up housekeeping in a district, every other living thing must get out—including elephants. When a king cobra rears up, he stands higher than the head of a kneeling man. They are unquestionably the most dangerous animal in the world today.

When Grace first got these monsters, she was unable to handle them as she would ordinary cobras; so she had to devise an entirely new method of working with them. When the kings first arrived, they were completely unapproachable. They reared up more than four feet, snorting and hissing, their lower jaws open to expose the poison fangs. "A very threatening look, indeed," Grace called it. She put them in a large cage with a sliding partition. Unlike other snakes, hamadryads are knowing enough to notice that when their keeper opens the door in the side of the cage to put in fresh water, he must expose his hand for a fraction of a second. These cobras soon learned to lie against the side of the cage and wait for Grace to open the door. She outwitted them by waiting until both of the hamadryads were on one side of the cage and then sliding in the partition before changing water pans. She did not dare to go near them with her bare hands; she used a padded stick to stroke them. Yet she was able to touch them four days after their arrival. "I petted the kings on their tails when their heads were far away," she told me. "Later in the day I had a little visit with them and told them how perfectly lovely they were, that I liked them and was sure we were going to be good friends."

A few weeks later, the king of kings began shedding his skin. Snakes are irritable and nervous while shedding and the hamadryad had trouble sloughing off the thin membrane covering his eyes. Grace wrote in her diary: "I stroked his head and then pulled off the eyelids with eyebrow forceps. He flinched a little but was unafraid. He put out his tongue in such a knowing manner! I mounted the eyelids and they looked just like pearls. What a pity that there have been nothing but unfriendly, aggressive accounts about this sweet snake. Really, the intelligence of these creatures is unbelievable."

The king of kings was so heavy that Grace was unable to lift him by herself. Jule offered to help her carry the snake outside for a picture. While Jule and Grace were staggering out the door with the monster reptile between them, the king suddenly reared and rapped Jule several times on her forehead with his closed mouth. "He's trying to tell you something!" exclaimed Grace. He was indeed. I saw that the Chinese crocodile had rushed out from under a table and grabbed the hamadryad by the tail. Jule relaxed her grip and the king dropped his head and gave a single hiss. The croc promptly let go and the ladies bore the cobra out into the sunlight. I was the only person who seemed upset by the incident.

Out of curiosity, I asked Grace if she ever used music in taming her snakes. She laughed and told me what I already knew: all snakes are deaf.[7] Grace assured me that the Hindu fakir[8] uses his flute only to attract a crowd and by swaying his own body back and forth the fakir keeps the snake swaying as the cobra is feinting to strike. The man times his music to correspond to the snake's

---

7. all snakes are deaf: Recently, scientists have found that snakes can hear some sounds.
8. fakir (fə-kîr′) n.: A Hindu holy man who charms snakes.

movements and it appears to dance to the tune. The fakir naturally keeps well outside of the cobra's striking range. Years later when I was in India, I discovered that this is exactly what happens. I never saw any Oriental snake charmer even approximate Grace's marvelous powers over reptiles.

Grace's only source of income was to exhibit her snakes to tourists, although she was occasionally able to rent a snake to a studio (she always went along to make sure the reptile wasn't frightened or injured), and sometimes she bought ailing snakes from dealers, cured them, and resold them for a small profit to zoos. While I was with her, a dusty car stopped and discharged a plump couple with three noisy children who had seen her modest sign: *Grace Wiley—Reptiles.* Grace explained that she would show them her collection, handle the poisonous snakes, call over the tame alligators, and let the children play with Rocky, an eighteen-foot Indian Rock python, which she had raised from a baby. The charge was twenty-five cents. "That's too much," the woman said to her husband, and they went back to the car. Grace sighed. "No one seems interested in my snakes. No one really cares about them. And they're so wonderful."

One day Grace telephoned me to say that she had gotten in a new shipment of snakes, including some Indian cobras from Siam. "One of them has markings that form a complete G on the back of his hood," she told me. "Isn't it curious that the snake and I have the same initial! I call him 'my snake.' " We laughed about this, and then Jule and I went out to Cypress to take a last set of pictures of Grace and her snakes for an article I was

doing about this remarkable woman.

When we arrived, Grace was talking to a couple of kids who had brought a pet turtle to show her. We set up our photographic apparatus, and after a while, I began to grow restless. "Couldn't we go ahead with our pictures?" I hinted. Grace replied gently, "These boys have come for miles on their bicycles to show me this turtle. They really seem to love reptiles and I can't send them away." We waited for more than an hour before the boys departed with their remarkable turtle.

We took several pictures and then I asked Grace to let me get a picture of the cobra with the G on the hood. "I didn't look very well in those other pictures," said Grace anxiously. "I'll comb my hair and put on another blouse." She was back in a few minutes. Jule and I had set up our cameras in the yard behind the barn, first removing several alligators and a big monitor lizard named Slinky to avoid any possibility of accidents. I wanted a shot of the cobra with spread hood, and Grace brought him out cradled in her arms. Before allowing me to take the picture, she removed her glasses, as she felt that she looked better without them. The cobra refused to spread, and Grace put him down on the ground and extended her flat palm toward him to make him rear—something I had often seen her do before, but never without her glasses.

I was watching through the finder of my camera. I saw the cobra spread and strike as I clicked the shutter. As the image disappeared from the ground glass of my Graflex, I looked up and saw the snake had seized Grace by the middle finger. She said in her usual quiet voice, "Oh, he's bitten me."

I dropped the camera and ran toward her, feeling an almost paralyzing sense of shock, for I knew that Grace Wiley was a dead woman. At the same time I thought, "Good Lord, it's just like the book," for the cobra was behaving exactly as textbooks on cobras say they behave; he was deliberately chewing on the wound to make the venom run out of his glands. It was a terrible sight.

Quietly and expertly, Grace took hold of the snake on either side of his jaws and gently forced his mouth open. I knew that her only chance for life was to put a tourniquet around the finger instantly and slash open the wound to allow the venom to run out. Seconds counted. I reached out my hand to take the snake above the hood so she could immediately start squeezing out the venom, but Grace motioned me away. She stood up, still holding the cobra, and walked into the barn. Carefully, she put the snake into his cage and closed the door.

This must have taken a couple of minutes and I knew that the venom was spreading through her system each moment. "Jule," said Grace, "call Wesley Dickinson. He's a herpetologist[9] and a friend of mine. He'll know what to do." Calmly and distinctly she gave Jule the telephone number and Jule ran to the phone. Then Grace turned to me. Suddenly she said, "He didn't really bite me, did he?" It was the only emotion I saw her show. I could only say, "Grace, where's your snakebite kit?" We both knew that nothing except immediate amputation of her arm could save her, but anything was worth a chance.

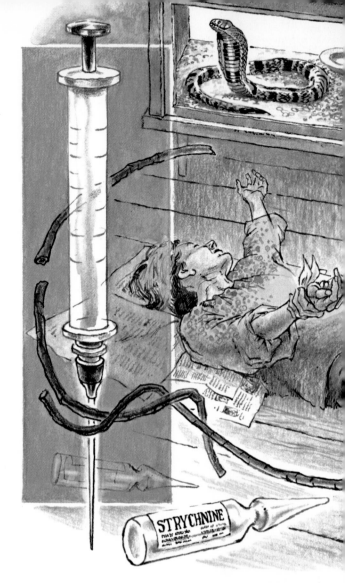

She pointed to a cabinet. There was a tremendous collection of the surgical aids used for snakebite, but I don't believe any of the stuff had been touched for twenty years. I pulled out a rubber tourniquet and tried to twist it around her finger. The old rubber snapped in my hands. Grace didn't seem to notice. I pulled out my handkerchief and tried that. It was too thick to go around her finger and I twisted it around her wrist. "I'll faint in a few minutes," said Grace.

---

9. herpetologist (hûr′pə-tŏl′ə-jĭst) n.: A scientist who studies reptiles.

"I want to show you where everything is before I lose consciousness."

Cobra venom, unlike rattlesnake, affects the nervous system. In a few minutes the victim becomes paralyzed and the heart stops beating. I knew Grace was thinking of this. She said, "You must give me strychnine injections to keep my heart going when I begin to pass out. I'll show you where the strychnine is kept. You may have to give me caffeine also."

She walked to the other end of the room, and I ran alongside trying to keep the tourniquet in place. She got out the tiny glass vials of strychnine and caffeine and also a hypodermic syringe with several needles. I saw some razor blades with the outfit and picked one up, intending to make a deep incision to let out as much of the venom as possible. Grace shook her head. "That won't do any good," she told me. Cobra venom travels along the nerves, so making the wound bleed wouldn't be very effective; but it was all I could think of to do.

Jule came back with a Mr. Tanner, Grace's cousin who lived next door. Tanner immediately got out his jackknife, intending to cut open the wound, but Grace stopped him. "Wait until Wesley comes," she said. Tanner told me afterward that he was convinced that if he had amputated the finger, Grace might have lived. This is doubtful. Probably nothing except amputation of her arm would have saved her then, and we had nothing but a jackknife. She probably would have died of shock and loss of blood.

Grace lay on the floor to keep as quiet as possible and slow the absorption of the venom. "You'd better give me the strychnine now, dear," she told Jule. Jule snapped off the tip of one of the glass vials, but the cylinder broke in her hands. She opened another tube and tried to fill the syringe; the needle was rusted shut. Jule selected another needle, tested it, and filled the syringe. "I'm afraid it will hurt," she told Grace. "Now don't worry, dear," said Grace comfortingly. "I know you'll do it very well."

After the injection, Grace asked Jule to put a newspaper under her head to keep her hair from getting dirty. A few minutes later, the ambulance, with Wesley Dickinson following in his own car, arrived. Wesley had telephoned the hospital and arranged for blood transfusions and an iron lung. As Grace was lifted into the ambulance, she called back to Tanner, "Remember to cut up the meat for my frogs very fine and take good care of my snakes." That was the last we ever saw of her.

Grace died in the hospital half an hour later. She lived about ninety minutes after being bitten. In the hospital, Wesley directed the doctors to drain the blood out of her arm and pump in fresh blood. When her heart began to fail, she was put into the lung. She had become unconscious. Then her heart stopped. Stimulants were given. The slow beating began again but grew steadily weaker. Each time stimulants were given, the heart responded less strongly, and finally stopped forever.

We waited with Mr. and Mrs. Tanner at the snake barn, calling the hospital at intervals. When we heard that Grace was dead, Mrs. Tanner burst into tears. "Grace was such a beautiful young girl— and so talented," she moaned. "There wasn't anything she couldn't do. Why did she ever want to mess around with those awful snakes?"

"I guess that's something none of us will ever understand," said her husband sadly.

Grace was born in Kansas in 1884. She studied entomology[10] at the University of Kansas, and, during field trips to collect insects, it was a great joke among Grace's fellow students that she was terrified of even harmless garter snakes. Later Grace turned with a passionate interest to the creatures she had so long feared. In 1923 she became curator of the Museum of Natural History at the Minneapolis Public Library but quarreled with the directors, who felt that her reckless handling of poisonous snakes endangered not only her own life but that of others. She went to the Brookfield Zoo in Chicago; here the same difficulty arose. Finally Grace moved to California, where she could work with reptiles as she wished.

An attempt was made by several of Grace's friends to keep her collection together for a Grace Wiley Memorial Reptile House, but this failed. The snakes were auctioned off and the snake that had killed Grace was purchased by a roadside zoo in Arizona; huge signboards bearing an artist's conception of the incident were erected for miles along the highways. So passed one of the most remarkable people I have ever known.

---

10. · entomology (ĕn'tə-mŏl'ə-jē) n.: The study of insects.

1. Grace Wiley based her technique on her knowledge of the physical and psychological differences in snakes. (a) Why could she allow a cobra to strike her open palm? (b) Why would she *not* allow a rattlesnake to strike her palm?

2. When handling the cobra, Grace depended on her practiced eye to determine a safe position for her hand. (a) Why did she remove her glasses when Daniel Mannix photographed her? (b) Why was this a tragic mistake?

3. (a) Why did Grace call the new Indian cobra from Siam "my snake"? (b) After reading the story's ending, what else do you think this name means?

Character

An author can tell you about a character in a story in five ways:
(1) By commenting directly on the character. For example, "But Grace was a perfectly honest person who was happy to explain in detail exactly how she could handle these terrible creatures."
(2) By describing what the character looks like.
(3) By revealing the character's thoughts and feelings. For example, ". . . she removed her glasses, as she felt that she looked better without them."
(4) By showing what other characters say about or think about the character.
(5) By showing you the character's actions, and letting you draw your own conclusions about that character.

1. List two things that made Grace one of the most remarkable people the author had ever met.

2. Reread the fourth paragraph in the story. Find the sentence that tells you what Grace Wiley looked like.

3. How did Grace Wiley feel about the hamadryads?

4. (a) How did Mrs. Tanner feel about Grace? (b) How did the directors of the Museum of Natural History at the Minneapolis Public Library feel about her?

5. On the basis of Grace Wiley's actions, do you think the directors' judgment of Grace was right? Why or why not?

Activities

1. List five facts you learned about snakes from this selection.

2. **Composition.** Write a paragraph about a remarkable person you know or have heard about.

A Running Brook of Horror   119

RELATIONSHIPS

Understanding Comparison and Contrast

A comparison shows how two or more things are alike. A contrast shows how they are different. Many story details can be connected through comparison or contrast. For example, "They (the crocodiles and alligators) don't mean anything by that (hissing), any more than a dog barking." This sentence shows that the hissing of a crocodile or alligator is like the barking of a dog because both are nonthreatening.

▶ Answer the question following each item below.

a. "Man-eating tigers are said to kill 600 natives a year, but cobras kill 25,000 people a year in India alone."

How are tigers different from cobras?

b. "The snake swayed like a reed in the wind, feinting for the strike."

How is the snake like a reed in the wind?

c. "As rapidly as an expert boxer drumming on a punching bag, the snake struck three times against Grace's palm, always, for some incredible reason, with his mouth shut."

How is the snake like an expert boxer?

d. "The cobra hesitated a split second, his reared body quivering like a plucked banjo string."

How is the snake's body like a plucked banjo string?

e. "Although the cobra is intrinsically a far more dangerous snake than the rattlesnake, Grace would never have attempted to handle a diamondback rattler in the manner she handled this cobra."

How is the cobra different from the rattlesnake?

WORD ATTACK

Using Context to Find the Meaning of Unfamiliar Words

The context of a word refers to the other words surrounding it. Often, the context helps you figure out the meaning of the unfamiliar word. For example, you may not know the meaning of *dexterity* in the following sentence.

He admired her smooth *dexterity* in handling the snake, and he realized that he had rarely seen a person work with such skillfulness.

The words *smooth, handling, work,* and *skillfulness* should help you figure out that *dexterity* means "skill in using one's hands."

1. Write the meaning of each *italicized* word. Use context to help you figure out the meaning. Then look up each word in a dictionary to check your answers.
   a. "Grace lives in a little house full of poisonous snakes *imported* from all over the world."
   b. "The cobra hesitated a split second, his reared body *quivering* like a plucked banjo string."
   c. "Because of the *deceptively* coiled S, no one can tell exactly how far a rattler can strike."
   d. "Grace knew snakes perfectly and could tell by tiny, *subtle* indications what the reptile would probably do next."
   e. "When a king cobra *rears* up, he stands higher than the head of a kneeling man."
   f. "Grace slid her open hand over his head and stroked his hood. The snake hissed again and struggled violently under her touch. Grace continued to *caress* him."
   g. "Because of his method of rearing, a cobra cannot strike directly upward (a rattler can strike up as easily as in any other direction), and Grace could actually touch the top of the snake's head. The snake became puzzled and frustrated. He felt that he was fighting an *invulnerable* opponent who, after all, didn't seem to mean him any harm."

2. Write an original sentence for each of the italicized words in Exercise **1.**

The Dying Detective

Michael and Mollie Hardwick

Adapted from a short story by Arthur Conan Doyle

Characters, in order of appearance:

Mrs. Hudson

Dr. Watson

Sherlock Holmes

Culverton Smith: "A great yellow face, coarse-grained and greasy, with heavy double chin, and two sullen, menacing gray eyes which glared at me from under tufted and sandy brows . . ."

Inspector Morton: Middle-aged, tough, dressed in plain clothes.

Scene One

(*Sherlock Holmes's bedroom at 221B Baker Street. The essential features are: a bed with a large wooden head, placed crosswise on the stage, the head a foot or two from one side wall; a small table near the bed-head, on the audience's side, on which stand a carafe of water and a glass, and a tiny metal or ivory box; a window in the back wall, the curtains parted; and, under the window, a table or chest of drawers, on which*

stand a green wine bottle, some wine glasses, a biscuit-barrel, and a lamp. Of course, there may be further lamps and any amount of furnishing and clutter: Holmes's bedroom was adorned with pictures of celebrated criminals and littered with everything from tobacco pipes to revolver cartridges.

There is daylight outside the window. Sherlock Holmes lies in the bed on his back, tucked up to the chin and evidently asleep. He is very pale. Mrs. Hudson enters followed by Dr. Watson, who is wearing his coat and hat and carrying his small medical bag. Mrs. Hudson pauses for a moment.)

Mrs. Hudson: He's asleep, sir.

(They approach the bed. Watson comes round to the audience's side and looks down at Holmes for a moment. He shakes his head gravely, then he and Mrs. Hudson move away beyond the foot of the bed. Watson takes off his hat and coat as they talk and she takes them from him.)

Watson: This is dreadful, Mrs. Hudson. He was perfectly hale and hearty when I went away only three days ago.

Mrs. Hudson: I know, sir. Oh, Dr. Watson, sir, I'm that glad you've come back. If anyone can save Mr. Holmes, I'm sure you can.

Watson: I shall have to know what is the matter with him first. Mrs. Hudson, please tell me, as quickly as you can, how it all came about.

Mrs. Hudson: Yes, sir. Mr. Holmes has been working lately on some case down near the river—Rotherhithe, I think.

Watson: Yes, yes. I know.

Mrs. Hudson: Well, you know what he is for coming in at all hours. I was just taking my lamp to go to my bed on Wednesday night when I heard a faint knocking at the street door. I . . . I found Mr. Holmes there. He could hardly stand. Just muttered to me to help him up to his bed here, and he's barely spoken since.

Watson: Dear me!

Mrs. Hudson: Won't take food or drink. Just lies there, sleeping or staring in a wild sort of way.

Watson: But, goodness gracious, Mrs. Hudson, why did you not send for another doctor in my absence?

Mrs. Hudson: Oh, I told him straightaway I was going to do that, sir. But he got so agitated—almost shouted that he wouldn't allow any doctor on the premises. You know how masterful he is, Dr. Watson.

Watson: Indeed. But you could have telegraphed for me.

(Mrs. Hudson appears embarrassed.)

Mrs. Hudson: Well, sir . . .

Watson: But you didn't. Why, Mrs. Hudson?

Mrs. Hudson: Sir, I don't like to tell you, but . . . well, Mr. Holmes said he wouldn't even have you to see him.

Watson: What? This is monstrous! I, his oldest friend, and . . . *(Holmes groans and stirs slightly.)* Ssh! He's waking. You go along, Mrs. Hudson, and leave this to me. Whether he likes it or not, I shall ensure that everything possible is done.

Mrs. Hudson: Thank you, sir. You'll ring if I can be of help.

(She exits with Watson's things.

Holmes *groans again and flings out an arm restlessly. Watson comes to the audience's side of the bed and sits on it.)*

Watson: Holmes? It's I—Watson.

Holmes *(sighs):* Ahh! Well, Watson? We . . . we seem to have fallen on evil days.

Watson: My dear fellow! *(He moves to reach for* Holmes's *pulse.)*

Holmes *(urgently):* No, no! Keep back!

Watson: Eh?

Holmes: Mustn't come near.

Watson: Now, look here, Holmes . . .!

Holmes: If you come near . . . order you out of the house.

Watson *(defiantly):* Hah!

Holmes: For your own sake, Watson. Contracted . . . a disease—from Sumatra. Very little known, except that most deadly. Contagious by touch. So . . . must keep away.

Watson: Utter rubbish, Holmes! Mrs. Hudson tells me she helped you to your bed. There's nothing the matter with her.

Holmes: Period of . . . incubation. Only dangerous after two or three days. Deadly by now.

Watson: Good heavens, do you suppose such a consideration weighs with me? Even if I weren't a doctor, d'you think it would stop me doing my duty to an old friend? Now, let's have a good look at you. *(He moves forward again.)*

Holmes *(harshly):* I tell you to keep back!

Watson: See here, Holmes . . .

Holmes: If you will stay where you are, I will talk to you. If you will not, you can get out.

Watson: Holmes! *(Recovering.)* Holmes, you aren't yourself. You're sick and as helpless as a child. Whether you like it or not, I'm going to examine you and treat you.

Holmes *(sneering):* If I'm to be forced to have a doctor, let him at least be someone I've some confidence in.

Watson: Oh! You . . . After all these years, Holmes, you haven't . . . confidence in me?

Holmes: In your friendship, Watson—yes. But facts are facts. As a medical man, you're a mere general practitioner, of limited experience and mediocre qualifications.

Watson: Well . . .! Well, really!

Holmes: It is painful to say such things, but you leave me no choice.

Watson *(coldly):* Thank you. I'll tell you this, Holmes. Such a remark, coming from you, merely serves to tell me what state your nerves are in. Still, if you insist that you have no confidence in me, I will not intrude my services. But what I shall do is to summon Sir Jasper Meek or Penrose Fisher, or any of the other best men in London.

Holmes *(groans):* My . . . dear Watson. You mean well. But do you suppose they—any of them—know of the Tapanuli Fever?

Watson: The Tap . . .?

Holmes: What do you yourself know of the Black Formosa Corruption?

Watson: Tapanuli Fever? Black Formosa Corruption? I've never heard of either of 'em.

Holmes: Nor have your colleagues. There are many problems of disease, many pathological possibilities, peculiar to the East. So I've learned during some of my recent researches. It was in the course of one of them that I contracted this complaint. I assure you, Watson, you can do nothing.

Watson: Can't I? I happen to know, Holmes, that the greatest living authority on tropical disease, Dr. Ainstree, is in London just now.

Holmes (beseeching): Watson!

Watson: All remonstrance is useless. I am going this instant to fetch him. (He gets up.)

Holmes (a great cry): No!

Watson: Eh? Holmes . . . my dear fellow . . .

Holmes: Watson, in the name of our old friendship, do as I ask.

Watson: But . . .

Holmes: You have only my own good at heart. Of course, I know that. You . . . you shall have your way. Only . . . give me time to . . . to collect my strength. What is the time now?

(Watson sits again and consults his watch.)

Watson: Four o'clock.

Holmes: Then at six you can go.

Watson: This is insanity!

Holmes: Only two hours, Watson. I promise you may go then.

Watson: Hang it, this is urgent, man!

Holmes: I will see no one before six. I will not be examined. I shall resist!

Watson (sighing): Oh, have it your own way, then. But I insist on staying with you in the meantime. You need an eye keeping on you, Holmes.

Holmes: Very well, Watson. And now I must sleep. I feel exhausted. (Drowsily.) I wonder how a battery feels when it pours electricity into a nonconductor?

Watson: Eh?

Holmes (yawning): At six, Watson, we resume our conversation.

(He lies back and closes his eyes. Watson makes as though to move, but thinks better of it. He sits still, watching Holmes. A slow blackout.)

Scene Two

(The stage lights up again, though more dimly than before, to disclose the same scene. Twilight is apparent through the window. Holmes lies motionless. Watson sits as before, though with his head sagging, half asleep. His chin drops suddenly and he wakes with a jerk. He glances round, sees the twilight outside, and consults his watch. He yawns, flexes his arms, then proceeds to glance idly about him. His attention is caught by the little box on the bedside table. Stealthily, he reaches over and picks it up.)

Holmes (very loudly and urgently): No! No, Watson, no!

Watson (startled): Eh? What?

(Holmes starts up onto his elbow.)

Holmes: Put it down! Down this instant! Do as I say, Watson!

Watson: Oh! All right, then. (Putting the box down.) Look here, Holmes, I really think . . .

Holmes: I hate to have my things touched. You know perfectly well I do.

Watson: Holmes . . .!

Holmes: You fidget me beyond endurance. You, a doctor—you're enough to drive a patient into an asylum!

Watson: Really!

Holmes: Now, for heaven's sake, sit still, and let me have my rest.

Watson: Holmes, it is almost six o'clock, and I refuse to delay another instant. *(He gets up determinedly.)*

Holmes: Really? Watson, have you any change in your pocket?

Watson: Yes.

Holmes: Any silver?

Watson *(fishing out his change)*: A good deal.

Holmes: How many half-crowns?

Watson: Er, five.

Holmes *(sighing)*: Ah, too few, too few. However, such as they are, you can put them in your watchpocket—and all the rest of your money in your left trouser pocket. It will balance you so much better like that.

Watson: Balance . . .? Holmes, you're raving! This has gone too far . . .!

Holmes: You will now light that lamp by the window, Watson, but you will be very careful that, not for one instant, shall it be more than at half flame.

Watson: Oh, very well. *(Watson goes to the lamp and strikes a match.)*

Holmes: I implore you to be careful.

Watson *(as though humoring him)*: Yes, Holmes. *(He lights the lamp, carefully keeping the flame low. He moves to draw the curtains.)*

Holmes: No, you need not draw curtains. *(Watson leaves them and comes back round the bed.)* So! Good. You may now go and fetch a specialist.

Watson: Well, thank heaven for that.

Holmes: His name is Mr. Culverton Smith, of 13 Lower Burke Street.

Watson *(staring)*: Eh?

Holmes: Well, go on, man. You could hardly wait to fetch someone before.

Watson: Yes, but . . . Culverton Smith? I've never heard the name!

Holmes: Possibly not. It may surprise you to know that the one man who knows everything about this disease is not a medical man. He's a planter.

Watson: A planter!

Holmes: His plantation is far from medical aid. An outbreak of this disease there caused him to study it intensely. He's a very methodical man, and I asked you not to go before six because I knew you wouldn't find him in his study till then.

Watson: Holmes, I . . . I never heard such a . . .!

Holmes: You will tell him exactly how you have left me. A dying man.

Watson: No, Holmes!

Holmes: At any rate, delirious. Yes, not dying, delirious. *(Chuckles.)* No, I really can't think why the whole ocean bed isn't one solid mass of oysters.

Watson: Oysters?

Holmes: They're so prolific, you know.

Watson: Great heavens! Now, Holmes, you just lie quiet, and . . .

Holmes: Strange how the mind controls the brain. Er, what was I saying, Watson?

Watson: You were . . .

Holmes: Ah, I remember. Culverton Smith. My life depends on him, Watson.

But you will have to plead with him to come. There is no good feeling between us. He has . . . a grudge. I rely on you to soften him. Beg, Watson. Pray. But get him here by any means.

Watson: Very well. I'll bring him in a cab, if I have to carry him down to it.

Holmes: You will do nothing of the sort. You will persuade him to come—and then return before him. *(Deliberately.)* Make any excuse so as not to come with him. Don't forget that, Watson. You won't fail me. You never did fail me.

Watson: That's all very well, Holmes, but . . .

Holmes *(interrupting):* Then, shall the world be overrun by oysters? No doubt there are natural enemies which limit their increase. And yet . . . No, horrible, horrible!

Watson *(grimly):* I'm going, Holmes. Say no more, I'm going!

(He hurries out. Holmes remains propped up for a moment, staring after Watson, then sinks back into a sleeping posture as the stage blacks out.)

Scene Three

(The stage lights up on the same scene. Holmes lies still. It is now quite dark outside. After a moment Watson bustles in, pulling off his coat. He pauses to hand it to Mrs. Hudson, who is behind him.)

Watson: Thank you, Mrs. Hudson. A gentleman will be calling very shortly. Kindly show him up here immediately.

Mrs. Hudson: Yes, sir.

(She exits. Watson approaches the bed.)

Holmes *(drowsily):* Watson?

Watson: Yes, Holmes. How are you feeling?

Holmes: Much the same, I fear. Is Culverton Smith coming?

Watson: Should be here any minute. It took me some minutes to find a cab, and I almost expected him to have got here first.

Holmes: Well done, my dear Watson.

Watson: I must say, Holmes, I'm only doing this to humor you. Frankly, I didn't take to your planter friend at all.

Holmes: Oh? How so?

Watson: Rudeness itself. He almost showed me the door before I could give him your message. It wasn't until I mentioned the name, Sherlock Holmes . . .

Holmes: Ah!

Watson: Quite changed him—but I wouldn't say it was for the better.

Holmes: Tell me what he said.

Watson: Said you'd had some business dealings together, and that he respected your character and talents. Described you as an amateur of crime, in the way that he regards himself as an amateur of disease.

Holmes: Quite typical—and surely, quite fair?

Watson: Quite fair—if he hadn't put such sarcasm into saying it. No, Holmes, you said he bears you some grudge. Mark my words, as soon as he has left this house, I insist upon calling a recognized specialist.

Holmes: My dear Watson, you are the best of messengers. Thank you again.

Watson: Not at all. Holmes, Holmes—let me help you without any of this nonsense. The whole of Great Britain will condemn me otherwise. Why, my cabmen both inquired anxiously after you; and so did Inspector Morton . . .

Holmes: Morton?

Watson: Of the Yard. He was passing our door just now as I came in. Seemed extremely concerned.

Holmes: Scotland Yard concerned for me? How very touching! And now, Watson, you may disappear from the scene.

Watson: Disappear! I shall do no such thing. I wish to be present when this Culverton Smith arrives. I wish to hear every word of this so-called medical expert's opinion.

Holmes (turning his head): Yes, of course. Then I think you will just find room behind the head of the bed.

Watson: What? Hide?

Holmes: I have reason to suppose that his opinion will be much more frank and valuable if he imagines he is alone with me. (We hear the murmur of Mrs. Hudson's and Culverton Smith's voices off stage.) Listen! I hear him coming. Get behind the bed, Watson, and do not budge, whatever happens. Whatever happens, you understand?

Watson: Oh, all right, Holmes. Anything to please you. But I don't like this. Not at all.

(He goes behind the bed-head and conceals himself. Mrs. Hudson enters, looks round the room and then at Holmes. Smith enters behind her.)

Mrs. Hudson (to Smith): Oh, Dr. Watson must have let himself out. No doubt he'll be back directly, sir.

Smith: No matter, my good woman. (Mrs. Hudson bristles at this form of address.) You may leave me alone with your master.

Mrs. Hudson: As you wish—sir.

(She sweeps out. Smith advances slowly to the bed and stands at the foot, staring at the recumbent Holmes.)

Smith (almost to himself): So, Holmes. It has come to this, then.

(Holmes stirs. Smith chuckles and leans his arms on the bed-foot and his chin on them, continuing to watch Holmes.)

Holmes (weakly): Watson? Who . . .? Smith? Smith, is that you?

Smith (chuckles).

Holmes: I . . . I hardly dared hope you would come.

Smith: I should imagine not. And yet, you see, I'm here. Coals of fire, Holmes—coals of fire!

Holmes: Noble of you . . .

Smith: Yes, isn't it?

Holmes: I appreciate your special knowledge.

Smith: Then you're the only man in London who does. Do you know what is the matter with you?

Holmes: The same as young Victor—your cousin.

Smith: Ah, then you recognize the symptoms. Well, then, it's a bad look-out for you. Victor was a strong, hearty young fellow—but a dead man on the fourth day. As you said at the time, it *was* rather surprising that he should contract an out-of-the-way Asiatic disease in the heart of London—a disease of which *I* have made such a very special study. *(Chuckles.)* And now, you, Holmes. Singular coincidence, eh? Or are you going to start making accusations once again—about cause and effect, and so on.

Holmes: I . . . I knew you caused Victor Savage's death.

(Smith comes round the bed.)

Smith *(snarling):* Did you? Well, proving it is a different matter, Holmes. But what sort of a game is this, then—spreading lying reports about me one moment, then crawling to me for help the next?

Holmes *(gasping):* Give . . . give me water. For . . . pity's sake, Smith. Water!

(Smith hesitates momentarily, then goes to the table and pours a glass from the carafe.)

Smith: You're precious near your end, my friend, but I don't want you to go till I've had a word with you.

(He holds out the glass to Holmes, who struggles up feebly to take it and drinks.)

Holmes *(gulping water):* Ah! Thank . . . thank you. Please . . . do what you can for me. Only cure me, and I promise to forget.

Smith: Forget what?

Holmes: About Victor Savage's death. You as good as admitted just now that you had done it. I swear I will forget it.

Smith *(laughs):* Forget it, remember it—do as you like. I don't see you in any witness-box, Holmes. Quite another shape of box, I assure you. But you must hear first how it came about.

Holmes: Working among Chinese sailors. Down at the docks.

Smith: Proud of your brains, aren't you? Think yourself smart? Well, you've met a smarter one this time. *(Holmes falls back, groaning loudly.)* Getting painful, is it?

(Holmes cries out, writhing in agony.)

Smith: That's the way. Takes you as cramp, I fancy?

Holmes: Cramp! Cramp!

Smith: Well, you can still hear me. Now, can't you just remember any unusual incident—just about the time your symptoms began?

Holmes: I . . . can't think. My mind is gone! Help me, Smith!

Smith: Did nothing come to you through the post, for instance?

Holmes: Post? Post?

Smith: Yes. A little box, perhaps?

Holmes *(a shuddering groan).*

Smith *(closer; deadly):* Listen! You *shall* hear me! Don't you remember a box—a little ivory box? *(He sees it on the table and holds it up.)* Yes, here it is on your bedside table. It came on Wednesday. You opened it—do you remember?

Holmes: Box? Opened? Yes, yes! There was . . . sharp spring inside. Pricked my finger. Some sort of joke . . .

Smith: It was no joke, Holmes. You fool! Who asked you to cross my path? If you'd only left me alone, I would never have hurt you.

Holmes: Box! Yes! Pricked finger. Poison!

Smith *(triumphantly):* So you do remember. Good, good! I'm glad indeed. Well, the box leaves this room in my pocket, and there's your last shred of evidence gone. *(He pockets it.)* But you have the truth now, Holmes. You can die knowing that I killed you. You knew too much about what happened to Victor Savage, so you must share his fate. Yes, Holmes, you are very near your end now. I think I shall sit here and watch you die. *(He sits on the bed.)*

Holmes *(almost a whisper)*: The . . . shadows . . . falling. Getting . . . so dark. I can't see. Smith! Smith, are you there? The light . . . for charity's sake, turn up the light!

(Smith laughs, gets up, and goes to the light.)

Smith: Entering the valley of the shadow, eh, Holmes? Yes, I'll turn up the light for you. I can watch your face more plainly, then. *(He turns the flame up full.)* There! Now, is there any *further* service I can render you?

Holmes *(in a clear, strong voice)*: A match and my pipe, if you please.

(He sits bolt upright. Smith spins round to see him.)

Smith: Eh? What the devil's the meaning of this?

Holmes *(cheerfully)*: The best way of successfully acting a part is to *be* it. I give you my word that for three days I have neither tasted food nor drink until you were good enough to pour me out that glass of water. But it's the tobacco I find most irksome. *(We hear the thud of footsteps running upstairs offstage.)* Hello, hello! Do I hear the step of a friend?

(Inspector Morton hurries in.)

Morton: Mr. Holmes?
Holmes: Inspector Morton, this is your man.

Smith: What is the meaning of . . .?
Morton: Culverton Smith, I arrest you on the charge of the murder of one Victor Savage, and I must warn you that anything you say . . .
Smith: You've got nothing on me! It's all a trick! A pack of lies!

(He makes to escape. Morton restrains him.)

Morton: Keep still, or you'll get yourself hurt!
Smith: Get off me!
Morton: Hold your hands out! *(They struggle. Morton gets out handcuffs and claps them on Smith's wrists.)* That'll do.
Holmes: By the way, Inspector, you might add the attempted murder of one Sherlock Holmes to that charge. Oh, and you'll find a small box in the pocket of your prisoner's coat. Pray, leave it on the table, here. Handle it gingerly, though. It may play its part at his trial.

(Morton retrieves the box and places it on the table.)

Smith: Trial! You'll be the one in the dock, Holmes. Inspector, he asked me to come here. He was ill, and I was sorry for him, so I came. Now he'll pretend I've said anything he cares to invent that will corroborate his insane suspicions. Well, you can lie as you like, Holmes. My word's as good as yours.
Holmes: Good heavens! I'd completely forgotten him!
Morton: Forgotten who, sir?
Holmes: Watson, my dear fellow! Do come out! *(Watson emerges with cramped groans.)* I owe you a thousand apologies. To think that I should have overlooked you!
Watson: It's all right, Holmes.

Would have come out before, only you said, whatever happened, I wasn't to budge.

Smith: What's all this about?

Holmes: I needn't introduce you to my witness, my friend Dr. Watson. I understand you met somewhat earlier in the evening.

Smith: You . . . you mean you had all this planned?

Holmes: Of course. To the last detail. I think I may say it worked very well—with your assistance, of course.

Smith: Mine?

Holmes: You saved an invalid trouble by giving my signal to Inspector Morton, waiting outside. You turned up the lamp.

(Smith and Watson are equally flabbergasted.)

Morton: I'd better take him along now, sir. *(To Smith.)* Come on. *(He bundles Smith roughly toward the door.)* We'll see you down at the Yard tomorrow, perhaps, Mr. Holmes?

Holmes: Very well, Inspector. And many thanks.

Watson: Goodbye, Inspector. *(Morton exits with Smith. Watson chuckles.)* Well, Holmes?

Holmes: Well, Watson, there's a bottle of claret over there—it is uncorked—and some biscuits in the barrel. If you'll be so kind, I'm badly in need of both.

(Watson goes to fetch them.)

Watson: Certainly. You know, Holmes, all this seems a pretty, well, elaborate way to go about catching that fellow. I mean, taking in Mrs. Hudson—and me—like that. Scared us half to death.

Holmes: It was very essential that I should make Mrs. Hudson believe in my condition. She was to convey it to you, and you to him.

Watson: Well . . .

Holmes: Pray do not be offended, my good Watson. You must admit that among your *many* talents, dissimulation[1] scarcely finds a place. If you'd shared my secret, you would never have been able to impress Smith with the urgent necessity of coming to me. It was the vital point of the whole scheme. I knew his vindictive nature, and I was certain he would come to gloat over his handiwork.

(Watson returns with the bottle, glasses, and barrel.)

Watson: But . . . but your appearance, Holmes. Your face! You really do look ghastly.

Holmes: Three days of absolute fast does not improve one's beauty, Watson. However, as you know, my habits are irregular, and such a feat means less to me than to most men. For the rest, there is nothing that a sponge won't cure. Vaseline to produce the glistening forehead; belladonna for the watering of the eyes; rouge over the cheekbones, and crust of beeswax round one's lips . . .

Watson *(chuckling):* And that babbling about oysters! *(He begins pouring the wine.)*

Holmes: Yes. I've sometimes thought of writing a monograph on the subject of malingering.[2]

---

1. dissimulation (dĭ-sĭm'yə-lā'shən) n.: Pretense; disguising the truth.

2. malingering (mə-lĭng'gər-ĭng) n.: Pretending to be ill.

Watson: But why wouldn't you let me near you? There was no risk of infection.

Holmes: Whatever I may have said to the contrary in the grip of delirium, do you imagine that I have no respect for your medical talents? Could I imagine that you would be deceived by a dying man with no rise of pulse or temperature? At four yards' distance I *could* deceive you.

(Watson *reaches for the box.*)

Watson: This box, then . . .

Holmes: No, Watson! I wouldn't touch it. You can just see, if you look at it sideways, where the sharp spring emerges as you open it. I dare say it was by some such device that poor young Savage was done to death. He stood between that monster and an inheritance, you know.

Watson: Then it's true, Holmes! You . . . you might have been killed, too!

Holmes: As you know, my correspondence is a varied one. I am somewhat on my guard against any packages which reach me. But I saw that by pretending he had succeeded in his design, I might be enabled to surprise a confession from him. That pretense I think I may claim to have carried out with the thoroughness of a true artist.

Watson (*warmly*): You certainly did, Holmes. Er, a biscuit? (*He holds out the barrel.*)

Holmes: On second thought, Watson, no thank you. Let us preserve our appetite. By the time I have shaved and dressed, I fancy it will just be nice time for something nutritious at our little place in the Strand.

(*They raise their glasses to one another and drink. The curtain falls.*)

Close Up

1. The first scene sets up the problem: Sherlock Holmes is dying from an exotic tropical disease. Why didn't Mrs. Hudson send for Dr. Watson as soon as she learned of Holmes's illness?

2. (a) Why does Holmes tell Watson that he has no confidence in Watson's medical ability? (b) How does Watson interpret this remark?

3. Holmes sends Watson for Mr. Culverton Smith. (a) Why does Smith have knowledge of this tropical disease? (b) At the end of Scene Two, what else does Holmes ask Watson to do?

4. (a) What is Watson's reason for hiding behind the head of the bed? (b) What is Holmes's real reason for having Watson hide there?

5. It turns out that Holmes has faked his illness in order to trap Smith into confessing to the murder of Victor Savage. (a) What steps did Holmes take to make himself look ill? (b) Find three statements he made that convinced others he was delirious.

Conflict

A conflict is a struggle between two opposing forces. One type of conflict is a struggle between the main character and another character in the story. For example, in "The Dying Detective," the struggle is between the main character, Sherlock Holmes, and Culverton Smith.

1. Sherlock Holmes wants to prove that Smith killed Victor Savage. (a) What does Smith want? (b) How does Smith plan to accomplish this goal?

2. Smith laughs and says, "I don't see you in any witness-box, Holmes. Quite another shape of box, I assure you." What does this statement mean?

3. Because of his elaborate trick, Holmes wins this conflict. (a) What personality traits does this trick reveal about Holmes (for example, cleverness)? (b) What personality trait causes Smith to fall into Holmes's trap?

Activities

1. **Composition.** Imagine you own a detective agency. Write a classified advertisement for a detective. Start with the words "Help Wanted—Detective."

2. Imagine you are a famous detective (for example, Ellery Queen, Nancy Drew, Nero Wolfe, or Miss Marple). Tell the class about one of your cases.

RELATIONSHIPS

Understanding Contrast Relationships

When you contrast two things, you show how they are different. For example, the following sentence shows how Holmes and Smith are different:

> Sherlock Holmes was smart, but Culverton Smith thought he was smarter.

Certain words signal a contrast relationship. For example,

although	in spite of	on the other hand
but	nevertheless	still
by contrast	nonetheless	while
however	on the contrary	yet

Notice that *while* can signal either a contrast relationship or time order. For example:

> Holmes was an amateur of crime, *while* Smith was an amateur of disease. (contrast)
> Holmes slept *while* waiting for Smith. (time order)

---

1. Find the word or words that signal a contrast relationship in each of the following items.
   a. Although he was not a doctor, Culverton Smith was the one person who knew everything about the disease.
   b. Holmes was delirious; however, he was not dying.
   c. Smith bore a grudge against Holmes. Still, he came at Holmes's request.
   d. Victor was a strong, hearty fellow; yet he died on the fourth day of his illness.
   e. Holmes was healthy in spite of his appearance.

2. Answer the question following each of the lettered items.
   a. Although Victor lived in the heart of London, he contracted a rare tropical disease.

   Where would you expect someone who contracted a tropical disease to live?

   b. Three days ago Holmes was perfectly hale and healthy; yet today he is weak and delirious.

   How was Holmes's health three days ago different from his health today?

WORD ATTACK

Finding the Meaning That Fits the Context

Many English words have more than one meaning. For example, *head* may mean (1) self-control, (2) leader or director, (3) the top or front part of something, or (4) the bony structure containing the brain. Now look at the following sentence: Dr. Watson concealed himself behind the *head* of the bed. Only the third meaning of *head* fits this context.

1. Read each sentence below. Then, for each *italicized* word, choose the meaning that fits the context.
    a. "Mrs. Hudson bristles at this form of *address*."
        (1) the place where a person lives
        (2) speech directed to an individual
        (3) the writing on an envelope
    b. "By the way, Inspector, you might add the attempted murder of one Sherlock Holmes to that *charge*."
        (1) accusation
        (2) the price of something
        (3) an attack
    c. "As you know, my *correspondence* is a varied one."
        (1) similarity
        (2) agreement
        (3) mail; letters or packages received and sent
    d. "I wonder how a *battery* feels when it pours electricity into a nonconductor?"
        (1) object used to knock down a wall
        (2) the pitcher and the catcher
        (3) a connected group of cells carrying an electrical charge
    e. "Such a remark, coming from you, merely serves to tell me what *state* your nerves are in."
        (1) condition
        (2) a political body
        (3) position in life

2. For each *italicized* word below, write an original sentence.
    a. *address*, meaning "the writing on an envelope"
    b. *charge*, meaning "the price of something"
    c. *correspondence*, meaning "mail"
    d. *battery*, meaning "a connected group of cells carrying an electrical charge"
    e. *state*, meaning "condition"

The Adventure of The Dying Detective

Isaac Asimov

Catastrophic! The great Holmes is dying.
Doctor Watson is desp'rately trying
    To protect his old friend
    From a terrible end.
(Can it be the detective is dying?)

Arthur

Ogden Nash

There was an old man of Calcutta,
Who coated his tonsils with butta,
Thus converting his snore
From a thunderous roar
To a soft, oleaginous mutta.

The Old Lady from Dover

Carolyn Wells

There was an old lady of Dover
Who baked a fine apple turnover.
    But the cat came that way,
    And she watched with dismay
The overturn of her turnover.

Activity

▶ **Composition.** A limerick is a humorous poem with only five lines. The first two lines and the last line are long; the third and fourth lines are short. The three long lines rhyme and the two short lines rhyme. Try writing your own limerick.

Big Red

Jim Kjelgaard

Danny knew that Old Majesty was bigger and fiercer than any other bear, but Danny and his dog Red had to hunt him.

Danny didn't look again at any of the men in the cabin. He took a canvas pack-sack from its hanger, packed into it a box of matches, a slab of bacon, a small package of coffee, five pounds of flour, two loaves of bread, and a first-aid kit. He hung a sheathed knife at his belt, put a box of cartridges in his pocket, took his gun from its rack, loaded it, and was ready for the Wintapi wilderness. Red trotted soberly over to sit beside him, and followed closely when Danny went out on the porch.

He stood there, feeling the warm spring breezes blow about his face and neck and ruffle his shirt. And it seemed to him that never before in his entire life had he been so calm, or known so exactly just what he was going to do.

Old Majesty must die, he was very sure of that. Not alone because he had killed Asa[1] and hurt Ross,[2] and probably would hurt or kill other men, but for an added reason. The Wintapi was wild and hard—ever ready with its threats and

dangers. Only those who could meet and parry its blows were entitled to live there, or could live there. Now Old Majesty had asserted his own supremacy over all of it, and, in attacking Ross, proclaimed that nothing could walk in the Wintapi unless he willed it. And Danny knew that he must meet the big bear's challenge, must go into the mountains and fight Old Majesty on his own grounds. This was not something that a man could forget or run from.

At the same time, he was fully aware of the risks he ran and the chances he took. First there was Red, the dog that, next to Ross, he loved better than anything else. In hunting Old Majesty, Red might be killed. Or, if he was not killed or even hurt, the fact that Danny must urge him to hunt a bear, a varmint, could easily make meaningless all the long hours that Danny had taken to teach him to hunt partridges alone. Lastly, Danny considered the fact that he himself might be hurt.

But he still knew that he had to go, that Ross expected him to go. Ross saw the Wintapi as Danny did, and knew that

1. Asa: A hound dog.
2. Ross: Danny's father.

he who quailed at any challenge it hurled was forever lost. Danny bit his lip. He was young, but old enough to know that life was seldom easy. And it seemed to him that in the future there would be a great many other bears to meet. How he met them depended in great measure on what he did now with Old Majesty. It had become his fight. Regardless of loss or sacrifice he must give everything to winning it.

He walked down the porch steps, averted his eyes from the dog kennels, and walked across the pasture into the beech woods. The sun sprayed its golden rays through their budding twigs, painted the forest floor beneath them. Red crowded close to his side, seeming, in some mysterious way, to know that this was no ordinary trip. Even when he reached the crest of Stoney Lonesome, Danny did not turn his eyes back for one last look at the cabin.

Danny walked around the rim of the big plateau, keeping out of the laurel that grew upon it in the scrub. There was no special hurry. Ross had left the scene of the battle yesterday afternoon, and since had been making his pain-racked journey home. Certainly he would no longer find a fresh trail away from that place where Old Majesty had killed the hounds, and he might be in the mountains many days before he had the final reckoning with the big bear. But he had to stay, and would stay, until the final hour of that reckoning.

Twilight fell, and Danny stopped beside a brawling little stream that tumbled down a wild mountain valley. He took a line and fishhook from the pack, turned over a rock and picked up the worms that crawled in the damp earth beneath it, and caught eight of the shin-ing little brook trout that swarmed in the stream and nibbled eagerly at his proffered bait. He broiled them on a stick, shared them with Red, and moved his fire to face a huge boulder. Sitting with his back to the boulder, he stared into the flames and caressed Red. And there in the still night it was as though some mysterious vessel poured into him a renewal of an old faith. First it was faith in himself, and then that in Red. His first judgment of the big setter had been that here was a dog with heart, courage, and brains, as well as beauty and near perfection. Somehow he knew now that that judgment had been the correct one.

He was awake with the first streaks of dawn, had caught and cooked more trout and started up the valley. Danny climbed the lost ridge at its head, and struck into the big pines that lined the ridge. The small pines wherein Ross and his hounds had had their tragic meeting with Old Majesty were scarcely two hours away. A warm wind eddied down the ridge to blow against his face, and Danny strode briskly. A pulsing eagerness crept through him, and he gripped the rifle more firmly. Red ranged out to hunt through a copse of brush at one side, and came running back.

Danny climbed the mountain where he and Ross had taken a snarling, spitting fisher from a cave two years before, and walked to its east slope to stand directly under what had been a fine chestnut tree. Now its branches were leafless and gray; its twigs broken and shapeless. He looked directly across the valley that yawned beneath him at a huge pine growing on the slope of the opposite mountain. The wind, playing up the valley, rippled the tops of the smaller pines down there and coaxed a soft song from them. Danny's roving eye laid out a straight line between the chestnut stub and the big pine, and, in the valley below him, he saw a cruising crow plane out of the air into the little pines. From the end of the valley another crow cawed raucously, and presently came winging down to alight where the first had descended. That was where the hounds lay.

Danny's eyes marked the spot from which he would have to start. Some day he would return, give what was left of Old Mike and the two pups a suitable burial, and mark something on their grave about the battle they had had. But that must wait. They had to be avenged first.

Danny sat beneath the chestnut stub, an arm about Red's neck and the rifle resting where he could instantly reach and bring it into play. His brow wrinkled in deep thought. He could go down into the valley, and work out Old Majesty's trail from the place where he had fought. But that might take hours or even days of painstaking effort.

"Where would he go, Red?" Danny asked softly. "Where would that old hellion of gone from here?"

Red whined, and turned his head to lick Danny's ear. Danny stared hard at the ground, saw a worm inching along it, and snapped his head erect. Insect eggs were hatching in the dead, damp logs, and they'd be full of grubs. Having failed in his bold attempt to raid the farms, Old Majesty had to take his living from the wilderness. And, at this season of the year, grubs were the most plentiful and easiest-to-get food in it.

Danny bent his head forward and closed his eyes, trying in his mind to reconstruct a picture of the country as he knew it. Certainly Old Majesty, bold enough to ambush the three hounds and Ross, had not fled in blind panic when he left the scene of the battle. Probably he had even waited around to see if he was going to be followed anymore. But he had had a long run, and would want to rest and eat after it. Two mountains away there were a great many fallen trees whose trunks were moss-encrusted and whose pulp was dozey.[3] Danny flipped a penny, and, when it fell heads-up, rose to quarter down the mountain. Before trying to work out a stale track, he would cross those two mountains and see if he could not find a fresh one.

Red padded behind him as he toiled up one mountain, down its other side, and up the mountain beyond. He paused on the summit to stare down the slope. Red edged around him, pricked up his ears, and raised his hackles. He growled, looked up and wagged his tail.

Danny squatted down, and clamped his hand over the big dog's muzzle as he strove to see past the trees in front of him. Wind shook a copse of brush, and Danny brought his rifle up with one hand on the breech, ready to cock it and shoot. He rose and walked slowly down the slope, passing the yellow, ripped stumps that marched in endless lines along it, and threading his way among the prostrate tree trunks. Some had been shredded by powerful claws; a bear had been at them.

It was where a little spring bubbled out of the mountainside and softened the earth about it that Danny found Old Majesty's track. He knelt to examine it, a huge thing longer than his own foot and wider than his spread hand. His guess,

---

3. dozey (dōz'ē) adj.: Full of decay or rot.

then, had been the correct one; Old Majesty had come here to feast on grubs. The track by the spring was scarcely two hours old. Danny grasped Red by the scruff of the neck, and shoved his nose down in the track.

"That's him," he said. "That's the varmint we got to find."

Red sniffed long and deeply at the track, and raised his head to look at Danny. He sat down, tail flat on the ground behind him, staring down the slope. Danny watched. Red never had been a trailing dog, and would not now become one. But if he could catch the body scent of Old Majesty, and was urged to the attack, he would chase the big bear and finally bring it to bay. Danny climbed back to the summit of the mountain and sat down. The wind was almost straight out of the west, blowing gently but steadily. Clouds scudded across the sky, and the feathered tips of the pine trees bent. For a long while Danny stared steadily into the valley, and looked from it to Red.

Old Majesty was not there now or Red would smell him and indicate his presence. But there was no sign that he had been alarmed and knew that another pursuer was on his trail. Danny looked back down to the spring where he had found the track. He could follow the trail if he wanted to, and eventually work it out, but he must wage a battle of wits as well as one of scientific woodcraft. Fresh as it was, it would still take a long while to puzzle out that trail on the hard, rocky ground. Danny looked again down the slope, at the vast number of decaying logs that lay undisturbed. All of them were full of grubs, and, if Old Majesty wanted to rest a few days, he would not stray far from this place. Probably he was resting now, and not far away. But exactly where was he and what was the best way to go about finding him?

Danny rose, and, with Red padding beside him, traveled straight up the top of the mountain. He crossed the valley at its head, crossed the next mountain to the one beyond, and swung down it. He came off its sloping nose into a forested valley, and struck due east. But all the while he had been both studying the ground beneath him and watching Red. The big setter had stalked away three or four times to hunt partridges that he had scented in the thickets. But not once had his nose gone to the ground, and Danny had seen no bear track leading away. Old Majesty, then, was somewhere within the circle he had made.

Danny walked due east, crossing the noses of the mountains whose heads he had walked around, and returned to the foot of the slope where the grub-ridden logs lay. He walked around it, up the valley that separated it from the next hill, and again sat down to ponder. He ate bread smeared with bacon grease, gave Red some, and sat down with his back against a boulder. Twilight came, and erratic bats swooped up and down the little stream before him. But pitch darkness had descended on the wilderness before Danny started up the mountain again.

He left his pack beside the stream, carrying only a three-cell flashlight and his rifle as he climbed. The wind still blew steadily from the west. A whippoorwill shrieked, and Red halted to peer toward the sound. Danny waited for the big dog to catch up with him. He was still a hundred feet below the mountain's crest when he stooped to crawl.

The back of his neck tingled, and lit-

tle shivers ran up and down his spine. Old Majesty, just twice in his whole terrible career, had been seen in daylight by men who carried rifles. Ross had missed his shot, and Danny had dared not shoot for fear that a wounded bear might injure Red. But, though the big bear had been hunted many times by day, as far as Danny knew, this was the first time anyone had ever thought of stalking him by night. He reached the summit of the mountain, and felt in the darkness for Red. His fingers found and clenched the big dog's fur.

Almost imperceptibly he felt Red stiffen, and Danny laid the rifle across his knees, while his other hand stole forth to clamp about the big setter's muz-

zle. He thrilled with pride. Again his guess had been the right one. Old Majesty had not wandered away, but, after eating his fill of grubs, had merely gone to sleep in some secluded thicket. Now he was back. From down the slope came the ripping sound of another log being torn apart. Then an eerie silence.

It was broken by the buzz of an insect in a nearby tree, and Danny snapped his head erect. A light wind blew out of the valley. Red maintained his tense stance. The wind eddied around, blowing from all directions, and Red shrank close to the earth. A clammy hand brushed Danny's spine. He let go of the dog's muzzle to pick up his rifle. He clutched it very tightly, wrapping his fingers about the breech with one hand on the trigger. Something was happening out there in the darkness, something that only Red could interpret, and in that moment Danny knew that he was afraid.

Red turned his head, and held it poised while he remained rooted in his tracks. Slowly he swung his body about, facing up the ridge now instead of into the valley. Inch by inch he continued to turn, facing down the other side of the razor-backed ridge, and swinging until he had made a complete circle and was staring into the valley again. Then, Danny understood. He bit his lip so hard that he felt the taste of blood in his mouth, and let go of Red's ruff to reach into his pocket for the flashlight.

They were hunting Old Majesty, but there in the black night the great bear was also hunting them. He had come back to feed on the grubs in the dead logs, scented Danny and Red, and, rather than run again, had elected to try conclusions in the darkness, the time that he favored most and that was most favorable to him. Danny swallowed hard as the complete realization of that was driven home to him, but he grasped it perfectly. Old Majesty was no ordinary bear, but bigger, wiser, fiercer, and more intelligent than any other bear that Danny had ever known. Beyond a doubt he remembered Red, and that Red had once brought him to bay. Even though he might now fear the dog, he still knew that he would have to fight it out sooner or later, and was selecting that fight to his own advantage.

In the darkness he had walked clear around them, nerving himself to the attack and trying to choose the best method for it. Now he was just a little

way down the hill, looking them over, reading them with his nose, and listening for their next move. Danny drew back the hammer of his rifle, and in the night its metallic little click was startlingly loud. He held it in his right hand, clutching the flashlight with his left, and spoke softly,

"Stay here, Red. Stay with me."

Down the slope pebbles rattled, and there was the scraping of a claw on a rock. Danny thought hard, trying in his mind to reconstruct an exact picture of the mountainside as he had seen it earlier that morning. The nearest big rock, he thought, was about sixty yards from where they stood now, and Old Majesty must have walked on it. Half tempted to flash the light and shoot, he hesitated. The bear might come nearer, present a fairer shot. If he did not, if instead of attacking he chose to run, Danny could always urge Red forward to follow him. Somewhere in the lost wilderness, Red would once again bring Old Majesty to bay.

Red was once more facing up the ridge, and had taken two stiff-legged steps forward. Danny poised the flashlight and rifle. Red did not turn his head again, so the bear was standing still. Danny snapped the light on. Its white beam traveled into the night to fall like a silver cage about something huge and black, something that stood scarcely twenty yards up the spine of the ridge. The wind blowing out of the valley eddied around it, curled the long hair that hung from its belly.

Danny raised the gun, supported it on the hand in which he gripped the light, and aimed in its uncertain glow. This, he thought, was not real or right. It was something that you did only in a dream, and awoke to find it a blurred memory. But the cold trigger about which his finger curled was real enough, as was the crack of the rifle and the little tongue of red flame that licked into the darkness. He heard the sodden little "splot" as the bullet struck and buried itself in flesh. Red's battle roar rang through the night, and, at almost exactly the same second, the big dog and Old Majesty launched themselves at each other.

Danny shot again and again, desperately working the lever of his gun and pumping bullet after bullet into the oncoming black mass. A feeling of hopelessness almost overwhelmed him. The bear kept coming. It was as though Old Majesty was a monstrous thing, an animated mass of something that had no more life than a stone or a rock, and upon which bullets had no effect. Wide-eyed, Danny saw it within thirty, then twenty feet of him, and in that moment he knew that he would have died if it had not been for Red.

The big setter met the charging bear, and closed with him. Old Majesty's paw flashed, raked down the dog's chest, and Red reeled away to roll over and over on the ground. His attention diverted from Danny, Old Majesty lunged after the dog.

Danny shook his head. He seemed still to be in a dream, in the throes of something terrible from which sane

awakening only could release him. Feverishly, he found himself ripping the box of cartridges apart, pumping more bullets into the rifle's magazine. His legs seemed to belong to someone else as he ran forward through the night, held the muzzle of his gun within two feet of Old Majesty's ear, and pulled the trigger. The big bear jerked convulsively, quivered, and settled down to stretch his great length on the earth.

For a moment Danny stood pale and trembling, the gun dangling by his side and the flashlight painting the unreal scene before him. He saw Red, whose coat was now stained with crimson, rise on three legs and prepare to renew the battle. He lunged at the bear, but stopped and turned toward Danny, his jaws very wide open, panting hard. Danny faltered, the rifle clattered to the ground, and tears rolled unashamed from his eyes. Red was everything Danny had thought him and very much more. Beautiful, courageous, strong—and noble. He would fight to the death if need be, but would not molest or disgrace a fallen enemy. Danny snapped back to reality.

"Red!"

The cry was wrenched from him. He ran forward to kneel beside the wounded dog. His hand strayed to Red's left chest and leg. Blood trickled through his fingers as he felt torn flesh and muscles. Even as he turned the light on, he knew that Red would never win another prize in a dog show. His left front leg was ripped half away. Danny picked the dog up, and carried him down the mountain to where he had left the pack. He knelt beside him, dusted the gaping wounds with sulfa powder, and wrapped a clean, white bandage around them. Danny took off his jacket, made of it a soft bed for the big setter, and built a fire.

Morning came slowly. The sun strove to break through the mists that blanketed the valley, and the little stream ran quarrelsomely on. Red lay stiffly on the coat, but raised his head to grin, and wagged his tail in the dawn's dim light. Danny unwrapped the blood-soaked bandage and looked at the wound. There was no infection. But it would be a long time before Red was able to travel. Danny rigged his fishline, and caught trout in the little stream. In the middle of the afternoon, he climbed back up the mountain, and looked at the still form of Old Majesty. Danny shuddered. Even now, if it was not for that giant, quiet thing, last night would be like a dream. But let the bear lie where it was; let it remain, a fallen king, in the wilderness it had once ruled.

Day followed day as they camped by the little stream. Red got up from his bed to walk stiffly about, and Danny watched with his heart in his eyes. Red's wounds were healing well, but an ugly scar showed and he would never again have much use of his left front leg. Danny gathered the dog to him, and hugged Red very tightly.

On the eighth day, with Red limping behind him, he started down the valley toward home. They camped that night in another little valley, under the shadow of Stoney Lonesome's laurel thickets. With Red's fine head pillowed on his lap, Danny sat before the leaping little fire he had built and stared into the darkness. Somehow he seemed to have changed. The old Danny Pickett had gone forth on the outlaw bear's trail, but a new one was returning. And the new one was a Danny Pickett able to do what he never could have done before.

Close Up

1. (a) What are the four reasons Danny gives for going into the Wintapi wilderness to fight Old Majesty? (b) Which reason do you think is the most important?

2. Danny thinks that how he will face bears in the future depends on how he faces Old Majesty now. What do you think the bear represents, or stands for, to Danny?

3. Danny uses both scientific woodcraft and his wits to track Old Majesty. (a) How does Danny find the bear's trail? (b) Why does Danny think Old Majesty is not too far from this spot?

4. Danny knows that the bear is near when he feels Red stiffen. (a) What does Danny realize the bear is doing? (b) Why is it a good time for the bear to do this?

5. (a) How does Red save Danny's life? (b) How does Danny save Red's life?

6. At the end of the story, how has Danny changed?

Conflict

A conflict is a struggle between two opposing forces. One type of conflict is a struggle between a person and nature. For example, this story centers on a struggle between Danny and the bear, Old Majesty.

1. How has Old Majesty proclaimed supremacy over all the Wintapi?

2. What three risks does Danny take when he sets out to fight Old Majesty?

3. (a) At what point in the story does it seem as though Old Majesty may win? (b) How does Danny finally win?

4. Danny thinks of the bear as "a fallen king." (a) Why is Danny glad that Red does not molest, or disturb, the fallen enemy? (b) What does he think this proves about Red?

5. Do you think Old Majesty is a good name for the bear? Why or why not?

Activities

1. Make a list of the attributes, or qualities, a person needs to go into the wilderness alone (for example, courage).

2. This story is from a novel by Jim Kjelgaard called *Big Red* (New York: Holiday House, 1975). Locate the novel and find out more about Danny and Red.

RELATIONSHIPS

Understanding Spatial Order

Spatial order tells you the location of something in relation to other things. For example, look at the following sentence. "Red trotted soberly over to sit beside him, and followed closely when Danny went out on the porch." This sentence tells you where Red is in relation to Danny.

▶ Read each item from the story and answer the questions that follow.

a. "Danny climbed the mountain where he and Ross had taken a snarling, spitting fisher from a cave two years before, and walked to its east slope to stand directly under what had been a fine chestnut tree."
   (1) In what direction did Danny walk?
   (2) Where did Danny end up in relation to the tree?

b. "The wind was almost straight out of the west, blowing gently but steadily. Clouds scudded across the sky, and the feathered tips of the pine trees bent."
   (1) From what direction was the wind coming?
   (2) In what direction were the trees bent?

c. "Danny sat beneath the chestnut stub, an arm about Red's neck and the rifle resting where he could instantly reach and bring it into play."
   (1) Where was Danny in relation to Red?
   (2) Where was Danny in relation to his rifle: eight to ten yards away or no more than arm's length away?

d. "Red turned his head, and held it poised while he remained rooted in his tracks. Slowly he swung his body about, facing up the ridge now instead of into the valley. Inch by inch he continued to turn, facing down the other side of the razor-backed ridge, and swinging until he had made a complete circle and was staring into the valley again."
   (1) Where was Red facing at the very beginning of this description?
   (2) Where was Red facing at the end of this description?
   (3) All the time, Red was facing the bear. How had the bear moved?

WORD ATTACK

Finding Root Words

A root is a word or word part that is used to form other words. For example, the root word *wild* is used to form the word *wilderness*—a place where things are in a natural, or wild, condition. The root word *crust* is used to form the word *encrusted*—covered over with a crust or hard covering. Sometimes you can use the root word to help you figure out the meaning of a larger word.

1. Find the root in each of the words below. Then use that root to figure out the meaning of the new word. Check the meaning in a dictionary.

   a. supremacy
   b. proffer
   c. mysterious
   d. renewal

   e. burial
   f. realization
   g. proclaim
   h. reckoning

2. Write an original sentence for each of the words above.

3. Find the root in each of the words below. Then use that root to figure out the meaning of the new word. Check the meaning in a dictionary.

   a. relation
   b. unashamed
   c. beautiful
   d. courageous
   e. reality

   f. monstrous
   g. metallic
   h. scientific
   i. lonesome
   j. meaningless

4. Write an original sentence for each of the words above.

5. The root *anima* means "the soul or mind." Use your dictionary to find five words built from the root *anima*.

The Wall

Noël Murchie

"Fear suddenly settled heavily just below my diaphragm. Even the most skilled climbers had accidents. What about the beginners like me?"

On weekends my parents always climbed mountains.

They went off with the University Outing Club and the New England Mountaineering Society and returned with fascinating tales of brand-new ropes that snapped like thread and people who missed breaking their necks because they had fingernails as strong as diamonds. Conversations around our house were never about the Hit Parade, politics, or whose grades were slipping, but more likely whose rope was slipping.

My mother would narrow her gray

eyes, gazing beyond the windowpanes, and say to my father, "Tom, your boots need oiling if we're going to do the Big Bulge next Sunday." Or, "I notice the half-inch Manila is slightly frayed in two places. Better replace it before someone gets killed." Or, "Remember the rock that smashed my left big toe? Well, the nail finally dropped off."

When I was ten, Daddy took me to Indian Bluffs and taught me the system of technical climbing. Besides scrambling up and belaying[1] correctly, this also involved tying knots that would never slip, splicing, and coiling the long, heavy ropes into efficient snakes. From Indian Bluffs, I graduated to the spindly, terrifying fire tower, where I rappelled[2] eighty feet off the concrete platform so many times that the sour taste of fear vanished from my mouth and I finally knew the exhilaration of propelling myself through free space.

For two years I kept waiting for my mother to say, "It's about time Jo did some real climbing with us." Maybe she still hoped that my anemic older brother, Will, would sprout sets of bulging muscles and become instantly obsessed with mountains. But I knew Will wasn't interested. So I waited for my parents to notice that I was coordinated, agile, and keenly interested.

One day in late summer my father said, "It's about time for Jo to climb the Wall with us, don't you think?" He was sprawled on the living-room floor, splicing a rope. My mother gave me a

vague look. She had black ink all over her hands and on her face. She was a writer, and every day she put on a sweater and skirt and ancient saddle Oxfords, jammed pink wax into both ears, and retreated to the attic, where she crouched for hours over a portable typewriter.

"How much do you weigh now, Jo?" my mother said. Her voice had an absent-minded tone, as though she'd just asked me, "What's your name?" as if I didn't live there, or something.

"About ninety-eight."

"Think you could hold me if I fell?" Daddy teased, wrapping neat strips of tape around the unraveled rope ends.

Before I could reply my mother said, "How tall are you?"

"How should I know? You haven't measured me for ages."

"Well, run get the yardstick from my dressing room."

I scampered up the stairs, hearing her voice following: "And get some pink butcher paper from the kitchen."

I paused on the landing. They had discussed the Wall all my life. It was a series of cliffs stacked on top of one another under the north face of Mount Adams. Leaning far over the railing, I imagined swinging down the Wall while icy winds threatened to send me hurtling hundreds of feet to my agonizing death. I shivered and raced on.

The yardstick leaned against the cane-seated rocker in my mother's dressing room. Pretending the wooden slat was my hiking staff, I rested my weight on it with both hands and studied the framed photograph on the wall behind the rocker. It was a photograph of my mother standing on some mountaintop, her dark hair swirling across her face and

---

1. belaying (bĭ-lā′ĭng) v.: Securing a rope by winding it around a rock or pin.

2. rappelled (ră-pĕld′) v.: Descended from a steep height by using a double rope passed under one thigh and over the opposite shoulder.

hiding her expression. I wondered what it would be like to stand on a summit with her.

There was also a framed certificate awarded my father for his rescue and survival work in Austria during World War Two. While he dug soldiers out of avalanches, my mother kept in shape by rapelling off buildings around our town, like the Congregational church, the city hall, and the shoe factory. I think people must have thought she was some kind of nut.

Standing in the center of my mother's dressing room, I wondered if reading the things she wrote would help me discover the secret of knowing her.

Her dressing table was an odd combination of corner drugstore and fancy boutique. On one side were bottles of Absorbine horse liniment and Sloan's rubbing mixture, tubes of chapped-lip and glacier creams, salt tablets, suntan lotions, little mounds of moleskin to prevent blisters, and a pedometer. Lined up like opposing forces across the way were a large bottle of French perfume, jars of rose-scented cold cream, monogrammed silver-backed hairbrushes and matching hand mirror, a pale-blue satin pincushion, a fountain pen with a solid gold point, and a Wedgewood knickknack box.

A shelf above was crammed with volumes on how to use a compass, surviving in the mountains in winter, first aid and identifying birds and flowers in the Alps, and an encyclopedia of mountain-climbing terms.

As I walked slowly back down the hall, I heard Will's cough rasping in his room, where, as usual, he was holed up with bronchitis, croup, or pneumonia, like one of those pale, tragic opera stars who cough to death just before the curtain drops. I could hear the rhythmic click and thump of his typewriter echoing between his snorting and hawking.

"Hey, Jo!" he called.

I stopped in his doorway. He didn't look one bit pale and tragic. Curled up in the middle of his disheveled bed in a glowing circle of lamplight, he looked flushed and important. Scattered all around him on the blankets were paints, papers, and books.

"Whaddyawant?" I said, lounging suspiciously just inside his door. The room smelled of eucalyptus from the cloud of steam whirling from the croup kettle.

"Come in and see my new book."

While I went skipping energetically off to school and was forced to learn dull old arithmetic and spelling, Will seemed to spend his entire childhood reclining on his pillows, creating volumes of stories and illustrating them. My mother spent a lot of time bending over his bed praising him and telling him how original and funny his creations were. Had he not been sick so much of the time, I am sure Will would have exposed himself gladly to some dread disease to keep from climbing mountains.

I approached his bed cautiously, wondering if there was a trick. He handed me a slim, homemade book.

"It's about some kids who take a steam engine across the desert." His black hair was standing in curly little wisps all around his head. "There's the girl who falls off and gets left behind to die. She's finally eaten by snakes."

"How old is she?" I asked skeptically. There was often a bratty girl in his stories who got into a lot of trouble and usually ended up dead.

"About your age, I'd guess. Around three years old." He flicked paint water at me with his brush.

"I'm twelve, you drip." I flipped the pages of the book, scanning them for the snake death scene. Then I put it down. "I'm going to climb the Wall. Mother's measuring me now to see if I'm tall enough."

"So? What's so good about that, twirp?" He made his hateful smirk.

"You stink. I hate your stories!" I darted out the door.

When I got downstairs my mother said, "What took you so long?"

"I had to go to the bathroom."

She pressed me against the living-room woodwork with her firm, chapped hand.

"Hey, stop sighing and twitching."

I held my breath. Even so, I could smell her French perfume and the horse liniment.

"Just a fraction under five feet tall." She unrolled a piece of butcher paper. "Now stand flat on it."

"What for?"

She didn't answer. Instead she traced outlines of my stocking feet.

"You're tickling me, Mother," I said, lifting one foot like a fly-ridden horse being shod.

"Now, listen here—this is serious. You can't climb the Wall without having a decent pair of lug boots."

That's when I really believed I would climb the Wall.

The outlines of my feet were mailed to Boston. My parents had their boots made in a special Italian leather shop there.

Two weeks later the boots arrived. The leather under my fingers was as soft as a horse's nose, and it smelled deli-

cious. There was special thick padding around the ankles, and the lugs were deep grooves.

"Better wear them every day," my father advised me. I clumped and squeaked around on the wide-planked wooden floors. Then I put the boots in the mountaineering closet in the front hall.

It seemed that our house had its heart in this special place. When you opened any other closet, umbrellas, books, clothes, and junk belched out in your face. The mountain closet was different. It had a nice, oil smell. There were hooks with neatly coiled ropes, summit packs, rucksacks, frames, and shiny karabiners[3] clipped together. Hanging close together like old elbow-rubbing pals were thick down parkas, Levi jackets, bandannas, sweaters, and slings. On the floor were efficient rows of well-oiled boots, prickly crampons,[4] flashlights, portable stoves, and neatly bagged tents and sleeping gear. There were ice axes and a box of hammers and pitons. Way in the back was a bag labeled "Survival Gear." Sometimes I used to hide in the closet when I needed a place to survive.

It was dark when I came down to breakfast on the Sunday we were going to scale the Wall. Like my parents, I wore dark-green knickers with leather patches on the seat and knees, and a turtle-necked jersey. Slung low around our hips were old World War Two pistol belts, and our sheath knives pressed

---

3. karabiners (kăr′ə-bē′nərz) n.: Steel rings that are snapped to the eyes of metal spikes. A rope is run through these rings.

4. crampons (krăm′pənz) n.: Iron spikes attached to shoes to prevent slipping.

The Wall **159**

against our thighs like sinister daggers. We padded softly in our colorful woolen knee socks, with the telltale lumps in the heels where moleskin was pressed on, as we made trips to the closet to assemble our gear.

The breakfast table was cluttered with my mother's special rib-sticking fare: raw nuts, heavy black bread smeared with honey, hard-boiled eggs, and fresh fruit. Mother was like a jack-in-the-box, nibbling breakfast for a second and then leaping up to fiddle with snacks, crackling little waxed-paper bags. There was never a peanut butter and jelly sandwich along when my parents climbed. It was always nibbles of dried fruit, lemon drops, beef jerky, and nuts. At times they dumped it all together into one bag and called it "gorp."

"Jack Holmes came out of his coma," said my mother, lighting momentarily like a butterfly on her chair. "He still has a big dent in his skull."

"What happened to him?" said Will, out of uniform in his maroon robe.

"His head was bashed in by a falling boulder," I said. Fear suddenly settled heavily just below my diaphragm. Even the most skilled climbers had accidents. What about the beginners like me?

"That's why people shouldn't climb mountains," Will said.

"You can die slipping in the shower," said Daddy.

"You guys are all nutty," said Will, pushing back his chair with a loud scrape. "I'm going to lug my guts over to the piano." He recently was saying things like "lug my guts" and "spur my dull revenge" because he was reading *Hamlet*.

"Look—you're taking a chance right now," Daddy said. "The piano cover could slam down and maim your hands."

Will sent his long, pale fingers dive-bombing down the keys with the opening chords of a Beethoven concerto. He looked like a messy old man, all hunched over and with murky glasses that he always forgot to clean. I liked him when he played.

"It's half past five," said Mother.

When we turned out of the driveway, I waved back at Will. He stood with his flannel bathrobe flapping in the chill early-morning wind, lifting his arm like a saluting general. I wondered if he'd be lonely.

We drove north for two hours through the gray, misty morning.

"Are we meeting the rest of the climbers up there?" I asked.

"You'll see," said my mother mysteriously.

There was a lone man standing with a topographical map in his hands when we drove into the meadow that lay in the shadow of Mount Adams.

"Well, well. Hello, Gunner," my mother said, shaking hands with him. He was a narrow, spidery man with a full gray beard. He was wearing a green felt hat with a beautiful enamel bird pinned to it.

"I want you to meet my daughter Josephine," my mother went on. "She's making her first real climb today." He must have been an important person for her to call me Josephine.

"Hallo, Josephine," the man said, crunching my hand. He pronounced it "Yosephine."

"How do you do," I said in a muffled voice.

"You know who he is, don't you?"

my father whispered, sticking his head into the open trunk of the car.

"No."

"Well, he's Gunner Benner. He's an Austrian and climbs all over the world. He also lectures and gives clinics on technical climbing."

"What's he doing here?"

"He lectured at the university last week, so I asked him to come along today. He's your climbing partner."

"He is?" I said stupidly, shivering and gazing up at Mount Adams, looming above. Where exactly was the Wall?

It took awhile to get organized. Before we actually started climbing, all the equipment had to be rechecked. Ropes were distributed and packs adjusted. I sat down on the hard ground and tried to tighten my boots. My fingers were cold and felt paralyzed. An army of butterflies performed stunts in my stomach. As I wound seven coils of Manila rope tightly around my torso to create the safety harness all climbers must wear to be belayed, I felt exhausted.

At last we were traipsing single file up a steep trail, through trees whose leaves were the brilliant color of flames.

Then Daddy shouted, "There it is!"

I glanced up. An expanse of dullest granite seemed to rise straight up and become part of the overcast sky.

"It's not as steep as it looks," my mother said. "The whole Wall is probably six hundred feet high, but its side pitches no more than one hundred and fifty feet at a stretch."

The highest cliff I'd negotiated was twenty-five feet, at Indian Bluffs.

"There are lots of ledges to rest on between pitches, too," said my father.

Gunner Benner came over and touched my shoulder blades. "Remember one thing, Yosephine. Women make better climbers than men because they must rely on *this*"—he poked my head— "not this." He thumped my arms and shoulders. "Women are agile and clever. They have no choice because they don't have the power in their upper body. You will see."

I didn't feel the slightest bit agile or clever, and what I hoped he wouldn't see was the way my heart was jumping under the safety harness. Inside my leather gloves, my hands were slippery.

"Mr. Benner," I mumbled, "could you call me Jo?"

"Okay. And you will call me Gunner then."

He smiled with his dark-blue eyes. I felt better. Overhead, the Wall loomed in an enormous hulk.

Gunner lashed the nylon belay rope to his summit pack. He was leading our rope team for the first pitch without belay. I sat down to watch until it was my turn.

As he went up, his boots seemed to be drawn magnetically to the rock. His hands and feet moved smoothly and automatically to find sure holds and bulges, and in fifteen minutes he was standing on a ledge about one hundred feet above me.

"Rope!" he yelled, and the heavy yellow-nylon belay rope crashed at my feet.

I stood up slowly and clipped the looped end into the karabiner on the front of my chest harness. I screwed the gate lock closed.

"Daddy, please check me."

"On belay," Gunner shouted from above.

"May I climb?" I yelled back.

"Climb!"

"Climbing," I said, and then, indeed, I was climbing.

As I faced the cold granite and took the first step up, Gunner's holds seemed to have vanished. My foot slipped out of the first crack. Somehow I kept jerking and lurching steadily upward, watching the slack rope wiggling reassuringly above me. I jammed my left boot into a crevice and searched for a place to put my right. Suddenly it seemed I was on a piece of highly waxed wood with no cracks, no bulges, not even a tiny cleft to put pressure on briefly, for balance, before lunging on. My boot lugs were useless.

Out of the corner of my eye, I saw a minute niche that maybe I could put my right knee into. I moved up.

"Don't ever let me catch you using your knees, Jo!" my father bellowed from below.

It was humiliating to be caught using my knees. Any dope knew better than that. I would never be a good climber.

One of my pigtails itched terribly, but I didn't dare scratch. My boots were two independent, two-ton bricks pulling my legs off the cliff. I thought I felt myself slipping. Frantically, I shouted to Gunner: "Secure, please!"

Immediately, the belay rope became taut and I rested. There was a loud, rasping sound, which I discovered was my breathing. Directly before my eyes was a clump of delicate wild violets, somehow clinging and surviving. I breathed deeply and shut my eyes.

When I opened them again I looked down between my legs. Space fell away in an awesome, limitless void. The earth

spun and twirled so that down and up were fused. The fear had left my stomach and moved into my bowels, adding new terror that I might lose complete control, like a baby. My giant sobs seemed to threaten to hurl me off the cliff, and I froze in a spread-eagle position.

"Don't hug the mountain, Jo. Relax!" my father shouted.

With clenched teeth I somehow managed to communicate to Gunner that once again I was going to climb. The belay rope slackened, and like a robot I moved up and on once more. I'd disgraced my parents and probably would never be asked to come again.

Then Gunner was there, reaching out a strong hand to pull me onto the ledge I didn't even know I'd got there.

"Good girl, Yo," he said. "Well done." I squatted, holding my knees. My throat was so tight that it seemed impossible for air to pass through.

Far below I heard my parents calling to each other as they made their arduous way up the Wall. Then they too reached the ledge, smiling and talking as if they'd just come in from the garden.

"I loathe this sport. I wish I'd never heard of mountains," I said to my father.

He looked at me with a question in his eyes and said nothing. Instead, he opened his pack and passed some gorp around.

"Yo, do you know why I started climbing?" asked Gunner.

"No," I said.

"When I was a small boy I went with my school class to the top of a tall building in Vienna. As we stood on the roof, admiring the view, another child playfully pushed me over the edge.

"It was many stories to the ground.

However, I didn't fall far. Just as I went over, my teacher grabbed my ankle and I hung upside down from his hand. I remember how busy the streets were as I dangled."

He was quiet for a minute. "I had to overcome my fear of heights, so I learned to climb. But even now I experience tremendous fears."

It was time to move up. My parents' rope led this time. Gunner and I perched on the ledge, waiting for a signal from above and hearing the clink of metal against rock as pitons were hammered into the Wall. I stared at the bird pin on Gunner's hat. Its feathers formed a fan of bright colors.

"What kind of bird is that?"

"Ah, that is my courage bird. It was given me by some village people for avalanche rescue work, to say thanks."

A rope swished onto the shelf from above.

"Now it's your lead," said Gunner, handing me the rope. Although I was technically leading our rope, I still needed the safety of being belayed from the ledge where my parents waited. Being on a belay is like having an umbilical cord attached to you, a lifeline, and I couldn't climb without it until I'd had more experience.

As I scaled the next pitch, I found the natural rhythm of climbing. Energy and agility were automatic. One boot pushed into a slot, a hand pressed around a knob, another boot balanced against a crack, and it worked.

When I reached my father's legs, hanging over the edge of the shelf, I used his boots as a final hold and hugged his legs.

"Climbing is great fun," I said, letting a sudden gust of wind whip the words from my mouth. My mother stood there, smiling.

With my parents' help I anchored myself to the rock at the back of the ledge. Taking one end of the belay rope, I yelled, "Rope!" and tossed it over the edge. Then I sat down on the extreme rim of the ledge, and jerked away from the cliff with all my strength to test whether I was securely tied on and ready to be Gunner's safety rope.

"On belay," I called down.

"Climbing." Gunner had one end of the rope snapped to his chest harness. The other end was drawn around the left side of my waist, across the back of my jacket—to create friction—and through my gloved right hand. As the slack built up from below, my mother piled it into a neat figure eight.

I peered over but couldn't see Gunner because he was under an outcropping. I suddenly thought, "We'll soon be at the top of the Wall." I imagined taking the final step and standing with my arms raised, like the picture in my mother's dressing room.

Without warning I heard his shout. "Falling!"

There was a scraping noise. For a brief minute the belay rope passed hotly and swiftly around my middle. So rapidly and automatically did my right hand jam down between my thighs to brake his fall that I wasn't aware of what I'd done until I realized I'd been jerked violently forward. I was still attached to the Wall from behind, but the nylon rope had stretched with the impact of Gunner's falling weight, and I was suspended over the lip of the ledge with nothing but air beneath me. The Manila from my anchor harness bit cruelly into my crotch and legs. My brake hand

remained motionless. Gunner's rope didn't move. Neither did my parents.

"Good girl, Jo," my father said heavily. "That was a fantastic job."

My mother looked at me with her distant expression and said, "I don't think I could have held him as well as that, Jo. Good job."

The rope began to quiver and move again as Gunner regained his balance and resumed climbing. I edged quickly back onto the shelf.

"Are you okay, Yo?" yelled Gunner.

"Yes." Only then did I become aware of a dull pain in my right arm.

Gunner heaved himself onto the ledge. "My God, what a strong girl you are! I'm a lucky man." His voice sounded thick and surprised. He hugged my shoulders. "The section I was traversing just cracked and fell away. You saved my life."

"Your jacket is torn," said Daddy, pivoting my right arm to expose a long gash where the rope had burned right through the cloth into the soft flesh of my inner arm.

"That's quite a rope burn you've got," said Mother.

"It's not that bad," I said.

Much later, after we'd finally swung down off the Wall, leaving the world of giddy heights and uncertain footholds far above in the eerie late-afternoon wind, Gunner came over to our car. Removing his old hat, he bowed to me and delivered a formal little speech.

"For many years I have climbed up and down mountains, wearing this hat. Always it has brought me good luck. Now I would like you to have it, and may it continue to bring you good fortune in your future climbs." He plunked the mellow green hat, branded with sweat stains, onto the crown of my head.

"Even the pin?"

"Ah, especially the pin for you, Yo," he said simply.

As we drove home, the air was filled with the smell of woodsmoke and apples. When the car turned into our driveway, the lights from the house cascaded across the lawn. Piano chords surged through the open living-room windows, dissecting the night with their reassuring sound. Will met me at the door, still clad in his bathrobe.

"Well, what was it like?"

"Scary. And fun." Wearily I plopped my armload of gear down in the hall by the closet. Will trailed me up the stairs with his leather bedroom slippers flapping. Stiffness and fatigue clung to my bones like glue. I wanted him to go away and leave me alone.

"Hey, how did you get this?" Will said, holding up my wrist and inspecting the crusted blood and the fibers of cloth embedded in the raw flesh of my arm. So, standing in the middle of my room, I told him about the Wall. He thought it would make a terrific story, and soon I heard the clatter of his typewriter.

I was still standing in the center of the room when my mother came in. She was drinking a bottle of cider.

"Here's some ointment for your rope burn. You may put your stuff away in the closet tomorrow." The rule in our house was that you put your climbing equipment away as soon as you came home from the mountains. She sat down and watched me unlace my boots.

"Jo," she said, swigging her cold cider. "I'm very proud of you." Her eyes were the color of the Wall, with a thin layer of mist across them. "For a long time my expectation was that Will would want to climb. But it turns out that you are the one." She didn't touch me, but then she rarely did.

I didn't know what to say, so I kept standing there.

"Sometimes I think I wasn't supposed to be a mother at all," she said wistfully.

I patted her shoulder awkwardly. "It's okay, Mother."

I watched her go quietly over to the window. She looked out for a while and then she said, "We're going to have fun climbing mountains together, Jo."

Later, lying in bed in the darkness, I remembered the smell of the wild violets that bloomed in the rock crannies. And then, turning over, I dropped off to sleep, hearing only the familiar sound of Will's typing down the hall.

Close Up

1. Jo is happy when her parents decide it's time to take her on a difficult climb. (a) What is the Wall? (b) How much climbing experience does Jo have?

2. Jo sees a photograph of her mother standing on a mountain-top. (a) What does Jo want to find out about her mother? (b) Why do you think she wants to climb with her mother?

3. Jo's parents ask Gunner Benner to be her climbing partner. How does their choice show that they want her climb to be successful?

4. (a) Why does Jo feel she has disgraced her parents during the first part of the climb? (b) What does she then say about climbing?

5. (a) How does Jo save Gunner's life? (b) How does Jo know that she has won her mother's respect?

6. How is Jo like the wild violets that cling to the rock?

Conflict

An internal conflict is a struggle that takes place within a character. For example, Jo must struggle with her fear and overcome it before she can climb the Wall.

1. At first, Jo is happy when her parents ask her to climb the Wall. How does she feel when she leans over the railing and imagines herself swinging down the Wall?

2. Why is Jo frightened when she learns about Jack Holmes's accident?

3. During the first part of the climb, Jo is overcome by fear and begins to sob uncontrollably. What does Gunner tell her that helps her overcome her fear?

4. (a) How does Jo prove her courage? (b) Why does Gunner give her his courage bird?

Activities

1. **Composition.** Imagine you are Jo. Write a letter to a friend telling about climbing the Wall.

2. Obtain a catalog from a sporting-goods store. Find each piece of equipment mentioned in this story in the catalog. Describe the function of each piece to the class.

3. **Composition.** Imagine you are Jo's mother. Write a diary entry telling about your hopes for your daughter.

RELATIONSHIPS

Understanding Listing

A list is a collection of items, all of which fit into a particular category. For example, a list of mountaineering equipment might include: rope, karabiners, summit packs, spikes, pitons, and crampons. Some lists are arranged in a significant order (e.g. from biggest to smallest, from nearest to farthest, from most important to least important).

1. Jo says that her mother's dressing table is an odd combination of corner drugstore and fancy boutique. (a) List all of the items on the dressing table that would fall into the category *corner drugstore*. (b) List all of the items that would fall into the category *fancy boutique*.

2. List all of the books on the shelf that would fall into the category *mountaineering books*.

3. List the objects in the mountain closet. Then divide this list in two, with one list for clothing and one list for equipment.

4. List all of the items that would fit into the category *gorp*.

5. Imagine you are going on a camping trip. List ten items you would include in your backpack. Arrange these items from most important to least important.

6. List ten items you have on the top of your bureau or chest of drawers. Arrange these items from biggest to smallest.

7. Imagine you are either Jo or Gunner. List five presents you would like to receive for your birthday. Arrange these items from least expensive to most expensive.

WORD ATTACK

Understanding Jargon

Jargon is the language—words and phrases—used by people in a special group or profession. For example, people who use CB radios may use words and phrases such as "ten-four," "Smokey Bear," and "tooling away."

▶ Use a dictionary to find the meaning of each of the following mountaineering terms.

a. orography
b. sling
c. chock
d. belay
e. gaiter
f. piton
g. timberline
h. escarpment
i. flume
j. bushwhack

REVIEW QUIZ

On the Selections

1. In "You Can't Take It with You," how does the family's stinginess backfire on them?

2. In "The Promised Visit," why are there white crosses along the highway?

3. How does the young man feel when he sees the girl standing along the side of the highway?

4. In "Say It with Flowers," what is Teruo's problem?

5. In "A Running Brook of Horror," what is Grace Wiley's special talent?

6. After Grace is bitten by the cobra, why does she ask for an injection of strychnine?

7. In "The Dying Detective," why is the little box that came through the mail important?

8. Why does Holmes ask Smith to turn up the light?

9. In "Big Red," the dog does not molest the bear after it has fallen. Why does this make Danny feel proud?

10. In "The Wall," Jo learns that Jack Holmes, an experienced climber, has had a serious accident. Why does this knowledge make her feel afraid?

On Relationships

1. In "You Can't Take It with You," why do the family think that Uncle Basil can't hear what they say about him?

2. In "Say It with Flowers," at first Teruo likes his job. What does he learn later that makes him change his mind?

3. (a) In "The Dying Detective," where is Watson when Smith confesses to the murder? (b) Where is Inspector Morton?

4. Think about "The Wall." (a) Write three sentences showing how Jo and her brother are alike. (b) Write three sentences showing how they are different.

5. Make a list of equipment Jo needs to climb the Wall.

On Plot and Character

▶ Decide whether the following statements are true or false.
   a. Usually, the *climax* of a story occurs at the beginning.
   b. One method of creating suspense is *foreshadowing*.
   c. A *dilemma* is a situation that involves a choice between two equally unpleasant alternatives.
   d. A writer always tells you exactly what each character thinks and feels.
   e. An *internal conflict* centers on a struggle between two characters.

COMPOSITION

Sentence Combining

You can show the relationship between two sentences by combining them with a signal word. For example, look at the following two sentences:

> Gunner gave Jo his good luck hat.
> They completed the climb. (after)

By using the signal word in parentheses, you can combine these sentences to show a time relationship.

> Gunner gave Jo his good luck hat after they completed the climb.

Now look at the next two sentences.

> Basil pretended to be deaf.
> He wanted to learn how his relatives really felt about him. (because)

By using the signal word in parentheses, you can combine these two sentences to show a cause-and-effect relationship.

> Basil pretended to be deaf because he wanted to learn how his relatives really felt about him.

Sometimes you need to use a punctuation mark with the signal word. Notice that the next two sentences are combined to show a contrast relationship.

> The young man wished he could drive Susan home.
> The road was too muddy. (, but)
> *becomes*
> The young man wished he could drive Susan home, but the road was too muddy.

▶ Combine each pair of sentences below by using the signal word contained in parentheses after the second sentence. (If a punctuation mark appears in parentheses, use this too.)

   a. When I looked at her, I almost drove off the road.
   She was the prettiest girl I had ever seen. (because)

   b. The family planned to inherit Basil's money.
   Basil had other plans. (; however)

   c. He stopped the car.
   He saw the girl standing by the side of the road. (when)

   d. Teruo sold the fresh flowers.
   Mr. Sasaki had asked him to sell the older ones.
   (, although)

BEFORE GOING ON

Scanning for Facts

How you read an article depends on your purpose in reading it. If your purpose is to prepare for a test, probably you will read the article slowly and carefully, pausing often to think about the information and to organize it in your mind. If, on the other hand, your purpose is to locate specific facts, probably you will scan the material until you find the information you want.

Scanning can save you a lot of time. When you scan, follow these steps:

1. Make a list of all the facts you want to find.
2. Start at the beginning of the selection. Let your eyes sweep across and down each page, looking for key words (for example, place names and numbers). These key words tell you where the fact you are looking for is located. Running your index finger down the middle of each page may help you focus on the lines of print and spot key words.
3. When you locate a key word, read around it to find the fact you are searching for.
4. Make notes as you read. This will help you remember the information you have found.

▶ Use these steps to help you find the following information.

a. Where does Kim Milburn do most of her skateboarding? (Look for a place name as you scan.)
b. What is the first trick Kim learned? (Scan for the key words, "first trick.")
c. What are "nose wheelies" and "tail wheelies"? (Scan for those names.)
d. How many degrees is the skateboard swung after each end-over? (Scan for the key word, "degrees.")
e. What are skateboards made of? (Scan for names of types of woods, metals, etc.)
f. What does Kim wear in competitions? (Scan for the key words, "wear" and "competitions.")
g. How much does it cost to skate in a skateboard park? (Scan for prices.)
h. Why is it good to be on a team? (Scan for the key word, "team.")
i. When might skateboarding be an Olympic sport? (Scan for the key word, "Olympics", and a date.)

Further Reading

Skateboarding

Karen Folger Jacobs

**An Interview with
Kim Milburn/14
Pacific Beach Junior High
San Diego, California**

For anyone who has the instincts of an Evil Knievel but lacks the funds for a motorized vehicle—or isn't old enough to drive legally—skateboarding is the ideal sport. The sixties skateboard fad became the new serious sport of the seventies. Safer equipment and better technology are partly responsible for the sales of over ten million skateboards a year.

When I spoke to her on the phone, fourteen-year-old Kim Milburn explained, "Skateboarding is not like tennis, where you just hit a ball around. You have to perfect skateboarding, perfect your tricks. It's neat!"

Down her driveway Kim Milburn skates; across the street she goes, heading for a crash into the curb. Just before the curb, she shifts to her back foot, the front wheels of the skateboard pop up, and Kim steps down on the front end and continues down the sidewalk. With her hands in her pockets, she sails downhill toward the Pacific Ocean. At the corner she flies off the curb and lands, still skating.

Kim turns onto a level street. Here she pushes off the ground with her left foot, keeping her right foot on the board. She takes a kneepad from her pocket, puts her left foot onto the board, steps her right foot through the pad, and adjusts it at her knee. Then, still coasting, she reties her shoelaces.

Soon after the next corner, Kim points down at a schoolyard and says, "This is Bay Park School, where I usually skate from 3:30 until it gets dark. When I don't have anything to do on weekends, I'm down here, too."

We approach the Cyclone fence surrounding the schoolyard. The gate to the ramp is locked; all that's available is a very steep flight of stairs. I cringe as Kim casually coasts off the top step.

In midair, she hops off onto the third step, grabs her board, and says, "I know every crack on this yard. Even though I didn't skateboard until I graduated from here, I used to roller-skate here every day. That takes balance, but it's not nearly as hard as skateboarding.

"Let me show you my tricks."

Kim wraps her fingers around the ends of her board and then runs sideways with it. While running, she puts the board on the asphalt and flips her body up into a handstand. She arches her back until her feet rest on her head!

She holds her feet on her head until she's almost at the fence. There, she straightens out her back and places her feet between her hands, stands, and pivots her board.

Shoving herself back to me with her left foot, she blurts, "That's the first trick I learned, and I can hold it for as long as I want. It was easy for me to learn because I already knew how to do a handstand and a backbend. A guy showed me how to hold the board to do a handstand. I arched my back up there, and somebody yelled, 'Kim, put your feet on your head!' So I did. I do it in every contest because hardly anybody else can do it, so I get a lot of points for it.

"This one's harder. Watch this!"

Kim folds her hands, put them in the center of her board, her elbows sticking over each end. Then, like a crab, she runs sideways, throws her body up into an armstand on the board, and again arches until her feet touch her forehead.

"I do nose wheelies and tail wheelies. That's when you stand on one end of your board and hold it on the back wheels only. I do walk-the-dog, too: That's when you step on one end, swing that tip, and the other end swings forward; then you step on that end and the other end swings forward; it makes you go zigzag. In end-overs, you go in a straight line by pivoting the back end around to the front. After each end-over, you swing your board 180 degrees, step on it, and swing it around again. It's *fun!*"

How was it when you were starting—frustrating?

"Oh, no! Kids help each other learn, like learning to ride a bike. There's only coaching—teaching—for advanced kids, kids on teams. But to get on a team, you've got to have your basic tricks down. Then the coaches help you perfect them and add style to them.

"To learn, you just have to stick with it and not give up. It takes awhile to get the hang of it. In the beginning, you're always falling. I guess it takes a lot of determination. It takes a lot of time to get good—but nothing like for gymnastics; that's about ten years. In skateboarding, it only takes a girl about three years. In another year I should be really good.

"Some kids on my block got boards for Christmas the year before last. I tried them out, and I liked skateboarding. But it's not as easy as it looks.

"My dad got me one when I was in seventh grade, after I kept saying, 'Get me a skateboard, get me a skateboard!' He got me one, and he got my sister one, too. She's six years younger than me. I tried to get her into it, but she always says, 'Oh, I'm afraid I'll fall!'

"My dad got into it, so now he has one. He keeps spare parts so he can fix boards; he's kind of a skateboard mechanic."

What do you need to skateboard?

"Well, to begin with, you usually buy your board and your wheels and your trucks separately. The truck is the suspension part, what holds the wheels to the board. Some people call them bases or mounts. You can adjust them tighter or looser. And the boards ride according to where the wheels are mounted. For free-style, you want the trucks closer together and the board shorter. For slalom—timed races around markers—you want your trucks farther apart and a longer board.

"You use smaller wheels for freestyle. And inside the wheels you have ball bearings or precision bearings. Precision bearings make the ride smoother and quieter, but they cost more.

"My board is made of plywood and coated with fiberglass. Some boards are aluminum, and some are all wood or all fiberglass. The surface of my board has grip tape on it, like on the bottom of a shower. That's so my foot or hand doesn't slip when I do tricks.

"The boards vary a lot. Really cheap boards are junky. You can't get a decent one for under forty dollars. Kids usually get them for a birthday or buy a used one from a friend, or they just save up their money—save up and save up.

"Some kids rip off skateboards. That's the quickest way; so you always have to keep your skateboard with you when you take it out of your house. One day I took mine to school and put it in my locker. Some kids tried to break in by using a bobby pin on my combination locker. A girl saw them trying and told me, so I gave my board to one of my teachers to lock in a closet until after school."

What do you wear for skating?

"You can skateboard in anything. For competitions, I always wear shorts and a shirt. I can't move in long pants. They're binding. So if it's cold I wear a warm-up outfit over my shorts until it's my turn.

"Up at Carlsbad Skateboard Park, they make you wear a lot of gear—helmet and kneepads and elbow pads. It's neat to skate up there. They have bowls. You can just fly around and feel weightless. It's built like a skiing hill—with concrete moguls. There are skateboard parks all over this country, and they're putting them in fast—not only in California, but in Florida and Texas and all along the East Coast. The owners make a lot of money. Up at Carlsbad, on weekends they charge you $3.00 to skate for 1½ hours. If you bring all the gear, it's still $2.25. They only let thirty people in at a time, so when you get there, you sometimes have to wait an hour or two to get in.

"I go up there about once a month. Some kids up there wear gloves and elbow pads, but I can't do my tricks then.

"I always wear shoes, though, to grip the board and to protect my toes. I never skate barefoot anymore. But, besides shoes, what I wear depends upon what team I'm on."

How can there be a team in such an individualized sport?

"You do skate alone. Except once I saw a picture of a guy skating with a chick on his shoulder. Other than that, it's all skating alone unless you catamaran; that's when two or more skaters sit on their boards with their feet on each other's boards.

"Teams are formed by manufacturers. If you're on a team, you've got to wear their jerseys, and they buy you everything for practice and contests. It advertises their products. Some kids skate independently, but if you skate on a team they help you practice, and you get more publicity.

"Once I get on another team and they give me a board, I'll use that board. Right now, I'm on a team that a kid in my neighborhood got me on. But I want to change teams because they haven't given me a skateboard yet. Every time I call them up, they say they're short on skateboards, short on stock. So far, all they gave me is a jersey that says their name."

What happens when teams compete?

"There's an audience and usually about five judges who score you on a system from one to ten points. They judge on the basis of the difficulty of each trick, how you blend from one to another, and how gracefully you do it all—like gymnastics, really.

"Once I did badly in a competition because of the team I was on. I was used to the board I owned, and then, the day before the contest, the manufacturer gave me a new board so they could advertise it. But it was a twenty-seven-inch board with a kicktail, so I couldn't do any handstands or headstands because the board came up at the ends. I only got third place out of six girls."

How do you feel going into competitions?

"Butterflies! They're in my stomach, but after a few seconds they go away. If I start the routine well, it usually goes well all the way through. I always do the hardest trick first, so once that's done I can relax more. My routine keeps changing because I keep adding new tricks when I learn them. I'm never scared about the tricks, though—just the audience.

"In Oceanside there were fifteen hundred people, but sometimes there are only twenty-five. It all depends on the publicity. People come to watch because they're curious about the sport, and they want to see somebody really do it well. Or they don't have anything better to do that afternoon.

"I like competition. I'm competitive. I like to be first. I just like to go to contests and to improve myself in sports. It's fun. I only went to my first competition

make the American team. That's why I'm staying amateur. If I turned pro, I couldn't compete for the USA. But right now my goal is to get into *Skateboard* magazine, get my picture in. And to win more contests.

"At contests, you see skateboarders you idolize like movie stars. Then you meet them, and you can walk up and talk to them. And they're just like you; you talk skateboarding. It's like a big family reunion.

"I compete against girls on other teams, not against guys unless no other girls show up. Sometimes they have to scrounge up girl contestants.

"Most guys think it's a guy's sport—especially if the girls are better than they are. Guys that aren't so good see you, and they say, 'That's a girl?' Most girls would rather not skate than hear that.

"There aren't many girls who compete, so girls have a better chance to succeed at skateboarding. We don't have to practice ten million hours a day like lots of guys do.

"The top guys have been skating since the sixties. Brad and Bruce Logan are about twenty-eight, and they've been skating for fifteen years! They're pros.

"Guys get more money, too! In the Long Beach contest, the first-place guy got $2,000, and the first girl got $600. Girls have better chances, but they can never win big like some guys do."

How does their skating compare? Do they do the same things, or are there separate styles or expectations?

"Guys are good in some things, and girls are good in other things. Not many guys are limber. Only one other girl can do the handstand I do, and no guys can. Guys usually don't do handstands;

about six months ago; I won that one, and it got me wired for more!

"I heard they're having skateboarding in the 1980 Olympics. I'd like to they're not as coordinated. Guys usually do more foot tricks and strength tricks like jumping. Girls usually have more grace and flexibility, so they use more gymnastics, more coordination stuff. You can tell which girls have done gymnastics by watching them on their boards. Ellen Berryman did a lot of gymnastics; she's the only other skateboarder who can do the spider, the trick where you put your feet on your head."

Did you study gymnastics?

"I did gymnastics from fourth grade until seventh grade, when I started skateboarding, and gymnastics seemed boring in comparison.

"I first took gymnastics in the YMCA of York, Pennsylvania. I spent my summers there with my grandparents. I wanted to continue it in San Diego, but there wasn't any good gymnastics place, so I took acrobatic classes at a dance studio. They weren't so good, so I quit.

"I used to dive, too. I was asked to be on the diving team for the York Y. Some people on that team went to the nationals. For diving, you need flexibility, and you need to twist and to know how to throw your arms.

"Diving helped me for skateboarding. I'm not scared to get upside down, like for headstands or handstands. I'm not even scared to pool ride."

Pool ride?

"Once you find a pool, an empty swimming pool, you can ride in it as long as the people who own it don't kick you out. Sometimes they're afraid you might sue them if you crash.

"Before I tried it the first time, I only felt a little bit scared, but now I never fall in pools. It's fun!

"Once I got really mad when I went to a pool with my friend Lynette. The guys skating there told us, 'You can't skate here. You'll hurt yourself, girls.' But we could skate as well as they could. It was a great pool to ride. The guys kept cutting in front of us and yelling, 'Step aside.' So we just said, 'Step aside yourself.' We skated fine, but one of those step-aside guys broke his wrist!

"You know, I think guys get hurt more than girls because they try to show off more. The most common break is in the wrist—if you try to break your fall with your hands. I've seen some nasty breaks, bones sticking out.

"After a break, you've got to wear a cast for a month or two. Then you can't skate well with a cast on. It changes your weight, makes you lopsided. When it comes off, you have to get used to rebalancing yourself.

"You just shouldn't do things that are too hard for you. Most people who have accidents aren't using safety equipment when they need it, or they're being plain stupid and trying to skate beyond their ability. Don't go overboard and try to show off."

Have you had any accidents?

"I've only skinned my knees and my chin. I do fall sometimes, but I'm used to falling, from doing gymnastics. When you fall you have to roll and keep rolling. That breaks the impact.

"My mom crashed! She saw me skating, and one day she took my board and said, 'It looks so easy I think I'll skate down the street!' She got going fast, out of control, and she fell on her knees. She said, 'Those things are dangerous!' That was a year and a half ago, and she'll never get on one again."

Is your mom into sports?

"No, not really. About the only sport she likes to do is jumping out of planes—skydiving. She has a pilot's license, too. She likes to fly—buzz around and do flips or circles in the air. She rents a plane when she can afford to.

"She hasn't flown in a long time because we have too many medical bills to pay. I was in the hospital for three days when I got paralyzed from doing a back layout half twist on the trampoline. That's when you throw yourself in a backflip, but you don't tuck—you stay flat out in layout—and then in the middle of it you throw your arms so you twist yourself around before you land.

"That time I twisted wrong, so I landed on my back. It didn't hurt much, so I thought I was okay. Then about two hours later I couldn't move on one side, and I couldn't see out of that eye. They took me to the hospital to run more tests on me. They stuck all these wires into my brain, and they fed me in my vein. It was weird! They took a lot of X-rays. The doctor decided that my back had a pinched nerve. The next day I felt all right, but that day I had *pain!* I still go on tramps, but I don't do back layout twists anymore."

What about at your school? Do your classmates know you skateboard? What do they think about it?

Kim lays down on the asphalt, cradling her skateboard as a pillow, and describes her situation. "Guys at my school don't mind that I skateboard. Some of them show me new tricks or make suggestions about improving my routine. Lynette's the only other girl at school who skates. One teacher, Mr. Cardenas, is super-interested in boards.

"Last year when I was in eighth grade, I wasn't too popular until our school had a skateboard contest and I won. Everybody was there. After that, people wanted to meet me, and everybody was nicer to me.

"Now, kids I never even knew come up to me at school and ask me what kind of board they should get. I just find out how they want to use it and tell them what I think they should buy.

"Next year, for tenth grade, I'll go to Mission Bay High. I'm not looking forward to it. I'm scared I won't know anybody, and it'll seem weird. I'm used to the groups in our school.

"The groups are the bikers and the surfers. You know, some people say that people who surf are just beach bums, but a lot of surfers get good marks in school, and a lot of our teachers surf, too. Our school is only four blocks from the ocean.

"Most of the people I hang around with surf. And most of them have skateboards, too. They skate for the fun of it; but surfing's more important to them. They skate to the beach, carrying their surfboards. And if there are no good waves, they can practice on their skateboards."

Are surfing and skateboarding alike?

"They say surfing is like skateboarding; you have to balance yourself. But surfboards are a lot more expensive than skateboards. They say skiing is like skateboarding, too—that it gives you the same feeling. But for skateboarding you don't want snow! Here in San Diego it never snows, so it's great for skateboarding. Pipe riding is supposed to be the most like surfing—skateboarding inside an empty fifteen-foot drainage pipe. They say it's like riding a tube in a wave, when the whole wave surrounds you, and you're shooting through it."

Do you surf? Or do you stick with your short, dry board?

"I never surfed. I'd like to. All I'd have to do is ask one of the guys I know. Any one of them would let me use his board and teach me. But I don't want to make a fool out of myself in front of them.

"Anyway, I can always think of other things to do after school—like skateboarding. Come to think of it, I can always think of other things to do instead of going to school, but I've got to finish high school to get a job. I want to be a stewardess."

Why?

"Stewardesses seem so independent! They just come and go with no strings attached. They get to go places and be in a big hurry. It would be fun, and I like clothes a lot!

"I've been flying by myself since I

was 5½, back and forth to Pennsylvania. The stewardesses babied me; they always let me help them.''

You'll probably be the first skateboarding stewardess.

"But I don't think the airlines would let me do my upside-down tricks. And I don't know if I want to keep skateboarding when I get older. I don't know how I'll feel then.

"Right now I like it a lot, and it's making me stronger and stronger. I eat junk food, though; my mom always brings home ice cream and cake. In seventh grade, my legs started to get pudgy, but now they're muscular. Skateboarding develops leg muscles, and it's made my arms a lot stronger, too. This year I've gotten thinner; I grew four inches, and I only gained five pounds. So, now I'm 5 feet 4 inches and 110 pounds.

"The strength in my legs is good for jumping. I can jump over a pole 2 feet 6 inches high and land back on my skateboard. That's high for a girl!

"I can do kickflips, too. That's where you stand on the edge of your board to make the board flip when you jump in the air. The board has to land on its wheels, and you have to land on top of it. Sometimes I can do doubles: make the board do two revolutions before I land on it. It's mainly guys that do doubles, but I'm strong.

"I want to show you my flying leap. It's really neat!"

Kim runs to the concrete benches and puts her skateboard on one end of the bench. She climbs onto her board. Pushing off with her left foot she skates rapidly down the length of the bench and sails off the end. Airborne, her hands stretch sideways for balance so that she looks like a tightrope walker. The inertia carries Kim and her board forward as gravity draws them toward earth. They land smoothly, coasting downhill.

Kim reaches down, grabs the ends of her board, and tosses herself into a headstand. She then lowers her feet to rest on her head. In that position she skates all the way across the schoolyard.

A letter recently arrived from Kim Milburn: "I'm on the team I wanted to join. We work out at the manufacturer's factory every Sunday. I'm not looking forward to high school and homework. I'd rather skateboard! Love, Kim."

PERSPECTIVES

Alone on the Hilltop

Lame Deer and Richard Erdoes

In this true story, Lame Deer tells of the vision he had that changed his life.

I was all alone on the hilltop. I sat there in the vision pit, a hole dug into the hill, my arms hugging my knees as I watched old man Chest, the medicine man who had brought me there, disappear far down in the valley. He was just a moving black dot among the pines, and soon he was gone altogether.

Now I was all by myself, left on the hilltop for four days and nights without food or water until he came back for me. You know, we Indians are not like some white folks—a man and a wife, two children, and one baby sitter who watches the TV set while the parents are out visiting somewhere.

Indian children are never alone. They are always surrounded by grandparents, uncles, cousins, relatives of all kinds, who fondle the kids, sing to them, tell them stories. If the parents go someplace, the kids go along.

But here I was, crouched in my vision pit, left alone by myself for the first time in my life. I was sixteen then, still had my boy's name, and, let me tell you, I was scared. I was shivering and not only from the cold. The nearest human being was many miles away, and four days and nights is a long, long time. Of course, when it was all over, I would no longer be a boy, but a man. I would have had my vision. I would be given a man's name.

Sioux men are not afraid to endure hunger, thirst, and loneliness, and I was only ninety-six hours away from being a man. The thought was comforting. Comforting, too, was the warmth of the star blanket which old man Chest had

wrapped around me to cover my nakedness. My grandmother had made it especially for this, my first *hanblechia*, my first vision-seeking. It was a beautifully designed quilt, white with a large morning star made of many pieces of brightly colored cloth. That star was so big it covered most of the blanket. If Wakan Tanka, the Great Spirit, would give me the vision and the power, I would become a medicine man and perform many ceremonies wrapped in that quilt. I am an old man now and many times a grandfather, but I still have that star blanket my grandmother made for me. I treasure it; some day I shall be buried in it.

The medicine man had also left a peace pipe with me, together with a bag of *kinnickinnick*—our kind of tobacco made of red willow bark. This pipe was even more of a friend to me than my star blanket. To us the pipe is like an open Bible. Some people need a church house, a preacher, and a pipe organ to get into a praying mood. There are so many things to distract you: who else is in the church, whether the other people notice that you have come, the pictures on the wall, the sermon, how much money you should give and did you bring it with you. We think you can't have a vision that way.

For us Indians there is just the pipe, the earth we sit on, and the open sky. The spirit is everywhere. Sometimes it shows itself through an animal, a bird, or some trees and hills. Sometimes it speaks from the Badlands, a stone, or even from the water. That smoke from the peace pipe, it goes straight up to the spirit world. But this is a two-way thing. Power flows down to us through that smoke, through the pipe stem. You feel that power as you hold your pipe; it moves from the pipe right into your body. It makes your hair stand up. That pipe is not just a thing; it is alive. Smoking this pipe would make me feel good and help me to get rid of my fears.

As I ran my fingers along its bowl of smooth red pipe-stone, red like the blood of my people, I no longer felt scared. That pipe had belonged to my father and to his father before him. It would someday pass to my son and, through him, to my grandchildren. As long as we had the pipe there would be a Sioux nation. As I fingered the pipe, touched it, felt its smoothness that came from long use, I sensed that my forefathers who had once smoked this pipe were with me on the hill, right in the vision pit. I was no longer alone.

Besides the pipe, the medicine man had also given me a gourd. In it were forty small squares of flesh which my grandmother had cut from her arm with a razor blade. I had seen her do it. Blood had been streaming down from her shoulder to her elbow as she carefully put down each piece of skin on a handkerchief, anxious not to lose a single one. It would have made those anthropologists[1] mad. Imagine, performing such an ancient ceremony with a razor blade instead of a flint knife! To me, it did not matter. Someone dear to me had undergone pain, given me something of herself, part of her body, to help me pray and make me stronghearted. How could I be afraid with so many people—living and dead—helping me?

One thing still worried me. I wanted to become a medicine man, a *yuwipi*, a healer carrying on the ancient ways of

---

1. anthropologists (ăn′thrə-pŏl′ə-jĭsts) n.: Scientists who study customs and social relationships.

the Sioux nation. But you cannot learn to be a medicine man like someone going to medical school. An old holy man can teach you about herbs and the right ways to perform a ceremony where everything must be in its proper place, where every move, every word has its own, special meaning. These things you can learn— like spelling, like training a horse. But by themselves these things mean nothing. Without the vision and the power this learning will do no good. It would not make me a medicine man.

What if I failed, if I had no vision? Or if I dreamed of the Thunder Beings, or lightning struck the hill? That would make me at once into a *heyoka*, a contrariwise, an upside-down man, a clown. "You'll know it, if you get the power," my Uncle Chest had told me. "If you are not given it, you won't lie about it, you won't pretend. That would kill you, or kill somebody close to you, somebody you love."

Night was coming on. I was still lightheaded and dizzy from my first sweat bath, in which I had purified myself before going up the hill. I had never been in a sweat lodge before. I had sat in the little beehive-shaped hut made of bent willow branches and covered with blankets to keep the heat in. Old Chest and three other medicine men had been in the lodge with me. I had my back against the wall, edging as far away as I could from the red-hot stones glowing in the center. As Chest poured water over the rocks, hissing white steam enveloped me and filled my lungs. I thought the heat would kill me, burn the eyelids off my face! But right in the middle of all this swirling steam I heard Chest singing. So it couldn't be all that bad. I did not cry out "All my relatives!"—which would

have made him open the flap of the sweat lodge to let in some cool air—and I was proud of this. I heard him praying for me: "Oh, holy rocks, we receive your white breath, the steam. It is the breath of life. Let this young boy inhale it. Make him strong."

The sweat bath had prepared me for my vision-seeking. Even now, an hour later, my skin still tingled. But it seemed to have made my brains empty. Maybe that was good, plenty of room for new insights.

Darkness had fallen upon the hill. I knew that *hanhepiwi* had risen, the night sun, which is what we call the moon. Huddled in my narrow cave, I did not see it. Blackness was wrapped around me like a velvet cloth. It seemed to cut me off from the outside world, even from my own body. It made me listen to the voices within me. I thought of my forefathers who had crouched on this hill before me, because the medicine men in my family had chosen this spot for a place of meditation and vision-seeking ever since the day they had crossed the Missouri to hunt for buffalo in the White River country some two hundred years ago. I thought that I could sense their presence right through the earth I was leaning against. I could feel them entering my body, feel them stirring in my mind and heart.

Sounds came to me through the darkness: the cries of the wind, the whisper of the trees, the voices of nature, animal sounds, the hooting of an owl. Suddenly I felt an overwhelming presence. Down there with me in my cramped hole was a big bird. The pit was only as wide as myself, and I was a skinny boy, but that huge bird was flying around me as if he had the whole sky to himself. I could hear his cries, sometimes near and sometimes far, far away. I felt feathers or a wing touching my back and head. This feeling was so overwhelming that it was just too much for me. I trembled and my bones turned to ice. I grasped the rattle with the forty pieces of my grandmother's flesh. It also had many little stones in it, tiny fossils picked up from an ant heap. Ants collect them. Nobody knows why. These little stones are supposed to have a power in them. I shook the rattle and it made a soothing sound, like rain falling on rock. It was talking to me, but it did not calm my fears. I took the sacred pipe in my other hand and began to sing and pray: "Tunkashila, grandfather spirit, help me." But this did not help. I don't know what got into me, but I was no longer myself. I started to cry. Crying, even my voice was different. I sounded like an older man, I couldn't even recognize this strange voice. I used long-ago words in my prayer, words no longer used nowadays. I tried to wipe away my tears, but they wouldn't stop. In the end I just pulled that quilt over me, rolled myself up in it. Still I felt the bird wings touching me.

Slowly I perceived that a voice was trying to tell me something. It was a bird cry, but I tell you, I began to understand some of it. That happens sometimes. I know a lady who had a butterfly sitting on her shoulder. That butterfly told her things. This made her become a great medicine woman.

I heard a human voice, too, strange and high-pitched, a voice which could not come from an ordinary, living being. All at once I was way up there with the birds. The hill with the vision pit was way above everything. I could look down even on the stars, and the moon was close to my left side. It seemed as though the earth and the stars were moving below me. A voice said, "You are sacrificing yourself here to be a medicine man. In time you will be one. You will teach other medicine men. We are the fowl people, the winged ones, the eagles and the owls. We are a nation and you shall be our brother. You will never kill or harm any one of us. You are going to understand us whenever you come to seek a vision here on this hill. You will learn about herbs and roots, and you will heal people. You will ask them for nothing in return. A man's life is short. Make yours a worthy one."

I felt that these voices were good, and slowly my fear left me. I had lost all sense of time. I did not know whether it was day or night. I was asleep, yet wide awake. Then I saw a shape before me. It rose from the darkness and the swirling fog which penetrated my earth hole. I saw that this was my great-grandfather, Tahca Ushte, Lame Deer, old man chief of the Minneconjou. I could see the blood dripping from my great-grandfather's chest where a white soldier had shot him. I understood that my great-grandfather wished me to take his name. This made me glad beyond words.

We Sioux believe that there is something within us that controls us, something like a second person almost. We call it *nagi*, what other people might call soul, spirit, or essence. One can't see it, feel it, or taste it, but that time on the hill—and only that once—I knew it was there inside of me. Then I felt the power surge through me like a flood. I cannot describe it, but it filled all of me. Now I knew for sure that I would become a *wicasa wakan*, a medicine man. Again I wept, this time with happiness.

I didn't know how long I had been up there on that hill—one minute or a lifetime. I felt a hand on my shoulder gently shaking me. It was old man Chest, who had come for me. He told me that I had been in the vision pit four days and four nights and that it was time to come down. He would give me something to eat and water to drink and then I was to tell him everything that had happened to me during my *hanblechia*. He would interpret my visions for me. He told me that the vision pit had changed me in a way that I would not be able to understand at that time. He told me also that I was no longer a boy, that I was a man now. I was Lame Deer.

1. Lame Deer's experience on the hilltop is part of a Sioux ritual. What is the purpose of this ritual?

2. Lame Deer tells you that the Sioux family is very close. (a) In what two ways does Lame Deer's grandmother help him feel her nearness during his first *hanblechia?* (b) Why does the pipe make him feel that he is not alone?

3. Why is Lame Deer worried that he will not receive a vision?

4. (a) When Lame Deer has his vision, what do the birds tell him? (b) What does his great-grandfather tell him?

5. (a) What is *nagi?* (b) Why does Lame Deer know he will become a medicine man when he discovers he has *nagi?*

Point of View

In a true story, often the author narrates, or tells about, his or her own experiences. This means that the story is told from the point of view, or angle of vision, of the author. The author uses the first-person pronoun *I* to identify himself or herself. For example, Lame Deer, the author of this story, says, "*I* was all alone on the hilltop." Usually, a true story told from the author's point of view is *subjective*, since it tells the author's personal thoughts and feelings.

1. (a) How does Lame Deer feel immediately after he is left alone in the vision pit? (b) How do you know how he feels?

2. (a) Why is the experience of being in the vision pit important to Lame Deer? (b) How does he feel about himself after this experience?

3. (a) Could anyone else accurately tell you what Lame Deer's feelings during his vision were like? Why or why not? (b) Do you think this story would have been less convincing if someone else had told it? Why or why not?

Activities

1. **Composition.** Have you decided what you want to be when you graduate from school? Write a paragraph telling about your decision.

2. Make a list of questions you would ask Lame Deer if you had the chance to interview him.

JUDGMENTS

Distinguishing Between Primary and Secondary Sources

When you tell about events and feelings you have experienced directly, or firsthand, you are a primary source of information. For example, you are a primary source when you tell what happened to you on your birthday or how you felt when you won an award. Lame Deer is a primary source of information about his vision-seeking experience.

When you tell about something that happened to someone else, something you have not experienced directly, you are a secondary source of information. For example, Lame Deer told Chest about his vision-seeking experience. Suppose Chest repeated the story to someone else. Chest would be a secondary source.

▶ Answer each of the questions below.

    a. Lame Deer tells you how the Sioux crossed the Missouri two hundred years ago. Is he a primary or a secondary source?

    b. Lame Deer says, "I felt feathers or a wing touching my back and head. This feeling was so overwhelming that it was just too much for me. I trembled and my bones turned to ice." Is he a primary or a secondary source?

    c. Lame Deer says, "I know a lady who had a butterfly sitting on her shoulder. That butterfly told her things." Is he a primary or a secondary source of information about the lady's experience?

    d. Lame Deer says, "Besides the pipe, the medicine man had also given me a gourd. In it were forty small squares of flesh which my grandmother had cut from her arm with a razor blade. I had seen her do it." Is he a primary or secondary source of information about this event?

WORD ATTACK

Using Direct Context Clues

Direct context clues tell you the exact meaning of a word. Sometimes authors use special words that are unfamiliar to their readers. They include direct context clues to deliver the meaning of these words. For example, Lame Deer says, "My grandmother had made it especially for this, my first *hanblechia*, my first vision-seeking." He knows that most readers won't know what *hanblechia* means, so he defines it in the same sentence, "my first *vision-seeking*."

Authors provide direct context clues in several ways. They may use commas to separate the word from its definition. They may use dashes to set it off. They may use a phrase such as "which mean" or "which we call." For example, "I knew that *hanhepiwi* had risen, the night sun, which is what we call the moon."

▶ Use direct context clues to find the definition of each of the *italicized* words below.

    a. "I wanted to become a medicine man, a *yuwipi*, a healer carrying on the ancient ways of the Sioux nation."

    b. "That would make me at once into a *heyoka*, a contrari-wise, an upside-down man, a clown."

    c. "The medicine man had also left a peace pipe with me, together with a bag of *kinnickinnick*—our kind of tobacco made of red willow bark."

    d. "We call it *nagi*, what other people might call soul, spirit, or essence."

    e. "Now I knew for sure that I would become a *wicasa wakan*, a medicine man."

The Contest

Paul Darcy Boles

My stepfather was driving me to the train through the winter day. It seemed strange to be out of high school on a weekday, and it caused a little guilt feeling. I kept looking at him when he wasn't expecting me to; he was doing the same thing to me. Don't get me wrong, I like him very much. But liking didn't make me agree with him or forget my own father, who'd died two years before.

For instance, when he said, a little line of worry coming across his forehead, "Joey, you'll be back Thursday night?" it meant more than he was asking. It meant he didn't approve of the whole trip to the state trumpet contest for high-school band-member soloists, and it meant that if he'd had his way, I'd never have gone.

So I couldn't keep from being a little sardonic. I said, "I'm pretty good at catching trains, planes, and buses. Honest, I always ask where they're going. I hardly ever end up in Utah or Florida."

He could have smiled at that. But didn't. "You'll have to make up the schoolwork you're missing."

"Did most of it ahead of time, except for some algebra," I said. "And I'll make that up this weekend. I know my grades haven't exactly catapulted me into the genius class, but I'm doing all right."

"Yes" was all he said. I don't have great ESP, but I knew he was thinking I'd get a lot better grades if I'd forget about playing the trumpet.

Which was impossible.

I'd been playing it since I was nine years old and it was part of me. He couldn't understand that. He seemed to think music was something I did the way other people collect stamps or work out on the parallel bars.

In the snow-rubbed day, gray as old steel, we passed the high school. Kids were just going in, hurrying up the hill before the last bell rang, and I saw Martha's red coat and her near-Gucci boots. I leaned out and yelled and waved, and she turned, gold hair floating out and hand shooting up as she waved back.

"Martha Connors," I explained to my stepfather. "Old friend. She wants me to win this contest."

He didn't say anything. He'd been married to my mother for three months, and, while we got along all right on the surface, there was always a tension underneath. It was as if everything he suggested was for my own good, which was a drag. How did he *know* my own good?

My mother went along with everything because she loved him. He was a fine man, not handsome, just quiet and tough. Sometimes, when he'd been in court all day, his face would look paper-gray. Those times, when I was practicing the horn, I'd stick in a Harmon mute and keep the noise level down to a whisper.

Now he swung the car into the station parking lot and I got out, swinging my traveling bag out and tucking the horn in its case under one arm.

"Well, as they say in the islands, aloha," I said.

He sat looking at me. "Joey——"

"Sir?"

He'd told me to call him Rob—he'd never asked me to call him Dad—but I couldn't bring myself to do that. Now he looked as if he'd like to roll up all the trouble—which hadn't even come out in the open—in his hands and toss it at me like a snowball.

"Joey. Good luck."

You can tell when people want to say a lot more than they can. It was all there.

For half a second, I, in turn, wanted to tell him to go ahead and get it off his chest. I just said, "Thanks a lot, Sir." And turned around and moved down the steps to the station. I looked out of one of the windows after I got inside, and he was still parked out there, as if he wanted to follow me and tell me some-

thing. After I'd bought my ticket for downstate I looked out again, but the car was gone.

In the train, when I'd settled down with a paperback and then tired of it, I offered it to a girl, Sue Langdon, who was from the next village. She was entered in the flute solo contest. She didn't look like a flutist, or even a flautist, which is what fancy people call flutists; matter of fact, she was pretty beautiful. She thanked me for the book but said she was too keyed up to read. She said she was doing selections from Debussy for her solo, and I told her I was doing the old standard *The Carnival of Venice*, which may be common but is hard to do. Harry James used to do it in a circus way, but if you take all the variations, it's a great workout.

She told me her parents had had a going-off party for her just before she caught the train, and I kept remembering, while she talked, how my real father had been. He'd encouraged my horn playing every chance he got. He'd played around in ricky-tick bands when he was my age and knew how it was. I guess I was thinking of him too hard, because all at once she stopped talking and said, "What's the matter? Am I boring you?"

"No," I said. "I was thinking of something else."

"You looked so far away . . . and sad."

"I'm not sad by nature," I told her. "In fact, I'm often known as the Clown of Glenport High. No, I was just thinking of a summer afternoon when the whole family was around the table, and the sun was falling a certain way, and people weren't talking importantly at all, just kind of chatting. In the next room, the hi-fi was playing Duke Ellington's *Rockin'* in *Rhythm*, with those beautiful brasses. Johnny Hodges was on alto, and everything was moving along as if it would always stay that way——"

She nodded. "Then why did you look so lost?"

"That's rough to explain," I said. "It's just . . . sometimes things *do* get lost, and I don't want them to. Now let's talk about your lip. Your embouchure. You practice a lot?"

She told me she did. She told me a lot about it.

By the time we got downstate we were good friends, good music-friends anyhow. I promised I'd check with her after all the solo contests were over the next day, so we could ride home together.

It was snowing, fresh and full of enchantment, by the time I got to the trumpet-registration building. Watching the snow fall on the old red brick of the university building, I got the feeling everything in the world was new. It's a crazy sensation I get sometimes, in all kinds of weather. I mean, I thought that in some secret way, from now on, nothing was going to be lost in the world or the nation; everything was going to get together and be the way it was always meant to be.

I still had the same feeling when I peeled off and went to the house where I was supposed to sleep that night. It was on a side street, and when I got there I was met by a little woman, about seventy or so, who told me to be sure to wipe my feet and not to make any noise after ten o'clock. She said she had a special TV show she always watched on Wednesday nights at ten o'clock. She had dyed gray-blue hair and sad eyes like the basset hound I'd been given by my father

and mother for my eighth birthday. The dog had been killed by a car about two years later. Remembering that, and feeling sorry for the little old lady who had the TV program and not much else to look forward to, I lost the feeling of newness and magic.

I looked in the small front room downstairs. It had a big TV set in it and a lot of lace doilies, along with a picture of a soldier in a silver frame. She saw me looking and said it was her grandson, killed in Vietnam two years before. That took away the last of the snow's magic, even though I sat on the edge of the bed when I got upstairs and watched the flakes fall for quite a while.

Then I took my horn out of its case and fingered all the variations of *Carnival of Venice*.

And gradually, the feeling that the world was still going to be fresh and wonderful and its true self came back. This time I held onto the feeling, even after I'd gone out and swallowed three hamburgers and a malt. I came back to the room to watch the snowflakes outside the window.

When I woke up, not only had the snow stopped, leaving everything high-shining in the morning, but it was a quarter to nine, and I was supposed to be at the trumpet-solo building at nine.

I skipped breakfast—eating just before playing makes you feel like a stuffed duck—and headed for the building. I was third on the program. There were nine other contestants from schools around Illinois.

They lined us up in the wings and told us to be quiet while the other people were playing. I leaned against a wall and warmed up my horn by blowing into it, making sure the valves were all loose and oiled and working freely. I took out the mouthpiece and held it cupped in my hand to keep it warm while I waited.

The first contestant was a lot taller than I and with his hair styled the way mine would never stay. He walked out carrying his music, played *The Three Deuces*, which has a lot of flashy triple-tonguing in it, high notes, and a nice low register. He did very well on the first section, but in the second he lost his place and just flurried around for a while, hitting a few prize clinkers. When he came off, he was red-faced and his hair style was slightly mussed. After him came someone about my own age, with a horn like mine. He played *The Arabian Nights* with a good tone, nice and sharp and never losing it. But when he hit the triple-tonguing, it sounded a little too slurred. Then he returned to the wings a lot cooler than the first man. It was my turn.

I couldn't see anything when the lights hit my eyes. I just kept on walking till I got to the piano, handed the accompanist my music and waited for the first introductory notes.

As soon as they came, in the right key, B flat, I knew everything would be all right, because all that could have stopped me was the piano breaking down and falling apart. I had the same feeling I'd had the afternoon before, that everything would be found and nothing lost at all, not a thing in creation. It's a feeling that comes out of the air and the light and the people listening. It doesn't have a lot to do with you. You have to know what you're doing, know where you're going, but the rest of it is riding a wave. Toward the end of the last varia-

tion, I lifted the horn and let the last notes sail out to the top limit, the high C coming up as if it happened to be the gold feather on the crest of a bird that could fly forever. I even remembered to bow when the judges and onlookers applauded. Then I walked off, in the right direction, even though I still couldn't see anything much.

I leaned against the wall as the next contestant went out. Then it was all over except the awards, and they were calling us all out to the stage.

We lined up out there. I still couldn't see anything but the glare of the lights. Then a judge came up the steps at the side and made the announcements. The third-prize medal was presented first. It went to the *Arabian Nights* guy. Then second was awarded to a small red-faced boy who'd played *Flight of the Bumblebee*. Then they were calling out my name, and I thought it was probably a mistake, until I remembered how I'd felt while I played. I stepped forward and knew it was true. The first-prize medal was gold, with a little laurel wreath around it. I stuck it in my pocket as the curtains shut. People were still applauding. Then I went back to the wings to get my trumpet, slung my coat over my shoulders, and went down the stairs and along the outside aisle.

I didn't even recognize my stepfather at first. I thought he was one of the judges or something. He was shaking my hand and standing there. My mother was behind him. He had a fairly good smile when he put his mind to it.

"Joey," he said, "I didn't know. I had to know. Can you see that?"

"Sure," I said, though I couldn't.

"No, I don't think you see." We were all going down the aisle toward the doors. "For wrong or right, I was raised strictly. Overstrictly. Entertainers, the arts, these were things to stay away from; hard work, a profession, that was the thing to cultivate. Maybe I can't say it all now, but I want you to know I'm proud of you. And this will never be a waste of your time."

I gave him a look. He'd meant it. I nodded and told him it had been nice of him to come all this way. Then he said we'd all better have some lunch.

While I ran along over the icy sidewalks back to the rooming house, I was thinking of the feeling that still held me up, the crazy, strange, noble feeling that nothing gets lost at all. I went in the house and upstairs and got my bag and then came down and looked into the front room again, the one with the doilies, the TV, and the silver-framed picture of the little old lady's grandson. She wasn't in the front room. I could hear her back in the kitchen. Then I found a piece of paper in my pocket and a pencil and wrote her a note and shoved it under one corner of the silver frame. The soldier in the picture, about five years older than I am, kept looking at me. I told the lady in the note that I wanted her to have the medal because it, by itself, couldn't mean as much to me as it could if I gave it to her. I just told her I wanted her to have it. I put it, in its small case, beside the note.

Then I went out. The kind of feeling I had didn't have anything to do with winning medals.

Over lunch, in the campus coffee shop, when my mother asked to see the medal, I told her and my stepfather about the way I felt. I said, "My girl, Martha Connors, back home, will feel the same way about it. Hope you do too."

My mother took a breath and said, "Yes."

"I agree, Joey. I agree fully," said my stepfather. He wasn't smiling now, but that didn't make any difference; he seemed to pack so much warmth into himself it made me think again of the way my father had been. Not an edgy remembering, just calm and quiet. For the flash of a second my own father might have been sitting there across from me.

About that time, Sue Langdon, the flutist, came floating in. She'd won a second and was five feet off the ground because of it. After I'd kissed her in a friendly musicianly way, I introduced her to my family. "This is my mother," I said, and then, "——this is Rob." I looked into his eyes, feeling there was nothing lost at all, and said, "I mean, this is my dad."

After which we all sat down to eat up a storm, and I started turning into the Clown of Glenport High.

1. (a) How does Joey's stepfather feel about the trumpet contest? (b) How does Joey think his real father would have felt?

2. Neither Joey nor his stepfather voices his feelings, but both are aware of tension between them. (a) Why does Joey resent his stepfather's suggesting things "for his own good"? (b) What does Joey mean when he says that his stepfather looks as though "he'd like to roll up all the trouble—which hadn't even come out in the open—in his hands and toss it at me like a snowball"?

3. When Joey reaches the house where he will spend the night, he goes upstairs and practices. (a) How does the music make him feel? (b) What does this tell you about the importance of music in his life?

4. Joey wants to become a professional musician. (a) Why is it difficult for his stepfather to understand this? (b) What happens that makes his stepfather realize how important music is to Joey?

5. Earlier on the train, Joey told Sue, "It's just. . .sometimes things *do* get lost, and I don't want them to." (a) Why does Joey give the old woman his medal? (b) Why does he come to feel that nothing gets lost at all?

Point of View

In fiction, a story may be told in the first person by a character who appears in it. This character is called the *narrator*, and the narrator refers to himself or herself by the pronoun *I.*

In a story told this way, you learn the narrator's personal thoughts and feelings, and you see the events unfold through the narrator's eyes. In fact, it seems as though you are standing in the narrator's shoes. You see other characters from the narrator's point of view, and you learn what the narrator thinks about them.

1. (a) Who is the author of this story? (b) Who is the narrator, the character who tells the story?

2. There are two important characters, Joey and his stepfather, Rob. About whose feelings do you learn more? Why?

3. Does the narrator tell you mostly about something that happened to him or something that happened to someone else?

4. Rob asks Joey if he'll be back Thursday night. (a) What does Joey think his stepfather means by this statement? (b) Do you think Joey is correct? Why or why not?

JUDGMENTS

Identifying Statements of Fact and Statements of Opinion

A statement of fact contains information that can be proved true or false. For example, Joey says, "I'd been playing it since I was nine years old." The information in this statement can be checked. You can find out if it is true or false.

A statement of opinion expresses a personal belief or attitude. It does not contain information that can be proved true or false. It tells how an individual perceives, looks at, or feels about some person, object, or situation. For example, Joey says, "I know my grades haven't exactly catapulted me into the genius class, but I'm doing all right." Joey believes he's doing all right, but his stepfather or teachers might disagree.

▶ Read the items below. Decide whether each statement is a statement of fact or a statement of opinion.
   a. "She didn't look like a flutist, or even a flautist, which is what fancy people call flutists; matter of fact, she was pretty beautiful."
   b. "I was third on the program."
   c. "He'd been married to my mother for three months . . . ."
   d. "He was a fine man, not handsome, just quiet and tough."
   e. "The dog had been killed by a car about two years later."
   f. ". . . eating just before playing makes you feel like a stuffed duck. . . ."
   g. "There were nine other contestants from schools around Illinois."
   h. "The first contestant was a lot taller than I. . . ."
   i. "He did very well on the first section. . . ."
   j. ". . . this will never be a waste of your time."

WORD ATTACK

Understanding Figurative Expressions

A figurative expression is a group of words that has a meaning all its own. The meaning of the expression has little to do with the meaning of the individual words. For example, Joey says, "I'd been playing it (the trumpet) since I was nine years old and *it was a part of me*." He means the trumpet is very important to him. He does not mean that the trumpet is a section of his body, like an arm or a leg.

1. Identify the figurative expressions in the sentences below.
   a. "For half a second I, in turn, wanted to tell him to go ahead and get it off his chest."
   b. "In the train, when I'd settled down with a paperback and then tired of it . . ."
   c. "She thanked me for the book but said she was too keyed up to read."
   d. "I still had the same feeling when I peeled off and went to the house where I was supposed to sleep that night."
   e. "You have to know what you're doing, know where you're going, but the rest of it is riding a wave."

2. Replace the figurative expressions in the sentences above with words that keep their basic meanings.

3. Write the meaning of each of the following italicized figurative expressions. Check your answers in the dictionary by looking up the word that is a part of the body.
   a. His stepfather liked to keep his feelings to himself; he didn't *wear his heart on his sleeve.*
   b. Things didn't always work out as she planned, but *her heart was always in the right place.*
   c. When he saw her, he fell *head over heels* in love.
   d. I have so much work to do, I'm having trouble *keeping my head above water.*
   e. During the contest, he *put his best foot forward.*
   f. My mother *put her foot down* about late hours.
   g. She had the answer *on the tip of her tongue.*
   h. They had *their hands full* running the contest.
   i. The noise had gotten *out of hand.*
   j. He knew his parents were angry, and he didn't want *to face the music.*

I Love All Gravity Defiers

Lillian Morrison

The vaulter suspended
on a slender pole
hangs in the air
before his fall.

5 The trapeze artist
tumbles through space
in split-second rescues
from the abyss.

Kids on swings
10 pumping to the sky
in a pendulum of pleasure,
fly.

Ski-jumpers, speed-propelled,
extended in flight
15 loop down
to land upright.

Hail gravity defiers,
jumpers, broad and high
and all non-jumpers
20 who will not drop, who try.

Somersaulters
on the trampoline,
battered boxers
up at the count of nine

25 Springboard athletes
jackknifing as they dive
and people who stand straight
and stay alive.

Close Up

1. Find at least five gravity defiers listed in this poem.

2. Reread lines 17–20. Why does the poet admire gravity defiers?

3. Someone who defies gravity will not be pulled or held down. Reread lines 25–28. Do you think this poem is really about all people who have the courage to defy life's problems? Why or why not?

Night Rider

Steven Otfinoski

He had been driving a truck for fifteen years, but he had never picked up a hitchhiker like Jake.

It was about quarter-past nine when I first saw him. I was tooling down Route 109 doing about fifty. He was standing along the side of the road, and I picked him up with my high beams. Route 109 is an old road, and few cars use it anymore. I thought it was odd that anyone would be trying to hitch a ride on it—especially at this hour!

My first reaction was to keep driving. I had a load of fresh vegetables to haul in, and I was already behind schedule. But somehow I felt sorry for him. I don't know why. Maybe I figured he'd be standing out there all night waiting for the next set of wheels to come along. So I slammed on the brakes and pulled over. That's how it all started.

"How far you going?" I asked as he climbed into the cab.

He just looked at me and said, "I'll tell you when we get there."

"Listen," I told him, "I know every town on this run, so don't . . ."

"Oh, it isn't a town," he broke in. "It's just a place."

"What kind of a place?"

"It's up there. I'll know it when we get there." He pointed a finger up into the darkness of the mountains. There

was nothing there but blackness. Not even the light of a single house.

I looked him over. He was just a kid—sixteen, maybe seventeen at the oldest. He was tall, thin, and very pale. He looked like any one of a thousand kids I've seen hitching. And yet there was something different about him. I couldn't put my finger on it.

"Are you sure you know where you're going, kid?" I asked him.

I expected him to get mad, but he didn't. He just turned two big, blue eyes on me and spoke very calmly. I'd never seen eyes that blue. They looked like the sea on a sunny day.

"My automobile broke down up there in the mountains. I had to get a part to fix it. If you take me back to my car, I will pay you for your trouble. I have money."

There was something about the way he talked. It sounded strange when he said *automobile* instead of *car*. It was as if he were a foreigner or something. He talked with a kind of funny accent, but one I had never heard before.

"I don't want your money," I told him. "I'm already late with this load. But if you think we can find your car without searching every hilltop from here to Bakerville, you've got yourself a ride."

He looked surprised but pleased. "I left a light on. It won't be hard to find. I promise you."

I took one hand off the wheel and offered it to him. "The name's Jake."

He just looked at my hand. Then finally he took it in his, but it wasn't natural. It was as though he did it because it was expected of him, not because he wanted to. His hand felt strangely warm for someone who'd been standing out in the night air.

I waited for him to speak. He didn't. Finally I said, "What's *your* name, kid? You *do* have a name, don't you?"

He looked puzzled, then scared. "This is very funny, but my name is Jake, too. Just like yours. Is that not funny?"

"Listen, kid," I said to him, "I've been driving a truck for fifteen years, and I've picked up just about every kind of person you can think of. Some of them are hitchhiking because they like it. Others do it because they have to. And some of them are running away from something. Now if that's what you're doing, it doesn't mean a thing to me. I just want to be sure that you don't have the law on your tail."

"Tail?" he asked. "What tail? I'm afraid I don't understand." It was as if I were talking in another language.

I was beginning to get just a little annoyed. "I think you know what I'm talking about all right."

"But my name really *is* Jake," he insisted, turning those unearthly eyes on me again.

"All right," I said. "Your name is Jake. Let's just drop the whole thing. OK?"

He didn't have time to answer, for just then I got a call on my CB radio.

"This is Bronco Bill heading west on Interstate 60," said a deep voice over the radio. "Do I have a copy?"

"Ten-four on that, Bronco Bill," I answered. "This is White Lightning coming up on you from Route 109. How's Smokey the Bear up there?"

"Not a Smokey in sight, White Lightning," spoke the voice. "All's clear up here. Over and out."

As I shut off the radio I could hear my passenger let out a gasp.

"What's the matter?" I asked him.

"Haven't you ever seen a CB radio before?"

I could see from the amazement in his eyes that he hadn't.

"I just asked that other trucker if there were any cops up ahead on the interstate," I explained. "We'll be coming up there in a few minutes, and I don't want to get picked up for speeding."

"But the way you talked to him . . ."

"CB slang. It saves a lot of yapping." I held out the radio mike to him. "Here, take a look at it. Try it out."

He picked up that radio and played with it like a kid with a new toy on Christmas morning. I couldn't help but smile. Maybe he was human after all.

We'd been on the interstate for about twenty miles when I sighted Lou's Place up ahead. Lou's is a truckers' diner and the owner makes the best hot cakes and coffee for 100 miles. The night you don't see that place surrounded by trucks you'll know there's either a truckers' strike or a new owner.

"Why are we stopping?" the kid asked as I pulled over.

"Just for a quick bite and some coffee," I told him. "From the looks of you, I'd say that wouldn't do you any harm at all."

"I'd rather we keep going," he answered, looking straight ahead into the night.

Any other trucker would have told him to get out and start walking, but I didn't. Sure I was mad, but I was even more curious about how this whole adventure was going to end.

"Stop worrying about your car and relax," I said. "We won't be long."

Whether he believed me or not, he got out. Inside, Lou was brewing a big pot of coffee as usual. Over by the jukebox, I spotted a bunch of drivers at a table. I gave them a friendly wave and pulled up a chair.

"What's the news, fellows?" I asked them.

"You mean you haven't heard?" said Charley, taking his pipe out of his wide mouth. "There's been an accident up in the mountains near Bakerville. Something fell out of the sky a few hours ago."

"What do you mean by 'something'?" I asked. "Was it an airplane?"

"Nobody knows what it was," said another trucker named Sam, "or who was in it when it hit. The state cops are up there looking for it. If you ask me, it's all pretty weird."

Charley laughed. "Maybe it was one of those flying saucers that flew too low!" he exclaimed.

"You hear that, kid?" I asked, turning in my chair. "You're not the only one who had trouble in the mountains tonight . . ." He wasn't there! I looked at Lou. "Where's the kid that came in with me?"

Lou shrugged his shoulders. "He just took off and ran right out the door."

I grabbed my cap and was gone. An untouched cup of hot steaming coffee sat on the table where I'd been. They must've thought I was off my rocker, but I didn't have time to worry about that.

I caught up with him about 100 yards down the highway. He was walking right down the middle of the road on the double yellow lines. I rolled down the window on the cab's passenger side.

"Do you want to get killed or something?" I called to him.

"They'll see me better if I walk in the middle," he said calmly.

"After they flatten you out like a pancake," I said, as I opened the door on his side. "Now get in here!"

He just kept walking. "That's all right. I'll get another ride."

"Like heck you will. Climb in, or I'll come out and get you."

He did. He sat there, not daring to look at me. I figured it was time I got some answers.

"Why did you run off without saying a word to me?"

"I didn't want to wait around. I told you that before."

"You're lying. It was something to do with that thing that fell from the sky tonight, wasn't it?"

"I don't know what you mean, Jake."

"Listen, I've put up with all the nonsense I'm going to put up with. You're going to start giving me some straight answers. What kind of car do you have up in those mountains?"

His wild eyes were darting back and forth. "It wasn't an automobile," he stuttered. "It was a truck like yours."

"I bet! You're saying that because you don't have any truck or car. Just like you said your name was the same as mine, because you don't have any name. Now just who are you, buddy, and what are you doing here?"

Well, that did it. He sat there looking at me, not moving a muscle. His eyes seemed to grow bigger and bigger. He didn't look scared anymore. Now I was the one who was scared.

"We don't have names where I come from, Jake," he said. "We are known by letters and numbers. I am XT-115."

My fingers tightly gripped the steering wheel. "What country do you come from?"

"Astrax."

"Astrax? I never heard of such a country."

"It's not a country, Jake. It's a planet."

The nightmare that every trucker dreams about happened. In the moment my eyes had left the road and turned to face those bright blue ones that sat next to me, the truck jumped off the road. Ahead of us was a giant boulder. I spun the wheel to miss it, but it was too late. In another second we would both be dead. Or so I thought.

Suddenly blue light filled the cab. It grew brighter and brighter until I thought the whole truck would explode with its brightness. I threw my hands up against my eyes. When I opened them, the light was gone and so was the boulder. It had vanished in thin air. I looked at XT-115. Two thin beams of light were coming from his eyes. I wanted to speak, but when I moved my mouth only one word would come out. "HOW . . . ?"

He only smiled. "You wouldn't understand, Jake. Someday, perhaps, but not now."

"Then you really are . . . " I couldn't finish. I didn't have to.

He nodded slowly. "Shall we go now?" he said. "I think we're both late."

I don't know how long I drove that night—one hour, maybe two hours. Time stood still inside the cab of that truck. He told me how he was riding around in his saucer when he hit a mountainside.

"I was flying too low," he said. "We don't have mountains on Astrax. I was taken by surprise."

There were many things I wanted to ask him, but I couldn't. It was as if I were dreaming and instead of sleepwalking, I was sleepdriving.

Suddenly I felt his warm hand on my shoulder. "There," he said, pointing a long finger toward a blue light shining out of the darkness in the mountains, "that's where I came down."

My truck slowly climbed the rocky mountain road toward the light. But before we could reach it, the red lights of a roadblock got in the way. I could make out a line of state troopers armed with rifles.

"It didn't take them long to find your saucer," I said. I was starting to come awake again.

"Stop the truck, Jake," he said softly. I did, and I wondered what he would do next. I knew the trooper wouldn't understand.

"Those men intend to harm me, Jake," he said. "I've got to get past them to my ship. Will you help me? I can't do it alone."

I was afraid. I didn't want to help him anymore. "But what about the blue light?" I asked. "Can't you use that to get away?"

"Yes, I could," he said very seriously. "But those men might be killed."

I looked up at them. They weren't bad men—just scared ones. People will sometimes do awful things when they're scared. I took a deep breath. "All right," I told him. "What do you want me to do?"

"Talk to them. Keep their attention on you while I get to my ship. I don't need much time to fix it."

Before I could say anything, he was out the door and gone. I drove the truck closer to the roadblock and came to a halt when the first trooper waved his rifle at me.

"A little off your regular route, aren't you, Mister?" he asked as I climbed out of the cab.

I had to talk fast. I could see my friend from Astrax creeping along a ledge of rock toward his spacecraft. "I just came up to see what was going on. Back down at Lou's they say you found a flying saucer. I'd sure like to see one of them."

Two more men with guns came toward me. "I'm sorry, but this area is closed off, Mister. You'll read all about it in tomorrow's newspaper."

The kid was halfway up the ledge. One of the troopers saw my eyes following him. "What are you looking at?" he demanded.

"That light up there," I spoke quickly. "I've never seen anything like it. What is it, anyhow?" A rock fell from the ledge. I heard a gun cock.

"You fellows sure are nervous. You think there was someone in that machine up there?"

They looked at each other, and then turned back to me. Had I said too much?

"Have you seen anybody on your way here, Mister?" the first trooper asked me. "Somebody walking along the road, maybe? Somebody who looks strange?"

"No." Had he made it? I had no way of knowing. "Not a soul. Do you think this saucer person is dangerous?"

"That's hard to say," said the trooper. "But if he *is* dangerous, we can't let him get away. Who knows what he'll bring back with him? Maybe thousands just like him to take over the earth."

That could happen, I thought. What did I know about Astrax except what XT-115 had told me? Maybe I would be sorry for helping him get away. But the only thing I knew for sure was that he had saved my life, and that had to be enough for me.

I wanted to keep talking, but they wouldn't let me waste anymore of their time. "Good luck XT, whoever you are," I whispered softly as I got back into the cab. "Good luck and goodbye."

It was a little past midnight when I saw the city lights of Bakerville up ahead on the highway. The man at the vegetable market would be mad because I was two hours late with his load. What could I tell him? That I picked up a man from outer space and got sidetracked? I began to wonder just what it was he had to fix on his machine. I'd guessed that would be one more unanswered question.

Suddenly a call came over the CB. I knew the voice at once.

"This is XT-115 heading west toward the Big Dipper. Do you copy me, White Lightning?"

I grabbed the mike and held it close to my face. My lips were trembling as I spoke. "Is that you, Jake?" I couldn't call him XT-115. It was too cold after all that had happened between the two of us that night.

"Ten-four on that, White Lightning. Just wanted you to know that I made it all right. The sky ahead is beautiful. There's not a meteor in sight." Then the voice spoke again, quieter and with warm friendship. "Thanks, Jake. I'll never forget what you did for me."

"I'll never forget you either, Jake!" I cried into the mike. "You come back down, you hear! You come back real soon! And be more careful where you land next time, huh?"

I don't know if he heard me. The radio clicked off. He was out of its range, somewhere beyond the Big Dipper.

Maybe it was all a dream. Maybe it never happened. But every time I come down old Route 109, I keep my hand near my CB and my eyes on those stars.

1. At the beginning of the story, the truck driver feels there is something odd about the hitchhiker. Find three things about the hitchhiker that seem unusual.

2. (a) At what point in the story does the truck driver suspect that the hitchhiker is from outer space? (b) Why does the truck driver follow the hitchhiker after he leaves the diner?

3. What do the truck driver and the hitchhiker do for each other that establishes their friendship?

Point of View

When a story is told in the first person, you learn directly what the narrator thinks and feels. You get to look inside the mind of the narrator, and you see other characters as the narrator sees them. You do not get to see into the minds of other characters.

1. (a) What is the truck driver's first reaction when he sees the hitchhiker? (b) Why does he finally decide to give him a ride?

2. Find two paragraphs in which the truck driver tells you what the hitchhiker looks like.

3. At the diner, Charley tells the truck driver, "There's been an accident up in the mountains near Bakerville. Something fell out of the sky a few hours ago." What do you suspect, that the truck driver does not yet suspect?

4. How do you think this story would have been different if XT-115 had told it?

Activities

1. **Composition.** Write a short statement telling why you do or do not believe the Earth has ever been visited by beings from other planets.

2. **Composition.** Extend the story "Night Rider" into the future. Imagine that XT-115 contacts Jake again. Write a paragraph telling what happens.

JUDGMENTS

Identifying Mixed Statements of Fact and Opinion

A statement of opinion expresses a person's belief or attitude. A statement of fact contains information that can be proved true or false. Notice the difference between the two kinds of statements in the following examples:

Fact: "I was tooling down Route 109 doing about fifty." (Jake could prove he was doing about fifty by checking his speedometer, and he could prove he was on Route 109 by checking a map or a road sign.)

Opinion: "Lou's is a truckers' diner and the owner makes the best hot cakes and coffee for 100 miles." (Whether or not Lou's hot cakes and coffee were the best is a matter of opinion. Tastes in hot cakes and coffee differ. No one could prove that Lou's were the "best.")

Sometimes you will come across a sentence that states both a fact and an opinion. For example, "It sounded strange when he said *automobile* instead of *car.*" The young man's saying *automobile* instead of *car* is a fact. However, the statement "It sounded strange" is an opinion. Two people might very well disagree about whether the use of *automobile* did or did not sound strange. You will better understand anything you read if you are able to distinguish statements of fact from statements of opinion.

▶ In each sentence below, decide which part contains a statement of fact and which part contains a statement of opinion.
  a. Route 109 was an old road, but it was more fun to drive on than the interstate.
  b. The night was scary because there was no moon in the sky.
  c. Truckers know the best places to eat, so Lou's parking lot was filled with trucks.
  d. Jake switched on his CB radio, the best invention ever made for truckers.
  e. The state troopers were on the scene, making all motorists feel a lot safer.
  f. Jake ran from the restaurant without even touching the best cup of coffee in the state.

WORD ATTACK

Understanding Jargon

Jargon is the special vocabulary—words or phrases—used by a particular group of people who share a job or a hobby. It develops as a more efficient, colorful, and meaningful way of talking about ideas or events that involve the group on a regular basis. For example, truckers do deal with state troopers on a regular basis, and many state troopers wear hats like Smokey the Bear. Someone made this association and began referring to a state trooper as Smokey. The term is now a regular part of truckers' jargon.

Jargon catches on and spreads. Writers often use jargon connected with a topic in order to add realism and interest. You will have a better grasp of what you read if you take time to notice and interpret jargon correctly. You will also gain some insight into how language originates and changes.

▶ Write the meaning for each of the *italicized* phrases below.
   a. "I was *tooling* down Route 109 doing about fifty."
   b. "Maybe I figured he'd be standing out there all night waiting for the next *set of wheels* to come along."
   c. " 'Do I have a *copy?*' '*Ten-four* on that, Bronco Bill,' I answered."
   d. "Not a *Smokey* in sight. . . ."
   e. "All's clear up here. *Over and out.*"

The Sin of Madame Phloi

Lilian Jackson Braun

From the very beginning Madame Phloi felt an instinctive distaste for the man who moved into the apartment next door. He was fat, and his trouser cuffs had the unsavory odor of fire hydrant.

They met for the first time in the decrepit elevator as it lurched up to the tenth floor of the old building, once fashionable but now coming apart at the seams. Madame Phloi had been out for a stroll in the city park, chewing city grass and chasing faded butterflies, and as she and her companion stepped on the elevator for the slow ride upward, the car was already half filled with the new neighbor.

The fat man and the Madame presented a contrast that was not unusual in this apartment house, which had a brilliant past and no future. He was bulky, uncouth, sloppily attired. Madame Phloi was a long-legged, blue-eyed aristocrat whose creamy fawn coat shaded into brown at the extremities.

The Madame deplored fat men. They had no laps, and of what use is a lapless human? Nevertheless, she gave him the common courtesy of a sniff at his trouser cuffs and immediately backed away, twitching her nose and breathing through the mouth.

"GET that cat away from me," the fat man roared, stamping his feet thunder-ously at Madame Phloi. Her companion pulled on the leash, although there was no need—the Madame, with one backward leap, had retreated to a safe corner of the elevator, which shuddered and continued its groaning ascent.

"Don't you like animals?" asked the gentle voice at the other end of the leash.

"Filthy, sneaky beasts," the fat man said with a snarl. "Last place I lived, some lousy cat got in my room and et my parakeet."

"I'm sorry to hear that. Very sorry. But you don't need to worry about Madame Phloi and Thapthim. They never leave the apartment except on a leash."

"You got TWO? That's just fine, that is! Keep 'em away from me, or I'll break their rotten necks. I ain't wrung a cat's neck since I was fourteen, but I remember how."

And with the long black box he was carrying, the fat man lunged at the impeccable Madame Phloi, who sat in her corner, flat-eared and tense. Her fur bristled, and she tried to dart away. Even when her companion picked her up in protective arms, Madame Phloi's body was taut and trembling.

Not until she was safely home in her modest but well-cushioned apartment did she relax. She walked stiff-legged to the sunny spot on the carpet where Thapthim was sleeping and licked the top of his head. Then she had a complete bath herself—to rid her coat of the fat man's odor. Thapthim did not wake.

This drowsy, unambitious, amiable creature—her son—was a puzzle to Madame Phloi, who was sensitive and spirited herself. She didn't try to understand him; she merely loved him. She spent hours washing his paws and breast and other parts he could easily have reached with his own tongue. At dinnertime she chewed slowly so there would be something left on her plate for his dessert, and he always gobbled the extra portion hungrily. And when he slept, which was most of the time, she kept watch by his side, sitting with a tall, regal posture until she swayed with weariness. Then she made herself into a small bundle and dozed with one eye open.

Thapthim was lovable, to be sure. He appealed to other cats, large and small dogs, people, and even ailurophobes[1] in a limited way. He had a face like a beautiful flower and large blue eyes, tender and trusting. Ever since he was a kitten, he had been willing to purr at the touch of a hand—any hand. Eventually he became so agreeable that he purred if anyone looked at him across the room. What's more, he came when called; he gratefully devoured whatever was served on his dinner plate; and when he was told to get down, he got down.

His wise parent disapproved this uncatly conduct; it indicated a certain lack of character, and no good would come of it. By her own example she tried to guide him. When dinner was served, she gave the plate a haughty sniff and walked away, no matter how tempting the dish. That was the way it was done by any self-respecting feline. In a minute or two she returned and condescended to dine, but never with open enthusiasm.

Furthermore, when human hands reached out, the catly thing was to bound away, lead them a chase, flirt a little before allowing oneself to be caught and cuddled. Thapthim, sorry to say, greeted any friendly overture by rolling over, purring, and looking soulful.

From an early age he had known the rules of the apartment:

No sleeping in a cupboard with the pots and pans.

Sitting on the table with the inkwell is permissible.

Sitting on the table with the coffeepot is never allowed.

The sad truth was that Thapthim obeyed these rules. Madame Phloi, on the other hand, knew that a rule was a challenge, and it was a matter of integrity to violate it. To obey was to sacrifice one's dignity. . . . It seemed that her son would never learn the true values in life.

To be sure, Thapthim was adored for his good nature in the human world of inkwells and coffeepots. But Madame Phloi was equally adored—and for the correct reasons. She was respected for her independence, admired for her clever methods of getting her own way, and loved for the cowlick on her white breast, the kink in her tail, and the squint in her delphinium-blue eyes. She was more truly Siamese than her son. Her

---

1. ailurophobes (ī-lûr′ə-fōbz′) n.: People who fear cats.

face was small and perky. By cocking her head and staring with heart-melting eyes, slightly crossed, she could charm a porterhouse steak out from under a knife and fork.

Until the fat man and his black box moved in next door, Madame Phloi had never known an unfriendly soul. She had two companions in her tenth-floor apartment—genial creatures without names who came and went a good deal. One was an easy mark for between-meal snacks; a tap on his ankle always produced a spoonful of cottage cheese. The other served as a hot-water bottle on cold nights, and punctually obliged whenever the Madame wished to have her underside stroked or her cheekbones massaged. This second one also murmured compliments in a gentle voice that made one squeeze one's eyes in pleasure.

Life was not all love and cottage cheese, however. Madame Phloi had her regular work. She was official watcher and listener for the household.

There were six windows that needed watching, for a wide ledge ran around the building flush with the tenth-floor windowsills, and this was a promenade for pigeons. They strutted, searched their feathers, and ignored the Madame, who sat on the sill and watched them dispassionately but thoroughly through the window screen.

While watching was a daytime job, listening was done after dark and required greater concentration. Madame Phloi listened for noises in the walls. She heard termites chewing, pipes sweating, and sometimes the ancient plaster cracking; but mostly she listened to the ghosts of generations of deceased mice.

One evening, shortly after the incident in the elevator, Madame Phloi was listening, Thapthim was asleep, and the other two were quietly turning pages of books, when a strange and horrendous sound came from the wall. The Madame's ears flicked to attention, then flattened against her head.

An interminable screech was coming out of that wall, like nothing the Madame had ever heard before. It chilled the blood and tortured the eardrums. So painful was the shrillness that Madame Phloi threw back her head and complained with a piercing howl of her own. The strident din even waked Thapthim. He looked about in alarm, shook his head wildly, and clawed at his ears to get rid of the offending noise.

The others heard it, too.

"Listen to that!" said the one with the gentle voice.

"It must be that new man next door," said the other. "It's incredible."

"I can't imagine anyone so crude producing anything so exquisite. Is it Prokofiev he's playing?"

"No, I think it's Bartók."

"He was carrying his violin in the elevator today. He tried to hit Phloi with it."

"He's a nut. . . . Look at the cats— apparently they don't care for violin."

Madame Phloi and Thapthim, bounding from the room, collided with each other as they rushed to hide under the bed.

That was not the only kind of noise which emanated from the adjoining apartment in those upsetting days after the fat man moved in. The following evening, when Madame Phloi walked into the living room to commence her listening, she heard a fluttering sound dimly through the wall, accompanied by highly conversational chirping. This was agreeable music, and she settled down on the sofa to enjoy it, tucking her brown paws neatly under her creamy body.

Her contentment was soon disturbed, however, when the fat man's voice burst through the wall like thunder.

"Look what you done, you dirty skunk!" he bellowed. "Right in my fiddle! Get back in your cage before I brain you."

There was a frantic beating of wings.

"GET down off that window, or I'll bash your head in."

This threat brought only a torrent of chirping.

"Shut up, you stupid cluck! Shut up and get back in the cage, or I'll . . ."

There was a splintering crash, and after that all was quiet except for an occasional pitiful "Peep!"

Madame Phloi was fascinated. In fact, when she resumed her watching the next day, pigeons seemed rather insipid entertainment. She had waked the family that morning in her usual way—by staring intently at their foreheads as they slept. Then she and Thapthim had a game of hockey in the bathtub with a ping-pong ball, followed by a dish of mackerel, and after breakfast the Madame took up her post at the living-room window. Everyone had left for the day, but not before opening the window and placing a small cushion on the chilly marble sill.

There she sat—Madame Phloi—a small but alert package of fur, sniffing the welcome summer air, seeing all, and knowing all. She knew, for example, that the person who was at that moment walking down the tenth-floor hallway, wearing old tennis shoes and limping slightly, would halt at the door of her apartment, set down his pail, and let himself in with a passkey.

Indeed, she hardly bothered to turn her head when the window washer entered. He was one of her regular court of admirers. His odor was friendly, although it suggested damp basements and floor mops, and he talked sensibly—indulging in none of that falsetto foolishness with which some people insulted the Madame's intelligence.

"Hop down, kitty," he said in a musical voice. "Charlie's gotta take out that screen. See, I brought you some cheese."

He held out a modest offering of rat cheese, and Madame Phloi investigated it. Unfortunately it was the wrong variety, and she shook one fastidious paw at it.

"Mighty fussy cat," Charlie laughed. "Well, now, you set there and watch Charlie clean this here window. Don't you go jumpin' out on the ledge, because Charlie ain't runnin' after you. No sir! That old ledge, she's startin' to crumble. Someday them pigeons'll stamp their feet hard, and down she goes! . . . Hey, lookit the broken glass out here. Somebody busted a window."

Charlie sat on the marble sill and pulled the upper sash down in his lap, and while Madame Phloi followed his movements carefully, Thapthim sauntered into the room, yawning and stretching, and swallowed the cheese.

"Now Charlie puts the screen back in, and you two guys can watch them crazy pigeons some more. This screen, she's comin' apart, too. Whole buildin' seems to be crackin' up."

Remembering to replace the cushion on the cool, hard sill, he then went on to clean the next window, and the Madame resumed her post, sitting on the very edge of the cushion so that Thapthim could have most of it.

The pigeons were late that morning, probably frightened away by the window washer. It was while Madame Phloi patiently waited for the first visitor to skim in on a blue-gray wing that she noticed the tiny opening in the screen. Every aperture, no matter how small, was a temptation; she had to prove she could wriggle through any tight space, whether there was a good reason or not.

She waited until Charlie had limped out of the apartment before she began pushing at the screen with her nose, first gingerly and then stubbornly. Inch by inch the rusted mesh ripped away from the frame until the whole corner formed a loose flap, and Madame Phloi slithered through—nose and ears, slender shoulders, dainty Queen Anne forefeet, svelte torso, lean flanks, hind legs like steel springs, and finally, proud brown tail. For the first time in her life she found herself on the pigeon promenade. She gave a delicious shudder.

Inside the screen the lethargic Thapthim, jolted by this strange turn of affairs, watched his daring parent with a quarter inch of his pink tongue hanging out. They touched noses briefly through the screen, and the Madame proceeded to explore. She advanced cautiously and with mincing step, for the pigeons had not been tidy in their habits.

The ledge was about two feet wide. To its edge Madame Phloi moved warily, nose down and tail high. Ten stories

below there were moving objects, but nothing of interest, she decided. Walking daintily along the extreme edge to avoid the broken glass, she ventured in the direction of the fat man's apartment, impelled by some half-forgotten curiosity.

His window stood open and un-screened, and Madame Phloi peered in politely. There, sprawled on the floor, lay the fat man himself, snorting and heaving his immense paunch in a kind of rhythm. It always alarmed her to see a human on the floor, which she considered feline domain. She licked her nose apprehensively and stared at him with enormous eyes, one iris hypnotically off-center. In a dark corner of the room something fluttered and squawked, and the fat man waked.

"SHcrrff! *GET* out of here!" he shouted, struggling to his feet.

In three leaps Madame Phloi crossed the ledge back to her own window and pushed through the screen to safety. Looking back to see if the fat man might be chasing her and being reassured that he wasn't, she washed Thapthim's ears and her own paws and sat down to wait for pigeons.

Like any normal cat, Madame Phloi lived by the Rule of Three. She resisted every innovation three times before accepting it, tackled an obstacle three times before giving up, and tried each new activity three times before tiring of it. Consequently she made two more sallies to the pigeon promenade and eventually convinced Thapthim to join her.

Together they peered over the edge at the world below. The sense of freedom was intoxicating. Recklessly, Thapthim made a leap at a low-flying pigeon and landed on his mother's back. She cuffed

his ear in retaliation. He poked her nose. They grappled and rolled over and over on the ledge, oblivious of the long drop below them, taking playful nips of each other's hide and snarling guttural expressions of glee.

Suddenly and instinctively Madame Phloi scrambled to her feet and crouched in a defensive position. The fat man was leaning from his window.

"Here, kitty, kitty," he was saying in one of those despised falsetto voices, offering some tidbit in a saucer. The Madame froze, but Thapthim turned his beautiful trusting eyes on the stranger and advanced along the ledge. Purring and waving his tail cordially, he walked into the trap. It all happened in a matter of seconds: the saucer was withdrawn, and a long black box was swung at Thapthim like a ball bat, sweeping him off the ledge and into space. He was silent as he fell.

When the family came home, laughing and chattering, with their arms full of packages, they knew at once something was amiss. No one greeted them at the door. Madame Phloi hunched moodily on the windowsill staring at a hole in the screen, and Thapthim was not to be found.

"Look at the screen!" cried the gentle voice.

"I'll bet he got out on the ledge."

"Can you lean out and look? Be careful."

"You hold Phloi."

"Do you see him?"

"Not a sign of him! There's a lot of glass scattered around, and the window's broken next door."

"Do you suppose that man . . . ? I feel sick."

"Don't worry, dear. We'll find him.

. . . There's the doorbell! Maybe someone's bringing him home."

It was Charlie standing at the door. He fidgeted uncomfortably. " 'Scuse me, folks," he said. "You missin' one of your kitties?"

"Yes! Have you found him?"

"Poor little guy," said Charlie. "Found him lyin' right under your windows—where the bushes is thick."

"He's dead!" the gentle one moaned.

"Yes, ma'am. That's a long way down."

"Where is he now?"

"I got him down in the basement, ma'am. I'll take care of him real nice. I don't think you'd want to see the poor guy."

Still Madame Phloi stared at the hole in the screen and waited for Thapthim. From time to time she checked the other windows, just to be sure. As time passed and he did not return, she looked behind the radiators and under the bed. She pried open the cupboard door where the pots and pans were stored. She tried to burrow her way into the closet. She sniffed all around the front door. Finally she stood in the middle of the living room and called loudly in a high-pitched, wailing voice.

Later that evening Charlie paid another visit to the apartment.

"Only wanted to tell you, ma'am, how nice I took care of him," he said. "I got a box that was just the right size. A white box, it was. And I wrapped him up in a piece of old blue curtain. The color looked real pretty with his fur. And I buried the little guy right under your window behind the bushes."

And still the Madame searched, returning again and again to watch the ledge from which Thapthim had disappeared. She scorned food. She rebuffed any attempts at consolation. And all night she sat wide-eyed and waiting in the dark.

The living-room window was now tightly closed, but the following day the Madame—after she was left by herself in the lonely apartment—went to work on the bedroom screens. One was new and hopeless, but the second screen was slightly corroded, and she was soon nosing through a slit that lengthened as she struggled out onto the ledge.

Picking her way through the broken glass, she approached the spot where Thapthim had vanished. And then it all happened again. There he was—the fat man—reaching forth with a saucer.

"Here, kitty, kitty."

Madame Phloi hunched down and backed away.

"Kitty want some milk?" It was that ugly falsetto, but she didn't run home this time. She crouched there on the ledge, a few inches out of reach.

"Nice kitty. Nice kitty."

Madame Phloi crept with caution toward the saucer in the outstretched fist, and stealthily the fat man extended another hand, snapping his fingers as one would call a dog.

The Madame retreated diagonally— half toward home and half toward the dangerous brink.

"Here, kitty. Here, kitty," he cooed, leaning farther out. But muttering, he said, "You dirty sneak! I'll get you if it's the last thing I ever do. Comin' after my bird, weren't you?"

Madame Phloi recognized danger with all her senses. Her ears went back, her whiskers curled, and her white underside hugged the ledge.

A little closer she moved, and the fat man made a grab for her. She jerked back a step, with unblinking eyes fixed on his sweating face. He was furtively laying the saucer aside, she noticed, and edging his fat paunch farther out the window.

Once more she advanced almost into his grasp, and again he lunged at her with both powerful arms.

The Madame leaped lightly aside.

"This time I'll get you, you stinkin' cat," he cried, and raising one knee to the windowsill, he threw himself at Madame Phloi. As she slipped through his fingers, he landed on the ledge with all his weight.

A section of it crumbled beneath him. He bellowed, clutching at the air, and at the same time a streak of creamy brown flashed out of sight. The fat man was not silent as he fell.

As for Madame Phloi, she was found doubled in half in a patch of sunshine on her living-room carpet, innocently washing her fine brown tail.

Close Up

1. Madame Phloi treats Thapthim with a great deal of love, even though they have different personalities. In what ways is Thapthim different from Madame Phloi?

2. (a) Why do people adore Madame Phloi? (b) Why do they adore Thapthim?

3. (a) Why does Madame Phloi try to get through the screens? (b) Later, after the screens have been repaired, Madame Phloi still manages to get out onto the ledge. What does this tell you about her personality?

4. At first, Madame Phloi waits for Thapthim to return. (a) When does she realize what has happened to him? (b) By what clever method does she trap the neighbor and take revenge?

Point of View

In some stories, the narrator does not appear as a character. The narrator disappears into one character and tells this character's story for him or her in the third person. For example, in "The Sin of Madame Phloi," the narrator disappears into Madame Phloi, and tells her story for her from the cat's point of view. The narrator uses third person pronouns (he, she, it) to refer to this character and to all other characters.

1. Since this story is told from the cat's point of view, you get a slightly different slant on life. Find three details that show that the way Madame Phloi sees the world is different from the way a human being sees the world. (For example, because Madame Phloi likes to sit in laps, she thinks people without laps are useless.)

2. What does Madame Phloi think is proper cat behavior?

3. Because Madame Phloi is a cat, she cannot tell anyone about what happened to Thapthim. (a) Why do you know what really happened to him? (b) Would you know this if one of Madame Phloi's owners had told the story? Why or why not?

Activities

1. **Composition.** Imagine you are Thapthim. Write a paragraph describing your mother, Madame Phloi.

2. **Composition.** Write a paragraph describing yourself from the point of view of your pet. (If you don't have a pet, make one up.)

JUDGMENTS

Recognizing Stereotypes

A stereotype is an opinion about a group of people that does not allow for individual differences. A stereotype is not based on proof and is dangerous because it can prevent you from seeing the worth of an individual. For example, do you think you can tell if someone's an athlete just by looking at him or her? Do you think you know what all schoolteachers are like; what's wrong with all teen-agers; how all rich people live? You can't answer any of these questions without forming stereotypes. Members of any group are very different from each other.

1. Which of the following statements are stereotypes?
   a. All heavyset people dislike animals.
   b. All ailurophobes are afraid of cats.
   c. Cats know by instinct how to clean themselves.
   d. Cats are nasty and haughty creatures.
   e. All people who own cats are genial and good-natured.
   f. All musicians are moody.
   g. All janitors take care of the buildings where they work.
   h. Violin players like birds, but they dislike cats.

2. Find advertisements in magazines or newspapers. Bring into class any that you think present people as stereotypes.

3. Which of the following statements are stereotypes?
   a. All truck drivers enjoy hockey and football.
   b. All secret agents are young, sophisticated, handsome men who enjoy fast cars and sophisticated gadgetry.
   c. All doctors have medical degrees.
   d. All nurses are young, beautiful women.
   e. All college professors are absent-minded.
   f. All college professors have graduated from one or more colleges.
   g. All waiters serve food.
   h. All private eyes are tough, quick-talking men of action.
   i. All actors are temperamental.
   j. All lawyers practice the law.

WORD ATTACK

Understanding Negative Prefixes

A prefix is a letter or combination of letters added at the beginning of a word or word root to change its meaning. A negative prefix acts like the word *not* and changes a word from its positive to its negative form. For example, un- is a frequently used negative prefix. Added to the word *usual,* un- changes the meaning to "not usual." Other frequently used negative prefixes are *dis-, il-, in-,* and *im-.*

To avoid serious misinterpretations readers should note the presence of negative prefixes. There is a large meaning difference between *usual* and *unusual.*

▶ The words with negative prefixes in the sentences below are printed in *italics*. Write the definition of each of these words.

a. "From the very beginning Madame Phloi felt an instinctive *distaste* for the man who moved into the apartment next door."

b. "And with the long black box he was carrying, the fat man lunged at the *impeccable* Madame Phloi, who sat in her corner, flat-eared and tense."

c. "This drowsy, *unambitious,* amiable creature—her son—was a puzzle to Madame Phloi who was sensitive and spirited herself."

d. "His wise parent *disapproved* this *uncatly* conduct; it indicated a certain lack of character, and no good would come of it."

e. "She was respected for her *independence,* admired for her clever methods of getting her own way . . . ."

f. "Until the fat man and his black box moved in next door, Madame Phloi had never known an *unfriendly* soul."

g. "They strutted, searched their feathers, and ignored the Madame, who sat on the sill and watched them *dispassionately* but thoroughly through the window screen."

h. "An *interminable* screech was coming out of that wall, like nothing the Madame had ever heard before."

Catalog

Rosalie Moore

Cats sleep fat and walk thin.
Cats, when they sleep, slump;
When they wake, pull in——
And where the plump's been
5   There's skin.
Cats walk thin.

Cats wait in a lump,
Jump in a streak.
Cats, when they jump, are sleek
10 As a grape slipping its skin——
They have technique.
Oh, cats don't creak.
They sneak.

Cats sleep fat.
15 They spread comfort beneath them
Like a good mat,
As if they picked the place
And then sat.
You walk around one
20 As if he were the City Hall
After that.

If male,
A cat is apt to sing upon a major
    scale:
This concert is for everybody, this
25 Is wholesale.
For a baton, he wields a tail.
(He is also found,
When happy, to resound
With an enclosed and private
    sound.)

30 A cat condenses.
He pulls in his tail to go under
    bridges,
And himself to go under fences.
Cats fit
In any size box or kit;
35 And if a large pumpkin grew under
    one,
He could arch over it.

When everyone else is just ready to
    go out,
The cat is just ready to come in.
He's not where he's been.
40 Cats sleep fat and walk thin.

Activity ▶ Write a short poem describing an animal.

How the Leopard Got Its Spots

Forbes Stuart

An African Folk Tale

Proud and handsome in his beautiful coat, the hyena went loping through the jungle. Suddenly he stopped, gazing down at the tortoise who stood in his way looking up at him plaintively. "Hyena, I am in need of your help. I cannot reach the fruit of this tree, but if you were to shake the branches, the fruit would fall down. Will you help me?"

"I'll do even more than you ask," replied the hyena. "I'll take you to the fruit!" Seizing the tortoise between his strong teeth, he jumped up into the tree and put the tortoise down in a fork of branches high above the ground. Then he leaped down again, laughing diabolically at the tortoise's plight before disappearing into the jungle.

Afraid to move, clinging to the branch, the tortoise stayed up there for hours, while the sun slowly dipped over to the west, lengthening the shadow of the tree. Every time he looked down at the ground far below, he felt dizzy and terrified, but he had to keep his eyes open for he knew that help wouldn't come from the skies. At last, with darkness falling and despair growing, the tortoise saw a leopard padding past the tree and cried for help. The leopard leaped gracefully into the tree and brought the frightened tortoise back to the ground. At his request, the leopard shook the branches so that the fruit fell to the ground for the tortoise to eat.

The leopard didn't wait to be thanked and was gliding into the gathering darkness when the tortoise called him back. "Leopard, listen to me before you go. You have been very good to me, and I would like to do something for you in return. If you let me paint black spots all over your tawny coat, you will be admired throughout the jungle. Come in the morning, when the sun gives us light."

The leopard's dull coat was completely transformed by the black spots that the tortoise painted in with care and artistic skill. And just as the artist had predicted, when the leopard swaggered through the jungle he was followed by the admiring glances of the other animals. The gray zebra was so impressed by the change in the leopard's appearance that he galloped as fast as he could to the tortoise, who was busy putting his paints away. "Tortoise," he panted, "give me spots too. Turn my coat into a spotted masterpiece like the leopard's." But the tortoise always had an artist's eye. "No," he replied, "spots are not for

you. You are lean and speedy, so I shall give you stripes instead of spots." When he had finished painting, he told the zebra to look at his reflection in the pond. The zebra was enchanted by what he saw, a transformation as complete as the leopard's, and went frisking through the jungle to show off his new coat.

Along the way, when he paused to nibble at a succulent bush, he heard a woman saying to her husband, "Look at that beautiful animal with the black stripes on its gray coat. Let's catch it and give it to the children as a pet. They will love playing with it."

Although flattered by this praise, the zebra kicked up his heels and galloped away, as zebras have been doing ever since, preferring the dangers of the jungle to sharing man's love with the goats, chickens, turkeys, geese, and ducks.

The animals were dazzled when they saw the zebra's new coat, but the hyena was jealous and decided that he would visit the tortoise, pretend to be sorry for tricking him the day before, and ask the artist to do for him what he had achieved for the leopard and the zebra. "Certainly I'll paint you, hyena," the tortoise drawled in his deep slow voice. "I'll see to it that your new coat will be the talk of the jungle." When he had finished, he urged the hyena to show the other animals his fine new coat without further ado.

When the hyena burst into the clearing where the animals stood, he shouted to them, strutting and prancing in his pride, "Look at this coat! Is it not even more magnificent than the leopard's and zebra's?" He couldn't understand, at first, why they looked at him as if they couldn't believe their own eyes, and then laughed and jeered derisively at

How the Leopard Got Its Spots **235**

him. But he knew why when he saw his reflection in the water of the pond, for his once handsome coat was splotched and muddy, dirty with big ugly spots. The tortoise had been avenged.

Ashamed, with his shoulders drooping, his head hanging down, and his tail trailing in the dust, the hyena slunk away into the jungle. And since that day, to avoid being mocked, hyenas have been coming out at night, when most of the animals are asleep and only the owl whistles in the dark. The Botswana people do not talk about "the laughing hyena" as others do, for they know that when he raises his head to the moon, his cry is a sad and lonely moan.

Close Up

1. What has the leopard done to make the tortoise eager to improve the leopard's appearance?

2. Why does the hyena want his coat painted?

3. Why does the tortoise make a fool of the hyena?

4. Why is the hyena's cry "a sad and lonely moan"?

Point of View

An omniscient narrator knows all. When a story is told in the third person by an omniscient narrator, you learn what each character in the story thinks and feels. You also receive information that the characters in the story do not have.

1. Although the tortoise is the main character, you learn how all the other characters think and feel, too. (a) How do the leopard and the zebra feel after the tortoise paints their coats? (b) How do the other animals react to the appearance of the leopard and the zebra?

2. The narrator takes time out from the action of the story to comment on, or explain, certain events. (a) According to the narrator, why do all zebras kick up their heels and gallop away when they see human beings? (b) Why do all hyenas come out only at night, when the other animals are asleep?

Activities

1. **Composition.** Write your own fable explaining some aspect of nature. (For example, explain how the turtle got its shell or how the elephant got its trunk.)

2. Use an encyclopedia to find a scientific explanation for why the leopard's coat has spots. Report your findings to your class.

JUDGMENTS

Identifying Loaded Words

A loaded word is one that is carefully chosen to create a certain kind of impression. The word *swaggered*, for example, is a loaded word. It tells not only how the leopard moved through the jungle, but also how he felt about himself. People who hear or read about someone who swaggered get the impression not only of movement, but also of pride and boastfulness.

Nobody wants to buy a cheap car, but everyone wants one that's reasonably priced. Most people would rather be called *mischievous* than *mean*, or *frugal* than *stingy*. The point is that a person who uses loaded words well influences other people's thinking.

Two questions you can ask yourself when you come across loaded words are: (1) What is the author trying to make me feel? and (2) Is the author giving me a general message or a loaded message?

▶ For each of the sentences below, tell whether the author is trying to make you admire the character, dislike the character, or feel sorry for the character.

   a. "Proud and handsome in his beautiful coat, the hyena went *loping* through the jungle."
   b. "Then he leaped down again, laughing *diabolically* at the tortoise's plight before disappearing into the jungle."
   c. "Afraid to move, *clinging* to the branch, the tortoise stayed up there for hours . . . ."
   d. "Every time he looked down at the ground far below, he felt dizzy and *terrified* . . . ."
   e. "The leopard *leaped gracefully* into the tree . . . ."
   f. ". . . when the leopard *swaggered* through the jungle . . ."
   g. ". . . he shouted to them, *strutting* and *prancing* in his pride . . . ."
   h. "Ashamed, with his shoulders *drooping*, his head hanging down and his tail *trailing in the dust*, the hyena *slunk* away into the jungle."
   i. "*Seizing* the tortoise between his strong teeth . . ."

WORD ATTACK

Using Context Clues

Using context clues is the most immediate and best strategy to use for getting the meaning of unfamiliar words when you don't have a dictionary. To get at the meaning of unfamiliar words, follow these steps:

1. Reread the sentence the word is in and perhaps the sentences before and after it.
2. Try substituting a more familiar word you think means about the same thing.
3. If the word you substituted makes sense, it probably has about the same meaning as the unfamiliar word and you can continue reading.

Using context clues to figure out unfamiliar words increases your vocabulary and strengthens word attack skills.

▶ The words *italicized* in the sentences below may be unfamiliar to you. Try substituting the more familiar words in the list under them until you find one that means about the same thing.

a. "Suddenly he stopped, gazing down at the tortoise who stood in his way looking up at him *plaintively.* 'Hyena, I am in need of your help.'"

b. "Then he leaped down again, laughing *diabolically* at the tortoise's *plight* before disappearing into the jungle."

c. "At last, with darkness falling and despair growing, the tortoise saw a leopard *padding* past the tree and cried for help."

d. "If you let me paint black spots all over your *tawny* coat, you will be admired throughout the jungle."

e. "The zebra was *enchanted* by what he saw, a *transformation* as complete as the leopard's, and went frisking through the jungle to show off his new coat."

yellow-brown	devilishly
walking softly	difficulty
delighted	pitifully
change	

REVIEW QUIZ

On the Selections

1. In "Alone on the Hilltop," why does Lame Deer spend four days and nights in a hole dug into the hill?

2. What will happen to Lame Deer if he has a vision?

3. In "The Contest," why does Joey's stepfather think that Joey's trumpet playing is a waste of time?

4. How do Joey's mother and stepfather feel when he tells them that he has given the medal away?

5. In "Night Rider," why does the hitchhiker run from the diner?

6. How does the hitchhiker save the truck driver's life?

7. In "The Sin of Madame Phloi," the cat is the official listener and watcher for the household. What sounds does Madame Phloi hear that the humans do not hear?

8. How does Madame Phloi wake up each of the members of the family?

9. In "How the Leopard Got Its Spots," why does the tortoise ask the hyena for help?

10. How does the tortoise get even with the hyena?

On Judgments

1. Is Lame Deer a primary or a secondary source of information when he tells about his first *hanblechia*? Why?

2. Which of the following are statements of fact and which are statements of opinion?
   a. Joey is the best trumpet player in the state.
   b. Joey won the trophy at the state trumpet contest.
   c. Joey wants to become a professional trumpet player.
   d. Joey will become a professional trumpet player.

3. Which part of the following sentence is a statement of fact and which part is a statement of opinion? The hitchhiker came from the planet Astrax and thousands like him will follow to take over the earth.

4. Which of the following statements is a stereotype?
   a. All truck drivers are talkative.
   b. All truck drivers need a driver's license.

5. Identify the loaded word in each pair below.
   a. doctor—sawbones
   b. lawyer—mouthpiece
   c. whine—cry
   d. criticize—attack
   e. discriminating—finicky
   f. blab—tell
   g. ruler—tyrant
   h. save—hoard
   i. old—antique
   j. slave—work

On Point of View

▶ Decide whether the following statements are true or false.
   a. The narrator is the person who tells the story.
   b. The narrator is always the main character in the story.
   c. When a story is told in the first person, the narrator refers to himself or herself by the pronoun *I*.
   d. An omniscient narrator is able to tell you about only one character.

COMPOSITION

Narration   **When you write narration, you tell a story.** Your story should have a beginning, a middle, and an end. In the beginning, you introduce your readers to the main character. In the middle, you tell what happens to this character and explain the conflict or struggle. In the end, you tell how the character feels about the way the conflict was resolved.

When you write narration, decide from what point of view you want to tell the story. If you decide to tell it in the first person, use the pronoun "I" to identify the narrator. If you decide to tell it in the third person, use the pronoun "he" or "she" to identify all characters.

▶   Write a narrative paragraph using one of the ideas below.

    a.   Imagine you are living on a planet in the far part of the galaxy. On your planet, teenagers take part in a special ceremony in order to receive an adult name. Write a paragraph telling how you received your adult name.

    b.   Write a paragraph telling about participating in a contest. Decide whether you want to write your paragraph in the first or third person. Try to begin with a sentence that will capture your readers' attention. For example, "I was certain I would win the contest until the curtain opened." At the end of the paragraph, tell how the main character feels about the way the contest ended.

    c.   Imagine you are the hitchhiker XT-115 in "Night Rider." Write a paragraph telling about how you crashed your saucer into the side of the mountain.

    d.   Write a paragraph telling about an event from an unusual point of view. For example, you might tell it from the point of view of an animal.

BEFORE GOING ON

Skimming

Skimming is the process by which your eyes sweep across and down printed pages to get a general idea about their content, or to look for specific information. Skimming is a skill to use when you need to determine quickly what the main points of a reading selection are or whether or not you want to read the selection more carefully and slowly.

Skimming is meant to give you only the highlights of a selection. It would be a poor way to read something you're going to be tested on or something you want to learn thoroughly. When you skim:

1. Read the title. It will give you some idea as to what the selection is about.
2. Read the first and last paragraphs. Knowing how a selection begins and ends often gives many clues to what's in between. (Note: Don't read the endings of books or stories you may want to read for pleasure. Instead read the first two or three pages.)
3. Flip through the pages quickly, reading any subtitles or other words in heavy print just as you read the title.
4. Run your index finger down the middle of the pages, letting your eyes sweep across the lines of print. Let your mind take in as many ideas as it can.
5. Pause for four or five seconds after every page or two and try to recall some of the ideas your mind took in.
6. When you have finished reading the last page, answer one or both of the following questions: Is this selection likely to have the information I want? Am I likely to enjoy reading this selection?

---

1. Skim "The Fastest Woman on Earth" according to the steps listed above. Then decide whether each of the statements below is true or false.
   a. Kitty O'Neil is a dramatic actress.
   b. Kitty O'Neil is deaf.
   c. Kitty was never able to excel in sports.
   d. Kitty succeeded without the help of either parent.
   e. Kitty's only sports are swimming and diving.
   f. Kitty gets her jobs because she is the best-qualified person.

2. List all the information you remember after just skimming.

Further Reading

The Fastest Woman on Earth

Phil Bowie

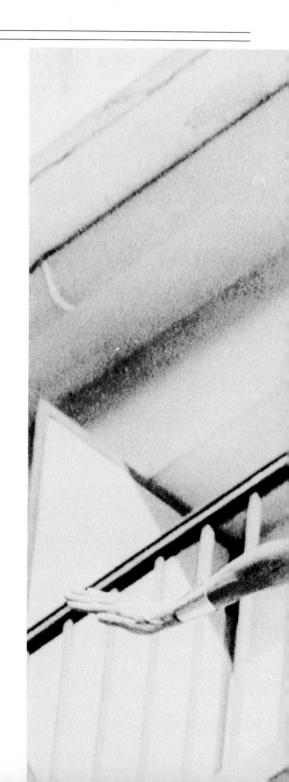

Under a sharp clear sky, high atop the windy roof of an apartment building, a woman struggled frantically with a man who was determined to fling her to her death. A crowd of millions looked on helplessly. The man, taller and obviously much stronger than the girl, forced her closer and closer to the edge. It was six stories down to the busy street below. They scuffled. The girl lost her footing on the gravel roof. She pitched over the side. In desperation, she twisted . . . falling . . . clawing . . . and caught the roof ledge with her hands. Fortunately, Robert Blake happened to be in the neighborhood. He appeared on the roof just in time to subdue the would-be killer and help the frightened young lady back to safety.

The millions of onlookers sighed and resumed munching their evening snacks.

Pretty twenty-eight-year-old Kitty O'Neil was only performing a routine stunt for an episode of the TV series "Baretta." Because her back was to the

camera throughout the incident, and because she was working as a double for actress Lana Wood, no one in the vast television audience knew who she really was. Had she missed the calculated grab for the roof ledge, a thin cable secretly harnessed to her would have saved her life, although it might have bruised her as it snubbed taut and swung her against the side of the building. Worse, the scene would have been completely ruined and she would have been faced with doing it over again.

Kitty has performed similar heart-stoppers on shows such as "Bionic Woman" and "Gemini Man," and she is featured for several critical moments in the Universal movie *Airport '77*. For the movie *Sundrops*, she fell 105 feet from a cliff into a river, the highest fall ever done on film by a woman. Two stunts in her lengthy résumé have never even been attempted by another woman: a crushing car roll-over triggered by a special explosive device, and a fully engulfed "fire gag," for which she was dressed in a protective suit, smeared with glue, and set aflame. The temperature within her suit reached 200 degrees F before the cameras nibbled up the required footage and she was extinguished. She emerged soaked with perspiration, but unscathed and smiling.

Kitty doesn't look like the most sought-after stunt woman in Hollywood. A petite five feet, two inches, she weighs only 105 pounds. There is just a hint of mischief in her blue-green eyes and only a suggestion of her grace and agility in the way she tosses her dark brown hair. Because there is something not quite right about her manner of speaking—an off-pitch slurring—most who meet her for the first time suspect that she has a

minor speech impediment, never realizing that she is totally deaf, as she has been since infancy.

Kitty was born in Corpus Christi, Texas. Not long after, her Irish father, John O'Neil, was killed in an airplane crash. When she was five months old, a trio of diseases attacked her concurrently—measles, mumps, and smallpox—and left her hearing destroyed. Kitty's mother, Patsy, a full-blooded Cherokee, moved with the child to Wichita Falls, Texas. Resolved that her daughter would lead a normal life despite the handicap, Patsy went through the University of Texas to earn her teaching credentials and learn the methods through which she could reach and teach her child. She began the tedious, often frustrating process of coaxing four senses to fill the void left by the useless fifth.

"She taught me to swim and to respond to directions when I was still just a baby," Kitty said. "Then she taught me how to read lips and speak." Patsy went on to teach other children with hearing defects, and eventually established the School of Listening Eyes in Wichita Falls.

Kitty was eight when she went out into the normal world—the world of laughter and whispered secrets and music—the world that she would never hear. She entered the regular public school system in the third grade, and at once began earning good marks. At Patsy's urging, Kitty took piano lessons. She also learned to play the cello, enjoying the feel of the resonant vibrations and keeping her notes true and pure by sensing minute changes in frequency level.

At twelve, she took up competitive swimming as a freestyle sprinter in the 100-meter event. She developed a mild interest in diving, but because hearing and balance are so closely related, her instructors doubted she would ever be capable of the precise aerial acrobatics necessary to compete effectively.

She surprised them and herself, at a swimming meet in Oklahoma. "One of our team's divers didn't show up," Kitty recalls. "I hardly knew one dive from another, but, on an impulse, I asked them to let me try." She captured a first-place gold medal at that meet and saw the spectators applauding for her. "It was my first real medal," she said, "so I gave up swimming competition right then to work only on diving."

Six months later, she won the AAU Southwest District Junior Olympics diving title in Texas, an achievement that made her a cover girl for the August, 1961, issue of *Times Features Magazine* and brought her to the attention of Dr. Sammy Lee, a two-time Olympic diving champion who operates a free school for exceptionally talented young divers in Anaheim, California.

At sixteen, Kitty moved to Anaheim to study with Dr. Lee. She attended Anaheim High School in the mornings, endured four rigorous hours of diving training each afternoon, and studied homework late into the evenings. She was forced to dig deeper in her textbooks than many of her classmates, because teachers would sometimes forget and talk to the blackboard rather than face the class. Unable to read their lips, Kitty would miss those portions of the lectures. She used the weekends to catch up.

Dr. Lee was impressed by her strength and stubborn determination, but he winced each time she slapped into the water wrong (at velocities up to forty miles an hour) after leaping from the ten-meter (thirty-three-foot) platform. For months she wore ugly pie-size bruises, but she shrugged off the punishment. Dr. Lee couldn't use his customary method of shouting to cue her exactly when to tuck or twist in her dives, so he began using a pistol loaded with blanks. Kitty would feel the concussions and respond in midair. "After a couple of trials with a new, complex dive," Dr. Lee said, "she would be oriented and from then on she would actually 'feel' her way through the sequence. After that, it was just a matter of polishing and perfecting."

In 1963, Kitty graduated from Anaheim High with honors. She was named "Young American of the Month" in the February issue of *American Youth Magazine*, published by General Motors. The article read, "Kitty snaps up diving awards like a hungry fish—five trophies and fifteen gold medals so far."

She was eighteen when she told a newspaper reporter, a bit defiantly, "I can do anything. I like to do things people say I can't do because I'm deaf. I have to work harder than some, but look at the fun I have proving they're wrong."

She went on to win the women's ten-meter diving championship at the 1964 AAU Nationals. Then, in a ten-meter dive during the Olympic qualifying trials, she failed to lock her thumbs tightly enough in the grip that divers use to punch an initial hole in the water for a clean high-speed entry. The force of impact drove one arm back against her forehead, breaking the wrist. She recovered, qualified, and placed eighth overall in the 1964 Tokyo Olympics. Dr. Lee was certain she could be a gold medalist in the 1968 Olympics coming up in Mexico,

but illness in her family forced her to give up the necessary constant training.

After winning thirty-eight blue ribbons, seventeen first-place trophies and thirty-one gold medals in her diving career, she began exploring the entire world of sports—the more dangerous an endeavor, the more irresistible it was to her. "I guess I like danger," she told me, "and thrills. But mostly I want always to have a goal, some dream that I can try for." She raced drag boats, top fuel dragsters and production sports cars. She tried sky diving, scuba diving, and high-speed water-skiing. In 1970, she set an official world's record as the fastest woman water-skier—at a phenomenal 104.85 mph.

She entered grueling off-road automobile and dune buggy events such as the Mint 400, the Baja 500, and the Mexican 1000, racing, and often winning, against such expert drivers as Mickey Thompson, Malcolm Smith, and Parnelli Jones. Cross-country motorcycle racing looked challenging, so Kitty studied the sport and then assaulted it. She soon achieved an American Motorcycle Association (AMA) expert rating. She is currently the only woman in the world to hold a professional license granted by the *Fédération Internationale Motorcycliste* (FIM, the world governing body for motorcycle speed records), qualifying her for international motorcycle competition.

At a motorcycle meet at Saddleback, California, she met competitor Duffy Hambleton. The muscular Hambleton, owner of World Wide Enterprises, a shop that specializes in motion-picture special-effects rigging and equipment rentals, was immediately impressed by Kitty O'Neil. "She was unbelievable," Duffy said. "I couldn't imagine being able to drive a motorcycle the way she could without hearing what gear the bike was in or knowing when a competitor was coming up behind her."

The admiration was mutual. Kitty and Duffy married. They live on a large ranch in Fillmore, California, surrounded by Valencia orange groves. Kitty settled down somewhat for the first few years of the marriage. She stayed in excellent physical condition by running eight to ten miles every morning and working out with light weights, a regimen she still maintains, but the routine life eventually became a bit too boring. Duffy had joined Stunts Unlimited, a fraternal organization of Hollywood's top stunt men, and was risking his neck regularly in movies and TV episodes. He had also signed on as Robert Blake's double for the "Baretta" series.

"Kitty was getting restless," Duffy recalls, "so I asked her what she'd like to do. She said, 'Well, why don't I just do what you do? Teach me how to do stunts.' She'd been coming to some of our practice sessions and she already knew a lot about the business, so we began teaching her how to fall and fake a fight and roll a car and so on. When she began actually doing all of it, she really razzled and dazzled them. I mean, I thought I knew what her capabilities were, but she far exceeded even my estimation. We would only have to explain something once and she'd do it. She's like a computer. She has tremendous powers of concentration."

In 1976, Universal Studios sponsored Kitty for her Screen Actors' Guild card, and she began stunting regularly on the TV series "Bionic Woman." She now receives so many job offers that she must turn many of them down for lack of time. Her credits include stunts on the NBC Mystery Movie series "Quincy," on the Spelling-Goldberg show "Family," and in the movie *9:30 '55*, the story of James Dean's death. The thirty-one members of Stunts Unlimited unanimously voted her in, solely on her talent and ability.

Winter Thunder

Mari Sandoz

A young school teacher is stranded with a group of children during a violent snowstorm. Will they survive or will they perish before help arrives? This short novel is based on the real-life experience of the author's niece.

Part 1

The snow began quietly this time, like an afterthought to the gray Sunday night. The moon almost broke through once, but toward daylight, a little wind came up and started white curls, thin and lonesome, running over the old drifts left from the New Year storm. Gradually the snow thickened, until around eight-thirty the two ruts of the winding trails were covered and undisturbed, except down in the Lone Tree district, where an old, yellow bus crawled heavily along, feeling out the ruts between the choppy sand hills.

As the wind rose, the snow whipped against the posts of a ranch fence across the trail, and caked against the bus windows, shutting in the young faces pressed to the glass. The storm increased

until all the air was a powdery white and every hill, every trace of road, was obliterated. The bus wavered and swayed in its direction, the tracks filling in close upon the wheels as they sought out the trail lost somewhere far back and then finally grasped at any footing, until it looked like some great snowy, bewildered bug seen, momentarily, through the shifting wind. But it kept moving, hesitating here, stalling there, in the deepening drifts, bucking heavily into them, drawing back to try once more while the chains spun out white fans that were lost in the driving snow which seemed almost as thick, as dense. Once the bus had to back down from a steep little patch that might have led into a storm-lost valley with a ranch house and warmth and shelter. It started doggedly around, slower now, but decisive, feeling cautiously for traction on the drifted hillside. Then the wheels began to slip, catch, and then slip again, the bus tipping precariously in the push of the wind, a cry inside lost under the rising noise of the storm.

For a long time, it seemed that the creeping bus could not be stopped. Even when all discernible direction or purpose was finally gone, it still moved, backing, starting again, this way and that, plowing the deepened slope, swaying, leaning, until it seemed momentarily very tall, and held from toppling only by the thickness of the flying snow. Once more a wheel caught and held under the thunder of the red-hot, smoking exhaust. It slipped, and held again, but now the force of the wind was too great. For a moment, the tilting bus seemed to lift. Then it pivoted into a slow skid and turned half around, broadside. Slowly it went over, almost as though without

weight at all, settling lightly against a drift, to become a part of it at that thickening place where the white storm turned to snowbanks, lost, except that there were frightening cries from inside, and a hiss of steam and smoke from the hot engine against the snow.

In a moment the door was forced outward, the wind catching a puff of smoke as dark, muffled heads pushed up and were white in an instant. They were children, mostly in snowsuits and in sheepskin coats, thrust down over the bus side, coughing and gasping as the force of the blizzard struck them, the older ones hunching their shoulders to shield themselves and some of the rest.

Once more the engine roared out, and the upper back wheel spun on its side, free and foolish in its awkward caking of snow. Then the young woman who had handed the children down followed them, her sheepskin collar up about her head, her arms full of blankets and lunch boxes.

"You'll have to give it up, Chuck," she called back into the smoking interior. "Quick! Bring the rest of the lunches——"

With Chuck, sixteen and almost as tall as a man, beside her, Lecia Terry pushed the frightened huddle of children together and hurried them away downwind into the wall of storm. Once, she tried to look back through the smother of snow, wishing that they might have taken the rope and shovel from the toolbox. But there was no time to dig for them on the underside now.

Back at the bus, thick smoke was sliding out the door into the snow that swept along the side. Flames began to lick up under the leaning windows, the caking of ice suddenly running from them. The glass held one moment and burst, and the flames whipped out, torn away by the storm as the whole bus was suddenly a wet, shining yellow that blistered and browned with the heat. Then there was a dull explosion above the roar of the wind, and down the slope, the fleeing little group heard it and thought they saw a dark fragment fly past overhead.

"Well, I guess that was the gas tank going," Chuck shouted as he tried to peer back under his shielding cap. But there was only the blizzard closed in around them, and the instinctive fear that these swift storms brought to all living creatures, particularly the young.

There was sobbing among the children now, a small one crying out, "Teacher! Teacher!" inside the thick scarf about her face, clutching for Lecia in her sudden panic.

"Sh-h, Joanie. I'm right here," the young woman soothed, drawing the six-year-old to her, looking around for the others already so white that she could scarcely see them in the powdery storm.

"Bill, will you help Chuck pack all the lunches in two, three boxes, tight, so nothing gets lost? Maggie's big syrup bucket'll hold a lot. Throw all the empties away. We'll have to travel light——" she said, trying to make it sound a little like an old joke.

"My father will be coming for me soon——" the eight-year-old Olive said primly. "So you need not touch my lunch."

"Nobody can find us here," Chuck said shortly, and the girl did not reply, too polite to argue. But now, one of the small boys began to cry. "I want my own lunch box too, Teacher," he protested, breathless from the wind. "I—I want to go home!"

His older brother slapped him across the earmuffs with a mittened hand. "Shut up, Fritz," he commanded. "You can't go home. The bus is——" Then he stopped, looked toward the teacher, almost lost only an arm's length away, and the full realization of their plight struck him. "We can't go home," he said, so quietly that he could scarcely be heard in the wind. "The bus is burned, and Chuck and Miss Lecia don't know where we are——"

"Sure we know!" Chuck shouted against him without looking up from the lunch-packing, his long back stooped protectively over his task. "Don't we know, Lecia? Anyway, it won't last. Radio this morning said just light snow flurries, or Dad wouldn't have let me take the bus out 'stead of him, even sick as he was." The tall boy straightened up, the lunch boxes strung to the belt of his sheepskin to bang together in the wind until they were snow-crusted. "Baldy Stever'll be out with his plane looking for his girlfriend soon's it clears a little, won't he, Lecia?" he said. "Like he came New Year's, with skis on it."

But the bold talk did not quiet the sobbing, and the teacher's nod was lost in the storm as she tied scarves and mufflers across the faces of the younger children, leaving only little slits for the eyes, with the brows and lashes already furred with snow. Then she lined up the seven, mixing the ages from six-year-old Joanie to twelve-year-old Bill, who limped heavily as he moved in the deepening snow. One of the blankets she pinned around the thinly dressed Maggie, who had only a short, outgrown coat, cotton stockings, and torn overshoes against the

January storm. The other blanket she tied around herself, ready to carry Joanie on her back, Indian fashion, when the short little legs were worn out.

Awkwardly, one after another, Lecia pulled the left arm of each pupil from the sleeve, buttoned it inside the coat, and then tied the empty sleeve to the right arm of the one ahead. She took the lead with little Joanie tied to her belt, where she could be helped. Chuck was at the tail end of the clumsy little queue, just behind Bill with the steel-braced ankle.

"Never risk getting separated," Lecia remembered hearing her pioneer grandfather say, when he told of burying the dead from the January blizzard of 1888 here, the one still called the schoolchildren's storm. "Never get separated and never stop moving until you find shelter——"

The teacher squinted back along the line, moving like some long, snowy, winter-logged animal, the segmented back bowed before the sharpening blizzard wind. Just the momentary turn into the storm took her breath and frightened her for these children, hunched into themselves, half of them crying softly, hopelessly, as though already lost. They must hurry. With not a rock anywhere and not a tree within miles to show the directions, they had to seek out the landmark of the ranch country—the wire fence. So the girl started downwind again, breaking the new drifts as she searched for valley ground where fences were most likely, barbed-wire fences that might lead to a ranch, or nowhere, except around some hay meadow. But it was their only chance the girl from the sand hills knew. Stumbling, floundering through the snow, she kept the awkward string moving, the eyes of the older ones straining through frozen lashes for even the top of one fence post, those of the small ones turned in upon their fear, as the snow caked on the mufflers over their faces and they stumbled blindly to the pull from ahead.

Once there was a bolt of lightning, milky white in the blizzard, and a shaking of thunder, ominous winter thunder that stopped the moving feet. Almost at once the wind grew sharper, penetrating even Chuck's heavy sheepskin coat, numbing the ears and feet as, panting, sobbing, the children plowed on again,

the new drifts soon far above Lecia's boots and no visibility, no way to avoid them.

With their hands so awkwardly useless, someone stumbled every few steps, but the first to fall was the crippled Bill, the others, the crying ones too, standing silent in the storm, not even able to slap one frozen hand against another while the boy was helped up. After that, others went down, and soon it was all that the teacher and the boy Chuck could do to keep the children moving, as they pushed through the chop hills and found themselves going up what seemed a long, wind-swept, wind-frozen slope, Lecia carrying Joanie on her back most of the time now. But they kept moving somehow, barely noticing even the jack rabbit that burst out among their feet and was gone into the storm. Otherwise, there was nothing.

After a long, long time, they reached what seemed a high ridge of hills standing across the full blast of the north wind that bent them low and blinded. Suddenly Chuck's feet slid off sideways into a hole, a deep-cupped blowout hidden by the storm. Before he could stop, he had drawn the rest tumbling in after him, with an avalanche of snow. Crying, frightened, the smaller ones were set to their feet and brushed off a little. Then they all crouched together under the bank to catch their breath, out of the wind, shivering, wet from the snow that had fallen inside their clothes, which were already freezing hard as board.

"With the blowouts always from the northwest to the southeast," Chuck shouted into the teacher's covered ear, "the wind's plainly from the north, so we're being pushed about due south. That direction there can't be a house for five, six miles, even if we could find it—unless we got clear out of our home country——"

The girl shivered, empty with fear. "—So that's why we haven't found a fence," she said slowly. "We're probably in the old Bar M summer range, miles and miles across. But we can't go any other direction——"

"I could alone; I could make it out alone!" Chuck shouted suddenly, angrily.

For a moment the teacher was silent, waiting, but when he added nothing more, she said: "You can't leave these little ones now, Chuck. Even if you were sure you could find a ranch——"

There was no reply, except that the crippled boy began to cry, a reddening from his ankle coming up through the snow that was packed into his overshoes around the brace. Others were sobbing, too, and shaking with cold, but the younger ones were very quiet now, already drowsing, and so the young teacher had to get to her feet and help lift the children out of the blowout. Slapping the muffler-covered cheeks, shaking the smaller ones so hard that the caked snow fell from them, she got the line moving again, but very slowly. She was worn out too, from the path-breaking and with Joanie in her arms to warm the child, keep her from the sleep of freezing that came upon her on Lecia's back, with only the thin blanket against the ice of the wind.

They seemed to be going down now, through a long, deep-drifted slope, plowing into buried yucca clumps, the sharp spears penetrating the snowsuits, even the boot tops. Here a few head of cattle passed them, less than three feet away and barely to be seen. They were run-ning, snow-caked, blinded, bawling, and Lecia squinted anxiously back into the storm for others, for a herd that might be upon them, trample them as surely as stampeding buffaloes. But there were no more now, and she could see that Chuck was shouting, "Little chance of its clear-ing up soon, with that snow thunder and those cattle already drifting so fast—all the way from the winter range!"

Yes, drifting fast with the force and terror of the storm, even hardy, thick-haired range cattle running!

Then suddenly, one of the younger boys cried out something. "Teacher!" he repeated, "I saw a post!"

But it must have been a trick of the wind, for there was only the driving snow, except that the sharp-eyed Maggie saw one too, ahead and to the right—a snowy post with only the upper foot or so out of the drifts, holding up a strand of gray wire, taut and humming in the cold.

For a moment Lecia could not see through the blurring of her eyes. At least this was something to follow, but which way? To her signal, Chuck lifted his arm and dropped it. He didn't recognize the fence either, and so the teacher took the easier direction, leftward, only sideface to the wind, although it might lead to the hills, to some final drift, as the fleeing cattle would end.

Moving slowly along the fence, Le-cia knew that it could not be much far-ther, anyway. Her arms were wooden with cold and the weight of the child, her legs so weary in the deepening drifts that, with each step, it seemed that she could never lift a snow-caked boot again.

Then suddenly Chuck was doubling up the line. "I think I know where we are! That old split post just back there's where we made a take-down running coyotes with Dad's hounds this fall. If I'm right, this is Miller's north meadow, and there's a strip of willows down ahead there, off to the right——"

For a moment, the girl set Joanie into the deep snow, panting, and even when she caught her breath, she was afraid to speak.

"How far to a house?" she finally asked, her lips frozen.

"There's no house along this fence if it's the Miller," Chuck had to admit. "It just goes around the meadow, three, four miles long."

"You're sure——" the teacher asked slowly, "—sure there's no crossfence to the ranch? You might get through, find help in time——"

The boy could only shake his snowy head and then, thinking that the storm hid this, he shouted the words on the wind. No, no crossfence, and the ranch was five miles south. Not even a hay-stack left in the valley here. Miller had had his hay balers in this fall, hauled it all out for his fancy Angus herd.

Then they must take a chance on the willows, with Bill hardly able to limp along, Joanie too heavy to carry, and several others worn out. So they wallowed through the drifted fence and tried to keep parallel to its direction, but far enough in the meadow to see any willows. There must be willows now.

Suddenly Lecia went down in what must have been a deep gully, the ground gone, the girl sinking into soft, powdery snow to her shoulder. Panting, choking, she managed to get Joanie and the rest back out and the frightened ones quieted a little. Then she swung off right along the barer edge of the gully, seeking a

place to cross. The wind was blowing in powerful gusts now, so that she could scarcely stand up. Bent low, she dragged at the line behind her, most of the children crawling in the trench she plowed for them. There was no crying now— only the slow, slow moving. Perhaps they should dig into the snow here, below the gully bank. Indians and trappers had done that and survived. But they had thick-furred buffalo robes to shut out the cold and snow, and they were grown men, tough, strong—not helpless, worn-out children, their frozen feet heavy as stone, with only an over-grown boy and a twenty-three-year-old girl to lead them, keep them alive.

More and more often Lecia had to stop, her head down, her arms dropping the weight of the little girl. But there seemed to be a shallowing in the gully now, and so it was time she tried to break a path through it and turned back toward the fence if they were not to wander, lost, as so many did that other time, long ago, when a teacher and her nine pupils were lost, finally falling to die on the prairie. They must cling to the fence here, if it went no farther than around the meadow. At least it was proof that something existed on the earth except the thick, stinging blizzard, with a white, freezing, plodding little queue caught in the heart of it, surrounded.

Once when the girl looked up from the running snow, it seemed there was something darkish off to the right, little farther than arm's reach away. She saw it again, something rounded, perhaps a willow clump, low, snow-filled, and possibly with more nearby. Signaling to Chuck, Lecia turned down to it—a wil-low covered as in sleep, but with at least two more bushes just beyond, larger, darker, and standing closer together, their longer upper arms snow-weighted, entwined over the drifts. There, between the clumps, out of the worst of the storm, she left the children squatted close, the blankets held over them. With the belts of her coat and Chuck's, they tied the longer brushy tops of the two clumps together as solidly as they could. Then, fighting the grasping wind, they managed to fasten the blankets across the gap between the willows, to hold awhile. Behind this protection, Lecia dug through the snow to the frozen ground while Chuck gathered deadwood. Inside a close little kneeling circle of children, they built a fire pile with some dry, inner bark and a piece of sandwich paper for the lighting. Awkwardly, with freezing hands, the teacher and Chuck hurried, neither daring to think about matches, dry ones, in any pocket after this stumbling and falling through the snow.

The two smaller children were dropping into the heavy sleep of exhaustion and cold and had to be held in their places by the older ones, while Chuck dug swiftly through his pockets, deeper, more awkwardly, then frantically, the circle of peering eyes like those of fearful young animals, cornered, winter-trapped.

Down to his shirt, Chuck found some in his pocket, six in a holder made of two rifle cartridges slipped together. Hurrying clumsily, he struck one of the matches. It sputtered and went out, the flames sucked away. They had to try again, making a closer circle, with the coattails of the children thrown up over their heads to shut out the storm. This time, the match caught on the waxed paper and the diamond willow began to snap and sizzle in the snow, throwing a

dancing light up to the circle of crouching children.

But it seemed even colder now that they had stopped walking, and Lecia thought of the night ahead, with the temperature surely down to twenty-five or thirty below zero. Beyond that she would not look now; but to get through this night they must have a great pile of wood, and they must have shelter, even to hold the fire.

"We can't both go out at one time," the teacher told Chuck in their planning, somehow making it seem as for a long, long time. "It's too risky for the children. We might not get back."

The boy looked around from the fire he was nursing, and upward, but there was still no thinning of the storm, the area of snowy visibility almost as small as the confines of their new meat-freeze room at the ranch. Even so, he gave the girl no sign of agreement.

Lecia set willow poles into the snowbanks as she went to look for wood, none farther apart than the outstretched reach of her arms. She found more willows, each clump sitting alone in the isolation of the driving storm, so cold now that the greenwood snapped off like glass. Each time, it was only by the row of sticks in the drifts that she managed to stagger her blinded and panting way back against the wind with her load of wood.

The brushier portions she piled behind the blankets of the shelter to catch the snow and shut out the wind. Some, long as fish poles, she pushed through the willow clumps and across the opening between, in a sort of lattice inside the bellying blankets that Eddie and Calla tried to hold in place. They were the first of the children to separate themselves from the snowy composite, the enforced coordinate that had been the queue driven by the storm, the circle that shielded the sprouting fire. Now they were once more individuals, who could move alone, hold the blankets from blowing inward, pile the dry, powdery snow from the ground against and between the sticks, trying to work it like plaster, building a wall between the clumps of willows. Even Bill helped a little, as far as he could reach without moving the bad ankle. They worked slowly, clumsily, pounding their freezing hands at the fire, but returning.

By one o'clock the north wind was cut off, so that the fire fattened and burned higher, softening the ice caked to the clothing until it could be knocked off, and softening the face of the drift reached by the wind-blown heat. The children packed this against the north wall too, and into the willow clumps both ways, drawing the rounded wall inward toward the top along the bend of the willows, making what looked like half of an Indian snow shelter or the wickiup Calla had seen at the county fair, just high enough at the center for a seven-year-old to stand up, the snow walls glistening rosy in the firelight as the wind was shut off.

"That's a good job!" Chuck shouted over the roar of the storm, as he tried to rub circulation into Joanie's waxen feet. The small girl was beginning to cry out of her sleep with the first pain; others began too, their ears and hands swollen and purpling, their toes painful as their boots thawed. But it seemed that the feet of nine-year-old Maggie must be lost, the ragged old overshoes and cotton stockings so frozen that she had to cut them away with Eddie's knife. Under them her

feet were like stone, dead white stone, although the girl was working hard to rub life into them. She worked silently and alone, as had become natural long ago, her thin face pinched and anxious with the pain and the alarm.

Of them all, only Olive seemed untouched. She was dry in her heavy, waterproofed snowsuit with attached rubber feet inside the snow boots. And she was still certain that her father would soon come for her.

"He would not care to leave me in such an unpleasant place——"

When they had the semicircular wall of the shelter drawn in as far as the snow would hold, Lecia decided to pull the blankets away from the outside and use one over the top, with the belt-tied willows sticking through a smoke hole cut in the center. But as the blankets came down, part of the loose snow wall was blown in by the force of the blizzard, the huddle of children suddenly white again, the fire almost smothered. So the wall had to be rebuilt, in discouragement, but with care, using more brush and sticks, more fire-softened snow to freeze in place as soon as it was struck by the storm. Lecia had to stop several times for her hands too, pounding them hard, holding them over the fire, the diamond sparkling. She tried to turn the ring off before the swelling became too great, and then gave it up. The wall must be finished, and when it was solid, Calla came to whisper under the roar of the wind. "Bill's been eating the lunch," she said.

"Oh, Bill! That's not fair to the others, to your own little sister Joanie!" Lecia cried. Suddenly not the good teacher, she grabbed up the containers and hung them on high branches, out in plain sight for watching, for reminders and derision from the other children. "Why, it may be days before we are found!" she scolded, in her exasperation saying what should have been kept hidden in silence.

Before the boy could defend himself with a plea of hunger or his usual complaint about the crippled foot, some realization of their plight had struck the others. Even little Fritz, with the security of an older sister and brother like Calla and Eddie along, began to sob. Only the round-cheeked Olive was calm, the others angered to see it, wanting to shout against her outsider's assurance, to tell her she was too stupid and green to know that her father could not come for her in such a blizzard, that he would never find her if he could get through. But they were silent under the teacher's admonitory eye. And, as in the schoolhouse and on the playground, Bill had withdrawn, except that now it could not be more than a foot or two.

As the frozen earth between the willow humps became soggy, Calla and Eddie helped move the others around so that there was room to draw the fire, first one way and then another, to dry and warm the ground. Lecia watched to see that they set no one afire, and then bowed her head out into the storm again. Chuck was dragging in willows for the night. They drove sticks into the hardening drifts around the front of the shelter and piled brush against them to catch the snow. It filled in as fast as they worked, until there was no more than a little crawling hole left. Then Chuck laid a mat of brushy sticks on the ground and packed soft snow into them to freeze, making a handled slab big enough to close the low doorway. Now, so long as the blanket with the smoke hole stayed tied over the top, they could be as warm as they wished in the little shelter that was scarcely longer than a tall man—a close cramping for the teacher, Chuck, and the seven pupils, but easily warmed with a few fingers of wood, an Indian fire. Safe and warm so long as the shelter stood against the rising ferocity of the blizzard, and the willows lasted.

By now, the cold stung the nose and burned the lungs, the snow turned to sharp crystals that drew blood from the bare skin. It drove the teacher and Chuck in to the fire, shaking, unable, it seemed, ever to be warmed-through again. Lecia opened her sheepskin coat, hung up her frozen scarf and cap, and shook out her thick brown hair that gleamed in the firelight. Even with her tawny skin red and swollen, her gold-flecked hazel eyes bloodshot, she was still a pretty girl, and the diamond on her hand flashed as she hunted for her stick of white salve to pass around for the raw, bleeding lips. It was all she could do.

Now they tried to plan for what was to come, but here they were as blind as in the flight through the storm. There would be sickness, with the noses already running, Joanie coughing deep from her chest, and, worst of all, Maggie's feet that seemed to be dying. Besides, the fire must be kept going and the food spread over three, perhaps four, days.

Here Bill raised his complaining voice. "You ain't our boss outside of school! We'll do what we want to. There ain't enough to eat for everybody."

"You mean *isn't*, not *ain't*," the teacher corrected firmly. "And talking like that—when you've barely missed one lunchtime!"

"You ain't never my boss," Chuck said casually, "—only about the kids while in the bus, like you do with my dad when he's driving. I sure can do what I want to here, and I'll do it."

Slowly the girl looked around the ring of drowsy, firelit eyes upon her, some uneasy at this bold talk to their teacher, but some smaller ones aping the defiance of the big boys. Chuck, who sat almost a head taller than Lecia, grinned down at the pretty young teacher, but with an arrogance that was intended to remind her he saw nothing here as his responsibility, nothing this side of the bus except saving himself.

Unable to reply in words that would not frighten the children more, the teacher looked past the fire into the boy's broad, defiant face, into his unblinking, storm-red eyes, the look commanding at first, then changing to something else in spite of herself, into a sort of public test, until it seemed she dared not turn her gaze away, or, at that instant, the sixteen-year-old boy must assert his victory by plunging out into the storm and perhaps destroy himself, perhaps bring death to all of them.

Before this silent, incomprehensible struggle, the children were uneasy and afraid, even the coughing stilled, so that the storm seemed very loud outside the smoke hole. But little Fritz was too young to be held so for long. "I'm hungry!" he shouted against the restraining hand of his sister. "I want my lunch!"

As though freed, released, Chuck sat back and grinned a little at the small boy. Matter-of-factly, the teacher washed her raw hands with snow and held them over the fire. Then she spread her napkin on her lap and set out all there was in the eight lunches now: fourteen sandwiches, most of them large, six pieces of Sunday cake, a handful of cookies, a few pieces of candy, and six apples and two oranges, frozen hard. There were two thermos bottles of milk, and these Lecia pushed away into the snow wall.

"If somebody gets sick and can't eat solid food," she said to the owners, their eyes following her hands in consternation. Even with the best management, there would be no food of any kind in a few days, but this the small owners could not yet understand.

The frozen fruit she handed to Chuck, and, without meeting the girl's eyes, he set it around the coals for toasting, to be eaten now because it would not keep well and might sicken leaner stomachs. In the meantime, Lecia set one lunch box filled with snow near the fire and packed away all, except four of the big sandwiches, into the others, the eyes of the children following her hands here too, even as she hung the containers back above her head. Then she divided the four sandwiches into halves and passed them around.

"Eat very slowly," she cautioned. "Blizzards usually last three days, so we must make what we have here last too, probably clear to Thursday, or longer."

But Bill seemed not to be listening. "Chuck's eating!" he suddenly protested. "He ain't, isn't, in on the lunches."

For a moment, the teacher looked sternly at the boy. "After Chuck carried them all from the bus, helped you through the bad places, and helped to make the shelter and the fire!" the girl said in astonishment. "Now, we'll have no more of this bickering and complaint. Here we are equal partners, and not one of us will get out of this alive unless we keep working together. Even your comic books should have taught you that much! And don't think this is play. You remember what the storm of 1888 was called in your history book—because so many schoolchildren died in it. That storm was short, not over two days most places, nothing for length like the one we had holiday time this year, and no telling about this one. Most of the children in 1888 died because somebody got panicky, didn't think, or they didn't stick together——"

There was silence all around the fire now, the storm seeming to rise, the children edging closer to each other, glancing fearfully over their shoulders as though toward night windows with terrible things stalking outside.

"Oh, we're OK," Chuck said optimistically. "We can last three days, easy, here——" the rebellion gone from him, or hidden for the moment.

Thinking of a five-day storm, the teacher looked around the frightened, sooty faces, the children coughing and sniffling, their pocket tissue gone, the few handkerchiefs hung to dry, and wondered if any, even the man-tall Chuck, would be here by then.

But Olive, the newcomer, was unconcerned. "I should like another sandwich, Miss Terry. From my own lunch, please," she said, with the formality of an old-fashioned boarding school for eight-year-olds. "I won't need the remainder. My father will come for me when it is time."

"He won't find you——" Maggie said as she rubbed at her feet, color seeping into them now, an angry, gray-splotched purple, with pain that twisted the thin face.

"My father will come," Olive repeated, plainly meaning that he was not like the fathers of the others here, particularly Maggie's, who had done nothing since the war except make a little South Pacific bug juice,[1] as he called it, for himself from chokecherries, wild grapes, or raisins, in the way they did in the war. He had only a little piece of copper tubing, and though he couldn't make more than enough for himself, yet he got into jail just the same, for crashing his old truck through the window of the county assistance office. But things had not been good before that. Often this fall, Maggie was at school when the bus arrived, not waiting at the stop near their crumbling old sod shack, but walking the three miles. Sometimes her face was bruised, but she was silent to any questioning. If Maggie lost her feet now, it was because she had no warm snowsuit and high boots like the others, only the short old coat above her skinny knees, the broken overshoes with the soles flopping.

But there was still a cheerful face at the fire. Although little Fritz's cheeks seemed swollen to bursting and his frosted ears stood away under the flaps of his cap, he could still show his gap-toothed grin in mischief.

"If we don't get home till Thursday, Teacher, Baldy'll be awful mad at you when he comes flying out Wednesday——"

The rest laughed a little, drowsily. "Maybe Baldy won't be flying around that soon," Eddie said, and was corrected by Calla's sisterly concern. "Don't say Baldy. Say Mr. Stever."

But the teacher busied herself hanging up everything loose. Then, with

---

1. South Pacific bug juice: A homemade alcoholic beverage.

Chuck's knife, she slit the remaining blanket down the middle and fastened half around each side against the snow wall, like a tepee lining. By the time the white blizzard darkness came, the smaller children had all been taken outside for the last time, and lay in fretful, uneasy sleep. Olive had been the last, waiting stubbornly for her father until she toppled forward. Calla caught her and made room for the girl still murmuring, "Papa——"

Finally, the last sob for parent and home was stilled, even Joanie asleep, her feverish head in the teacher's lap, her throat raw and swelling, with nothing except hot snow water to ease the hollow cough. There were half a dozen lozenges in Lecia's pocket, but these must be saved for the worse time that would surely come.

The children were packed around the fire like little pigs or puppies on a very cold night. Chuck was at the opposite side from Lecia, the boys on his side, the girls on hers, with Calla and her brothers around the back. The older ones lay nearer the wall, their arms over the younger to hold their restlessness from the fire.

But Bill was still up, drawn back under the willows, his head pulled into his sheepskin collar, his ankle bent to him. He watched the teacher doze in fatigue, met her guilty waking gaze sullenly. But finally, he reached down into his pocket and drew out something in waxed paper.

"I didn't eat the piece you gave me——" he said, holding out his half of the sandwich.

"Bill! That was fine of you," the girl said, too worn out for more as she reached up to put it away.

"No—no, you eat it. I guess you didn't take any."

A moment Lecia looked at the boy, but he avoided her as he edged himself around Chuck closer to the fire, turning his chilled back to the coals, and so she ate the buttered bread with the thick slice of strengthening cold beef, while more snow was driven in through the smoke hole and settled in sparkling dust toward the little fire. There were white flashes too, and the far rumble of winter thunder.

"Is—is there lots of willows left?" the crippled boy asked.

The teacher knew what he meant—how many clumps, and if so far out that someone might get lost.

"I think there are quite a few," she replied, needing to reassure the boy, but unable to make it a flat lie.

A long time he sat silent. Finally, he pulled his cap off and shook the long, yellowish hair back from his petulant face. "I wonder what Mother's doing——" he said slowly, looking away, his hand seeking out the tortured ankle. Lecia motioned him to hold it over to her, and so she did not need to reply, to ask what all the mothers of these children must be doing, with the telephone lines still down from the other storm and surely nobody foolish enough to try bucking this one, unless it might be Olive's father, the new Eastern owner of the little Box Y ranch.

With snow water heated in the lunch tin, Lecia washed the poor stick that was the boy's ankle, gently sponging the bone laid almost bare where the frozen snow and the iron brace wore through the scarred and unhealthy skin.

"It looks pretty bad, Bill, but you probably won't have to put the brace back on for days——" Lecia started to comfort, but it was too late, and she had to see fear and anger and self-pity darken the face in the firelight. Because nothing could be unsaid, the girl silently bandaged the ankle with half of the boy's handkerchief. "Now get a little sleep, if you can," she said gently.

The boy crawled in next to Eddie as though Ed were the older, and, for a long time, the teacher felt the dark eyes staring at her out of the shadowy coat collar as though she had deliberately maneuvered this plunge into the blizzard.

Close Up

1. (a) Why is the teacher, Lecia Terry, in a hurry to get the children out of and away from the bus? (b) What supplies does she manage to save from the bus?

2. (a) How does Lecia prevent the children from getting separated and lost? (b) Why does she place herself at the front of the line of children and Chuck at the back?

3. Why does Lecia think that the storm will last a long time?

4. (a) How does Lecia build the shelter in the willow clumps? (b) What does she do to keep the wind from cutting through the blankets that form the walls of the shelter?

5. Although Lecia is often frightened, she acts calmly and decisively. (a) What decision does she make about the food? (b) Find two other instances where she acts calmly and decisively.

6. Chuck and some of the children rebel against Lecia's authority. (a) How does Lecia regain control of the group? (b) Find two reasons why she wants Chuck to stay with the group.

7. (a) Why does Lecia try to make the children aware of the danger of the storm? (b) Why does she also try to assure them that they will be all right?

Part 2

Several times before midnight the girl started to doze, but jerked herself awake at the frozen creak of the willow shelter, to push the out-tossed arms back and replenish the fire.

Eddie's cough began to boom deep, as from a barrel. He turned and moaned, digging at his chest, Calla helpless beside him, her sleep-weighted eyes anxious on the teacher. Maggie, too, was finally crying now. Her feet had puffed up and purpled dark as jelly bags, with the graying spots that would surely break and slough off, perhaps spread in gangrene.[2] Yet all Lecia could do was turn the girl's feet from the fire and push them behind the blanket against the snow to relieve the pain and itching a little. Perhaps only freeze them more. Lecia touched the girl's forehead to calm her, but felt her stiffen and start to pull away from this unaccustomed kindly touch. Then Maggie relaxed a little, and as the teacher stroked the hot temples, she wondered how many days it might be before help could get through. Suddenly their plight here seemed so hopeless, the strength and wisdom of her twenty-three years so weak and futile, that she had to slip out into the storm for calm. And finally Maggie slept, worn out, but still tearing at her feet.

To the weary girl watching, half asleep, at the fire, the roar of the storm rose and fell like the panting of a great live thing, sometimes a little like many great planes warming up together. If only she had married Dale Stever New Year's,

they would be in the Caribbean now, these children all safe at home, with probably no other teacher available so soon. Once, Lecia turned her swollen hand to the fire, watching the ring catch and break the light into life, and tried to recall the fine plans Dale had made for them. He wasn't a rancher's son, like those who usually took her to parties and dances—like Joe, or Wilmo, or even Ben, of the local bank. Dale had come from outside last summer and bought up the sale pavilion in town. Since then, he flew all around the surrounding ranch country in a plane the color of a wild canary rising from a plum thicket, gathering stock for the sales. Fairtime, he took Lecia and her friend Sallie down to the state fair, and several times on long trips since, to Omaha to the ballet and to Denver. At first it seemed he was all jolly big-talk, with windy stories of his stock in an oil company down in Dallas and in a Chicago commission house. He had a touch of gray at his temples that he thought made him look distinguished when he had his hat on, and to their fathers he called himself the Dutch uncle of the two girls. But, gradually, he concentrated on Lecia, and at Christmas there was the big diamond and the plane ready to fly south. He even took her to the school board to ask for a release from her contract.

"No," the old school director told the girl. "Bill Terry was a friend of mine, brought me into the country. I can't help his granddaughter marry no man in a rush hurry."

Dale laughed confidently and put his arm about the girl's shoulder as they left, but, somehow, Lecia couldn't break her contract. They must wait until school was out. Dale had been angry.

---

2. gangrene (găng′grēn′) n.: Tissue decay caused by lack of blood.

"This is no life for a girl as pretty as you," he said. Truly he was right. Today it was no life for any girl.

Soon after midnight, Lecia was startled out of a doze by the sound of cattle bawling somewhere in the roar of the storm, like the herds that passed her home in the night of the May blizzard three years ago, when so many died in the drifts and lakes that the whole region was a stench far into the summer. Then, suddenly, the girl realized where she was, and hurried bareheaded out into the storm. The bawling was very close; any moment hundreds of storm-blinded cattle might be running over the little willows, over their own two clumps.

Lecia dragged burning sticks from the fire, but in an instant, the storm had sucked their flame away. So, with her arms up to shield her eyes from the snow that was sharp as steel dust, she stood behind the shelter shouting the "Hi-ah! Hi-ah!" she had learned when she helped the cowboys push cattle to market. It was a futile, lost little sound against cattle compelled to run by an instinct that could not be denied,

compelled to flee for survival before the descent of the arctic storm, never stopping until trapped in some drift or boldly overtaken in some open fence corner to freeze on their feet, as Lecia had seen them stand.

Realizing her danger as a warmth crept over her, the girl stumbled back into the shelter and crouched at the fire. She barely noticed the sting of returning blood in her ears and face while she listened until the drifting herd was surely past, made more afraid by the knowledge of this thing that drove cattle galloping through the night, the power of it, and how easily it could overcome the little circle of children here if it were not for the handful of fire, for the walls of the storm's own snow.

Toward morning, the weary girl knew that she could not keep awake. She had stirred Chuck to sit up awhile, but he was unable to shake off the weight of sleep so heavy on an overgrown boy. Trying to remember how the Indians carried their fire—something about moss and damp, rotted wood—Lecia pulled old dead roots from the willow butts and laid them into the coals with the ends sticking far out. Even with waxed paper handy, it would be a desperate chance. Willows burned fast as kindlings, and there were only five matches, including the one from Eddie's pocket, and no telling how many spoiled by dampness.

Even so, it was sweet to let herself sink into darkness, but it seemed that she awoke at once, stiff and cold from the nightmare that reached into the waking black, even the ashes of the fire-spot cold. With the waxed paper held ready, the girl blew on the ends of the unburnt roots her hands found, carefully, breathless in her fear. At last a red spark glowed deep in one, and when the fire was going again, she slipped outside for calm in the cold that was like thin, sharp glass in the nose.

There was still no earth and no sky, only the white storm of late dawn blowing hard. But the wood had lasted, and now Lecia put on a few extra sticks and heated water to wash the goose mush from the inflamed eyes of the children. She started a rousing song: "Get up! Get up, you sleepyhead!" but even before it was done, Joanie began to whimper, "I'm hungry——"

So the teacher laid out four sandwiches on sticks over the coals, and then added another half for herself when she saw Bill watching. "There won't be anything more today except a pinch of cake unless the sun breaks through."

"If it does, we can stomp out a message on the snow," Calla said cheerfully.

"Yes, even if people can't travel for a whole week, Baldy'll come flying over to see about his girlfriend," Bill said, boldly.

The younger boys laughed a little, but Chuck was more serious. "If the sky lightens at all and there's no blowing, I'll do the stomping before I leave."

"You'd run away now?" the teacher asked softly, as she combed at Joanie's fine brown hair.

"Somebody's got to get help," he defended, in loud words.

The children around the fire were suddenly quiet, turning their eyes to follow the tall boy as he pulled up his sheepskin collar and crawled out into the storm. And silent a long time afterward—all except Joanie, who sobbed softly, without understanding. Even Olive looked up once, but Maggie grated

her feet hard along the snow wall and tore at their congestion as though she heard nothing.

Then suddenly there was stomping outside, and Chuck came back in, snowy, thick frost all over his collar and cap, his brows and lashes in ice, the children pushing over toward him, as to one gone, lost. He brought more wood, and the teacher seemed to have forgotten that

he had said anything about leaving. But the children watched him now, even when they pretended they didn't, and watched Lecia too, for suspicion had come in.

The teacher started as for a school day, except that the arithmetic was rote learning of addition and multiplication tables, and a quick run through some trick problems: "If I had a fox, a goose, and some corn to get across a river in a boat——" and then, "If I had a dollar to buy a hundred eggs—no, I should take something that won't make us hungry."

"Like a hundred pencils?"

"Well, yes, let's take pencils. I want to buy a hundred for a dollar. Some are five cents each, poor ones two and a half cents, and broken ones half a cent. How many of each kind must I buy?"

In history and nature study, they talked about the Indians that still roamed the sand hills when Lecia's grandfather came into the country. They lived the winter long in skin tepees something like the shelter here, and almost as crowded, but with piles of thick-furred buffalo robes for the ground and the beds. The girls sat on one side, the boys on the other.

"Like we are here——" Fritz said, his eyes shining in the discovery. "We're Indians. Whoo-oo-oo!" he cried, slapping his mouth with his palm.

They talked about the food too, the piles of dried and pounded meat, the winter hunts, how the village and lodges were governed, and what the children did, their winter games, one almost like "button, button." The boys learned from the men—such things as arrow-making, and later bullet-making, hunting, fighting; and, particularly, the virtues of resourcefulness, courage, fortitude, and responsibility for all the people. A girl learned from the women—beading, tanning hides, and all the other things needed to live well with modesty, steadfastness, and generosity, and with courage and fortitude and responsibility too, for it was thought that the future of the people lay in the palms of the women, to be cherished or thrown away.

"What does that mean, Teacher?"

Fritz asked, hitting out in mischief at his brother Eddie despite Calla and the teacher both watching, then shouting he was hungry again.

The rest tried to laugh a little as Calla whispered to her small brother, trying to make herself heard against the storm, while Lecia taught them a poem about Indians. Even Joanie repeated a few lines for her, although the child leaned weak and feverish against Calla, while Bill comforted his bound ankle and Maggie tried hard to pull herself out of the curious drowsiness that had the teacher frightened.

After a while the children played "button, button," and tried to tell each other poems. When Eddie got stuck on "Snowbound,"[3] Bill nudged Fritz, and they laughed as easily at his discomfiture as at school, perhaps because Chuck was back and this was the second day of the storm, with tomorrow the third. Then it would clear up and somebody with a scoop shovel would get his horse along the barer ridges to a telephone.

"Maybe somebody'll just come running over the hills to find us," Eddie teased, looking at Olive, turning his face from the teacher.

"Well, even if nobody came and Baldy couldn't find a place to land with skis on his plane, he would have sacks of food and blankets and stuff dropped like in the movies and the newspapers."

"I saw it in a movie once, I did," Joanie cried.

So they talked, pretending no one was looking up at the hanging lunch buckets, or sick and afraid. But Lecia did not hear them.

---

3. "Snowbound": A poem written by John Greenleaf Whittier (1807–1892).

"Oh-oo, Teacher's sleeping like one of those Indian women up to Gordon, just sitting there!" Eddie exclaimed.

"Sh-h," Calla said, in her way. "Let her stretch out here;" and with a polite smile, Olive moved aside.

That night Joanie was delirious, and once, Maggie slipped past the teacher out into the storm to relieve the fire of her feet. By midnight she couldn't stand on them, and the grayish spots were yellow under the thick skin of a barefoot summer, the swelling creeping above the girl's thin ankles, with red streaks reaching almost to the knees. Her eyes glistened, her cheeks were burning, and she talked of wild and dreadful things.

Lecia tried to remember all that she had read of frostbite, all that her grandfather had told, but she knew that the inflammation spreading past the frozen area was like the cold overtaking the fleeing cattle, and she had to make a desperate decision. She dug two holes deep into the snow wall and laid Maggie with her feet in them almost to her knees, wishing they had something waterproof for covering. The cold would probably freeze the girl more, but it would numb the nerves and perhaps slow the congestion and tissue starvation. Later, when the girl was restless again and crying, Lecia found the yellow spots spreading, painful and hard as boils. She burned the end of a safety pin and, while Maggie's frightened eyes became caverns in her thin face, Lecia opened one of the spots. Bloody pus burst down over her hand. Holding the foot aside, she wiped it away on the snow, from her ring too, and then slipped the ring from her shrunken finger and hung it on a twig overhead, where it swayed a little, like a morning dewdrop, while she opened the rest of the festering.

When the girl's feet were bathed and bound in the sleeves torn from Lecia's white-shirt blouse, she thrust them back into the snow. Then she gave Maggie half a cup of the milk, very quietly, hoping none would awaken to see, although none needed it more. Almost at once the girl was asleep, to rest until the pus gathered again. But the first time Lecia returned with firewood, she saw the thermos bottle half out. She jerked it from the hole. The milk was all gone, and across the little fire Olive stared at her teacher.

"It was mine," the girl said flatly.

So the time had come when the little food left must be hidden. Now, with all but Olive sleeping, was the time. When Lecia came back in, the girl held out something—the ring that had been left hanging on the twig and forgotten.

The next day and the next were the same, only colder, the drifts deeper and harder along the willows, the wind so sharp with snow that it froze the eyeballs. Lecia and Chuck covered their faces as they fought their way back against it, the wood dragging from their shoulders, tied by a strap of cloth cut off around the bottom of Lecia's coat. One at a time they went out and came back, a hand stretched ahead feeling for the next guide pole in the snow before the other let go of the last, the covered face turned from the storm to save the breath from being torn away by the wind.

All the third day, there was watching out of the smoke hole for the sky that never appeared. When night finally came without star or stillness, even Lecia, who had tried to prepare herself for this eventuality, felt that she could not face another day of blizzard. Maggie no longer sat up now, and both Joanie and Eddie were so sick—their fever high, their chests filling—that the teacher had to try something. She seemed to remember that the early settlers used willow bark to break a fever, so she steeped a handful in Maggie's tin cup until the liquid was strong and dark. She made the two children drink it, first experimentally, then more, and after a while they began to sweat. When they awoke, they were wet, their hair clinging to their vulnerable young foreheads, but they seemed better all the next day, except weak. Then, at night, it was the same with Joanie.

The fourth day was like the rest, colder, with the same white storm outside, the children hunching silent upon themselves inside. Sometimes a small one sobbed a little in sickness and hunger, but it was no more than a soft moaning now, even when Lecia divided most of the little food that was left. The children, even Chuck, took it like animals, and then sat silent again, the deep-socketed eyes watching, some slyly gnawing at willow sticks and roots hidden in the palm.

Everybody around the fire was coughing and fevered now, it seemed to Lecia, the bickering going beyond childish things to quarrels about real or fancied animosities between their families. Once, even Calla spoke angrily to Bill, defending her brothers.

"At least they aren't mama babies like you!"

"Mama babies! I wouldn't talk if everybody knew that my family got a start in cattle by stealing calves——"

"You can't say such things!" Calla cried, up and reaching for Bill, caught without his brace and unable to flee into the storm, Joanie crying, "Don't! Don't hit my brother!"

When Lecia returned, Chuck was holding the two apart, shaking them both. The teacher spoke in anger and impatience too, now, and Bill's face flushed with embarrassment and shame, the sudden red-like fever in his hunger-grayed cheeks.

Only Maggie, with her poor feet, was quiet, and Olive, sitting as though stunned or somewhere far away. The teacher knew that she should do something for this girl, only eight yet apparently so self-contained. Olive never spoke of her father now, as none of the boys teased Lecia about Baldy anymore. Olive was as remote about him as everything else since the night she drank the milk, and found the ring on a twig.

Too weary to think about it, and knowing she must keep awake in the night, Lecia stretched out for a nap. When she awoke, Olive was sitting exactly the same, but the places of Chuck and Eddie were empty—Eddie out in the blizzard after his night of sweating. Then the boys returned with wood—weak, dragging, almost frozen—and with something that Lecia had to be told outside. There seemed only one willow clump left.

One clump? Then they must start digging at the frozen butts, or even pull down their shelter to keep the fire alive, for now the boys, too, were believing that the storm would blow forever. Yet, toward evening, there was a thinning above the smoke hole, the sun suddenly there like a thin disk of milky ice from the bottom of a cup. It was almost a promise, even though the storm swept the sun away in a few minutes and the wind shifted around to the south, whipping in past the block the boys had in the hole of the shelter. The children shivered, restless. Once Eddie rose from his sleep and fought to get out, go home. When he finally awakened, he lay down in a chill, very close to the fire, and would not move until a stench of burning cloth helped rouse him. Then he drank the bitter willow-bark tea, too, and finally he slept.

Friday morning the sun came out, again toward ten o'clock, the same cold, pale disk, with the snow still running along the earth, running higher than the shelter or Chuck, shutting out everything except the veiled sun. The boy came in, looked around the starved, listless circle at the fire, at the teacher too, with her face that had been so pretty Monday morning gaunt and sooty now.

He laid two red-tipped matches, half of all he had, in the girl's lap. "I'm getting out," he said, and without a protest from anyone, crawled through the hole and was gone.

The children were almost past noticing his desertion now, barely replying when spoken to. If the colds got worse or pneumonia struck, it would be over in a few hours. Maggie hadn't sat up since yesterday, lying flat, staring at the white storm blowing thin above the smoke hole. If any of them wondered how Lecia could keep the fire going alone, with nothing much except the willow butts left, none spoke of it. The teacher sat with her arms hanging between her knees, hopeless.

She finally stirred and put the matches away in waxed paper in her shirt pocket where her ring lay, buttoning the flap down carefully now. Joanie

started to cough again, choking, turned red and then very white under the grime and grayness of her face, lying very still. Now Bill made the first gesture toward his small sister.

"Come here, Doll," he said gently, drawing her awkwardly from Lecia's lap, the child lifting her head slowly, holding herself away, looking up at him as a baby might at a stranger, to be weighed and considered. Then she snuggled against him and in a moment, she was asleep.

After a long time there seemed a dull sound outside, and then Chuck was suddenly back, crawling in almost as though he had not left, panting, in his weakness, from the fight against the wind that had turned north again, and colder.

"Scared an eagle off a drift out there," he finally managed to say. "And there's a critter stuck in the snow— beyond the far willows. Small spring calf. Froze hard, but its meat——"

Then the realization that Chuck was back struck the teacher. She was not alone with the children, and he, too, was safe for now. But there was something more. The boy who had resented them and his involvement in their plight—he had escaped and come back.

"Oh, Chuck!" the girl exclaimed. Then what he said reached her mind. "A calf? Maybe we could build a fire there so we can cut some off, if we can't get it all out." She reached for her boots. "But we'll have to go work at it one at a time ——" looking around the firelit faces that were turned toward her as before, but the eyes alert, watching, as though a morsel might be dropped, even thrown.

"I'll go with Chuck, Miss Lecia," Bill said softly. "He can show me and I'll show you. Save time hunting——"

The teacher looked at the crippled boy, already setting Joanie gently aside and reaching for his brace. She felt pride in him, and unfortunate doubt.

"He can probably make it," Chuck said, a little condescending. "It's not over an eighth of a mile, and I found more willows farther along the way, the drifts mostly frozen hard too. I blazed the willows beyond our poles——"

"You'll be careful—mark everything," the girl pleaded.

"We've got to. It's snowing again, and the sun's gone."

It seemed hours since the boys went out, and finally the teacher had to go after them, appalled that the younger ones had to be left alone; yet it must be done. She moved very carefully, feeling her way in the new storm, going sideways to it, from pole to pole. Then she came to a place where the markers were gone, probably blown down and buried by the turning wind. The boys were out there, lost, in at least fifteen, perhaps twenty, below zero. Without sticks to guide her way back, the girl dared go no farther, but she crouched there, bowed before the wind, cupping her mouth with her mittens, shouting her hopeless: "Boys! Chuck! O-hoo!" the wind snatching it away. She kept calling until she was shaking and frozen and then, to a frightening warmth.

But now she had to keep on, for it seemed that she heard something, a vague, smothered sound, and yet a little like a reply. Tears freezing on her face, she called again and again, until suddenly the boys were at her feet, there before she could see them, so much like the snow, like white dragging animals, one bowed, half carrying the other. For a few minutes they crouched together in desperate relief, the snow running over them as something immovable, like an old willow butt. Then, together, they pulled themselves up and started back. When they finally reached the shelter, out of breath and frozen, they said nothing of what had happened, nor spoke at all for a while. Yet all, even little Joanie, seemed to sense that the boys had almost been lost.

As soon as the teacher was warmed a little, she started out alone, not certain that she could make it against the storm, but knowing that she must try to get meat. She took Chuck's knife, some dry bark, waxed paper, the two matches in her shirt pocket, and a bundle of poles pulled from their shelter. Moving very carefully beyond the gap in the willow markers, she set new sticks deep, and tipped carefully with the new storm. She found the farther willow clumps with Chuck's blazing, and the brush pile the boys had made, and beside it, the ice-covered head of the calf still reaching out of the snow. The hole they had dug around the red hindquarters was drifted-in loosely, but easily dug out. Lecia set a fire pile there and felt for a match with her numb fingers, fishing in the depths of her pocket; something round in the way, her ring. But she got the match, and lighted the fire under her shielding sheepskin coat. For a long time she crouched protectively over the flame, the wind carrying away the stench of burning calf hair. As the skin thawed, she hacked at it the way Indians must have done here a thousand years ago, their stone knives sharper and more expertly handled.

At a sound, she looked over her shoulder and saw a coyote not three feet away, gaunt-bellied too, and apparently no more afraid than a hungry dog. But

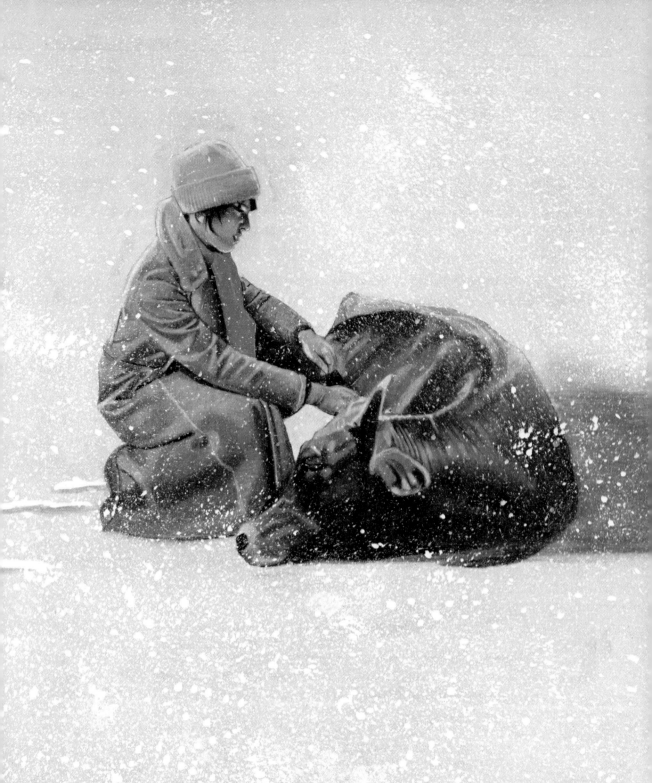

suddenly he caught the human smell, even against the wind, and was gone. He would have made a soft rug at the fire, Lecia thought, and wondered if he might not return to watch just beyond the wall of storm. But she was too busy to look. As the heat penetrated the meat, she cut off one slice after another, until she had a little smoky pile—not much for nine people who had lived five days on one lunch apiece, but enough to bring tears that were not all from the storm. In this meat, perhaps three pounds, might lie the life of her pupils.

Lecia scattered the fresh ashes over the calf to keep the coyotes away, and piled brush into the fire hole. Then she headed sideways into the storm, so violent that it was a good thing she had the strength of a little cautious meat inside her, for it seemed no one could face the wounding snow. Numb and frightened, she managed to hold herself, not get hurried, panicked, never move until the next broken willow, the next marker was located. So she got back, to find Chuck out near the shelter digging wood from the old clumps, watching, uneasy.

It was hard for the children to wait while the thinner slices of meat roasted around the sticks. When the smell filled the little shelter, Lecia passed out toasted bits to be chewed very slowly and well. It tasted fine, and none asked for bread or salt—not even Olive, still silent and alone. She accepted the meat, but returned only distant gravity for the teacher's smile.

By now, the white blizzard darkness was coming back, but before they slept, there was a little piece of boiled veal for each and a little hot broth. It was a more cheerful sleeping time, even a confident one, although in the night they were struck by the diarrhea that Lecia had expected. But that was from the fresh meat and should not last.

By now Lecia could build a coal bed with rotten wood and ashes to hold a fire a long time, even with diamond willows, and so she dressed Maggie's feet, the girl light as a sack of bird bones, and prepared the night fire. For a while, Chuck and Eddie kept each other awake with stories of coyote hunts and with plans for another morning of storm—the sixth. The two boys met the day with so much confidence that Lecia had to let them go out into the storm. Eddie, only ten, suddenly became a little old man in his seriousness as he explained their plans carefully. They would make a big brush pile so that they could settle out of the wind and work the fire until they got a whole hindquarter of the calf hacked off. So the teacher watched them go out very full of hope, the hope of meat, one of the half blankets along to drag their prize in over the snow, like great hunters returning.

Bill had looked sadly after the disappearing boot soles, but without complaint. He helped Lecia with the smaller children, washing at the grime of their faces that would never yield, except to soap, and took them out into the storm and back while the teacher soaked Maggie's great, swollen feet and tried to keep the girl from knowing that the bone ends of her toes could be seen in the suppurating[4] pits of dying flesh. There were holes on the tops of the toes too, along the edges of her feet, and up the heels as high as the ankle. But above there the swelling seemed looser, the red streaks perhaps no farther up the bony legs. Once Bill

---

4. suppurating (sŭp′yə-rāt′ĭng) adj.: Festering; forming pus.

looked over the teacher's shoulder and then, anxiously, into her face. Others had chilblains—his own feet were swollen from yesterday—but not like this.

"Will she lose——" he started to whisper, but he could not put the rest into words, not with a crippled foot himself.

The air was thick and white with new snow whipped by a northwest wind when Lecia went out for a little wood and to watch for the boys. But they were, once more, within touching distance before she could see them—very cold and backing awkwardly into the storm through the soft, new drifts, but dragging a whole hindquarter of the calf. It was a lot of meat, and surely the wind must finally blow itself out, the clouds be drained.

By the time Eddie and Chuck were warm, they knew they had eaten too much roasted veal while they worked. Next, Olive became sick and Fritz, their deprived stomachs refusing the sudden meat, accepting only the broth. During the night, the nausea struck Lecia too, and left her so weak that she could scarcely lift her head all the next day. That night Chuck lost his voice for a while, and Joanie was worse again, her mind full of terrors, the cough so deep, so exhausting, that Bill made a little tent over her face with the skirt of his coat to carry steam from a bucket of boiling snow water to her face. Then sometime toward morning, the wind turned and cut into the southeast corner of the shelter, crumbling the whole side inward.

The boys crawled out to patch it with brush and snow softened at the fire, Lecia helping dry off the children as much as she could. Then when they were done and she laid her swimming head down, she heard a coyote's thin, high howl and realized that the wind was dying. Through the smoke hole she saw the running snow like pale windrows of cloud against the sky, and between them stars shining, far pale stars. As one or another awoke, she directed sleepy eyes to look up. Awed, Joanie looked a second time. "You mean they're really stars——?"

"Yes, and maybe there will be sunshine in the morning."

Dawn came early that eighth day, but it seemed that nothing could be left alive in the cold whiteness of the earth that was only frozen scarves of snow flung deep and layered over themselves. The trailing drifts stretched down from the high ridge of hills in the north, so deep that they made a long, sliding slope of it far over the meadow and up the wind-whipped hills beyond, with not a dark spot anywhere to the horizon—not a yucca or fence post or willow above the snow. In the first touch of the sun, the frozen snow sparkled in the deep silence following a long, long storm. Then out of the hills a lone grouse came cackling over the empty meadow, gleaming silver underneath as she flew, her voice carrying loud in the cold stillness.

But the meadow was not completely empty, for out of a little white mound of drifted willows a curl of smoke rose, and spread thin and blue along the hill. There was another sound too, farther, steadier than the cackle of the grouse, a sound seeming to come from all around and even under the feet.

"A plane!" Chuck shouted hoarsely, bursting out into the blinding sunlight.

Several other dark figures crept out behind him into the frosty air, their

breath a cloud about them as they stood looking northward. A big plane broke from the horizon over the hills, seeming high up, and then another, flying lower. Foolishly, Chuck and Eddie started to shout. "Help! Hello! Help!" they cried, waving their arms as they ran toward the planes, as though to hasten their sight, their coming.

But almost at once the sky was empty, the planes circling and gone. For a long time, the boys stared into the broad, cold sky, pale, with nothing in it except wind streaks that were stirring along the ground too, setting feather curls of snow to running.

"Quick! Let's make a big smudge!" Lecia called out, her voice loud in the unaccustomed quiet, and fearful. She threw water on the fire inside, driving smoke out of the hole, while the boys set the snowy woodpile to burning.

Before the smoke could climb far, there were planes up over the north hills again, coming fast. Now even Fritz got out into the stinging cold—everybody except Joanie, held back by Lecia, and Olive, who did not move from her place. Maggie was lifted up by the teacher to watch through the smoke hole as something tumbled from the higher plane, came falling down. Then it opened out like the waxy white bloom of the yucca, and settled toward the snow, with several other smaller chutes, bright as poppies, opening behind.

There was shouting and talk outside the shelter, and while Lecia was hurrying to get the children into their caps and boots, a man came crawling into the shelter with a bag—a doctor. In the light of the fire and a flashlight, he looked swiftly at Joanie and then at Olive, considered her unchanging face, lifted the lids of her eyes, smiled, and got no response. Then he examined the poor feet of Maggie, the girl like a skin-bound skeleton in this first sharp light, her eyes dark and fearful on the man's face.

The doctor nodded reassuringly to Lecia, and smiled down at Maggie.

"You're a tough little girl!" he said. "Tough as the barbed wire you have out in this country. But you're lucky somebody thought to try snow against the gangrene——" He filled a little syringe and fingered cotton as he looked around to divert the child.

"All nine of you alive, the boys say. Amazing! Somebody got word to a telephone during the night, but we had no hope for any of you. Small children lost eight days without food, with fifty inches of snow at thirty-eight below zero. Probably a hundred people dead through the country. The radio in the plane picked up a report that six were found frozen in a car stalled on the highway—not over five miles from town. I don't see how you managed here."

The doctor rubbed the punctured place in the child's arm a little, covered it, smiling into her fearful eyes, as men with a stretcher broke into the front of the shelter.

When they got outside, the air was loud with engine roar, several planes flying around overhead, two with skis already up toward the shelter, and a helicopter, hovering like a brownish dragonfly, settling. Men in uniform were running toward the children, motioning where they should be brought.

They came along the snow trail broken by the stretcher men, but walking through it as through the storm. Lecia, suddenly trembling, shaking, her feet unsteady on the frozen snow, was still in the lead, the others behind her, and Chuck once more at the end. Bill, limping awkwardly, carried little Joanie, who clung very close to her brother. They were followed by Calla and Eddie, with Fritz between them, and then the stretcher with Maggie. Only Olive, of all the children, walked alone, just ahead of Chuck, and brushing aside all help.

There were men running toward the bedraggled, sooty little string now, men with cameras, and others, among them some who cried, joyous as children, and who must be noticed, must be acknowledged soon—Olive's father and Dale Stever of the yellow plane——

But for now, for this little journey back from the smoke-holed shelter of snow, the awkward queue stayed together.

Close Up

1. When Lecia awakens in the middle of the night, she hears cattle bawling. Why does this frighten her?

2. Lecia's knowledge of woodcraft helps her to face two crises. (a) Why does she place Maggie's legs in two deep holes in the snow wall? (b) Why does she give Joanie and Eddie a drink made from willow bark?

3. Why does Lecia feel hopeless after Chuck deserts the group?

4. (a) Why does Chuck change his mind and come back to the group? (b) Do you think this decision shows that he has matured? Why or why not?

5. **Composition.** After eight days the group is rescued. Select one character and write a paragraph telling how this character changed during the eight days.

VISTAS

Beware of the Dog

Roald Dahl

During World War II, Peter Williamson bails out of his plane over the English Channel. On one side of the Channel is England, but on the other side is Nazi-occupied France.

Down below there was only a vast, white, undulating sea of cloud. Above there was the sun, and the sun was white like the clouds, because it is never yellow when one looks at it from high in the air.

He was still flying the Spitfire. His right hand was on the stick, and he was working the rudder bar with his left leg alone. It was quite easy. The machine was flying well, and he knew what he was doing.

Everything is fine, he thought. I'm doing all right. I'm doing nicely. I know my way home. I'll be there in half an hour. When I land I shall taxi in and switch off my engine and I shall say, help me to get out, will you. I shall make my voice sound ordinary and natural and none of them will take any notice. Then I shall say, someone help me to get out. I can't do it alone because I've lost one of my legs. They'll all laugh and think that I'm joking, and I shall say, all right, come and have a look. Then Yorky will climb up onto the wing and look inside. He'll probably be sick because of all the blood and the mess. I shall laugh and say, for heaven's sake, help me out.

He glanced down again at his right leg. There was not much of it left. The cannon shell had taken him on the thigh, just above the knee, and now there was nothing but a great mess and a lot of blood. But there was no pain. When he looked down, he felt as though he were seeing something that did not belong to him. It had nothing to do with him. It was just a mess which happened to be there in the cockpit—something strange and unusual and rather interesting. It was like finding a dead cat on the sofa.

He really felt fine, and because he still felt fine, he felt excited and unafraid.

I won't even bother to call up on the radio for the blood wagon, he thought. It isn't necessary. And when I land I'll sit there quite normally and say, "Some of you fellows come and help me out, will

Beware of the Dog **285**

you, because I've lost one of my legs." That will be funny. I'll laugh a little while I'm saying it, I'll say it calmly and slowly, and they'll think I'm joking. When Yorky comes up onto the wing and gets sick, I'll say, "Yorky, have you fixed my car yet?" Then when I get out I'll make my report and later I'll go up to London. I won't say much until it's time to go to bed. Then I'll say, "Bluey, I've got a surprise for you. I lost a leg today. But I don't mind, so long as you don't. It doesn't even hurt. We'll go everywhere in cars." I always hated walking, except when I walked down the street of the coppersmiths in Baghdad, but I could go in a rickshaw. I could go home and chop wood, but the head always flies off the ax. Hot water, that's what it needs, put it in the bath and make the handle swell. I chopped lots of wood last time I went home, and I put the ax in the bath. . . .

Then he saw the sun shining on the engine cowling[1] of his machine. He saw the rivets in the metal, and he remembered where he was. He realized that he was no longer feeling good; that he was sick and giddy. His head kept falling forward onto his chest because his neck seemed no longer to have any strength. But he knew that he was flying the Spitfire, and he could feel the handle of the stick between the fingers of his right hand.

I'm going to pass out, he thought. Any moment now I'm going to pass out.

He looked at his altimeter. Twenty-one thousand. To test himself he tried to read the hundreds as well as the thousands. Twenty-one thousand and what?

---

1. cowling (kou'lĭng) n.: The engine's removable metal covering.

As he looked, the dial became blurred, and he could not even see the needle. He knew then that he must bail out; that there was not a second to lose, otherwise he would become unconscious. Quickly, frantically, he tried to slide back the hood with his left hand, but he had not the strength. For a second he took his right hand off the stick, and with both hands he managed to push the hood back. The rush of cold air on his face seemed to help. He had a moment of great clearness, and his actions became orderly and precise. That is what happens with a good pilot. He took some quick deep breaths from his oxygen mask, and as he did so, he looked out over the side of the cockpit. Down below there was only a vast white sea of cloud, and he realized that he did not know where he was.

It'll be the Channel, he thought. I'm sure to fall in the drink.

He throttled back, pulled off his helmet, undid his straps, and pushed the stick hard over to the left. The Spitfire dipped its port wing, and turned smoothly over onto its back. The pilot fell out.

As he fell he opened his eyes, because he knew that he must not pass out before he had pulled the cord. On one side he saw the sun; on the other he saw the whiteness of the clouds, and as he fell, as he somersaulted in the air, the white clouds chased the sun and the sun chased the clouds. They chased each other in a small circle; they ran faster and faster, and there was the sun and the clouds and the clouds and the sun, and the clouds came nearer until suddenly there was no longer any sun, but only a great whiteness. The whole world was white, and there was nothing in it. It was so white that sometimes it looked black, and after a time it was either white or black, but mostly it was white. He watched it as it turned from white to black, and then back to white again, and the white stayed for a long time, but the black lasted only for a few seconds. He got into the habit of going to sleep during the white periods, and of waking up just in time to see the world when it was black. But the black was very quick. Sometimes it was only a flash, like someone switching off the light, and switching it on again at once, and so whenever it was white, he dozed off.

One day, when it was white, he put out a hand and he touched something. He took it between his fingers and crumpled it. For a time he lay there, idly letting the tips of his fingers play with the thing which they had touched. Then slowly he opened his eyes, looked down at his hand, and saw that he was holding something which was white. It was the edge of a sheet. He knew it was a sheet because he could see the texture of the material and the stitchings on the hem. He screwed up his eyes, and opened them again quickly. This time he saw the room. He saw the bed in which he was lying; he saw the gray walls and the door and the green curtains over the window. There were some roses on the table by his bed.

Then he saw the basin on the table near the roses. It was a white enamel basin, and beside it there was a small medicine glass.

This is a hospital, he thought. I am in a hospital. But he could remember nothing. He lay back on his pillow, looking at the ceiling and wondering what had happened. He was gazing at the smooth grayness of the ceiling which was so clean and gray, and then suddenly he saw a fly walking upon it. The sight of this fly, the suddenness of seeing this small black speck on a sea of gray, brushed the surface of his brain, and quickly, in that second, he remembered everything. He remembered the Spitfire and he remembered the altimeter showing twenty-one thousand feet. He remembered the pushing back of the hood with both hands, and he remembered the bailing out. He remembered his leg.

It seemed all right now. He looked down at the end of the bed, but he could not tell. He put one hand underneath the bedclothes and felt for his knees. He found one of them, but when he felt for the other, his hand touched something which was soft and covered in bandages.

Just then the door opened and a nurse came in.

"Hello," she said. "So you've waked up at last."

She was not good-looking, but she was large and clean. She was between thirty and forty and she had fair hair. More than that he did not notice.

"Where am I?"

"You're a lucky fellow. You landed in a wood near the beach. You're in Brighton.[2] They brought you in two days ago, and now you're all fixed up. You look fine."

"I've lost a leg," he said.

"That's nothing. We'll get you another one. Now you must go to sleep. The doctor will be coming to see you in about an hour." She picked up the basin and the medicine glass and went out.

But he did not sleep. He wanted to

---

2. Brighton (brīt'n) n.: A city in southern England.

keep his eyes open because he was frightened that if he shut them again everything would go away. He lay looking at the ceiling. The fly was still there. It was very energetic. It would run forward very fast for a few inches, then it would stop. Then it would run forward again, stop, run forward, stop, and every now and then it would take off and buzz around viciously in small circles. It always landed back in the same place on the ceiling and started running and stopping all over again. He watched it for so long that after a while it was no longer a fly, but only a black speck upon a sea of gray, and he was still watching it when the nurse opened the door, and stood aside while the doctor came in. He was an Army doctor, a major, and he had some last war ribbons on his chest. He was bald and small, but he had a cheerful face and kind eyes.

"Well, well," he said. "So you've decided to wake up at last. How are you feeling?"

"I feel all right."

"That's the stuff. You'll be up and about in no time."

The doctor took his wrist to feel his pulse.

"By the way," he said, "some of the lads from your squadron were ringing up and asking about you. They wanted to come along and see you, but I said that they'd better wait a day or two. Told them you were all right, and that they could come and see you a little later on. Just lie quiet and take it easy for a bit. Got something to read?" He glanced at the table with the roses. "No. Well, nurse will look after you. She'll get you anything you want." With that he waved his hand and went out, followed by the large clean nurse.

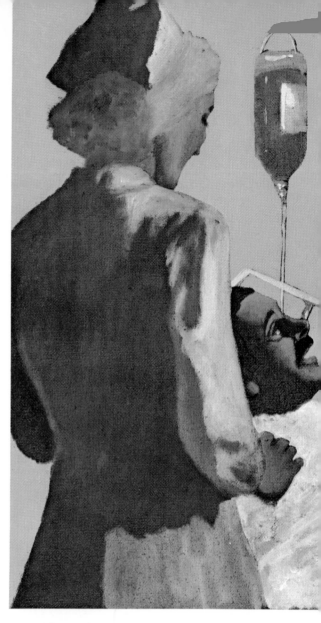

When they had gone, he lay back and looked at the ceiling again. The fly was still there, and, as he lay watching it, he heard the noise of an airplane in the distance. He lay listening to the sound of its engines. It was a long way away. I wonder what it is, he thought. Let me see if I can place it. Suddenly he jerked his head sharply to one side. Anyone who has been bombed can tell the noise of a

where were the sirens, and where the guns? That German pilot had a nerve coming near Brighton alone in daylight.

The aircraft was always far away and soon the noise faded away into the distance. Later on there was another. This one, too, was far away but there was the same deep, undulating bass and the high, singing tenor, and there was no mistaking it. He had heard that noise every day during the battle.

He was puzzled. There was a bell on the table by the bed. He reached out his hand and rang it. He heard the noise of footsteps down the corridor, and the nurse came in.

"Nurse, what were those airplanes?"

"I'm sure I don't know. I didn't hear them. Probably fighters or bombers. I expect they were returning from France. Why, what's the matter?"

"They were JU-88's. I'm sure they were JU-88's. I know the sound of the engines. There were two of them. What were they doing over here?"

The nurse came up to the side of his bed and began to straighten the sheets and tuck them in under the mattress.

"Gracious me, what things you imagine. You mustn't worry about a thing like that. Would you like me to get you something to read?"

"No, thank you."

She patted his pillow and brushed back the hair from his forehead with her hand.

"They never come over in daylight any longer. You know that. They were probably Lancasters or Flying Fortresses."

"Nurse."

"Yes."

Junkers 88. They can tell most other German bombers for that matter, but especially a Junkers 88. The engines seem to sing a duet. There is a deep vibrating bass voice and with it there is a high-pitched tenor. It is the singing of the tenor which makes the sound of a JU-88 something which one cannot mistake.

He lay listening to the noise, and he felt quite certain about what it was. But

"Could I have a cigarette?"

"Why certainly you can."

She went out and came back almost at once with a packet of Players and some matches. She handed one to him and when he had put it in his mouth, she struck a match and lit it.

"If you want me again," she said, "just ring the bell," and she went out.

Once toward evening he heard the noise of another aircraft. It was far away, but even so he knew that it was a single-engined machine. But he could not place it. It was going fast; he could tell that. But it wasn't a Spit, and it wasn't a Hurricane. It did not sound like an American engine either. They make more noise. He did not know what it was, and it worried him greatly. Perhaps I am very ill, he thought. Perhaps I am imagining things. Perhaps I am a little delirious. I simply do not know what to think.

That evening the nurse came in with a basin of hot water and began to wash him.

"Well," she said, "I hope you don't still think that we're being bombed."

She had taken off his pajama top and was soaping his right arm with a flannel. He did not answer.

She rinsed the flannel in the water, rubbed more soap on it, and began to wash his chest.

"You're looking fine this evening," she said. "They operated on you as soon as you came in. They did a marvelous job. You'll be all right. I've got a brother in the RAF,"[3] she added. "Flying bombers."

He said, "I went to school in Brighton."

---

3. RAF: Royal (British) Air Force.

She looked up quickly. "Well, that's fine," she said. "I expect you'll know some people in the town."

"Yes," he said, "I know quite a few."

She had finished washing his chest and arms, and now she turned back the bedclothes, so that his left leg was uncovered. She did it in such a way that his bandaged stump remained under the sheets. She undid the cord of his pajama trousers and took them off. There was no trouble because they had cut off the right trouser leg, so that it could not interfere with the bandages. She began to wash his left leg and the rest of his body. This was the first time he had had a bed bath, and he was embarrassed. She laid a towel under his leg, and she was washing his foot with the flannel. She said, "This wretched soap won't lather at all. It's the water. It's as hard as nails."

He said, "None of the soap is very good now and, of course, with hard water it's hopeless." As he said it he remembered something. He remembered the baths which he used to take at school in Brighton, in the long stone-floored bathroom which had four baths in a room. He remembered how the water was so soft that you had to take a shower afterward to get all the soap off your body, and he remembered how the foam used to float on the surface of the water, so that you could not see your legs underneath. He remembered that sometimes they were given calcium tablets because the school doctor used to say that soft water was bad for the teeth.

"In Brighton," he said, "the water isn't . . ."

He did not finish the sentence. Something had occurred to him; something so fantastic and absurd that for a moment he felt like telling the nurse about it and having a good laugh.

She looked up. "The water isn't what?" she said.

"Nothing," he answered. "I was dreaming."

She rinsed the flannel in the basin, wiped the soap off his leg, and dried him with a towel.

"It's nice to be washed," he said. "I feel better." He was feeling his face with his hands. "I need a shave."

"We'll do that tomorrow," she said. "Perhaps you can do it yourself then."

That night he could not sleep. He lay awake thinking of the Junkers 88's and of the hardness of the water. He could think of nothing else. They were JU-88's, he said to himself. I know they were. And yet it is not possible, because they would not be flying so low over here in broad daylight. I know that it is true, and yet I know that it is impossible. Perhaps I am ill. Perhaps I am behaving like a fool and do not know what I am doing or saying. Perhaps I am delirious. For a long time he lay awake thinking these things, and once he sat up in bed and said aloud, "I will prove that I am not crazy. I will make a little speech about something complicated and intellectual. I will talk about what to do with Germany after the war." But before he had time to begin, he was asleep.

He woke just as the first light of day was showing through the slit in the curtains over the window. The room was still dark, but he could tell that it was already beginning to get light outside. He lay looking at the gray light which was showing through the slit in the curtain, and, as he lay there, he remembered the day before. He remembered the Junkers 88's and the hardness of the water; he remembered the large pleasant nurse and the kind doctor, and now the small grain of doubt took root in his mind and it began to grow.

He looked around the room. The nurse had taken the roses out the night before, and there was nothing except the table with a packet of cigarettes, a box of matches, and an ashtray. Otherwise, it was bare. It was no longer warm or friendly. It was not even comfortable. It was cold and empty and very quiet.

Slowly the grain of doubt grew, and with it came fear, a light, dancing fear that warned but did not frighten; the kind of fear that one gets not because one is afraid, but because one feels that there is something wrong. Quickly the doubt and the fear grew so that he became restless and angry, and when he touched his forehead with his hand, he found that it was damp with sweat. He knew then that he must do something; that he must find some way of proving to himself that he was either right or wrong, and he looked up and saw again the window and the green curtains. From where he lay, that window was right in front of him, but it was fully ten yards away. Somehow he must reach it and look out. The idea became an obsession with him, and soon he could think of nothing except the window. But what about his leg? He put his hand underneath the bedclothes and felt the thick bandaged stump which was all that was left on the right-hand side. It seemed all right. It didn't hurt. But it would not be easy.

He sat up. Then he pushed the bedclothes aside and put his left leg on the floor. Slowly, carefully, he swung his body over until he had both hands on the floor as well; and then he was out of bed, kneeling on the carpet. He looked at the

Beware of the Dog **291**

stump. It was very short and thick, covered with bandages. It was beginning to hurt and he could feel it throbbing. He wanted to collapse, lie down on the carpet and do nothing, but he knew that he must go on.

With two arms and one leg, he crawled over toward the window. He would reach forward as far as he could with his arms, then he would give a little jump and slide his left leg along after them. Each time he did, it jarred his wound so that he gave a soft grunt of pain, but he continued to crawl across the floor on two hands and one knee. When he got to the window he reached up, and one at a time he placed both hands on the sill. Slowly he raised himself up until he was standing on his left leg. Then quickly he pushed aside the curtains and looked out.

He saw a small house with a gray tiled roof standing alone beside a narrow lane, and immediately behind it there was a plowed field. In front of the house there was an untidy garden, and there was a green hedge separating the garden from the lane. He was looking at the hedge when he saw the sign. It was just a piece of board nailed to the top of a short pole, and because the hedge had not been trimmed for a long time, the branches had grown out around the sign so that it seemed almost as though it had been placed in the middle of the hedge. There was something written on the board with white paint, and he pressed his head against the glass of the window, trying to read what it said. The first letter was a G, he could see that. The second was an A, and the third was an R. One after another he managed to see what the letters were. There were three words, and slowly he spelled the letters out loud

to himself as he managed to read them. G-A-R-D-E A-U C-H-I-E-N. *Garde au chien.*[4] That is what it said.

He stood there balancing on one leg and holding tightly to the edges of the windowsill with his hands, staring at the sign and at the whitewashed lettering of the words. For a moment he could think of nothing at all. He stood there looking at the sign, repeating the words over and over to himself, and then slowly he began to realize the full meaning of the thing. He looked up at the cottage and at the plowed field. He looked at the small orchard on the left of the cottage and he looked at the countryside beyond. "So this is France," he said. "I am in France."

Now the throbbing in his right thigh was very great. It felt as though someone was pounding the end of the stump with a hammer, and suddenly the pain became so intense that it affected his head, and for a moment he thought he was going to fall. Quickly he knelt down again, crawled back to the bed, and hoisted himself in. He pulled the bedclothes over himself and lay back on the pillow exhausted. He could still think of nothing at all except the small sign by the hedges, and the plowed field and the orchard. It was the words on the sign that he could not forget.

It was some time before the nurse came in. She came carrying a basin of hot water and she said, "Good morning, how are you today?"

He said, "Good morning, nurse."

The pain was still great under the bandages, but he did not wish to tell this woman anything. He looked at her as she

---

4. Garde au chien: French words meaning, "Beware of the dog."

busied herself with getting the washing things ready. He looked at her more carefully now. Her hair was very fair. She was tall and big-boned, and her face seemed pleasant. But there was something a little uneasy about her eyes. They were never still. They never looked at anything for more than a moment, and they moved too quickly from one place to another in the room. There was something about her movements also. They were too sharp and nervous to go well with the casual manner in which she spoke.

She set down the basin, took off his pajama top, and began to wash him.

"Did you sleep well?"

"Yes."

"Good," she said. She was washing his arms and his chest.

"I believe there's someone coming down to see you from the Air Ministry after breakfast," she went on. "They want a report or something. I expect you know all about it. How you got shot down and all that. I won't let him stay long, so don't worry."

He did not answer. She finished

GARDE AU CHIEN

washing him, and gave him a toothbrush and some tooth powder. He brushed his teeth, rinsed his mouth, and spat the water out into the basin.

Later she brought him his breakfast on a tray, but he did not want to eat. He was still feeling weak and sick, and he wished only to lie still and think about what had happened. And there was a sentence running through his head. It was a sentence which Johnny, the Intelligence Officer of his squadron, always repeated to the pilots every day before they went out. He could see Johnny now, leaning against the wall of the dispersal hut with his pipe in his hand, saying, "And if they get you, don't forget, just your name, rank, and number. Nothing else. For God's sake, say nothing else."

"There you are," she said as she put the tray on his lap. "I've got you an egg. Can you manage all right?"

"Yes."

She stood beside the bed. "Are you feeling all right?"

"Yes."

"Good. If you want another egg, I might be able to get you one."

"This is all right."

"Well, just ring the bell if you want any more." And she went out.

He had just finished eating, when the nurse came in again.

She said, "Wing Commander Roberts is here. I've told him that he can only stay for a few minutes."

She beckoned with her hand and the Wing Commander came in.

"Sorry to bother you like this," he said.

He was an ordinary RAF officer, dressed in a uniform which was a little shabby, and he wore wings and a DFC.[5] He was fairly tall and thin with plenty of black hair. His teeth, which were irregular and widely spaced, stuck out a little even when he closed his mouth. As he spoke, he took a printed form and a pencil from his pocket, and he pulled up a chair and sat down.

"How are you feeling?"

There was no answer.

"Tough luck about your leg. I know how you feel. I hear you put up a fine show before they got you."

The man in the bed was lying quite still, watching the man in the chair.

The man in the chair said, "Well, let's get this stuff over. I'm afraid you'll have to answer a few questions so that I can fill in this combat report. Let me see now, first of all, what was your squadron?"

The man in the bed did not move. He looked straight at the Wing Commander and he said, "My name is Peter Williamson. My rank is Squadron Leader, and my number is nine seven two four five seven."

---

5. DFC: Distinguished Flying Cross.

1. Peter Williamson fights to remain calm and alert while flying back to base. Do you think his thoughts show that he is really calm or do they show that he is frightened and confused? Why?

2. (a) Why does Peter decide to bail out of the plane? (b) Why does he turn the Spitfire over on its back?

3. When Peter wakes up, he thinks that he is in a hospital in Brighton. (a) Why does the sound of the Junkers 88 overhead make him suspicious? (b) Why are Peter's suspicions further aroused when the nurse complains about the hard water?

5. (a) Where does Peter begin to suspect he is? (b) What finally confirms his suspicions?

6. (a) Why do the nurse and doctor lie to Peter? (b) Why does Peter tell the Wing Commander only his name, rank, and serial number?

Setting

The setting of a story is where and when it occurs. This means that the setting consists of the place and the time of the story. In "Beware of the Dog," Roald Dahl tells you the time, but he keeps you uncertain about the place until near the end of the story.

1. The time of this story is during World War II. Use a dictionary or an encyclopedia to find out when World War II occurred.

2. How does the fact that Peter bails out over the Channel keep you uncertain about the place of the story?

3. List the setting details that make Peter believe he is in Brighton. For example, when Peter wants a cigarette, the nurse gives him a package of Players, a brand of cigarettes popular in England.

4. List the setting detail that convinces Peter he is really in France.

Activities

1. **Composition.** This story is told entirely from the point of view of Peter Williamson. Write a paragraph telling about one incident that occurs in the hospital. Tell about it from the point of view of the nurse, the doctor, or the Wing Commander.

2. Use an encyclopedia to find information about World War II fighter planes. Share this information with your classmates.

INFERENCES

An inference is an intelligent guess based on evidence, or proof.
At the beginning of this story, you probably inferred that Peter is
returning from a bombing mission in France. You based your
inference on the following evidence: Peter is flying a Spitfire,
which is a British fighter plane; he is flying home after being hit;
he is over the English Channel.

1. Use evidence from the story to help you answer each of the
following questions.
   a. Why does Peter take some quick, deep breaths from his
   oxygen mask before he bails out of the plane?
   b. The doctor tells Peter that some lads from his squadron
   have called and asked about him. Why does the doctor
   also say that he told them to wait a few days before coming to visit?
   c. Peter falls asleep thinking about the JU-88's and the hardness of the water. Why does his room feel unfriendly to
   him when he wakes up the next day?
   d. When Peter crawls back into bed after reading the sign
   that says, "*Garde au chien*," his leg throbs painfully. Why
   doesn't he tell the nurse about the pain?
   e. Why does the Wing Commander ask Peter the name of his
   squadron?

2. The author does not tell you how much time Peter spends in
the hospital before he regains consciousness. Reread the last
paragraph on page 286. Find evidence that shows that at least
several days have passed.

3. Find evidence that shows that the nurse is part of the enemy's
plan to get information from Peter.

WORD ATTACK

Understanding Words Used as Nouns and Verbs

A noun is a word that names a person, place, thing, or idea. For example, *parachute*, *hospital*, *pilot*, and *loyalty* are nouns. **A verb is a word that expresses action or a state of being.** For example, *flew*, *throbbed*, and *is* are verbs. Some words may be used as either nouns or verbs. For example, in the following sentence, *slit* is used as a noun that means "a long, narrow opening."

> The light of day was showing through the *slit* in the curtain.

In the next sentence, *slit* is used as a verb that means "to cut."

> They *slit* the leg of his pajamas so that it would not interfere with the bandages.

The meaning of a word in a particular sentence sometimes depends on whether it is used as a noun or a verb.

▶ Read each sentence below. First decide if the word in *italics* is used as a noun or as a verb. Then find its meaning in your dictionary. Write this meaning on a separate piece of paper.

a. After landing, Peter would *taxi* in and turn off the engine.
b. Peter planned to go everywhere in a car or in a *taxi*.
c. He did not *voice* his fears to the nurse.
d. He wanted to make his *voice* sound ordinary.
e. Peter noticed the *rivet* in the engine cowling of the plane.
f. The words on the sign *rivet* his eyes.
g. Parachute jumpers sometimes *somersault* in the air.
h. Peter jumped from the plane and did a *somersault*.
i. Each movement would *jar* his leg and cause him pain.
j. There was a *jar* of medicine on the table.
k. Peter held on to the *edge* of the windowsill.
l. Peter tried to *edge* forward.
m. The Wing Commander wanted Peter to fill out a combat *report*.
n. Peter would *report* only his name, his rank, and his serial number.
o. He attempted to *hoist* himself up onto the bed.
p. They used a *hoist* to load the plane.

Otero's Visitor

Manuela Williams Crosno

Every night they heard footsteps walking back and forth in the room, but when they opened the door, they found no one there.

Many years ago there came to this country from Spain, a noble family named Otero. Many sons there were with much gold claimed from conquest, so that the family was able to establish itself well in the new world. Handsome were the señors and beautiful the señoritas. One of the sons, Adolfo, built for himself a beautiful hacienda, and furnished it with possessions the family had brought with them from Spain. The walls of the long, low building were made of adobe and were four-feet thick. The rooms were built about a patio and many of the doors opened out to it. These doors were of heavy, hand-hewn wood. There were lace curtains at the windows, and the highest of luxuries, an organ, stood in one corner of the long living room near the fireplace. It was beautifully made of

carved wood and was supported with heavy carved legs. The organ had been brought from Spain by way of Mexico City and a long three-months' journey northward on an ox-cart.

There were many sons and daughters born in the hacienda of Adolfo Otero, and it became a place of laughter and song and music. Young people and old for miles about found it a place in which to make merry, and always there was about it the feeling of warm hospitality. Happy indeed were they who dwelled within its walls.

As Don Adolfo grew older and could no longer count the white hairs among the black, but could more easily count the black ones among the white, he thought that life had given him all that he could desire. One by one the sons and daughters had married and established haciendas for themselves, and now Don Adolfo lived alone except for his wife and two servants. But still there came to the house many who were friends, and some who were strangers, for the weary traveler who had heard about the open hospitality was accustomed to stop here on his journeys and spend the night.

Now this is a country of many winds. Sometimes the soft winds blow from the southwest and travel close to the ground. They are the winds that sing songs in the yucca[1] and grasses that grow on the mesa. But sometimes the hard winds blow from the east and bring snow, if it is winter, or sand. The sand blows hard into the face of the traveler and beats against his horse so that he is driven to seek shelter. One day, there came such a wind. All day it beat about

---

1. yucca (yŭk'ə) n.: A plant that grows in the Southwest; the state flower of New Mexico.

the hacienda of Don Otero and blew the white sands and the brown sands in piles against the doors and windows. No one ventured out on this day, and even when the sun vanished behind the mountains, leaving a trail of smoldering fire, the wind did not abate. In the darkness of the night, it seemed even worse than it had been in the daytime.

The two servants and Doña Otero retired early, but Don Adolfo remained in the living room. Two or three times he paced back and forth, back and forth, with an assuring step, as if to tell the elements he was calm and at peace. Then he seated himself before the fireplace, where he sat looking into the embers, dreaming who-knows-what dreams. A handsome figure he made sitting there, smoking his pipe, his hair falling down to his shoulders in the soft whiteness like snowbanks in the early morning. His eyes were black and still much alive with the vitality of living. Like coals they glowed as the light before him flickered and threw shadows upon the wall. He wore a black jacket, trimmed in fine black satin, and black trousers. About his waist was tied a sash of bright colors. Suddenly his revery was interrupted by a hasty pounding on his door. Don Adolfo pulled back the heavy bars that formed the lock, and the great carved door swung open to admit a stranger. He seemed in great agitation and would not remove his hat; nor would he partake of the warmth before the fire, or wait for some of the wine Otero offered to bring for him. He was a young man, well formed. His black beard stood out in sharp contrast to the white face beneath it.

"They are coming," he said, seeming to assume that Don Adolfo knew who "they" might be. "This they must not find!" And he drew from his coat a small box of carved wood and thrust it into the hand of Don Adolfo.

"You shall hide it for me and when I come again you shall give it to me! Guard it with your life! Hide it carefully and tell no one!" With these words, the man turned, opened the door, and it closed quickly behind him. In a moment, Don Adolfo heard the sound of horse hoofs as the stranger rode quickly away.

Amazed, Otero stood and held the little carved box. Then he walked closer to the firelight and examined it. It was curiously carved, but whether or not it was locked, Otero never knew, for he was a Spanish gentleman—a caballero! Then, recalling the command of his visitor, he walked over to the old organ, opened a secret panel in one of the heavy wooden legs, and here he carefully inserted the box and closed the panel. Don Adolfo smiled to himself with satisfaction, because he had been able to hide the box so well. Even his wife did not know of this place.

He went back and sat down before the fire. Soon there was a clatter of hoofs, and three armed men stood in his doorway.

"Has someone stopped here?" they asked, glancing around the room. "Have you heard anyone pass?"

Otero held his head to one side as if thinking. "A few minutes ago I heard horse hoofs flying down the road in a great hurry!" he said.

The years continued to throw their days across the path of Don Adolfo, but he did not forget the stranger who had placed a box in his keeping, nor did he forget to guard the trust that had been given him. He waited for the return of the man, and, indeed, he never thought to open the secret panel, until the stranger should return to claim his property. And one day Don Adolfo died, taking with him the secret of the little carved box and its hiding place. His estate was settled by his sons, and all of his obligations known to them were dutifully discharged.

The eldest son, Reyes, moved into the hacienda with his wife, in order to be with his mother, who was also grown quite old. Reyes was much like his father, an honorable man, but times were different. With the oncoming of American civilization, ranchos sprang up along the old road, which was now repaired often, and here and there little villages grew, so that it was no longer necessary for strangers to seek hospitality in the open countryside. For days at a time, however, the hacienda would ring with the laughter of young people and of old, when Reyes would call them there for a fiesta to honor the old days. And the good people would sit about with lighted faces, speaking of Don Adolfo, and the many fine times they had enjoyed under that very roof. The younger ones would gather about the old organ, standing in one corner of the long living room where it had always stood, and sing songs.

"It is a fine instrument," said Don Reyes, in praise of the organ. "Each day its tone becomes more and more mellow!"

One moonlight night, when the wind was blowing, Carla, the wife of Reyes, was awakened by a sound in the house. She arose quickly and walked to the living-room door. Just outside the room she listened. Yes, she was sure of it! There were footsteps walking slowly up and down the room, back and forth, back and forth! Quiet, assured footsteps!

They sounded as if they knew where they were going! She opened the door, but could see no one in the moonlighted room. She walked across to the organ and back, but no one was there.

The next morning she told her husband, and that night, he, too, listened, but they heard nothing. Smiling at her, he told her he thought she had been mistaken, but she implored him to listen with her again. On this night, too, they heard nothing. For six nights they listened, and on the seventh night, when the wind was blowing, they heard the footsteps walking back and forth, back and forth, the full length of the living room and then pausing before the organ. But when they entered the room, no one was there. Soon they learned to expect the footsteps just before ten o'clock each night that the wind blew, and promptly at ten-thirty they would cease and not be heard again. Reyes and Carla might have been frightened, but there was a reassurance in the walk that quieted their fears.

They said nothing to the old Doña, the wife of Don Adolfo, thinking that it would alarm her. Great was the surprise of Don Reyes, therefore, on a certain morning, to come upon his mother, walking back and forth in the living room, back and forth, back and forth. For a moment he thought it might have been she whom he and his wife had heard, but his mother's footsteps were much lighter, and besides, she could not have disappeared so quickly. He and his wife had never been able to intercept their visitor.

So he asked, "Mamacita, what do you do here?"

She looked at him a moment, quietly. "Don Adolfo, your father, walks in this room many nights," she said. "I am trying to find what is disturbing his spirit!"

There was conviction upon her face, and Don Reyes knew then that the footsteps he had heard were as the footsteps of his father. Many times had he heard him walk in just this fashion; and that, he thought, was why the footsteps did not frighten or alarm him. They were familiar ones! He needed time to think about this thing! So he said to his mother, "Do not be perturbed, Mamacita! My father was a good man. We will find out what is disturbing him. I will help you!" And he patted her gently upon her stooped shoulders.

So Don Reyes remained alone in the living room each evening when the wind brought sand, and he sat quietly before the fireplace, looking almost like his father. But nothing happened, although Don Reyes sat there for many evenings, hearing the footsteps.

One Friday, there came a sandstorm. All day the wind beat sand and whirled it in heaps about the hacienda; there was a constant pelting of sand against the windows—the white sands and the brown sands. No one ventured to leave the house. After the sun had set, the wind seemed to increase in its fury. But before the fireplace sat Don Reyes waiting for he knew not what—hoping only to assuage the concern of his mother for his father.

Suddenly there came a quick knock at the door and he opened it to admit a stranger. The man looked at him uncertainly in the dim light. Reyes closed the door and pushed the heavy bars against it to keep out the wind and sand. The stranger seemed greatly agitated. He was a middle-aged man, well formed. A black

beard stood out in sharp contrast to his white face.

Without sitting down, he began, "But I thought you were Otero—Señor Adolfo Otero! As I came past the window and saw you sitting there, I thought——"

And Reyes added, "He was my father."

The man hesitated, as if weighing in his mind whether to inform Reyes of the purpose of his visit. Then he spoke, "A son of Adolfo Otero could not be other than trustworthy. I come for a box left in the keeping of your father."

"Come," said Reyes, "sit here."

And he pointed the stranger to a

chair before the fireplace. The man sat down without removing his coat, as one in a daze, and said something under his breath in a queer mumble that Reyes did not understand.

"Come," Reyes said again, "make yourself comfortable. You are but chilled from the wind! I do not know where my father left your box, but I will try to think where it might be. Let me bring some wine for you."

The stranger did not answer. He sat stooped over in his chair toward the fire, in a disconsolate manner.

As Reyes reached the door leading out of the room, he heard the footsteps. That the man by the fireplace heard them also, he knew by the startled look in his eyes as he arose quickly to his feet and stared at Reyes.

Reyes smiled. "Do not be alarmed," he said reassuringly.

The footsteps had walked over to the organ, and stopped. Reyes closed the door behind him, and went to bring the wine. In a short time, he returned.

The outside door stood open. The stranger had disappeared. As Reyes stood in the room and looked about him, his eyes saw a small panel in the leg of the organ slide softly shut. Then he heard the footsteps for the last time. The wind from the entrance blew the door open leading to the patio, and the curtains parted as if someone walked through them and closed them gently.

Reyes Otero closed the outer door against the fury of the wind, and hastened to the organ, where he stooped to examine the place in which he had seen the opening close. When his fingers found the secret panel and slid it open, he knew that his father's last trust had been honorably discharged. The little enclosure was empty!

Close Up

1. (a) Why does the young man ask Don Otero to hide the box for him? (b) What are his exact instructions?

2. A caballero is a gentleman—a man of honor. How does the fact that Don Otero is a caballero help explain why he doesn't know whether or not the box is locked?

3. How does Don Otero fulfill his duty, even after death?

Setting

The author of a story helps you see and feel the setting by using description. For example, in "Otero's Visitor," the author helps you experience the setting by including specific details and creating vivid impressions.

1. Which of the following details describe Don Otero's hacienda?
   a. A long, low building made of adobe.
   b. Furnished in a modern style.
   c. Rooms built around a patio.
   d. Doors of heavy, hand-hewn wood.
   e. A gloomy, cheerless place.
   f. Lace curtains on the windows.

2. This passage creates a vivid impression of the setting:

   "Now this is a country of many winds. Sometimes the soft winds blow from the southwest and travel close to the ground. They are the winds that sing songs in the yucca and grasses that grow on the mesa."

   Find three other statements that help you to picture the setting and feel as though you are there.

Activities

1. Imagine you are producing this story as a radio drama. List sound effects you will need to use.

2. **Composition.** Write a paragraph describing a room. (You might want to describe a messy brother's room, a gym room, a kitchen, etc.) Be sure to include many details to create a vivid impression.

INFERENCES

Making Inferences About Characters

When you make an inference about a character, you make an intelligent guess about what that character is like based on clues in the story. For example, you probably made the inference that Don Otero dresses carefully and well, although the author does not tell you this directly. You based your inference on the following evidence: (1) Don Otero is the descendant of a noble and wealthy family, and (2) his house is furnished tastefully and beautifully. Therefore, it seems to follow that Don Otero dresses carefully and well.

1. To answer the following questions, use evidence from the story to make inferences about Don Otero.
   a. Do you think Don Otero is an unhappy man or a contented man? Why?
   b. Do you think Don Otero's word is respected in his community? Why or why not?
   c. Do you think Don Otero's children honor and respect him? Why or why not?
   d. Do you think Don Otero values his Spanish heritage? Why or why not?

2. The stranger who comes for the box makes an inference about Reyes. He says, "A son of Adolfo Otero could not be other than trustworthy." On what knowledge or evidence does he base his inference?

WORD ATTACK

Using Context to Understand Words from Spanish

English borrows words and phrases from several different languages. One of these languages is Spanish. When you read a Spanish word in a sentence, try to use its context to figure out its meaning. For example, look at the word *hacienda* in the following sentence: "One of the sons, Adolfo, built for himself a beautiful *hacienda*, and furnished it with possessions the family had brought with them from Spain." The rest of the words in the sentence should help you figure out that a *hacienda* is a house.

▶ Use context clues to match the *italicized* Spanish words in the sentences below with the definitions under them.

    a. "Handsome were the *señors* and beautiful the *señoritas*."

    b. "The walls of the long, low building were made of *adobe* and were four-feet thick."

    c. "They are the winds that sing songs in the yucca and grasses that grow on the *mesa*."

    d. "It was curiously carved, but whether or not it was locked, Otero never knew, for he was a Spanish gentleman—a *caballero!*"

    e. "For days at a time, however, the hacienda would ring with the laughter of young people and of old, when Reyes would call them there for a *fiesta* to honor the old days."

    (1) a gentleman

    (2) sun-dried brick used for building houses

    (3) a feast or big party

    (4) plateau or flat land with steep walls of rock

    (5) men

    (6) a large state

    (7) women

The Sea

James Reeves

The sea is a hungry dog,
Giant and gray.
He rolls on the beach all day.
With his clashing teeth and shaggy jaws
5 Hour upon hour he gnaws
The rumbling, tumbling stones,
And "Bones, bones, bones, bones!"
The giant sea-dog moans,
Licking his greasy paws.

10 And when the night wind roars
And the moon rocks in the stormy cloud,
He bounds to his feet and snuffs and sniffs,
Shaking his wet sides over the cliffs,
And howls and hollos long and loud.

15 But on quiet days in May or June,
When even the grasses on the dune
Play no more their reedy tune,
With his head between his paws
He lies on the sandy shores,
20 So quiet, so quiet, he scarcely snores.

Close Up ▶ Make a list of things the sea and a dog have in common.

Back There

Rod Serling

An episode from
The Twilight Zone

Characters

Corrigan, a young skeptic who learns better, and panics

William, an attendant; a calm gentleman who could be either a servant or a millionaire

Captain of Police, incorruptibly dense

Policeman, average

Wellington, tall and authoritative; cape and moustache

Police officer, young and sympathetic

Jackson, clubman

Millard, clubman

Whitaker, clubman

Attendant

Mrs. Landers, a fussy landlady

Lieutenant ⎫ two handsome
His girl ⎭ young people

Landlady

Attendant Two

Two voices

Narrator

Act One

SCENE 1. *Exterior of club at night.*

(Near a large front entrance of double doors is a name plaque in brass which reads "The Washington Club, Founded 1858." In the main hall of the building is a large paneled foyer with rooms leading off on either side. An attendant, William, carrying a tray of drinks, crosses the hall and enters one of the rooms. There are four men sitting around in the aftermath of a card game. Peter Corrigan is the youngest, then two middle-aged men named Whitaker and Millard, and Jackson, the oldest, a white-haired man in his sixties, who motions the tray from the attendant over to the table.)

Jackson: Just put it over here, William, would you?

William: Yes, sir. *(He lays the tray down and walks away from the table.)*

Corrigan: Now what's your point? That if it were possible for a person to go back in time, there'd be nothing in the world to prevent him from altering the course of history—is that it?

Millard: Let's say, Corrigan, that you go back in time. It's October, 1929. The day before the stock market crashed. You know on the following morning that the securities are going to tumble into an abyss. Now, using that prior knowledge, there's a hundred things you can do to protect yourself.

Corrigan: But I'm an anachronism[1]

back there. I don't really belong back there.

Millard: You could sell out the day before the crash.

Corrigan: But what if I did and that started the crash earlier? Now history tells us that on October 24th, 1929, the bottom dropped out of the stock market. That's a fixed date. October 24th, 1929. It exists as an event in the history of our times. It *can't* be altered.

Millard: And I say it can. What's to prevent it? What's to prevent me, say, from going to a broker on the morning of October 23rd?

Corrigan: Gentlemen, I'm afraid I'll have to leave this time travel to H. G. Wells. I'm much too tired to get into any more metaphysics[2] this evening. And since nobody has ever gone back in time, the whole blamed thing is much too theoretical. I'll probably see you over the weekend.

Whittaker: Don't get lost back in time now, Corrigan.

Corrigan: I certainly shall not. Good night, everybody.

Voices: Good night, Pete. Good night, Corrigan. See you tomorrow.

(Corrigan walks out into the hall and heads toward the front door.)

William *(The attendant; going by)*: Good night, Mr. Corrigan.

Corrigan: Good night, William. *(Then he looks at the elderly man a little more closely.)* Everything all right with you William? Looks like you've lost some weight.

William *(With a deference built of a*

---

1. anachronism (ə-năk′rə-nĭz′əm) n.: Something that doesn't belong to the time period.

2. metaphysics (mĕt′ə-fĭz′ĭks) n.: A branch of philosophy that studies existence and reality.

forty-year habit pattern): Just the usual worries, sir. The stars and my salary are fixed. It's the cost of living that goes up.

(Corrigan smiles, reaches in his pocket, starts to hand him a bill.)

William: Oh no, sir, I couldn't.

Corrigan *(Forcing it into his hand):* Yes, you can, William. Bless you and say hello to your wife for me.

William: Thank you so much, sir. *(A pause.)* Did you have a coat with you?

Corrigan: No. I'm rushing the season a little tonight, William. I felt spring in the air. Came out like this.

William *(Opening the door):* Well, April *is* spring, sir.

Corrigan: It's getting there. What is the date, William?

William: April 14th, sir.

Corrigan: April 14th. *(Then he turns, grins at the attendant.)* 1965—right?

William: I beg your pardon, sir? Oh, yes, sir. 1965.

Corrigan *(Going out):* Good night, William. Take care of yourself. *(He goes out into the night.)*

SCENE 2. *Exterior of the club.*

(The door closes behind Corrigan. He stands there near the front entrance. The light from the street light illuminates the steps. There's the sound of chimes from the distant steeple clock. Corrigan looks at his wristwatch, holding it out toward the light so it can be seen more clearly. Suddenly his face takes on a strange look. He shuts his eyes and rubs his temple. Then he looks down at his wrist again. This time the light has changed. It's a wavery, moving light, different from what it had been. Corrigan looks across toward the light again. It's a gaslight now. He reacts in amazement. The chimes begin to chime again, this time eight times. He once again looks at the watch, but instead of a wristwatch there is just a fringe of lace protruding from a coat. There is no wristwatch at all. He grabs his wrist, pulling at the lace and coat. He's dressed now in a nineteenth-century costume. He looks down at himself, looks again toward the gaslight that flickers, and then slowly backs down from the steps staring at the building from which he's just come. The plaque reads "Washington Club." He jumps the steps two at a time, slams against the front door, pounding on it. After a long moment the door opens. An attendant, half undressed, stands there peering out into the darkness.)

Attendant: Who is it? What do you want?

Corrigan: I left something in there. *(He starts to push his way in and the attendant partially closes the door on him.)*

Attendant: Now here you! The Club is closed this evening.

Corrigan: The devil it is. I just left here a minute ago.

Attendant *(Peers at him):* You did what? You drunk, young man? That it? You're drunk, huh?

Corrigan: I am not drunk. I want to see Mr. Jackson or Mr. Whitaker, or William. Let me talk to William. Where is he now?

Attendant: Who?

Corrigan: William. What's the matter with you? Where did you come from? *(Then he looks down at his clothes.)* What's the idea of this? *(He looks up. The door has been shut. He pounds on it again, shouting.)* Hey! Open up!

Voice *(From inside)*: You best get away from here or I'll call the police. Go on. Get out of here.

(Corrigan backs away from the door, goes down to the sidewalk, stands there, looks up at the gaslight, then up and down the street, starts at the sound of noises. It's the clip-clop of horses' hooves and the rolling, squeaky sound of carriage wheels. He takes a few halting, running steps out into the street. He bites his lip, looks around.)

Corrigan *(Under his breath)*: I'll go home. That's it. Go home. I'll go home. *(He turns and starts to walk and then run down the street, disappearing into the night.)*

SCENE 3. *Hallway of rooming house.*

(There is the sound of a doorbell ringing. Mrs. Landers, the landlady, comes out from the dining room and goes toward the door.)

Mrs. Landers: All right. All right. Have a bit of patience. I'm coming.

Mrs. Landers *(Opening door)*: Yes?

Corrigan: Is this 19 West 12th Street?

Mrs. Landers: That's right. Whom did you wish to see?

Corrigan: I'm just wondering if . . . .

(He stands there trying to look over her shoulder. Mrs. Landers turns to look behind her and then suspiciously back toward Corrigan.)

Mrs. Landers: Whom did you wish to see, young man?

Corrigan: I . . . I used to live here. It's the oldest building in this section of town.

Mrs. Landers *(Stares at him)*: How's that?

Corrigan *(Wets his lips)*: What I mean is . . . as I remember it . . . it was the oldest——

Mrs. Landers: Well now really, young man. I can't spend the whole evening standing here talking about silly things like which is the oldest building in the section. Now if there's nothing else——

Corrigan *(Blurting it out)*: Do you have a room?

Mrs. Landers *(Opens the door just a little bit wider so that she can get a better look at him. She looks him up and down and appears satisfied)*: I have a room for acceptable boarders. Do you come from around here?

Corrigan: Yes. Yes, I do.

Mrs. Landers: Army veteran?

Corrigan: Yes. Yes, as a matter of fact I am.

Mrs. Landers *(Looks at him again up and down)*: Well, come in. I'll show you what I have.

(She opens the door wider and Corrigan enters. She closes it behind him. She looks expectantly up toward his hat, and Corrigan rather hurriedly and abruptly removes it. He grins, embarrassed.)

Corrigan: I'm not used to it.

Mrs. Landers: Used to what?

Corrigan *(Points to the hat in his hand)*: The hat. I don't wear a hat very often.

Mrs. Landers *(Again gives him her inventory look, very unsure of him now)*: May I inquire as to what your business is?

Corrigan: I'm an engineer.

Mrs. Landers: Really. A professional man. Hmmm. Well, come upstairs and I'll show you.

(She points to the stairs that lead off the hall, and Corrigan starts up as an army officer with a pretty girl comes down them.)

Mrs. Landers *(Smiling)*: Off to the play?

Lieutenant: That's right, Mrs. Landers. Dinner at The Willard and then off to the play.

Mrs. Landers: Well, enjoy yourself. And applaud the President for me!

Lieutenant: We'll certainly do that.

Girl: Good night, Mrs. Landers.

Mrs. Landers: Good night, my dear. Have a good time. This way, Mr. Corrigan.

(*The lieutenant and Corrigan exchange a nod as they pass on the stairs. As they go up the steps, Corrigan suddenly stops and Mrs. Landers almost bangs into him.*)

Mrs. Landers: Now what's the trouble?

Corrigan (*Whirling around*): What did you say?

Mrs. Landers: What did I say to whom? When?

Corrigan: To the lieutenant. To the officer. What did you just say to him?

(*The lieutenant has turned. The girl tries to lead him out, but he holds out his hand to stop her so that he can listen to the conversation from the steps.*)

Corrigan: You just said something to him about the President.

Lieutenant (*Walking toward the foot of the steps*): She told me to applaud him. Where might your sympathies lie?

Mrs. Landers (*Suspiciously*): Yes, young man. Which army *were* you in?

Corrigan (*Wets his lips nervously*): The Army of the Republic, of course.

Lieutenant (*Nods, satisfied*): Then why make such a thing of applauding President Lincoln? That's his due, we figure.

Mrs. Landers: That and everything else, may the good Lord bless him.

Corrigan (*Takes a step down the stairs, staring at the lieutenant*): You're going to a play tonight?

(*The lieutenant nods.*)

Girl (*At the door*): We may or we may not, depending on when my husband makes up his mind to get a carriage

in time to have dinner and get to the theater.

Corrigan: What theater? What play?

Lieutenant: Ford's Theater, of course.

Corrigan (*Looking off, his voice intense*): Ford's Theater. Ford's Theater.

Lieutenant: Are you all right? I mean do you feel all right?

Corrigan (*Whirls around to stare at him*): What's the name of the play?

Lieutenant (*Exchanges a look with his wife*): I beg your pardon?

Corrigan: The play. The one you're going to tonight at Ford's Theater. What's the name of it?

Girl: It's called "Our American Cousin."

Corrigan (*Again looks off thoughtfully*): "Our American Cousin" and Lincoln's going to be there.

Corrigan (*Looks from one to the other, first toward the landlady on the steps, then down toward the soldier and his wife*): And it's April 14th, 1865, isn't it? Isn't it April 14th, 1865? (*He starts down the steps without waiting for an answer. The lieutenant stands in front of him.*)

Lieutenant: Really, sir, I'd call your actions most strange.

(*Corrigan stares at him briefly as he goes by, then goes out the door, looking purposeful and intent.*)

SCENE 4. *Alley at night.*

(*On one side is the stage door with a sign over it reading "Ford's Theater." Corrigan turns the corridor into the alley*) at a dead run. He stops directly under the light, looks left and right, then vaults over the railing and pounds on the stage door.)

Corrigan (*Shouting*): Hey! Hey, let me in! President Lincoln is going to be shot tonight! (*He continues to pound on the door and shout.*)

Act Two

SCENE 1. *Police station at night.*

(*It's a bare receiving room with a police captain at a desk. A long bench on one side of the room is occupied by sad miscreants awaiting disposition. There is a line of three or four men standing in front of the desk, with several policemen in evidence. One holds onto Corrigan, who has a bruise over his eye and his coat is quite disheveled. The police captain looks up to him from a list.*)

Captain: Now what's this one done? (*He peers up over his glasses and eyes Corrigan up and down.*) Fancy Dan with too much money in his pockets, huh?

Corrigan: While you idiots are sitting here, you're going to lose a President!

(*The captain looks inquiringly toward the policeman.*)

Policeman: That's what he's been yellin' all the way over to the station. And that's what the doorman at the Ford Theater popped him on the head for. (*He nods toward Corrigan.*) Tried to pound his way right through the stage door. Yellin' some kind of crazy things about President Lincoln goin' to get shot.

Corrigan: President Lincoln *will* be shot! Tonight. In the theater. A man named Booth.

Captain: And how would you be knowin' this? I suppose you're clairvoyant[3] or something. Some kind of seer or wizard or something.

Corrigan: I only know what I know. If I told you *how* I knew, you wouldn't believe me. Look, keep me here if you like. Lock me up.

Captain (*Motions toward a turnkey, points to cell-block door*): Let him sleep it off.

(*The turnkey grabs Corrigan's arm and starts to lead him out of the room.*)

Corrigan (*Shouting as he's led away*): Well, you boobs better hear me out. Somebody better get to the President's box at the Ford Theater. Either keep him out of there or put a cordon of men around him. A man named John Wilkes Booth is going to assassinate him tonight!

(*He's pushed through the door leading to the cell block. A tall man in cape*

3. **clairvoyant** (klâr-voi'ənt) *adj.*: Able to predict the future or see things beyond the range of normal vision.

and black moustache stands near the open door at the other side. He closes it behind him, takes a step into the room, then with a kind of very precise authority, he walks directly over to the captain's table, shoving a couple of people aside as he does so with a firm gentleness. When he reaches the captain's table, he removes a card from his inside pocket, puts it on the table in front of the captain.)

Wellington: Wellington, Captain. Jonathan Wellington.

(The captain looks at the card, peers at it over his glasses, then looks up toward the tall man in front of him. Obviously the man's manner and dress impresses him. His tone is respectful and quiet.)

Captain: What can I do for you, Mr. Wellington?

Wellington: That man you just had incarcerated. Mr. Corrigan I believe he said his name was.

Captain: Drunk, sir. That's probably what he is.

Wellington: Drunk or . . . (He taps his head meaningfully.) Or perhaps, ill. I wonder if he could be remanded in my custody. He might well be a war veteran and I'd hate to see him placed in jail.

Captain: Well, that's real decent of you, Mr. Wellington. You say you want him remanded in your custody?

Wellington: Precisely. I'll be fully responsible for him. I think perhaps I might be able to help him.

Captain: All right, sir. If that's what you'd like. But I'd be careful of this one if I was you! There's a mighty bunch of crackpots running the streets these days

and many of them his like, and many of them dangerous too, sir. (He turns toward turnkey.) Have Corrigan brought back out here. This gentleman's going to look after him. (Then he turns to Wellington.) It's real decent of you sir. Real decent indeed.

Wellington: I'll be outside. Have him brought out to me if you would.

Captain: I will indeed, sir.

(Wellington turns. He passes the various people who look at him and make room for him. His walk, his manner, his positiveness suggest a commanding figure, and everyone reacts accordingly. The Captain once again busies himself with his list and is about to check in the next prisoner, when a young police officer alongside says——)

Police Officer: Begging your pardon, Captain.

Captain: What is it?

Police Officer: About that Corrigan, sir.

Captain: What about him?

Police Officer: Wouldn't it be wise, sir, if——

Captain (Impatiently): If what?

Police Officer: He seemed so positive, sir. So sure. About the President, I mean.

Captain (Slams on the desk with vast impatience): What would you have us do? Send all available police to the Ford Theater? And on what authority? On the word of some demented fool who probably left his mind someplace in Gettysburg. If I was you, mister, I'd be considerably more thoughtful at sizing up situations or you'll not advance one half grade the next twenty years. Now be good enough to stand aside and let me get on with my work.

Police Officer (*Very much deterred by all this, but pushed on by a gnawing sense of disquiet*): Captain, it wouldn't hurt.

Captain (*Interrupting with a roar*): It wouldn't hurt if what?

Police Officer: I was going to suggest, sir, that if perhaps we placed extra guards in the box with the President——

Captain: The President has all the guards he needs. He's got the whole Federal Army at his disposal and if they're satisfied with his security arrangements, then I am too and so should you. Next case!

(*The young police officer bites his lip and looks away, then stares across the room thoughtfully. The door opens and the turnkey leads Corrigan across the room and over to the door. He opens it and points out. Corrigan nods and walks outside. The door closes behind him. The young police officer looks briefly at the captain, then puts his cap on and starts out toward the door.*)

SCENE 2. *Lodging house, Wellington's room.*

(*Wellington is pouring wine into two glasses. Corrigan sits in a chair, his face in his hands. He looks up at the proffered drink and takes it.*)

Wellington: Take this. It'll make you feel better. (*Corrigan nods his thanks, takes a healthy swig of the wine, puts it down, then looks up at the other man.*) Better?

Corrigan (*Studying the man*): Who are you anyway?

Wellington (*With a thin smile*): At the moment, I'm your benefactor and apparently your only friend. I'm in the Government service, but as a young man in college I dabbled in medicine of a sort.

Corrigan: Medicine?

Wellington: Medicine of the mind.

Corrigan (*Smiles grimly*): Psychiatrist.

Wellington (*Turning to him*): I don't know the term.

Corrigan: What about the symptoms?

Wellington: They *do* interest me. This story you were telling about the President being assassinated.

Corrigan (*Quickly*): What time is it?

Wellington: There's time. (*Checks a pocket watch.*) A quarter to eight. The play won't start for another half hour. What gave you the idea that the President would be assassinated?

Corrigan: I happen to know, that's all.

Wellington (*Again the thin smile*): You have a premonition?

Corrigan: I've got a devil of a lot more than a premonition. Lincoln *will* be assassinated. (*Then quickly.*) Unless somebody tries to prevent it.

Wellington: I shall try to prevent it. If you can convince me that you're neither drunk nor insane.

Corrigan (*On his feet*): If I told you what I was, you'd be convinced I *was* insane. So all I'm going to tell you is that

I happen to know for a fact that a man named John Wilkes Booth will assassinate President Lincoln in his box at the Ford Theater. I don't know what time it's going to happen . . . that's something I forgot—but——

Wellington *(Softly)*: Something you forgot?

Corrigan *(Takes a step toward him)*: Listen, please——*(He stops suddenly, and begins to waver. He reaches up to touch the bruise over his head.)*

Wellington *(Takes out a handkerchief and hands it to Corrigan)*: Here. That hasn't been treated properly. You'd best cover it.

Corrigan *(Very, very shaky, almost faint, takes the handkerchief, puts it to his head, and sits back down weakly)*: That's . . . that's odd. *(He looks up, still holding the handkerchief.)*

Wellington: What is?

Corrigan: I'm so . . . I'm so faint all of a sudden. So weak. It's almost as if I were——

Wellington: As if you were what?

Corrigan *(With a weak smile)*: As if I'd suddenly gotten drunk or some —— *(He looks up, desperately trying to focus now as his vision starts to become clouded.)* I've never . . . I've never felt like this before. I've never—— *(His eyes turn to the wine glass on the table. As his eyes open wide, he struggles to his feet.)* You . . . you devil! You drugged me, didn't you! *(He reaches out to grab Wellington, half struggling in the process.)* You drugged me, didn't you!

Wellington: I was forced to, my young friend. You're a very sick man and a sick man doesn't belong in jail. He belongs in a comfortable accommodation where he can sleep and rest and regain his . . . *(He smiles, a little apologetical-*

ly.) . . . his composure, his rationale. Rest, Mr. Corrigan. I'll be back soon.

(He turns and starts toward the door. Corrigan starts to follow him, stumbles to his knees, supports himself on one hand, looks up as Wellington opens the door.)

Corrigan: Please . . . please, you've got to believe me. Lincoln's going to be shot tonight.

Wellington *(Smiling again)*: And that's odd! Because . . . perhaps I'm beginning to believe you! Good night, Mr. Corrigan. Rest well. *(He turns and goes out of the room, closing the door behind him. We hear the sound of the key being inserted, the door locked.)*

(Corrigan tries desperately to rise and then weakly falls over on his side. He crawls toward the door. He scrabbles at it with a weak hand.)

Corrigan *(Almost in a whisper)*: Please . . . please . . . somebody . . . let me out. I wasn't kidding . . . I know . . . the President's going to be assassinated! *(His arm, supporting him, gives out and he falls to his face; then in a last effort, he turns himself over so that he's lying on his back.)*

(There is a sound of a heavy knocking on the door. Then a landlady's voice from outside.)

Landlady: There's no need to break it open, Officer. I've got an extra key. Now if you don't mind, stand aside.

(There's the sound of the key inserted in the lock and the door opens.

The young police officer from earlier is standing there with an angry-faced landlady behind him. The police officer gets down on his knees, props up Corrigan's head.)

Police Officer: Are you all right? What's happened?

Corrigan: What time is it? *(He grabs the officer, almost pulling him over.)* You've got to tell me what time it is.

Police Officer: It's ten-thirty-five. Come on, Corrigan. You've got to tell me what you know about this. You may be a madman or a drunk or I don't know what—but you've got me convinced, and I've been everywhere from the Mayor's office to the Police Commissioner's home trying to get a special guard for the President.

Corrigan: Then go yourself. Find out where he's sitting and get right up alongside of him. He'll be shot from behind. That's the way it happened. Shot from behind. And then the assassin jumps from the box to the stage and he runs out of the wings.

Police Officer *(Incredulous)*: You're telling me this as if, as if it has already happened.

Corrigan: It *has* happened. It happened a hundred years ago and I've come back to see that it *doesn't* happen. *(Looking beyond the police officer.)* Where's the man who brought me in here? Where's Wellington?

Landlady *(Peering into the room)*: Wellington? There's no one here by that name.

Corrigan *(Waves a clenched fist at her. He still holds the handkerchief)*: Don't tell me there's no one here by that name. He brought me in here. He lives in this room.

Landlady: There's no one here by that name.

Corrigan *(Holds the handkerchief close to his face, again waving his fist)*: I tell you the man who brought me here was named——*(He stops abruptly, suddenly caught by something he sees on the handkerchief. His eyes slowly turn to stare at it in his hand. On the border are the initials J.W.B.)*

Corrigan: J.W.B.?

Landlady: Of course! Mr. John Wilkes Booth, who lives in this room, and that's who brought you here.

Corrigan: He said his name was Wellington! And *that's* why he drugged me. *(He grabs the police officer again.)* He gave me wine and he drugged me. He didn't want me to stop him. He's the one who's going to do it. Listen, you've got to get to that theater. You've got to stop him. John Wilkes Booth! He's going to kill Lincoln. Look, get out of here now! Will you stop him? Will you——

(He stops abruptly, his eyes look up. All three people turn to look toward the window. There's the sound of crowd noises building, suggestive of excitement, and then almost a collective wail, a mournful, universal chant that comes from the streets, and, as the sound builds, we suddenly hear intelligible words that are part of the mob noise.)

Voices: The President's been shot. President Lincoln's been assassinated. Lincoln is dying.

(The landlady suddenly bursts into tears. The police officer rises to his feet, his face white.)

Police Officer: Oh my dear God! You

were right. You *did* know. Oh . . . my . . . dear . . . God!

(He turns, almost trance-like, and walks out of the room. The landlady follows him. Corrigan rises weakly and goes to the window, staring out at the night and listening to the sounds of a nation beginning its mourning. He closes his eyes and puts his head against the windowpane, and with fruitless, weakened smashes, hits the side of the window frame as he talks.)

Corrigan: I tried to tell you. I tried to warn you. Why didn't anybody listen? Why? Why didn't anyone listen to me? *(His fist beats a steady staccato on the window frame.)*

SCENE 3. *The Washington Club at night.*

(Corrigan is pounding on the front door of the Washington Club. Corrigan is standing there in modern dress once again. The door opens. An attendant we've not seen before appears.)

Attendant Two: Good evening, Mr. Corrigan. Did you forget something, sir?

(Corrigan walks past the attendant, through the big double doors that lead to the card room as in Act One. His three friends are in the middle of a discussion. The fourth man at the table, sitting in his seat, has his back to the camera.)

Millard *(Looking up):* Hello, Pete. Come on over and join tonight's bull session. It has to do with the best ways of amassing a fortune. What are your tried-and-true methods?

Corrigan *(His voice is intense and shaky):* We were talking about time travel, about going back in time.

Jackson *(Dismissing it):* Oh, that's old stuff. We're on a new tack now. Money and the best ways to acquire it.

Corrigan: Listen . . . listen, I want to tell you something. This is true. If you go back into the past you can't change anything. *(He takes another step toward the table.)* Understand? You can't change anything.

(The men look at one another, disarmed by the intensity of Corrigan's tone.)

Jackson *(Rises, softly):* All right, old man, if you say so. *(Studying him intensely.)* Are you all right?

Corrigan *(Closing his eyes for a moment):* Yes . . . yes, I'm all right.

Jackson: Then come on over and listen to a lot of palaver from self-made swindlers. William here has the best method.

Corrigan: William?

(He sees the attendant from Act One but now meticulously dressed, a middle-aged millionaire obviously, with a totally different manner, who puts a cigarette in a holder with manicured hands in the manner of a man totally accustomed to wealth. William looks up and smiles.)

William: Oh, yes. My method for achieving security is far the best. You simply inherit it. It comes to you in a beribboned box. I was telling the boys here, Corrigan. My great grandfather was on the police force here in Washington on the night of Lincoln's assassination. He went all over town trying to warn people that something might happen. *(He holds up his hands in a gesture.)* How he figured it out, nobody seems to know. It's certainly not recorded any place. But because there was so much publicity, people never forgot him. He became a police chief, then a councilman, did some wheeling and dealing in land and became a millionaire. What do you say we get back to our bridge, gentlemen?

(Jackson takes the cards and starts to shuffle. William turns in his seat once again.)

William: How about it, Corrigan? Take a hand?

Corrigan: Thank you, William, no. I think I'll . . . I think I'll just go home.

(He turns very slowly and starts toward the exit. Over his walk we hear the whispered, hushed murmurings of the men at the table.)

Voices: Looks peaked, doesn't he? Acting so strangely. I wonder what's the matter with him.

(Corrigan walks into the hall and toward the front door.)

Narrator's Voice: Mr. Peter Corrigan, lately returned from a place "Back There"; a journey into time with highly questionable results. Proving, on one hand, that the threads of history are woven tightly and the skein of events cannot be undone; but, on the other hand, there are small fragments of tapestry that *can* be altered. Tonight's thesis, to be taken as you will, in The Twilight Zone!

Close Up

1. Millard claims that if people could go back in time, they would be able to alter the course of history. Why does Corrigan disagree with Millard?

2. Corrigan leaves the Club on the night of April 14, 1965. (a) List three things that occur as he stands outside the Club that make you think Corrigan has traveled back in time. (b) How does the attendant's behavior support this idea?

3. Before renting a room to him, Mrs. Landers asks Corrigan if he is an army veteran. Which army does she mean?

4. Why is Corrigan upset when he learns that President Lincoln will attend Ford's Theater that night?

5. (a) What reason does Wellington give the police for taking Corrigan into his custody? (b) What is his real reason?

6. Peter Corrigan isn't able to change history in a large way by saving President Lincoln. How is he able to change history in a small way?

Setting

The time of a story may be an important part of the setting. In "Back There," the place where the events in the play occur remains the same, but the time changes from the present to the past.

1. The place where the events in this play occur is Washington, D.C. (a) When do the events in Act One, Scene 1 occur? (b) When do the events in Act One, Scene 2 occur?

2. Corrigan tells Mrs. Landers that her house is the oldest building in this section of town. (a) Why does she think that this statement is strange? (b) Find one other statement Corrigan makes to Mrs. Landers that shows he is from another time.

3. Imagine that you are going to record this play as a radio drama. (a) List the sound effects you would use to indicate the present. (b) List the sound effects you would use to indicate the past.

Activities

1. **Composition.** If you could travel in time, what time period would you visit? Write a paragraph explaining your answer.

2. Imagine that you are opening a time-travel agency. Make up a television commercial for it.

INFERENCES

Making Inferences About a Character's Feelings

When you make inferences about a character's feelings, you reach conclusions about this character based on clues in the story. These clues include gestures and facial expressions, actions and reactions, and what a character says and how the character says it. For example, the author doesn't tell you how Corrigan feels in the following passage.

> "Corrigan looks at his wristwatch, holding it out toward the light so it can be seen more clearly. Suddenly his face takes on a strange look. He shuts his eyes and rubs his temple. Then he looks down at his wrist again."

Based on clues in the passage, you probably inferred that Corrigan feels uncertain and surprised.

▶ Read each of the following passages. Pay special attention to clues to feelings. Then make an inference about how Corrigan feels in each passage.

a. "Corrigan backs away from the door, goes down to the sidewalk, stands there, looks up at the gaslight, then up and down the street, starts at the sound of noises. . . . He takes a few halting, running steps out into the street. He bites his lip, looks around."

b. "He stops suddenly and begins to waver. He reaches up to touch the bruise over his head."

c. "(Corrigan) waves a clenched fist at her. He still holds the handkerchief. (He says,) 'Don't tell me there is no one here by that name. He brought me here. He lives in this room.' "

d. "He stops abruptly, suddenly caught by something he sees on the handkerchief. His eyes slowly turn to stare at it in his hand."

e. "Corrigan rises weakly and goes to the window, staring out at the night and listening to the sounds of a nation beginning its mourning. He closes his eyes and puts his head against the windowpane, and with fruitless, weakened smashes, hits the side of the window frame as he talks."

WORD ATTACK

Understanding Adverbs

An adverb is a word that modifies a verb, an adjective, or another adverb. Usually, an adverb answers one of the following questions: How? When? Where? How much? How often? Often, adverbs help you to visualize, or see, how the character performs the action. Many adverbs are formed by adding *-ly* to an adjective. For example:

> She did a *thorough* job. (adjective)
> She did the job *thoroughly*. (adverb)

When you use a dictionary to find the meaning of an adverb formed this way, drop the *-ly* ending and look up the adjective form of the word.

1. Use a dictionary to find the meaning of each of the *italicized* adverbs below.
   a. William answers Corrigan's questions *deferentially*.
   b. The door was *partially* closed.
   c. Mrs. Landers looked at Corrigan *suspiciously*.
   d. She glanced at his hat *expectantly*.
   e. Corrigan pounded on the door *intently*.
   f. The captain glanced *inquiringly* toward the officer.
   g. Wellington was dressed *elegantly*.
   h. The police captain slammed his fist on the desk and spoke *impatiently*.
   i. Corrigan tried *desperately* to focus his eyes.
   j. Wellington smiled *apologetically* at him.

2. Read each sentence above, but leave out the adverbs. How do the sentences change?

3. For each sentence in Exercise 1, replace the *italicized* adverb with an adverb that means the opposite, or nearly the opposite.

Storm Ending

Jean Toomer

Thunder blossoms gorgeously above our heads,
Great, hollow, bell-like flowers
Rumbling in the wind,
Stretching clappers to strike our ears . . .
5 Full-lipped flowers
Bitten by the sun
Bleeding rain
Dripping rain like golden honey——
And the sweet earth flying from the thunder.

Nocturne

Gwendolyn Bennett

This cool night is strange
Among midsummer days . . .
Far frosts are caught
In the moon's pale light,
5 And sounds are distant laughter
Chilled to crystal tears.

Close Up

1. In "Storm Ending," the poet creates a vivid picture of thunder by comparing it to bell-like flowers. How is the sound of thunder like the sound of a bell?

2. Lightning is followed by thunder. Why do you think the poet describes thunder as blossoming into flowers?

3. (a) Find four lines that give you a vivid picture of rain. (b) How does this picture help you to know that the storm is ending, rather than beginning?

Crime on Mars

Arthur C. Clarke

Danny Weaver would have stolen Mars' greatest treasure, if it hadn't been for a piece of fantastically bad luck.

"We don't have much crime on Mars," said Detective-Inspector Rawlings, a little sadly. "In fact, that's the chief reason I'm going back to the Yard. If I stayed here much longer, I'd get completely out of practice."

We were sitting in the main observation lounge of the Phobos Spaceport, looking out across the jagged sun-drenched crags of the tiny moon. The ferry rocket that had brought us up from Mars had left ten minutes ago and was now beginning the long fall back to the ocher-tinted globe hanging there against the stars. In half an hour we would be boarding the liner for Earth—a world on which most of the passengers had never set foot, but which they still called "home."

"At the same time," continued the Inspector, "now and then there's a case that makes life interesting. You're an art dealer, Mr. Maccar; I'm sure you heard about that spot of bother at Meridian City a couple of months ago."

"I don't think so," replied the plump, olive-skinned little man I'd taken for just another returning tourist. Presumably the Inspector had already checked through the passenger list; I wondered how much he knew about me, and tried to reassure myself that my conscience was—well, reasonably clear. After all, everybody took *something* out through Martian Customs——

"It's been rather well hushed up," said the Inspector, "but you can't keep these things quiet for long. Anyway, a

jewel thief from Earth tried to steal Meridian Museum's greatest treasure—the Siren Goddess.''

"But that's absurd!" I objected. "It's priceless, of course—but it's only a lump of sandstone. You couldn't sell it to anyone—you might just as well steal the Mona Lisa.''

The Inspector grinned, rather mirthlessly. "*That's* happened too," he said. "Maybe the motive was the same. There are collectors who would give a fortune for such an object, even if they could only look at it themselves. Don't you agree, Mr. Maccar?"

"That's perfectly true," said the art dealer. "In my business you meet all sorts of crazy people."

"Well, this chappie—name's Danny Weaver—had been well paid by one of them. And if it hadn't been for a piece of fantastically bad luck, he might have brought it off."

The Spaceport P.A. system apologized for a further slight delay owing to final fuel checks, and asked a number of passengers to report to Information. While we were waiting for the announcement to finish, I recalled what little I knew about the Siren Goddess. Although I'd never seen the original, like most other departing tourists I had a replica in my baggage. It bore the certificate of the Mars Bureau of Antiquities, guaranteeing that "this full-scale reproduction is an exact copy of the so-called Siren Goddess, discovered in the Mare Sirenium by the Third Expedition, A.D. 2012 (A.M. 23)."

It's quite a tiny thing to have caused so much controversy. Only eight or nine inches high—you wouldn't look at it twice if you saw it in a museum on Earth. The head of a young woman, with slightly oriental features, elongated earlobes, hair curled in tight ringlets close to the scalp, lips half parted in an expression of pleasure or surprise—and that's all.

But it's an enigma[1] so baffling that it has inspired a hundred religious sects, and driven quite a few archeologists out of their minds. For a perfectly human head has no right whatsoever to be found on Mars, whose only intelligent inhabitants were crustaceans[2]—"educated lobsters," as the newspapers are fond of calling them. The aboriginal Martians never came near to achieving space flight, and in any event, their civilization died before men existed on Earth.

No wonder the Goddess is the Solar System's Number One mystery. I don't suppose we'll find the answer in my lifetime—if we ever do.

"Danny's plan was beautifully simple," continued the Inspector. "You know how absolutely dead a Martian city gets on Sunday, when everything closes down and the colonists stay home to watch the TV from Earth. Danny was counting on this when he checked into the hotel in Meridian West, late Friday afternoon. He'd have Saturday for reconnoitering the museum, and undisturbed Sunday for the job itself, and on Monday morning he'd be just another tourist leaving town. . . .

"Early Saturday he strolled through the little park and crossed over into Meridian East, where the museum stands. In case you don't know, the city gets its name because it's exactly on longitude one-eighty degrees; there's a big

---

1. enigma (ĭ-nĭg′mə) n.: A puzzle or mystery.
2. crustaceans (krŭ-stā′shənz) n.: Aquatic, or water, animals that have shells.

stone slab in the park with the Prime Meridian engraved on it, so that visitors can get themselves photographed standing in two hemispheres at once. Amazing what simple things amuse some people.

"Danny spent the day going over the museum, exactly like any other tourist determined to get his money's worth. But at closing time he didn't leave; he'd holed up in one of the galleries not open to the public, where the museum had been arranging a Late Canal Period reconstruction but had run out of money before the job could be finished. He stayed there until about midnight, just in case there were any enthusiastic researchers still in the building. Then he emerged and got to work."

"Just a moment," I interrupted. "What about the night watchman?"

"My dear chap! They don't have such luxuries on Mars. There weren't even any burglar alarms, for who would bother to steal lumps of stone? True, the Goddess was sealed up neatly in a strong glass-and-metal cabinet, just in case some souvenir hunter took a fancy to her. But even if she were stolen there was nowhere the thief could hide, and of course all outgoing traffic would be searched as soon as the statue was missed."

That was true enough. I'd been thinking in terms of Earth, forgetting that every city on Mars is a closed little world of its own beneath the force-field that protects it from the freezing near-vacuum. Beyond those electronic shields is the utterly hostile emptiness of the Martian Outback, where a man will die in seconds without protection. That makes law enforcement very easy; no wonder there's so little crime on Mars....

"Danny had a beautiful set of tools, as specialized as a watchmaker's. The main item was a microsaw no bigger than a soldering iron; it had a wafer-thin blade, driven at a million cycles a second by an ultrasonic power-pack. It would go through glass or metal like butter—and leave a cut only about as thick as a hair. Which was very important for Danny, as he could not leave any traces of his handiwork.

"I suppose you've guessed how he intended to operate. He was going to cut through the base of the cabinet and substitute one of those souvenir replicas for the genuine Goddess. It might be a couple of years before some inquisitive expert discovered the awful truth, and long before then the original would have been taken to Earth, perfectly disguised as a copy of itself. Pretty neat, eh?

"It must have been a weird business, working in that darkened gallery with all those million-year-old carvings and unexplainable artifacts around him. A museum on Earth is bad enough at night, but at least its—well, *human*. And Gallery Three, which houses the Goddess, is particularly unsettling. It's full of bas-reliefs showing quite incredible animals fighting each other; they look rather like giant beetles, and most paleontologists[3] flatly deny that they could ever have existed. But imaginary or not, they belonged to this world, and they didn't disturb Danny as much as the Goddess, staring at him across the ages and defying him to explain her presence here. She gave him the creeps. How do I know? He told me.

"Danny set to work on that cabinet

---

3. **paleontologists** (pā′lē-ŏn-tŏl′ə-jĭstz) n.: Scientists who study fossils and ancient life forms.

as carefully as any diamond cutter preparing to cleave a gem. It took most of the night to slice out the trapdoor, and it was nearly dawn when he relaxed and put down the saw. There was still a lot of work to do, but the hardest part was over. Putting the replica into the case, checking its appearance against the photos he'd thoughtfully brought with him, and covering up his traces might take a good part of Sunday, but that didn't worry him in the least. He had another twenty-four hours, and would positively welcome Monday's first visitors so that he could mingle with them and make his inconspicuous exit.

"It was a perfectly horrible shock to his nervous system, therefore, when the main doors were noisily unbarred at eight thirty and the museum staff—all six of them—started to open up for the day. Danny bolted for the emergency exit, leaving everything behind—tools, Goddesses, the lot.

"He had another big surprise when he found himself in the street: it should have been completely deserted at this time of day, with everyone at home reading the Sunday papers. But here were the citizens of Meridian East, as large as life, heading for plant or office on what was obviously a normal working day.

"By the time poor Danny got back to his hotel we were waiting for him. We couldn't claim much credit for deducing that only a visitor from Earth—and a very recent one at that—could have overlooked Meridian City's chief claim to fame. And I presume you know what *that* is."

"Frankly, I don't," I answered. "You can't see much of Mars in six weeks, and I never went east of the Syrtis Major."

"Well, it's absurdly simple, but we shouldn't be too hard on Danny—even the locals occasionally fall into the same trap. It's something that doesn't bother us on Earth, where we've been able to dump the problem in the Pacific Ocean. But Mars, of course, is all dry land; and that means that *somebody* is forced to live with the International Date Line. . . .

"Danny, you see, had planned the job from Meridian West. It was Sunday over there all right—and it was still Sunday there when we picked him up at the hotel. But over in Meridian East, half a mile away, it was only Saturday. That little trip across the park had made all the difference! I told you it was rotten luck."

There was a long moment of silent sympathy, then I asked, "What did he get?"

"Three years," said Inspector Rawlings.

"That doesn't seem very much."

"Mars years—that makes it almost six of ours. And a whopping fine which, by an odd coincidence, came to exactly the refund value of his return ticket to Earth. He isn't in jail, of course—Mars can't afford that kind of nonproductive luxury. Danny has to work for a living, under discreet surveillance. I told you that the Meridian Museum couldn't afford a night watchman. Well, it has one now. Guess who?"

"All passengers prepare to board in ten minutes! Please collect your hand baggage!" ordered the loudspeakers.

As we started to move toward the airlock, I couldn't help asking one more question.

"What about the people who put Danny up to it? There must have been a lot of money behind him. Did you get them?"

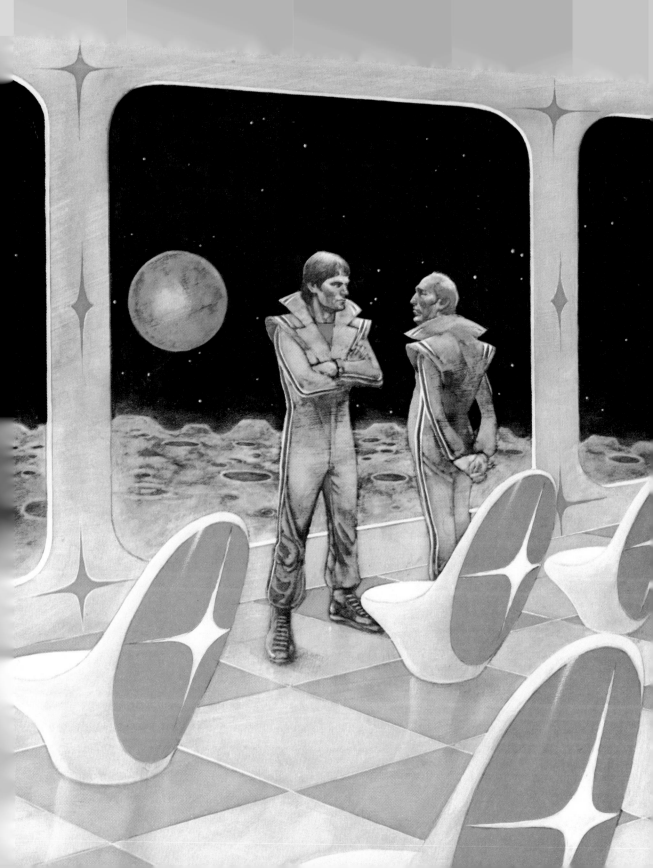

"Not yet; they'd covered their tracks pretty thoroughly, and I believe Danny was telling the truth when he said he couldn't give us a lead. Still, it's not my case. As I told you, I'm going back to my old job at the Yard. But a policeman always keeps his eyes open—like an art dealer, eh, Mr. Maccar? Why, you look a bit green about the gills. Have one of my space-sickness tablets."

"No, thank you," answered Mr. Maccar, "I'm quite all right."

His tone was distinctly unfriendly; the social temperature seemed to have dropped below zero in the last few minutes. I looked at Mr. Maccar, and I looked at the Inspector. And suddenly I realized that we were going to have a very interesting trip.

Close Up

1. Inspector Rawlings tells the narrator and Maccar about the crime. Why does he mention the fact that an art collector had paid Danny Weaver to steal the Siren Goddess?

2. (a) What is the Siren Goddess? (b) Why is the statue a puzzle to archeologists?

3. (a) How did Weaver plan to get away with the theft? (b) What mistake did he make?

4. (a) What happens to Weaver? (b) Why is this ironic, or just the opposite of what he had planned?

5. At the end of the story, why does the narrator think he is going to have an interesting trip home?

Setting

The setting of the story can affect the plot. It can influence the characters' actions and force certain events to occur. For example, the ending of "Crime on Mars" would have been very different if the story had taken place somewhere else.

1. How did Meridian City get its name?

2. Danny checked into a hotel on Friday afternoon. (a) Where was the hotel located? (b) Where was the museum located?

3. Why didn't the museum have a night watchman or burglar alarms?

4. (a) Why was Danny surprised when the Museum's doors were unbarred and the staff walked in? (b) How did the location of the museum upset Danny's plan?

Activities

1. Write a headline for a newspaper story telling how Danny Weaver got caught.

2. **Composition.** Write a paragraph giving your explanation for the puzzle of the Siren Goddess.

INFERENCES

Making Inferences About Realistic and Fantastic Details

A fantastic detail exists only in fancy or imagination. It is unreal or strange and wondrous. It does not exist in reality. For example, "We were sitting in the main observation lounge of the Phobos Spaceport, looking out across the jagged sun-drenched crags of the tiny moon."

A realistic detail is true to life. In many stories, the author mixes realistic details with fantastic details.

---

1. Which of the following sentences contain fantastic details?

   a. "The ferry rocket that had brought us up from Mars had left ten minutes ago and was now beginning the long fall back to the ocher-tinted globe hanging there against the stars."

   b. "It bore the certificate of the Mars Bureau of Antiquities, guaranteeing that 'this full-scale reproduction is an exact copy of the so-called Siren Goddess, discovered in the Mare Sirenium by the Third Expedition, A.D. 2012 (A.M. 23).'"

   c. "You know how absolutely dead a Martian city gets on Sunday, when everything closes down and the colonists stay home to watch the TV from Earth."

   d. "Danny spent the day going over the museum, exactly like any other tourist determined to get his money's worth."

   e. "I'd been thinking in terms of Earth, forgetting that every city on Mars is a closed little world of its own beneath the force-field that protects it from the freezing near-vacuum."

   f. "He was going to cut through the base of the cabinet and substitute one of those souvenir replicas for the genuine Goddess."

   g. "It took most of the night to slice out the trapdoor, and it was nearly dawn when he relaxed and put down the saw."

   h. "And Gallery Three, which houses the Goddess, is particularly unsettling. It's full of bas-reliefs showing quite incredible animals fighting each other; they look rather like giant beetles, and most paleontologists flatly deny that they could ever have existed."

2. Make a list of ten fantastic details in this story.

WORD ATTACK

Using Context Clues

You may be unfamiliar with the word *brogan*. Sounding it out won't help you get its meaning. However, using context clues may help. For example, "He slipped his tired feet into his brogans and stood up, ready for another day of digging in the jagged crags of Mars." Brogans are heavy-duty work shoes.

Notice how context clues in the following sentence help you figure out that *elongated* means "stretched out" or "out of proportion because of too much length":

> "The goddess had *elongated* ears that stretched from the top of her head to her lower lip."

When you come across a word you don't know, look for context clues in the rest of the sentence or the sentences around it.

▶ Use context clues to help you select the correct definition for the *italicized* word in each sentence below.

a. "Although I'd never seen the original, like most departing tourists I had a *replica* in my baggage. It bore the certificate of the Mars Bureau of Antiquities, guaranteeing that 'this full-scale reproduction is an exact copy of the so-called Siren Goddess . . . .' "
  (1) perfect copy of the original
  (2) something older than the original
  (3) something either smaller or larger than the original

b. "Beyond those electronic shields is the utterly *hostile* emptiness of the Martian Outback, where a man will die in seconds without protection."
  (1) friendly, peaceful
  (2) ancient
  (3) unfriendly, threatening

c. "The main item was a *microsaw* no bigger than a soldering iron; it had a wafer-thin blade . . . ."
  (1) a very small saw
  (2) a very sharp saw
  (3) a saw for cutting up microscopes

d. "Danny set to work on that cabinet as carefully as any diamond cutter preparing to *cleave* a gem."
  (1) smash
  (2) cut
  (3) explode

R. Higginbotham

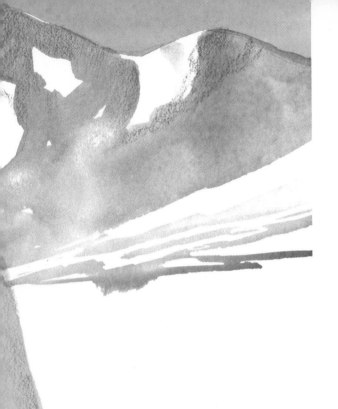

Avalanche

Robb White

"Scotty fought the thing. With his arms around his head, he kept fighting to keep the snow cleared away from his face, fighting to make a hole of air around his head."

Part One

The sunballs rolling down the vast expanse of unmarked snow were beautiful—and as threatening as a pit full of poisonous snakes.

Scotty watched them for a moment, then looked up at the top of this mountain where the enormous mass of snow hung above him. He had never seen so much snow here, and even the oldest men in his village were awed and frightened by it, for they, in all their long lives, had never known such a winter.

Scotty turned to watch the man who had hired him as a guide, as the man kept on climbing, his expensive boots sinking into the fresh snow.

During the long trip up the mountain, Scotty had lost all respect for this man, and now, watching his dogged ascent, he knew why. What the man was doing on this now very serious mountain, the reason for his being here, was trivial. The purpose of this climb—at great risk to his life and to Scotty's—wasn't important.

To get his picture on TV and his name, in small print, in a paperback book of records, this man was climbing straight into an avalanche.

"Hey, Marick!" Scotty called up to him. "Hold it a minute."

Without looking back Marick said, "Try to keep up. That's what I'm paying you for."

"*Hold* it!" Scotty yelled at him, then drove his own feet into the snow and caught up with him. "Don't these sunballs tell you anything?"

Marick looked at him, his fanatical eyes as bright and shallow as a bird's. "They tell me we'd better get to the top while there's still light for the TV cameras to see me coming down."

"Is that all they tell you?"

"Yeah," Marick said. "So *move.*"

Scotty, whose entire life had been influenced by the daily—even hourly—moods and changes, the violence and tranquility of this mountain, was appalled by this outsider's lack of understanding of the warning the mountain was giving them. This mountain was telling them, in plain language, what its next mood, next change was going to be.

"There's been a 10-degree rise in temperature in the last hour," Scotty said. "Does *that* tell you anything?"

"It tells me that I've got thousands of dollars worth of TV cameras and crews waiting for me to ski down this mountain."

Some of the globes of snow rolling fast down the steep slope were now the size of basketballs, and they were leaving warning trails in the snow.

"If we don't get out of the way, the only thing your TV crew will film will be two people being buried under about a million tons of snow," Scotty said.

Marick ignored him. "I'm going to start from that mogul[1] over there." Then he turned and grinned. "From the valley, that'll look like the summit." Then his tone changed, growing threatening. "And nothing you can say later will change what those cameras see."

"Look up there!" Scotty said, his voice thin with fury. "Look at that mountain of snow. It's just hanging there, man, waiting. It's going to kill us if we don't get out of the way."

"That snow is why I'm here," Marick said coldly. "This is the first time in a hundred years that there's been enough snow for a man to ski down this mountain." He stopped and looked with those cold, brilliant eyes at Scotty. "I've spent years preparing for this, studying this mountain; I've spent a small fortune. Now the time has come and I'm going to do it. Understand?"

Scotty's fury changed to a cold, still anger. "Usually this mountain doesn't give you much warning. But this time it's giving us plenty. The heavy snowfall awhile ago, the hot wind, the sunballs leaving trails. It's telling us, Marick."

Marick raised his arms to heaven and looked upward. "Of all the guides in your village, why am I afflicted with this gutless wonder?" Then he looked at Scotty. "How old are you?"

"Eighteen."

---

1. mogul (mō′gəl) n.: A slightly raised pile of earth on a ski slope.

"I've been skiing bigger mountains than this for longer than you've been alive, kid, so stop giving me advice and start helping me with my gear."

In silence Scotty steadied Marick as he took off the climbing boots and put on the rigid ski boots. Scotty slung the boots around his neck and then helped Marick unstrap the long Alpine downhill racing skis from his back. As he got down on his knees in the snow to clamp Marick's feet into the bindings, he said quietly, "You've got the tension on the releases set up pretty high, Mr. Marick. You may need to get out of these bindings a lot faster than these will let you."

"I said knock off with the advice," Marick told him as he pulled the cover off the aerosol canisters mounted in a rack on his back.

"It isn't advice," Scotty said, handing him the ski poles. "It's just wondering why you're risking your life."

Marick rammed the poles down into the snow and then stared coldly at Scotty. "Kid, when you try to accomplish big things, you've got to take big risks. If you ever understand that, maybe you'll amount to something. But I doubt it."

Scotty wondered whether getting your picture on TV for a few seconds was a big accomplishment. *Big enough,* he wondered, *to die for?*

Then, suddenly, Scotty realized that you had to risk your life just to cross the street. Was anything on the other side of the street as important as your life?

Scotty felt a little ashamed as he helped Marick uncover the canisters. As he brought the release cords around under Marick's arms he said, "I'm sorry. I'd forgotten that what you do on this mountain is none of my business."

"That's right. So try one of the canisters. Just a short shot to be sure it's clear. I don't want to alert them down there until I'm ready."

Scotty tapped the aerosol release valve gently, and a little cloud of bright red dust shot up into the air and hung there, brilliant against the overhanging snow, until it was blown away by the wind. "Works OK," he said.

"Of course, it does. I do my homework." Then Marick turned to stare at him. "You think there's going to be an avalanche, don't you?"

"Yes, I do."

"And you're scared stiff, right?"

"I'm scared," Scotty told him.

"You want to run and hide."

"I want to get out of the way of it."

"That's the difference between you and me," Marick said. "You're scared of it, but I—*want*—it! I *want* an avalanche to come down on me."

He poked Scotty in the chest with his finger. "Because, kid, I'm going to outrun it! Out-ski it! I'm going to go all the way down this mountain in front of an avalanche with all those TV cameras catching every bit of it. What a *picture!* It'll be the greatest thing you'll ever see on the tube."

Sure will," Scotty said, "if you make it."

"I'll make it. So you run on and hide, kid. Hide real, real good."

"Thanks," Scotty said. "And goodbye—in case I don't see you again."

"You won't," Marick told him. "I'll leave your money with the banker in the village."

"Don't bother," Scotty said. "I don't get paid if I don't bring people up here and bring them down again—alive."

As Marick pushed off, herringboning toward the mogul, Scotty turned and looked for anything that would give him even a little protection from an avalanche. The only thing he could see that offered him a small degree of safety was a low, black ridge of rock protruding from the mantle of snow. He started toward it, his boots driving into the loose, powdery snow as he pulled himself along with both his and Marick's ice axes.

About halfway to the stone ridge, Scotty stopped for a second to get his breath. He looked back and saw that Marick had reached the mogul and was standing on top of it, facing into the valley 12,000 feet below.

And as Scotty looked, a brilliant red cloud of the aerosol dust burst around Marick, the particles glittering in the sunlight. The wind carried them like a banner across the white expanse of snow.

As Scotty turned to go on, he grinned a little. *That idiot might just make it,* he thought. *If he took off from the mogul now, he just might make it.*

But, Scotty thought, glancing back again, *if he stands there posing in his red dust, making sure that his TV cameras are getting a picture of him, he just might not.*

The explosion was first a sharp, distinct CRACK—like the sound of a cannon and then, like thunder, it spread, and rolled, and shook the earth.

For a moment, Scotty was overwhelmed by the sheer pressure of the sound, but then he jerked around and looked up at the mountain.

The smooth, curving contour of the snowcap had been broken. There was a ragged gap in it now, and the slab of snow which had broken away was sliding down the slope, losing its distinct

shape as it created a cloud of loose snow billowing around the front of it.

It was not a great avalanche. Most of the enormous mass of snow up there was still in place, motionless. Scotty stood, almost paralyzed, watching, and hoping that the slab which had broken loose would be enough to relieve the tension in the remaining mass so that it would hang there in place at least long enough for him—and Marick—to reach safety.

For Marick was now skiing down the mountain directly ahead of the moving slab. A red streamer of dust seemed to pursue him and, Scotty thought, it must be making a beautiful picture for the TV cameras in the valley.

He turned away from this great spectacle and started driving with all his strength toward the ridge, clawing with the axes, pounding with his feet, driving himself as the constant and increasing thunder of the avalanche poured around him.

The stone ridge was still fifty yards distant when, with no warning at all, the mountain erupted.

The sound of it went beyond sound and became a tremendous pressure on him as the enormous mass of snow broke loose all the way across the summit. Looking back, Scotty saw a gigantic wave, towering above the slope, the front of it lost in the clouds of snow foam which the increasing wind lashed into the air.

And now the terrifying rumbling of a great avalanche started as the tons of snow catapulted down the slope, looking as though the entire mountain was collapsing upon itself.

For Scotty, now, there was nowhere to go, no place to hide.

He looked once for Marick and, for a second, saw the man racing ahead of the mass, but then Scotty lost sight of him in the cloud of snow foam flowing ahead of the solid body of the avalanche. In that blizzard of blowing snow, Marick could still be moving ahead, his speed perhaps greater than that of the avalanche.

And then the avalanche was upon Scotty and he had no more time to think of Marick. Afraid the ice axes would stab him, he threw them away, then ripped Marick's boots from around his neck and dropped them. Then he crouched, facing the roaring, tumbling wall descending on him, the muscles of his legs taut, his whole body ready.

And then it s time and, like a spring letting go, Scotty leaped up as high as he could toward the oncoming mass. As he moved upward through the snow cloud, he twisted around so that his back was toward the solid wall of the avalanche, his head toward the summit. When he felt the moving wave of snow hit him, he began to flail his arms and legs, clawing his way up the moving face of snow almost like a swimmer trying to master a towering wave.

It was no use. No matter how hard he fought it, he could not keep the enormous mass from slowly grasping him and holding him helpless. In a motion that felt to him almost slow, the avalanche threw him face forward and down. He saw the blue sky disappear and then, for a fraction of a second, he was in the gray gloom of the snow foam, but that too, disappeared, and he was in darkness.

The moving wall of snow rolled him over and over, burying him deep within itself.

Scotty fought the thing. With his arms around his head, he kept fighting to keep the snow cleared away from his face, fighting to make a hole of air around his head.

Slowly the avalanche stopped moving him as it rammed him deeper and deeper into its mass. And, slowly, the terrifying sound of it faded away: that sound replaced by a profound, heavy silence.

At last he was motionless, his body in a ball with his legs drawn up against his chest, his arms still working to push back the snow.

The onslaught of the avalanche had been so violent, so fast, and so overpowering that he had lost all reaction, all feeling. It was as though the thing had taken away his strength and—his mind.

But now in the silent stillness, he slowly began to feel his body again. With one hand, he touched his face.

His helmet and snow goggles had been ripped off and were gone, and his face was encased in snow.

Gently he scraped the snow away until he could breathe and then open his eyes.

He might as well have left them shut for the darkness was absolute. There was no light of any kind; just a heavy, black, velvety, cold darkness.

It frightened him, and he started to shake with fear. And, he began to hear a strange, rhythmic sound and recognized it finally as his own frantic panting.

He could not afford this fear; it was using up the small amount of air he had. Almost saying it out loud, Scotty talked to himself. "Cut it *out! Stop* this!"

And his breathing slowed, and his body stopped shaking, and he went on with his investigation.

At first, he couldn't believe that through all the violence and onslaught of the snow, it had failed to hurt him. But, as he slowly moved, ramming his legs down, nothing *hurt*. His body was not broken anywhere. Nothing hurt.

This knowledge flooded him with excitement, almost jubilation. It gave him a feeling of victory. He had *triumphed* over the most awful avalanche he had ever seen.

Scotty felt *great!* Nothing to it!

Just get out of this snow and go on about my business, he thought.

Aloud, his voice strong with victory, he said, "I beat it! It couldn't even hurt me! Let's get out of here."

But—which way?

Which way was out?

Which way was up?

All his triumph, his victory, drained away and fear took its place. He could not hold it back, for now he knew that even if he could find out which way was up, there was no way to know—*how far?*

All he had left now was a few cubic feet of air in the hole he had made around his head. How long would that last? Long enough to find which way was up? Then enough more to let him dig his way out?

And then a thought simply overwhelmed him. *I am buried alive,* he thought. *Buried alive.*

Part Two

The avalanche that had overrun the eighteen-year-old Scotty and buried him he knew not how deep under the snow, had destroyed his grasp on reality.

The insanity and violence of the avalanche seemed to him as though nature had suddenly gone crazy. All the natural laws by which he had lived had been broken in that instant when the avalanche had started, with quiet, soft snow suddenly exploding with the sounds of thunder, and of awful bombardment, and of terrible grinding of rock upon rock. And the sudden turning of a vast expanse of silent, unruffled snow into a sea of wildly surging waves and breakers, with a foam of snowy surf surrounding them, was simply insane.

For Scotty, now, nothing was real anymore. There were no rules to follow, no logic to work with. He was buried, his body encased in snow, with only a small pocket of air around his head—air which he knew he was using up with no way to obtain more. This was the only reality he could grasp: that he was dying in this grave of snow, buried alive in it.

His mind, affected by the growing poison of the air he was breathing, began to drift, and he idly wondered if this was the feeling of death. This almost peaceful drifting.

But then his mind drifted back again to the avalanche and, slowly, he began to realize that no laws had been broken, that nature had not, as he had thought, gone insane. All the natural laws of cohesion, of tension and pressure, had been obeyed. There had been, finally, too much snow piled on the mountain, and the warming temperature had finally broken the icy cohesion of millions of tiny snowflakes which had held it there.

The slope of the mountain had simply been too steep, the tension of the enormous weight too great, and so the natural laws of gravity had been obeyed and the inevitable result had been the avalanche that had buried him alive.

There was small consolation for Scotty in this realization that the laws of nature still worked. His problem was that his supply of air was running out,

and he would die here if he could not dig his way out of this icy grave. A simple problem in itself, but now complicated by the fact that he did not know which way to dig; he did not know where, with relation to the ground and the surface of the snow, he was lying. Was he upside down so that if he dug head-first through the snow, he would eventually reach the solid rock of the mountain—where there was no air at all?

Or was he lying parallel to the ground so that if he dug his way along, his effort and lack of air would soon kill him?

Which way was up?

Scotty didn't know and didn't know how to find out.

And then he thought: If nature is still sane and the laws still work, then the law of fluid pressure will also work and would, if he himself were sane enough, tell him what he had to know to save himself from death.

He began to move his arms and legs, moving them slowly and with the least amount of effort, to keep his lungs from wasting the air he had.

And as he moved, turning his body slowly around in a circle like a diver doing a slow flip, his mind monitored the pressure of the blood against his skull.

His motions were almost those of a swimmer, except that he was swimming in some thick, but yielding fluid, as he worked his way around through the soft, almost dry-feeling snow.

And then he reached a point where the pressure of the blood in his skull seemed to diminish as he moved beyond a certain spot.

Going back to that place in his circle, he felt the pressure increase again. And now he knew.

For the second time in this grave he felt excitement, almost jubilation, and a small feeling that, although he had not yet been victorious over this avalanche, he was still fighting it. He had not given up and simply let the thing kill him.

If the pressure of blood in his head was greatest here, then the way up was where his feet were, for, if the law of gravity still worked, he was now upside down, his head pointing straight down toward the center of the earth.

Scotty, conserving his scant air, worked his body around through 180 degrees, feeling the pressure in his face and head decreasing, until he reasoned that he was now pointing up toward the surface of the snow.

Again like a swimmer working his way to the top, Scotty began a slow swimming motion with his arms and legs, stopping regularly to clear the snow from around his face. And as he moved upward it seemed to him that the air he breathed was growing fresher; his mind seemed now to be clearer and keener.

That was caused by a law of nature also, for, he reasoned now, the heaviest, most dense snow of the avalanche would have worked its way down, leaving light, powdery snow of the last fall on the surface; snow that was porous enough to admit some air.

Suddenly one arm, reaching up to pull downward, found no resistance.

With his body still encased in snow, with only his head and one arm free of it, he stayed motionless for a long time, gulping in the fresh, cold, clear air.

All the violence, all the roaring and grinding and booming of the avalanche had died, and there was around him now a total, cold silence.

Working his way up until he was standing on the surface, Scotty looked slowly around.

The world he had known only a few minutes ago was gone. The great white, smooth, unmarked blanket of snow upon the mountain had been clawed and torn and ripped apart, so that it seemed to him as though he were standing on some distant, unknown planet with an awful surface of tortured rock protruding through a layer of dirty, gray-brown snow.

Looking up, he saw the summit of the mountain now almost unmarked by snow; the rocks almost as clean as they had been in July.

And Scotty turned again and gazed out over the terrible terrain toward where he had last seen Marick, flying on those long Alpine skis, the cloud of red dust erupting from the aerosol canister on his back. Scotty remembered how, like a fade-out on television, Marick had disappeared in the wind-blown clouds of light snow preceding the body of the avalanche.

Almost saying it aloud, Scotty thought: "I am now alone here on this mountain."

And he thought: *I beat it! I'm alive! I'm out of that grave.*

And all I've got to do now is get out of this mess, find my snowmobile, and chug on home.

They won't believe it in the village; they won't believe that I lived through that avalanche. But I don't care whether they do or not—I'm alive!

It was a beautiful afternoon. The sun was in a cloudless sky and there wasn't a sound anywhere. Only when he looked down at the destruction the avalanche had caused, the great raw scars it had made on the face of the mountain, was his feeling of peacefulness disturbed.

Scotty was turning toward where they had parked the snowmobile when he suddenly stopped. There was time, he decided, to at least go over to where he had last seen Marick and, from there, check on that red dust. There should be a line of it for as far down the mountain as he could see.

It'll make me feel better, Scotty decided, to know that Marick made it. Then he grinned. He probably made it, probably accomplished his crazy dream of skiing down this mountain. But Scotty doubted if those expensive TV cameras in the valley had been able to photograph it. For, Scotty figured, Marick would have been obscured in that cloud of free snow for most of his long journey. But at least he'll get his name in the book of records.

Scotty worked his way across the steep slope, coming at last to a trace of the red dust on the grayish snow. Since it was lighter than snow and propelled by the aerosol gas, Scotty could see now a broken, but distinct line of the dust leading straight downward.

Then, abruptly, the red line ended in an area of almost clean, white snow, which, when Scotty reached it, he found to be light and powdery.

Standing there in the cold silence, Scotty somehow knew that the name of Marick was not going to appear in the book of records, nor was Marick going to be shown on the evening TV news. For, Scotty knew now, Marick was buried here just as he had been.

The man could not live long in this deep snow. A few minutes; an hour at the most—*if* the snow had not so compressed his body that he could not expand his lungs to breathe whatever air might be in it.

Standing there, a sad weariness seemed to drain his strength. Scotty wondered if there was anything he could do. He thought of the rescue chopper and dismissed the idea. It would take hours just to get a message down the mountain.

Was there any use trying to dig down into this snow, looking for a body?

None. Marick's body could be *anywhere* in this desolate area.

The only thing he could do was mark this place so that sometime people could come here and search.

He could not risk taking off any of his clothes to use as a marker, so he began to search for something in the snow, and, as he searched, he suddenly saw the rack of canisters half buried in the snow.

For a moment Scotty just stared at them, his mind too stunned by his own experience to function. But slowly he realized that if the canisters had been ripped off Marick by the first impact of the avalanche, then the man might be buried close to them. And on a line between them and the summit.

If he dug a trench along that line, perhaps he'd be lucky and find a ski pole that he could use to probe down into the snow in search of a body. It was a faint chance; useless really, but Scotty could not simply walk away from a man buried alive. Not even a man like Marick.

It was slow, hard digging, the cold seeping through his gloves and numbing his hands, but he kept on, foot after foot, opening a narrow trench parallel to the line of red dust.

Finally, defeated and afraid that darkness would trap him on the mountain, Scotty measured off one more foot to go and decided that, at the end of it, he would abandon what he had known from the beginning was a useless search.

He had dug perhaps six of the last twelve inches when his hands met solid resistance. Scraping the snow away from whatever had stopped him, he slowly recognized it as the waxed bottom of a ski.

Scotty became unreasonably irritated when something prevented him from pulling the ski out of the snow. It must, he figured, be wedged under something, for certainly when the avalanche hit Marick, the force would have released the clamps of his bindings and freed his foot from this ski.

But the bindings had not let go, and, as Scotty freed up the whole length of the ski, he knew that Marick's foot was still attached to it.

There was something terribly wrong. The ski turned in his hands as though on a swivel. And he suddenly knew that, below the ski, Marick's leg was broken—totally broken.

Fumbling down through the snow, Scotty found the binding release handle and forced it open. Now he lifted the ski clear and, using it both as pick and shovel, began attacking the snow, digging it out from around Marick's legs, then his hips, until Scotty could reach down and grasp the leather belt.

Bracing himself, Scotty pulled the body up and out of the snow and laid it face up on the surface.

Marick was still alive! Unconscious, his leg broken, his face covered with blood and snow, he was still breathing.

Cleaning the snow away from his nose and mouth, Scotty covered his chest with his jacket and then began working on the broken leg. With his belt and Marick's, he strapped the dangling leg to the ski so that when he lifted the man, the leg hung down almost straight.

The walk across the terrible slope was a nightmare, Marick's weight on his back seeming to increase with every step he took. But at last he saw his blue snowmobile parked at the foot of the cliff. It was covered with snow, but untouched by the brutal avalanche.

With the seat belts and rope, he strapped Marick along the top of the snowmobile and then, since there was no room left, Scotty walked along beside it, steering it down the side of the mountain.

During the whole trip, the last half hour of it in darkness, Marick never spoke. Occasionally Scotty thought that he had died, but then Marick would groan or gasp for air, and they went on.

As he passed familiar landmarks in the dark, Scotty began looking ahead for the lights of his village to guide him. But there were no lights, and as he went on his apprehension grew. The old men of the village had been warning people for weeks that when the avalanche came, it could be great enough to sweep completely over the village, burying it and burying the people stupid enough to stay there.

The old men had been right. Where there had been a little village, there were now only a few scattered humps which Scotty recognized as rooftops covered with snow.

The only familiar thing that finally appeared in the headlights was the rectangular shape of the hospital, which was the only two-story building in town. The avalanche had buried the ground floor, and the level of snow now stood a foot or so higher than the bottom of the second-story windows.

Dim, flickering, yellow light shone from some of the windows, and, as Scotty steered the snowmobile slowly along, he finally came to the wide, immovable window of the operating room. Stopping there he could dimly see through the frosted glass that the whole room was crowded with people. A few flashlights were feebly glowing, and there were some candles burning yellow

on the tops of tables and cabinets.

The people were motionless, speechless and, for a second, Scotty thought that they were all dead. Frozen perhaps, or suffocated. But dead.

He moved the snowmobile on to one of the room windows where, inside, he could see more people; these also motionless, dead, sitting and lying around on the floor.

But when he tapped on the glass, he saw a few people raise their heads and look at him, their faces blank, their eyes uncomprehending.

Scotty motioned for someone to open the window and, at last, a man walked slowly to it and stood, staring blankly out.

Scotty motioned violently for him to open the window, and the man finally understood and pulled it slowly down. Then, in a dead voice, the man said, "What do you want?"

"Help me get this man inside," Scotty said. "He's got a broken leg."

The man started to close the window as he said in that strange, lifeless voice, "No use. We haven't got any light or heat or anything."

Scotty dragged the window open again. "Help me!" he demanded, and with his other hand, he began unstrapping Marick.

Other men, walking like zombies, came slowly to the window and slowly dragged Marick into the room.

"Where's the doctor?" Scotty asked.

A woman he knew slowly looked up at him and said wearily, "He can't do anything."

Scotty climbed through the window and stood looking at these people he had known all his life. And now he realized that they had been so stunned and shocked by the onslaught of the avalanche that they were, indeed, acting like zombies.

Closing the window, he made his way to the operating room.

The doctor was sitting on the floor in the dimly lit room, his hands lying helplessly in his lap, his head covered with a sheepskin hood. Scotty stooped down in front of him and said, "I've got a man who's almost dead."

The doctor didn't even raise his head. "I can't do anything," he said helplessly, his eyes in the dim candlelight almost in tears. "I have no light."

Scotty took the doctor's hands and pulled him to his feet. "You get the man on the table and I'll get you light," he told him.

Going back to Marick, Scotty told the men to take him to the operating room. Then he climbed back out the window and made his way to the snowmobile.

Maneuvering it around until it was pointed toward the wide, solid window of the operating room, Scotty nosed it up until it almost touched the glass. Then he switched on the headlights and watched the people inside the room slowly turn to stare at them.

As the men shuffled in with Marick, Scotty went to the window and began scraping the frost off with his cold, gloved hands. Then he stood in the snow and watched as the doctor began cutting away the cloth around Marick's leg.

It was then that the ice-cold weariness hit Scotty, and it took all his strength just to drag himself into the snowmobile and sit there, slumped over the steering wheel.

Now, he thought, *I'm a zombie like them,* his mind growing numb and slow. *A zombie.*

The voice sounding above the steady thrumming of the motor surprised Scotty, and he dragged his head up to see a man standing beside him in the darkness.

"Is that Marick?" the man asked in a slow, dead voice.

"Yeah."

"Is he alive?"

"Barely."

The man leaned wearily against the snowmobile, and his voice was vague as he said, "It's too bad."

Scotty stared slowly at him, confused and lost. "That he's alive?" he asked. "What do you mean, 'too bad'?"

"Oh no," the man said slowly. "Not that. Just too bad that we never got a picture of him. Did he make it?"

"Well," Scotty said, trying to force his mind to function, "He's in there."

"That's too bad," the man said in that vague voice. "Because my camera's gone. Buried. I don't guess I'll ever find it."

Scotty lowered his head to let it rest in his hands on the steering wheel.

"That's too bad," he said.

Close Up

1. (a) Why has Scotty lost respect for Marick? (b) Why is Marick angry with Scotty?

2. (a) What signs warn Scotty of the avalanche? (b) How does Marick interpret each of these signs?

3. (a) Why does Scotty head for the black stone ridge? (b) Why does he throw away his ice axes?

4. Scotty is able to act with calm and control in the face of impending disaster. (a) What does Scotty do to prevent his being buried by the avalanche? (b) What does he do to keep from being smothered by the snow and ice? (c) Find one other instance where his ability to remain calm saves his life.

5. Why does Scotty try to save Marick's life, even though he does not like him?

Setting

The setting of a story can bring out the best or the worst in characters. It can force them to make decisions that affect their lives and the lives of others. For example, in "Avalanche," the life-threatening setting forces Scotty to prove his courage and make certain decisions.

1. When the avalanche buries him, Scotty seems to lose all reaction, all feeling. (a) How does the "heavy, black, velvety, cold darkness" eventually force him to feel? (b) What does he do to overcome this feeling?

2. (a) Why doesn't Scotty know which way to dig in order to get out of his icy grave? (b) How does he find which way is up?

3. When Scotty escapes he thinks, ". . . all I've got to do now is get out of this mess, find my snowmobile, and chug on home." (a) Why does he change his mind and decide to search for Marick? (b) How do the red dust and the aerosol canisters help him to locate Marick?

4. At the beginning of the story, Marick called Scotty "a gutless wonder." Do you think Scotty's saving Marick's life proves his courage? Why or why not?

Activities

1. Make a list of items you think a person would need to survive for twenty-four hours on a snow-covered mountain.

2. **Composition.** Write a paragraph defining courage. Try to use specific examples to illustrate your points.

INFERENCES

Making Inferences About Future Actions and Events

An inference is an intelligent guess you form by using hints in the story; that is, by reading between the lines. The author may not tell you in so many words that something is going to happen or that someone is going to do something, but the author may give you hints. By paying close attention to these hints, you can infer what will happen next. When you begin reading a story, you have very little, if any, idea of how it will end. However, as you get further into the story, you begin to suspect certain outcomes.

A good habit to get into as you read is to pause periodically and ask yourself what's going to happen next or how the story seems likely to end. Making inferences and then reading to discover whether or not you inferred correctly helps you better understand what you read, and it also adds excitement.

---

1. As you read "Avalanche" you might have inferred that Marick was headed for trouble. Which details below helped you make that inference?
   a. He was an excellent skier.
   b. He was boastful and vain.
   c. He was careless.
   d. He made fun of Scotty's warnings.
   e. He didn't know much about the danger of avalanches.
   f. He wore expensive boots.
   g. He wanted glory at any risk.

2. Which of the following details support the inference that Scotty will escape from his snow prison?
   a. Scotty is familiar with mountains and avalanches.
   b. Scotty is a strong man.
   c. Scotty did not like Marick.
   d. Scotty is eighteen years old.
   e. Scotty is intelligent and resourceful.

WORD ATTACK

Understanding Compound Words

A compound word is made up of two smaller words. For example, look at the word *sunball*. It is made up of the words *sun* and *ball*. You may not have known the meaning of the word *sunball* before you read this story. By looking at the meaning of the two individual words (*sun* and *ball*), you probably guessed that a sunball is a ball of snow formed when the sun melts some of the snow on a mountainside.

When you read a word you do not know, check to see if it is a compound word. If it is, look at the two smaller words that it contains. Putting their meanings together may help you find the meaning of the compound word.

1. First decide which of the following words are compound words. Then, for each compound word, write the two words that make up the larger word.
    - **a.** yelled
    - **b.** paperback
    - **c.** outside
    - **d.** thousands
    - **e.** overpower
    - **f.** snowfall
    - **g.** catapult
    - **h.** candlelight
    - **i.** bombardment
    - **j.** basketball

2. For each of the compound words above, write an original sentence.

3. A snowmobile is a vehicle used for traveling through snow. Use your dictionary to find out how this word was formed.

Crow Call

Lois Lowry

It was morning, early, barely light, cold for November. I was nine and the war was over. At home, in the bed next to mine, my older sister still slept, adolescent, her blond hair streaming over the edge of the sheet. I sat shyly in the front seat of the car next to the stranger who was my father, my blue-jeaned legs pulled up under the too-large wool shirt I was wearing, making a bosom of my knees.

"Daddy," I said, the title coming uncertainly, "I've never gone hunting before. What if I don't know what to do?"

"Well," he said, "I've been thinking about that, and I've decided to put you in charge of the crow call. Have you ever operated a crow call?"

I shook my head. "No."

"It's an art," he said. "No doubt about that. But I'm pretty sure you can handle it. Some people will blow and blow on a crow call and not a single crow will even wake up or bother to listen, much less answer. But I really think you can do it. Of course," he added, chuckling, "having that shirt will help."

I glanced over quickly to see if he was laughing at me, but his smile was

inclusive; I chuckled too, hugging my shirt around me.

My father had bought the shirt for me. In town to buy groceries, he had noticed my hesitating in front of Kronenberg's window. The plaid hunting shirts had been in the store window for a month—the popular red and black and green and black ones toward the front, clothing ruddy mannequins holding guns and duck decoys; but my shirt, the rainbow plaid, hung separately on a wooden hanger toward the back of the display. I had lingered in front of Kronenberg's window every chance I had since the hunting shirts had appeared.

My sister had rolled her eyes in disdain. "Daddy," she pointed out to him as we entered Kronenberg's, "that's a *man's* shirt."

The salesman had smiled and said dubiously, "I don't quite think . . . "

"You know," my father had said to me as the salesman wrapped the shirt, "buying this shirt is probably a very practical thing to do. You will never *ever* outgrow this shirt."

Now, as I got out of the car in front of the diner where we were going to have breakfast, the shirt unfolded itself downward until the bottom of it reached my knees; from the bulky thickness of rolled-back cuffs my hands were exposed. I felt totally surrounded by shirt.

My father ordered coffee for himself. The waitress, middle-aged and dawn-sleepy, asked, "What about your boy? What does he want?"

My father winked at me, and I hoped that my pigtails would stay hidden inside the plaid wool collar. Holding my head very still, I looked at the menu. At home, my usual breakfast was cereal with honey and milk. My mother kept honey in a covered silver pitcher. The diner's menu, grease-spotted and marred with penciled notations and paper-clipped addenda, seemed not to include honey.

"What's your favorite thing to eat in the whole world?" asked my father.

I smiled at him. If he hadn't been away for so long, he would have known. It was a family joke in a family that hadn't included him. "Cherry pie," I admitted.

My father handed back both menus to the waitress. "Three pieces of cherry pie," he told her.

"Three?" She looked at him sleepily, not writing the order down. "You mean two?"

"No," he said, "I mean three. One for me, with black coffee, and two for my hunting companion, with a large glass of milk."

She shrugged.

We ate quickly, watching the sun rise now across the Pennsylvania farm lands. Back in the car, I flipped my pigtails out from under my shirt collar and giggled.

"Hey, boy," my father said to me in an imitation of the groggy waitress' voice, "you sure you can eat all that cherry pie, boy?"

"Just you watch me, lady," I answered in a deep, I thought boyish, voice, pulling my face into stern, serious lines. We laughed again, driving out into the gray-green hills of the early morning.

Grass, frozen after its summer softness, crunched under our feet; the air was sharp and supremely clear, free from the floating pollens of summer, and our words seemed etched and breakable on the brittle stillness. I felt the smooth wood of the crow call in my pocket, moving my fingers against it for warmth, memorizing its ridges and shape. I stamped my feet hard against the ground now and then as my father did. I wanted to scamper ahead of him like a puppy, kicking the dead leaves and reaching the unknown places first, but there was an uneasy feeling along the edge of my back at the thought of walking in front of someone carrying a gun. Carefully, I stayed by his side.

It was quieter than summer. There were no animal sounds, no bird-waking noises; even the occasional leaf that fell within our vision did so in silence, spiraling slowly down to blend in brownly with the others. But most leaves were already gone from the trees; those that remained seemed caught there by accident, waiting for the wind that would free them. Our breath was steam.

"Daddy," I asked shyly, "were you scared in the war?"

He looked ahead, up the hill, and rubbed the stock of his gun thoughtfully with one hand and said after a moment, "Yes. I was scared."

"Of what?"

"Lots of things. Of being alone. Of being hurt. Of hurting someone else."

"Are you still?"

He glanced down. "I don't think so. Those kind of scares go away."

"I'm scared sometimes," I confided.

He nodded, unsurprised. "I know," he said. "Are you scared now?"

I started to say no, and then answered, "Maybe of your gun, a little."

I looked quickly at his gun, his polished, waxed prize, and then at him. He nodded, not saying anything. We walked on.

"Daddy?"

"Mmmmmm?" He was watching the sky, the trees.

"I wish the crows didn't eat the crops."

"They don't know any better," he said. "Even people do bad things without meaning to."

"Yes, but . . ." I paused and then told him what I'd been thinking. "They might have babies to take care of. Baby crows."

"Not now, not this time of year," he said. "By now their babies are grown. It's a strange thing, but by now they don't

even know who their babies are." He put his free arm over my shoulders for a moment.

"And their babies grow up and eat the crops too," I said and sighed, knowing it to be true and unchangeable.

"It's too bad," he acknowledged. We began to climb the hill.

"Can you call anything else, Daddy? Or just crows?"

"Sure," he said. "Listen. Mooooooooo. That's a cow call."

"Guess the cows didn't hear it," I teased him when we encountered silence.

"Well, of course, sometimes they choose not to answer. I can do tigers too. Rrrrrrrrrrrr."

"Ha. So can I. And bears. Better watch out, now. Bears might come out of the woods on this one. Grrrrrrrrrrrrr."

He looked at me arrogantly. "You think you're so smart, doing bears. Listen to this. Giraffe call." He stood with his neck stretched out, soundless.

I tried not to laugh, wanting to do rabbits next, but couldn't keep from it. He looked so funny with his neck pulled away from his shirt collar and a condescending, poised, giraffe look on his face. I giggled at him and we kept walking to the top of the hill.

From where we stood we could see almost back to town. We could look down on our car and follow the ribbon of road through the farm lands until it was lost in trees. Dark roofs of houses lay scattered, separated by pastures.

"Okay," said my father, "you can do the crow call now. This is a good place."

I saw no crows. For a moment the fear of disappointing him struggled with my desire to blow into the smooth, pol-

ished tip of the crow call. But he was waiting, and I took it from my pocket, held it against my lips, and blew softly.

The harsh, muted sound of a sleepy crow came as a surprise to me, and I smiled at it, at the delight of having made that sound myself. I did it again, softly.

From a grove of trees on another hill came an answer from a waking bird. Just one, and then silence.

Tentatively, I called again, more loudly. The branches of a nearby tree rustled, and crows answered, fluttering and calling crossly. They flew briefly into the air and then settled on a branch—three of them.

"Look, Daddy," I whispered. "Do you see them? They think I'm a crow!"

He nodded, watching them.

I moved away from him with confidence and stood on a rock at the top of the hill and blew loudly several times. From all the trees rose crows. They screamed with harsh voices and I responded, blowing again and again as they flew from the hillside in circles, dipping and soaring, landing speculatively, lurching from the limbs in afterthought, and then settling again with resolute and disgruntled shrieks.

"Listen, Daddy! Do you hear them? They think I'm their friend! Maybe their baby, all grown up!"

I ran about the top of the hill and then down, through the frozen grass, blowing the crow call over and over. The crows called back at me, and from all the trees they rose, from all the hills. They circled and circled, and the morning was filled with the patterns of calling crows as I looked back, still running. I could see my father sitting on a rock, his gun leaning against him, and I could see he was smiling.

My crow calling came in shorter and shorter spurts as I became breathless; finally I stopped and stood laughing at the foot of the hill, and the noise from the crows subsided as they circled irritably and settled back in the trees. They were waiting for me.

My father came down the hill to meet me coming up. He carried his gun carefully; and though I was grateful to him for not using it, I felt that there was no need to say thank you, for I felt that he knew. The crows would always be there and they would always eat the crops; and some other morning, on some other hill, he would shoot them.

I blew the crow call once more, to say good morning and goodbye and everything that goes in between. Then I put it into the pocket of my shirt and reached over out of my enormous cuffs and took my father's hand. We stood there, he and I, halfway up the November hillside, and the newly up sun was a pink wash across the Pennsylvania sky. The brown grass and curled leaves were thick around our feet, and above our heads the air was filled with the answering sound of the circling crows.

Close Up

1. At the beginning of this story, the girl feels awkward with her father. (a) Where has he been for the last few years? (b) Why does this make him seem like a stranger to her?

2. The father takes his daughter hunting so that he can get to know her again. (a) What reason does he give for buying her a shirt that is too large for her? (b) What is his real reason?

3. When her father asks her what is her favorite thing to eat, the girl thinks, "If he hadn't been away for so long, he would have known. It was a family joke in a family that hadn't included him." Why do you think the father orders two pieces of cherry pie for his daughter?

4. (a) How does the daughter feel when the crows answer her call? (b) Why does the father decide not to shoot the crows?

Mood

The mood of a story is the impression it creates and the emotions it arouses in the reader. In "Crow Call," the author creates a mood of quiet happiness through her choice of setting, specific details and images, and words and phrases.

1. When the girl wakes up, it is barely light outside and cold for November. (a) Why does her shirt make her feel surrounded by warmth? (b) How do the shirt's colors create a happy feeling?

2. Find three words or phrases that create a vivid picture of the cold November woods. (For example, notice the *italicized* words and phrases in the following sentence: "Grass, *frozen after its summer softness, crunched* under our feet.")

3. When the girl blows the crow call in the cold woods, she feels surrounded by the warmth of friendship. Why?

4. Sounds are important in creating the mood of this story. Find three sounds that fill the November morning and help create the mood of happiness (for example, the sound of laughter).

5. Reread the last paragraph of the story. (a) Find the sentence that describes the November sky. (b) Do you think this image adds to the mood of the story? Why or why not?

Activity

▶ **Composition.** Choose a time of day or a place that makes you feel a particular way. Write a paragraph about it and see if another student can identify the mood you wanted to create.

INFERENCES

Identifying Valid Inferences

An inference is an intelligent guess you make based on evidence. For example, if you see a man in the woods carrying a gun and a crow call, you might infer that he is hunting for crows. You have not seen him hunting, but based on the evidence (the gun and the crow call), you infer that he is hunting. The more evidence you use to make your inference, the more likely it is that your inference will be valid; that is, that it will turn out to be true.

1. Which of the inferences below were valid and which were not?
   a. The father inferred that his younger daughter would love the hunting shirt, even though it was too large.
   b. The waitress inferred that the father was with his son.
   c. The waitress inferred that the father meant to order two pieces of pie.
   d. The father inferred that his daughter did not want him to shoot the crows.

2. At the end of the story, the girl infers that her father will shoot the crows sometime in the future. Do you think her inference is valid? Why or why not?

WORD ATTACK

Using a Dictionary to Break Words into Syllables

A syllable is a word or word part that stands for a complete sound unit. A syllable contains at least one vowel. Each syllable is set off by a space, a hyphen, or dot in the dictionary. For example, syl·la·ble.

Breaking long words into syllables often will help you to pronounce them correctly.

▶ Find the following words in a dictionary and divide them into syllables.

a.	grateful	k.	adolescent
b.	dubious	l.	operate
c.	enormous	m.	inclusive
d.	memorize	n.	mannequin
e.	waitress	o.	linger
f.	Pennsylvania	p.	practical
g.	cereal	q.	notation
h.	companion	r.	addendum
i.	imitation	s.	condescend
j.	brittle	t.	arrogant

Crows

David McCord

I like to walk
And hear the black crows talk.

I like to lie
And watch crows sail the sky.

5   I like the crow
That wants the wind to blow:

I like the one
That thinks the wind is fun.

I like to see
10 Crows spilling from a tree,

And try to find
The top crow left behind.

I like to hear
Crows caw that spring is near.

15 I like the great
Wild clamor of crow hate

Three farms away
When owls are out by day.

I like the slow
20 Tired homeward-flying crow;

I like the sight
Of crows for my good night.

Haikai II

Sadakichi Hartmann

Butterflies a-wing—
  Are you flowers returning
To your branch in Spring?

Cynthia in the Snow

Gwendolyn Brooks

It SHUSHES.
It hushes
The loudness in the road.
It flitter-twitters,
5 And laughs away from me.
It laughs a lovely whiteness,
And whitely whirs away,
To be
Some otherwhere,
10 Still white as milk or shirts.
So beautiful it hurts.

Activity

▶ **Composition.** Did you notice that each sentence in "Crows" begins with the words "I like"? Write your own poem about something you like to do.

One Alaska Night

Barrett Willoughby

"There was something distinctly sinister in the very quality of the silence that hung over the cabin—a feeling as if death brooded there."

A root tripped me and threw me flat in the trail that led through the blueberry thicket. For a moment I was too tired to stir. I lay there, face on my arms, feeling that I'd been foolhardy to start out alone on a ten-mile hike across an unfamiliar peninsula. Yet I comforted myself with the thought that it could not be much farther to the coast fox-ranch which was my destination. There Lonnie, a schoolmate of mine, was spending the summer with her father, who owned the place.

Suddenly, nose to the ground, I became aware of a rank, musky odor that brought my head up with a jerk. Something queerly crawling touched my cheek. I slapped my hand over it, and, with a chill of premonition, looked at what I'd caught—a long tuft of coarse brown hair dangling from a twig above.

One startled glance told me it had been raked from the side of an Alaskan brown bear—the largest carnivorous animal that walks the world today. With the tuft of hair clutched in my hand and sudden alarm sharpening my senses, I looked closely at the path leading forward under the leafy tunnel in which I lay.

All along it, evenly spaced in the damp, brown mold, were deep depressions, round and large as dinner plates.

The truth came with a shock—I had been following a bear trail! It was already getting dark, and I was unarmed.

I'm not a hunter. I'm not even a brave woman. And I'd never before been alone in a bear-infested forest with night coming on. I recalled that bears do most of their traveling after dark—and I was lying flat in the middle of one of their thoroughfares.

I leaped to my feet, turned off the trail, and began plowing through the brush, intent only on putting all possible distance between me and that place before dark.

Almost at once the bushes thinned out, and I was able to make good time through stretches of short ferns; but the light was fading fast. Oddly, it was only now, when I was safely away from the bear trail, that it dawned on me that I had no idea which way to go.

I was lost.

In that instant of realization all my strength seemed to ooze out of me. Then panic came upon me. I had a senseless, almost uncontrollable impulse to dash madly through the trees, regardless of direction, bears, or anything else. But I got hold of myself, decided on a course, and with forced calmness went forward, watching tensely for that breaking away of the timber which foretells an approach to the sea.

Every step took me deeper into the darkening wilderness. There was no wind. Not a thing moved except myself—not a leaf, not a twig.

The very silence began to frighten me. I found myself stepping furtively, trying not to make any noise, and straining to hear the slightest sound. I kept glancing back over my shoulder. Every few feet I'd stop suddenly, holding my breath while I studied a moss-grown log or the long arm of a thorny shrub which I was sure had stirred a second before.

I was groping with my feet, my gaze fixed ahead, when out of the tail of my eye I saw a blurred stirring in the shadows under the hemlocks. I jerked my head around to look.

Nothing moved.

I wondered if the "woods-madness" that seizes lost persons was coming upon me so soon.

And then I paused to stare at a murky clump which I hoped was only bushes. The clump, big as a truck horse, started toward me. It kept coming, slowly, heavily, swinging a great, low head. Brush rattled under its shambling tread. I smelled the rank, musky odor of bear.

The next instant I had turned from the monster and was running madly through the semidarkness of the forest.

I was nearly exhausted when I burst through the timber and saw the log cabin. I was running toward this refuge with all the speed left in me, when something in the look of the place caused me to slow up. I came to a stop and peered fearfully through the dusk.

There was something distinctly sinister in the very quality of the silence that hung over the cabin—a feeling as if death brooded there. The boarded windows on each side of the closed door stared back at me like eye sockets in a brown and weathered skull.

My recoil from the place was so

strong that I turned to go back, but after one glance back into the black forest, I changed my mind. I slipped my belt ax from its sheath, grasped it firmly, and moved forward.

At the edge of the dooryard I came upon a stump and again hesitated. My fingers, absently exploring the stump's broad top, felt a crosshatch of ax marks. A block for chopping firewood, I thought, glancing at the nearby stack of dead hemlock boughs.

For some reason, this evidence of human workaday activity heartened me. I moved on and paused before the closed door. It was a homemade door of heavy, rough planks, silvered by the beating of many storms. In place of a knob, it had a rawhide latch-thong hanging outside. The thong had curled up into a hard, dry knot.

Obviously, no one had drawn this latchstring for many months. Yet when I gave it a pull, I leaped back, expecting—I don't know what.

The creaking door swung in of its own weight, revealing an interior so dark I could make out no details. I listened. All was silent. I sniffed. The place gave off the faint rancid odor that clings to a cabin in which raw furs have been dried.

Suddenly impatient at my senseless hesitancy, I plunged inside and bumped against a crude table in the middle of the floor. My outflung hand touched a bottle with dribbles of wax on the side. I struck a match, lighted the candle stub, and turned to inspect my shelter. Clearly, this was the very ordinary dwelling of some trapper who had abandoned it for other fields. There was nothing here to alarm even the most fearful woman, yet I continued to feel uneasy.

The sensible thing to do now was build a fire and then eat a sandwich. Luckily I had a couple remaining from lunch. I would go on to the fox ranch in the morning. A trail must lead out from here; and I knew I could find it when the sun came up. As I raked the ashes from the stove, I began searching my memory for all I had heard of this region.

The first thing that popped into my mind was the story of five prospectors who, a few years before, had vanished on this peninsula without leaving a trace. Rumor had it that they had met foul play at the hands of a crazy trapper—"Cub Bear" Butler. I didn't even know whether the mystery had ever been solved. But—a crazy trapper . . . I glanced back over my shoulder, wishing I hadn't thought about that.

A moment later, ax in hand, I reluctantly went out-of-doors to the chopping block to cut some wood for the stove. In nervous haste I chopped an armload of wood, then began piling the sticks on my arm. As I was reaching for the last stick, which had fallen in the bear weed, my groping fingers touched something which made me recoil so violently that all my wood fell to the ground. Hurriedly I struck a match, and, leaning forward, lowered it until the tiny light fell on the thing which lay half-concealed under the moonlit leaves.

It was a fleshless, skeleton hand, cut off at the wrist.

The match burned my fingers. I dropped it. I was backing away when my eyes, now adjusted to the darkness, fell on another set of bony fingers thrust out from under a round leaf of bear weed. Then, just beyond that, a third skeleton hand took shape in the gloom.

My brain went into a sickening tailspin. I tried to scream, but could make no sound. I tried to run, but my legs seemed turned to water. Then the hope that my eyes had tricked me in the dim light brought back a measure of calmness. I struck another match and, sweeping aside the weeds with my foot, bent to look.

They were there—all three of them.

I don't know how I nerved myself to make a thorough search of the ground around that ax-marked stump, but I did. And in the dense bear weed I saw twelve skeleton hands, all cut off at the wrist. There wasn't a skull or bone of any other kind.

Somehow I got back inside the candlelit cabin with an armload of wood, and, shoving the door shut, latched it. The fastening was an unusually sturdy bar of wood. The only way to lift and lower the bar from the outside was by means of the latch-thong. I pulled this through its small hole, grateful that the door was strong and that no one could enter unless I lifted the bar.

But I was hollow with dread. My mind kept swirling about Cub Bear Butler, the crazy trapper, and the five prospectors who had vanished. The men were last seen on this peninsula when Butler was living in the vicinity running his trap lines. Was it possible that I had stumbled onto Cub Bear's cabin? Could those skeleton hands belong to——

"But there were only *five* prospectors." I was startled to find I had spoken aloud. There were six pairs of fleshless hands out there. To whom did the sixth pair belong?

I was so unstrung by these thoughts that even after the fire was going I couldn't eat a sandwich. Instead, after

making sure that the door was still barred, I snuffed the candle, knowing it would soon burn out anyway. With my wadded jacket for a pillow, I lay down in the bare bunk, my little ax handy by my side.

I didn't intend to go to sleep, but gradually fatigue began to triumph over nerves.

I don't know what awakened me; but suddenly I found myself sitting bolt upright, heart pounding, ears straining. In the sooty darkness I could see nothing except a streak of moonlight lancing in through a knothole in one of the slats over the window. The stillness was intense. Yet, I knew that some sound had penetrated my sleep.

I was about to get up to light the candle when it came again: *Thump!* . . . *Thump-thump-thump!* Someone was knocking to get in!

I chilled to the pit of my stomach, for the summons was curiously muffled, as if the visitor were rapping not with firm knuckles, but with——I shoved the horrible thought from me.

"Who—who's there?" I called unsteadily.

Silence.

Ax in hand, I eased out of the bunk, lighted the candle, and turned to inspect the door. It was barred. Everything in the dim room was just as it had been when I fell asleep.

"Who is it?" I demanded in a firmer voice.

I knew that anyone knocking at this hour of the night would identify himself—unless he were a——

Again I put from me the thought of a dead man with no hands. I do not believe in ghosts.

I was trying to convince myself that

the knocking had been born of my over-wrought nerves when——*Thump!* . . . *Thump-thump-thump! Thump!* . . . *Thump-thump-thump!* It was like the fleshy stub of an arm hammering on wood.

Leaden with fright, I managed to reach the door and press my ear against it. "Who—what do you want? Answer me!"

I heard a faint rustling, as of a loose garment brushing against the rough log wall outside. After a dozen seconds, I had a sudden, desperate impulse to end the suspense. I lifted the bar, flung open the door, and looked out.

Nothing.

The high moon lighted the clearing with a brilliance almost like that of day, but there was neither movement nor sound in the breathless northern night.

Puzzled as well as frightened, I went back inside.

No sooner had I dropped the bar in place than it came again——*Thump!* . . . *Thump-thump-thump!* Instantly I jerked open the door.

No one was there. But the slithering sound, plainer than before, seemed to come from the corner to the right, as if someone had knocked and then run, to play a joke on me.

A flash of anger banished my fear. I darted out and ran all the way around the cabin.

There was no one.

The nearest cover—a tall hemlock—was fully fifty feet away. Nothing human, no matter how fleet, could possibly have covered that distance in the second between the last knock and my abrupt opening of the door. No creature larger than a rabbit could have concealed itself in the meadow surrounding the cabin.

Then gooseflesh broke out all over me. With a rush of terror came the thought that I was gazing on no ordinary wild meadow. Under the bear weed were skeleton hands—so many of them that this was literally a meadow of the dead.

I was trembling, and though it was not from cold, I wanted the comfort of a fire—a great, flaming fire. I dragged the pile of dead limbs over to the hut and kindled a roaring blaze just outside the door. The crackling and the warmth of it put new courage into me. I sat in the doorway and watched the clearing.

Nothing further disturbed me. After a while I began to nod.

I woke with a start, thinking I heard laughter and someone calling my name. Late-morning sun flooded the clearing. Then I saw a slim, blonde young woman in breeches and a windbreaker, running across the meadow toward me. Lonnie, my friend of the fox ranch! Behind her strode her father, a lean, sourdough Alaskan who had, as I well knew, no very high opinion of a woman's ability to take care of herself in the woods.

I was so overjoyed to see them that I could have rushed upon them and fallen to embrace their knees. But pride kept me from betraying myself to the quizzical eyes of Lonnie's father, whom I always called "Dad." I assumed a nonchalant manner and strolled out to greet them.

"There, Dad!" said Lonnie, laughing. "I told you she'd be cool as a cucumber!" She gave me a hug. "I knew you'd be all right, but Dad had a fit when you failed to show up last night."

"A woman," declared Dad, "should never go into the woods alone. Women are always getting lost." He readjusted the heavy holster on his hip. "I was afraid you'd run into a bear—there are a lot of brownies around this summer. You can thank your lucky star you stumbled onto Butler's cabin."

Butler's cabin! But even as a shivering thrill ran through me, Dad's I-told-you-so manner nettled me.

"It's not only women who get lost," I retorted. "How about those five prospectors who disappeared in these woods a few years ago?"

"Oh, those chaps! It's likely they were drowned in the tiderips off the Cape."

"No, they weren't, Dad," I said quietly. "They were killed—murdered— right here at Butler's cabin."

He and Lonnie stared at me as if they thought I had gone insane. Then Dad began to laugh. "Now, Sis, don't try to put over any of your writer's imaginings on an old fellow like me."

"It's not imagination. Come. I'll show you."

I led the way to the chopping block, and, brushing aside the bear weed with my foot, one by one revealed the skeleton hands, stark white in the sunlight.

Dad looked grave. "By George," he muttered. "This looks bad. I remember there was some talk about Cub Bear Butler, but——" He stooped and picked up one of the bony things.

After a moment's inspection he tossed it back into the weeds, and brushed his hands together. "Just like a woman!" he drawled, grinning at me. "Those are not human hands, Sister. They're the skeleton paws of cub bears."

I must have looked uncommonly foolish for he patted my shoulder consolingly. "Nine men out of ten would have made the same mistake. You see, the skeleton of a bear's paw, particularly a cub's, is almost identical with that of the human hand."

"But—why are there no other bones here?"

"Cub Bear Butler, like all other trappers, skinned his catch at the traps in the woods—all except the feet, which need a good deal of care. He brought the pelts back here to his cabin to skin the paws. He trapped only cubs, yearlings. That's how he got his nickname."

Feeling very much deflated, I followed him into the cabin.

"Poor old Cub Bear," he said. "They finally got him."

"Who got him?" I asked, remembering that Butler had been called "the crazy trapper."

"Bears. Some Indians round here swear it was the Great She-Bear, the Spirit Bear, who took revenge on him for killing so many cubs. At any rate he was found crumpled down right there"— Dad pointed to a spot just outside the door—"killed as a bear kills a man. He'd been dead only a couple of days and the tracks of a big brownie were still visible in the dooryard."

"But why didn't he shoot the beast if it jumped him in his own yard?"

"Couldn't reach his gun. When they found him, his rifle, his ax, and a fresh cub pelt were all here in the cabin, and the door was barred and the latch-thong broken off."

"What a strange thing!"

"Nothing strange about it. What happened was plain enough. Cub Bear must have come in from his trap line with the pelt. He dropped it when he put his rifle on the table, and then went out—for water, likely—shutting the

door behind him. Possibly the mother of the cub he'd just killed did follow him home, and—well, an angry she-brownie is just about the most terrifying creature a man can run up against. When she went for him, he ran for his cabin to get his rifle. In his haste, he jerked the latch-thong so hard he broke it off. Then he couldn't open the door. And it is so heavy he couldn't break it in. So—the beast got him."

"How terrible—and ironic!" I shuddered as I pictured what had happened.

"Tough luck, all right. Bert Slocum, one of my ranch hands now, spent a couple of months here afterward, trapping mink. He came out with a fine, large tale about Cub Bear's ghost hanging around here, and——"

"Ghost," I started, and turned to stare at the spot where Butler must have stood frantically beating on the heavy plank door trying to get in.

"Yes, so Bert claims." Dad chuckled. "But Bert's the biggest liar in Alaska. The way he tells it, Cub Bear——"

Thump! . . . Thump-thump-thump! With the door wide open it came, and before I knew it I had leaped to my feet.

"What in heck's the matter with you, Sis?" inquired Dad.

I looked from the empty door to the faces of my companions. "Didn't you hear it?" I demanded.

"Hear what?"

"That knocking."

"Oh, those pesky flying squirrels," drawled Dad. "The country's getting overrun with 'em. On a moonlight night a man can't get a wink of sleep, the way they play humpty-dumpty on the roof. They——"

"Flying squirrels," I interrupted, doubtingly. "I'd like to see one—playing."

"No trouble. Just stand there inside the door, sort of hidden, and keep your eye on that lone hemlock out in front."

I took up the position he indicated.

After a moment, sure enough, a small, furry form soared out from the top of the tree and, with little legs outspread, came gliding down to land with that soft, solid *thump!* on the roof. Then, quickly, *thump-thump thump!* it bounded down to the eaves, and off, racing back toward the tree.

"What a cunning little creature," I observed, turning around with what must have been a sickly smile.

As I did so, my attention was caught by the door, swung in so that the outside of it was very close to me. Years of Alaska weather—beating rain and wind and snow, alternating with hot summer sun—had worked the rough grain of the unfinished planks into a coarse, light gray nap. Visible now on the sunstruck surface, and about even with the top of my head were curious marks—depressions in the weathernap of the wood, such as might have been made by the edge of heavily pounding fists.

"What are you staring at now, Sis?" Dad broke in on my thoughts.

"Those marks on the door."

He laughed. "You must have been pretty excited when you got here last night—knocking that hard. But that's just like a woman—never able to tell whether a cabin's deserted or not." He picked up my jacket from the bunk and held it for me. "Come, now. Slip into this. It's time we were moving. I'm hungry enough to eat boiled owl, and it's eight miles to the ranch."

A few minutes later, as we were walking away across the sunny clearing, I fell a step behind the other two and turned to look back at the cabin in which I had spent the most terrifying night of my life.

I was remembering that two days ago there had been a heavy southeast gale which must have beat directly on that closed door. Yesterday's sun drying out the planks would have raised the wood-nap, obliterating any depressions that might have been there before I reached the cabin. Yet marks were there, as if two fists had pounded on the door. Dad thought I had made them.

I looked down at my hands, and, though I don't believe in ghosts, I had a queer feeling in the pit of my stomach. The marks were there, plainly visible when the sun struck the door just right. But I knew that my two small fists had never made them.

For I had never knocked, or even thought of knocking, on the door of that grim, deserted cabin in the clearing.

Close Up

1. The young woman who tells this story sets out on a ten-mile hike to her friend's fox ranch. Why does she leave the trail?

2. When the woman first sees the cabin, she feels there is something sinister, or evil, about it. (a) What does she find by the chopping block that further frightens her? (b) Why does this discovery convince her that the cabin belongs to Bear Cub Butler?

3. In the middle of the night, she is awakened by a thumping on the door. (a) What does the woman find when she looks outside? (b) Why does this frighten her?

4. In the morning, Dad accuses her of letting her writer's imagination get away from her. (a) How does he explain the skeleton hands and the thumping on the door? (b) Why do the marks on the door suggest a different explanation?

5. The woman says that Dad has "no very high opinion of a woman's ability to take care of herself in the woods." Find three instances in this story where the woman proves her competence, or ability.

Mood

Some stories create a mood of terror. They make you feel frightened. "One Alaska Night" creates a mood of terror by foreshadowing, or hinting at, events and by using specific details.

1. Find two statements that foreshadow, or hint at, the danger to come. (For example, "Something queerly crawling touched my cheek. I slapped my hand over it, and, with a chill of premonition, looked at what I'd caught—a long tuft of coarse brown hair dangling from a twig above.")

2. Make a list of details that add to the mood of terror. (For example, darkness.)

3. The author uses body signals to indicate terror. (For example, "I chilled to the pit of my stomach. . .") Find three other body signals that indicate terror.

4. Make a list of descriptive words and phrases that help create terror. (For example, the author describes the meadow as "a meadow of the dead.")

Activity

▶ **Composition.** Imagine you are the woman in this story. Write a note to leave in the cabin for the next person who uses it.

INFERENCES

Making Inferences About Past Events

When you make an inference about a past event, you make an intelligent guess about something that happened earlier. For example, the woman in this story sees large footprints and some torn fur, and she smells the musky odor of bear. Therefore, she makes the inference that bears have used this trail earlier.

1. The woman makes several inferences about past events. Find evidence that supports each of these inferences.
   a. No one had opened the door of the cabin for many months.
   b. The skeleton hands were the hands of the five missing prospectors and one other person.
   c. The cabin had belonged to a trapper.
   d. The cabin had been abandoned.
   e. The meadow was the site of foul murders.

2. Which two inferences above are not valid; that is, do not turn out to be true? What evidence had the woman overlooked?

WORD ATTACK

Understanding Similes

A simile is a comparison of two unlike objects. For example, the following simile compares a bear to a locomotive. "The bear was coming toward me like a charging locomotive." Usually, a simile contains the words *like* or *as*.

▶ Find the simile in each sentence below. Then tell what two objects are being compared.

a. "All along it, evenly spaced in the damp, brown mold, were deep depressions, round and large as dinner plates."

b. "The boarded windows on each side of the closed door stared back at me like eye sockets in a brown and weathered skull."

c. "I tried to convince myself that the knocking had been born of my overwrought nerves when——Thump!. . . Thump-thump-thump! Thump!. . .Thump-thump-thump! It was like the fleshy stub of an arm hammering on wood."

d. "I told you she'd be cool as a cucumber."

The Night the Ghost Got In

James Thurber

The ghost that got into our house on the night of November 17, 1915, raised such a hullabaloo of misunderstandings that I am sorry I didn't just let it keep on walking, and go to bed. Its advent caused my mother to throw a shoe through a window of the house next door and ended up with my grandfather shooting a patrolman. I am sorry, therefore, as I have said, that I ever paid any attention to the footsteps.

They began about a quarter past one o'clock in the morning, a rhythmic, quick-cadenced walking around the dining-room table. My mother was asleep in one room upstairs, my brother Herman in another; grandfather was in the attic, in the old walnut bed which once fell on my father. I had just stepped out of the bathtub and was busily rubbing myself with a towel when I heard the steps. They were the steps of a man walking rapidly around the dining-room table downstairs. The light from the bathroom shone down the back steps, which dropped directly into the dining room; I could see the faint shine of plates on the plate rail; I couldn't see the table. The steps kept going round and round the table; at regular intervals a board creaked, when it was trod upon. I sup-posed at first that it was my father or my brother Roy, who had gone to Indianap-olis but were expected home at any time. I suspected next that it was a burglar. It did not enter my mind until later that it was a ghost.

After the walking had gone on for perhaps three minutes, I tiptoed to Her-man's room. "Psst!" I hissed, in the dark, shaking him. "Awp," he said, in the low, hopeless tone of a despondent beagle—he always half suspected that something would "get him" in the night. I told him who I was. "There's something down-stairs!" I said. He got up and followed me to the head of the back staircase. We lis-tened together. There was no sound. The steps had ceased. Herman looked at me in some alarm: I had only the bath towel around my waist. He wanted to go back to bed, but I gripped his arm. "There's something down there!" I said. Instantly, the steps began again, circled the dining-room table like a man running, and started up the stairs toward us, heavily, two at a time. The light still shone palely down the stairs; we saw nothing coming; we only heard the steps. Herman rushed to his room and slammed the door. I slammed shut the door at the stairs top and held my knee against it. After a long

minute, I slowly opened it again. There was nothing there. There was no sound. None of us ever heard the ghost again.

The slamming of the doors had aroused mother: she peered out of her room. "What on earth are you boys doing?" she demanded. Herman ventured out of his room. "Nothing," he said, gruffly, but he was, in color, a light green. "What was all that running around downstairs?" said mother. So she had heard the steps, too! We just looked at her. "Burglars!" she shouted, intuitively. I tried to quiet her by starting lightly downstairs.

"Come on, Herman," I said.

"I'll stay with mother," he said. "She's all excited."

I stepped back onto the landing.

"Don't either of you go a step," said mother. "We'll call the police." Since the phone was downstairs, I didn't see how we were going to call the police— nor did I want the police—but mother made one of her quick, incomparable decisions. She flung up a window of her bedroom, which faced the bedroom windows of the house of a neighbor, picked up a shoe, and whammed it through a pane of glass across the narrow space that separated the two houses. Glass tinkled into the bedroom occupied by a retired engraver named Bodwell and his wife. Bodwell had been for some years in rather a bad way and was subject to mild "attacks." Most everybody we knew or lived near had *some* kind of attacks.

It was now about two o'clock of a moonless night; clouds hung black and low. Bodwell was at the window in a minute, shouting, frothing a little, shaking his fist. "We'll sell the house and go back to Peoria," we could hear Mrs. Bodwell saying. It was some time before mother "got through" to Bodwell. "Burglars!" she shouted. "Burglars in the house!" Herman and I hadn't dared to tell her that it was not burglars but ghosts, for she was even more afraid of ghosts than of burglars. Bodwell at first thought that she meant there were burglars in his house, but finally he quieted down and called the police for us over an extension phone by his bed. After he had disappeared from the window, mother suddenly made as if to throw another shoe, not because there was further need of it, but, as she later explained, because the thrill of heaving a shoe through a window glass had enormously taken her fancy. I prevented her.

The police were on hand in a commendably short time: a Ford sedan full of them, two on motorcycles, and a patrol wagon with about eight in it and a few reporters. They began banging at our front door. Flashlights shot streaks of gleam up and down the walls, across the yard, down the walk between our house and Bodwell's. "Open up!" cried a hoarse voice. "We're men from Headquarters!" I wanted to go down and let them in, since there they were, but mother wouldn't hear of it. "You haven't

a stitch on," she pointed out. "You'd catch your death." I wound the towel around me again. Finally, the cops put their shoulders to our big, heavy front door with its thick beveled glass and broke it in: I could hear a rending of wood and a splash of glass on the floor of the hall. Their lights played all over the living room and crisscrossed nervously in the dining room, stabbed into hallways, shot up the front stairs, and finally up the back. They caught me standing in my towel at the top. A heavy policeman bounded up the steps. "Who are you?" he demanded. "I live here," I said. "Well, whattsa matta, ya hot?" he asked. It was, as a matter of fact, cold; I went to my room and pulled on some trousers. On my way out, a cop stuck a gun into my ribs. "Whatta you doin' here?" he demanded. "I live here," I said.

The officer in charge reported to mother. "No sign of nobody, lady," he said. "Musta got away—whatt'd he look like?" "There were two or three of them," mother said, "whooping and carrying on and slamming doors." "Funny," said the cop. "All ya windows and doors was locked on the inside tight as a tick."

Downstairs, we could hear the tromping of the other police. Police were all over the place; doors were yanked open, drawers were yanked open, windows were shot up and pulled down, furniture fell with dull thumps. A half-dozen policemen emerged out of the darkness of the front hallway upstairs. They began to ransack the floor: pulled beds away from walls, tore clothes off hooks in the closets, pulled suitcases and boxes off shelves. One of them found an old zither that Roy had won in a pool tournament. "Looky here, Joe," he said, strumming it with a big paw. The cop named Joe took it and turned it over. "What is it?" he asked me. "It's an old zither our guinea pig used to sleep on," I said. It was true that a pet guinea pig we once had would never sleep anywhere except on the zither, but I should never have said so. Joe and the other cop looked at me a long time. They put the zither back on a shelf.

"No sign o' nuthin'," said the cop who had first spoken to mother. "This guy," he explained to the others, jerking a thumb at me, "was nekked. The lady seems historical." They all nodded, but said nothing; just looked at me. In the small silence we all heard a creaking in the attic. Grandfather was turning over in bed. "What's 'at?" snapped Joe. Five or six cops sprang for the attic door before I could intervene or explain. I realized that it would be bad if they burst in on grandfather unannounced, or even announced. He was going through a phase in which he believed that General Meade's men, under steady hammering by Stonewall Jackson, were beginning to retreat and even desert.

When I got to the attic, things were pretty confused. Grandfather had evidently jumped to the conclusion that the police were deserters from Meade's

army, trying to hide away in his attic. He bounded out of bed wearing a long flannel nightgown over long woolen underwear, a nightcap, and a leather jacket around his chest. The cops must have realized at once that the indignant white-haired old man belonged in the house, but they had no chance to say so. "Back, ye cowardly dogs!" roared grandfather. "Back t' the lines, ye——lily-livered cattle!" With that, he fetched the officer who found the zither a flat-handed smack alongside his head that sent him sprawling. The others beat a retreat, but not fast enough; grandfather grabbed Zither's gun from its holster and let fly. The report seemed to crack the rafters; smoke filled the attic. A cop cursed and shot his hand to his shoulder. Somehow, we all finally got downstairs again and locked the door against the old gentleman. He fired once or twice more in the darkness and then went back to bed. "That was grandfather," I explained to Joe, out of breath. "He thinks you're deserters." "I'll say he does," said Joe.

The cops were reluctant to leave without getting their hands on somebody besides grandfather; the night had been distinctly a defeat for them. Furthermore, they obviously didn't like the "layout"; something looked—and I can see their viewpoint—phony. They began to poke into things again. A reporter, a thin-faced wispy man, came up to me. I had put on one of mother's blouses, not being able to find anything else. The reporter looked at me with mingled suspicion and interest. "Just what the——is the real lowdown here, Bud?" he asked. I decided to be frank with him. "We had ghosts," I said. He gazed at me a long time as if I were a slot machine into which he had, without results, dropped a nickel. Then he walked away. The cops followed him, the one grandfather shot holding his now-bandaged arm, cursing and blaspheming. "I'm gonna get my gun back from that old bird," said the zither-cop. "Yeh," said Joe. "You—and who else?" I told them I would bring it to the station house the next day.

"What was the matter with that one policeman?" mother asked, after they had gone. "Grandfather shot him," I said. "What for?" she demanded. I told her he was a deserter. "Of all things!" said mother. "He was such a nice-looking young man."

Grandfather was fresh as a daisy and full of jokes at breakfast next morning. We thought at first he had forgotten all about what had happened, but he hadn't. Over his third cup of coffee, he glared at Herman and me. "What was the idee of all them cops tarryhootin' round the house last night?" he demanded. He had us there.

1. When the narrator first hears the footsteps, he thinks they might belong to his father or brother returning from Indianapolis. What does he finally realize the footsteps are?

2. The narrator and his brother Herman do not want to alarm their mother, but she has heard the footsteps also. To whom does she think they belong?

3. The mother wants to call the police, but the telephone is downstairs. (a) Why is she afraid to go downstairs? (b) How does she signal her neighbors to call the police?

4. (a) Why does Grandfather think the police are deserters from Meade's army? (b) How does he manage to expel them from the attic?

5. The police are reluctant to leave without taking somebody into custody since they do not like the "layout." What things might seem strange to them?

6. (a) What does Grandfather ask the narrator and his brother at breakfast? (b) Why does this surprise them?

Mood

Mood is the feeling created by a story or novel. The author builds a particular mood by including selected events, using precise language, and depicting very specific scenes.

1. In the opening paragraph of the story, Thurber briefly recounts the events of the night the ghost got in his house. What feeling does the opening paragraph help create?

2. (a) What has Herman always suspected would happen in the night? (b) What kind of picture does this give of Herman?

3. How do the mother's actions, especially in the scene about the shoe, help create the mood of the story?

4. Without the strange collection of characters that make this a humorous story, the events would not have happened. How does Grandfather's character help add to the humorous mood?

Activities

1. James Thurber is also a cartoonist. Choose a story scene that would make a good cartoon and sketch it.

2. Identify the two or three sentences that you think are the funniest in this story.

INFERENCES

Making Inferences About Tone

When you make an inference about tone, you make an intelligent guess about the author's attitude, or feelings, toward what he or she has written. Some words that describe tone are *amused, sarcastic, bitter,* and *light-hearted.*

▶ Which of the items below set an amused tone for "The Night the Ghost Got In"? Two do not set this tone.

  a. "Its advent caused my mother to throw a shoe through a window of the house next door and ended up with my grandfather shooting a patrolman."

  b. ". . . grandfather was in the attic, in the old walnut bed which once fell on my father."

  c. "They were the steps of a man walking rapidly around the dining-room table downstairs."

  d. ". . . I tiptoed to Herman's room. 'Psst!' I hissed, in the dark, shaking him. 'Awp,' he said, in the low, hopeless tone of a despondent beagle . . ."

  e. "I stepped back onto the landing."

  f. "Bodwell was at the window in a minute, shouting, frothing a little, shaking his fist."

  g. "They caught me standing in my towel at the top."

  h. "He bounded out of bed wearing a long flannel nightgown over long woolen underwear, a nightcap, and a leather jacket around his chest."

  i. " 'What was the idee of all them cops tarryhootin' round the house last night?' "

WORD ATTACK

Understanding Figurative Expressions

Authors use figurative expressions to create word pictures that vividly convey ideas and feelings. For example, Herman did not really say, " 'Awp' *in the low, hopeless tone of a despondent beagle.*" A boy's voice cannot be the same as a dog's. However, the figurative expression gives readers a good picture of how sad Herman sounded.

Figurative expressions are not meant to be taken literally. They add color to literature by contrasting or comparing seemingly unlike things.

▶ Which of the items below contain figurative expressions and which do not?

a. " 'Nothing,' he said, gruffly, but he was, in color, a light green."

b. "Bodwell was at the window in a minute, shouting, frothing a little, shaking his fist."

c. "Bodwell at first thought that she meant there were burglars in his house . . ."

d. " 'You haven't a stitch on,' she pointed out. 'You'd catch your death.' "

e. "Their lights played all over the living room and crisscrossed nervously in the dining room, stabbed into hallways, shot up the front stairs and finally up the back."

f. " 'All ya windows and doors was locked on the inside tight as a tick.' "

g. "Police were all over the place . . ."

h. "They all nodded, but said nothing, just looked at me."

i. "They began to poke into things again."

j. "He gazed at me a long time as if I were a slot machine into which he had, without results, dropped a nickel."

REVIEW QUIZ

On the Selections

1. In "Beware of the Dog," why does the nurse hide her nationality from Peter?

2. Why is Peter confused when the nurse complains about the hardness of the water?

3. In "Otero's Visitor," why doesn't Otero tell the three armed men about his visitor?

4. At the beginning of "Back There," Corrigan is described as a skeptic. How has he changed by the end of the play?

5. When does Corrigan learn Wellington's true identity?

6. In "Crime on Mars," why is Rawlings returning to Earth?

7. In "Avalanche," who is more cautious—Scotty or Marick?

8. In "Crow Call," why does the father put the girl "in charge of the crow call"?

9. At the beginning of "One Alaska Night," the woman feels "a chill of premonition." This premonition—or look into the future—warns her of what creature?

10. In "The Night the Ghost Got In," what event begins the confusion?

On Inferences

1. (a) In "Beware of the Dog," how do you think the nurse feels when Peter says he heard a Junkers 88 overhead? (b) Why would she feel this way?

2. Find three details in "Otero's Visitor" that tell you the family is prosperous.

3. Find three details in "Crime on Mars" that tell you this story takes place in the future.

4. In "Avalanche," when Scotty is buried alive, how does he infer which way is up?

5. In "One Alaska Night," what inference does the woman make when she wakes and hears a pounding on the door?

On Literature Skills

▶ Decide whether the following statements are true or false.
   a. The setting of "Beware of the Dog" is Brighton during World War II.
   b. All the events in "Otero's Visitor" take place during one day.
   c. The setting of a story can affect its plot.
   d. The mood of a story is the impression it creates and the emotions it arouses in the reader.
   e. "Back There" creates a mood of humor.

COMPOSITION

Description　A good descriptive paragraph helps you form a clear picture of something. It makes you feel as though you are *actually* seeing the thing that is being described.

When you write a descriptive paragraph, follow these steps. First, include only the most important details. For example, if you wish to write about a room, don't describe everything in the room (from the smallest speck of dust on the floor to each item in the closet to the lamp on the ceiling). Select the details you consider important.

Second, arrange these details in a logical order. For example, you might describe how the room looks from right to left or from top to bottom. You might describe the biggest objects in the room first and then proceed to the smallest.

Third, try to make your description appeal to the five senses. How does the room smell? How does the rug on the floor feel? Is the room quiet or is it filled with street noises?

Fourth, choose your words carefully. You can create a strong impression by using precise adjectives and verbs. For example, instead of saying it was a *nice* room, you could say it was a *spacious* room, or a *sunny* room, or a *cheerful* room. Instead of saying a woman *walked* into the room, you could say she *strutted*, or she *strolled*, or she *trudged* in.

▶ Write a descriptive paragraph using one of the ideas below.

　　a. In "Back There," Corrigan finds himself on a familiar street one hundred years in the past. Imagine you have traveled one hundred years into the future. Write a paragraph describing the street you live on.

　　b. In "Crime on Mars," the detective mentions that most of his fellow passengers have never seen Earth. Imagine you are one of those passengers. Write a paragraph telling about your first impression of Earth.

　　c. In "Avalanche," Robb White creates a vivid picture of a snow-covered mountain. Imagine you have a pen pal in Tahiti. This person has never seen snow. Write a paragraph for your pen pal describing a snow-covered landscape.

　　d. In "Crow Call," Lois Lowry creates a vivid picture of the nine-year-old girl in her bright plaid shirt. Write a paragraph creating a vivid impression of a person.

BEFORE GOING ON

Outlining

When you outline, you organize the important information. To do this, you divide and then subdivide the information.

First, you divide the essay into major parts, or topics—for example, "The history of balloons," "The history of zeppelins," and "The uses of balloons today." (Remember that a topic is not a complete sentence.) Next, you divide these topics into subtopics. For example, under the topic "The history of balloons," you would have the subtopics "Hot air balloons" and "Hydrogen balloons." Then, you list specific information you find about each of these subtopics.

You indicate a major part, or topic, by a roman numeral (I, II, III). You indicate a subtopic by a capital letter (A, B, C). You indicate specific information you find about each of these subtopics by arabic numerals (1, 2, 3).

► After you finish reading "How People Flew Before Airplanes Were Invented," copy the outline below on a separate piece of paper. Then fill in the missing subtopics and specific information about these subtopics.

   I. The history of balloons
      A. Hot Air Balloons
          1. Made by Étienne and Joseph Montgolfier
          2. Worked on principle that hot air rises
      B. Hydrogen balloons
          1. Contained gas that is lighter than air
          2.
  II. The history of zeppelins
      A. The first zeppelins
          1.
          2.
      B. The Graf Zeppelin
          1.
          2.
      C. Reasons why zeppelins lost popularity
          1.
          2.
 III. The uses of balloons today
      A.
      B.
      C.

Reading Graphs

A graph is a diagram showing how certain sets of facts or statistics are related. One important type of graph is the bar graph. This graph shows the relationship of information with graphs of different sizes.

Exercise 6. Study the graphs below. Then, on a separate piece of paper, answer each of the following questions.

Questions

1. The three graphs below show the reasons why the Japan National Railways is in trouble. These reasons are soaring losses, mounting debt burden, and static ridership. Study the graph labeled *Soaring Losses*. In which year did Japan National Railways experience the greatest losses?
2. What was the net loss for the railways in 1981?
3. In what year did the railways experience a net loss of 3.4 billion dollars?
4. Study the graph labeled *Mounting Debt Burden*. What was the debt for the railways in 1982?
5. In what year did the railways have the lowest debt?
6. In what year did the railways have the greatest debt?
7. Study the graph labeled *Static Ridership*. How many passengers rode the railways in 1980?
8. How many rode in 1981?
9. How many rode in 1982?
10. Why is *Static Ridership* a good title for this graph?

Troubles for the Japan National Railways

Financial results translated from yen at current exchange rate

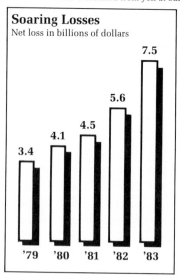

Soaring Losses
Net loss in billions of dollars

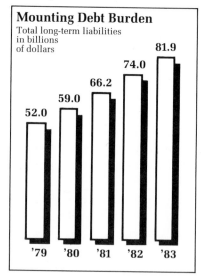

Mounting Debt Burden
Total long-term liabilities in billions of dollars

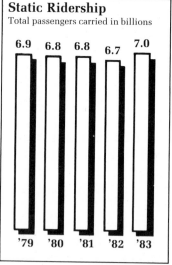

Static Ridership
Total passengers carried in billions

The New York Times / Nov. 26, 1984

Further Reading

How People Flew Before Airplanes Were Invented

Robert Miller

In 1783, when he was in Paris, France, trying to get French support for the American Revolution, Benjamin Franklin saw men fly—almost 120 years before airplanes were invented. With thousands of French people, he saw a balloon lift up from the ground and carry two men into the air. A spectator standing near Franklin muttered, "What good is it?"

And Franklin, who was one of the world's leading scientists as well as an expert diplomat, is supposed to have replied, "What good is a baby when it is born?"

A few years after that flight in Paris, President George Washington and other leaders of our new nation watched the famous French balloonist, Jean-Pierre Blanchard, make his first balloon flight in the United States. Before his flight, President Washington had presented the French visitor with a passport to land anywhere in the United States.

The first balloons were made by two French brothers, Étienne and Joseph Montgolfier. These balloons worked on the simple principle that hot air rises. When the balloons were filled with hot air, they went up. When the air inside the balloons cooled, they settled back to earth. And, if the balloons were large enough, men could ride in wicker baskets that had been hung under the balloons and carefully attached by nets. Some balloons had small stoves in the basket where the flyers stood. By burning bundles of hay, more hot air could be put into the balloon—but sometimes the flames from the stoves went too high, and the balloons caught fire. These early flights in hot air balloons could be frightening and did not last very long or go very far.

Then in the late 1700s, people decided to try filling balloons with gases that were lighter than air, such as hydrogen. Hydrogen balloons could lift more weight than hot air balloons of the same size, but there was one serious drawback to using the gas—hydrogen catches fire even more quickly than the gasoline used in today's cars. Just one spark could turn a balloon into a raging ball of fire.

Despite all the dangers, balloon flying became very popular. Some of the early French hydrogen balloons were able to carry fifty people into the air at once. Balloons were popular in the United States, too. They were used in the American Civil War by both the North and the South, carrying observers high into the sky to spy on the other army.

The early balloons could go up and come down at the wishes of the *aeronaut*, which is what balloon flyers are called. But, once in the air, the balloons could only go where the wind blew them. Inventors struggled with this problem and came up with many strange-looking devices to control the balloons' movement, but none of them worked very well.

Then, during the early 1900s, a German named Count Von Zeppelin designed and built a huge *dirigible*—a lighter-than-air craft that could be steered. This dirigible, called a Zeppelin after its designer, was shaped like a huge sausage, 420-feet long and about 38-feet wide and high. It was made of an aluminum frame covered with waterproofed cotton cloth. Inside the cylinder-shaped craft were seventeen large balloons filled with hydrogen.

Many people at that time thought of the air as a kind of sea, and they regarded dirigibles as aerial boats. Count Zeppelin's first models actually had two boat-like gondolas suspended below the cylinder, one toward the front and one near the back. The engines that powered the dirigibles were located at the rear of these gondolas, which also provided a place for the crew to stay during flights.

Because existing engines were too small to power the propellers on his dirigibles, Count Zeppelin started an engine manufacturing company that produced very reliable and powerful engines. Each of these new engines was more powerful than ten of the automobile engines used in today's cars. But the faster the dirigibles could go, the harder they were to steer, and Count Zeppelin soon realized that the steering methods used on the earlier, smaller dirigibles would not work on his large airships.

To make the first dirigibles turn to the right or left, designers often used small sails. The sails were turned to catch or deflect the wind, thus causing the airships to turn. But this system was useless for the larger Zeppelins. Sometimes the sails broke loose or the cloth ripped, leaving the aeronaut no choice but to valve off his hydrogen and sink slowly to earth.

Keeping his dirigibles horizontally level was also a problem for Zeppelin. At first, he tried to raise or lower the nose of the airship by attaching a heavy weight to a cable running down the center of the cylinder, moving the weight forward to tip the nose down and backward to tip it

up. But sometimes the weight got stuck on the cable, forcing the airship into a crash-landing. And the heavy weight and cable meant the dirigible could carry less in the way of cargo, passengers, or engine fuel.

Finally Count Zeppelin discovered that by simply adding a tail to one end of his dirigibles, he could help keep them flying level and in the right direction. The dirigible tail looked like two wings, one vertical and the other horizontal. These wings, similar to the tails on today's airplanes, were called stabilizers, because they kept the aircraft flying level. Hinged flaps attached to the stabilizers were used to steer the airships up or down and to the right or left.

As they learned more and more about dirigibles, the Zeppelin people built bigger and more successful airships. Some of the later ones were over two football fields long and higher and wider than most school gymnasiums. These great ships of the sky could carry cargo and many crewmen and passengers, and could fly long distances without stopping.

By the late 1920s, many nations had become interested in dirigibles, but the Germans maintained the lead in building these airships. One of their best, the *Graf Zeppelin*, was used to establish regular passenger and cargo service between Europe and North and South America. The *Graf Zeppelin* also made a spectacular trip around the world and, on another occasion, safely carried a scientific expedition into the Arctic.

American designers were hard at work on dirigibles during this time. Two of their largest were converted into aircraft carriers, and one of them, the *Macon*, carried five airplanes. The planes landed in midair by flying under the dirigibles and at the same speed. The pilot guided the airplane so that a hook on top of each wing caught on a trapezelike bar that hung below the airship. The pilot then turned off the motor, and both the trapeze bar and the airplane were hauled up into the dirigible. The planes were launched by reversing this procedure.

Airships began losing their popularity just when they seemed to be providing the ideal long-range air transportation. The two plane-carrying American dirigibles crashed, a British dirigible went down during a long trip to India, and then, in 1937, the German airship named the *Hindenburg* burst into flames as it was getting ready to land in New York after a trans-Atlantic flight.

Although most of the crew and passengers escaped, the airship quickly became a pile of charred aluminum girders. The *Hindenburg* was the largest airship ever built. It was over 800 feet long, 138 feet wide, and 138 feet high. That would make it almost three football fields long, as high as a fourteen-story building, and as wide as a very long school hall.

The explosion of the *Hindenburg* proved that one problem with airships remained unsolved. The *Hindenburg* used hydrogen, like the early balloons, and after its crash people decided that hydrogen balloons were not safe.

Today many people remember the *Hindenburg* disaster and believe the era of the balloon has passed. But balloons are still very much in use, though they now use helium—a gas that, like hydrogen, is lighter than air, but one that does not catch fire or explode.

Scientists have turned to that first aerial vehicle, the balloon, to gain more knowledge about space travel. In the

1960s, huge balloons made of lightweight plastic and filled with helium carried people higher than they had ever gone before. The spacesuits now worn by astronauts were first tested by balloonists.

Just as important are the weather balloons. Each day scientists all over the nation send up balloons carrying special instruments. These balloons range from ones about the size of a birthday party balloon to those as big as a small house. Once up in the sky, the balloons burst, and the instruments parachute back to earth. These instruments measure atmospheric conditions and help scientists predict what the weather will be like.

It is possible that dirigibles will return to play an important part in the future. These large airships do not pollute the skies or make much noise. They don't need airports that use valuable space because they take off and land much like helicopters. And finally, they don't use much fuel to power their engines.

Some people believe that modern plastics, lightweight metals, better engines, and helium can be combined to make dirigibles completely safe. They claim that dirigibles have always had a good safety record, even during the days when hydrogen was used. Back in the first years of this century, a German dirigible cargo and passenger line flew over 100,000 miles without a passenger being hurt. Other dirigibles such as the *Graf Zeppelin* flew thousands of miles without an accident.

Balloons are making quite a comeback in this country today. During football season, an American manufacturing company has a dirigible circling over some of the stadiums. Television camera crews in the airship provide an aerial view of the games, and the airship flies thousands of miles safely every year. And all over the United States there are clubs for people who have discovered the fun of flying in simple hot air balloons much like the one Benjamin Franklin saw in 1783. So, even though people talk about traveling by jet from New York to Paris in three hours, or about traveling in space at 25,000 miles per hour, the earliest balloons have not been forgotten. They may be just now coming into their own.

MOSAIC

On the Edge

Robert Russell

The deep valley stretched out before him in the June sunshine. Five hundred feet below, the tops of the evergreens sloped sharply to the Little Salmon River that wound like a silver thread through the purple shadows. It looked as if he could reach out and pick up that thread.

"Distances are tricky in the mountains, very tricky," he could almost hear the voice of Mr. Johnson, the climbing instructor. "That's why nobody, but *Nobody*, goes into the mountains alone."

Well, Frank Summers had. Mr. Johnson knew a lot about mountains, but he didn't seem to understand that sometimes a boy—no! He was sixteen. Sometimes a man needed to be alone. So on this last morning of the training camp, Frank had crept from the sleep-filled cabin into the dawn stillness, and climbed Old Baldy. Now, he sat on the peak gazing into those tricky distances, and he didn't even have that sagging sensation in his stomach that he used to have on the ladder when he was helping Dad paint the garage. He felt good, but he was tired. Drowsy . . . The silver thread glinted far below, spreading out into a shadowy blur that rose and grew and grew until . . . suddenly he found himself slipping down the steep slope on which he sat.

The bang and scrape of granite, fingers clawing at rounded stone, arms and legs flailing, the thud of body against a dwarf pine, his right arm hooking, then left hand clenched right, and for one second he swung, a crazy pendulum, then the drop—four more feet to a ledge where, shuddering, he clung to a naked rock wall. Huddled there, his mind tried to explain to his quivering flesh that he was still alive.

"Oh," he moaned. "Oh—oh. I'm here and I'm—I'm not—not going to move—until—until *what?*" Another moan. "Did I break anything? Am I OK?" Afraid to move, he asked each arm, each leg if it was OK.

Slowly turning his head, he examined the ledge. It was about eighteen inches wide. He dared not look down. Three feet to his right it widened a little. If he could creep over there—if he could hang on somehow, shuffle sideways—

there would be room to sit down to get himself together.

He ordered his legs to stop shaking, spread his arms and body against the cliff, and inched his way to the platform. Then he sank down and cried.

Then he pounded his thigh. "No! Stop! You're all right. What's the matter with you, Frank Summers? Bawling's not going to get you out of this!" *That's funny,* he thought. *I haven't even yelled.*

He shouted: "Help! Help! Help!" His call soared over the empty valley, which threw back three faint cries, mocking his weakness. *Weak? Frank Summers!* What about all those push-ups? Why, nobody in school could come close to him. But, then, he wasn't in school now. He was in the mountains, and mountains didn't care if he could do a thousand push-ups or even ten thousand.

"Nobody"—Mr. Johnson's voice echoed in Frank's mind. "That means *nobody* goes into the mountains alone." Frank understood now. If he had had a partner up there with a rope—but nobody was there.

He studied the cliff. He had fallen only about twelve feet. But even twelve feet *down* means twelve feet *up*. It might as well be miles. There were a few gentle bulges, but nothing big enough for a foothold or a handhold, and his gear was up on top. Near the top, a crack zigzagged along.

If I could get back up to that crack, he thought, *I could make it.*

"You've got to learn to read the mountains"—Mr. Johnson's voice came back again. "Anybody can look, but not everyone can read."

Frank studied the face of rock. He could see nothing promising. *That must be ten or eleven feet to the crack, and from there I could reach the top.* It looked like twelve miles. The crack ran diagonally down, but it looked only about an inch wide.

He sighed. If he had only left his rope buckled to his belt! But what good would a rope do? He couldn't just toss the end up into the air and then climb up. It would have to be tied to something at the top, and that meant there'd have to be someone up there to tie it. So what was the use? Still, he continued staring at the narrow slit.

If I tied a big enough knot in the end, I could toss it up there and jam the knot so that it wouldn't pull through. That might work.

His eyes opened wide at the idea. But would he have the nerve to try it? Reaching into his jeans pocket, his fingers closed on the familiar knife.

"All right," he said, "that's what I'll do." He laid his knife on the ledge and unlaced and removed his shoes. He took off his jeans, and cut them into long, even strips, tying them carefully together, testing each knot.

The big knot was going to be a problem. He wouldn't have enough line for a knot that he could be sure would jam in the crack. It would have to be heavy enough, too, or he wouldn't be able to throw it accurately. He hunted about the ledge for a loose stone or a dead branch, but there was nothing except his shoes. *Why not?* Picking up his right shoe, he flexed the heavy leather. *Perfect!*

With his makeshift rope, he made two tight loops around the shoe between the heel and where the sole widened, then tied a firm knot. Then he made it more secure by using both shoelaces to tie the line to the shoe. Having made certain that the shoe would not slip through, he swung it around. *Good.* It was heavy enough to carry the rope accurately.

Coiling the material with trembling fingers, he thought: *I've got my equipment, but have I got the nerve? Maybe I should wait? They must be looking for me.* The sun was beginning to dip. *But if I don't go now,* his mind pressed, *if I wait and have to spend the night here, I'll be too tired tomorrow. I've got to try—and now!*

He got to his feet and started along the ledge toward the overhanging trunk. "Whoops!" he cried, "if I make it, I'd better have that other shoe." He went back, picked it up, and flung it toward the edge above. It landed with a thud and did not

roll back. Cautiously, he made his way along the ledge until he stood under the bad edge of the crack in the rock wall.

Afraid to rest, afraid to think, he eased the line from beneath him, took the end in his right hand, gathered the rest in his left, and swung the shoe. It landed on top, but the line missed the crack, so the shoe came tumbling back when he pulled. On the third try, the line disappeared, and Frank guessed that the shoe was two or three feet back from the edge. He pulled. The shoe scuffed on the rock, then stuck. Harder and harder he tugged, until he pulled himself off his perch. Then he climbed for his life—up and up—clawed his way over the edge to safety.

He lay gasping, partly with relief, partly with fear, and partly with shame, but with a new sense of how beautiful it was to be alive. And how dangerous.

Close Up

1. What does Frank want to prove to himself by going into the mountains alone?

2. (a) Why is Frank afraid to look down from the ledge? (b) What does he plan to do first?

3. After Frank overcomes his first fears, he understands why Mr. Johnson had said that no one should go into the mountains alone. How would having a partner have helped Frank?

4. (a) Since Frank is without a rope or any of his gear, what does he use to save himself? (b) What does this show about Frank's ability to think under pressure?

Theme

The theme of a story is its central insight into life. One way to discover the theme of a story is to look at what the main character learns.

1. Frank feels he has to prove he is a man. When he disregards Mr. Johnson's advice, do you think his behavior is more like a boy's than a man's? Why?

2. After Frank falls from the cliff, why does he wish another person were with him?

3. Frank is filled with mixed emotions as he lies gasping on the edge of the slope. (a) Why does he feel shame? (b) What does this experience teach him about needing people?

4. Which of the following statements best expresses the theme of this story?
   a. Needing other people can be a strength, rather than a weakness.
   b. People have to learn how to get along without help from anyone else.
   c. Climbing mountains can be dangerous.

Activities

1. **Composition.** Do you think Frank told his friends about his narrow escape when he returned to the cabin? Write a paragraph explaining your answer.

2. List the sports that require teamwork. Then list the sports you can do on your own. Compare your lists with your classmates' lists.

MAIN IDEA

Finding Topic Sentences

The topic sentence expresses the most important idea in a paragraph. It helps you read the paragraph with greater understanding. The topic sentence may appear at the beginning, the middle, or the end of a paragraph. In the following paragraph, the topic sentence is the first sentence. Notice that the two other sentences give you additional information about the topic sentence.

"The deep valley stretched out before him in the June sunshine. Five hundred feet below, the tops of the evergreens sloped sharply to the little Salmon River that wound like a silver thread through the purple shadows. It looked as if he could reach out and pick up that thread."

1. Find the topic sentence in each of the paragraphs below.
   a. "Slowly turning his head, he examined the ledge. It was about eighteen inches wide. He dared not look down. Three feet to his right it widened a little. If he could creep over there—if he could hang on somehow, shuffle sideways—there would be room to sit down to get himself together."
   b. "He shouted: 'Help! Help! Help!' His call soared over the empty valley, which threw back three faint cries, mocking his weakness. *Weak? Frank Summers!* What about all those push-ups? Why, nobody in school could come close to him. But, then, he wasn't in school now. He was in the mountains, and mountains didn't care if he could do a thousand push-ups or even ten thousand."
   c. "The big knot was going to be a problem. He wouldn't have enough line for a knot that he could be sure would jam in the crack. It would have to be heavy enough, too, or he wouldn't be able to throw it accurately. He hunted about the ledge for a loose stone or a dead branch, but there was nothing except his shoes. *Why not?* Picking up his right shoe, he flexed the heavy leather. *Perfect!*"

2. Write a paragraph for each of the topic sentences below.
   a. Frank was foolish to go into the mountains alone.
   b. People shouldn't be ashamed to admit they need other people.
   c. Admitting your weaknesses can be a sign of strength.
   d. Mountain climbers need to rely on their wits as well as their physical prowess.

WORD ATTACK

Understanding Words Used as Nouns and as Verbs

A noun is a word that names a person, place, idea, or object. For example, in the sentence, "Sometimes a *man* needed to be alone," *man* is a noun. **A verb is a word that expresses an action or state of being.** For example, in the sentence, "He *dared* not look down," *dared* is a verb. Some words can be used as both nouns and verbs. For example, "He *dared* not take the *dare*." The meaning of words that can be either nouns or verbs depends on their use in a particular sentence.

▶ Read each of the *italicized* words in the sentence pairs below. Then decide whether the word is used as a noun or a verb. Find the dictionary definition that fits how that word is used in the sentence.

   a. The trees *sloped* sharply to the river.
   Frank slipped down the steep *slope*.

   b. Frank tried to *thread* his gaze through the cracks in the rock.
   The river looked like a silver *thread*.

   c. If he had his belt, he would *buckle* it to his shoe.
   He could have used the *buckle* on his belt.

   d. He pulled himself off his *perch*.
   He *perched* on the narrow ledge.

   e. He tried to *edge* his way along the side.
   The shoe hit the *edge* and fell back down.

My First Life Line

Maya Angelou

"She was one of the few gentlewomen I have ever known, and has remained, throughout my life, the measure of what a human being can be."

For nearly a year, I sopped around the house, the Store, the school, and the church, like an old biscuit, dirty and inedible. Then I met, or rather got to know, the lady who threw me my first life line.

Mrs. Bertha Flowers was the aristocrat of Black Stamps. She had the grace of control to appear warm in the coldest weather, and on the Arkansas summer days it seemed she had a private breeze which swirled around, cooling her. She was thin without the taut look of wiry people, and her printed voile dresses and flowered hats were as right for her as denim overalls for a farmer.

Her skin was a rich black that would have peeled like a plum if snagged, but then no one would have thought of getting close enough to Mrs. Flowers to ruffle her dress, let alone snag her skin. She didn't encourage familiarity. She wore gloves, too.

I don't think I ever saw Mrs. Flowers laugh, but she smiled often. A slow widening of her thin black lips to show even, small white teeth, then the slow, effortless closing. When she chose to smile on me, I always wanted to thank her. The action was so graceful and inclusively benign.

She was one of the few gentlewomen I have ever known, and has remained, throughout my life, the measure of what a human being can be.

Momma had a strange relationship with her. Most often when she passed on the road in front of the Store, she spoke to Momma in that soft yet carrying voice, "Good day, Mrs. Henderson." Momma responded with "How you, Sister Flowers?"

Mrs. Flowers didn't belong to our church, nor was she Momma's familiar. Why on earth did she insist on calling her Sister Flowers? It didn't occur to me for many years that they were as alike as sisters, separated only by formal education.

Although I was upset, neither of the

women was in the least shaken by what I thought an unceremonious greeting. Mrs. Flowers would continue her easy gait up the hill to her little bungalow, and Momma kept on shelling peas or doing whatever had brought her to the front porch.

Occasionally, though, Mrs. Flowers would drift off the road and down to the Store and Momma would say to me, "Sister, you go on and play." As I left I would hear the beginning of an intimate conversation. Momma persistently using the wrong verb, or none at all.

"Brother and Sister Wilcox is sho'ly the meanest——" "Is," Momma? "Is"? Oh, please, not "is," Momma, for two or more. But they talked, and from the side of the building where I waited for the ground to open up and swallow me, I heard the soft-voiced Mrs. Flowers and the textured voice of my grandmother merging and melting. They were interrupted from time to time by giggles that must have come from Mrs. Flowers (Momma never giggled in her life). Then she was gone.

She appealed to me because she was like people I had never met personally. Like women in English novels who walked the moors (whatever they were) with their loyal dogs racing at a respectful distance. Like the women who sat in front of roaring fireplaces, drinking tea incessantly from silver trays full of scones and crumpets. Women who walked over the "heath" and read morocco-bound books and had two last names divided by a hyphen. It would be safe to say that she made me proud to be black, just by being herself.

She acted just as refined as whitefolks in the movies and books and she was more beautiful, for none of them could have come near that warm color without looking gray by comparison.

One summer afternoon, sweet milk fresh in my memory, she stopped at the Store to buy provisions. Another black woman of her health and age would have been expected to carry the paper sacks home in one hand, but Momma said, "Sister Flowers, I'll send Bailey up to your house with these things."

She smiled that slow dragging smile, "Thank you, Mrs. Henderson. I'd prefer Marguerite, though." My name was beautiful when she said it. "I've been meaning to talk to her, anyway." They gave each other age-group looks.

Momma said, "Well, that's all right then. Sister, go and change your dress. You going to Sister Flowers's."

The chifforobe was a maze. What on earth did one put on to go to Mrs. Flowers' house? I knew I shouldn't put on a Sunday dress. It might be sacrilegious. Certainly not a house dress, since I was already wearing a fresh one. I chose a school dress, naturally. It was formal without suggesting that going to Mrs. Flowers' house was equivalent to attending church.

I trusted myself back into the Store.

"Now, don't you look nice." I had chosen the right thing, for once.

"Mrs. Henderson, you make most of the children's clothes, don't you?"

"Yes, ma'am. Sure do. Store-bought clothes ain't hardly worth the thread it take to stitch them."

"I'll say you do a lovely job, though, so neat. That dress looks professional."

Momma was enjoying the seldom-received compliments. Since everyone we knew (except Mrs. Flowers, of course) could sew competently, praise was rarely handed out for the commonly practiced craft.

"I try, with the help of the Lord, Sister Flowers, to finish the inside just like I does the outside. Come here, Sister."

I had buttoned up the collar and tied the belt, apronlike, in back. Momma told me to turn around. With one hand she pulled the strings, and the belt fell free at both sides of my waist. Then her large hands were at my neck, opening the button loops. I was terrified. What was happening?

"Take it off, Sister." She had her hands on the hem of the dress.

"I don't need to see the inside, Mrs. Henderson, I can tell . . ." But the dress was over my head and my arms were stuck in the sleeves. Momma said, "That'll do. See here, Sister Flowers, I French-seams around the armholes." Through the cloth film, I saw the shadow approach. "That makes it last longer. Children these days would bust out of sheet-metal clothes. They so rough."

"That is a very good job, Mrs. Henderson. You should be proud. You can put your dress back on, Marguerite."

"No ma'am. Pride is a sin. And 'cording to the Good Book, it goeth before a fall."

"That's right. So the Bible says. It's a good thing to keep in mind."

I wouldn't look at either of them. Momma hadn't thought that taking off my dress in front of Mrs. Flowers would kill me stone dead. If I had refused, she would have thought I was trying to be "womanish" and might have remembered St. Louis. Mrs. Flowers had known that I would be embarrassed and that was even worse. I picked up the groceries and went out to wait in the hot sunshine. It would be fitting if I got a sunstroke and died before they came outside. Just dropped dead on the slanting porch.

There was a little path beside the rocky road, and Mrs. Flowers walked in front swinging her arms and picking her way over the stones.

She said, without turning her head, to me, "I hear you're doing very good schoolwork, Marguerite, but that it's all written. The teachers report that they have trouble getting you to talk in class." We passed the triangular farm on our left and the path widened to allow us to walk together. I hung back in the separate unasked and unanswerable questions.

"Come and walk along with me, Marguerite." I couldn't have refused even if I wanted to. She pronounced my name so nicely. Or more correctly, she spoke each word with such clarity that I was certain a foreigner who didn't understand English could have understood her.

"Now no one is going to make you talk—possibly no one can. But bear in mind, language is man's way of communicating with his fellow man and it is language alone which separates him from the lower animals." That was a totally new idea to me, and I would need time to think about it.

"Your grandmother says you read a lot. Every chance you get. That's good, but not good enough. Words mean more than what is set down on paper. It takes the human voice to infuse them with the shades of deeper meaning."

I memorized the part about the human voice infusing words. It seemed so valid and poetic.

She said she was going to give me some books and that I not only must read them, I must read them aloud. She suggested that I try to make a sentence sound in as many different ways as possible.

"I'll accept no excuse if you return a book to me that has been badly handled." My imagination boggled at the punishment I would deserve if, in fact, I did abuse a book of Mrs. Flowers'. Death would be too kind and brief.

The odors in the house surprised me. Somehow I had never connected Mrs. Flowers with food or eating or any other common experience of common people. There must have been an outhouse, too, but my mind never recorded it.

The sweet scent of vanilla had met us as she opened the door.

"I made tea cookies this morning. You see, I had planned to invite you for cookies and lemonade so we could have this little chat. The lemonade is in the icebox."

It followed that Mrs. Flowers would have ice on an ordinary day, when most families in our town bought ice late on Saturdays only a few times during the summer to be used in the wooden ice-cream freezers.

She took the bags from me and disappeared through the kitchen door. I looked around the room that I had never in my wildest fantasies imagined I would see. Browned photographs leered or threatened from the walls, and the white, freshly done curtains pushed against themselves and against the wind. I wanted to gobble up the room entire and take it to Bailey, who would help me analyze and enjoy it.

"Have a seat, Marguerite. Over there by the table." She carried a platter covered with a tea towel. Although she warned that she hadn't tried her hand at baking sweets for some time, I was cer-

tain that, like everything else about her, the cookies would be perfect.

They were flat round wafers, slightly browned on the edges and butter-yellow in the center. With the cold lemonade, they were sufficient for childhood's life-long diet. Remembering my manners, I took nice little ladylike bites off the edges. She said she had made them expressly for me and that she had a few in the kitchen that I could take home to my brother. So I jammed one whole cake in my mouth, and the rough crumbs scratched the insides of my jaws, and if I hadn't had to swallow, it would have been a dream come true.

As I ate she began the first of what we later called "my lessons in living." She said that I must always be intolerant of ignorance but understanding of illiteracy. That some people, unable to go to school, were more educated and even more intelligent than college professors. She encouraged me to listen carefully to what country people called mother wit. That in those homely sayings was couched the collective wisdom of generations.

When I finished the cookies, she brushed off the table and brought a thick, small book from the bookcase. I had read *A Tale of Two Cities* and found it up to my standards as a romantic novel. She opened the first page and I heard poetry for the first time in my life.

"It was the best of times and the worst of times . . . " Her voice slid in and curved down through and over the words. She was nearly singing. I wanted to look at the pages. Were they the same that I had read? Or were there notes, music, lined on the pages, as in a hymn book? Her sounds began cascading gently. I knew from listening to a thousand preachers that she was nearing the end of her reading, and I hadn't really heard, heard to understand, a single word.

"How do you like that?"

It occurred to me that she expected a response. The sweet vanilla flavor was still on my tongue, and her reading was a wonder in my ears. I had to speak.

I said, "Yes, ma'am." It was the least I could do, but it was the most, also.

"There's one more thing. Take this book of poems and memorize one for me. Next time you pay me a visit, I want you to recite."

I have tried often to search behind the sophistication of years for the enchantment I so easily found in those gifts. The essence escapes but its aura remains. To be allowed, no, invited, into the private lives of strangers, and to share their joys and fears, was a chance to exchange the Southern bitter wormwood for a cup of mead with Beowulf or a hot cup of tea and milk with Oliver Twist. When I said aloud, "It is a far, far better thing that I do, than I have ever done . . . " tears of love filled my eyes at my selflessness.

On that first day, I ran down the hill and into the road (few cars ever came along it) and had the good sense to stop running before I reached the Store.

I was liked, and what a difference it made. I was respected, not as Mrs. Henderson's grandchild or Bailey's sister, but for just being Marguerite Johnson.

Childhood's logic never asks to be proved (all conclusions are absolute). I didn't question why Mrs. Flowers had singled me out for attention, nor did it occur to me that Momma might have asked her to give me a little talking to. All I cared about was that she had made tea cookies for me and read to me from her favorite book. It was enough to prove that she liked me.

Close Up

1. In this true story, Maya Angelou tells about the woman who helped her at an important point in her life. (a) Write three sentences describing Mrs. Flowers. (b) List three things Marguerite admires about her.

2. (a) Why is Marguerite embarrassed when her mother calls Mrs. Flowers "sister"? (b) What does she come to realize about her mother and Mrs. Flowers?

3. Marguerite considers herself unimportant and she refuses to speak. What simple things does Mrs. Flowers do to show that she values Marguerite?

4. Mrs. Flowers tells Marguerite, "Words mean more than what is set on paper. It takes the human voice to infuse (fill) them with the shades of deeper meaning." What do you think this statement means?

5. (a) Why do you think Mrs. Flowers reads aloud to Marguerite? (b) How does Marguerite show that she is grateful?

Theme

Sometimes a character in a story makes a statement that points to theme. For example, in "My First Life Line," Mrs. Flowers makes a statement that serves as Marguerite's "lesson in living." This statement helps you find the theme, or insight into life, of the story.

1. Marguerite's problem is her self-concept, the way she feels about herself. Find two things Marguerite does that show she feels inferior and unimportant.

2. Marguerite feels inferior because she is poor and her family has not had much schooling. (a) Go back to the story and find what Mrs. Flowers tells Marguerite about ignorance and mother wit. (b) Paraphrase these words; that is, put them into your own words.

3. Write a statement that you think expresses the theme of this selection.

Activities

1. **Composition.** Write a paragraph describing a person you admire.

2. Mrs. Flowers reads the following sentence to Marguerite: "It was the best of times and the worst of times . . . " Read this sentence aloud as you think she said it.

MAIN IDEA

Distinguishing Between the Topic and the Main Idea

The topic of a paragraph is the paragraph's subject; that is, what it is about. For example, a paragraph may be about a person, a dog, or learning to ride a bicycle. **The main idea of the paragraph is the most important thing it says about the topic.** For example, the main idea may be that it is easy to learn to ride a bicycle or that dogs make good companions.

1. State the topic of each paragraph below. Then, in your own words, state the main idea—what the paragraph says about the topic.

   a. "Mrs. Bertha Flowers was the aristocrat of Black Stamps. She had the grace of control to appear warm in the coldest weather, and on the Arkansas summer days it seemed she had a private breeze which swirled around, cooling her. She was thin without the taut look of wiry people, and her printed voile dresses and flowered hats were as right for her as denim overalls for a farmer."

   b. "The chifforobe was a maze. What on earth did one put on to go to Mrs. Flowers' house? I knew I shouldn't put on a Sunday dress. It might be sacrilegious. Certainly not a house dress, since I was already wearing a fresh one. I chose a school dress, naturally. It was formal without suggesting that going to Mrs. Flowers' house was equivalent to attending church."

   c. "As I ate she began the first of what we later called 'my lessons in living.' She said that I must always be intolerant of ignorance but understanding of illiteracy. That some people, unable to go to school, were more educated and even more intelligent than college professors. She encouraged me to listen carefully to what country people called mother wit. That in those homely sayings was couched the collective wisdom of generations."

2. For the topic of your paragraph, choose a part-time job. (a) Write a paragraph expressing the following main idea: _____ is the best way to earn extra money. (b) Keep the same topic, but write a paragraph expressing the opposite main idea: _____ is the worst way to earn extra money.

WORD ATTACK

Understanding Vivid Compound Words

A compound word is made up of two words that have been joined together. Some compound words are joined by a hyphen (for example, *tongue-twister*). To find the meaning of a compound word, look up the meaning of the two individual words. Some compound words function as adjectives and give you a vivid picture of what is being described.

▶ Find the meaning of the compound word *italicized* in each sentence below.

   a. "But they talked, and from the side of the building where I waited for the ground to open up and swallow me, I heard the *soft-voiced* Mrs. Flowers and the textured voice of my grandmother merging and melting."

   b. "Women who walked over the 'heath' and read *morocco-bound* books and had two last names divided by a hyphen."

   c. "One summer afternoon, *sweet-milk* fresh in my memory, she stopped at the Store to buy provisions."

   d. "They gave each other *age-group* looks."

   e. "*Store-bought* clothes ain't hardly worth the thread it take to stitch them."

Portrait by a Neighbor

Edna St. Vincent Millay

Before she has her floor swept
  Or her dishes done,
Any day you'll find her
  A-sunning in the sun!

5 It's long after midnight
  Her key's in the lock,
And you never see her chimney smoke
  Till past ten o'clock!

She digs in her garden
10 With a shovel and a spoon,
She weeds her lazy lettuce
  By the light of the moon,

She walks up the walk
  Like a woman in a dream,
15 She forgets she borrowed butter
  And pays you back cream!

Her lawn looks like a meadow,
  And if she mows the place
She leaves the clover standing
  And the Queen Anne's lace!

Who Am I?

Miguel Leon-Portilla

Who am I?
As a bird I fly about,
I sing of flowers;
I compose songs,
5 butterflies of song.
Let them burst forth from my soul!
Let my heart be delighted with them!

Close Up ▶
List the reasons the poet enjoys having the woman in the first poem as a neighbor.

Mike and the Grass

Erma Bombeck

When Mike was three he wanted a sandbox and his father said, "There goes the yard. We'll have kids over here day and night and they'll throw sand into the flower beds and cats will make a mess in it and it'll kill the grass for sure."

And Mike's mother said, "It'll come back."

When Mike was five, he wanted a jungle gym set with swings that would take his breath away and bars to take him to the summit and his father said, "Good grief. I've seen those things in backyards and do you know what they look like? Mud holes in a pasture. Kids digging their gym shoes in the ground. It'll kill the grass."

And Mike's mother said, "It'll come back."

Between breaths, when Daddy was blowing up the plastic swimming pool, he warned, "You know what they're going to do to this place? They're going to condemn it and use it for a missile site. I hope you know what you're doing. They'll track water everywhere and you'll have a million water fights and you won't be able to take out the garbage without stepping in mud up to your neck, and when we take this down, we'll have the only brown lawn on the block."

"It'll come back," smiled Mike's mother.

When Mike was twelve, he volunteered his yard for a campout. As they hoisted the tents and drove in the spikes, his father stood at the window and observed, "Why don't I just put the grass seed out in cereal bowls for the birds and save myself the trouble of spreading it around? You know for a fact that those tents and all those big feet are going to trample down every single blade of grass, don't you? Don't bother to answer," he said. "I know what you're going to say, 'It'll come back.' "

The basketball hoop on the side of the garage attracted more crowds than the Winter Olympics. And a small patch of lawn that started out with a barren spot the size of a garbage-can lid soon grew to encompass the entire side yard.

Just when it looked like the new seed might take root, the winter came and the sled runners beat it into ridges and Mike's father shook his head and said, "I never asked for much in this life . . . only a patch of grass."

And his wife smiled and said, "It'll come back."

The lawn this fall was beautiful. It was green and alive and rolled out like a sponge carpet along the drive where gym shoes had trod . . . along the garage where bicycles used to fall . . . and around the flower beds where little boys used to dig with iced teaspoons.

But Mike's father never saw it. He anxiously looked beyond the yard and asked with a catch in his voice, "He will come back, won't he?"

Close Up

1. At the beginning of this selection, Mike's father seems very concerned about the grass. What does Mike's mother mean when she says, "It will come back"?

2. At the end of the story, what does the father say that shows he cares much more about Mike than about the grass?

The Little Lizard's Sorrow

Mai Vo-Dinh

There was once a very rich man whose house was immense and filled with treasures. His land was so extensive that, as the Viet-Namese say, "Cranes fly over it with outstretched wings," for cranes do so only over very long distances. Wealth breeding vanity, one of the rich man's greatest pleasures was beating other rich men at a game he himself had invented. One player would announce one of his rare possessions; the other would counter the challenge by saying that he, too—if he really did—owned such a treasure. "A stable of fifty buffalos," one man would say. The other would reply, "Yes, I also have fifty of them." It was then his turn to announce, "I sleep in an all-teak bed encrusted with mother-of-pearl." The first player would lose if he slept on simple cherry planks!

One day, a stranger came to the rich man's house. Judging from his appearance, the gatekeeper did not doubt that the visitor was a madman. He wanted, he said, to play the famous game with the mansion's master. Yet, dressed in clothes that looked as if they had been mended hundreds of times, and wearing broken straw sandals, the stranger appeared to be anything but a wealthy man. Moreover, his face was gaunt and pale as if he had not had a good meal in days. But there was such proud, quiet dignity to the stranger that the servant did not dare shut the gates in his face. Instead, he meekly went to inform his master of the unlikely visitor's presence. Intrigued, the man ordered that the pauper be ushered in.

Trying to conceal his curiosity and his surprise, the rich man offered his visitor the very best chair and served him hot, perfumed tea.

"Well, stranger, is it true that you have come here to play a game of riches with me?" he began inquiringly.

The visitor was apparently unimpressed by the rich surroundings, giving them only a passing, casual look. Perfectly at ease, sipping his tea from a rare porcelain cup, he answered in a quiet, though self-assured, voice, "Yes, sir, that is if you, too, so wish."

"Naturally . . . naturally." The rich man raised his hand in a sweeping motion. "But, may I ask, with your permission, where you reside and what is your honorable occupation?"

The stranger was amused. "Sir, would you gain any to know about these? I came here simply to play your game; only, I have two conditions, if you are so generous as to allow them."

"By all means! Pray, tell me what they are," the rich man readily inquired.

The visitor sat farther back on the brocaded chair, his voice soft and confidential. "Well, here they are. A game is no fun if the winner does not win anything and the loser does not lose anything. Therefore, I would suggest that if I win, I would take everything in your possession—your lands, your stables, your servants, your house and everything contained in it. But if you win——" Here the stranger paused, his eyes narrowed ever so slightly, full of humorous malice, "If you win, you would become the owner of everything that belongs to me." The stranger paused again. "What belongs to me, sir, you will have no idea of. I am one of the most fortunate men alive, sir. . . . And besides that," he added, "I would remain in this house to serve you the rest of my life."

For a long moment, the rich man sat back in silence. Another long moment went by; then the rich man spoke, "That's agreed. But, please tell me your other condition."

Eyes dreamy, the stranger looked out of the window. "My second condition, sir, is not so much a condition as a request. I hope you would not mind giving me, a visitor, an edge over you. May I be allowed to ask the first question?"

The rich man thought for a long second, then said, "That is also agreed. Let's begin."

"Do I really understand that you have agreed to both my conditions?" the stranger asked thoughtfully.

Something in the visitor's manner and voice hurt the rich man's pride. He was ready to stake his very life on this game that he himself had created. There was no way out. "Yes," he said. "Yes, indeed I have. Now tell me, please, what do you have that I have not got?" The stranger smiled. Reaching to his feet, he took up his traveling bag, a coarse cotton square tied together by the four ends. Opening it slowly, ceremoniously, he took out an object and handed it to his host without a word. It was an empty half of a coconut shell, old and chipped, the kind poor people use as a container to drink water from.

"A coconut-shell cup!" the rich man exclaimed. One could not know whether he was merely amused or completely shattered.

"Yes, sir, a coconut-shell cup. A *chipped* shell cup. I use it to drink from on my wanderings. I am a wanderer," the visitor said quietly.

Holding the shell between his thumb and his forefinger and looking as if he had never seen such an object before, the rich man interrupted, "But,

but you don't mean that I do not have a thing like this?"

"No, sir, you have not. How could you?" the stranger replied.

Turning the residence upside down, the man and his servants discovered odds and ends of one thousand and one kinds, but they were unable to produce a drinking cup made from a coconut shell. In the servants' quarters, they found a few such cups, but they were all brand new, not chipped. The servants of such a wealthy man would not drink from a chipped cup. Even a beggar would throw it away.

"You see, sir," the stranger said to the rich man once they were again seated across the tea table, "you see, I am a wanderer, as I have said. I am a free man. This cup here is several years old and my only possession besides these poor clothes I have on. If you do not think me too immodest, I would venture that I treasure it more than you do all your collections of fine china. But, from this day, I am the owner and lone master of all that belongs to you."

Having taken possession of the rich man's land, houses, herds, and all his other treasures, the stranger began to give them away to the poor and needy people. Then, one day, taking up his old cotton bag, he left the village and no one ever saw him again.

As for the once rich man, it is believed that he died of grief and regret and was transformed into this small lizard. Curiously, one sees him scurrying about only indoors. Running up and down the walls, crossing the ceiling, staring at people and furniture, he never stops his "Tssst, Tssst." Children are very fond of him, for he looks so harassed, so funny.

But, oh, such sorrow, such regret, such self-pity.

Close-Up

1. (a) In the rich man's game, what does one player have to do when the other player announces one of his rare possessions? (b) When does a player lose?

2. Why is the rich man curious about the wanderer?

3. (a) The wanderer requests two conditions before they play. What are they? (b) By asking the first question, what does the wanderer force the rich man to do?

4. Why does the rich man lose?

Theme

A symbol is something that is a real object, but that also stands for something else. For example, in this story, the coconut-shell cup is a real object, but it also symbolizes, or stands for, freedom. A symbol often points to the theme of a story. The theme of the story is a generalization about life. It deals with human beings in general, not with the characters in the story in particular.

1. The rich man cares so much about his possessions, that he loses sight of other things. (a) What does he think symbolizes, or stands for, wealth? (b) What does the wanderer think is more important than possessions?

2. (a) Why is the chipped coconut shell more valuable to the wanderer than all the rich man's fine china? (b) What do you think determines the value of something?

3. Why does the wanderer give away all of the rich man's possessions?

4. What do you think is the theme of this story? (Think about what it says about wealth and freedom. Which should people value more?)

Activities

1. **Composition.** This folktale explains why the lizard never stops saying, "Tsst, tsst." Write your own imaginative explanation for this.

2. **Composition.** What do you think makes a person wealthy? Write a paragraph explaining your answer.

MAIN IDEA

Finding Supporting Details

The main idea of a paragraph is the most important thing it says about the topic, or subject, of a paragraph. Usually, the main idea is backed up by supporting details. For example, the main idea of the first paragraph of this story is that the man is very wealthy. This idea is backed up by the following supporting details: (1) his house is immense, (2) he owns many treasures, and (3) his land is extensive.

1. The following are main ideas from paragaphs in "The Little Lizard's Sorrow." Under these main ideas are supporting details from the story. Identify the details that support each main idea.

   Main Ideas
   a. The visitor was obviously a poor man.
   b. The visitor was not impressed by the rich man's wealth.
   c. The rich man did not have a chipped coconut-shell drinking cup in his house.

   Supporting Details
   (1) The visitor was dressed in mended clothes.
   (2) The visitor gave the rich surroundings only a passing, casual look.
   (3) The visitor looked as if he had not had a meal in days.
   (4) Even the servants in the rich man's house would not drink from a chipped cup.
   (5) The visitor answered the rich man in a proud, self-assured voice.
   (6) The visitor was perfectly at ease sipping tea from a rare porcelain cup.
   (7) The servants searched the entire house for a chipped, coconut-shell cup.

2. Find three supporting details to back up each of the following main ideas.
   (a) The very rich man was vain.
   (b) The rich man did not believe the stranger would win the game.
   (c) The stranger valued his freedom above worldly possessions.

WORD ATTACK

Finding Synonyms

A synonym is a word that has the same or almost the same meaning as another word. For example, *rich* and *wealthy* have similar meanings, in certain contexts; so they are synonyms.

▶ Match each word in Column **A** with its synonym in Column **B**.

A	**B**
a. immense	(1) cherish
b. wealth	(2) home
c. owner	(3) sadness
d. treasure	(4) huge
e. pauper	(5) possessor
f. usher	(6) riches
g. residence	(7) guide
h. inquire	(8) beggar
i. sorrow	(9) ask

436

The Baroque Marble

E. A. Proulx

Late autumn rain again. Sister Opal woke up in a Polaroid yellow light with her head hanging off the bed all sideways. Down in the street children's voices slid under the window muffled and changed by the damp morning. Sister Opal thought the children sounded as if they were speaking Russian or Basque—some queer, garbled language. She pretended she was in another country where she didn't know a word of the language and where she would have to make signs to get breakfast in a few minutes when she went downstairs. False panic began to rise in her, then subsided. From her position of suspension over the edge of the bed, the furniture looked darker, and the unfamiliar angle gave it a sinister look. The bureau loomed, a skyscraper in dull, dark varnish. Perhaps there were tiny people and offices inside. The chair arms seemed to have clenched hands at their ends, like brown old men sitting anxiously in the doctor's office waiting to hear the bad news.

Sister Opal twisted her head around toward the yellow window. On the sill was a square glass jar of marbles, reddish brown, yellow, and white glassies and a very large blue one. Most of them were mob marbles, as much alike as the faces of the crowd to a dictator on his balcony. Off to one side of the jar there was a white marble, deformed and not a true round—a lopsided freak of a marble— her favorite one. When this marble sat alone on the splendor of Sister Opal's blue-velvet best dress, it took on a silver, translucent glow. In the jar, it was dirty-white, opaque, and with more space around it than the other marbles, as if they avoided getting too close to it.

The jar of marbles was a kind of wealth. It was the most Sister Opal owned. Eight hundred and forty-three marbles. She took a miser's satisfaction in pouring them out onto the bed, watching them roll into the valleys, gathering up their heavy, glassy weight, cold but soon warming in her hand. Each marble was individually beautiful. A kind of classic Greek perfection shone in their roundness. Under Sister Opal's father's magnifying glass, the perfect marbles disclosed blemishes, pits, and scratches. Sister Opal liked them unmagnified; in their smallness she found their greatest value.

She touched the shade and it leaped up, startled, to the top of the wooden roller where it chattered a few seconds in fright, and then clung, tightly wound. Her warm breath made a milky fog on the window glass and her warm finger wrote, "All the sailors have died of scurvy, yours truly, Opal Foote."

Downstairs, Sister Opal's family sat at the table. Dark and sullen, they crunched toast, stabbed at their eggs, and made whirlpools in their coffee, with spoons. Except for Sister Opal, it was a bad-tempered family in the mornings, and the only conversations were mumbles to each other to pass the sugar or salt. By noontime the family would be chatty and warm, and by suppertime everyone was in high spirits. Sister Opal's four brothers (except for Roy, who worked on the night shift at GE) were very jovial at suppertime, when Sister Opal was weary. This morning Sister Opal's father asked about homework. Sister Opal thought of homework as yellow leaves dropping softly down, like the yellow blank pages she had dropped into the wastepaper basket last night. Guilty, Sister Opal went outside with jammy toast, hearing something from her father about being home right after school to make up Roy's dinner pail and to start supper because Mama had to work late. Sister Opal sang a private song as she walked along the wet sidewalk hopping the shallow puddles which were out to ruin her good shoes.

> Sailors died of scurvy, oh,
> They threw them in the sea.
> Pack Roy's dinner pail tonight
> With a thermos bottle of tea.

The rain outside had transmuted to yellow light and threatened afternoon lightning. Somewhere Sister Opal had read that yellow was the favorite color of insane people. The woman down the street had had a nervous breakdown last summer only a week after her husband had painted their house yellow. Across the street some white boys from Sister Opal's class at school were walking in the same direction. They pushed and shoved each other. One of them yelled, "Hey, turkey!" at Sister Opal. Sister Opal laughed because their faces looked yellow. Immediately they became hostile, thinking she was laughing at their existence, their being. Sister Opal's dignity did not allow her to hear their jeers.

At three-thirty Sister Opal was not on her way back home to pack up Roy's dinner pail. Instead, she was walking thoughtfully down Essex Street, peering into all the windows of the silver and antique shops. Art class that afternoon had completely enthralled Sister Opal. Mrs. Grigson had shown a film about ordinary people who started art collections with inexpensive things that became rare and valuable as time went by. Sister Opal envisioned herself someday in her own apartment with rare items of art in glass cases and white walls hung with glowing works of great artists which she, Sister Opal, had picked up years before for just a song. Even though she had only a few dollars in her savings account (a birthday present from her grandmother), and little hope of getting more, she was looking for something really good and fine on Essex Street. The film had indicated that all the people who built up enviable art collections had started off with the things they really liked. This was Sister Opal's primary mission: to find something she really liked. Then she would face the money

problem. She had quite forgotten about Roy's empty dinner pail, the cold stove, and Mama working late.

As she splashed through the puddles of Essex Steet, she dismissed old silver, all lumpy with twisted roses and crests, and dark with tarnish. She rejected the idea of collecting glass—too space-consuming and bothersome. She didn't really like sculpture, and she didn't know where she could buy real paintings or prints. The rain began again and Sister Opal's shoes were sodden and squishy. Past shops with small, dirty windows she went, discarding ceramics, carved wooden figures, vases, chandeliers, toy soldiers, andirons, dog-grates, lacquerware, and crystal.

Then, in the window of R. Sonnier's, she saw it. On a piece of blue velvet, quite like Sister Opal's best dress, there lay a large, glowing, misshapen marble. Sister Opal drew in her breath and exhaled slowly. This was it. She would collect marbles, rare ones from China, ancient ones from Peru, Roman marbles, marbles Genghis Khan had played with, marbles from Napoleon's cabinets, from Istanbul and Alexandria, marbles of solid gold, of azure, of lapis lazuli, of wood and stone and jewel. And she would begin with the marble in this very window! In she marched, a thin black girl with wet shoes, whose older brother was going to go supperless on the night shift.

The shop inside was crowded with objects stacked on shelves, in corners or looming down from the ceiling, crumpled, dusty dark things. A fat, middle-aged white man was reading a book in a leather chair behind the counter. He looked up when the door opened and then back to his book. Sister Opal did not waste time looking around the shop. She marched briskly up to R. Sonnier, or as briskly as one can march with wet shoes.

"Excuse me, how much is that marble in the window, and do you have any other kinds?"

"*What* marble in the window? I haven't got any marble that I know of in there. This is an antique shop, not a toy store." Sister Opal went to the curtain that hung behind the window to give a background for the objects displayed and pulled it aside.

"There," she said simply, pointing to the fat, lucent sphere.

"Young lady," said R. Sonnier, highly amused, "that is *not* a marble. That is a baroque pearl, an antique baroque pearl, and even though I am letting it go at an unbelievably low price, I doubt you could afford it." He looked her up and down, seeing the wet shoes, the cotton dress in late October, the brown skin and thinness that was Sister Opal. "It is for sale for four hundred and fifty dollars. A bargain for those who can afford such things. Marbles, I believe, you'll find at Woolworth's."

Sister Opal felt a horrible combination of shame, embarrassment, anger, pride, and sadness rise in her. She carried as a memory for the rest of her life R. Sonnier's knowing look that dismissed her as a person of no importance at all. Sister Opal, in a burst of pride and fantasy, said in a haughty voice, "I prefer to think of baroque pearls as marbles. And I would definitely like *that* marble. Please save it for me because it might be quite a while before I can pick it up. My name is Opal Foote."

R. Sonnier digested this information and repeated, "Then you want me to

save this baroque pearl for you? You intend to buy it?"

"Yes," said Sister Opal. "Opal Foote is the name." She gave him her address and then left with her shoes squelching softly. She was committed to the baroque marble which R. Sonnier was saving for her. Suddenly she remembered Roy's dinner pail and the gloomy apartment without one picture or really nice thing in it. There were only the family photographs kept in an old candy box and a plastic vase filled with plastic flowers.

She ran home hoping that Roy hadn't left for work yet.

At the table that night Sister Opal's father looked on her with disfavor. His cheerful supper face was cloudy, and Sister Opal knew the storm would break before she poured out his coffee. Roy had had to go to work without any dinner, supper had been late, and Opal had broken three eggs by slamming the old refrigerator door so hard that the eggs had shot out of their aluminum nest and run all over everything inside. Sister Opal's father finished the last bit of mashed potato on his plate and leaned back, glaring at Sister Opal.

"Well, girl, how come you didn't get home to fix your brother's dinner pail or start the supper? Everybody in this family's got to do his part. Now I'm waiting to hear."

There was no escape. Sister Opal took a deep breath and began telling about the art class and Essex Street and the baroque pearl in R. Sonnier's shop.

Her father's face was first incredulous, then angry, then sad. He said nothing for a long time. Opal sat miserably waiting for the lecture. Her brother Andrew got up and poured the coffee and patted Opal's shoulder as he passed behind her chair. Her father began to speak, slowly at first.

"Well, Sister, I think for a family in the kind of situation we got, where we all work to keep some kind of decency in our lives, and where we are trying to work toward an education for all you kids, an education of *some* kind, that any ideas about collecting art are just plain *crazy*. We are poor people and it's no use you pretending otherwise. Maybe someday your children, or more likely, grandchildren can collect art, but right now, girl, we can't gather enough money together to collect milk bottles! Wait!" (Sister Opal had uttered a furious "But!")

"Now just wait! I don't want to crush you down like a pancake. I *know* how you felt when that antique man looked you up and down and made his remarks. Every person in this family knows how you felt. And I understand how you answered him back pridefully about how you'd *get* that pearl or marble or whatever it is. But now, Opal, you got to swallow your pride and forget that marble, or else you got to do something about it. You got any ideas? Because I personally do not."

"I am old enough and able enough to get a job after school in the evenings and earn enough money to *buy* that baroque pearl myself, and I am going to do it!" Opal spoke slowly.

Her father looked at Opal, sadder than ever, and said, "If you are old enough to get a job, Sister Opal, you are old enough to save that job money for college or for helping this big family to get along. How would it be if I decided to save the money I make at Quadrant for buying myself a Picasso or something? Or suppose Roy decided not to kick in money for groceries and things but to buy himself a—a—harpsichord or a statue?" The idea of big, quiet Roy, clumsy and inarticulate, buying himself a harpsichord or a statue sent half the table snorting with laughter. "Besides," continued her father, "who's going to pack up Roy's dinner pail and start the supper while you are at some job?"

Sister Opal's brother Andrew stood up. "I am sick and tired of hearing about Roy's dinner pail. I expect the sun isn't going to come up and set anymore—no, it's going to be Roy's dinner pail! I say that if Sister Opal sees more in life than groceries and trying to get along, she should at least have the chance to try. I can get home a little earlier and start supper myself, and Roy can pack up his *own* dinner pail. You've told us yourself, Papa, that if a person wants something bad enough, and works hard enough *for* it, he'll get it. I'm willing to see Opal get that baroque pearl. I wouldn't mind seeing a few nice things around here myself."

The great argument broke out and raged around the supper table and took on fresh vigor when Sister Opal's mother came in, tired and with a sharp edge to her tongue. The final resolution, near midnight, was that if Sister Opal got a job, she could save half the money for the baroque pearl and half for college. Sister Opal felt triumphant and like a real art collector.

It took her three days to find a job. She was to work at Edsall's drugstore after school until ten-thirty from Monday to Friday and all day Saturday. She dipped out ice cream, made sodas and cherry Cokes, mixed Alka-Seltzer for gray-faced men, sold cigars and newspapers, squeezed her homework in between customers, and wiped off the sticky counter with a yellow sponge (Mr. Edsall had bought five hundred yellow sponges at a bargain sale the year before and Sister Opal got to despise those yellow sponges). She made change for people to use in the phone booth, she cleaned out the Pyrex coffeepots and made fresh coffee a thousand times a day, sold cough drops and throat lozenges all through the winter, and dispensed little plastic hats to ladies when the spring rains came. She got home at eleven o'clock each night with aching legs and red eyes, and Sunday mornings she slept late, catching up. In little ways, her mother showed an extra tenderness for her only daughter's great desire for a beautiful object. Her father surprised Sister Opal by Scotch-taping a reproduction of a Picasso painting over the kitchen calendar. He had cut *The Three Musicians* out of an old magazine. When Roy said "What's that!?" Sister Opal's father remarked loftily, "I always did like Picasso."

"Yeah," said Andrew to Roy, "at least he doesn't go in for harpsichords and statues." This joke about harpsichords and statues was one that Roy had never quite fathomed, and he eventually grew so confused on the matter that he was convinced that he really did take an extraordinary interest in keyboard music and sculpture. It was even suspected by the family that on his night off he had once gone, not to a night baseball game, but to a concert.

Sister Opal's weeks turned into months, and the long drugstore nights dragged through winter into spring. She had two bank accounts, one for college money and one for the baroque pearl. In March on a Friday night, she had four hundred dollars in the school account, and four hundred fifty in the pearl account. It was enough. She got permission from Mr. Edsall to take the next day off to go to R. Sonnier's to buy the pearl.

Early in the morning Sister Opal woke to pale yellow spring sun. She leaped up with her heart beating hard and dressed the part of a baroque-pearl buyer. Something special was needed. Her blue-velvet best dress had been outgrown and remade during the winter into a blue-velvet best skirt. She put it on and borrowed her mother's white silk blouse. She shined her shoes until the cracks didn't show and rushed downstairs to breakfast. Everybody knew she was going to buy the pearl that day but nobody said anything. The whole family was shy and quiet with anticipation. Andrew sat breathing quietly on his coffee.

At nine o'clock Sister Opal was walking along Essex Street. She went past the dusty windows displaying lumpy silverware, ceramic mugs with gold decorations, wooden candelabra from Spain, and then she came to R. Sonnier's shop. In his window there was a display of silver and gold watches and clocks under glass bells. Sister Opal smiled, thinking of the baroque pearl hidden secretly in a box, waiting for Sister Opal all those long months. She went inside. R. Sonnier sat in his chair behind the counter, reading a book. Nothing had changed. Stuff was still stacked to the ceiling, stuff still hung down to the floor.

R. Sonnier looked up. His eyes were flat, incurious.

"Can I help you?"

"It's me, Mr. Sonnier. Opal Foote. I've come to get my baroque marble that you've been saving for me."

"What marble? I don't have any marbles."

Patiently Sister Opal explained about the baroque pearl she had asked him to save for her last fall, and then she expectantly waited for the shock of recognition, the rummaging in a desk drawer, and the uncovering of the baroque pearl. She hadn't even yet seen it up close or held it. R. Sonnier looked annoyed.

"Listen, young lady, I had a baroque pearl last fall, and I sold it to a very nice lady who comes in here often to buy things. I never save anything except for my good customers. This lady paid me by check right away. I don't run any layaway plan here, and that baroque pearl was priced at almost five hundred dollars."

"You sold it? But it was supposed to be *mine!* I worked after school all fall and winter long, and I earned the money for it!" Sister Opal pulled out her wad of money. R. Sonnier looked astounded.

"Little lady, how was I to know you were serious? We get people in here every day saying they like something and they'll be back the next day or next week. They never show up, never! So when somebody comes in and says, I'll take that ring or that vase, here, here's the money, why I *sell* it to them. I'd go out of business if I believed everything people tell me. But since you've worked all that time, maybe you'd like to see some nice earrings I've got, jade and . . ."

"No. I was starting a famous marble collection. I don't want anything else." Sister Opal tucked her worthless money away in her old purse and went out with her back straight and stiff.

She walked around downtown all day long, looking into bookstores, department stores, stationery shops, jewelry stores, boutiques, but nothing seemed attractive to her. She thought it was strange that all the times she hadn't had any money hundreds and hundreds of things in the store windows had looked so great and she had really wanted them. Now that she had a lot of money nothing interested her. She stared at the most exotic clothes without even a twinge of desire. Her beautiful baroque pearl belonged to somebody else; she didn't want any other thing. She put off going home as long as possible, but when the lights began to come on she knew it was time to go back.

The family was at supper. Every head turned to Sister Opal as she came in and slumped into her chair.

"Well!" boomed Roy, who didn't work Saturday nights. "Let's see that solid gold marble you got!" Sister Opal's mother, who saw something was wrong, said, "Well, what's the trouble, Sister? Was the store closed?" Sister Opal, who had not cried, or even felt much of anything except emptiness and loss, burst into a howl she didn't even know was inside her.

"He sold it to somebody else a long time ago-o-oo-o!" Between sobs, hiccups, and tears dripping into her plate, Sister Opal told the family about R. Sonnier and how he had sold the pearl. Andrew was indignant and declared that if he was ever in the market for a baroque pearl, he would rather die in the gutter than buy it from R. Sonnier. But Sister Opal's father said judiciously, "Well, Sister, he didn't do it out of spite and meanness. He was just being business-like. If you were a store man and somebody breezed in and said, 'Here, you hold on to that stuffed elephant for me, I'll be back someday and pay for it,' and a week later somebody else came in and said, 'Here, here's a thousand dollars for that stuffed elephant,' you *know* you are going to sell that elephant right there and then. Sister Opal, you should have checked back with that R. Sonnier every week or so, so that he'd know you were really serious about buying it. I know you're disappointed. I'm disappointed myself. I was looking forward to seeing that baroque pearl and knowing somebody in our family owned it." This brought a fresh howl from Sister Opal, which her father silenced by continuing.

"As I see it, Sister, you can either curl up and die because you didn't get your fancy marble, or you can hurry up and quit crying and think about the future. Probably you should take that pearl money and put it with the college money so that you can study up on baroque pearls when you get to college. So you got to adopt a long range plan now and think about education and a career. . . ."

Sister Opal heard her father talking on in a kindly way about his favorite subject, education and getting knowledge and getting ahead and having a career. She knew that most of what he was saying was sensible, but she had heard it all so many times she didn't want to hear it again. Her father didn't *know* how it felt to be a girl and to want a beautiful thing very badly. Sister Opal excused herself

from the table and went up to her room. She flung herself on the bed sideways and dangled her head off the edge, looking at the pale rectangle of the window. The marble jar was dark in the twilight and it glittered along one side from the reflected light of the street lamp. Sister Opal reached out for the marble jar, tipped the contents onto the bed with a rich, sensuous, rolling sound. Her thin hand slid through the marble pile in the darkening room until she touched the familiar lopsided marble. Warming it in the hollow of her hand, she could just make out its ephemeral glow, its waxy luster against the darkness of her hand and the darkness of the oncoming night. She rolled it slightly in her palm and said softly to the warmed, heavy marble, "Oh, what a beautiful baroque pearl."

Close Up

1. (a) Why does Opal start thinking about collecting beautiful things? (b) How does she picture herself someday?

2. (a) Why does Mr. R. Sonnier dismiss Opal as a person of no importance? (b) How does his dismissal make her feel and what does it make her do?

3. (a) What steps does Opal take to obtain the pearl? (b) How do the members of her family help her work toward her goal?

4. How does Opal's father show that he approves of Opal's desire to buy the pearl?

5. Opal's father tells her that Mr. Sonnier wasn't being mean or malicious when he sold the pearl, just "businesslike." Do you agree with this statement? Why or why not?

6. At the end of the story, Opal pretends that the lopsided marble is the baroque pearl. Do you think this story ends on a hopeful note or a sad note? Why?

Theme

In literature, a symbol is an object that stands for an idea, feeling, or belief. Often, in stories, objects take on symbolic meanings. In many instances, these symbols point to the theme of the story.

1. (a) Why does Opal think of her jar of marbles as a kind of wealth? (b) Why does she especially value the deformed white marble?

2. Why doesn't Opal like to look at her marbles under a magnifying glass?

3. What does the baroque marble represent to Opal?

4. Think about what the baroque marble means to Opal. Then write a statement that you think best expresses the theme of this story.

Activities

1. Make a list of things teenagers can do to earn money for something they want.

2. Create a sign for Mr. R. Sonnier's window advertising the baroque pearl.

MAIN IDEA

The main idea of a paragraph is the most important thing said about its topic, or subject. The main idea is always expressed as a complete sentence. For example, read the following paragraph.

> "She walked around downtown all day long, looking into bookstores, department stores, stationery shops, jewelry stores, boutiques, but nothing seemed attractive to her. She thought it was strange that all the times she hadn't had any money hundreds and hundreds of things in the store windows had looked so great and she had really wanted them. Now that she had a lot of money nothing interested her. She stared at the most exotic clothes without even a twinge of desire. Her beautiful baroque pearl belonged to somebody else; she didn't want any other thing. She put off going home as long as possible, but when the lights began to come on she knew it was time to go back."

The main idea is: Opal did not want anything but the beautiful, baroque pearl.

▶ In your own words, state the main idea of each of the following paragraphs.

a.   " 'Well, Sister, I think for a family in the kind of situation we got, where we all work to keep some kind of decency in our lives, and where we are trying to work toward an education for all you kids, an education of *some* kind, that any ideas about collecting art are just plain *crazy*. We are poor people and it's no use you pretending otherwise. Maybe someday your children, or more likely, grandchildren can collect art, but right now, girl, we can't gather enough money together to collect milk bottles! Wait!' "

b.   "Sister Opal's brother Andrew stood up. 'I am sick and tired of hearing about Roy's dinner pail. I expect the sun isn't going to come up and set anymore—no, it's going to be Roy's dinner pail! I say that if Sister Opal sees more in life than groceries and trying to get along, she should at least have the chance to try. I can get home a little earlier and start supper myself, and Roy can pack up his *own* dinner pail. You've told us yourself, Papa, that if a person wants something bad enough, and works hard enough *for* it, he'll get it. I'm willing to see Opal get that baroque pearl. I wouldn't mind seeing a few nice things around here myself.' "

c.   "The jar of marbles was a kind of wealth. It was the most Sister Opal owned. Eight hundred and forty-three marbles. She took a miser's satisfaction in pouring them out onto the bed, watching them roll into the valleys, gathering up their heavy, glassy weight, cold but soon warming in her hand. Each marble was individually beautiful. A kind of classic Greek perfection shone in their roundness. Under Sister Opal's father's magnifying glass, the perfect marbles disclosed blemishes, pits, and scratches. Sister Opal liked them unmagnified; in their smallness she found their greatest value."

WORD ATTACK

Understanding Comparisons

Comparisons are groups of words or complete statements that show how people or objects are alike. For example, "I don't want to crush you down like a pancake." This sentence compares how Opal would look to a pancake.

▶ Tell what is being compared to what in each passage below.

a.   "The bureau loomed, a skyscraper in dull, dark varnish."

b.   "The chair arms seemed to have clenched hands at their ends, like brown old men sitting anxiously in the doctor's office waiting to hear the bad news."

c.   "Sister Opal thought of homework as yellow leaves dropping softly down, like the yellow blank pages she had dropped into the wastepaper basket last night."

d.   "On a piece of blue velvet, quite like Sister Opal's best dress, there lay a large, glowing, misshapen marble."

e.   "At the table that night Sister Opal's father looked on her with disfavor. His cheerful supper face was cloudy, and Sister Opal knew the storm would break before she poured out his coffee."

Where the Sidewalk Ends

Shel Silverstein

"Where the Sidewalk Ends" by Shel Silverstein [from *Where the Sidewalk Ends: The Poems and Drawings of Shel Silverstein.*]

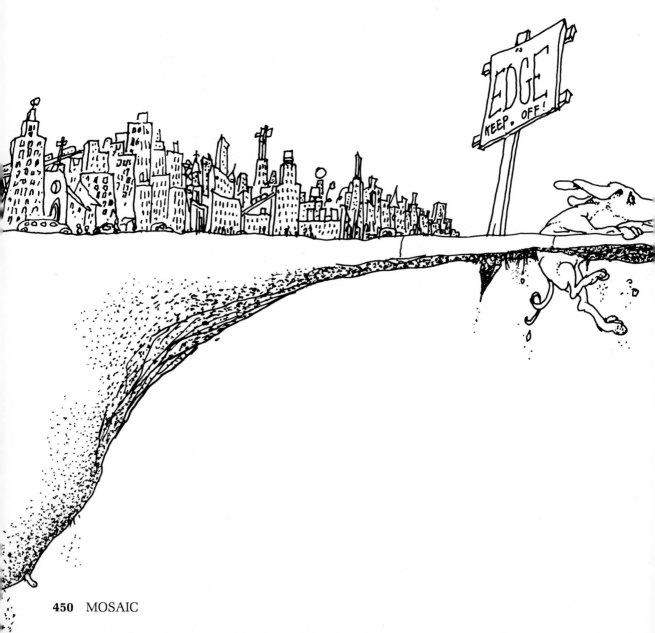

There is a place where the sidewalk ends
And before the street begins,
And there the grass grows soft and white,
And there the sun burns crimson bright,
5   And there the moon-bird rests from his flight
To cool in the peppermint wind.

Let us leave this place where the smoke blows black
And the dark street winds and bends.
Past the pits where the asphalt flowers grow
10   We shall walk with a walk that is measured and slow,
And watch where the chalk-white arrows go
To the place where the sidewalk ends.

Yes we'll walk with a walk that is measured and slow,
And we'll go where the chalk-white arrows go,
15   For the children, they mark, and the children, they know
The place where the sidewalk ends.

Close Up

1. Why does the poet want to leave this place?
2. What makes the place where the poet wants to go magical?

REVIEW QUIZ

On the Selections

1. In "On the Edge," what event first makes Frank feel fear?

2. How does Frank use his shoe to save himself?

3. In "My First Life Line," why does Mama ask Marguerite to take off her dress?

4. Find two things Mrs. Flowers does in order to make Marguerite feel special.

5. In "Mike and the Grass," why does the father object to his son's having a sandbox?

6. In which country does "The Little Lizard's Sorrow" take place?

7. Why does the rich man agree to see the stranger who appears at his door?

8. In "The Baroque Marble," why does Opal favor the white marble in her collection?

9. At first, why does Opal's father object to her getting a job after school to pay for the baroque marble?

10. In Shel Silverstein's poem, what is special about the place where the sidewalk ends?

On Main Idea

1. What is the topic of the paragraph below?

> Mountain climbers should follow three important rules. First, they should never go into the mountains alone. This way, if one person gets into trouble, someone else is there to help. Second, they should carry necessary equipment. A rope, a compass, and a knife can help climbers get out of tight spots. Third, they should learn to read the mountains. Spotting a safe foothold or handhold can save a life.

2. What is the topic sentence in the paragraph above?

3. Write a topic sentence for a paragraph that would include the following details.
   (a) He was wearing broken straw sandals.
   (b) His clothes looked as if they had been mended hundreds of times.
   (c) He looked as though he had not eaten in days.

4. List three points supporting the following main idea: Language separates human beings from the lower animals.

On Theme ▶ Decide whether the following statements are true or false.
   a. The theme of a story is its central insight into, or generalization about, life.
   b. In "My First Life Line," Mama makes a very important statement about sewing that points to the theme.
   c. A symbol is never a real object.
   d. A symbol can help you discover the theme of a story.

COMPOSITION

Exposition

Exposition is the act of expounding or explaining. You write exposition when you give information or explain something.

An expository paragraph often contains a topic sentence which may appear at the beginning of the paragraph. Sometimes it appears in the middle or at the end of the paragraph. The rest of the paragraph contains information that supports the main idea expressed in the topic sentence. This information may take the form of facts or examples or an incident.

A good expository paragraph has unity. This means it contains only information that relates to the main idea of the paragraph.

1. Write an expository paragraph about one of these topics.
   a. Building a collection
   b. How _____ changed my life
   c. The value of having a hobby
   d. What freedom means to me

2. Use one of the following topic sentences to begin an expository paragraph.
   a. There are several rules to follow when playing marbles.
   b. In my spare time I like to _____.
   c. _____ was a day I shall never forget.
   d. My typical day is quite hectic.

BEFORE GOING ON

Reading for Main Ideas

You can improve your comprehension of an essay by reading for main ideas. After you read each paragraph, stop and ask yourself, "What is the topic and what is the main idea about this topic?"

1. Read paragraphs 1–5 of "Gifts of the Indians."
   a. Which statement expresses the main idea of paragraph 1?
      (1) Christopher Columbus set sail from Spain in search of the East Indies.

       (2) Ever since Columbus, there have been many misconceptions about the first Americans.

   b. Which statement expresses the main idea of paragraph 2?

       (1) Most students know little about the first Americans.

       (2) Most students enjoy studying about the Huns under Attila.

   c. Which statement expresses the main idea of paragraph 3?

       (1) The first Americans had to be removed before Western culture could develop in the New World.

       (2) The reason many people know so little about the first Americans may be that they incorrectly assume "everything in the twentieth-century Americas came from Europe."

   d. Which statement expresses the main idea of paragraph 4?

       (1) Americans are impressed by statistics concerning money.

       (2) The first Americans developed the products that account for more than half of America's cash farm crop.

   e. Which statement expresses the main idea of paragraph 5?

       (1) The first Americans developed corn, which is the most valuable crop grown in the United States.

       (2) Popcorn sweetened with maple sugar is called "crackerjack."

2. Read paragraphs 6–10. If the statement below expresses the main idea of the paragraph, label it true. (Statement **a** is for paragraph 6, **b** for 7, etc.) If it does not, write a sentence stating the main idea.

   a. Sweet potatoes and some types of yams are of American origin.

   b. A large number of valuable crops are of American origin.

   c. South-American Indians made rubber toys for their children.

   d. The scientific study of biology and medicine is indebted to the medicinal knowledge of American Indians.

   e. Sixteenth-century Europeans did not bathe often.

3. Read paragraphs 11–15. For each paragraph, write a statement expressing the main idea.

4. Write a statement expressing the main idea of the entire essay.

Further Reading

Gifts of the Indian

C. Fayne Porter

Nearly five centuries ago, a hardy old salt named Christopher Columbus set sail from Spain, outward bound for the East Indies. When he made his earth-shaking landfall at San Salvador in the Bahamas, he immediately dubbed the native Arawaks there "Indians," and Indians the residents of the New World have been ever since. Of course they had nothing to do with India, so the term was a misnomer from the beginning. Misconception has been piled on top of misconception ever since, so that today much of our thinking about the first Americans is cloudy.

Ask any moderately good student who has had a course or two in world

history to comment on the rise and fall of Carthage, or the invasion of the Huns under Attila, or the life and times of King Alfred, and that student could give a halfway intelligent answer. Ask about the rise and fall of the Ho-de-no-sau-nee, or the Trail of Tears, or the life and times of Chief Joseph of the Nez Perces, and that student would be: (1) completely stumped for an answer, and (2) quite sure that you were strange for asking such a question in the first place.

Now why should this be? Perhaps much of it is because people fall into the grave error of thinking that everything in the twentieth-century Americas came from Europe—that the Stone Age Indian in the New World was a minus factor who had to be moved out of the way before a Western culture could flourish, that he contributed nothing except opposition. Then let's look at the record.

Americans today have something of a reputation for being impressed by statistics concerning money, so try this one: The United States is, of course, the world's leading agricultural nation; but more than half of the cash farm crop of this country comes from products the Indian developed! This makes him certainly the greatest of the Stone Age farmers.

Today's domestic tillers of the soil realize about $3,000,000,000 annually from corn, the most valuable crop grown in the United States. Corn has been called the greatest natural resource of our country, and a bumper corn crop will equal the total value of all wheat, potatoes, barley, rye, rice, tobacco, beans, and sweet potatoes grown yearly. Science is still puzzled as to how the Indians ever developed it in the first place, because no wild corn has ever been

found. It is by now so thoroughly domesticated that it has lost the power of self-propagation in an untended state. It grows only where man plants it and is totally helpless without man's care. Other cereal grains—wheat, barley, rice, oats, rye—will thrive by themselves, but not corn; its origin is shrouded in mystery. Scientists have improved corn, true, *but all of the main types now grown were developed by the time of Columbus.* (This includes popcorn. It was often served sweetened with maple sugar. The tasty confection of crackerjack or caramelcorn, then, is a few thousand years old.)

And let's add the Irish potato, one of the world's most widely grown vegetables. Irish it is not; it came first from the high plateau country of Peru and Bolivia. The world embraced it, and its total production of over eight billion bushels yearly makes it an easy winner on the world scene. Its annual value surpasses that of all the gold and silver mined yearly throughout the world. While we're on the subject of potatoes, add the sweet potato and some types of yams as of American origin—the three from different families and representing different kinds of domesticated vegetables.

To this list add tomatoes, the lead-ing crop canned in the United States today; tobacco, base of a billion-dollar-a-year industry, plus the related uses of nicotine in insecticide and medicine; table beans, both the dry (kidneys and limas) and the string beans or green beans; the castor bean used for medicinal castor oil and a wide variety of commercial needs; the peanut, and its vast range of by-products; the pumpkins and the related squash families; the green or bell peppers and the red chile pepper (not the black table variety, however); pineapples; avocados; eggplant; wild rice; cassava (from which our tapioca comes); native grape strains; strawberries; blackberries; raspberries and on and on the list might go.

Then, too, quite an industry has been built around what the Indians of South America once called *cahuchi* (the weeping tree). The Indians would make cuts in the bark and gather the "tears" from this tree, which would be compressed into balls and used as toys and playthings. Today we know "the weeping tree" as the rubber tree, and the rubber industry is a giant one. In the United States alone, rubber and rubber goods production is in the five-billion-dollar-a-year class.

Where would the scientific study of biology and medicine be without the guinea pig, domesticated by the South American aborigines? In the field of medicine, consider curare, quinine, cocaine, cascara, arnica, petrolatum, ipecac, and wintergreen, a few of the curative substances understood and utilized by the Indians. So skillful were the Indians in the knowledge of natural remedies, that in 1952 Felix S. Cohen could write "... in the four hundred years that the European physicians and botanists have been analyzing and examining the flora of America, they have not yet discovered a medicinal herb not known to the Indians."

In fact, the Indians whom the first settlers found had a far better conception of what constituted good health and how to maintain it than did the settlers themselves. They were a scrupulously clean people, unlike the Europeans who first came to their shores. Columbus took back the news of how often the Indians bathed, and one of the first dictates set down by Queen Isabella of Spain was to the point, if misdirected: "They are not to bathe as frequently as hitherto."

Columbus took back another idea which he got from the Arawaks, one which would become synonymous with ships that sail the sea and the men who sail them. That idea also concerned a tree, called the *hamaca*, whose bark was used to make a swinging bed, hung by vine ropes between two supports. This, of course, became the hammock, dearly beloved of old sailors and do-it-yourself gardeners.

American soldiers who coursed over the world in World War II were greeted by small fry (and some fry not so small) in the most remote and inaccessible corners of the earth with the same classic query: "Got any gum, Yank?" Chewing gum, along with cigarettes and chocolate candy, became the *wampum* for Yanks everywhere. Cigarettes were of American Indian origin, as was chocolate—and chewing gum. The Indians used numerous tree gums for chewing as well as the Central American *chicle*, which is the "chewy" base of all gum made today.

As a small boy from the remote hill country of Northern California, I used to thrill to the cry of the "peanut-butchers" at carnivals and circuses and ball games. I can see them yet, with their red-and-white hats and their precious wares in a tray slung from around their necks, and I can hear their stirring cry of "POPcorn, PEAnuts, CRACKerjack, CHEWing gum! POPcorn, PEAnuts, CRACKerjack, CHEWing gum!" To a country boy with a few small coins clutched tightly in a sometimes not-too-clean hand, they represented all that was opulent and desirable in the world. I did not know then, as I know now, that they were hawking small-boy delights that had tempted countless generations of Indians before me. Perhaps it would not have seemed important to me then anyway, but I think it would have.

The white comers to the New World found themselves in an environment and in a land so foreign to them as to be almost incomprehensible. There was only one way in which the white man could survive, and that was by emulating the Indian who knew and understood the land and its ways. So the newcomers took nearly all that the Indian had to offer—they took his means of transportation, like the canoe and the snowshoe; they took his buckskin dress for life on the frontier; and they took his foods, like cornbread, and persimmon bread, and hominy, and succotash, and the corn tortilla of the Southwestern Pueblo dwellers. As an interesting aside here, the poor starving Pilgrims at Plymouth Rock, with the centuries of supposedly superior occidental learning behind them, refused to eat the plentiful clams of that area because they thought them to be poisonous. We can thank the Wampanoags of Massachusetts for introducing the Pilgrims to the fine old Indian tradition of the clambake.

They took, too, the Indian's names for the rich and varied land upon which he lived. Probably in every county in the United States today (exclusive of Hawaii) there is an Indian place-name—of a stream or a mountain or a city—whispering of the time when another people lived and worked and played here. The sonorous roll of the old Indian names is indelibly stamped into the fabric of the land—Mississippi and Monongahela, Narragansett and Natchez, Savannah and Seattle, Tishomingo and Taos, Winnemucca and Wichita—and half of our fifty states bear names which stem from Indian words.

The Hobbit

J. R. R. Tolkien
Dramatized by Patricia Gray

Characters

Bilbo Baggins, a Hobbit

Gandalf, a great Wizard

Dwalin and Balin ⎫
Kili and Fili ⎪
Dori, Nori, and Ori ⎬ Dwarves
Oin and Gloin ⎪
Bifur and Bofur ⎪
Bombur ⎭

Thorin, Leader of the Dwarves

Grocery Boy, a Hobbit lad

Burt ⎫
Essie ⎬ Trolls
Tom ⎭

The Great Goblin ⎫ Goblins
Attendant Goblin ⎭

Gollum, a slimy creature

The Elven-Queen ⎫ Wood-elves
Two Elf Guards ⎭

Smaug, the Dragon

Other Hobbits, Goblins, Elves, etc. may be added as desired, or the number may be easily reduced.

PLACE: From Underhill, through the Wilderland, to the Lonely Mountain.

TIME: Long ago in the quiet of the world.

Act One

SCENE 1: [*The house lights dim. The lights come up in front of the curtain, revealing an imaginary part of the world called Middle Earth. We are in the Shire, Underhill, home of the hobbits. It is a pleasant morning. The Shire is the picture of rural perfection.*

At L sits a well-appointed little hobbit by the name of Bilbo Baggins, Esq. He is sitting on the stoop outside his round green door, which has a shiny-yellow brass doorknob in the exact middle. At the side is a mailbox with several letters in it. Before him is a turntable or lazy Susan, laid with four complete breakfasts. Bilbo has just eaten the first of these and lets out a deep sigh of satisfaction. He carefully dabs his mouth with a huge napkin. Emitting another sigh, he turns the table so that breakfast number two is before him. He digs in with determination after a brief hesitation over which ham to spread his muffin with.

From R an extraordinary old man (Gandalf) enters. He is tall, with a flowing white beard and bushy black brows, out of which gleam deep, piercing eyes. On his head is a tall, peaked hat covered with strange designs. He wears a long gray cloak, a silver scarf, and immense black boots, and carries a staff.]

Gandalf (*regarding the scene with relish, taking a deep breath of the sparkling air*): Ah, the Shire! How delicious the morning is in this part of the world! The air is *stuffed* with comfort. It feels like nothing exciting has happened here for ages—all green and still—— (*Crosses to Bilbo, who is well into his third break-*

fast.)——rather like the inside of one of those fresh eggs you're eating—don't you think?

Bilbo (*looking up, startled*): Oh! I wouldn't know. It's hard to look at a place from the outside when you live in the inside! But then you're a stranger here. Welcome! I still have a breakfast or two left if you'd care for some.

Gandalf: Thank you, I haven't the time—and I am not a stranger anywhere, unless, of course, I choose to be.

(*A hobbit with a green, pointed cap peeks down at them from a window flap in the curtain. Immediately, two more hobbits pop out from the two sides of the curtain.*)

Bilbo (*confused*): Oh, yes? Well, how do you do, sir—— (*Offering his hand.*)

Gandalf (*ignoring the gesture*): Magnificently, of course! (*Slowly and deliberately.*) But at the moment, I am looking for someone to share a great adventure—— (*Pauses to see Bilbo's reaction, which is sheer horror.*)——a stupendous adventure that I'm arranging—and it's very difficult to find anyone—— (*The three hobbits who have been listening suddenly vanish. We hear sounds of doors and shutters slamming offstage.*) What was that?

Bilbo (*standing up, taking from his pocket a long wooden pipe and tapping it impatiently*): That was neighbors slamming doors and shutters.

Gandalf (*sadly*): On adventure. Tch, tch.

Bilbo: You, sir, are in the neighborhood of hobbits.

Gandalf (*feigning ignorance*): Hobbit? Hobbit? What's a hobbit?

Bilbo: We're just plain folk—have no use for adventures. *(Shudders.)* Nasty, uncomfortable things! Adventures make you late for dinner! Can't think what anybody sees in them! *(Gandalf continues to stare at Bilbo with a strangely disturbing gleam in his eye. Bilbo nervously crosses to the mailbox and removes some letters. He sits on the stoop and examines them.)* Good morning, we don't want any adventures here. You might try across The Hill or over The Water. *(Bilbo devotes himself to his letters.)*

Gandalf: You should be ashamed of yourself, *Bilbo Baggins!*

Bilbo *(sitting up alertly):* That's my name! How did you know——

Gandalf *(cutting in):* You know mine, too, although you don't know that I belong to it. I am Gandalf, and Gandalf means me! To think that I should have lived to be good-morninged by Belladonna Took's son—as if I were selling buttons at the door!

Bilbo *(beside himself with excitement):* Gandalf! Gandalf! Good gracious! Not the wandering wizard who used to tell such wonderful tales at parties about dragons and giants and goblins——

Gandalf *(merely yawning):* The same, dear boy.

Bilbo: And about the rescue of princesses and the unexpected luck of widows' sons! And the fireworks! I remember those! Old Grandpa Took used to send them up on Midsummer's Eve. What a display!

Gandalf: Naturally.

Bilbo: Up they rose, like great lilies and snapdragons, and hung in the twilight all evening, falling at last like silver and gold rain! . . . Dear me! Are you the same Gandalf who led so many of our quiet lads and lasses off on mad adventures? Bless me, life used to be quite inter—— I mean, you used to upset things quite badly in these parts! I beg your pardon, but I had no idea you were still in business.

Gandalf: Where else should I be? Tch, tch. Well, for your Grandfather Took's sake and for the sake of your poor mother, Belladonna, I'll give you what you asked for.

Bilbo: But I haven't asked for anything!

Gandalf: Yes, you have. My pardon—I give it to you. In fact, I will be so kind as to send you on an adventure—very amusing for me, very good for you—and profitable too, *if* you live through it.

Bilbo: *If I live through it?* Sorry. No adventures, thank you. Good morning! *(Starts for his door, then remembers his manners.)* I'd ask you in to tea but——

Gandalf: How kind of you to ask me—I hate to think alone! *(Propelling him through the door.)* You go along in and fix the tea. I'll be in shortly—I have a little business to attend to. *(Gives Bilbo a final shove through the door, then chuckles slyly to himself, rubs his hands, and hangs a large, colorful sign on the door. The sign reads: BURGLAR WANTS GOOD JOB. PLENTY OF EXCITEMENT AND REASONABLE REWARD. He looks off R.)* Ah, here they come! *(Goes through door.)*

(The curtain opens to reveal the main hall at Bag-End, residence of B. Baggins, Esquire. UC is a large round door with a mat in front. To the left of it is a pegged coat rack. Downstage is a long table, with benches. To the right of the table is a fireplace with a stool before it.

Gandalf, at C, looking around the room, calls off to Bilbo.)

Gandalf: A fine place you have here, Bilbo.

(Bilbo bustles on L with tea trolley.)

Bilbo: Yes, I love my quiet home.

Gandalf: I haven't been this way for a long time—not since your grandfather Took passed on——

Bilbo: Yes, well, I don't expect there's much to amuse you around here——

Gandalf: True—but you hobbits make a relaxing change from those dwarves and elves with their hard-headed hustle and light-headed bustle. Do you know the most amazing thing about hobbits?

Bilbo: No, what?

Gandalf: That you remain gentlefolk in spite of everything. I mean, I just dropped in and yet you *insisted* I stay to tea.

Bilbo *(protesting weakly):* Well— *(Doorbell rings. Bilbo starts in surprise.)*

Gandalf: You expecting someone?

Bilbo *(crossing to door):* No—oh, maybe the groceries.

[Bilbo opens the door UC, and in pops a dwarf (Dwalin) with a blue beard neatly tucked into his golden belt. He wears a dark green hood.]

Dwalin *(executing a low, sweeping bow):* Dwalin, at your service!

Bilbo *(baffled, looking for groceries):* Why—Bilbo Baggins, at yours! Ummm—I was expecting groceries.

Dwalin: I was told you set a great table.

Gandalf: Ask the fellow in to tea, why don't you?

Bilbo: Yes, yes, certainly. Uh, would you care to join us? The kettle's on the boil——

Dwalin: Delighted! *(Hangs his hood on a peg and seats himself expansively at table.)*

Bilbo *(sitting down beside Dwalin):* Well, now! *(Laughs nervously.)* Tell me—— *(The doorbell rings again.)* Oops, excuse me. *(Goes to the door, saying while opening it:)* I have no idea *who* it could—— Oh!

[There stands an elderly dwarf (Balin) with a white beard and scarlet hood.]

Balin *(hobbling inside, gesturing at the coat rack with his cane):* Ha! I see they have begun to arrive already! *(Hangs his hood next to Dwalin's.)* Balin, at your service! *(It is difficult for him to execute a bow. He groans.)*

Bilbo: Thank you. Uh, you said "They have begun to arrive"?

Gandalf *(calling):* Groceries, Bilbo?

Bilbo: Actually, no—— *(Taking a deep breath, to Balin)* Won't you join us for tea?

Balin: A glass of buttermilk would suit me better, if it's all the same to you, my good sir. But I don't mind some cake—seed cake, if you have any. *(Crosses to table.)*

Bilbo *(automatically):* Oh, lots! Excuse me. *(Hurries off L to get the cake.)*

Dwalin: No hurry. *(To Balin.)* Fine lodgings here, eh, brother?

Balin *(seating himself):* Ummm. These hobbits have the cream. A big thing this is we're setting out for.

(Doorbell rings, bringing on Bilbo from L with platter of cakes.)

Dwalin: But dangerous. Terribly dangerous!

Bilbo: Not again!

Gandalf (crossing to Bilbo): Allow me to unburden you—— (Takes platter from Bilbo and passes platter to others. Dwalin takes two cakes and downs them rapidly and is shortly back for more. Balin takes one and nibbles at it and puts it down on small table. Later Balin eats it unnoticed.)

[Bell rings again. Bilbo rushes to the door and opens it. There stand two dwarves (Kili and Fili), look-alikes with blue hoods, silver bells, and yellow beards. Each carries a bag of tools and spades.]

Kili: Kili!

Fili: Fili! (Both sweep off their hoods and bow.)

Kili and **Fili** (together): At your service!

Bilbo: Baggins, here—— (Weakly.) At yours . . . uh, and your families!

Kili: Dwalin and Balin here already, I see. Let us join the throng! (Kili and Fili hang up their hoods, cross to table, and sit down.)

Bilbo (horrified): Throng!

Gandalf: Why, Bilbo, I really am surprised! I didn't think that hobbits mixed with dwarves.

Bilbo: They don't!

Gandalf: No? That's odd, since you have so many dwarf friends.

Bilbo (confidentially, to Gandalf): I've never laid eyes on them before! If my neighbors knew, they'd be scandalized! Dwarves here! At Bag-End! (Bell rings, and then there is the lively rat-a-tat of a stick on the door.)

Dwalin: That'll be Dori, Nori, Ori, Oin, and Gloin!

Bilbo (horrified, crossing to door): Who? (Hurrying to the door as the rat-a-tat continues.) The nerve!

(Bilbo opens the door and there stand no less than five dwarves, Dori, Nori, Ori, Oin, and Gloin, their broad hands stuck in their gold and silver belts. They bow upon introducing themselves.)

Dori (has a blond beard, dark purple hood, and gold belt; doffing his hood): Dori!

Nori (has a blond beard, pale purple hood, and silver belt; doffing his hood): Nori!

Ori (has a brown beard, orange hood, and gold belt; doffing his hood): Ori!

Oin (has an auburn beard, brown hood, and a gold belt; doffing his hood): Oin!

Gloin (has a gray beard, gray hood, and a silver belt; doffing his hood): Gloin!

Bilbo: Oh!

Dori, Nori, Ori, Oin, and **Gloin** (together): At your service! (They hang up their hoods.)

Bilbo: Where do you all come from? (Crossing to Gandalf, frantically.) There's just no end to them! I must be having a nightmare! (Gandalf pinches Bilbo.) Ouch!

Gandalf: You're awake. (Dwarves have been whispering among themselves.)

Bilbo (coughing importantly to get the dwarves' attention): Ahem, ahem. Honored Dwarves, I'm sorry, but I'm afraid you've mistaken this for a restaurant. This is a private home. (Dwarves laugh politely at what they think is an attempt at humor.)

Dori (slapping Bilbo on the back good-naturedly): Oh-ho, jolly good! Bring out the food.

Ori: Hot cocoa for me, please.

Dwalin (from the table): And more cakes! We're fresh out. Please! (Shows empty plate. There is a terrific banging on the door.)

Bilbo (fuming): Stop that pounding! What are you trying to——

[Bilbo pulls the door open with a jerk, and in tumble four dwarves (Bifur, Bofur, Bombur, and Thorin), one on top of the other.]

Gandalf (laughing): Careful, careful! It's not like you, Bilbo, to keep friends waiting on the mat, and then open the door like a popgun!

(The dwarves pick themselves up and bow as they announce themselves, except for Thorin, who was at the bottom of the heap, directly under Bombur, the fattest of the lot.)

Bifur (has a very slight chestnut beard and pale yellow hood; he is the youngest of the dwarves): I'm Bifur!

Bofur (has a gray beard and a dark yellow hood and a silver belt): Bofur!

Bifur and **Bofur** (together): At your service!

Bombur (Has a light blue beard and a pale green hood. He is the fattest of the dwarves and is a natural clown. He scrambles off Thorin and bows deeply): Bombur, at your service! (He indicates Thorin, who was at the bottom of the heap and who stands apart brushing himself off indignantly.) Our great leader, Thorin.

(Thorin has a black beard and a sky-blue hood with a long silver tassel.)

Thorin (snarling at Bombur): Sir! (Bombur cringes. They all hang up their hoods.)

Bilbo (interceding): My fault. I'm terribly sorry.

Thorin (grunting): Don't mention it. (Gazes regally up at the ceiling, looking at row of thirteen hoods.) I see we are all here.

Gandalf: Quite a merry gathering! (Doorbell rings.)

Thorin: Who can that be?

Bilbo: Well, I certainly wouldn't know!

(Bilbo crosses to door, and opens it, and there stands a hobbit boy with a box of groceries.)

Grocery Boy: Your groceries, Mr. Baggins.

Bilbo (quickly): Thank you, lad. I'll take them—— (Takes box and attempts to shut door on boy.)

Grocery Boy (peering over Bilbo's shoulder): Having a party, Mr. Baggins?

Bilbo: Humph.

Grocery Boy: Dwarves! Cheez, Mr. Baggins—hundreds of 'em! Wait till they hear of this down the road. Dwarves! Like locusts!

(Bilbo shuts the door rudely on the boy.)

Bilbo (*sadly*): Oh, dear!

Thorin (*crossing to table with new arrivals*): I trust there's food for the late-comers.

Bilbo (*tight as a coil*): Well—I may have a little tea left.

Gandalf: Tea? No, no, thank you. A little red wine and some cold chicken and pickles.

Thorin: And for me.

Bifur: Apple pie—and coffee, if you don't mind.

Bofur: And mince pie with cheese!

Bombur (*already seated at the table, drumming on it with zest*): Pork pie and salad! (*Thorin gives Bombur a disgusted look.*)

Bifur: And raspberry jam and muffins.

Gandalf: Put on a few eggs, there's a good fellow.

Dori (*from table*): Cold tongue!

Nori: A side of ham!

Ori: Cupcakes!

Oin: Assorted cheeses—if you please!

Dwalin: More cakes and ale!

Bilbo (*dumbfounded*): More! (*Sarcastic.*) Oh, certainly, dig in, dig in! (*Heading L for the kitchen with box of groceries.*) Don't stint yourselves! (*Grumbling to himself as he goes off.*) Seem to know as much about the inside of my kitchen as I do! (*Calling back.*) I could use some help!

Thorin: Bifur! Nori! (*Bifur and Nori go off L to help Bilbo.*) Now! Lower the lamp, Balin. (*Balin pulls down the lamp, which hangs over the table. The lights dim.*)

Dwalin (*rubbing his palms together*): Dark for dark business!

Balin: Hush! Let Thorin speak!

Thorin (*at head of table; standing and clearing his throat importantly*): Gandalf, dwarves, and Mr. Baggins!

(*Bilbo, Bifur, and Nori bustle on L, laden with huge platters of food and drink.*)

Bilbo: Why so dark?

Fili: We like the dark. (*Fili notices Bilbo is not serving himself and begins to fill a plate for him.*)

Dwarves: Shh——

Thorin: We are met together in the house of our friend and fellow conspirator——

Bilbo (*protesting*): No, no!

Thorin: ——this wise and brave hobbit——

Bilbo (*flattered*): Dear me!

Thorin: May the hair on his toes never fall out! All praise to his food. (*The dwarves raise their mugs.*)

Dwarves (*toasting*): Hear, hear! (*Bilbo has slunk over to his stool in front of the fire, where he sits clutching his toes protectively. Fili brings him a plate of food, but Bilbo shakes his head. His appetite is completely gone. Fili returns to his own place.*)

Thorin: We are met to discuss our plans. We shall start before dawn on a long, hard journey, so dangerous that some may not live through it or they may reach the misty mountain only to be eaten by the dragon—— (*Bilbo lets out a piercing shriek, falling off the stool to the floor, where he lies shaking and twitching wildly. The dwarves spring up and stare at him in dismay.*)

Gandalf (*producing[1] a blue light at end of his staff and crossing to Bilbo, prodding him with his foot*): Come,

---

1. Gandalf produces this effect by using camera flash equipment.

come. He's an excitable little fellow. He gets these queer fits, but he's fierce as a dragon in a pinch!

Bilbo (*shrieking*): I'm struck by lightning! Struck by lightning! (*Dwarves circle Bilbo curiously.*)

Gloin (*the doubter, snorting*): Humph! It's all very well for you to talk . . . but one shriek like that in a moment of danger might wake the dragon and all his kin. They'd eat the lot of us fast as you'd swallow a dozen cupcakes.

Thorin: It *did* sound more like fright than excitement. In fact, but for the sign on the door, I'd have thought we'd come to the wrong house.

Balin: Why, he just turned to jelly right before our eyes! He looks more like a grocer than a burglar!

Bilbo (*raising himself up with all the dignity he can muster*): Pardon me, but I couldn't help overhearing your insults. Am I allowed a few words?

Thorin (*condescendingly*): By all means.

Bilbo: First, I don't know what you're talking about. There isn't any sign on my door—unless, of course, you're referring to the dents from all your banging!

Gandalf: Of course there's a sign. I put it there myself.

Thorin: My good sir, the sign says: "Burglar wants good job, plenty of excitement and reasonable reward." Read it yourself. (*Opens door and shows sign.*)

Bilbo: So! I've been deceived!

Gandalf (*to Thorin*): You asked me to find a fourteenth man for your expedition—and I chose Mr. Baggins here——

Bilbo (*incensed*): Oh, you did, did you? Well, if you think that I——

Gandalf: ——but I'm afraid I've made a sad mistake. This can't be the chap! No, no, I was looking for a member of the famous Took family. Imagine! I mistook *him* for a *Took!* (*Glowers at Bilbo.*)

Bilbo (*stung*): But I *am* a Took!

Gandalf: Really? Tch, tch, the blood must have thinned then.

Bilbo: Why, my great-uncle, Bull-Roarer Took——

Gloin (*cutting in*): Yes, yes, but we're talking about you!

Gandalf (*melodramatically*): I said to myself, now *here* is a hobbit with desires beyond his next cup of tea—but alas, he's just an ordinary run-of-the-Shire hobbit. When adventure knocks, he locks his door and hides under the bed.

Bilbo (*highly insulted, standing up*): Really, this is too much!

Gandalf (*to dwarves*): Well, dwarves, you can go back to shoveling coal. The hobbit is afraid to go and you certainly can't set out with thirteen! That's too unlucky!

Bilbo (*with great dignity*): Sir, I must tell you that to uphold the honor of the Took family, I would cross mountains and deserts and fight a hundred dragons! I would——

Gandalf (*cutting in*): Splendid! Mr. Baggins is with us! (*Shakes Bilbo's hand.*) Now, Thorin—— (*Crosses to Thorin.*)

Bilbo (*mumbling to himself*): Now why did I say that? Bilbo, you're a fool! Now you *have* put your foot in it!

Thorin (*to Gandalf*): But are you sure he'll do? You, yourself, said that he——

Gandalf (*interrupting*): If I say he's a burglar, a burglar he is—or will be when the time comes. There's more to him than you guess or he has any idea of himself. You'll live to thank him, and to thank him that you live.

Thorin: Let us hope so! (*Turns to others.*) Well, now to get on with the plans. It's late. (*All walk over to the table and sit with Thorin at the head, Bilbo at his right, and Bombur next to Bilbo.*)

Gandalf (*spreading a large map on the table before Thorin*): Let's have some light on this. (*Bombur adjusts the overhanging lamp. Lights come up. To Thorin.*) This is a map of the Lonely Mountain. It was left by your grandfather, King Thrain.

Thorin: Ah, yes?

Bilbo: What mountain?

Bombur (*giving Bilbo a friendly nudge*): Where the *treasure* is! And the dragon. (*Makes a gruesome face and hisses alarmingly at Bilbo.*)

Thorin (*studying the map*): I don't see that this will help much—— I remember the mountain well enough and the lands about it—— (*Pointing them out.*) Mirkwood—the Withered Heath——

Bombur: That's where the great dragons breed! (*Makes clawlike, threatening gestures and hisses at Bilbo, who manages a sickly smile in spite of being terrified.*)

Thorin: There's the dragon— marked in red. Well, we're not likely to miss *him*, are we! (*Laughter from company. Bilbo's laughter lingers on. Dwarves look at him curiously.*)

Bilbo (*nervously*): Oh ho ho ha! The—— (*Stops, embarrassed.*) Dragon! I'm not overfond of dragons, but then I've never actually known any.

Gandalf (*dismissing Bilbo's chatter*): You will, you will. (*To Thorin.*)

Look here, Thorin. This circle on the map marks the secret entrance in the mountain—here! (*Points to spot on map.*)

Thorin: Ha! But is it still secret? That's the question!

Balin: By now the dragon must know these caves from top to bottom.

Gandalf: Not the secret entrance. It's so well hidden it looks exactly like the side of the mountain. And, by the way, I've a key that goes with the map. Here it is. (*Hands Thorin a key.*) Keep it safe!

Thorin: Indeed I will! (*Fastens it on a gold chain that hangs about his neck, and speaks with great satisfaction.*) Well, now, things begin to look more hopeful. A secret entrance! What luck!

Bombur (*to Bilbo*): Arrrgh! Hear him roar? It's almost dinner time. The dragon's hungry for some nice roasted burglar! (*Bilbo hides his face in his hands and moans. The other dwarves chuckle and nudge each other.*)

Thorin (*turning to Bilbo with mock politeness*): Suppose we ask our burglar expert to give us his ideas and suggestions——

Bilbo (*confused and shaky*): Well, first off, I should like some information. I mean, about the dragon and the treasure and how it got there and who it belongs to, and so on——

Thorin (*wearily*): Oh, very well——

Bilbo: And I'd also like to know about risks, out-of-pocket expenses, time required, wages, etc.

Balin: He wants to know his chances of coming back alive and how much gold he'll get.

Thorin: His chances are as good as ours. The circumstances are briefly these: Long ago, when my grandfather

was king, the dwarves settled here——
(Points at map.)——under the Lonely
Mountain, and they built the merry town
of Dale. Those were the happy days!
They made beautiful things just for the
fun of it. Not to sell, as we do now. When
they needed more gold or emeralds or
rubies, they just dug them out of the
mountain. There was no end to the supply. But that brought the dragon. Good
times always bring dragons. History
illustrates——

Gandalf *(interrupting)*: Be brief,
won't you?

Thorin *(insulted)*: Very well. There
was an especially wicked dragon called
Sm—sm—sm—— *(Apologetically.)* —
his name seems to stick in my
throat——

Gandalf *(helpfully)*: Smaug!

Thorin: Yes, curse him! He flew
from the east and burned the town. Only
a few escaped, my father among them.

Bilbo *(thrilled)*: And then?

Thorin: The dragon ate all the
dwarves and took their treasure. The
fiend! *(Pounds on the table.)* So now we
mean to get back what is rightfully ours,
and bring our curses home to Sm—sm—
sm——

Gandalf *(helping)*: Smaug!

Thorin: Death to all dragons—especially Sm—sm—sm——

Dwarves *(banging their mugs and
roaring it out)*: Smaug!

Bilbo *(weakly)*: Hear, hear!

Dwarves: Hear what?

Bilbo *(flustered)*: Hear what I've got
to say!

Gandalf: Go ahead. Say it!

Bilbo: I think you ought to go first to
the secret entrance and look around—
dragons must sleep sometimes. And now
I'm off to bed. You have my blessing.

Uh—is there anything I can get you
before you go?

Thorin: Before *we* go, I suppose you
mean. You're the burglar, and getting
inside the entrance is *your* job.

Dwarves *(thundering applause)*:
Thorin!

Bilbo: But—but, you see, I may have
spoken a little hastily just now. It's an
inconvenient time to——

Gandalf *(dismissing it)*: It's nearly
dawn. Time to clear up and start. *(Bilbo
tries to attract his attention by pulling at
his sleeve, but Gandalf ignores him, and
he is equally unsuccessful in attracting
Thorin's attention. Bilbo finally gives
up, shaking his head gloomily. The
dwarves jump up and begin to make tall
stacks of the plates and glasses. Gandalf
and Thorin remain seated, looking over
the map.)*

Bilbo *(squeaking with fright)*: Please
be careful! *(Spinning around the room.)*
Please don't trouble! I can take care of
everything after you've all gone!

Dwarves *(chanting while clearing
table)*:
Chip the glasses, and crack the plates!
  Blunt the knives and bend the forks!
That's what Bilbo Baggins hates——
  Smash the bottles and burn the
corks!

Bilbo *(shrieking)*: My best china!
Please be careful!

Dwarves *(chanting)*:
Cut the cloth and tread on the fat!
  Pour the milk on the pantry floor!
Leave the bones on the bedroom mat!
  Splash the wine on every door!
That's what Bilbo Baggins hates!
So, carefully! carefully with the plates!

*(The dwarves exit with the glasses,
platters, etc., Bilbo whirling around*

madly. Offstage there is a tremendous clatter as the curtain falls.

Lights come up in front of the curtain. The dwarves are lined up on the apron, sticks with bundles over their shoulders, ready to start. Thorin is at the head.)

Thorin *(pacing impatiently)*: Well, where's the hobbit? Where's our burglar?

(Bilbo runs on L, puffing profusely.)

Bifur: Here he is! Bravo!

Thorin: Humph!

Bilbo *(very put out, catching his breath)*: Oh, my! Oh, my! The way the morning starts decides the day! It's going to be a miserable day! Hunting dragons! At my age! What a fool I am. Everyone expecting me to be ready at the drop of a hat! *(Feels his head. No hat.)* My hat! My coat, my brolly, my pocket hankie—my purse——

Thorin *(cutting in)*: Stop fussing!

Bilbo *(searching his pockets)*: Where's my diary? If the dragon eats me there'll be no record! My friends 'back home won't know what happened! And I've got no money——

Thorin *(disgusted)*: Get a grip on yourself, Baggins!

Dwalin *(grimly)*: You'll learn to do without small comforts before we reach journey's end.

Gloin *(disgusted, acting it out)*: Where's his money? Imagine! Our burglar hasn't any money! *(Capers about, imitating Bilbo's fluster. The dwarves laugh derisively.)*

Bombur *(helpful but mocking)*: I've a spare hood. The lining is fireproof. It'll keep your hair from being burned when Smaug spits fire at you.

Bilbo *(politely)*: Thank you, Bombur, much obliged. *(Tries it on. It is very large.)* I wish it fitted closer, but the fireproof lining is great. Very great.

(Gandalf strides on from L.)

Gandalf: Are we all ready to start? Ah, Bilbo, I believe you forgot these. *(Hands Bilbo a handkerchief, a pipe and tobacco pouch, a leather-bound journal, and a hat.)*

Bilbo *(delighted, stowing them away)*: Oh, thank you! And my diary! How kind of you! *(Bilbo is puzzled by the hat. He replaces the hood with the hat and looks regretfully at the lining of the hood. Then, with decision, he replaces the hood on his head, looks uncertainly at the hat, and then tosses it offstage.)*

Dwarves *(approvingly)*: Bilbo! Long live our Burglar!

Gandalf: And I remembered you, Bombur. *(Hands over a string bag of small, hard cakes.)*

Bombur: Cakes! Thank you! Where did you get them?

Gandalf: From a friend of mine. He lives far from here. You may yet meet him.

Bombur *(eating one)*: It tastes of honey.

Gandalf: Yes, my friend keeps bees. *(Bombur starts to take another.)* You'll need these cakes. Don't eat them right away.

Bombur *(stowing the cakes away)*: Need them? With all the food we're taking! But, as you say, Gandalf.

Thorin: Our marching song! *(Thorin leads the dwarves off L. They march off*

heavily, in step, chanting in gloomy tones.)

> Far over the misty mountains cold
> To dungeons deep and caverns old
> We must away, ere break of day,
> To seek the pale enchanted gold!

(*Gandalf and Bilbo follow closely after dwarves.*)

Bilbo (*to Gandalf*): Couldn't they sing something cheery?

Gandalf: Such as——

Bilbo (*firmly*): Such as "Home, Sweet Home." (*As they exit, Gandalf puts his arm around Bilbo and laughs.*)

SCENE 2: (*In the forest several months later. The curtain rises to reveal a nearly bare stage that is divided into three playing areas. At R there is a platform approximately a foot-and-a-half high that extends in from the right side to about one-quarter of the way across the stage. A similar platform extends the same distance from L.*)

At Rise of Curtain: (*Lights come up on the platform at L. Bilbo is discovered sitting on a log at the edge, legs crossed, writing thoughtfully in his journal with a long quill pen. Behind him, the dwarves, except for Fili and Kili, are sprawled out, resting. The only sound is that of Bombur's heavy snoring. Bilbo finishes with a flourish, blows on script, holds it off admiringly, and reads aloud.*)

Bilbo (*reading his entry*): Have just stopped to rest and let Fili and Kili water our ponies. Thought for today: "Adventures are not all Sunday strolls in May sunshine." That's really well put. (*Lays down book and massages his feet.*) Covered with burrs! (*Picks at burrs.*) And soaked with these nasty May rains. Bother burgling! I wish I was home with the kettle just beginning to sing!

Bofur (*rousing and leaning on an elbow*): You'll wish that again before we're out of this mess. But go on, I like to hear you read about our adventures.

Bilbo: Thanks. (*Resumes reading.*) At first, I thought adventures were much like picnics. We traveled past pretty farms, and the people seemed friendly. But things have changed lately. See thought for today. We've seen no one all day and there's nothing ahead but black, rainy mountains. As soon as Fili and Kili are back, we should move ahead and make an early camp and have some hot supper.

Bombur: Sound idea! (*Takes out bag of honey cakes and looks at them. He glances about to see if anyone is noticing, and then slips a cake in his mouth.*)

Bifur (*rousing*): Did someone say supper?

Thorin (*rousing*): We should be going on. Where are Fili and Kili? (*Offstage cries are heard.*)

Bilbo (*jumping up*): I hear something.

Dori (*rising*): It's Fili.

Nori (*rising*): And Kili.

Bifur (*struggling to his feet*): They're shouting for help!

(*Fili and Kili enter. They are drenched, breathless, and gasping.*)

Thorin: Where are the ponies? What's happened?

Kili: We lost them. (*The dwarves*

press forward around them excitedly ad-libbing questions: "Lost them!" "How could you?" "Did they run away?" etc.)

Thorin *(sternly)*: Silence, dwarves. Kili, what happened?

Kili: We took them down to water like you said. But the stream bed was almost dry and they wandered out into it drinking at some of the little pools. *(Pauses, gulping breath.)*

Thorin *(sternly)*: Did you stay with them?

Kili *(uncomfortably)*: I did, until they were settled drinking water. Then I—well, I went along the bank looking for mushrooms to eat.

Thorin: You mean you left them!

Kili: But Fili was watching them from the bank and I ran back the minute I heard him shout.

Thorin: What happened, Fili?

Fili: A great wall of water came thundering out of the mountains. I shouted, but it was over the ponies in a moment. They just tumbled over and over like logs and were gone!

Thorin: All of them!

Fili: Yes.

Thorin: And the food bags?

Kili: On the ponies. *(Thorin turns away with a gesture of despair.)*

Bilbo: But then we've nothing to eat.

Bifur: We've got the honey cakes.

Dwalin: Wise Gandalf. He knew we'd need them!

Thorin: But maybe we'll have greater need of them later. This isn't a real emergency. We're not starving.

Bombur: I am.

Thorin: After all, we've got our burglar here. *(To Bilbo.)* It's up to you, burglar. Burgle us some food.

Bilbo: Up to me. I like that! Out here in the middle of nowhere! It needs a magician to find food here. Besides, maybe this is the time Gandalf meant us to eat the honey cakes. Why don't you ask him?

Galin: He's right. Ask Gandalf. *(There is a general murmur of agreement from the dwarves.)*

Thorin: You may be right. *(Glances around.)* Where's Gandalf?

Balin: Asleep, probably. I'll wake him up. *(Calls.)* Gandalf! *(No answer. Louder.)* Gandalf!

Dori: He's gone!

Ori: Gone! Oh, no!

Gloin: Smartest thing he ever did!

Balin: If I was a wizard, I'd vanish, too.

Thorin: Yes—well, I'm sure he had his reasons. We'll have to go on without him.

Dwarves *(ad-libbing groans, etc.)*: Oh, no!

Thorin *(proudly)*: We dwarves have always stood alone. Our forefathers didn't depend on magic.

Gloin: And look what happened—a dragon ate them!

Bifur: Speaking of eating——

Thorin *(crossly)*: Oh, very well! Bombur, share out the cakes. *(Bombur rapidly passes out the cakes, starting with Thorin. He comes to Bilbo last. Bilbo takes the cake Bombur hands him. He sees the bag is empty.)*

Bilbo: But there's none left for you! *(All the dwarves turn to look at Bombur.)*

Bombur *(embarrassed)*: Never mind. I had mine.

Bilbo: But you didn't. You just passed them out.

Bombur: I ate mine before.

Bilbo: You mean that time when Gandalf gave them to you? That doesn't count.

Bombur (blurting it out miserably): I ate one just before Fili and Kili came back. I'm sorry!

Gloin (indignant): You broke into our supplies?

Bilbo (calmly): They weren't ours, they were Bombur's. Gandalf gave the cakes to him. Besides, we thought we still had our supplies then.

Gloin: I still think——

Bilbo: After all, I'm the only one concerned. You all had your share, and I say Bombur had the right to eat all the cakes if he wanted to. They were his. (Breaks his cake in two.) Take half of this one, Bombur.

Bombur: I couldn't——

Bilbo (thrusting it in his hand): Then you'll be wasting food as well as the time we're all wasting, for the cake will just crumble away. Come on— together. (Bilbo and Bombur each pop the half cake in their mouths, smile, and clasp hands in a brief handshake.)

Balin: The burglar's right. We're wasting time. What's your plan, Thorin?

Thorin: Look over there—— (Gestures L. All look off.)

Bilbo: Is that where Smaug, the dragon——

Thorin (cutting in): Of course not. But fierce trolls live there. (All shudder.)

Bilbo: What are trolls?

Thorin: Huge creatures, too big for us to fight! They eat dwarves—and hobbits.

Bilbo (aghast): But shouldn't we run? Do we go on right up to where they are?

Thorin: We have to. That's the only way. (Encouragingly.) But there's one way to get the better of a troll. They're night creatures. Sunlight kills them. Turns them to stone.

Balin: I've heard of that. The thing to do is trick them into staying out of their cave until a ray of sunlight hits them.

Bilbo (more cheerfully): That shouldn't be so hard.

Gloin: But the trolls know this will happen. They're hard to fool. Chances are, they've got you frying in a pan while you're still trying to trick them. (Bombur has been sneaking up on Bilbo from the rear. He grabs him.)

Bombur: Got you! I'm a troll. (Bilbo lets out a shriek.)

Thorin (sharply): Order. (To Bombur.) No more tricks till we're safely out of here! (To Bilbo.) Be quiet. Do you want to bring a band of trolls down on us?

Balin (pointing to platform R): Look, there's a light over there!

(The platform R is now dimly lit with a reddish glow. We can make out three large figures. They are trolls: Bert, Tom, and Essie. They are seated on the ground, toasting mutton on long spits of wood and licking the gravy off their fingers. There is a large wine jug.)

Thorin: So there is! Fili, Kili, you look. Your eyes are sharpest. (Fili and Kili strain to see.)

Fili: It looks like——

Kili: It's trolls! Three of them.

Dwarves (ad-lib): Trolls! Ugh! Ich! Oh! (The dwarves huddle together, except Thorin, who stands apart.)

Bombur (sniffing the air deliciously): I can smell mutton cooking! (All sniff the air.)

Thorin: It *does* smell like mutton.

Dwarves *(ad-lib):* Ummm! Sure does! I could do with some mutton! With mint.

Bombur: Mutton with garlic. I'm never wrong about that!

Oin: It's a pity it belongs to the trolls.

Gloin: Yeh. But . . . wait a minute . . . we have a *burglar* with us!

Bilbo *(sarcastically):* Ah! So you've finally noticed!

Gloin *(rubbing his hands together):* Yes, indeed, a burglar! Bilbo, your chance has come at last!

Bilbo *(warily):* It has?

Oin *(to Thorin):* It's the burglar's turn.

Bilbo: It is?

Gloin: Now you can show your stuff. *(Moves closer to Bilbo, until they are nose to nose.)* Gandalf said that hobbits were especially clever at quietly sneaking up——

Bilbo *(incredulously):* You can't mean—the trolls? You want *me* to burgle trolls?

Thorin *(nodding):* Exactly.

Bilbo *(desperately):* But I—I thought I was only supposed to burgle the *dragon!*

Thorin: Later, later. Bring back as much mutton as you can carry. We're hungry, remember. If you run into any difficulty, hoot twice like a barn owl, and we'll come.

Bilbo *(exploding):* What! Are you out of your mind?

Thorin *(icily):* I beg your pardon?

Bilbo *(indignantly):* Hobbits never hoot! But, no matter. No matter. Forward, Bilbo! *(He draws himself up to his full height and walks grandly off the platform.)*

Dwarves: Careful, now! Don't come back empty-handed! Good luck!

Bilbo *(crawling stealthily toward the trolls, turning his head toward dwarves):* Hush! Stop the racket! You'll spoil everything. *(Muttering to himself, he continues to crawl toward the trolls.)* Dwarves!

(Lights dim on platform L and come up on platform R as Bilbo approaches the trolls' campfire.)

Bert *(disgusted):* Ugh! I'm sick to death o' mutton, Essie! It's coming out me ears! Mutton yesterday, mutton today, and blimey, if it don't look like mutton again tomorrer! *(Turns his back to the fire and tosses his mutton over his shoulder in Bilbo's direction.)*

Tom: Never a blinking bit o' man-flesh or a nice shoulder of dwarf have we had for a long time! *(Faces front, also tossing his mutton over his shoulder.)*

Essie: Aw, git off! Times been up our way when yer'd have said, "Thank yer, Essie," for a nice bit o' fat valley-mutton like what this is.

Bert *(taking a healthy pull at the jug):* Ugh! No more'n a dribble o'drink left! *(Tom grabs the jug.)* What we was a-thinkin' of to come into these parts beats me! *(Tom takes a pull at the jug. Bert gives him a jab in the ribs, causing Tom to choke.)*

Tom *(coughing):* We ain't done badly. We've et a village and a half between us since we come.

Bert *(whining):* Them villages was barely bite-sized. *(Bilbo has made his way to the fire and is just about to make off with the discarded mutton when Essie spots him.)*

Essie *(wheeling around, catching*

Bilbo by the scruff of his neck and holding fast): Blimey, boys, look what I've copped!

Bert *(jumping up):* 'Ere, wot's it?

Tom *(eyeing Bilbo):* Lumme if I know. *(To Bilbo, prodding him in the belly.)* What are yer? Man? *(Bilbo shakes his head wildly)*——dwarf? *(Bilbo shakes his head again.)*

Bilbo *(stuttering):* Ha—ha—ha—hobbit!

Tom: A hahahahobbit? Can't say I tasted 'em. Can yer cook 'em, Essie?

Essie *(pinching Bilbo like a soup chicken):* Yer can try. Won't make above a mouthful, though—not once he's skinned and boned. Now if there was four-and-twenty of 'em I might make a pie!

Bert: Hey, you! Any more o'your sort a-sneakin' in these here woods, yer nasty little rabbit!

Bilbo *(correcting him politely):* Hobbit, not rabbit. Yes, lots—no—none at all!

Bert *(scratching his head):* What d'yer mean?

Bilbo *(collecting his scattered wits):* What I say. *(To Essie.)* There's no need to pinch me, madam.

Essie: Shut yer mouth! I can always serve you on toast—minced!

Bilbo *(pleading):* Oh, please don't cook me, kind ma'am and sirs! I'm a good cook myself and cook better than I cook, if you see what I mean. Besides I like it here with you.

Bert *(suspiciously):* What's 'e say? *(Grabs Bilbo by the hair.)*

Bilbo: Ow!

Essie *(softening):* Ah, poor little blighter, let him go.

Tom: Not till 'e says what 'e means by *lots* and *none at all.* I don't want me

throat slit in me sleep! *(Grabs for Bilbo's feet.)* I'll hold his toes in the fire till 'e talks!

(Gandalf's head appears from behind a tree. There is a flash of blue fire from his staff, which the trolls do not notice.)

Tom: No! There isn't time. We have to get back to our cave before sun-up.

Essie *(hanging on):* Give him back. He's mine.

Tom: Well, I'm boss.

Gandalf *(sticking his head out and calling in a voice mimicking Essie's):* Tom, yer a fat fool!

Tom *(taken aback):* Essie! Watch what you say!

Gandalf *(sticking his head out, mimicking Tom):* Yer a swag-belly, Essie!

Essie *(shrieking):* What? I'll give you what for! *(Kicks Tom in the shins.)*

Tom *(howling):* Oww! *(Releases Bilbo and hops about. Bilbo runs and hides behind a tree.)*

Bert *(scratching his head; slow on the uptake):* You insult the missus, Tom? *(Advancing menacingly on Tom.)*

Tom *(baffled):* What? I didn't say nothing——

Bert *(putting his fist in Tom's eye):* Liar!

Tom *(hopping around in pain):* Yeow!

Gandalf *(mimicking Tom):* Big skunk!

Essie *(coming up behind Tom and hitting him on the head with a dummy club):* Take *that!*

Tom *(howling and rubbing his head):* Ow! Ow! What did you do that for! *(Picks up club and hits Bert on the head.)*

Bert (stunned): Gosh! Ouch! (A bird calls, and other birds chime in.)

Gandalf (stepping out from behind tree, holding his staff high with blue fire coming from it; loudly): Dawn take you all, and be stone to you! (The trolls look at one another agape, and turn toward the voice. The twittering of birds rises to a climax of bird calls, and a great shaft of light strikes the trolls.)

Trolls: Wha'? Huh? Ugh! (Suddenly they freeze into statues.)

Gandalf (walking around the trolls, waving his hand in front of their faces, touching Bert's hair, etc.): Excellent! Museum pieces!

Bilbo (*capering wildly*): They're stone! They've turned to stone!

Gandalf: Where are the dwarves?

Bilbo: Waiting for me to return with some food or to hoot like an *owl*.

Gandalf (*hooting*): Whoo! Whoo!

Thorin (*at platform L, springing up*): The signal! To the rescue, dwarves! (*They all groan and follow reluctantly. Thorin runs up to Bert with bravado, brandishing his sword.*) On guard, Troll! (*Bert does not stir; Thorin lunges fiercely.*) Aha! (*Still no reaction; Thorin, completely baffled, kicks Bert in the knee.*) Yeow! (*Holds his foot, hopping in pain. Bilbo and Gandalf laugh uproariously. Thorin is startled.*) Gandalf!

Dwarves (*circling the trolls curiously; ad-lib*): Stone! Horrid! What a trio! Solid rock! etc.

Gandalf: A fine pickle you left your burglar in, Thorin!

Thorin: And where were you, if I may ask?

Gandalf: I went to look ahead.

Thorin: And what brought you back?

Gandalf: Looking behind——

Thorin: Exactly! But could you be more plain?

Gandalf: I went on to spy out our road. It will soon become much more dangerous. I had not gone very far when I met some elf friends—they were hurrying along for fear of trolls. I had a feeling I was needed here and I hurried back. So now you know.

Thorin: We thank you! Pack up the food, dwarves——

Gandalf (*picking up two swords from the ground*): And don't leave *these* behind! Hmmm, these were not made by the trolls—the workmanship is much too good. The trolls must have stolen these. Why, these are elvish blades— with the ancient runes engraved on them. The elves have cleaved many a goblin with these, I'll warrant. (*Hands one to Thorin and one to Bilbo.*)

Bilbo: For me? Why, thank you!

Thorin: I will keep this sword in honor. May it soon cleave goblins again!

Bilbo: Oh, dear!

Gandalf: A wish that will soon be granted.

Bilbo: I didn't wish a thing!

Gandalf: Come, let's head for the Misty Mountains. You must keep to the proper path, or you'll get lost and have to come back. Remember that: stick to the path!

Thorin: We will, Gandalf.

Elves (*offstage, burst of laughter, then singing*):

O! Where are you going
With beards all a-wagging?
No knowing, no knowing
What brings Mister Baggins,
And Balin and Dwalin
down into the valley
in June
ha, ha!

Thorin: Elves! Humph!

(*First elf peeks around the left curtain.*)

First Elf: Well, well! Just look! Bilbo, the hobbit, on an adventure with dwarves! Isn't it delicious!

(*Second elf peeks around the curtain R.*)

Second Elf: Most astonishingly wonderful!

Thorin: Silly fools!

Third Elf (*off*): Mind you don't step on your beard, Thorin! (*Burst of laughter from elves, off.*)

Gandalf: Hush, hush, my friends! Valleys have ears, and some elves have over-merry tongues. We must go quietly. There is a grave danger ahead. (*They all exit as curtain falls.*)

SCENE 3: (*A cave in the Misty Mountains. Lightning flashes. Sounds of thunder.*)

At Rise of Curtain: (*Lights come up on platform at stage L. The dwarves and Gandalf are huddled together, talking in hushed tones. Bilbo sits downstage on platform, writing in his diary. He scribbles industriously, then holds book off and reads impressively.*)

Bilbo (*reading his entry*): This is the first chance I've had to write in ages. We've been driven before the storm for twelve days and nights. (*There is a distant roll of thunder and more lightning.*) The mountain path is steep and long. We are now resting in a smelly cave. (*He again scribbles rapidly.*)

Thorin (*in a low voice*): This is awful!

Gloin (*holding his nose*): Phew!

Balin: At least it's dry!

Gandalf (*to Thorin*): If you know a better place, take us there!

Bilbo (*holding his script off and reading again*): We don't dare to talk too loud—there are goblins in these mountains. All this misery for their gold—and my pride—hardly seems worthwhile. The next time anyone calls me a coward, I'll agree with him and stay home. I'd gladly trade my share of the treasure this minute for a steaming bowl of mutton soup!

Gandalf: Keep your voices down! Thorin, look, your blade glows—that means goblins are nearby. Keep your eyes and ears open. Goblins are swift as weasels in the dark and make no more noise than bats. (*They huddle together, peering in all directions; lightning flashes and sounds of thunder.*) Are your guards posted?

Thorin (*nodding*): Four of them, Gloin north, Bofur south, Oin east, and Ori west.

(*Lights dim on platform L and come up on platform R. Drumbeats are heard off. The Great Goblin steps out on the platform, followed by an attendant.*)

Great Goblin (*bellowing in a stony voice*): Who are those miserable persons?

Attendant Goblin (*bowing and scraping*): Dwarves, I believe, O Truly Tremendous One.

Great Goblin: What are they doing in my domain?

Attendant Goblin (*shaking*): I'll go and ask them, O Truly Tremendous One.

Great Goblin (*with an awful howl of rage*): Ask them? (*Kicks the attendant goblin and bats him over the head.*) Beat them! Gnash them! Squash them! Smash them! (*Gesturing L.*) After them!

(*The drumbeats increase as many goblins rush on R with bloodcurdling cries. As they reach C, the lights come up on platform L.*)

Oin (*reporting*): Goblins coming.

Ori: I think they're going to rush us!

Goblins *(chanting and cracking whips):*

> Swish, smack! Whip, crack!
> Clash, crash! Crush, smash!

Thorin *(drawing his sword):* Ready, my Goblin-cleaver! *(He stands on the edge of the platform.)* Ready, dwarves— and Mr. Baggins. *(Gandalf, arms folded, stands aloof watching intently. The goblins rush at the dwarves. Thorin stabs one with his blade. The other dwarves back up Thorin, and there are hand-to-hand conflicts. Bilbo trips up a goblin who is about to stab Thorin from behind. Thorin stabs another. All conflicts must be rehearsed with extra care so that the tempo is very fast. The goblins fall, howling.)*

Goblins *(ad-lib):* Aie! He's got a Goblin-cleaver! Watch out! Stay back! *(The goblins back off in terror.)*

Gandalf *(to dwarves and Bilbo):* Quick. Now's our chance! Everyone follow me! *(Runs off L. Others follow. Bilbo last. From off.)* Quicker, quicker! *(Goblins run after them, howling and hooting.)*

BLACKOUT

(Lights come up very dimly in cave. Bilbo is discovered lying on the ground DC.)

Bilbo *(sitting up, holding his head in pain):* Oooh! My head! Where am I! My head—I must have run into a tree! *(Groping.)* It's so dark in here I can't see a thing. *(Calls loudly.)* Anyone here?

Echo *(getting progressively fainter):* Here—here—here.

Bilbo *(getting frightened):* Who's that?

(Now gleams appear in the darkness. They prove to be always in pairs, of yellow or green or red eyes. They seem to stare awhile and then slowly fade out and disappear and shine out again in another place. Sometimes they shine down from above. Some of them are bulbous.)

Bilbo: Now I remember. The goblins!

Echo: 'Oblins, 'oblins—'oblins— 'oblins.

Bilbo: And what are those awful eyes watching me for? *(Lowers voice.)* I was on Dori's back and someone tackled him and he dropped me!

Echo: 'Opped me—'opped me—'opped me—'opped me.

Bilbo *(frightened, to the eyes):* Keep away from me, eyes! I wonder what happened to the dwarves? I hope the goblins didn't get them! *(Gasps.)* My sword! *(Holding it up.)* It hardly glows. That means the goblins aren't near and yet they're still around. Ugh! What a nasty smell! Go away, you horrible eyes! *(Realizing, stage whisper.)* I know where I am. I'm still in the goblin's cave! They smell that way and these may be just the eyes of bats and mice and toads and slimy things like that. *(More naturally.)* Cheer up, Bilbo. Fear always helps the thing you're afraid of. You're alive and you've been in holes before. You live in one. This is just an ordinary, black, foul, disgusting hole. So blah! *(The eyes begin to flicker out, pair by pair, until all are gone. Bilbo brightens further.)* If this place were aired and decorated, it would be nice and cozy. So now I'll just figure out how to get out of here. (*Bilbo crawls around on his hands and knees toward stage R.*) Seems to be a lake over here—no use heading that way. Ouch! Something hurt my knee—— (*Picks up small object.*) It's a ring! Someone's lost a ring. Well, finders keepers. I'll just stick it in my pocket so I don't lose it myself. (*Pockets ring. Lights come up a little.*) I can see better now. (*Stands and turns toward stage L.*)

(*An unobtrusive black rubber float is pulled on stage R. On it sits a slimy creature, dressed in black tights or a shiny rubber diving suit, touched up with vaseline to make it glisten, complete with cap, goggles painted a pale watery green. He sits with a leg dangling over each side of the raft, or with knees bent, and holds a short paddle as if rowing.*)

Gollum (*making a swallowing sound as he is pulled on*): Gollum! Gollum!

Bilbo (*whirling around*): What's that!

Gollum: It's me—Gollum!

Bilbo (*peering nervously in Gollum's direction*): Who's there?

Gollum (*in full view now*): Bless us and splash us, my preciousss! Here's something to eat! (*Guttural.*) Gollum!

Bilbo (*brandishing his blade, while shaking and backing off*): Stay back!

Gollum (*swaying his head from side to side as he talks*): What's he got in his handses, hmmm?

Bilbo (*as fiercely as possible*): A sword, an elvish blade! It came out of Gondolin.

Gollum (*taken aback, hissing*): S-s-s-s. What *iss* he, my preciousss? Hic!

(*More politely.*) Whom have we the pleasure of meeting?

Bilbo (*rapidly*): I am Mr. Bilbo Baggins, a hobbit. I've lost the dwarves and the wizard and I don't know where I am—but then I don't want to know where I am. The only thing I want to know is how to get out of here!

Gollum (*hissing*): S-s-s-s-s s'pose we sits here and chats with it a bitsy, my preciousss—A Bagginsess! (*Rubs his stomach.*) It likes riddles, p'raps it does, does it? S-s-s-s.

Bilbo: You mean me?

Gollum: Yesssss——

Bilbo: Well, I'd love to, but I'm expected somewhere else—— (*To himself.*) I hope. (*To Gollum.*) So if you'd kindly direct me to the nearest exit——

Gollum (*cutting in*): S-s-s-s-s stop. First a riddle, yesss?

Bilbo (*resigned*): Very well, if you insisssst! After you——

Gollum: S-s-s-s-s say,
What has roots as nobody sees,
Is taller than trees,
Up, up it goes,
And yet never grows?

Bilbo: Easy! Mountain. Now if you'll kindly——

Gollum (*cutting in*): S-s-s-s-s so does it guess easy? It must have a competition with us, my preciouss. If we wins we eats it—it tastes better if we earns it. If it wins we shows it the way out. Yessss.

Bilbo (*resigned*): Well—all right. Only, how many of them are you? Who's this "Precious" you keep talking to?

Gollum: Our Preciousss Self! We has to talk to someone, doesn't we? We are alone here—forever.

Bilbo: So, I see. It's a dreadful place.

The Hobbit **485**

Gollum: We likes it! We generally passes the time feasting on fishesss and gobbling goblins. S-s-s.

Bilbo: Goblins! Ick! I didn't think anyone ate *them!*

Gollum: We acquired the taste. Hic! S-s-s-s-s. *(Impatient.)* Your turn. Riddle! Riddle!

Bilbo: Just a minute—— *(Thinking hard.)* Ah!——

Thirty white horses on a red hill,
First they champ,
Then they stamp,
Then they stand still.

Gollum: Easy! Teethes! Teethes! My preciouss, but we has only *six.* Now! Ssssss.

Voiceless it cries,
Wingless flutters,
Toothless bites,
Mouthless mutters.

Bilbo: Half a moment! *(Straining.)* Wind! Wind, of course!

Gollum *(disappointed)*: Ssssssss. Your turns!

Bilbo: Uh——

A box without hinges, key or lid,
Yet golden treasure inside is hid.

Gollum *(having great difficulty)*: S-s-s-s-s. *(Whispers.)* What iss it? Sssssss.

(Takes a fish out of his pocket and wipes his brow with it.)

Bilbo: Well—what is it? The answer's not a kettle boiling over, as you seem to think from the noise you are making!

Gollum: Give us a chance; let it give us a chance, my preciousss——

Bilbo: Well?

Gollum *(wiping his brow with fish; suddenly)*: Eggses! Eggses it is! Sssssssss—here's a choice one!

Alive without breath,
As cold as death;
Never thirsty, ever drinking,
All in mail, never clinking!

Bilbo *(stumped)*: Ahem—ahem—well now. Just a minute——

Gollum *(starting to emerge from the raft)*: S-s-s-s-s-s.

Bilbo *(panic-stricken)*: Wait! I gave you a long time to guess!

Gollum *(settling back in raft, hissing with pleasure)*: Is it nice, my preciousss? Is it juicy? Is it crunchable?

Bilbo *(stalling for time)*: Actually, I never gave a thought to how I'd taste cooked until I set out on this horrid adventure. But I'm sure I'd be terribly indigestible. *(False laughter.)* Ha, ha!

Gollum: S-s-s-s-s—the riddle, answer it! It must make haste. We is hungry! *(Wipes his brow with the fish.)*

Bilbo *(pointing wildly at the fish)*: Fish! That's the answer! Fish!

Gollum *(angry)*: S-ss-ss—rotten luckses! It's got to ask us a question, my preciouss, yes, yess, just *one* more, yesss. Ask uss!

Bilbo *(frantic)*: Oh, dear! I can't think——*(Grabs for his sword, puts his hand in his pocket. To himself.)* What have I got in my pocket?

Gollum *(taking this for the question)*: Ssss—not fair! Not fair, my preciousss, to ask us what it's got in its nasty little pocketses!

Bilbo *(explaining)*: But I—— *(Thinks better of it.)* Well, why not? *(Boldly.)* What have I got in my pocket?

Gollum: S-s-s-s-s. It must give us three guesseses, my preciouss, three!

Bilbo: Very well! Guess away!

Gollum: Handses!

Bilbo: Wrong. Guess again!

Gollum: S-s-s-s-s—knife!

Bilbo: Wrong! Last guess!

Gollum *(wiggling and squirming, hissing and sputtering, rocking sideways and slapping his feet on the floor)*: S-s-s-s-s-s.

Bilbo *(trying to sound bold and cheerful)*: Come on! I'm waiting! Time's up!

Gollum *(shrieking)*: String or nothing!

Bilbo *(relieved)*: Both wrong. *(Brandishes his sword.)*

Gollum *(eyeing the sword)*: S-s-s-s-s.

Bilbo *(shivering)*: Well? Show me the way out. You promised!

Gollum: Did we say so, preciouss? Show the nassty little Baggins the way out, yes, yess. But what's it got in its pocketses, eh? *(Starts to get up.)* Not string, preciouss, but not nothing. Oh, no! Gollum!

Bilbo: Never you mind. A promise is a promise!

Gollum: Cross it is. The Baggins is getting cross, preciouss, but it must wait, yes, it must. We can't go up the tunnels so hasty. We must go and get somethings first, yess, things to help us. My birthday present, that's what we wants now—then we'll be quite safe! *(He steps out of* his raft and waddles UR.) We slips it on and it won't see us, will it, my preciouss. No, it won't see us and its nasty little sword will be useless, yess——Sssss. (Exits R.)

Bilbo (calling): Hurry up!

Gollum (off, letting out a horrible shriek): Aaaaaah! Where iss it! Lost! Lost!

Bilbo: What's the matter?

Gollum (offstage, wailing): Gone—must find it! Lost! Lost!

Bilbo: Well, so am I!

(Gollum waddles on from R, on his hands and knees, searching wildly.)

Gollum: Cursesss! Must find it!

Bilbo: You can look for whatever it is later. You never guessed my riddle. You promised!

Gollum: Never guessed—never guessed——(Light dawns.) What has it got in its pocketses? Tell us! (Advances toward Bilbo.)

Bilbo: What have you lost?

Gollum: We guesses, we guesses, precious, only guesses. He's got it and the goblinses will catch it and take the present from it. (Makes a lunge at Bilbo.) They'll find out what it can do. The Baggins doesn't know what the present can do. It'll just keep it in its pocketses. It's lost itself, the nasty, nosey thing.

Bilbo: I better put that ring on or I'll lose it. (Puts his hand into his pocket and slips the ring on his finger and holds it up.) This?

Gollum (rushing right past Bilbo, wailing): Cursess, the Baggins is gone—my precious. It has my ring! The ring of power!

Bilbo (alone onstage): He ran right past—as if he didn't see me—as if I weren't there. . . . Maybe I'm not! The ring! I wonder if it made me invisible? (Inspects himself.) I can still see me.

(Gollum rushes on again from L.)

Gollum: Give it back like a good Baggins! Where isss it? (Rushes off R.)

Bilbo: A magic ring! I've heard of such things in Gandalf's stories—but to find one! What luck!

Gollum (offstage, shrieking): Thief!

Bilbo: I could stab him with my blade, but that would be wrong when he can't see me.

(Gollum waddles on R, worn out and weeping.)

Gollum (sitting downstage): It's gone! (Guttural sobs.) Gollum! Gollum! Thief! Thief Baggins! We hates it, we hates it, hates it forever! S-s-s-s-s. (Recovering.) But he doesn't know the way out—he said so. (Bilbo nods silently and sits beside him.) But he's tricksy. He doesn't say what he means—like what was in his pocketses—he knows! He knows a way in. He must know a way out! Yesss—he's off to the back door, that's it! (Springs up.) After him! Make haste! (Runs off L.) Gollum! Gollum!

Bilbo: I'll follow him to the exit. Then with luck I can slip out the door! (Runs off L after Gollum.)

SCENE 4: In Front of Curtain: *(Outside the cave entrance. Bilbo's head pops out of the center of the curtain. He looks around warily.)*

Bilbo: Whew! A narrow escape! *(Comes DC, looking himself over.)* Torn my cloak! Burst my buttons! But I've got spare buttons at home. I wonder where I am? *(Looks off.)* Good heavens. This must be the other side of the Misty Mountains! I don't see Gandalf and the dwarves. Maybe the goblins got them. I'd have to go back in there after them—I guess—— *(Shudders.)* But at least I have Gollum's ring—— *(Holds finger up.)* Why, I must be invisible this very moment! Fancy!

Balin *(calling, from offstage)*: Mr. Baggins! Mr. Baggins! Where are you?

Bilbo *(overjoyed)*: Balin!

(Balin pops his head around curtain R. Bilbo goes to greet him with outstretched arms; of course he is invisible.)

Balin: He's not here. But I'm sure I heard him call my name!

Thorin *(offstage)*: Are you certain? *(Bilbo puts his hand to his mouth and doubles up with silent laughter.)*

(Balin walks on R, followed by Thorin, Gandalf, and the dwarves.)

Thorin: Confound the hobbit! Still lost!

Gandalf: Keep looking. We can't go on without him. I feel responsible for him.

Ori: Pity you didn't pick someone with more sense!

Thorin: He's been more trouble than he's worth. *(Bilbo draws himself up, offended.)*

Oin: Why couldn't he stick with us?

Gloin *(testily)*: That's right. I refuse to go back into those awful tunnels to look for the little blighter, drat him! *(Bilbo kicks his leg.)* Ouch!

Thorin: What's the matter?

Gloin: Dunno—felt as if someone kicked my leg!

Gandalf *(to Gloin)*: Serves you right if someone did. *(Angrily, to all.)* Now, either you help me look for him or I leave you here to get out of this mess as best you can. Why didn't you stay with him, Dori?

Dori: Good heavens! Can you ask? Goblins fighting and biting—everybody falling over bodies and hitting one another! You shouted "Follow me, everybody!"—I thought everybody had——

Thorin: And here we are, minus a burglar. Drat him! *(Bilbo steps down in the middle of them and slips off the ring. He is now visible.)*

Bilbo: And here's the Burglar!

Dwarves *(jumping; ad-lib)*: What! Bilbo! Mr. Baggins! Where did you come from?

Gandalf: Bilbo, my boy! What a relief!

Thorin *(to Balin)*: A fine lookout you are, Balin!

Balin: Well, it's the first time that even a mouse has crept by me. I take my hood off to you, Mr. Baggins! *(He does, and bows.)* You're a great burglar. Balin, at your service——

Bilbo *(bowing)*: Your servant, Baggins.

Dwarves *(ad-lib)*: How'd you escape? What happened? Tell us!

Gandalf: He can tell us on the way. We must leave at once. *(Dwarves groan.)*

Bilbo: But I'm so dreadfully hungry——

Fili: Me, too——

Kili: And me——

Bombur: Me most of all!

Gandalf: Forget it. Hundreds of goblins will be out after us as soon as it gets dark. So tighten your belts and let's go. Better no supper than *be* supper.

Dwarves: Hear, hear!

Thorin: But where are we going? *(Takes out his map.)*

Gandalf: Through Mirkwood Forest. *(Groans from the dwarves.)* It is dark and dangerous but it won't be too bad if you can only remember one thing: the path is clearly marked and you *must stay on it.* Don't let anything tempt you to leave it even for a moment.

Thorin: But aren't you coming with us?

Gandalf: Impossible. I have pressing business in the South.

Thorin: But you *can't* desert us now!

Gandalf: We may meet again before all is over and then again we may not. That depends on your luck and courage and good sense. But I am sending Mr. Baggins with you, and there's more to him than meets the eye. *(Bilbo groans.)* Cheer up, Bilbo, don't look so glum. Cheer up, Thorin and Company. Think of the treasure at the end!

Bilbo: Do we really have to go through Mirkwood! Isn't there some safer way 'round it?

Gandalf: There are no safe ways in this part of the world. You are over the Edge of the Wild now, and there's danger everywhere.

Thorin *(studying map, irritably):* You said someabout a forest path——

Gandalf: Yes. Straight through the forest is your way now. Don't stray off the path. If you do, it's a thousand to one you'll never find it again and never get out of Mirkwood. And then, I suppose, you'll all be eaten by goblins and I shall never see you again!

Thorin *(sourly):* Very consoling you are, to be sure.

Gandalf: Come now, enough delay. These woods will soon be thick with goblins! *(Gandalf exits R. His voice is heard faintly in the distance.)* Don't leave the path! *(The dwarves and Bilbo trudge glumly off L.)*

Close Up

1. Make a list of facts you learn about hobbits at the beginning of this play. (For example, hobbits do not like adventure.)

2. (a) As the dwarves arrive, why does Bilbo invite each one in to tea? (b) Why does Bilbo decide to join the dwarves on their adventure?

3. Gandalf says of Bilbo, "There's more to him than you guess or he has any idea of himself." (a) How does Bilbo prove his bravery when the dwarves lose their supplies? (b) How does Gandalf help him escape being cooked?

4. After the battle with the goblins, Bilbo is lost in a dark cave. (a) Find two ways in which Bilbo's cleverness helps him escape. (b) How does the ring he finds aid him?

Act Two

SCENE 1: (Mirkwood Forest, weeks later. The stage is dimly lit. On the platform at stage L are huge gnarled tree trunks. Vines trail the forest floor. On a tree a sign is posted reading "MIRKWOOD. Proceed at your own risk." Along the front, signs are placed at intervals: "The Path." The dwarves and Bilbo trudge on L in single file, with Thorin at their head.)

Thorin (pausing on the path): There's just no end to this accursed forest. (Shakes his fist.) I hate Mirkwood more than I hate the goblin tunnels.

Balin: Misery me! It goes on forever!

Oin: And ever!

Gloin: And ever.

Bofur: Gandalf said, "Cheer up, I'm sending Mr. Baggins with you. He has more about him than you guess. You'll find that out before long." (Turns sharply to Bilbo.) Well, Mr. Baggins? It's been long enough——

Gloin (angrily): What good's a hobbit? Gandalf left us with a hobbit to help us! Hah!

Bilbo: That's right, Gloin. Blame it all on me! I wanted to come on this adventure! I begged you to let me come!

Thorin (placatingly): Now, now, this won't do. We must all stick together.

Bombur (slapping his own face): Ouch! Mosquitos biting! Sticky vines wrapping 'round my throat, roots pulling at my feet! I can't go another step. Go on if you must. I'm going to lie down here and sleep—— (Sits.)—— and dream of food, if I can't get it any other way. (Curls up, yawns sleepily.) The treasure? I'll be too starved to enjoy it—— (Swats at a mosquito. There is a sudden flash of light.)

Bifur (jumping): What was that?

Balin: Those flashes of light again! We'd better circle away from them.

Bilbo: But if we circle away, we'll have to leave the path!

Thorin: So?

Bilbo: Gandalf warned us not to.

Balin: Bilbo's right.

Kili: So he is.

Nori: Gandalf did say we musn't leave the path. But he didn't know all that was going to happen.

Bilbo: I think he had a pretty good idea, all the same.

Thorin: We're all hungry.

Ori: And tired.

Oin: I can't go any further.

Bilbo: We must go on. Maybe we'll find some berries.

Gloin: Find berries in the spring—that's a hobbit for you!

Dori: It's time to rest and eat.

Bilbo: Let's stick to the path awhile longer. (The lights flash again.)

Bombur: I can smell meat roasting.

Thorin: Fili and Kili, go and investigate. But be careful.

Fili and Kili: Yes, sir. (Fili and Kili go out R.)

Bilbo: They've left the path. Gandalf said——

Thorin: Gandalf should have stayed with us if he expected to run things.

Balin: But he did say don't leave the path.

Thorin: Well, we haven't left it. Only Fili and Kili have.

Bilbo: Curious—it's so quiet—as

horribly quiet as it is before something awful happens.

Balin (*looking off R*): Fili and Kili are coming back.

(*Fili and Kili come on R and rush up to Thorin.*)

Fili and Kili (*together*): It's elves! They've got food!

Others: Elves! (*The following speeches are said in such rapid succession it is as if one person were talking.*)

Fili: We crept up——

Kili: To the lights——

Fili: What a sight!

Kili: In a clearing——

Fili: Lots of elves sitting 'round a fire.

Balin: What luck!

Kili: Laughing!

Fili: Eating!

Kili: We couldn't bear it. We ran up to beg some food and poof! The lights went out.

Fili: As if by magic!

Kili: Somebody kicked the fire and it went up——(*Gestures widely.*) ——in glittering sparks——

Fili: And they all vanished!

Thorin: Those were wood-elves.

Bombur: Friendly elves! And they've got food!

Thorin: No, no, the wood-elves aren't very friendly. They don't like strangers. Mirkwood breeds distrust. (*There is another flash of light.*)

Bilbo: The lights again!

Bombur: Let's all go to the feast!

Dwarves (*ad-lib*): Whoopee! Let's go! (*They start to go, leaving the path at an angle.*) Come on, Bilbo.

Bilbo (*standing fast*): Wait! A feast will be no good if we don't get back alive from it.

Bombur: Well, I'm going. We won't last much longer without food anyway.

Bilbo: That's true—I guess.

Bifur: Come on, Bilbo. (*Bilbo reluctantly follows the others off the path.*)

(*The Elven-Queen and several of her attendant lords and ladies enter from L. The Queen wears a trimly fitted garment of forest green and a crown of oak leaves and berries. She carries a wand of carved oak. Her attendant ladies carry bows and arrows.*)

Elven-Queen: Halt! (*Dwarves and Bilbo freeze in surprise.*)

Thorin: By whose authority do you bid us halt?

Elven-Queen: I am the Elven-Queen. Who are you that trespass on my domain?

Thorin (*stage whisper to Bilbo*): Quick, Bilbo, make yourself invisible. Put on your ring. (*Bilbo does so, and from then on he is ignored by all.*)

Elven-Queen (*imperiously*): Speak.

Thorin (*stepping forward proudly*): I am Thorin Oakenshield, son of Thrain, son of Thror, King under the Mountain!

Elven-Queen (*disdainfully*): A dwarf all the same. Why did you and your folk attack my people?

Thorin: We did not attack them, Your Majesty. We came to beg because we are starving.

Elven-Queen: What are you doing in Mirkwood?

Thorin: We are looking for food and drink.

Elven-Queen (*impatiently*): But why are you here at all? (*Thorin remains silent.*) Come now! (*Thorin remains silent.*) Very well! You shall all go to my dungeons where you shall remain until

you tell me the truth—if it takes a thousand years! Seize them! *(The elf guards grab Thorin and surround the others. To the guards.)* How many are there?

Guard: Thirteen, O Queen.

Elven-Queen: Away with them. *(She exits L.)*

First Guard: Step lively, dwarves!

Second Guard: March! *(The elves march the dwarves off L.)*

Bilbo *(taking off his ring and speaking to it.).* Well, my friend, thanks to you I'm still free. We should have stayed on the path as Gandalf warned us. And now they'll all be shut up in a stone dungeon. That's a hard thing! Somehow I must get them out! *(Bilbo runs off L.)*

SCENE 2: *[The dungeon of the Elven-Queen's palace. At rise, the dwarves are discovered behind the bars of a large prison cell in the center section of the stage. They are seated on wooden stools in attitudes of despondency. Thorin occupies a private cell to their right. On the platform at R there are a table and chairs. On the platform L are a pile of straw and four wine barrels. Also in this section, somewhere in the background, are various possessions of the dwarves: bags containing tools (drills and hammers); jackets; pad and pencil.]*

At Rise of Curtain: *(Bilbo sits against one of the barrels, writing busily in his journal. As lights come up on platform L, Bilbo finishes writing and holds up his diary to see better.)*

Bilbo *(reading impressively):* Well, so far I haven't come up with a plan of escape. I might as well be locked up with my friends. Being invisible day after day is driving me mad. This is without a doubt the dreariest, dullest part of this wretched adventure. At least the dwarves are eating well. I have to steal my scraps of food from the kitchen. *(Nods approval and scribbles again.)*

Thorin *(calling softly to Bilbo):* Psst!

Bilbo *(ignoring him, reading again, impressively):* I'm like a burglar that can't get away but must go on miserably burgling the same house day after day! *(Snaps journal shut.)*

Thorin *(louder):* Psst, Mr. Baggins!

Bilbo: Shhh—— *(Gets up, looks around, and crosses cautiously to Thorin's cell.)* What is it, Thorin? The guards will be coming any minute with your food.

Thorin: Then put on your ring. Why aren't you wearing it?

Bilbo: I don't like to wear it when I don't have to. It makes me feel funny. What did you want?

Thorin: Did you get off the message to Gandalf?

Bilbo: I don't know where to send it.

Thorin: Of course. I get more stupid every day.

Bilbo: Me, too. It's hard to concentrate when I'm invisible so much. It's as if I'm not all there.

Thorin: At least do *something.* You're a burglar. Steal! *(The other dwarves have gathered at the front of their cage and are listening eagerly.)*

Bilbo: Well, I could steal the keys— that's not so hard.

Thorin *(brightening):* You could? Wonderful!

Dwarves: Bilbo!

Bilbo: But how would we get past

the guards? One invisible ring isn't much good among fourteen.

Thorin: We might escape—somehow.

Bilbo: But we couldn't possibly get out of the main gate.

Thorin: Why not?

Bilbo: Sealed by elf magic.

Thorin (*deflated*): Oh. (*There is the sound of a key turning in a lock.*)

Bilbo (*hushed tones*): The guards are coming. Talk up and distract them! I'll see what I can do about the keys.

Thorin (*urgently*): Put on your ring, you stupid hobbit! (*Bilbo smites his brow at his forgetfulness, pulls out ring, and puts it on.*)

(*The guards enter from R. The first guard has a large ring of keys fastened by a chain to her belt. The second guard carries a tray with a bowl of soup and end of a loaf of bread. The first guard takes up her stand by the door, guarding it. The second guard brings the tray of food to Thorin.*)

Second Guard: Food for you, Thorin Oakenshield. Thanks to our gracious queen. (*Bilbo, walking on tiptoe, begins to cross very cautiously toward the first guard.*)

Thorin (*taking the tray*): I thank the Elven-Queen and hope to return her hospitality when I have recaptured my castle. Its dungeons are deep.

First Guard: What's that he says?

Second Guard: He threatens our queen.

First Guard: That's treason! Write it down! Write down every word he says!

Second Guard: I've nothing to write with.

First Guard (*rushing forward and barely missing colliding with the tiptoeing Bilbo, who leaps aside to avoid him*): Here, take this. (*Gives him a pencil.*)

Second Guard: Now, are you ready to answer the questions of our Elven-Queen?

Thorin: I refuse to answer questions under duress.

First Guard (*leaning forward, excitedly*): More treason. Write that down! (*Bilbo is now crouched by the side of the first guard, ready to start removing keys from her key ring.*)

Second Guard (*writing busily on pad*): Prisoner defies our Elven-Queen.

Thorin: *Now,* Bilbo!

First Guard: What's that he's saying?

Second Guard: Sounded like he said Bilbo. Dwarves are stupid. Let's get out of here. (*Bilbo has begun removing the key ring. He is very cautious but his hands are shaking and the keys clink. The first guard moves uneasily and Bilbo freezes. The first guard fumbles for her keys. Doesn't find them. She fumbles again. Bilbo extends the keys so that she touches them. She is satisfied and returns her attention to second guard.*)

First Guard: He hasn't eaten yet and the others haven't had their food.

Second Guard: Let them do without. (*To Thorin.*) The tray. Let me have it.

Thorin (*throwing it at her feet*): Gladly.

Dwarves (*roaring approval*): Thorin!

Second Guard: If it weren't forbidden, I'd make you suffer for that! But wait and see how you like your dinner—*when* it comes! It'll be *well* salted. I promise you that.

First Guard: There's a big feast tonight and *we'll* be eating like kings! (*The guards *stalk out with a clanking of the door.)*

Thorin *(excitedly):* Did you get the keys?

Bilbo: I did. *(He unlocks the cage door.)*

Thorin: My word! Gandalf spoke true. You're a fine burglar when the time comes! We're all forever in your service! *(Thorin steps out and bows as Bilbo unlocks the door.)*

Dwarves: Bravo! Mr. Baggins—*(All bow.)*—at your service!

Bilbo: Thank you. At yours. *(He bows.)* But now what? We're still stuck here in the dungeon, and, if we got out, the guards will grab us and put us right back in! *(Bilbo crosses despondently and sits on one of the barrels.)*

Dwarves *(ad-lib, uneasily):* That's true. He's got a point there, all right, etc.

Dwalin *(prodding Balin):* Speak to him, Balin.

Balin: Why me?

Dwalin: You're the oldest.

Balin: Uh, Thorin——

Thorin *(warily):* Yes, Balin?

Balin: We were thinking that— umm, maybe it might be best to tell the Elven-Queen about our quest—the treasure and all that.

Dwalin *(putting in):* Maybe if she knew, she might even help us. After all, the dragon has stolen elf treasure, too. They took the elven crown jewels even!

Thorin *(outraged):* Tell the Queen? And right away she'd ask for a share! Just because you're cowards, you want me to ransom you all with *my* treasure! A share? What's to stop her from taking it all?

Gloin: Let's not fight about who gets the treasure until we're out of here.

Bilbo *(suddenly jumping up, excitedly):* I've got it! *(Taps the wine barrel.)* And to think they've been here all the time! *(Crosses to Thorin.)* I've got a plan! You won't like it, but it's our only chance! *(To the others.)* Follow me and all keep together. *(The dwarves look at each other blankly.)*

Bofur: We can't see you, Bilbo.

Thorin: Take off your ring.

Bilbo *(slipping off ring):* Sorry.

Bifur: There he is.

Bilbo: Over here! *(Dwarves ascend platform L.)* Balin, guard the door in case anyone comes.

Balin: Right. *(Crosses and listens at door.)* Not a sound. *(Takes up watch, his back against door.)*

Bilbo: Now. *(Coming down eagerly to Thorin.)* As you know, we can't escape through the gates. But there is another way out.

Thorin: There is?

Bilbo: There's a stream under the wine cellar that joins the river further east, and when the wine barrels are empty like these—*(Taps one.)*—the guards dump them through a trapdoor just outside here—*(Gestures L.)*—and they float away.

Bifur: How do you know?

Bilbo: I've watched them. Lots of times. They go bobbing down the river and the current carries them along to Laketown. *(Excitedly.)* And where is Laketown?

Thorin: At the foot of the Lonely Mountain.

Bilbo *(triumphantly):* Our exact destination.

Thorin: Interesting, but it doesn't help us.

Bilbo: Can't you see? We hide ourselves in the empty barrels and the elves dump us through the trapdoor along with the empties. We simply ride down to Laketown. *(The dwarves hear this with complete dismay.)*

Dwarves *(ad-lib)*: No, no. Not me.

Thorin: Bilbo, no! This is madness!

Gloin: We'd be battered to pieces!

Nori: Or drowned like kittens!

Dwalin: Who'll let us out? We'll starve to death nailed up in those things. *(Kicks a barrel scornfully.)*

Bilbo: No, no! Don't worry! We'll pack the barrels with straw and seal them airtight, and I'll see that everyone gets out.

Thorin: Great! And just how do we breathe?

Bilbo: Air holes.

Bombur: You're not getting *me* into one of those! I won't fit, thank goodness!

Bilbo: Yes, you will, Bombur. We'll shove you in. *(Dwarves all turn away, muttering among themselves; Bilbo is annoyed and downcast.)* Oh, very well! Then go back to your cozy cells. I'll lock you all in again, and you can figure out a better plan for escape.

Thorin *(soothingly)*: Now, Mr. Baggins, be reasonable.

Bilbo: But I doubt I can ever get hold of the keys again. *(Dwarves groan.)*

Thorin: It seems we have no choice. We'll try your plan. It just might work.

Balin: But there aren't enough barrels.

Bilbo: Most of them are piled out there. *(Gestures offstage L.)*

Dwalin: I still feel the risk is too great——

Bilbo *(ignoring him)*: We'll have to act at once. Time's passing.

Balin *(excitedly)*: I hear them. Hurry!

Bilbo: Are they coming?

Balin: Not yet. They're down the corridor. Hear them singing? *(Balin slightly opens door R.)*

Elves *(chanting offstage R)*:
Roll—roll—roll—roll,
Roll-roll-rolling down the hole!
Heave ho! Splash plump!
Down they go, down they bump!
Down the swift dark stream you go
Back to lands you once did know.

Balin: They'll be along for our barrels soon.

Thorin: Line up the barrels. Kili and Fili, bore holes. Gloin, make a list and check every dwarf off as he goes in. Bifur, collect straw from our cells to pad the barrels. Bofur, collect jackets and stuff them with straw to leave in the cells.

Bofur: Whatever for?

Thorin: Make it look as if we're all asleep. They'll finally figure out how we got away, but the longer they think we're still here, the better for us.

Nori *(approvingly)*: Pretty smart! *(A scene of great activity follows. Kili and Fili pull tools out of their bags and go from barrel to barrel pretending to bore holes in them while Bofur brings out armfuls of straw and pokes them into the barrels. Gloin, with pad and pencil, checks off the dwarves as they go into the barrels. Oin has gone off L.)*

Oin *(speaking from offstage)*: Fili, Kili, don't forget we've got barrels off here, too.

Fili and Kili: In a minute. We're coming.

Bofur *(busily stuffing jackets with straw)*: I hate to leave these good jackets behind.

The Hobbit **497**

Thorin: Nori, you and Ori start packing dwarves in. Start with Bombur. He'll be the hardest. *(Nori and Ori march the protesting Bombur to a barrel.)*

Bombur: Not me! Let someone else go first!

Thorin: Dwalin, Dori, Oin, you're after Bombur. Line up the rest. Into those barrels, fast! Kili and Fili, as soon as you finish boring air holes, head up barrels. Close those outside first.

Kili and Fili *(putting aside their drills and picking up hammers):* But who'll head up our barrels?

Bilbo: I'll do it! *(There is a frantic scene of dwarves hopping into barrels. Some of this supposedly goes on offstage, to make the process faster. Bilbo is everywhere at once. Fili and Kili go out L, and there is a sound of hammering.)*

Balin *(warningly):* I think they're coming. They just said, "That's the last of that lot."

Thorin: Leave the door. Over here, quick. Into your barrel.

Bilbo: Balin, outside. *(Balin goes out L.)* You're next, Thorin.

Thorin: The leader should go last.

Bilbo: No time to argue. Into the barrel, Thorin! *(Calling offstage.)* Everybody in out there? Hurry!

Kili: Just heading up Balin.

Fili: We're coming!

Thorin: But who'll be last?

(Kili and Fili enter L and thrust the protesting Thorin into a barrel.)

Bilbo: I'll be last. Hurry, Kili and Fili. *(They put the barrel head in place. Offstage shouts are heard.)* In with you, Kili and Fili.

Fili: But we can't both fit in one barrel.

Bilbo: Into it. *(Bilbo pushes the protesting pair in and closes the barrel. Suddenly he realizes that there is no one to close his.)* But what about me? Well, I'll just have to catch a loose barrel and ride on it. *(At the very last he suddenly remembers his journal. He dashes back*

and grabs it.) Now into the river! (*Holds his nose firmly.*)

(*As Bilbo seems to leap off into the river, the guards come surging through the door chanting:*)

Guards: Roll—roll—roll—roll——

SCENE 3: In Front of Curtain: [*Lights come up in front of curtain to reveal Dwalin, Bofur, Bifur, Dori, Ori, Nori, Oin, and Gloin in various stages of exhaustion and saturation. Thorin and Bilbo are sitting at C stage, back to back. Behind them are three of the wine barrels (fronts, indicated by cardboard props). They contain Balin, Kili, Fili, and Bombur.*]

Thorin (*groaning*): I've never felt worse than at this moment!
Bilbo (*nudging Thorin*): But are you alive or dead?
Thorin: Achoo!
Bilbo: Are you still in prison or are you free? If you want food and if you want to get on with this silly adventure of yours, you'd better slap your arms and legs and try to help me get the others out while there's a chance! (*Stands up.*)
Thorin: Uh-huh—— (*Gets up painfully.*) Ooooh! My knees! My elbows! (*Thorin goes over to a barrel and removes the lid.*) It's Balin! Come on, old friend.

(*Balin's head pops out. He pulls some straws from his draggled beard.*)

Balin (*groaning*): Oooh! I'm too old for this sort of thing.
Bilbo (*removing lid from another barrel*): It's Kili—and Fili!

(*Their heads pop out, and then Kili and Fili crawl out of the barrel.*)

Kili: Aaaa——
Fili: Choo!
Thorin (*removing the lid from the last barrel*): This one's packed solid— must be Bombur.

Bombur (wailing from inside): Pull me out!

Thorin: I need help over here. (Bilbo, Bofur, and Bifur go over to barrel. They all reach in and pull.) Push, Bombur.

Bombur (still inside): Oooooh! Ugh!

(Bombur pops out of the barrel.)

Bombur: Ah! I hope I never smell the smell of apples again! My barrel was full of it. To smell apples when you can scarcely move and are sick and cold with hunger is torture! I could eat anything in this wide world now for hours on end— but not an apple!

Thorin: Well, that's all of us. It could be worse—and then again, it could be a good deal better.

Bilbo: I'm going into Laketown for food.

Bombur: Good thinking!

Thorin: Then, we'll make camp and wait for you here. In the morning we can start for the Lonely Mountain to drive the dragon from his cave. (Bilbo slips his ring on his finger and goes off.)

Gloin: Maybe he's dead by now. (There is a tremendous, distant, bellowing roar.)

Dwarves (ad-lib): He's alive. That's Smaug. Now our burglar will steal the treasure for us! (Again the dragon roars.)

SCENE 4: [The Lonely Mountain, outside the entrance to the dragon's cave. The stage is barren except for a few blackened tree stumps. A few broken mining tools may be lying about at stage R. The mountain is indicated by a ³⁄₄ frame drop, with a practical doorway left of C. Left of the door, the remaining quarter of the drop is scrim (gauze) so that when lights are brought up in front and up behind the scrim portion, you can play the scene in the cave. If this is not possible, travelers may be employed to the same purpose. A scrim, of course, lends more magic to the scene. It is almost sunset and the sky is reddening in the west.]

At Rise of Curtain: (Bilbo is discovered busily writing in his journal. He is sitting on the stoop before the cave entrance. Dragon smoke belches from under the entrance. The dwarves glumly pace around the stage, hands behind their backs.)

Bilbo (holding script off and reading it): And so we have come at last to the Lonely Mountain. What a desolate spot! But Thorin remembers when it was green and fair. According to his map, I am now sitting on the very doorstep of the secret entrance to the dragon's cave. But despite our best efforts, the door remains mysteriously sealed. (Resumes writing silently.)

Thorin (stopping before the door, shaking his fist passionately): Come out and get us then! I'd rather face ten thousand of you than stand here doing nothing.

Bilbo (reading from journal again): I don't say so, but our predicament may be a blessing in disguise. I'm not looking forward to burgling old Smaug. No, actually, I prefer just sitting—— (Stops writing and hums pleasantly to himself.)

Gloin: All that treasure in there! Just waiting to be burgled, and *what* is our burglar doing for us?

Thorin (*approaching Bilbo*): Just what are you doing, Mr. Baggins?

Bilbo (*who has been humming happily*): Hmmm? You said sitting on the doorstep and thinking would be my job, so I'm sitting and thinking. Come join me. This is certainly the warmest spot on the mountain.

Thorin (*angry*): Mr. Baggins!

Bilbo: That certainly is a fine-looking key Gandalf gave you, Thorin.

Thorin: But there's no keyhole! (*Flicks at the key about his neck.*)

Bilbo: Let's have another look at your map.

Thorin: Again! What for?

Bilbo: I just thought maybe——

Thorin: Oh, very well. (*Pulls out and opens map. Bilbo joins him in scanning it. Droning*): The runes tell us to stand by the gray stone——we've been doing that, all right! And the setting sun by the last light of Durin's Day will——

Thorin and Bilbo (*together*):——shine upon the keyhole——

Bilbo (*cheerily*): Well, perhaps today is Durin's Day.

Bombur: Wake me when something happens. (*Lies down.*)

Thorin: Durin's Day! I never heard of it. I've lost track of time altogether——

Dwalin: Our beards will grow 'til they hang down the cliff into the valley before anything happens here! (*Suddenly a red ray of sunset-light falls upon the cave entrance.*)

Dwarves: Look! The setting sun shines on the door!

Bilbo: This must be the sign!

Thorin: Push! Hard! (*The dwarves push against the door.*)

Nori: It won't budge!

Bilbo: The keyhole! Look for the keyhole! (*Spots it.*) Here it is! The key! Quick, Thorin, try your key while the light still shines on the keyhole.

Thorin (*removing the key from around his neck and trying it*): It fits! It fits! (*Turns the key.*) The door is unlocked.

Dwarves: Hooray!

Thorin (*standing on the stoop and addressing company*): And now is the time for our esteemed Mr. Baggins to perform the service for which he was included in our company. Now is the time for him to earn his reward—by being first to enter the secret door.

Dwarves: Hear! Hear! Bilbo first!

Bilbo: Well, I don't think I'll refuse. Perhaps I've begun to trust my luck more than I used to.

Gloin: Well, well, look at our burglar now! Is this the same safe fellow who was lost without his pocket hankie?

Thorin: Mr. Baggins, this is your opportunity.

Bilbo: I have no doubt it's an opportunity, but who's coming in with me? (*The dwarves look the other way, embarrassed. They cough self-consciously and shuffle their feet. Bilbo stands to one side.*) Any volunteers?

Thorin: Now, that isn't quite fair of you, Mr. Baggins. You know we would go with you if it would do any good. But the moment the dragon sees us, he will kill us. Since he can't see you, you'll be safe.

Bilbo: I'll lend you the ring.

Thorin: But then you'd be seen. No, no, you better wear it. We'll stand by out here.

Bilbo: Hmmmm! In that case, stand by the door. (*Slips his ring on.*)

Thorin: Good luck, Bilbo, my friend! (*Reaches for Bilbo's hand but winds up*

shaking the air; tries again and misses.)
Mr. Baggins?

Bilbo *(clasping Thorin's hand):* Here I am, Thorin.

Thorin *(laughing and shaking Bilbo's hand):* Oh! Good luck!

(The Elven-Queen, accompanied by two attendants, rushes on from R. She is followed by a number of her elves armed with bows and arrows.)

First Attendant: Halt! In the name of the Elven-Queen. *(The dwarves groan as the elves surround them.)*

Elven-Queen *(stepping forward):* So, Thorin Oakenshield, we meet again! Of course, I knew I would find you here. Where is the burglar?

Thorin: What burglar?

Elven-Queen: Don't try to deceive me. *He* may be invisible, but the treasure isn't! Well, now that we are all here, we can discuss matters. How shall we divide the treasure?

Thorin: No elf has a claim to the treasure of my people! I will not parley with armed elves.

Elven-Queen: But the wealth of the elves is mingled in Smaug's hoard. Let us discuss that.

Thorin: We will give you nothing! Not a single gold coin. We look on you as foes and thieves!

Elven-Queen: So you claim treasure that is not really yours. Then how are you better than Smaug? Besides, you need my aid.

Bilbo *(stepping up to the Elven-Queen and removing his ring):* Have you a better plan than ours, Your Majesty?

Elven-Queen *(startled):* Ah, the burglar has decided to show himself! But you're not a dwarf—what are you?

Bilbo: A hobbit, ma'm. Allow me to introduce myself. Bilbo Baggins, Esquire, companion to Thorin Oakenshield. At your service. *(Bows cordially.)*

Thorin *(furious):* Mr. Baggins! Will you please not interfere——

Elven-Queen: A hobbit? Then maybe you'll listen to reason. Certainly I have a better plan. Dragons have to be *slain.* Then we should share the treasure. Part of it belongs to us. The dragon stole it from us.

Bilbo: Well, slaying dragons is not at all in my line. I was engaged as a burglar. But if part of the treasure belongs to you, I favor giving it to you.

Thorin: I will not share the treasure. I, myself, will slay the dragon.

Elven-Queen: With what?

Thorin: With this! *(Draws his battered sword.)*

Elven-Queen: You ruined that sword when you struck the troll, not knowing he had turned to stone. Behold the sword of the elves. *(Claps her hands.)*

(Two elves enter carrying a gleaming sword on a purple pillow. They stand before the Elven-Queen.)

Elven-Queen: This blade was forged to slay Smaug. Agree to give us our rightful share of the treasure and you shall use it.

Thorin: I will not give up so much as one gold piece of the treasure. All of it belongs to me.

Bilbo: But, Thorin, if part of it is really hers——

Thorin *(thrusting him aside):* Silence, traitor!

Balin: Thorin, we know the crown jewels of the elves are in the hoard.

Thorin: I no longer call you friend, Balin.

Bilbo: It's a bitter thing if our adventure ends this way. I wish Gandalf could help us now!

(Gandalf enters behind Bilbo.)

Gandalf *(lifting his staff majestically, with the blue light shining):* Gandalf is here!

Bilbo: Gandalf!

Thorin *(sourly):* Well, I never expected to see you again. I expect you're coming around for a share, too?

Gandalf: You are not cutting a very splendid figure, Thorin. But things may change yet. Instead of destroying each other, you should destroy Smaug together so that Middle Earth can again thrive in peace and plenty. I bring with me certain knowledge that you will need in order to vanquish him. But I will not reveal it unless you and the Elven-Queen agree to join forces. *(The Elven-Queen and Thorin hesitate and then approach one another and clasp hands, at first reluctantly and then with warmth.)*

Dwarves: Hurrah for the wood-elves! *(They toss their hats in the air.)*

Elves: Hurrah for the dwarves! *(They drum with their arrows on their bows.)*

Gandalf: Excellent!

Dwarves *(bowing to elves):* At your service!

Elves *(returning the bows):* At yours! *(Elvish laughter.)*

Gandalf: The dragon cannot be wounded except for one spot! He wears a diamond waistcoat that protects him from danger, but there is a bare spot just over his heart.

Thorin *(excited):* Then that's the place to strike.

Gandalf: Quite so. You will only have one chance—if any—and you must use the elven blade and no other.

Elven-Queen: He shall have it. *(Claps her hands. The attendants offer Thorin the sword.)*

Thorin *(taking it):* Many thanks, O Elven-Queen. *(Brandishes sword.)* Blade! I shall not disgrace you! I shall drive you home to your destiny! *(Suddenly realizing.)* But how?

Gandalf: Quite simple. Bilbo, you will go in first, wearing your ring. Thorin, you follow, but only as far as the inside of the door, and don't move a muscle or Smaug will see you. Once inside, Bilbo must somehow get Smaug to expose his bare patch.

Bilbo: How?

Gandalf: You'll find a way.

Bilbo: But——

Gandalf *(cutting in):* And when you do, signal to Thorin, who will fall upon Smaug and slay him. Good luck to you both. *(Bilbo slips on his ring and is no longer visible to them.)*

Bilbo: I'm going in now, Thorin.

Thorin *(gesturing to Bilbo):* I follow, Mr. Baggins. *(Bilbo steps inside the door, followed by Thorin.)*

(Lights dim down in front as they come up in the cave behind the scrim. The den is bathed in a golden-red light. The walls and ceiling are covered with every kind of treasure: crowns, coats of silver mail, jeweled goblets, shields, etc. Smaug lies asleep on a vast pile of precious gems. Bubbling noises and vapors emanate from him. Bilbo enters from R. He is dazzled by the light and glittering jewels and rubs his eyes. Suddenly he sees Smaug and jumps.)

Smaug *(stirring, in a thundering*

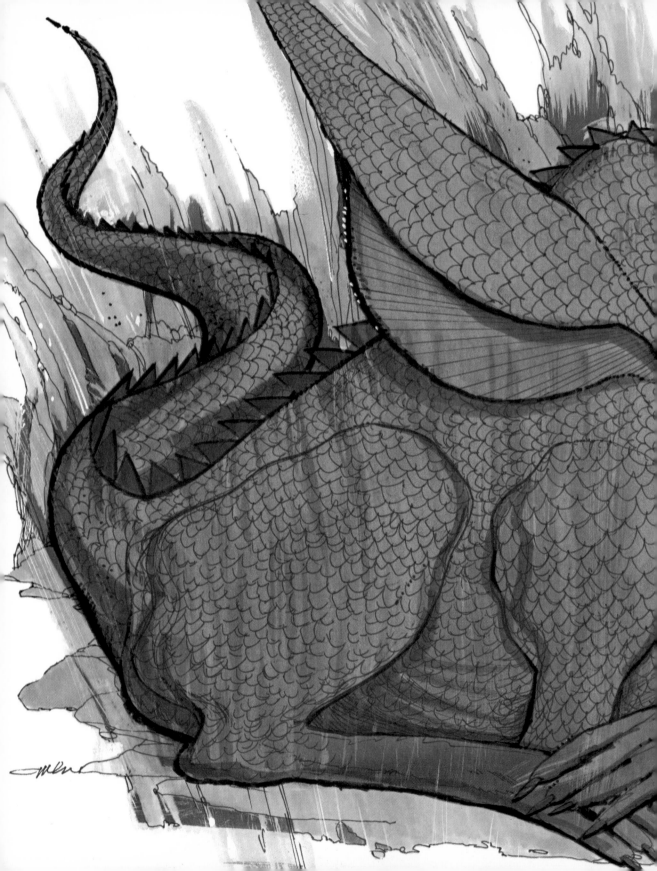

voice): Thief! I know you're there. I smell you and I hear your breath. Thought you'd catch me napping, did you? *(Vapors and bubbles increase.)*

Bilbo *(summoning up all his courage)*: Oh, no, O Smaug. I did not come to rob you. I only wished to have a look at you and see if you were truly as great as tales say. I did not believe them——

Smaug *(somewhat flattered)*: Do you now?

Bilbo: Truly, songs and tales fall far short of the reality! You are the greatest of calamities.

Smaug: Nice manners for a thief and a liar. Come closer so I can eat—I mean, see you.

Bilbo: I don't think that would be wise, O Smaug.

Smaug: Hmmm, you seem familiar with my name, but I don't remember smelling you before. Who are you? Where do you come from?

Bilbo *(trying to sound formidable)*: I come from under the hill and over the hills. I am he that walks unseen. I am Barrel-rider and Ringbearer and Luck-wearer, and I am here to reclaim the rightful treasure of the King under the Mountain.

Smaug *(snorting and belching smoke)*: The King under the Mountain is dead, and I have eaten his people as a wolf eats sheep. I laid low the warriors of old, when I was young and tender. Now I am old and strong! Thief in the shadows!

Bilbo: I am the clue finder, I am he that buries his friends alive and drowns them and draws them alive again from the water. I am Ring-winner and Luck-wearer and Barrel-rider!

Smaug *(gloating)*: My armor is like tenfold shields, my teeth are swords, my claws spears, the shock of my tail is a thunderbolt, my wings are as a hurricane, and my breath is death!

Bilbo *(in a frightened squeak):* I have always understood that dragons are softer underneath, especially in the region of the, er, chest, but that you are guarded by a diamond waistcoat, if those are real diamonds. I hear they are only fakes.

Smaug *(snapping):* Your information is false and the jewels are real. Look at them, fool. My waistcoat is made entirely of diamonds, which no blade can pierce! *(Smaug rears up and displays the glittering waistcoat. There is a black spot over the heart, bare of diamonds.)*

Bilbo *(calling off):* Now, Thorin!

(Thorin rushes on from R and plunges his sword into Smaug's chest. Smaug thrashes about wildly, emitting bubbling noises and thick smoke, then collapses and lies still.)

Bilbo: Well done, Thorin, well done!

Thorin: What a treasure! *(He looks at it and removes a magnificent golden coat from the wall.)* Mr. Baggins, here is the first payment of your reward! Cast off your old cloak and put on this. It was my grandfather's. *(Bilbo removes his cloak, and Thorin helps him into the gold coat.)*

Bilbo: Thank you! My, my, I feel magnificent! But I expect I look rather absurd. How they would laugh back home in the Shire. Still, I wish there was a looking glass handy!

Thorin *(surveying the treasure):* Dividing all this will be a long task.

Bilbo: I'll miss all that. I must be going home.

Thorin: But yours is a large share. Very large. Wait for it.

Bilbo: How would I get a large share safely back to the Shire, and what would I do with it when I got there? The coat is enough for me.

Thorin: At least take this casket of gold coins. No one can question your right to that. Perhaps you may find good use for it on your return. Things change, and not always for the better.

Bilbo *(accepting the small casket Thorin offers):* I thank you, Thorin Oakenshield, and await the day when you rap again on the door of your faithful burglar.

Thorin: And the Queen—— *(Glances around, and his eyes light on a richly encrusted robe of state.)* This robe is not dwarf treasure. *(Takes it up.)* And here is the ancient Crown of the Elves! *(Picks up a jeweled crown.)* Help carry them, Bilbo.

Bilbo: Now let us leave this place. *(They leave the cave and join the others. Lights come up again in front.)*

Dwarves and Elves *(ad-lib):* Thorin! Mr. Baggins! Hooray!

Thorin: Rejoice, my friends! Smaug is dead!

All: Bravo, Thorin. Bravo, Mr. Baggins!

Thorin *(to the Elven-Queen):* Madam, your robe. *(He puts it over her shoulders. Her ladies adjust it.)* Your crown. *(Places it on her head.)*

Dwarves and Elves: Hail Queen of the Elves!

Elven-Queen: I thank you all. You have grown in stature, Thorin Oakenshield. Dwarves, you have a brave and honorable chief.

Thorin: It was your sword that felled the dragon, Great Queen.

Elven-Queen *(smiling):* But your hand that wielded it!

Gandalf: Excellent! *(Crosses R and slips out unnoticed.)*

Elven-Queen: I must return to my kingdom. Farewell, and may dwarves and elves ever live in friendship. And you, Bilbo Baggins, I name Elf Friend forever. *(All bow as Thorin, holding her hand high, escorts her off R.)*

Bilbo: I, too, must start the long journey home. Farewell, friends. *(Smiles at them.)* Remember, a certain burglar will always be listening for the sound of a dwarf staff beating on his door! *(He exits R.)*

Dwarves *(waving and laughing):* Goodbye, Mr. Baggins. We shall miss you!

Close Up

1. (a) What happens to the dwarves when they stray from the path through Mirkwood Forest? (b) Why doesn't this happen to Bilbo?

2. (a) How does Bilbo show he is a good burglar when the dwarves are locked in the dungeon? (b) What does his plan for escaping from the dungeon show about Bilbo? (For example, it shows that he is daring.)

3. How does the dragon's vanity help Bilbo to defeat it?

4. **Composition.** Why do you think Gandalf chose a hobbit, rather than a dwarf, to go on this adventure? Write a paragraph explaining your answer.

WRITING PROCESS

HANDBOOK

Most people won't realize that writing is a craft. You have to take your apprenticeship in it like anything else.

—Katherine Anne Porter

Writing is a craft, but one you can learn to master. It is helpful to think of this craft as consisting of a series of on going, interconnected activities. These activities form the steps in a process that involves prewriting, writing, and revision.

Prewriting

Prewriting is the planning and inventing stage of writing. It consists of the decisions you make and the activities you do before you write in order to get off to a good start. It is a period during which you can get yourself in the mood to write and can play with thoughts and ideas. Unfortunately, many of us spend too little time at this stage. We rush ahead to the writing stage, face a blank piece of paper, and find we have nothing to say.

Making Choices

Before you write, you must make two choices which will guide your writing. These choices involve audience and purpose.

Audience

I don't think it ever hurt the writer to sort of stand back now and then and look at his stuff as if he were reading it instead of writing it.

—James Jones

Unless you are writing in your diary or journal, what you write is most likely meant to be read by others. Your audience consists of the person or group of people who will be reading what you write. To write effectively, you must have a clear picture of your audience. Therefore, before you start to write, ask yourself, "Who is my audience and what do I know about this person or group of people that matters?"

In much of the writing you do in school, you assume your audience is your teacher, and you keep in mind your teacher's expectations and standards when you write. However, not all teachers are alike.

Just like other people, they vary in experience and attitudes. For example, your mathematics teacher would no doubt know a lot more about and be more interested in mathematics than your English teacher. If you were writing a composition about Archimedes for your science teacher, you might concentrate on Archimedes' theories and principles. If you were writing this composition for your English teacher, you might concentrate on his life.

Other audiences vary even more. For example, imagine you are away at summer camp. You have just won a prize for your science experiment. You write a letter home to your eight-year-old brother. Obviously, you would not describe your experiment in detail but would simply try to give your brother a general idea of what you did. You would keep your sentences short and your language simple. You would try not to use any scientific terms, but if you found you needed to use them, you would define these terms.

How different this letter would be from the one you would write to your best friend, who is a member of the young scientists' club back home. For her, you would describe your experiment in detail, feeling comfortable using as much scientific terminology as necessary. In addition, you would not feel it important to keep your sentences particularly short or your language simple.

Activity 1. In "A Running Brook of Horror," Daniel Mannix describes the physical and psychological differences between rattlesnakes and cobras. This description begins on page 109, column **b,** paragraph 2 and ends on page 112, column **a,** paragraph 2. Read this description carefully. What words would a ten-year-old probably not know? Write them on a separate piece of paper.

Activity 2. Imagine your audience is a group of ten-year olds. Using the information on pages 109 to 112, write a short composition explaining the physical and psychological differences between rattlesnakes and cobras.

Purpose

Your purpose is your reason for writing. It is what you want to accomplish as a result of your writing. For example, do you want your audience to be better informed? Then your purpose will be to provide information. On the other hand, your purpose may be to persuade someone or even to impress someone. It may be to entertain or to amuse or to defend a position. Sometimes you have more than one purpose. You may want not only to give information but also to amuse your readers.

To some extent, your purpose depends on your audience. For your composition on Archimedes for your mathematics teacher, your purpose might be to show how much you know. For your composition on Archimedes for your English teacher, your purpose might be to show how well you write.

In addition, your purpose affects not only what you say but how you say it. If you were writing a composition on the effects of exercise on health to show your teacher how much you know about this subject, you would try to make your composition sound formal and impersonal. You would not use slang, dialect, or contractions or many of the personal pronouns I, me, or my. However, if you were writing a composition about a weekend trip to amuse a sick friend, you would make your tone informal and personal.

Activity 3. In "The Story of Tuffy, the Dolphin Who Was Trained to Save Lives," on pages 68–71, Margaret Davidson's primary purpose is to give information about Tuffy and the Sealab II project. Imagine you are writing a composition about this project. Your audience consists of your classmates. Your purpose is to persuade them to work for increased funding for this project. On a separate piece of paper, list five facts or opinions you would use in your composition. (Hint: Your facts should show advantages or benefits of such a project.)

Activity 4. In "The Night the Ghost Got In" (pages 384–388) James Thurber's primary purpose is to amuse. Imagine you were the police officer on duty. Write a report of this incident for your police captain. Your main purpose is to give information.

Choosing a Topic

Writing comes more easily if you have something to say.

—Sholem Asch

Before you can begin writing effectively, you must decide on a topic to write about. Often your teacher provides you with a topic for your composition. However, sometimes in shool, and usually in other writing situations, you can choose the topic yourself. Here are three strategies for choosing a topic.

Personal Interests

One strategy for choosing a topic is to find something that interests you. For example, James Herriot, who wrote "Cat-About-Town" (pages 3–14), is a veterinarian. In his many books, he writes about a subject that interests him deeply – animals.

Activity 5. Take an inventory of your interests. On a separate piece of paper, answer each of the questions below.

1. What is your favorite sport?
2. What do you talk about with your friends?
3. What clubs do you belong to?
4. How do you make pocket money?
5. Who is your favorite writer?
6. What type of books do you like to read?
7. Who is your favorite actor?
8. What type of movies do you like to watch?
9. What type of music do you enjoy?
10. What would you like to know more about?

Activity 6. Write ten more questions to ask yourself to inventory your interests. Then answer your questions. Compare your questions with those of your classmates. Compile a questionnaire with twenty-five questions for you and all your classmates to answer.

Personal Experiences
Most of the basic material a writer works with is acquired before the age of fifteen.

Willa Cather

Another strategy for choosing a topic for writing is to write about something you have done, an experience you have had. For example, in "Alone on the Hilltop" (pages 186–192), Lame Deer writes about an experience he had that changed his life.

Activity 7. The following questions should help you recall experiences you might like to write about. On a separate piece of paper, answer each of these questions.

1. The first event I remember is _____.
2. The funniest thing I ever saw was _____.
3. The smartest decision I ever made was _____.
4. The hardest decision I ever made was _____.
5. The loneliest time in my life was when _____.
6. The happiest time in my life was when _____.
7. The bravest thing I ever did was _____.
8. The most unusual thing I ever saw was _____.
9. The best job I ever had was _____.
10. The luckiest thing that ever happened to me was _____.

Journals

In a very real sense, the writer writes in order to teach himself, to understand himself, to satisfy himself.

—Alfred Kazin

A third strategy for choosing a topic is to keep a journal. Your journal is for your eyes only. It is a private place where you can record your thoughts and experiences, where you can keep interesting articles from newspapers and magazines, where you can store photographs that have captured your imagination. It is a place where you can be free to experiment, to explore ideas, and to discover yourself. Obviously, your journal is a storehouse of topics for writing. When the time comes to choose a topic for formal writing, usually you can easily find one that interests you merely by flipping through the pages of your journal.

Activity 8. It is good practice to write in your journal regularly. Choose one of the items below. On a regular basis, write in your journal on this item. You do not have to write every day and you may write more than once a day. However, write at least seven entries. In addition, include in your journal any clippings and photographs from newspapers and magazines that relate to this item.

1. I felt good today when I _____.
2. The most unusual thing I heard about today is _____.
3. During lunch today, my friends talked about _____.
4. The most interesting thing I did today was _____.
5. The thing that worried me most today was _____.

Developing Ideas About the Topic

Whatever our theme in writing, it is old and tired. Whatever our place, it has been visited by the stranger, it will never be new again. It is only the vision that can be new, but that is enough.

—Eudora Welty

Once you have chosen a topic, you are ready to warm up your mind, to get your thoughts perking. Allow yourself plenty of time to mull over your topic. Let your special point of view, or vision, take over. If you have selected a topic that interests you, no doubt you already have many ideas about it. The following strategies will help you turn up these ideas and get them out into the open where you can later analyze them and choose from them.

Making Lists

Most people like to make lists. They make shopping lists, lists of things to be done, lists of their favorite movies, lists of just about anything they can think of. The amazing thing about lists is their ability to grow. You may have five things in your mind that you want to jot down in a list. However, by the time you have written down the fifth item, you've thought of five more, and once you've written down these five, even more have come to mind.

To compile a list of information and associations about your topic, you need to get yourself in a freewheeling frame of mind. List-making is a way of exploring a topic. Relax. Turn off your internal critic, that part of yourself that says no to ideas before they are fully formed. No one is going to mark your list; no one is going to judge it. Let your mind roam freely. Look at your topic from every angle. What do you know about it? How would you describe it? How do you feel about it? What opinions do you have about it? Jot down all your thoughts as they come to mind, no matter how unimportant they may now seem.

Here is a list that might have been developed on the topic of dolphins.

Dolphins

Communicate with each other
People studying whether they can communicate with human
  beings
Mammals
Affectionate, playful
The Island of the Blue Dolphin
Save lives
May have been mistaken for mermaids
Used by the Navy
Sociable
Saw some at Sea World
Can be trained to do tricks
Whales are their natural enemies
Fun to watch
Not porpoises

Activity 9. Choose one of the following topics. On a separate piece of paper, make a list of all the information, thoughts, and associations that come to mind about this topic. Be sure to include at least ten items about your topic.

1. snakes
2. video games
3. friendship
4. fads
5. rock music
6. football
7. money
8. cars
9. television
10 patriotism

Asking Questions

Asking and answering questions is another strategy for generating ideas about a topic. Once you ask the question, you may find that you already know the answer, that you need to look up the answer, or that you need to turn to other people for the answer. The most common questions to ask begin with the words *who, what, where, when, why,* and *how.* For example:

> *Who* is training dolphins?
> *What* can dolphins be trained to do?
> *Where* is this training taking place?
> *When* do dolphins learn best?
> *Why* were dolphins chosen?
> *How* do you train a dolphin?

Here are some other types of questions you can ask about your topics:

> How are dolphins like porpoises? (comparison)
> How are dolphins different from porpoises? (contrast)
> What is the first step in training a dolphin? (time order)
> What makes dolphins easy to train? (cause/effect)
> When training a dolphin, where should the trainer be in relation to the dolphin? (spatial order)

Activity 10. For the topic you chose in Activity 9, make a list of ten questions to which you would like to find answers. Then find the answers to these questions.

Activity 11. A written interview is a type of composition largely developed by asking someone questions. Study the questions Karen Folger Jacobs asked Kim Milburn in "Skateboarding" on pages 175–183. Then write ten questions you would ask your favorite television or sports figure, writer, or musician during an interview.

Brainstorming

Brainstorming is an activity that is often best done in a group. Like list-making, it gives you the opportunity to think freely and widely about a topic. However, unlike list-making, it also gives you the opportunity to bounce your thoughts off the thoughts of others. It allows you not only to generate ideas, but also to receive ideas from others.

To brainstorm, get together a group of friends or fellow students. Have someone act as secretary or, if possible, have a tape recorder going. Write the topic on the chalk board. Then have the group throw out ideas about this topic as they come to mind. Look at the topic from every angle possible. Take a break. Bring in refreshments. The purpose is to come up with as many ideas as possible. The critic is not welcome at a brainstorming session; the imaginative person is.

Here is the beginning of a list on jazz developed through brainstorming:

> Mellow sound, sometimes so sad
> Syncopated rhythm, gets under my skin
> Blues singers – Billie Holiday, Ella Fitzgerald, Della Reese, Sarah Vaughn
> Making an instrument of your voice
> King of jazz – Miles Davis
> Who is Wynton Marsalis?
> Why are the singers women and the musicians men?
> Dixieland
> The Big Band Era
> How did jazz influence rock and roll?
> Louis Armstrong
> Nicknames: Satchmo, the Bird, Lady Day
> American sound, roots in Africa

Activity 12. With a group of other students, brainstorm on one of the following topics.

1. superstitions
2. school lunches
3. earning extra money
4. hobbies
5. rock videos

Clustering

Clustering is like list-making or brainstorming. You can perform it alone or in a group. However, instead of listing ideas in a random fashion, you cluster or group relate ideas. First write your topic in the middle of your paper or chalk board. Next write your ideas around the topic as though they were the spokes of a wheel. Then form subclusters around each of these ideas.

Here is a list of ideas and associations about horror movies developed through clustering.

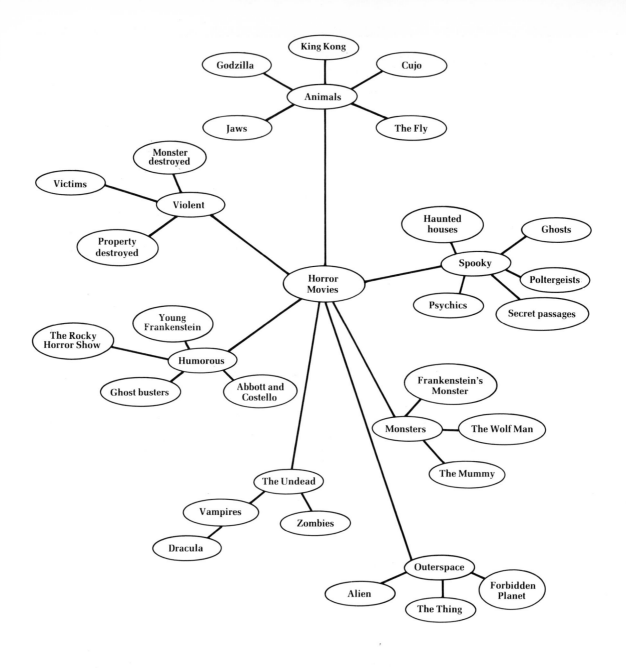

Activity 13.   Choose one of the following topics. Develop your ideas about this topic through clustering.

1.   the Loch Ness monster
2.   collecting stamps
3.   heroism
4.   skiing
5.   camping

Writing

Writing is like driving at night. You can see only as far as the highlights, but you make the whole trip that way.

—E. L. Doctorow

Writing is the stage of the process where the most people become stumped. They sit down to blank piece of paper and feel overwhelmed. They set standards for themselves that are too high. They expect to have every word of their composition already in their heads, and to be able to put these words down on paper without any mistakes. When they can't to this, they think they have failed and will never be able to write. Looking failure in the face, they become blocked. Even most professional writers can't write under this kind of pressure. They make their job easier by breaking the writing stage into steps.

Planning

Now that you have a topic and ideas about this topic, what do you do with them? You formulate a plan showing which ideas you will use and how you will use them. Of course, while you are planning, you may find you need to go back to the prewriting stage to generate even more ideas. Remember that in writing you do not shut the door on any stage of the process but move about freely as needed.

Narrowing the Topic

No one who cannot limit himself has ever been able to write.

—Nicholas Boileau

Whittle your topic down to a manageable size. For example, you probably would find the topic *animals* too large to cover well in one short composition. However, you could do quite a nice job on the topic *cruelty to animals* or *unusual pets*. Here is one of the places where your list-making and brainstorming come in handy. For example, the list developed for dolphins points out several manageable topics. One good one to write about might be *how dolphins communicate*.

Activity 14. Review the lists you developed through list-making, asking questions, brainstorming, and clustering. Then for each list, decide on a manageable topic for a composition.

Activity 15. When George Laycock wrote the article on pages 36–40, he narrowed the topic to "Unforgettable Grizzly Bears." Start with the larger topic *bears*. Then brainstorm with a group of your classmates. Finally review your list and decide on a manageable topic for your composition.

Writing the Topic Sentence

The topic sentence contains the main idea you wish to express about your topic. This is the idea that you wish to develop in your paragraph or composition. (If the sentence contains the main idea of your entire composition, it is called the thesis statement.) This idea is usually expressed by a word or words that describe the topic, make a judgment on the topic, or arouse strong feelings. For example, imagine your topic is *hot air ballooning*. Your topic sentence might be *If proper precautions are taken, hot air ballooning is actually quite a safe sport.* In this topic sentence, the words *safe sport* express the idea you would develop about *hot air ballooning*. Your topic sentence might be *Hot air ballooning is making a comeback today*. In this topic sentence, the words *comeback today* expresses the idea you would develop about *hot air ballooning*.

Activity 16. For each of the topics below, write a topic sentence for a paragraph.

1. How young people are portrayed in movies
2. Getting an after-school job
3. The annual family vacation
4. What makes a good teacher
5. The value of cliques

Activity 17. Choose one of the manageable topics from Activities 14 and 15. Then decide what idea you wish to develop in a composition about this topic. Finally write a thesis statement.

Outlining

Outlines clarify your ideas perhaps, but you must govern the outline, not let the outline govern you.
—Max J. Herzberg

Outlining is a planning strategy that helps you to organize your information. The first stage of outlining can be quite informal, while the final stage is very formal.

Before you begin to write, develop a rough outline, or scratch outline. This outline should contain the important points you wish to cover and the order in which you want to deal with them. In a way, it is like a quick sketch for a painting. It includes the essentials, but it also leaves out a lot.

A scratch outline is flexible. You can use your first draft of it to get started writing and add to it as you continue writing. Remember that writing is a process. Know where you are going but be flexible enough to grow as you write.

Here is a scratch outline for the topic "How People Flew Before Airplanes Were Invented."

Hot Air Balloons
>The Montgolfier brothers
>Blanchard

Hydrogen Balloons
>In France
>In the United States

Dirigibles
>Zeppelins
>American aircraft carriers
>The *Hindenburg*

The scratch outline leads to a more detailed and formal outline, which you can construct before you begin writing your first draft or when you are a little further along in the writing process. Two types of formal outlines are the topic outline and the sentence outline. Turn to page 395. Here you will see a topic outline and instructions for preparing it.

A sentence outline is like a topic outline. However, in a sentence outline, each topic and subtopic is written and punctuated as a sentence. Here is part of the outline on page 395 rewritten as a sentence outline.

I. The history of ballooning in the Western world dates back to the eighteenth century.
>A. It began with hot-air balloons
>>1. The first hot-air balloons were made by Étienne and Joseph Montgolfier.

Activity 18.   Write a rough outline for a composition you would write using the thesis statement you developed in Activity 17.

Activity 19.   Write a topic outline for a composition you would write using the thesis statement you developed in Activity 17. (You may leave blanks in your outline for information you would need to find before writing your composition.)

Activity 20.   Turn the topic outline you wrote in Activity 19 into a sentence outline.

The First Draft

> I must write it out, at any cost. Writing is thinking.
> —Anne Morrow Lindbergh

Your first draft is just that, a first attempt. Consider it thinking aloud on paper. Following your outline, you should write your first draft as carefully as you can, but remember it is open to change and revision. Writers, unlike speakers, are lucky. They have the chance to go back and correct their mistakes before anyone sees them. No one expects your first draft to be perfect. However, your final draft should be polished and correct.

Writing Effective Sentences

A sentence is a group of words with a subject and a predicate that expresses a complete thought. You can make your writing more effective by varying the method you use to construct your sentences and by emphasizing appropriate details.

Variety. No one wants to read something written in a monotonous style. Achieve variety in your writing by varying the way you begin your sentences and the length of your sentences. Study the following ways to begin your sentences.

Start with the subject:
Watson feared that his friend was dying.

Start with and adjective:
Undaunted, Bilbo continued on his quest.

Start with an adverb:
Tenderly, the mother held her newborn baby.

Start with a prepositional phrase:
At the top of the slope, the skier patiently awaited her turn.

Start with a participial phrase:
Balancing the tray on one hand, the waiter walked cautiously toward our table.

Start with an infinitive phrase:
To protect her farm, the woman hunted the renegade bear.

Now review pages 66 and 172. These pages show how to combine two or more sentences into one sentence, a technique that helps you to vary the length of your sentences.

Emphasis. You can emphasize an important element in your sentence by the way you arrange the sentence. Study the following ways for providing emphasis. (The information being emphasized is printed in italics.)

Place the information you want to emphasize at the beginning of the sentence:

Comfort was what Bilbo desired most.

Place the information you want to emphasize at the end of the sentence following a colon or dash:

She found out something about herself: *She was not afraid.*

The prisoner discovered something long buried now growing in his heart—*love.*

Arrange details so that the most important ones come last:

His parents felt that the sport was too time-consuming, too expensive, and *too dangerous.*

Write in the active not the passive voice:

Not: The boy *was thrown* by the horse.

But: *The horse threw* the boy.

Activity 21.   Rewrite each of the sentences below by following the directions at the end of it.

1.   The speaker spoke for two hours. (Begin with an adverb.)
2.   The pictures fell from the wall. (Begin with a prepositional phrase.)
3.   The new teacher walked into the room. (Begin with an adjective.)
4.   You have to answer ninety percent of the questions correctly. (Begin with an infinitive phrase.)
5.   She saw that it was going to rain. (Begin with a participial phrase.)

Activity 22.   Each of the sentences below is written in the passive voice. Rewrite each sentence in the active voice.

1.   The pies were baked by the members of the home economics class.
2.   The food was donated by the club.
3.   Transportation was provided by the students.
4.   The solo was sung by Marie.
5.   Harry was rewarded by the principal.

Writing Effective Paragraphs

A paragraph is a group of sentences working together to express one main idea about a topic. Indent the first line of each new paragraph. If you are writing by hand, indent this line about one inch. If you are using a typewriter or a computer, indent this line five spaces.

Topic Sentence.   Write a clear and well-developed topic sentence. Your topic sentence helps you organize your paragraph, since in it you clearly state the idea you will develop in that paragraph. You can place your topic sentence at the beginning of your paragraph, in the middle of your paragraph, or at the end of your paragraph. (See page 410).

When you place your topic sentence at the beginning of the paragraph, you help your readers identify immediately your topic and your main idea. For example, read paragraph 2 on page 38, column **b** from the article "Unforgettable Grizzly Bears" by George Laycock. This paragraph begins with a topic sentence which tells you that the topic of the paragraph is *grizzly bears and people* and the main idea is that *they have never made good neighbors*. The rest of the sentences in this paragraph support this idea.

When you place your topic sentence at or near the middle of the paragraph, you delay stating your main idea. Usually, you place your topic sentence here in order to arouse your readers' curiosity before driving home your main idea or to form a bridge between the thoughts in the first part of the paragraph and those in the last. For example, read paragraph 4 on page 36, column **a** from the article "Unforgettable Grizzly Bears" by George Laycock. The topic sentence is the fourth sentence. The topic is *Old Two Toes* and the main idea is that *this bear was beginning a long career of big trouble for the cow country*. This topic sentence forms a bridge between the first story about Old Two Toes and the second.

When you place your topic sentence at the end of the paragraph, you let your details build up to a climax or you let your topic sentence summarize the information or show the logical conclusion or result of the information. For example, read paragraph 3 on page 398, column **a** from the article "How People Flew Before Airplanes Were Invented" by Robert Miller. The last sentence in this paragraph is the topic sentence. It shows the result of the information in the previous sentences.

If you choose not to state the topic sentence, then the details in the paragraph must make your main idea clear to your reader. (See page 448.) For example, read paragraph 2 on page 456, column **a** from the article "Gifts of the Indian" by C. Fayne Porter. This paragraph does not contain a topic sentence. However, the information in the paragraph makes clear the main idea: *Although we spend much time studying in detail the history of other nations, we spend little time studying the history of our own native people, the American Indians.*

Support.   The rest of the sentences in your paragraph must clearly support your topic sentence. (See page 434.) There are many ways to develop your support. Three common ways are through examples, through reasons, and through facts or statistics.

For example, read paragraph 4 on page 224, column **a** from the short story "The Sin of Madame Phloi" by Lilian Jackson Braun. The main idea of this paragraph is that Madame Phloi lived by the Rule of Three. This main idea is supported by examples.

Now read paragraph 2 on page 401, column **a** from the article "How People Flew Before Airplanes Were Invented" by Robert Miller. The main idea of this paragraph is that dirigibles may play an important role in the future. This main idea is supported by reason.

Finally read paragraph 3 on page 458, column **a** from the article "Gifts of the Indian" by C. Fayne Porter. The main idea of this paragraph is that one gift of the Indians is the most valuable crop grown in the United States, corn. This main idea is supported by facts and statistics.

Arrangement. Arrange the information in each paragraph in a logical way. There are several organizational patterns you can use. Which one you choose depends to some extent on your purpose.

When your purpose is to relate a sequence of events or ideas or the steps in a process, organize your paragraph through time order. For example, read paragraph 2 on page 112, column **a** from "A Running Brook of Horror" by Daniel Mannix. This paragraph is arranged according to time order. It shows the sequence of steps Grace Wiley followed in order to be able to handle a cobra confidently.

When your purpose is to show spatial position or to describe where certain people or objects are in relation to others, organize your paragraph through spatial order. For example, read paragraph 2 on page 292, column **a** from the short story "Beware of the Dog" by Roald Dahl. This paragraph describes what the flyer sees as he looks out the window of his hospital room. The details are arranged according to spatial order.

When your purpose is to build up to a dramatic or powerful conclusion, organize your paragraph through climactic order, or order of importance. For example, read again paragraph 2 on page 292 column **a.** Notice that the most important, and startling detail is saved for last.

When your purpose is to show the causes behind certain effects or the reasons for certain results, orgainize your paragraph through cause and effect. For example, read paragraph 1 on page 400, column **b** from "How People Flew Before Airplanes Were Invented" by Robert Miller. The first sentence provides the result. The rest of the paragraph shows the reasons for this result.

When your purpose is to show the similarities or the differences between two things, organize your paragraph through comparison and contrast. For example, read paragraph 2 on page 108, column **b** from the article "A Running Brook of Horror" by Daniel Mannix. Each sentence contrasts the cobra with another creature.

Activity 23. Choose one of the topic sentences you developed in Activity 16. Decide on your method of development and of arrangement. Write a paragraph with this topic sentence at the beginning.

Activity 24. Choose one of the topic sentences you developed in Activity 16. Decide on your method of development and of arrangement. Write a paragraph with this topic sentence in the middle.

Activity 25. Choose one of the topic sentences you developed in Activity 16. Decide on your method of development and of arrangement. Write a paragraph with this topic sentence at the end.

Writing Effective Compositions

A composition has three parts: an opening paragraph, the paragraphs that form the body of the composition, and the concluding paragraph. Each part has a different function.

Introduction. Your introductory paragraph should tell your readers the topic of the composition and the main point you are going to develop about this topic. This information is contained in your thesis statement, which usually appears at the end of the paragraph. (Remember that your thesis statement is like a topic sentence that guides the entire composition.) Your opening paragraph should also arouse your readers' interest and make them want to find out what you have to say about the topic. There are many strategies for arousing your readers' interest. Some particularly useful ones are the following: Tell an amusing anecdote or tale related to your topic. Begin with a quotation. Ask a question that you will answer in the composition. Start with an unusual fact. For example, read the introductory paragraph for the article "Gifts of the Indian" by C. Fayne Porter on page 456. Porter begins with a little story telling how Columbus misnamed the Indians. This story leads to his main point, which is that much of our thinking about the first Americans is cloudy and filled with misconceptions. This point is expressed in the thesis statement at the end of the paragraph.

The Body. The body of your composition should contain paragraphs that develop and support the main idea of the essay. Each paragraph should have its own topic sentence or the details in the paragraph should be so strong that the main idea will be clear to your readers.

Look again at your outline. What are the main divisions of the outline (those indicated by a Roman numeral)? Your paragraphs should develop your main divisions. The subdivisions should provide the support.

Conclusion.   Your concluding paragraph should bring your composition to a logical conclusion and summarize or clinch the points you made in the body of the composition. For example, read the concluding paragraph on page 401 of the article "How People Flew Before Airplanes Were Invented" by Robert Miller. This paragraph gives information about how ballooning is making a comeback. It then connects this information to other information in the article about the history of ballooning and draws a conclusion.

Activity 26.   Following the outline you developed in Activity 20, write a first draft of a composition.

Revising and Proofreading

In baseball, you only get three swings and you're out. In rewriting, you get almost as many swings as you want and you know, sooner or later, you'll hit the ball.
—Neil Simon

Revising

Once you have completed your first draft, you are ready to rewrite it and polish it. You may find you need to rewrite it only once. You may find you need to rewrite it three times, or five, or twenty. Be hard on yourself. Remove yourself from the composition. Let it sit for a few days. Now read it with a critic's eye. Imagine that you did not write it. Would you understand it? Would you think it good? How would you improve it? Read it aloud. How does it sound? Should you improve any sentences? Should you change any words? The revision process gives you a chance to make your writing shine.

Keep in mind the following questions when revising your composition.

Overall Concerns

1.   Is your composition appropriate for your intended audience?
2.   Does your composition accomplish your purpose?
3.   Is your thesis statement well constructed?
4.   Does your introductory paragraph arouse your readers' interest?

5. Do the paragraphs in the body of your composition support and develop your thesis statement?
6. Does your concluding paragraph bring your composition to a logical conclusion?

Paragraphs

1. Does each paragraph have a topic sentence, or, if it doesn't, is the main idea clear from the details?
2. Does the information in each paragraph support the main idea?
3. Is each paragraph well developed?
4. Is each paragraph well organized?

Sentences

1. Is each sentence grammatically correct?
2. Is each sentence complete and well developed?
3. Are the beginnings of your sentences varied?
4. Are the sentences varied in length?
5. Is the emphasis within each sentence correct?

Language

1. Is your word choice appropriate for your audience and your purpose?
2. Have you chosen the correct words?

Focus on Special Sentence Problems

Sentence Fragments. A sentence fragment is a sentence part written as though it were a complete sentence. Usually a sentence fragment is missing a subject or a complete verb or both or it doesn't express a complete thought. You can correct a sentence fragment by rewriting the fragment as a complete sentence or by connecting it to a complete sentence. Study the following examples.

Fragment:	Completed my homework on time.
Sentence:	I completed my homework on time.
Fragment:	A strange sound in the middle of the night.
Sentence:	A strange sound awoke him in the middle of the night.
Fragment:	On the top shelf in the closet.
Sentence:	The equipment was on the top shelf in the closet.
Fragment:	The writer usually working on her novel.
Sentence:	The writer is usually working on her novel.
	or
Sentence:	The writer usually works on her novel.
Fragment:	Because it was an enigma.
Sentence:	It was an enigma.

or

> Sentence: The Siren Goddess was considered valuable because it was an enigma.
>
> Fragment: Hunting in the woods with his dog.
> Sentence: Danny was hunting in the woods with his dog.
>> or
> Sentence: Hunting in the woods with his dog, Danny spotted the tracks of the bear.

Activity 27. Each item below is a fragment. On a separate piece of paper, correct each fragment by rewriting it as a complete sentence or by connecting it to a complete sentence that you provide.

1. Because they defy gravity.
2. Sherlock Holmes always outwitting the criminal.
3. For example, trolls, goblins, and dwarves.
4. That are interested in training dolphins.
5. On the first page of this book.
6. Returning only to discover that the town had changed.
7. Forgot my books at the movie theater.
8. A moan from the patient in the bed.
9. The woman jogging in the park.
10. Since he wanted to become a medicine man.

Run-on Sentences. A run-on sentence consists of two or more sentences written as though they were one sentence with only a comma or no punctuation at all between them. There are four common methods for correcting a run-on sentence: (a) Place a period (or other appropriate end mark) between the two sentences and begin the second sentence with a capital letter; (b) if the sentences are closely related, place a semicolon between them; (c) place a comma and a coordinating conjunction (*and, but, or, nor, for, yet*) between the two; or (d) turn one into a dependent clause. Try not to choose one method of correcting run-on sentences all of the time. Vary your style. Play with the sentence. Usually you will find that different methods work best for different sentences.

Study the following examples carefully.

> Run-on: Jamie heard footsteps coming up the stairs in the middle of the night, his brother heard nothing.
> Corrected: Jamie heard footsteps coming up the stairs in the middle of the night. **His** brother heard nothing.
>> or
> Corrected: Jamie heard footsteps coming up the stairs in the middle of the night; his brother heard nothing.
>> or

Corrected: Jamie heard footsteps coming up the stairs in the middle of the night, **but** his brother heard nothing.

or

Corrected: **Although Jamie heard footsteps coming up the stairs in the middle of the night,** his brother heard nothing.

Run-on: Grace could not judge the distance accurately she was not wearing her glasses.

Corrected: Grace could not judge the distance accurately. **She** was not wearing her glasses.

or

Corrected: Grace could not judge the distance accurately; she was not wearing her glasses.

or

Corrected: Grace could not judge the distance accurately, **for** was was not wearing her glasses.

or

Corrected: Grace could not judge the distance accurately, **since she was not wearing her glasses.**

Run-on: The hitchhiker signalled the driver stopped to pick him up.

Corrected: The hitchhikder signalled. **The** driver stopped to pick him up.

or

Corrected: The hitchhiker signalled; the driver stopped to pick him up.

or

Corrected: The hitchhiker signalled, **and** the driver stopped to pick up him.

or

Corrected: **When the hitchhiker signalled,** the driver stopped to pick him up.

Activity 28. On a separate piece of paper, correct each of the following run-on sentences.

1. Tommy tried to be a good florist, Teruo wanted to be a good florist, too.
2. Thapthim came whenever he was called Madame Phloi considered this uncatly behavior.
3. At first, Corrigan doesn't believe in time travel, by the end of the story, he has learned better.
4. Frank turned his head slowly to examine the ledge he saw it was about eighteen inches wide.

5. In the Shire the air is filled with comfort, in the woods it is filled with danger.
6. An adventure is not the thing for Bilbo he would rather stay home where he is comfortable.
7. The bushmaster is the deadliest snake in the world, what a terrible creature to be loose aboard a ship!
8. Basil had found gold in the Transvaal now he was rich.
9. Holmes claimed that he had contracted a rare disease from Sumatra, can he be dying?
10. The morning was gray and threatening it promised to storm before noon.

Focus on Special Language Problems

Appropriate Word Choice. A composition you write for school or for any other formal situation should be written in standard English. This is the language that you are taught in school, that you read in most books, newspapers, and national magazines, and that you hear spoken by announcers on television and the radio. It is a language that follows the rules and conventions that you are taught in your grammar and composition textbook.

Nonstandard English, on the other hand, is language that does not follow these conventions. More than likely, it is the language that you hear on the street and that you use with close friends. It includes slang, dialect (regional expressions), and jargon (see pages 169 and 217). Nonstandard English is appropriate for very informal situations, but it is not appropriate for most of the writing you do in school.

Activity 29. Rewrite each sentence below in standard English. Replace each example of slang, dialect, or jargon, printed in italics, with an appropriate word or group of words.

1. Watson felt *in the pits* as he looked at his dying friend.
2. The way he could play the trumpet was simply *awesome*.
3. The speaker made a *massive goof* in the middle of his talk.
4. The novelist's first book was a *flop*.
5. *T'aint nobody's* business what you *done*.
6. The Current Events Club meets every Wednesday at 3:15 to *shoot the breeze*.
7. Club members must *shell out* five dollars to attend the annual party.
8. The candidate's remarks made a *big splash* in the newspapers.
9. Students should learn to *utilize* their resources to *the maximum degree*.
10. Everything is *A-OK*.

Clarity. Clarity means that your words say exactly what you want them to say. Many words have more than one meaning. Page 81 explains that when you try to find a synonym for a word, you must choose the synonym that has the same meaning as the meaning you intend for that word. For example, *attractive* is a synonym for *pretty* when you intend *pretty* to mean "pleasing." *Attractive* is not a synonym when you intend *pretty* to mean "somewhat": She is a *pretty* good dancer.

Many words sound a lot alike or are commonly confused. For example, *allusion* and *illusion* sound a lot alike. However, *allusion* means "an indirect reference to something." *Illusion* means "a false belief." *Infer* and *imply* are commonly confused. *Infer* means "to conclude from details." *Imply* means "to suggest." Do not be careless with words. If you are not certain which word to use, look the word or words up in a dictionary.

Activity 30. For each word below, write a sentence. Then rewrite each sentence using a synonym for this word. Write your sentences on a separate piece of paper.

1.	dull	**3.**	difference	**5.**	rule	**7.**	road	**9.**	dream
2.	bland	**4.**	ideal	**6.**	fault	**8.**	nice	**10.**	care

Activity 31. The words in each item below are commonly confused. First look up each word in your dictionary. Then, on a separate piece of paper, write a sentence using each word.

1. principle – principal		**6.**	all together – altogether
2. among – between		**7.**	raise – rise
3. lay – lie		**8.**	quote – quotation
4. farther – further		**9.**	teach – learn
5. borrow – lend		**10.**	desert – dessert

Activity 32. Reread your first draft of your composition. Following the guidelines for revision, rewrite your composition.

Proofreading Once you are satisfied that your composition accurately says what you want it to say as well as you can say it, read it through again. This time, look for and correct any errors in punctuation, capitalization, and spelling.

Capitalization

Make sure your composition follows the capitalization rules below. (If you do not find a rule here that suits your particular problem, consult your grammar and composition textbook.)

1. Begin the first word of each sentence with a capital letter.

   After the treaty was signed, he went back to his room. Now he would lead a nation at peace with its neighbors.

2. Capitalize proper nouns, proper adjectives, the pronoun **I**, and the interjection **O**.

Maria	Canadian border
Ms. Perkins	Shakespearian play
San Francisco	National Council of Scientists
Oak Street	Boston Tea Party

3. Capitalize a title or a word showing a family relationship when it comes before a person's name. However, capitalize a title that is used alone or that comes after a name only when it refers to a high official or to someone to whom you wish to show respect.

Mr. Gleason	Aunt Eileen
Mr. Cerriti	the President
Doctor Papalou	Elizabeth II, the Queen of England

4. Capitalize the first and last words and all other important words in titles of books, magazines, newspapers, movies, television shows, and the like.

All Quiet on the Western Front	All in the Family
"Otero's Visitor"	Hill Street Blues

5. Capitalize the names of specific courses.

World Literature	History I	Home Economics

6. Capitalize all words referring to the diety.

God	the Lord	may His will be done

7. In general, do not capitalize words preceded by the articles *a* or *an* or by a personal pronoun.

a mayor	an empire	his father
a history course	my aunt	the gods of ancient Greece

However, this rule does not apply to proper nouns or proper adjectives.

an English course	Chevrolet	a Disney movie
a Texas barbecue	a Swede	a Mexican

Activity 33. Correct the capitalization problems in each sentence below. Write your answers on a separate piece of paper.

1. we vacationed at yellowstone national park.
2. ronald reagan, the president of the united states, will address the nation at six o'clock this evening.
3. mr. and mrs. sampson announced the engagement of their daughter, may louise, a lawyer with the firm of verderber and lewis.
4. who is the current prime minister of india?
5. the pershing high school explorer's club took a trip to washington, d.c.

Activity 34. Proofread your composition for errors in capitalization.

Punctuation

In writing, punctuation plays the role of body language. It helps readers hear you the way you want to be heard.

—Russell Baker

Make sure your composition follows the punctuation rules below. (If you do not find a rule here that suits your particular problem, consult your grammar and composition handbook.)

End Marks

1. End a statement with a period.

    The Tigers won the game.

2. End a question with a question mark.

    Did the Tigers win the game?

3. End an exclamation or a statement that expresses strong emotion with an exclamation point.

    Wow! The Tigers won!

Commas

1. Separate items in a series with a comma.

    Chris enjoyed playing tennis, baseball, soccer and football.

    Notice that a comma is not needed before the word *and*. However, do place a comma before the word *and* if the meaning would be unclear without it:

Unclear:	For the class picnic the cook made thirty each of the following sandwiches: turkey, roast beef, chicken, ham and cheese. (Did the cook prepare four or five types of sandwiches?)
Clear:	For the class picnic the cook made thirty each of the following sandwiches: turkey, roast beef, chicken, ham, and cheese.

2. Separate with a comma two or more adjectives preceding a noun.

    He heard a lonely, haunting, melodic song.

    If you cannot logically place the word *and* between the adjectives or if you cannot change their position, do not place a comma between them.

    Do not touch the hot coffee pot.

3. Separate with a comma independent clauses joined by *and, but, or, nor, for,* or *yet.*

   In the O'Henry story she sells her hair to buy a chain for her husband's watch, but her husband sells his watch to buy a comb for her hair.

4. Set off the nonessential elements with commas.

   "The Gift of the Magi," written by O'Henry, is still widely read today.

5. Set off appositives or appositive phrases with commas.

   Charlene Gillis, the famous singer, will speak to our group today.

6. Use a comma at the end of two or more prepositional phrases.

   In the middle of the night, Jamie heard footsteps coming up the stairs.

7. Use a comma at the end of an introductory adverb clause.

   Since he had missed the bus, he was late for his appointment.

8. Use a comma at the end of a introductory participial phrase.

   Hearing her sister open the door, Nancy ran down the stairs to greet her.

9. Use a comma at the end of introductory words such as *well, yes, no, oh,* and *why.*

   Yes, I want this job.

10. Use a comma or commas to set off a word or words used in direct address.

    Ricky, have you heard my new album?
    The cookies you baked, Uncle Gene, were just wonderful.

11. Use a comma or commas to set off a word or words used parenthetically.

    To tell the truth, I really don't understand this poem.
    We do not know, however, who actually fired the first shot.

12. Use a comma to separate elements in dates and addresses.

    He was born on Monday, July 7, 1947, in a small hospital at 102 East 20th Street, New York, New York 10003.

13. Use a comma at the end of a salutation in a friendly letter and at the end of the closing.

    Dear Mike,   Truly yours,

14. Use a comma after a name followed by an abbreviation such as Jr., Sr., MD., or D.D.S.

    Gerald Rubin, Jr.   Harold Thompson, M.D.

Semicolons

1. Use a semicolon between closely related independent clauses not joined by *and, but, or, nor, for,* or *yet.*

   The days are warm and sunny; the nights are cool and clear.

2. Use a semicolon between independent clauses joined by transitional words or expressions such as *however, therefore, nevertheless, consequenty, otherwise, for example, for instance.*

   Today Columbus is honored; when he died he was considered a failure.

3. Use a semicolon between items in a series when the items themselves contain commas.

   The three teams consist of the following players: Mike, Anita, Sally; Kate, Joel, Ricardo; Mai, Nicholas, Harry.

Colons

1. Use a colon to introduce a list.

   Her dressing table was littered with many items: horse liniment, chapped-lip cream, glacier creams, salt tablets and suntan lotion.

   However, do not use a colon immediately after a verb or preposition.

   On her dressing table are horse liniment, chapped-lip cream, glacier creams, salt tablets and suntan lotion.

2. Use a colon to introduce a long, formal quotation or statement.

   Kenneth Bird once defined humor in the following way: "Humor is falling downstairs if you do it in the act of warning your wife not to."

3. Use a colon at the end of the salutation of a business letter.

   Dear Mr. Garcia: Dear Supervisor:

Dashes and Parentheses

1. Use dashes for a sudden break in thought.

   I wish I had remembered – oh, how I wish I had remembered – your birthday.
   "The name of the culprit is –" the detective said before he was interrupted.

2. Use parentheses to set off added explanations or qualifications that are not of major importance to the sentence.

   Theodore Roethke (1908–1963) was born in Saginaw, Michigan.

Quotation Marks

1. Use quotation marks to enclose a speaker's exact words. (See also page 16.)

    "Never risk getting separated," Lucia's pioneer grandfather had warned.
    "Good luck XT," Jake whispered, "whoever you are."
    "Is Marick alive?" the journalist asked.

2. Use single quotation marks to enclose a quotation within a direct quotation.

    "Do you know who said 'A learned blockhead is a greater blockhead than an ignorant one'?" inquired Carmen.
    The detective warned, "Remember the English proverb that claims 'Opportunity makes the thief.'"

3. Use quotation markes to enclose titles of short works such as short stories, poems, articles, songs, short plays, chapters and other parts of books.

    In his poem "The Sea," James Reeves compares the sea to a hungry dog.
    Have you read "Avalanche" by Robb White?

Italics

1. Use italics (or underlining) for titles of long works such as books, full-length plays, movies, magazines, journals, works of art, and long musical compositions.

    Patricia Gray dramatized J. R. R. Tolkien's *The Hobbit*.

    "Otero's Visitor" first appeared in *New Mexico Quarterly*.
    "Back There" was an episode of *The Twilight Zone*.

2. Use italics (or underlining) for words used as words, figures used as figures, and letters used as letters, and for foreign words.

    How many *i*'s are in the word *Mississippi*?
    Is this a *7* or a *1*?
    Lame Deer wanted to become a *yuwipi*, a medicine man.

Apostrophes

1. Use an apostrrophe followed by an *s* to form the possessive of a singular noun.

    Jake's truck   the boy's dog   today's assignment

2. Use only an apostrophe to form the possessive of a plural noun ending in *s*.

    the students' workbooks   the girls'   the actors' cafe

3. Use an apostrophe followed by *s* to form the possessive of a plural noun that does not end in *s*.

the oxen**'s** yoke   women**'s** gloves   the geese**'s** squawks

4. Use an apostrophe followed by *s* to form the possessive of an indefinite pronoun.

everyone**'s** score   either**'s** cooking   somebody**'s** coat

5. Use an apostrophe to indicate a missing letter in a contraction. (See also page 63.)

isn't   she'd   it's   we're

6. Use an apostrophe followed by *s* to form the plural of letter, numbers, symbols, and words used as words.

three *8***'s**   five *a***'s**   two +**'s**   too many *I***'s**

Hyphens

1. Use a hyphen to indicate the division of a word at the end of a line.

As they explored the island, the found many ex–
otic flowers.

2. Use a hyphen to connect the prefixes *ex–*, *self–*, and *all–* and the suffix *–elect* to the base word.

ex–player   self–made   all–star   President–elect

3. Use a hyphen to connect a suffix to a base word beginning with a capital letter.

un–American   post–Nixon   pre–Revolutionary

4. Use a hyphen to connect the parts of compound numbers from twenty-one to ninety-nine and fractions used as adjectives.

fifty–seven students   a two–thirds majority   eighty–six letters

---

Activity 35. Correct the punctuation problems in each sentence below. Write your answers on a separate piece of paper.

1. Janet asked, "Bill did you borrow my book last week.
2. Wow thats a great idea.
3. Nancys ancestors came to America in preRevolutionary times.
4. Because he didnt know the answer Ron tried to avoid the teachers eye.
5. June asked, do you know who said "No man is an island?"
6. The three squads were made up of the following members, James, Harry and Jean, Marilyn, Maura and Sidney, George, Herman and Susan
7. Carol couldnt find her homework assignment, therefore, she

called Annette to find out which poem in the book An American Anthology of Poetry to read.

8. Annette said, "Tonights assignment is to read the poem Annabelle Lee by Edgar Allan Poe.
9. Poe 1809–1849 died mysteriously in Baltimore Maryland
10. Although some might disagree many critics consider Poe the most important American poet before Walt Whitman.

Activity 36. Proofread your composition for errors in punctuation.

Spelling

Proofread your composition carefully for spelling errors. If you are not absolutely sure of the spelling of a word, look it up in your dictionary. Be careful not to use an incorrect homophone, a word that sounds like the word you intend, but that has a different spelling and a different meaning (see page 103). In addition, keep the following spelling rules in mind.

ie or ei   Write i before e, except after c, or when sounded like a, as in neighbor or weigh.

i before e	except after c	sounded like a
field	receive	freight
achieve	ceiling	reign
niece	receipt	beige

Exceptions: counterfeit, either, financier, foreign, forfeit, height, leisure, neither, protein, seize, science, weird.

Final e   Drop the final e from the base word when adding a suffix beginning with a vowel.

dance + ing = dancing   live + able = livable
sincere + ity = sincerity   continue + ation = continuation

Exceptions: mileage, singeing, dyeing, (tinting).
However, do not drop the final e from base words ending in ce or ge when adding a suffix beginning with a or o.

peace + able = peaceable   advantage + ous = advantageous

notice + able = noticeable   courage + ous = courageous

Final y   If final y is preceded by a consonant, change the y to i when adding a suffix with any letter other than i.

busy + ness = business   beauty + ful = beautiful
rely + ance = reliance   hurry + ed = hurried

Exceptions: (1) Some one-syllable words, for example, dying, lying, crying, shyness, spryness; (2) the words lady and baby, for example, ladylike, babyish.

Doubling the Final Consonant For a one-syllable word ending in a consonant-vowel-consonant, double the final consonant when adding a suffix beginning with a vowel.

> run + ing = ru**nn**ing   pop + ed = po**pp**ed
> swim + ing = swi**mm**ing   stop + ed = sto**pp**ed

For a word of more than one syllable in which the last syllable is accented and ends in a consonant-vowel-consonant, double the final consonant when adding a suffix beginning with a vowel.

> rebel + ed = rebe**ll**ed   permit + ing = permi**tt**ing
> begin + er = begi**nn**er   propel + ed = prope**ll**ed

Activity 37. Proofread your composition for errors in spelling. If you are not sure how to spell a word, look it up in the dictionary.

Additional Writing Assignments

Paragraphs

Review the steps in the writing process. Use these steps to help you complete the assignments that follow. Assume that your audience consists of your classmates.

Time Order

Write a paragraph explaining the first ten things you do when you come home from school. Begin your paragraph with a topic sentence. Then arrange your details according to time order, starting with the thing you do first.

Spatial Order

Write a paragraph describing what you see as you look from your classroom window. Begin your paragraph with a topic sentence. Then arrange your details according to spatial order, moving from left to right.

Order of Importance

Take a position on one of the following topics: lengthening school days, shortening summer vacations, allowing students to choose their own courses. Begin your paragraph with a topic sentence. Then support your position. Arrange your support according to order of importance.

Cause and Effect

Your purpose to explain the causes for a certain effect or result: for example, why the sky appears blue. First use prewriting techniques to find a topic. Then write a topic sentence explaining the result. Finally write supporting sentences showing the reasons for this result.

Comparison and Contrast

Your purpose is to compare or to contrast two pets: for example, parakeets and dogs. First use prewriting techniques to find a topic. Then write a topic sentence. Finally write supporting sentences comparing or contrasting these two pets.

Compositions

Review the steps in the writing process. Use these steps to help you complete the following assignments. Choose an audience for each assignment. Indicate your audience at the top of your paper.

Informative

Your purpose is to provide information. Write a five-paragraph composition explaining the development of something. You may select your own topic or choose one of the following topics: newspapers in the United States, the alphabet, lending libraries in the United States, the home computer. You will probably find it helpful to gather information in the library before you start to write.

Narrative

Your purpose is to tell an amusing story. Write a five-paragraph composition about something that actually happened to you or make up an incident.

Descriptive

Your purpose is to provide an accurate description of someone who means a lot to you. Write a five-paragraph composition. In your first paragraph, introduce the person you will be writing about. In each of the next three paragraphs, describe one special characteristic of this person: For example, one paragraph might deal with the person's sense of humor, another with this person's kindness, and another with this person's generosity. In your last paragraph, reach a conclusion about this person.

Persuasive

Look through current newspapers and magazines until you find an issue about which you feel strongly. Write a five-paragraph composition persuading your readers to agree with your stand. In your first paragraph, introduce the topic and your position. In each of the next three paragraphs, support your stand. In the last paragraph, sum up your position.

STUDY SKILLS

HANDBOOK

Reading is to the mind, what exercise is to the body.
—Joseph Addison

Reading is a tool for learning. It not only helps you to find out how to do things, it also helps you to discover more about yourself and other people and about the world. Certain reading skills help you to become better students. (Review pages 67, 173, 243, 395, and 454.) These skills, which we will call study skills, help you complete assignments accurately and well.

Following Directions

Directions are instructions for how to do something. Some directions are spoken; others are written. If the directions are spoken, you must listen carefully. Too often with spoken instructions we hear only part of what is said. However, we proceed as though we had heard the complete instructions and often do the wrong thing. For example, your teacher gives you directions for taking a test. Because your mind is on an argument you had with a friend last night, you are not listening carefully. You don't hear all of the teacher's words, but you do hear him say to write your answers in complete sentences. You go ahead as though you'd heard the complete instructions. You write all your answers in complete sentences on the test paper itself. Unfortunately, the part of the directions you missed was very important. Your teacher said to write your answers on a separate piece of paper, since the actual test papers will be given to another group of students.

If the directions are written, you must read carefully. For example, imagine that the directions for making a soup say to add a teaspoon of pepper. The soup would taste very odd indeed if you misread the directions and added a tablespoon of pepper.

Exercise 1. Read the recipe below for preparing chicken soup. Study the directions carefully. Then answer the questions that follow the recipe.

Ingredients

2½ lbs stewing chicken
4 large carrots
4 stalks of celery, diced
2 large or 4 small onions, cubed

1 cup club soda
1 teaspoon salt
1 teaspoon pepper
4 sprigs parsley

Place chicken in large kettle, with water to cover. Add club soda. Bring the water to a boil. Then lower heat. Cut the carrots and onions into cubes. Add them to water. Dice the celery. Add to water. Add salt and pepper. Simmer until the meat falls off the bone, adding water as needed. Remove bones. Add parsley and serve.

Questions.   Number your paper from 1 to 10. If the direction below is accurate based on the recipe, write *True* on the paper. If the direction is inaccurate, write *False*.

1. Add enough water to cover the chicken.
2. Bring the water to a boil before you add the club soda.
3. Add the carrots and onions to the water before it boils.
4. Cut the carrots and onions into cubes.
5. Use either 2 small onions or 4 large onions.
6. Cut the celery into cubes.
7. Add 1 tablespoon of salt.
8. Add 1 teaspoon of pepper.
9. Cook until the meat falls off the bone.
10. Do not add any extra water.

Understanding the Parts of a Book

Most of us become very familiar with what is in the body of a book. However, sometimes we overlook two very useful parts of the book, the front matter and the back matter.

The Front Matter

The front matter contains the title page, the copyright page, and the table of contents. Sometimes it contains other material as well, such as a preface or a foreword. The title page tells you the title of the book, the author, the publisher, and the place of publication. The copyright page, which appears on the reverse side of the title page, tells you when the book was copyrighted and by whom. It also lists acknowledgments, credits for published material, if there are any. The table of contents lists the main divisions of the book. At times, it also lists sections within this division. It also provides page numbers telling you where each section begins.

Exercise 2. Follow the directions below. Then write your answers on a separate piece of paper.

1. Turn to the title page of this book. It is a two-page spread appearing before page iv. Since this book is part of a series, it has a series title, which appears on the left-hand page. What is the series title?

2. The book title appears on the right-hand page. What is it?

3. Two professors helped to prepare this book and are listed under Curriculum and Writing. What are their names?

4. Who is the publisher of the book?

5. Now turn to page iv, the copyright page. In what year was this book copyrighted?

6. The acknowledgments give credit for the selections used from other publications. How many pages of acknowledgments are there?

7. Now turn to page vii. This page gives thanks to people who helped to evaluate, or judge, the material in this book. How many people are listed?

8. Now turn to page viii, the start of the table of contents. How many selections are in the chapter *Woodnotes*?

9. In the table of contents, find the selection "I Love All Gravity Defiers" by Lillian Morrison. On what page does this selection begin?

10. Pages xiv–xvii provide an outline of skills for this book. On what page will you find the inference skill *making inferences about past events*?

Back Matter The back matter may include a glossary and an index. The glossary is a dictionary of words in the book that the reader may not know. The index is an alphabetical listing of topics and the pages on which they appear. Sometimes the back matter contains other information as well.

Exercise 3. Follow the directions below. Then write your answers on a separate piece of paper.

1. Turn to page 545. The glossary in this book begins with a chart. What is this chart?

2. The glossary is arranged alphabetically. On what page do you find an entry for the word *inertia*?

3. On what page do you find an entry for the word *boutique*?

4. This book contains two types of indexes. Turn to page 556. What index is provided here?

5. How many types, or categories, of selections does this index list?

6. How many selections do you find under *Poetry*?

7. Look under *Drama*. On what page would you find the selection "The Dying Detective"?
8. On what page would you find the selection "Crime on Mars"?
9. What index do you find on page 557?
10. According to this index, on what page in the body of the book would you find a selection by Langston Hughes? On what pages would you find selections by Gwendolyn Brooks?

Using Reference Books

Reference books are invaluable sources of information. There are several types, and each type provides somewhat different information. An **encyclopedia** provides detailed information on a wide range of subjects. However, some specialized encyclopedias, such as an encyclopedia of engineering, provide detailed information on only one subject.

A **dictionary** provides detailed information about words. It gives their meaning, their spelling, their pronunciation, and usually their origin. Like encyclopedias, some dictionaries, for example, a dictionary of word origins, are specialized and provide only one type of information about words.

An **atlas** provides detailed information about places. Usually it is a bound collection of maps that may also contain lists of statistics about places.

An **almanac** is a yearly record including lists, charts, and tables of information about unrelated fields. A typical almanac will contain sports records, lists of Presidents, facts about states, the flags of the world, and the latest census findings.

These reference books can help you find answers to questions and facts you may need for writing compositions. Become familiar with them and learn to use them comfortably.

Exercise 4. Use reference books to answer each of the questions below. Write your answers on a separate piece of paper. Indicate the type of reference book you used for each type of question.

1. From what language did the word *patio* come into English?
2. What is the capital of Colorado?
3. When were mirrors first invented?
4. What country borders Poland on the east?
5. According to the latest census, how many people live in the United States?
6. What is the postal abbreviation for Texas?

7. The French and Indian War was part of a larger world conflict. What conflict was this?
8. What body of water borders Florida to the west?
9. How is the word *sincerity* divided into syllables?
10. When did Gerald Ford become President of the United States?

Reading Tables

A table is a list of numbers, facts, or items arranged for easy reference, usually organized in categories. Learn to read tables, since they can be an invaluable source of quick information.

Exercise 5. Study the table below. Then, on a separate piece of paper, answer each of the questions following the table.

Primary Teeth	Average Age of Appearance	Order of Appearance
Central incisors	6 to 8 months	1
Lateral incisors	9 to 11 months	2
First molars	14 to 17 months	3
Eye teeth	18 to 20 months	4
Second molars	24 to 26 months	5
Adult Teeth		
First molars	6 to 7 years	1
Central incisors	7 to 8 years	2
Lateral incisors	8 to 9 years	3
First premolars	10 to 12 years	4
Second premolars	10 to 12 years	5
Canines	12 to 14 years	6
Second molars	12 to 16 years	7
Third molars	17 to 21 years	8

Questions
1. How many types of primary teeth do we have?
2. How many types of adult teeth do we have?
3. Look at the category *Primary Teeth*. At what age do the first molars appear?
4. At what age do the lateral incisors appear?
5. What is the first type of primary teeth to appear?
6. Look at the category *Adult Teeth*. What is the last type of adult teeth to appear?
7. What is the second type to appear?
8. At what age do the premolars appear?
9. At what age do the central incisors appear?
10. At what age do the second proemolars appear?

GLOSSARY

From *The American Heritage Dictionary of the English Language.*
© 1979 by Houghton Mifflin Company. Reprinted by permission of
Houghton Mifflin Company.

Pronunciation Key

ă	pat		ŏ	pot
ā	pay		ō	toe
âr	care		ô	paw, for
ä	father		oi	noise
b	**bib**		ŏŏ	took
ch	**church**		ōō	boot
d	**deed**		ou	**out**
ĕ	pet		p	**pop**
ē	bee		r	**roar**
f	**fife**		s	**sauce**
g	**gag**		sh	**ship, dish**
h	**hat**		t	**tight**
hw	**which**		th	**thin, path**
ĭ	pit		th	**this, bathe**
ī	pie		ŭ	**cut**
îr	pier		ûr	**urge**
j	**judge**		v	**valve**
k	**kick**		w	**with**
l	**lid, needle**		y	**yes**
m	**mum**		z	**zebra, dismal, exile**
n	**no, sudden**		zh	vision
ng	**thing**		ə	**about, item, edible, gallop, circus**

Abbreviation Key

adj.	adjective	*n.*	noun	*prep.*	preposition
adv.	adverb			*v.*	verb

A

a bate (ə-bāt′) *v.*: To let up; to ease or become less strong.

ab do men (ăb′də-mən, ăb-dō′mən) *n.*: The lower body cavity which contains the digestive organs.

ab o rig i nal (ăb′ə-rĭj′ə-nəl) *adj.*: Very ancient; dating to the time before written records or history.

ab surd (ăb-sûrd′, ăb-zûrd′) *adj.*: Silly, foolish.

a byss (ə-bĭs′) *n.*: A bottomless pit; a profound depth.

ac curs ed (ə-kûr′sĭd, ə-kûrst′) *adj.*: Terrible, hateful, abominable.

ac ro bat ic (ăk′rə-băt′ĭk) *adj.*: Pertaining to balancing or tumbling techniques.

ad den dum (ə-děn′dəm) *n.*: An entry attached or tagged on to the end of something. [*Addenda* (ə-děn′də) is the plural form.]

a dorn (ə-dôrn′) *v.*: To decorate.

ad vent (ăd′věnt) *n.*: The arrival or start of something.

aer o sol (âr′ə-sôl′, âr′ə-sŏl′, âr′ə-sōl′) *n.*: A spray container. —*adj.*: Pertaining to aerosol.

a gape (ə-gāp′, ə-găp′) *adv.*: With the mouth wide open in amazement.

ag ile (ăj′əl, ăj′īl) *adj.*: Nimble; quick and sure-footed.

a gil i ty (ə-jĭl′ə-tē) *n.*: Quickness of movement, nimbleness.

ag i tate (ăj′ə-tāt′) *v.*: To excite, disturb, or upset. —**ag i tated,** *adj.* —**ag i ta tion,** *n.*

al ter nate (ôl′tər-nāt′, ăl′tər-nāt′) *v.*: To pass from one to another and back again; to take turns.

am pu tate (ăm′pyŏŏ-tāt′) *v.*: To cut off. —**am pu ta tion,** *n.*

an ces try (ăn′sĕs′trē) *n.*: The line of descendents from one generation to the next.

a ne mic (ə-nē′mĭk) *adj.*: Suffering from a lack of iron in the blood; sickly, easily tired.

an tiq ui ty (ăn-tĭk′wə-tē) *n.*: A very old and historical object or piece of art.

ap er ture (ăp′ər-chŏŏr′, ăp′ər-chər) *n.*: An opening or hole.

ap pre hen sion (ăp′rĭ-hĕn′shən) *n.*: A vague sense of fear or uneasiness.

aq ua naut (ăk′wə-nôt′, ä′kwə-nôt′) *n.*: An explorer of underwater life; a diver.

ar du ous (är′jŏŏ-əs) *adj.*: Difficult; demanding great physical strength.

ar ro gant ly (ăr′ə-gənt-lē) *adv.*: Snobbishly, haughtily; in a superior, or condescending, fashion.

ar se nic (är′sə-nĭk) *n.*: A deadly poison (often used to kill rats).

ar ti fact (är′tə-făkt′) *n.*: Any tool, piece of art, or other object which comes from an ancient civilization.

as phalt (ăs′fôlt′) *n.*: The black material used to pave roads; blacktop.

as suage (ə-swāg′) *v.*: To lessen or ease.

as tro naut (ăs′trə-nôt′) *n.*: A person trained to travel and explore outer space.

au ra (ôr′ə) *n.*: A halo-like effect or light; a glow.

av a lanche (ăv′ə-lănch′, ăv′ə-länch′) *n.*: A rockslide or snowslide on a mountain. —*adj.*: Pertaining to an avalanche.

a vert (ə-vûrt′) *v.*: To turn away; to turn aside.

B

ba roque (bə-rōk′) *adj.*: Irregular in shape.

bas-re lief (bä′rĭ-lēf′) *n.*: A type of sculpture in which figures stand out in relief against a flat background.

be hest (bĭ-hĕst′) *n.*: A command or instruction.

bel la don na (bĕl′ə-dŏn′ə) *n.*: A medical preparation made from the poisonous berries of plants.

ben e fac tor (bĕn′ə-făk′tər) *n.*: Someone who takes care of the needs of another person; especially, one who offers financial aid.

be nign (bĭ-nīn′) *n.*: Gentle; friendly

bev el (bĕv′əl) v.: To cut or slope at any angle other than a right angle. —**bev eled,** adj.

bob by pin (bŏb′ē pĭn) n.: A thin metal clip used to curl or hold hair.

bou tique (boo-tēk′) n.: A small shop which usually sells fancy clothing or gifts.

bran dish (brăn′dĭsh) v.: To wave or flourish in a menacing way.

breech (brēch) n.: The part of a gun directly behind the barrel.

bridge (brĭj) n.: The raised section at the front of a ship where the navigator sits. —adj.: Pertaining to the bridge.

brol ly (brôl′ē) n.: A slang expression for an umbrella.

bron chi tis (brŏng-kī′tĭs) n.: A disease characterized by a deep cough and a build-up of fluid in the tubes leading to the lungs.

bul bous (bŭl′bəs) adj.: Rounded and bulging out.

C

ca denced (kā′dənsd) adj.: Having a beat or rhythm.

caf feine (kă-fēn′, kăf′ē-ĭn) n.: The ingredient in coffee or tea which helps keep people awake; a stimulant.

ca lam i ty (kə-lăm′ə-tē) n.: A disaster or great misfortune.

ca per (kā′pər) v.: To dance or leap around; to frolic.

ca rafe (kə-răf′) n.: A wide-necked bottle or decanter.

car niv o rous (kär-nĭv′ər-əs) adj.: Meat-eating.

car toon (kär-toon′) n.: A humorous drawing.

cas cade (kăs-kād′) v.: To tumble down; to fall, especially from one level to another.

cat a pult (kăt′ə-pŭlt′) v.: To launch or hurl.

churl (chûrl) n.: A person who hoards money; a miser.

clam my (klăm′ē) adj.: Unpleasantly cold and damp.

cleave (klēv) v.: To cut in half.

co he sion (kō-hē′zhən) n.: The force which causes particles to cling to each other or stick together.

col league (kŏl′ ēg′) n.: A follower of the same profession; an associate.

co ma (kō′mə) n.: A state of prolonged unconsciousness resulting from injury or sickness.

com mend a bly (kə-mĕnd′ə-blē) adv.: Admirably; in a way deserving of praise.

com pan ion way (kəm-păn′yən-wā′) n.: A stairway between decks on a ship.

com po sure (kəm-pō′zhər) n.: Self-possession, or calmness of mind.

con cep tion (kən-sĕp′shən) n.: 1. An interpretation of an event. 2. An idea or notion.

con cer to (kən-chér′tō) n.: A musical arrangement for an orchestra and one or more soloists.

con cur rent ly (kən-kûr′ənt-lē) adv.: Simultaneous with; at the same time.

con cus sion (kən-kŭsh′ən) n.: The vibration of the shock wave which travels through the air after a gun has been fired. (Normally, a severe blow or impact.)

con de scend (kŏn′dĭ-sĕnd′) v.: To act as if granting a favor; to look down upon.

con so la tion (kŏn′sə-lā′shən) n.: A feeling of relief from a burden; comfort.

con sol ing ly (kən-sōl′ĭng-lē) adv.: Comfortingly; in a way that eases pain or sorrow.

con spir a tor (kən-spîr′ə-tər) n.: One who joins in a plot; a partner in crime.

con sti tute (kŏn′stə-toot′, kŏn′stə-tyoot′) v.: To make up; to compose.

con tour (kŏn′toor) n.: The outer surface or shape.

con tro ver sy (kŏn′trə-vûr′sē) n.: An argument or clash of opinion.

co or di nate (kō-ôr′də-nāt′) v.: To have good muscular control. —**co or di nated,** adj.

copse (kŏps) n.: A thicket; a small cluster of bushes.

cor don (kôr′dən) n.: Group forming a barrier.

cor ral (kə-răl′) n.: Pen.

cor rob o rate (kə-rŏb′ə-rāt′) v.: To back up; to agree with or support (a story or alibi).

cra dle (krād′l) v.: To hold gently and carefully.

craft y (krăf′tē, kräf′tē) adj.: Sly or underhanded; sneaky. —**craft i ly,** adv.

crag (krăg) n.: A mountain peak or ridge.

crank y (krăng′kē) adj.: Cross.

cre ma tion (krĭ-mā′shən) n.: A form of burial in which the body is burned to ashes.

croup (kro͞op) n.: A children's disease characterized by a hacking cough and respiratory difficulty. —adj.: Pertaining to croup.

cur mudg eon (kər-mŭj′ən) n.: A mean, miserly person; a tightwad.

cus toms (kŭs′təmz) n.: A tax levied on certain goods taken out of or brought into a country. —adj.: Pertaining to customs.

D

de cep tive ly (dĭ-sĕp′tĭv-lē) adv.: In a misleading fashion.

def er ence (dĕf′ər-əns) n.: An attitude of respect or courteous regard toward others.

de fi ant ly (dĭ-fī′ənt-lē) adv.: In a challenging manner; in a boldly rebellious way.

de flate (dĭ-flāt′) v.: To puncture or let the air out of; to let down. —de flated, adj.

de lir i ous (dĭ-lîr′ē-əs) adj.: Out of one's mind with fever; hallucinating.

de ment ed (dĭ-mĕn′tĭd) adj.: Crazy, insane.

de ri sive ly (dĭ-rī′sĭv-lē) adv.: Mockingly or scornfully.

des o late (dĕs′ə-lĭt) adj.: Barren; deserted; bleak.

de spon den cy (dĭ-spŏn′dən-sē) n.: Depression or sadness.

de spon dent (dĭ-spŏn′dənt) adj.: Hopelessly sad; in despair. —de spon dent ly, adv.

dex ter i ty (dĕk-stĕr′ə-tē) n.: Skill in using the hands.

di a bol i cal ly (dī′ə-bŏl′ĭ-kəl-lē) adv.: In a devilish, wicked, or evil fashion.

di a phragm (dī′ə-frăm′) n.: The muscles and tendons lying between the chest and the stomach.

dip lo mat (dĭp′lə-măt′) n.: An appointed official of a nation who tries to maintain friendly government relations with other nations.

dis arm (dĭs-ärm′) v.: To put at ease; to rid of hostility or suspicion.

dis con so late (dĭs-kŏn′sə-lĭt) adj.: Sad, disappointed; beyond consolation; dejected.

dis creet (dĭs-krēt′) adj.: Subtle, tactful, or cautious.

dis dain (dĭs-dān′) n.: Scorn or disgust. —dis dain ful ly, adv.

dis grun tle (dĭs-grŭnt′l) v.: To annoy or upset. —dis gruntled, adj.

di shev eled (dĭ-shĕv′əld) adj.: Messy or disordered.

dis pas sion ate ly (dĭs-păsh′ən-ĭt-lē) adv.: In a calm or unconcerned fashion; unemotionally.

dis per sal (dĭs-pûr′səl) n.: The act of distributing widely or of scattering. —adj.: Pertaining to dispersal.

dis po si tion (dĭs′pə-zĭsh′ən) n.: A decision or judgment; a settlement of affairs.

dis qui et (dĭs-kwī′ĭt) n.: A feeling that something is wrong; uneasiness.

dis sim u la tion (dĭ-sĭm′yə-lā′shən) n.: Faking or pretending.

dis traught (dĭs-trôt′) adj.: Upset from worry and confusion; extremely agitated or crazed.

doff (dôf, dŏf) v.: To remove or take off.

dol phin (dŏl′fĭn, dôl′fĭn) n.: A large salt-water mammal.

do mes ti cate (də-mĕs′tĭ-kāt′) v.: 1. To tame. 2. To grow under careful cultivation. —do mes ti cated, adj.

dour (do͝or, dour) adj.: Grim; unsmiling or sullen.

driv el (drĭv′əl) n.: Meaningless talk; nonsense.

drone (drōn) v.: To speak in a dull, unchanging tone.

du bi ous ly (do͞o′bē-əs-lē, dyo͞o′bē-əs-lē) adv.: Uncertainly; in an unsure manner.

du ress (do͝o-rĕs′, dyo͝o-rĕs′, do͝or′ĭs, dyo͝or′ĭs) n.: 1. Pressure or strain. 2. Imprisonment.

E

ed dy (ĕd′ē) v.: To swirl against the current.

ee rie (îr′ē) adj.: Scary; strangely frightening.

e ma ci ate (ĭ-mā′shē-āt′) v.: To waste away; to become very thin. —e ma ci ated, adj.

em a nate (ĕm′ə-nāt′) v.: To radiate; to come or flow forth from.

em bou chure (äm′bo͝o-sho͝or′) n.: The formation of the mouth and lips when playing a wind instrument.

em u late (ĕm′yə-lāt′) v.: To imitate; to follow someone's example.

en coun ter (ĕn-koun′ tər, ĭn-koun′ tər) v.: To meet with; to experience.

en crust (ĕn-krŭst′, ĭn-krŭst′) v.: To cake on, as with jewels; to cover. **—en crus ted,** adj.

en deav or (ĕn-dĕv′ ər, ĭn-dĕv′ ər) n.: An attempt; a project.

en sue (ĕn-sōō′, ĭn-sōō′) v.: To follow in time; to come after. **—en suing,** adj.

en thrall (ĕn-thrôl′, ĭn-thrôl′) v.: To captivate, or hold spellbound; to capture the imagination.

e phem er al (ĭ-fĕm′ ər-əl) adj.: Lasting only an instant; fleeting.

e quiv a lent (ĭ-kwĭv′ ə-lənt) adj.: Equal to; the same as.

er go (ûr′ gō, âr′ gō) conj.: Therefore.

er rat ic (ĭ-răt′ ĭk) adj.: In a wandering manner.

e rupt (ĭ-rŭpt′) v.: To gush forth, as if by explosion.

es teem (ĕ-stēm′, ĭ-stēm′) v.: To consider worthy; to think highly of. **—es teemed,** adj.

etch (ĕch) v.: To scratch in with fine lines.

eu ca lyp tus (yōō′kə-lĭp′təs) n.: A fragrant, menthol-like medicine often used to soothe coughs.

ex hil a ra tion (ĕg-zĭl′ə-rā′ shən, ĭg-zĭl′ə-rā′ shən) n.: Joyous excitement; delight.

ex ot ic (ĕg-zŏt′ ĭk, ĭg-zŏt′ ĭk) adj.: Strikingly unusual or strange.

ex pan sively (ĕk-spăn′ sĭv-lē) adv.: In an open and generous fashion.

F

fal set to (fôl-sĕt′ ō) n.: High-pitched and abnormal voice tones. **—adj.:** Pertaining to falsetto.

ta nat i cal (fə-năt′ ĭ-kəl) adj.: Unreasonably enthusiastic or overzealous; intense.

fas tid i ous (fă-stĭd′ ē-əs, fə-stĭd′ ē-əs) adj.: Discriminating, or choosy; hard to please.

fath om (făth′ əm) v.: To understand or comprehend.

feint (fānt) v.: To fake movement in one direction in order to confuse an opponent.

fi ber glass (fī′ bər-glăs′, fī′ bər-glâs′) n.: A strong but light construction material made from threads of glass.

flail (flāl) v.: To make wild waving motions.

flour ish (flûr′ ĭsh) n.: A sweeping motion of the arm.

foi ble (foi′ bəl) n.: A weakness; a tendency toward foolishness.

foot hill (foot′ hĭl′) n.: The lower, gently rolling slope at the start of a mountain range.

for mi da ble (fôr′ mə-də-bəl) adj.: Awesome; overpowering; difficult to defeat.

froth (frôth, frŏth) v.: To foam or bubble.

frus trate (frŭs′ trāt′) v.: To defeat or cause to fail. **—frus trating,** adj.

fur tive ly (fûr′ tĭv-lē) adv.: Sneakily.

G

gal ley (găl′ ē) n.: The kitchen of a ship. **—adj.:** Pertaining to a galley.

gang plank (găng′ plăngk′) n.: A movable ramp for boarding or leaving a ship which is docked.

gau dy (gô′ dē) adj.: Brightly colored and showy.

gaunt (gônt) adj.: Extremely thin and bony.

ghast ly (găst′ lē, gäst′ lē) adj.: Terrible; awful-looking.

glut ton (glŭt′ n) n.: One who can never get enough of something; someone with a tremendous appetite.

gnarled (närld) adj.: Knobby and twisted.

gon do la (gŏnd′ l-ə, gŏn-dō′ lə) n.: The basket-like passenger section of a hot air balloon.

grub (grŭb) n.: Food.

gru el ing (grōō′ ə-lĭng) adj.: Torturous, exhausting.

gut tur al (gŭt′ ər-əl) adj.: Having a harsh or rasping vocal quality.

H

hack les (hăk′ əls) n.: The hairs on the back of a dog's neck.

hap less (hăp′ lĭs) adj.: Unlucky, unfortunate.

har ass (hăr′ əs, hə-răs′) v.: To annoy; to upset. **—har assed,** adj.

har mo nize (här′ mə-nīz′) v.: To fit together pleasingly; to be in agreement with.

har ry (hăr′ ē) v.: To worry, harass, or burden. **—harried,** adj.

hatch (hăch) n.: A doorway or hinged opening on a ship.

ho gan (hō′gôn′, hō′gən) *n.*: A type of dirt-covered building in which Navajo Indians live.

hos pi tal i ty (hŏs′pə-tăl′ə-tē) *n.*: **1.** Welcome or greeting. **2.** The act of warmly receiving guests into one's home.

hul la ba loo (hŭl′ə-bə-loo′) *n.*: A commotion; a great deal of excitement.

hy po der mic (hī′pə-dûr′mĭk) *adj.*: Pertaining to a type of needle used to inject substances under the skin.

I

i dol ize (īd′l-īz′) *v.*: To worship; to admire greatly.

ig no rance (ĭg′nər-əns) *n.*: Stupidity, lack of knowledge.

il lit er a cy (ĭ-lĭt′ər-ə-sē) *n.*: The inability to read or write.

im pec ca ble (ĭm-pĕk′ə-bəl) *adj.*: Perfectly groomed.

im ped i ment (ĭm-pĕd′ə-mənt) *n.*: A problem or obstruction to be overcome.

im pe ri ous ly (ĭm-pîr′ē-əs-lē) *adv.*: In a commanding manner.

im plore (ĭm-plôr′, ĭm-plōr′) *v.*: To beg; to plead with someone.

in ac ces si ble (ĭn′ăk-sĕs′ə-bəl) *adj.*: Difficult or impossible to reach or find.

in ar tic u late (ĭn′är-tĭk′yə-lĭt) *adj.*: Unable to speak clearly or effectively.

in car cer ate (ĭn-kär′sə-rāt′) *v.*: To put in jail; to lock up.

in ces sant ly (ĭn-sĕs′ənt-lē) *adv.*: Continuously.

in cip i ent (ĭn-sĭp′ē-ənt) *adj.*: In its early stages; just beginning.

in clu sive (ĭn-kloo′sĭv) *adj.*: Taking everything into account; all-encompassing. **—in clu sive ly,** *adv.*

in com pa ra ble (ĭn-kŏm′pər-ə-bəl) *adj.*: Never to be equaled or surpassed.

in com pre hen si ble (ĭn′kŏm-prĭ-hĕn′sə-bəl, ĭn-kŏm′prĭ-hĕn′sə-bəl) *adj.*: Incapable of being understood or fathomed.

in con spic u ous (ĭn′kən-spĭk′yoo-əs) *adj.*: Not noticeable; not attracting any attention.

in cred u lous (ĭn-krĕj′ə-ləs) *adj.*: Disbelieving; unconvinced. **—in cred u lous ly,** *adv.*

in cu ba tion (ĭn′kyə-bā′shən, ĭng′kyə-bā′shən) *n.*: The time between exposure to a disease and the appearance of symptoms.

in del i bly (ĭn-dĕl′ə-blē) *adv.*: Permanently; in a way that cannot be erased or removed.

in di gest i ble (ĭn′dī-jĕs′tə-bəl, ĭn′dī-jĕs′tə-bəl) *adj.*: Difficult to digest, or to be consumed and broken down by the body.

in dig nant (ĭn-dĭg′nənt) *adj.*: Angry; annoyed by someone's words or actions. **—in dig nant ly,** *adv.*

in dul gent ly (ĭn-dŭl′jənt-lē) *adv.*: Fondly and willingly excusing or overlooking faults.

in ed ible (ĭn-ĕd′ə-bəl) *adj.*: Not fit to eat.

in er tia (ĭn-ûr′shə) *n.*: The tendency of an object to keep moving in the same direction once it has started to move.

in ev i ta ble (ĭn-ĕv′ə-tə-bəl) *adj.*: Unavoidable.

in fu ri ate (ĭn-fyoor′ē-āt′) *v.*: Anger, enrage.

in fuse (ĭn-fyooz′) *v.*: To add to the original composition; to instill.

in no va tion (ĭn′ə-vā′shən) *n.*: A new way of doing something; a change.

in quis i tive (ĭn-kwĭz′ə-tĭv) *adj.*: Curious, questioning.

in sip id (ĭn-sĭp′ĭd) *adj.*: Unexciting, bland.

in stinct (ĭn′stĭngkt′) *n.*: A natural tendency or impulse; a sense.

in teg ri ty (ĭn-tĕg′rə-tē) *n.*: Honor; quality of being true to one's principles, or code of behavior; strength of character.

in ter mi na ble (ĭn-tûr′mə-nə-bəl) *adj.*: Never-ending; seeming to go on forever.

in ter val (ĭn′tər-vəl) *n.*: A space in time between two events.

in ter vene (ĭn′tər-vēn′) *v.*: To step inbetween; to interrupt.

in tol er ant (ĭn-tŏl′ər-ənt) *adj.*: Angry at; not understanding of.

in tri cate (ĭn′trĭ-kĭt) *adj.*: Complicated or involved.

in trigue (ĭn′trēg′, ĭn-trēg′) *v.*: To make curious; to excite with an idea. **—in trigued,** *adj.*

in trin si cal ly (ĭn-trĭn′sĭ-kəl-lē) *adv.*: Innately; by nature.

in va lid (ĭn′və-lĭd) *n.*: A sickly person; someone of delicate health.

in ven to ry (ĭn′ vən-tôr′ē, ĭn′ vən-tōr′ē) n.: A careful noting of every detail and item. —*adj.*: Pertaining to inventory.

in vul ner a ble (ĭn-vŭl′ nər-ə-bəl) *adj.*: Impossible to kill or defeat; indestructible.

irk some (ûrk′ səm) *adj.*: Aggravating, annoying.

J

ju bi la tion (jōō′bə-lā′ shən) n.: Joy; bubbling excitement.

ju di cious ly (jōō-dĭsh′ əs-lē) *adv.*: Wisely, prudently, justly.

K

kit (kĭt) n.: A baby fox.

knick ers (nĭk′ ərz) n.: Knickerbockers, or short, knee-length pants which fit snugly around the knees.

knick-knack (nĭk′ năk′) n.: A small, decorative object; a trinket or ornament. —*adj.*: Pertaining to a knick-knack.

L

le thal (lē′thəl) *adj.*: Capable of causing death.

le thar gic (lə-thär′jĭk) *adj.*: Sleepy, lazy.

lin i ment (lĭn′ə-mənt) n.: A preparation which is rubbed on muscles or skin to relieve soreness.

loathe (lōth) v.: To hate, detest, or despise.

loll (lŏl) v.: To hang or droop.

lore (lôr, lōr) n.: The tales and legends of a particular group of people or of a particular region.

lu cent (lōō′sənt) *adj.*: Full of light; lit up.

lug (lŭg) v.: To drag, pull, or haul.

lug (lŭg) n.: A leather piece attached to mountain-climbing boots. —*adj.*: Pertaining to a lug.

lu gu bri ous (lŏō-gōō′brē-əs) *adj.*: Extremely sad or mournful.

M

maim (mām) v.: To cripple or damage severely.

ma lar i a (mə-lâr′ē-ə) n.: A tropical disease spread by mosquitoes and marked by recurrent attacks of chills, fever, and sweating.

mal ice (măl′ĭs) n.: Evil intentions; a desire to hurt or destroy or to see others suffer: ill will.

ma lin ger (mə-lĭng′gər) v.: To pretend illness.

man tle (măn′ təl) n.: A covering, as in a cloak or blanket.

maul (môl) v.: To claw savagely.

med ley (mĕd′ lē) n.: A mixture or combination; a jumble.

men ace (mĕn′ ĭs) v.: To threaten; to alarm. —**men acing,** *adj.*

me rid i an (mə-rĭd′ ē-ən) n.: Any imaginary semicircle drawn on a planet's surface from its north to its south pole. (Meridians are used in measuring longitude.)

me thod i cal (mə-thŏd′ ĭ-kəl) *adj.*: Orderly and precise; proceeding according to a plan, one step at a time (having a method or procedure.)

mill (mĭll) v.: Move about aimlessly.

mince (mĭns) v.: To step carefully or daintily. —**mincing,** *adj.*

min us cule (mĭn′ ə-skyōōl′, mĭ-nŭs′ kyōōl) *adj.*: Extremely small; tiny. (Also **miniscule.**)

mis cre ant (mĭs′ krē-ənt) n.: A wrongdoer; someone who has committed a crime.

mis no mer (mĭs-nō′ mər) n.: A title or name that does not suit the topic at hand. (Literally, a "wrong name.")

mo gul (mō′ gəl) n.: A bump or small mound on a ski slope or race course.

mole skin (mōl′ skĭn′) n.: A heavy, cotton-like material.

mon goose (mŏng′ gōōs′, mŏn′ gōōs′) n.: A small, longtailed animal which can kill cobras or other poisonous snakes.

mon i tor (mŏn′ ə-tər) v.: To watch closely; to take careful note of.

mon o gram (mŏn′ ə-grăm′) v.: To decorate with a set of initials. —**mon o grammed,** *adj.*

musk y (mŭsk′ ē) *adj.*: Smelling like the strong glandular secretions of certain animals.

mute (myōōt) v.: To soften the sound; to make less harsh. —**muted,** *adj.*

myth (mĭth) n.: A traditional story, usually about gods, heroes, etc., often offering an explanation of something in nature or of past events.

N

nes tle (nĕs′ əl) v.: To snuggle; settle cozily.

niche (nĭch) n.: A small space or hole; an indentation.

nom i nal (nŏm′ ə-nəl) *adj.*: Small or trifling.

non cha lant (nŏn′shə-länt′) *adj.*: Carefree and unconcerned.

nuz zle (nŭz′əl) *v.*: To push or rub with the nose; to nestle or cuddle.

O

o bliv i ous (ə-blĭv′ē-əs) *adj.*: Totally unaware.

ob scure (ŏb-skyŏŏr′, əb-skyŏŏr′) *v.*: To conceal or hide.

ob sess (əb-sĕs′, ŏb-sĕs′) *v.*: To fascinate; to preoccupy greatly; to haunt or possess.

ob ses sion (əb-sĕsh′ən, ŏb-sĕsh′ən) *n.*: An overpowering idea; a single, driving ambition.

oc ci den tal (ŏk′sə-dĕn′təl) *adj.*: Western, or pertaining to Western thought. (Western refers to countries west of Asia, especially those of Europe and the Americas.)

om i nous (ŏm′ə-nəs) *adj.*: Foreboding, or threatening; full of a feeling that something bad is about to happen.

on slaught (ŏn′slôt′, ôn′slôt′) *n.*: The beginning or advent; the first attack.

op u lent (ŏp′yə-lənt) *adj.*: Rich and luxurious.

o ri ent (ôr′ē-ənt, ôr′ē-ĕnt′, ōr′ē-ənt) *v.*: To make one's self familiar with a situation or circumstance.

o ver ture (ō′vər-chŏŏr′) *n.*: An opening move or friendly gesture.

P

pa lav er (pə-lăv′ər, pə-lä′vər) *n.*: Nonsense talk; useless information; chitchat or small talk.

par a lyt ic (păr′ə-lĭt′ĭk) *n.*: One who suffers from a loss of movement or sensation; a cripple.

par a lyze (păr′ə-līz′) *v.*: To make unable to move; to cripple.

par ley (pär′lē) *v.*: To discuss or confer with.

par si mo ni ous (pär′sə-mō′nē-əs) *adj.*: Stingy; thrifty, or careful with money.

path o log i cal (păth′ə-lŏj′ĭ-kəl) *adj.*: Pertaining to pathology, the study of the nature of disease.

pe dom e ter (pĭ-dŏm′ə-tər) *n.*: A device attached to the foot to measure the distance walked (it registers the number of steps taken.)

pel vis (pĕl′vĭs) *n.*: The bone structure at the base of the spine which provides support and forms the hip sockets.

pen du lum (pĕn′jŏŏ-ləm, pĕn′dyə-ləm, pĕn′də-ləm) *n.*: Something that swings back and forth.

pe nin su la (pə-nĭn′syə-lə, pə-nĭn′sə-lə) *n.*: Land that is surrounded by water on three sides.

per turb (pər-tûrb′) *v.*: To upset or disturb.

pi ton (pē′tŏn′) *n.*: A steel spike which is hammered into the rock of a mountain to provide a hand or foothold.

piv ot (pĭv′ət) *v.*: To turn in one direction on an axis; to rotate.

pla cate (plā′kāt′, plăk′āt′) *v.*: To comfort or appease; to ease tension between those having an argument.—**pla cat ing ly**, *adv.*

plain tive ly (plān′tĭv-lē) *adv.*: In a sad, pleading, mournful fashion.

ply wood (plī′wŏŏd′) *n.*: A building material comprised of several very thin layers of wood that have been glued tightly together.

pneu mo nia (nŏŏ-mōn′yə, nyŏŏ-mōn′yə) *n.*: A disease characterized by a deep racking cough and a build-up of fluid in the lungs.

po rous (pôr′əs, pōr′əs) *adj.*: Having small holes or gaps that allow air or water to pass through.

port (pôrt, pōrt) *n.*: The left side of a ship (as you face front).—*adj.*: Pertaining to port.

port (pôrt, pōrt) *n.*: A harbor or bay where ships dock.

pox (pŏks) *n.*: Any disease leaving sores on the skin (e. g., chickenpox, smallpox).

pre cede (prĭ-sēd′) *v.*: To come before; to be ahead of.

pre dic a ment (prĭ-dĭk′ə-mənt) *n.*: A troublesome situation.

pre mo ni tion (prē′mə-nĭsh′ən, prĕm′ə-nĭsh′ən) *n.*: A feeling in advance that something bad is about to happen; a forewarning, or a glimpse of some future event.

pre sum a bly (prĭ-zŏŏ′mə-blē) *adv.*: Probably; most likely.

prof fer (prŏf′ər) *v.*: To offer; to extend or hold out.—**prof fered**, *adj.*

pro found (prə-found′, prō-found′) *adj.*: Very deep; awesome or overpowering.

pro lif ic (prō-lĭf′ĭk) *adj.*: Capable of reproducing quickly and having many offspring; fertile.

prop a ga tion (prŏp′ə-gā′shən) *n.*: Reproduction or fertilization.

prov o ca tion (prŏv′ə-kā′shən) n.: A challenge or action intended to cause a strong reaction or attack.

psy cho log i cal (sī′kə-lŏj′ĭ-kəl) adj.: Having to do with the mind or emotions.

Q

quail (kwāl) v.: To cower or cringe in fear.

quake (kwāk) v.: To tremble or shake with fear.

quak er (kwā′kər) n.: One who trembles or shakes.

quar rel some ly (kwôr′əl-səm-lē) adv.: In an agitated or troubled fashion.

quar ter (kwôr′tər) v.: To travel over an area in a zigzag fashion.

R

ran cid (răn′sĭd) adj.: Smelling like something that has rotted or spoiled.

ran sack (răn′săk′) v.: To "turn things upside down" while searching for something; to tear apart or destroy.

re buff (rĭ-bŭf′) v.: To reject or refuse sharply or rudely.

reck on ing (rĕk′ən-ĭng) n.: A showdown or confrontation to settle a dispute.

re con noi ter (rē′kə-noi′tər, rĕk′ə-noi′tər) v.: To explore a place; to look around carefully.

re cum bent (rĭ-kŭm′bənt) adj.: Lying down; in a reclining position.

re mand (rĭ-mănd′) v.: To hand over or send back.

re mon strance (rĭ-mŏn′strəns) n.: An argument or protest.

rend (rĕnd) v.: To tear or break; to rip.—n.: The act or quality of rending something.

ren e gade (rĕn′ə-gād′) n.: An outlaw or killer.

rep tile (rĕp′tĭl, rĕp′tīl′) n.: Any cold-blooded, egg-laying animal, such as a snake or lizard.

res o lute (rĕz′ə-loot′) adj.: Characterized by firmness and determination.

res o nant (rĕz′ə-nənt) adj.: Resounding or re-echoing.

rev er ie (rĕv′ər-ē) n.: A daydream.

ruck sack (rŭk′săk′, rook′săk′) n.: A canvas bag, similar to a knapsack, usually used for carrying supplies.

rud dy (rŭd′ē) adj.: Rosy; reddish.

ruff (rŭf) n.: The collar-like fur around the neck of some dogs.

rune (roon) n.: Any of the letters of an ancient alphabet (of the Scandinavians, Anglo-Saxons, and other early Germanic peoples.)

S

sac ri le gious (săk′rə-lē′jəs) adj.: Contrary to the laws of a religion; sinful, irreverent.

sage brush (sāj′brŭsh′) n.: A green shrub which grows in desert regions.

sal ly (săl′ē) n.: A trip or expedition.

sanc tu ar y (săngk′choo-ĕr′ē) n.: A place of refuge or safety.

sar cas tic (sär-kăs′tĭk) adj.: Mocking or making fun of, typically by saying the opposite of what one really means.

sar don ic (sär-dŏn′ĭk) adj.: Sarcastic, or cutting or mocking in tone.

sat u ra tion (săch′ə-rā′shən) n.: The condition of being drenched, or soaked with water.

saun ter (sôn′tər) v.: To stroll casually.

scan (skăn) v.: To look over quickly.

scan dal ize (skăn′də-līz′) v.: Shock; disgrace.

scru pu lous ly (skroo′pyə-ləs-lē) adv.: Conscientiously; painstakingly.

scud (skŭd) v.: **1.** To move, run, or fly swiftly; to skim along. **2.** In sailing, to be pushed along by a strong wind.

scur vy (skûr′vē) n.: A disease resulting from a lack of vitamin C and characterized by sores and bleeding gums.

seethe (sēth) v.: To boil over with excitement or fear.

sen su ous (sĕn′shoo-əs) adj.: Pleasant or appealing to the senses.

sham ble (shăm′bəl) v.: Walk awkwardly.—Pl. n.: Complete disorder.

sheathe (shēth) v.: To enclose within an outer covering; to encase.—**sheathed**, adj.

shrike (shrīk) n.: A fierce bird of prey which feeds on insects and small animals.

sin is ter (sĭn′ ĭ-stər) *adj.*: Evil, wicked.

sin u ous (sĭn′ yo͞o-əs) *adj.*: **1.** Smoothly winding or twisting. **2.** Supple, flexible, or limber.

skein (skān) *n.*: A quantity of yarn or thread wound into a loose, long coil or loop.

skep ti cal ly (skĕp′ tĭ-kəl-lē) *adv.*: In a doubting, questioning, or disbelieving manner.

slough (slŭf) *v.*: To shed.

smite (smīt) *v.*: To strike a blow; to hit.

smol der (smōl′ dər) *v.*: To smoke like a fire that is not quite extinguished.—*adj.*: Pertaining to smolder.

so ber ly (sō′ bər-lē) *adv.*: Seriously; somberly or gravely.

sod den (sŏd′ n) *adj.*: Soaked through; soggy.

so nar (sō′ när′) [So (und) Na(vigation) R(anging)] *n.*: The technique or ability to locate underwater objects by sending out high-frequency sound waves and then picking up their echoes.

so no rous (sə-nôr′ əs, sə-nōr′ əs, sŏn′ ə r-əs) *adj.*: **1.** Rich sounding. **2.** Impressive.

so phis ti ca tion (sə-fĭs′tĭ-ka′ shən) *n.*: An understanding and knowledge of the ways of the world.

spec u la tive ly (spĕk′ yə-lə-tĭv-lē) *adv.*: In an uncertain fashion.

stac ca to (stə-kä′ tō) *n.*: A series of short, sharp noises.

stance (stăns) *n.*: The posture or position that a hunting dog is trained to take.

stat ure (stăch′ ər) *n.*: **1.** Height or physical build. **2.** Status, or level of importance.

stealth i ly (stĕlth′ ĭ-lē) *adv.*: Sneakily or cautiously.

steer (stîr) *n.*: A young ox.

stew ard (sto͞o′ ərd, styo͞o′ ərd) *n.*: The staff member in charge of food and provisions on a ship.

stri dent (strīd′ ənt) *adj.*: Loud and harsh.

strych nine (strĭk′ nīn′, strĭk′ nən, strĭk′ nĕn′) *n.*: A poison which is prescribed in small doses as a stimulant to the nervous system.—*adj.*: Pertaining to strychnine.

sub due (səb-do͞o′, səb-dyo͞o′) *v.*: To defeat or overcome.

suc cu lent (sŭk′ yə-lənt) *adj.*: Juicy; full of sap.

su per sti tion (so͞o′pər-stĭsh′ ən) *n.*: An unreasonable belief, one that has absolutely no basis in fact or logic.

sur veil lance (sər-vā′ ləns) *n.*: **1.** Supervision. **2.** A watch placed on someone; close observation of a person under suspicion.

sus pen sion (sə-spĕn ′shən) *n.*: The supporting framework of springs that keeps a vehicle upon its axles—*adj.*: Pertaining to a suspension.

su ture (so͞o′ chər) *v.*: To stitch together; to sew, as a wound.

svelte (svĕlt) *adj.*: Thin and graceful.

swag ger (swăg′ ər) *v.*: To strut; to walk proudly and boastfully.

swat (swät) *v.*: To slap.

T

taut (tôt) *adj.*: Stretched tight.

tech ni cal (tĕk′ nĭ-kəl) *adj.*: Scientific; requiring specialized knowledge or skills.—**tech ni cal ly**, *adv.*

tem per a ment (tĕm′ prə-mənt, tĕm′ pər-ə-mənt) *n.*: A person's disposition, nature, or emotional makeup.

ten ta tive ly (tĕn′ tə-tĭv-lē) *adv.*: Hesitatingly, uncertainly.

ter rain (tə-rān′, tĕ-rān′) *n.*: The surface features of a land or region.

the o ret i cal (thē′ə-rĕt′ ĭ-kəl) *adj.*: Having to do with thoughts and guesses rather than facts.

the sis (thē′ sĭs) *n.*: An idea or statement which must be examined and proved either true or false; a hypothesis or proposition.

thick et (thĭk′ ĭt) *n.*: A clump of dense bushes or underbrush.

throe (thrō) *n.*: The grip; the clutches of something.

thyme (tīm) *n.*: A spice or seasoning.

top o graph i cal (tŏp′ə-grăf′ ĭ-kəl) *adj.*: Pertaining to the physical features of a region.

top side (tŏp′ sīd′) *adv.*: On the top deck.

tour ni quet (to͝or′ nĭ-kĭt, to͝or′ nĭ-kā′, tûr′ nĭ-kĭt) *n.*: A rope, cloth, or band which is tied so tightly that it stops the flow of blood.

traipse (trāps) *v.*: To walk or march.

tram po line (trăm′ pə-lēn′) *n.*: A piece of canvas attached with springs to a metal frame and used for tumbling.

tran quil i ty (trăn-kwĭl′ ə-tē) *n.*: Peacefulness, calmness.

tran si tion (trăn-zĭsh′ən, trăn-sĭsh′ən) n.: A change from one thing to another. (In stage directions, "transition" indicates a scene change.)

trans mute (trăns-myo͞ot, trănz-myo͞ot′) v.: To change in form from one thing to another.

trav erse (trăv′ərs, trə-vûrs′) v.: To cross; to move in a diagonal way.

trough (trôf, trŏf) n.: A long, narrow bin for holding water or feed for animals.

twitch (twĭch) v.: To move jerkily.

u

um bil i cal cord (ŭm′bĭl′ĭ-kəl kôrd) n.: The tough, rope-like tissue that connects an unborn child to its mother. (It carries food to, and removes waste from, the unborn child.)

u nan i mous (yo͞o-năn′ə-məs) adj.: In total agreement.—**u nan i mous ly,** adv.

un can ny (ŭn′kăn′ē) adj.: Strange, eerie, weird, so remarkable or mysterious that it causes uneasiness or fear.

un couth (ŭn′ko͞oth′) adj.: Lacking manners; rude.

un du late (ŭn′jo͞o-lāt′, ŭn′dyə-lāt′, ŭn′də-lāt′) v.: To roll smoothly, like a wave.—**un du la ting,** adj.

un ob tru sive (ŭn′əb-tro͞o′sĭv) adj.: Not attracting attention; hardly noticeable.

un or tho dox (ŭn′ôr′thə-dŏks′) adj.: Unusual; contrary to the established way of doing things.

un sa vor y (ŭn′sā′və-rē) adj.: Unpleasant, foul.

un scathed (ŭn′skāthd′) adj.: Unharmed; untouched.

u su rer (yo͞o′zhər-ər) n.: Someone who charges extremely high rates of interest on the money that he or she lends.

V

van quish (văng′kwĭsh, văn′kwĭsh) v.: To conquer; to defeat.

var mint (vär′mənt) n.: A pest or troublemaker; vermin, or vile and loathsome creatures.

veer (vîr) v.: To turn sharply; to change direction.

ve loc i ty (və-lŏs′ə-tē) n.: Speed.

ven i son (věn′ə-sən, věn′ə-zən) n.: Deer meat.

ven om (věn′əm) n.: The poison which a snake injects through its fangs into its victims.

ven tral (věn′trəl) adj.: The bottom or underside.

vin dic tive (vĭn-dĭk′tĭv) adj.: Spiteful; anxious to seek revenge.

vin tage (vĭn′tĭj) n.: The year or season in which a wine was bottled.

vi tal i ty (vī-tăl′ə-tē) n.: Strength, energy, force.

vix en (vĭk′sən) n.: A female fox.

void (void) n.: Empty space; nothingness.

W

wharf (hwôrf) n.: A dock or pier.

wire less (wīr′lĭs) n.: A message sent by telegraph.

wisp y (wĭsp′ē) adj.: Thin and fragile.

wran gler (răng′glər) n.: A ranch hand responsible for the care of horses; a cowboy.

writhe (rīth) v.: To twist and turn from side to side, as if to escape pain.

INDEX OF CONTENTS BY TYPE

INDEX OF AUTHORS AND TITLES

A 5
B 6
C 7
D 8
E 9
F 0
G 1
H 2
I 3
J 4